D1339317
000000770269

'Adam Zamoyski conclusively proves his case against the reactionary European Legitimist monarchy-dictatorships, and he does so with appropriately aristocratic panache. In so doing he leads an entire herd of sacred cows to the abattoir of history' ANDREW ROBERTS

'Both very enjoyable and timely. Elegantly written, its subject matter is the response of governments across Europe to the violent eruption of the French Revolution and its aftermath'

JEREMY JENNINGS, *Standpoint*

'With characteristic flair and elegance, Adam Zamoyski dissects the paranoia, suspicion, and conspiracy theories which followed in the wake of the French Revolution. He sketches out the birth of the modern police state in this era, as well as the origins of European totalitarianism and the beginnings of what we would later come to call class struggle. *Phantom Terror* is a timely and original history book, a brilliant guide to the past which will inspire reflections about the present as well' ANNE APPLEBAUM

'This substantial work offers a fast-paced engaging history of the frequently ludicrous lengths to which the fear of revolution carried the political elite of Europe in the sixty years after 1789'

DAVID ANDRESS, *BBC History Magazine*

'A sweeping history of the rise of state control in Europe from 1789 to 1848 ... Mr Zamoyski demonstrates an impressive command of political history and international relations as he chronicles the practices of state-sponsored censorship, surveillance and brutality that, in his view, ultimately prompted the revolutions they were intended to prevent' LAURA AURICCHIO, *Wall Street Journal*

'Zamoyski, who writes with flair and an eye for amusing detail, is particularly good on things Russian'

DAVID A. BELL, *Atlantic Magazine*

'Zamoyski documents, in indisputable detail, a system that relied on bumblers and fumblers, "security agents" so inept as to make the Keystone Cops look like Sherlock Holmes in comparison … [A] work of serious history' JOSEPH C. GOULDEN, *Washington Times*

By the same author

CHOPIN: A BIOGRAPHY

THE BATTLE FOR THE MARCHLANDS

PADEREWSKI

THE POLISH WAY

THE LAST KING OF POLAND

THE FORGOTTEN FEW:
THE POLISH AIR FORCE IN THE SECOND WORLD WAR

HOLY MADNESS: ROMANTICS, PATRIOTS
AND REVOLUTIONARIES, 1776–1871

1812: NAPOLEON'S FATAL MARCH ON MOSCOW

RITES OF PEACE: THE FALL OF NAPOLEON
AND THE CONGRESS OF VIENNA

WARSAW 1920: LENIN'S FAILED CONQUEST OF EUROPE

POLAND: A HISTORY

CHOPIN: PRINCE OF THE ROMANTICS

Phantom Terror

The Threat of Revolution and the Repression of Liberty 1789–1848

ADAM ZAMOYSKI

William Collins
An imprint of HarperCollins*Publishers*
1 London Bridge Street
London SE1 9GF
WilliamCollinsBooks.com

First published by William Collins in 2014
This William Collins paperback edition published 2015
1

A catalogue record for this book is
available from the British Library

ISBN 978-0-00-728277-7

Printed and bound in Great Britain by
Clays Ltd, St Ives plc

Contents

Illustrations

The Radical's Arms by George Cruikshank, published 13 November 1819 by George Humphrey. (© The Trustees of the British Museum)

Drawing of an 'anti-cavalry machine'. (The National Archives, Kew. TS II/200)

The Duke of Wellington, arch-reactionary and apologist for the 'Peterloo Massacre'. Attributed to Thomas Lawrence. (Huntington Library/Superstock)

The Peterloo Massacre, 16 August 1819. By George Cruikshank, published 1 October 1819 by Richard Carlile. (Manchester Art Gallery/Bridgeman Images)

Radical Parliament!! 1820. By George Cruikshank, c.1820. (© The Trustees of the British Museum)

The murder of the duc de Berry on 13 February 1820. By Louis Louvel. (RA/Lebrecht Music & Arts)

A document purporting to be a copy of the hieroglyphs used by a secret society. (Documents from Archives nationales, Paris, F/7 Police Générale 6684, Sociétés secrètes, Dossier 4)

A meeting of the Carbonari, as imagined by a contemporary illustrator. (Private Collection/Archives Charmet/Bridgeman Images)

A drawing supplied to the French police by an informer, supposedly of daggers being forged by French and Italian secret societies for the murder of European monarchs. (Documents from Archives nationales, Paris, F/7 Police Générale 6684, Sociétés secrètes, Dossier 4)

General Alexei Arakcheev, by an anonymous artist, 1830s. (© Fine Art Images/AGE Fotostock)

Russian political prisoners in the dungeons of the Schlusselburg fortress. (Everett Collection Historical/Alamy)

The Peter and Paul fortress in St Petersburg. (RIA Novosti)

Count Alexander von Benckendorff, head of the notorious Third Section. Portrait by Yegor Bottman. (Fine Art Images/AGE Fotostock)

Europe in 1789
GREAT BRITAIN
Glasgow
Edinburgh
North Sea
Belfast
Atlantic Ocean
Dublin
DENMA
Bantry Bay
Manchester
Birmingham
Norwich
London
NETHERLANDS
Boulogne
Brussels
Austrian Netherlands
Koblen
Frankfurt
Main
Paris
Strasbourg
WÜRTTEMBERG
BADEN
FRANCE
Bay of Biscay
SWIS
CONF
Geneva
Lyon
Milan
Turin
Genoa
PORTUGAL
SPAIN
KINGDOM OF SARDINIA
Madrid
Lisbon
CORSICA
SARDINIA
Trafalgar
Mediterranean Se

SWEDEN
St Petersburg
Baltic Sea
Moscow
Mittau
RUSSIAN EMPIRE
Friedland
PRUSSIA
Berlin
POLAND
Warsaw
SAXONY
Pillnitz
Jena
Krakow
EMPIRE
BAVARIA
Vienna
AUSTRIA
Buda
Pest
HABSBURG POSSESSIONS
HUNGARY
Venice
Black Sea
OTTOMAN EMPIRE
Adriatic Sea
Constantinople
Rome
Naples
KINGDOM OF NAPLES AND SICILY
Palermo
Malta

Europe in 1815
GREAT BRITAIN
Glasgow
Edinburgh
North Sea
Atlantic Ocean
Belfast
Dublin
Manchester
Birmingham
Bristol
London
The Hague
HOLLAND
Brussels
Aix-la-
Paris
Saumur
FRANCE
BADEN
Belfort
La Rochelle
Bay of Biscay
Geneva
Lyon
Bordeaux
SAVOY
PIEDMONT
Turin
Grenoble
Marseille
PORTUGAL
SPAIN
Madrid
Lisbon
CORSICA
SARDINIA
Cádiz
Mediterranean

St Petersburg
SWEDEN
Dorpat
Moscow
Baltic Sea
RUSSIAN EMPIRE
Vilna
Danzig
PRUSSIA
Posen
Warsaw
Berlin
KINGDOM OF POLAND
GALICIA
Kharkov
Kiev
SAXONY
Töplitz
Karlsbad
Troppau
Krakow
Pressburg
Vienna
AUSTRIA
Buda
Pest
AUSTRIAN EMPIRE
HUNGARY
Transylvania
MOLDAVIA
Odessa
Laibach
Venice
Bologna
WALLACHIA
Black Sea
Macerata
LE MARCHE
Adriatic Sea
OTTOMAN EMPIRE
Constantinople
Rome
Naples
KINGDOM OF THE TWO SICILIES
Janina
MOREA
Palermo
Malta

Preface

The Battle of Waterloo, Napoleon's final nemesis, also marked the defeat of the forces unleashed by the French Revolution of 1789. This had challenged the foundations of the whole social order and every political structure in Europe. It had opened a Pandora's Box of boundless possibilities, and horrors: the sacred was profaned, the law trampled, a king and his queen judicially murdered, and thousands of men, women and children massacred or guillotined for no good reason. The two and a half decades of warfare that followed saw thrones toppled, states abolished and institutions of every sort undermined as the Revolution's subversive ideas swept across Europe and its colonies.

The reordering of the Continent by those who triumphed over Napoleon in 1815 was intended to reverse all this. The return to a social order based on throne and altar was meant to restore the old Christian values. The Concert of Europe, a mutual pact between the rulers of the major powers, was designed to ensure that such things could never happen again.

Yet the decades that followed were dominated by the fear that the Revolution lived on, and could break out once more at any moment. Letters and diaries of the day abound in imagery of volcanic eruption engulfing the entire social and political order, and express an almost pathological dread that dark forces were at work undermining the moral fabric on which that order rested. This struck me as curious, and I began to investigate.

The deeper I delved, the more it appeared that this panic was, to some extent, kept alive by the governments of the day. I also became aware of the degree to which the presumed need to safeguard the political and social order facilitated the introduction of new methods of control and repression. I was reminded of more recent instances where the generation of fear in the population – of capitalists, Bolsheviks, Jews, fascists, Islamists – has proved useful to those in power, and has led to restrictions on the freedom of the individual by measures meant to protect him from the supposed threat. A desire to satisfy my curiosity about what I thought was a historic cultural phenomenon gradually took on a more serious purpose, as I realised that the subject held enormous relevance to the present.

I have nevertheless refrained from drawing attention to this in the text, resisting the temptation, strong at times, to suggest parallels between Prince Metternich and Tony Blair, or George W. Bush and the Russian tsars. Leaving aside the bathos this would have involved, I felt readers would derive more fun from drawing their own.

In order to avoid cluttering the text with distracting reference numbers, I have placed all notes relating to quotations and facts contained in a given paragraph under a single one, positioned at the end of that paragraph. For the sake of simplicity, I have used the Gregorian calendar throughout when referring to Russian events and sources. I have not been as consistent on the transliteration of Russian names, using those versions with which I believe the reader will be most familiar – the Golitsyn family have appeared in Latin script for over three hundred years as Galitzine, and I have therefore stuck to that spelling, which they still use themselves. Translations of quotations from books in languages other than English are mine, with some assistance in the case of German.

Lack of time prevented me from spending as much of it in archives as I would have liked, and I was therefore obliged to seek the assistance of others. I should like to thank Pauline Grousset for following up some of my leads at the Archives Nationales in Paris; Veronika Hyden-Hanscho for pursuing various trails in the Viennese archives on my behalf; Philipp Rauh for reading through a large number of books in German; Thomas Clausen for his enthusiastic trawl through the archives in Stuttgart, Wiesbaden and Darmstadt; Hubert Czyżewski for his diligent work in the National Archive at Kew; Sue Sutton for further searches on my behalf at Kew; and Jennifer Irwin for her research in the Public Record Office of Northern Ireland.

I would also like to extend my thanks to Chris Clark for his guidance on matters German, to Michael Burleigh for moral support at a moment when the surrealism of my subject began to make me doubt my own sanity, to Charlotte Brudenell for drawing my attention to the eruption of Mount Tambora, and to Shervie Price for reading the manuscript.

I owe a great debt of gratitude to my editor Arabella Pike, for her patience and her extraordinary faith in and enthusiasm for my work; to Robert Lacey, whose meticulous and intelligent editing is unmatched; and to Helen Ellis, who makes the uphill task of promoting books a pleasure. I am also deeply indebted to my agent and friend Gillon Aitken, for his unflagging support. Finally, I would like to thank my wife Emma for her patience and understanding, and her love.

Adam Zamoyski
May 2014

traced officers [illegible] [illegible] [illegible] [illegible] [illegible] [illegible] [illegible] [illegible] up [illegible] of my finds in the Archives Nationales in Paris. [illegible] [illegible] [illegible] [illegible] various [illegible] in the [illegible] [illegible] [illegible] [illegible] [illegible] [illegible] [illegible] [illegible] [illegible] [illegible] in Germany. Then [illegible] for [illegible] [illegible] the archives in [illegible] [illegible] and [illegible]. Hubert [illegible] for his diligent work in the National Archive at Kew, [illegible] [illegible] for further [illegible] on my behalf at Kew, and [illegible] for his research in the [illegible] [illegible] of [illegible] Ireland.

I would like to extend my thanks to [illegible] for [illegible] [illegible] [illegible] Michael [illegible] for [illegible] support and [illegible] [illegible] [illegible] [illegible] [illegible] [illegible] [illegible] [illegible] [illegible] [illegible] [illegible] my [illegible] to the [illegible] [illegible] [illegible] [illegible] for reading the manuscript.

I owe a great debt of gratitude to my editor, [illegible] [illegible], for her [illegible] and her extraordinary [illegible] [illegible] [illegible] [illegible] [illegible] [illegible] intelligent [illegible] [illegible] [illegible] [illegible] [illegible] [illegible] [illegible] [illegible] [illegible] [illegible] [illegible] [illegible] [illegible] [illegible]. Finally, I would [illegible] [illegible] [illegible] [illegible] [illegible] [illegible] [illegible].

[illegible] Adam [illegible]
[illegible]

1

Exorcism

On Wednesday, 9 August 1815, HMS *Northumberland* weighed anchor off Plymouth and set sail for the island of St Helena in the South Atlantic, bearing away from Europe the man who had dominated it for the best part of two decades. All those who had lived in fear of the 'Ogre' heaved sighs of relief. 'Unfortunately,' wrote the philosopher Joseph de Maistre, 'it is only his person that has gone, and he has left us his morals. His genius could at least control the demons he had unleashed, and order them to do only that degree of harm that he required of them: those demons are still with us, and now there is nobody with the power to harness them.'[1]

The man in question, Napoleon Bonaparte, former Emperor of the French, had said as much himself. 'After I go,' he had declared to one of his ministers, 'the revolution, or rather the ideas which inspired it, will resume their work with renewed force.' As he paced the deck with what the captain of the seventy-four-gun man-of-war, Charles Ross, described as 'something between a waddle and a swagger', he appeared untroubled by any thought of the demons he was leaving behind. He was more concerned with his treatment at the hands of the British to whom he had surrendered, who refused to acknowledge his title. He was addressed as 'General Buonaparte', and accorded no more than the honours due to a prisoner of that rank. Two days earlier, protesting vigorously, he had been unceremoniously transferred from HMS

Bellerophon, which had brought him to the shores of England, to the *Northumberland*, in which Rear-Admiral Sir George Cockburn, commander of the flotilla that was to convey him to his new abode, had hoisted his flag. He had been subjected to a thorough search on coming aboard and his baggage was turned over – Captain Ross noted that he had 'a very rich service of Plate, and perhaps the most costly and beautiful service of porcelain ever made, a small Field Library, a middling stock of clothes, and about Four Thousand Napoleons in Money', which was confiscated and sent to the British Treasury. Dignity had never been Napoleon's strong suit, and his attempts to elicit the honours due to his imperial status were doomed. Nor did he elicit much sympathy outside the group of devoted followers who had elected to share his captivity. On first meeting him, Captain Ross found him 'sallow' and 'pot-bellied', and thought him 'altogether a very nasty, priest-like looking fellow'. Closer acquaintance as they set sail did nothing to soften his view. Admiral Cockburn described his habit of eating with his fingers and his manners in general as 'uncouth'.[2]

Napoleon and six of his entourage, which, with domestics and the children of some of his companions, totalled twenty-seven, dined at the captain's table, along with the admiral and the colonel of the regiment of foot which was to guard him. He soon abandoned his efforts to 'assume improper consequence' by, for instance, trying to embarrass the British officers into removing their hats when he did, or into leaving the dinner table when he rose. After dinner he would play chess with members of his own entourage, and whist or vingt-et-un with the British officers, from whom he took English lessons and whom he willingly entertained with accounts of the more sensational episodes of his life, particularly his Egyptian and Russian campaigns, often going into lengthy explanations and self-justifications. He was sometimes listless and absent, and occasionally indisposed through seasickness or the other discomforts of shipboard life, but on the whole he was cheerful and gave the impression of having left behind not only his ambitions, but all concern for the future of the continent he had held in thrall for so long. On the evening of 11 September, five weeks into the voyage and less than three months since he had stood at the head of a formidable army on the field of Waterloo, he read aloud for over two hours to the assembled company from a book of Persian tales.[3]

That same evening, the man who had contributed most to his downfall, Tsar Alexander of Russia, was giving thanks to the Lord at the end of what he professed had been the most beautiful day of his life. On a plain beside the small town of Vertus in the Champagne region of France, he had staged an extravagant display of military might and religious commitment, meant to herald the dawning of a new era of universal peace and harmony. It had commenced the day before, with a parade of over 150,000 of his troops and 520 pieces of artillery which went through their paces 'with all the precision of a machine', according to the Duke of Wellington. This was followed by a gargantuan dinner prepared by the famous chef Carême, lent to the tsar for the occasion by the gourmet prince de Talleyrand. The three hundred guests, who included the Emperor of Austria and the King of Prussia, as well as a glittering array of diplomats, generals and ministers, sat down at trestle tables under a marquee in the garden of a local physician, Dr Poisson, in whose house Alexander had set up his quarters. As the locality had been ravaged by war, the food for the banquet and the victuals for the troops had to be carted in from Paris.[4]

On 11 September, the feast of the patron saint of Russia St Alexander Nevsky and the tsar's nameday, the troops reassembled and formed squares around seven altars erected on the same plain overnight on the pattern of a Greek Orthodox cross. Alexander rode up to the central one, dismounted and bowed his head. At this, the priests officiating at all seven altars began a Mass conducted in unison lasting more than three hours. Alexander went from altar to altar, led by the sentimental novelist turned religious mystic Baroness Julie von Krüdener, theatrically clad in a long black robe. He was entirely absorbed in the service, and 'his attitude bore the appearance of a real devotedness and the humility of an earnest Christian', according to an English lady present.[5]

Alexander saw the parade and the service as an event of cosmological significance, marking not only victory over the devils conjured by the Revolution and Napoleon, but also the death of the old world and the birth of a new one. He had been on a long spiritual odyssey, and had reached a point at which he recognised the absolute primacy of God. The parade on the plain of Vertus was a demonstration of both his own physical might and its submission to the Divine Will. He mentally associated himself and the two other monarchs who had vanquished Napoleon, the Emperor Francis I of Austria and King Frederick William III of Prussia, with the three wise kings of the Epiphany recognising the sovereignty of Christ. He wanted to give substance to this by engaging them, and all rulers, to confront the evils of the day with a new kind of government, one based on a legitimacy derived from the Word of God. Leaving aside the mechanics of this for later elaboration, he proposed that they all sign an undertaking to govern in a new spirit, a Holy Covenant ('*Sainte Alliance*' has traditionally been rendered in English as 'Holy Alliance', but the French word actually refers to the scriptural Holy Covenant) binding them to acknowledge the kingdom of God on earth.[6]

The original draft, couched in apocalyptic language, envisaged a fusion of Europe into a Christian federation, effectively 'one nation' with 'one army'. This was amended at the insistence of Francis and Frederick William, but the final version nevertheless proclaimed that the sovereigns had 'acquired the conviction that it is necessary to base the direction of policy adopted by the Powers in their mutual relations on the sublime truths taught by the eternal religion of God the redeemer'. They professed their 'unshakable determination to take as the rule of their conduct, both in the administration of their respective States as in their political relations with all other governments, only the precepts of that holy faith, the precepts of justice, charity and peace, which, far from being applicable only to private life, should on the contrary have a direct influence on the decisions of princes and guide all their actions'.[7]

The Emperor Francis was sceptical; Frederick William thought it ridiculous; the British foreign secretary Lord Castlereagh and the Duke of Wellington had difficulty in controlling their mirth when the tsar showed it to them. They were all nevertheless prepared to humour what they saw as a harmless whim, 'a high-sounding nothing' in the words of the Austrian foreign minister Prince Metternich. The document was not a public act, and they hoped it would remain buried in the archives of their chancelleries, fearing that publication would make them appear ridiculous. It was duly signed on 26 September, the eve of the anniversary of his coronation, by Alexander, Francis and Frederick William. With time, on the tsar's insistence, it would be signed by every monarch in Europe except King George III of England (on constitutional grounds) and the pope (on doctrinal ones). What none of them fully appreciated was how much importance the tsar attached to it.[8]

Alexander was the only European ruler of his time to have received an education worth speaking of. It was an unusual education, ill suited to his predestined role as autocrat of a huge empire, and it added to the contradictions inherent in his position and set him apart from his brother monarchs. His grandmother, the Empress Catherine II, had taken great care in selecting tutors and meant to direct his educational programme herself, but Alexander's French-language teacher, the Swiss philosopher Frédéric César de La Harpe, soon took over. La Harpe inculcated his own view of the world in the young prince, refuting the notion of Divine Right and teaching him that all men were equal.[9]

Catherine had hoped to cut her son and Alexander's father, Paul, out of the succession, and therefore insisted that the boy spend most of his time at her court rather than with his parents. Not only his education but his personal inclination made him detest this corrupt and immoral, typically eighteenth-century court, and he valued all the more the brief moments he could spend with his mother and father, whose establishment at the palace of Gatchina was homely and, given that they were, respectively, wholly and three-quarters

German by blood, comfortingly *gemütlich*. While his grandmother primed him for the exercise of power, he dreamed of leading a quiet life as a private citizen somewhere in Germany.

Catherine had been afraid that Alexander would be chased by women and might turn into a libertine, so she insisted that he be brought up in total ignorance of 'the mysteries of love'. His entourage was sworn to prudery, and when out on a walk one day the teenage Alexander encountered two dogs coupling, the tutor accompanying him explained that they were fighting. Yet he was married off at an early age, to a German princess, and although he fell in love with his child bride, he found it difficult to consummate the marriage. His subsequent love life was dogged by feelings of guilt, and he would come to see the early deaths of all his children as God's punishment.[10]

When Catherine died in November 1796, her son Paul ascended the throne and promptly embarked on a course that was to make him one of the most unpopular rulers in Russian history. He banned almost the entire canon of French literature, and established censorship offices at every port to scour imported goods for subversion. He proscribed foreign music and the use of words such as 'citizen', 'club', 'society' and 'revolution'. Russians were forbidden to study abroad. He issued imperial decrees, which he frequently revised, governing manners and mealtimes, hairstyles, the wearing of moustaches, beards and sideburns, and clothes. People would suddenly learn that the style of their garments had been banned, and would have to frantically cut off tails and lapels, add or remove pockets, and pin hats into the prescribed shape before they could go out.

Gradually, Alexander came to realise that he must assume the responsibility fate had reserved for him. 'I believe that if my turn to rule ever came, instead of going abroad, I would do better to work at making my country free and thereby to preserve it from being in the future used as a plaything by lunatics,' he wrote to La Harpe. He began to see his life's task as that of transforming the Russian autocracy into a constitutional monarchy and freeing the serfs. His turn came in

1801, following Paul's assassination, in which he was passively complicit. He liberated political prisoners, repealed much of his father's repressive legislation, lifted censorship and restrictions on travel, brought in educational reforms, founded universities, set up a commission to codify the laws, and commissioned his friend Aleksandr Vorontsov to draw up a charter for the Russian people modelled on the French Declaration of the Rights of Man.[11]

In 1804, when negotiating an alliance with Britain, he put forward a project for the transformation of Europe into a harmonious federation that would make war redundant. In 1807, when he signed a treaty with Napoleon at Tilsit, he believed that he was entering into a grand alliance of the Continent's superpowers to ensure peace and progress. He gradually changed his view, and came to see the Emperor of the French as evil. He endured Napoleon's invasion of Russia in 1812 with readings from the Bible and fervent prayer as his army was defeated and Moscow burned, and celebrated the French army's expulsion with thanks to the Lord. Instead of making peace with Napoleon, a peace he could have dictated to great advantage for Russia (as many in his entourage wished), Alexander prosecuted the war. 'More than ever, I resign myself to the will of God and submit blindly to His decrees,' he announced in January 1813 as he set out to liberate Europe from the French 'ogre': he was convinced that he was merely a tool in the hands of the Almighty. Once he had achieved his purpose of forcing Napoleon to abdicate, he demonstrated (in a way that was to cost the allies dear in 1815) the spirit of Christian charity by granting him generous terms and sovereign status on the Mediterranean island of Elba.[12]

While he continued to hold Orthodox services, Alexander sometimes combined them, as on 10 April 1814, when according to both the Julian and the Gregorian calendars Easter fell on the same day, with Catholic and Protestant ones. In London, which the victorious allies visited following the defeat of Napoleon, he attended Bible Society meetings and communed with Quakers. In Baden on his way back to Russia he was introduced to the German Pietist Johann Heinrich Jung

Stilling, with whom he held long discussions on how to bring about the kingdom of God on earth.

Over the next months Alexander would follow a path he believed to be dictated by God. He was frustrated by the practical difficulties he encountered at the Congress of Vienna, and believed that Napoleon's escape from Elba was God's punishment for the venial behaviour of its participants, himself included. At Heilbronn, on his way to join Wellington before Waterloo, he met Baroness Krüdener, who convinced him that he was the elect of God, and that he must concentrate on carrying out His will. Alexander was at the time absorbed in a book by the German philosopher Eckartshausen, which put forward the thesis that some people were 'light-bearers' endowed with the capacity to see Divine Truth through the clouds obscuring it from the multitude. That and the baroness's words only reinforced his sense of being marked out by the Almighty. They knelt together to give thanks on hearing news of Napoleon's defeat at Waterloo, and she followed him to Paris afterwards, moving into a house next door to the Élysée Palace where he took up his quarters. They saw each other every day, praying and holding often bizarre services, culminating in the spiritual jamboree on the plain of Vertus.[13]

Wellington, Castlereagh and many others thought the tsar had gone a little mad. Metternich had long regarded him as a child in thrall to dangerous enthusiasms. A cynical pragmatist, the Austrian foreign minister had no time for such nonsense, confident as he was that with Napoleon removed from the scene everything would return to normal. But in 1815 Alexander was probably the only one among the Continent's monarchs and chief ministers who understood something of the longings and anxieties agitating European minds, and that many wanted something more than just peace, order and a full stomach.

His Holy Alliance was a genuine attempt to put the world to rights. He believed that only a system built on Christian morality could hope to bind the wounds opened up by the events of the past quarter of a century and restore harmony to a profoundly fragmented world. And although his approach may have been naïve and his solution half-baked, he alone among the monarchs and ministers who fashioned the Vienna settlement appreciated that no peace treaty, however equitable, could alone hope to bridge the chasm that had opened up in 1789.

2

Fear

News of the fall of the Bastille on 14 July 1789 had had an electrifying effect as it travelled across Europe and beyond, over the Atlantic to the United States and the European colonies of the Americas. Although the event did not in itself amount to much more than an alarming outbreak of rioting, mutiny and mob rule, it was universally interpreted as standing for something else, and accorded immense significance. The English statesman Charles James Fox declared it to be 'the greatest event that ever happened in the World'. Rather than wait and observe further developments before reaching an opinion, most educated people immediately took up one of two diametrically opposed positions. It was as though they had seen a long-awaited signal.[1]

To those who identified with the ideological canon of the eighteenth-century European Enlightenment, the grim old fortress (which was largely redundant) was an emotionally charged symbol of the oppressive and iniquitous *ancien régime* whose institutions and practices were unacceptable to the modern mind. It stood for everything that was wrong with the world. Its fall was therefore seen as the harbinger of a new age, immeasurably more just and moral in every way than the existing one. There was nothing logical or reasoned about their response.

'Although the Bastille had certainly not been a threat of any sort to any inhabitant of Petersburg,' noted the French ambassador to the

Russian court, 'I find it difficult to express the enthusiasm aroused among the shopkeepers, merchants, townsfolk and some young people of a higher class by the fall of this state prison.' He went on to describe how people embraced in the street as though they had been 'delivered from some excessively heavy chain that had been weighing them down'. Even the young Grand Duke Alexander greeted the news with enthusiasm.[2]

From London, the barrister and legal reformer Sir Samuel Romilly wrote to his Genevan friend Étienne Dumont: 'I am sure I need not tell you how much I have rejoiced at the Revolution that has taken place. I think of nothing else, and please myself with endeavouring to guess at some of the important consequences which must follow throughout Europe ... the Revolution has produced a very sincere and very general joy here ... even all the newspapers, without one exception, though they are not conducted by the most liberal or the most philosophical of men, join in sounding forth the praises of the Parisians, and in rejoicing at an event so important for mankind.'[3]

This view was echoed in Germany, where poets such as Klopstock and Hölderlin hailed the Revolution as the greatest act of the century, and numerous Germans flocked to Paris to breathe the air of freedom. 'If the Revolution should fail, I should regard it as one of the greatest misfortunes that had ever befallen the human race,' wrote the Prussian civil servant Friedrich von Gentz in a letter to a friend on 5 December 1790. 'It is philosophy's first practical triumph, the first instance of a form of government based on principles and on a coherent and consistent system. It is the hope as well as the consolation for so many of the old evils under which humanity groans.'[4]

To the young in particular, the sudden explosion of energy in the French capital held enormous appeal, and it set their collective imagination on fire. 'A visionary world seemed to open up' to the young poet Robert Southey, and according to Mary Wollstonecraft 'all the passions and prejudices of Europe were instantly set afloat'. The news from Paris was greeted with almost religious fervour, and William Wordsworth spoke for many of his generation when he wrote: 'Bliss was it in that dawn to be alive'. The Second Coming could hardly have elicited greater ecstasy.[5]

The excitement was driven by emotions of an essentially spiritual nature – similar to those which would drive so many young people in the second half of the twentieth century to embrace without questioning a 'socialism' they were usually at a loss to define, but which they believed held out the promise of a better world. Convinced as they were that it was the 'right' way forward for humanity, many of those who hailed the French Revolution would not only seek to justify its worst atrocities, they would brand those who did not share their faith as 'enemies of the people'.

To these, news of the upheaval in Paris came not only as a terrible shock, but as confirmation that a long-prepared onslaught on the ideological basis of their universe had begun. Monarchs reacted with predictable outrage. The British *chargé d'affaires* in Vienna reported that the Austrian Emperor went into 'transports of passion' and uttered 'the most violent Menaces of Vengeance' when he heard the news. The King of Sweden had not been able to sleep after reading reports of the goings-on in Paris, and the Empress of Russia had stamped her foot in rage.[6]

Barely more measured were the reactions of many who had less to lose. 'If the French delirium is not properly repressed, it may prove more or less fatal to the heart of Europe,' the philosopher Baron Melchior Grimm warned, 'for the pestilential air must inevitably ravage and destroy everything it approaches.' In England, Edmund Burke thundered against the 'Venom' being spewed out by 'the Reptile Souls moving in the Dirt of the Obscure Vices in which they were generated', as he described the French revolutionaries. Even in far-away North America the news from France divided those who, in the words of Edmund Quincy of Massachusetts, saw it 'as another Star in the East – the harbinger of peace and good-will on earth', from those for whom it was 'a baleful comet that "from its horrid hair shook pestilence and war", shed its influences for good or evil upon the New World as well as the Old'. 'It inspired terror or joy, according as the eyes which watched its progress looked for its issues of life or of death in faith or in fear,' he concluded.[7]

A notable feature of the gulf which had opened up was that while the discussion, if one can call it that, was conducted between people of considerable intellectual standing, it was carried on along almost entirely irrational lines. While partisans of the Revolution praised its vices as well as its virtues in poetic and quasi-religious terms, its enemies responded in the language of the Inquisition.

In his *Reflections on the Revolution in France*, published in 1790, Edmund Burke warned that everything being perpetrated in Paris violated fundamental laws and undermined the twin pillars of religion and property on which the social order of Europe rested. History would vindicate his prediction that the road the revolutionaries had taken would lead them to commit untold horrors and to the eventual emergence of a brutal dictatorship. But long before this happened, his tone would change and his diatribes against the Revolution degenerate into hysterical rants.

Another prominent defender of the *ancien régime*, the Savoyard nobleman, lawyer, diplomat and philosopher Joseph de Maistre, propounded a spiritual view of the events. A devout Catholic, he had in his youth been an enthusiastic supporter of the American Revolution, and even welcomed the fall of the Bastille before identifying the evil lurking behind it. He now condemned the entire canon of the Enlightenment, arguing that God presided over a natural order of things, departure from which was perverse, and that the Catholic faith was 'the mother of all good and real knowledge in the world'. He believed the eighteenth century would come to be seen by posterity 'as one of the most shameful epochs in the history of the human mind'. As for the French Revolution, it was, according to him, an 'inexplicable delirium', 'an atrocity', 'an impudent prostitution of reason' and an insult to the concepts of justice and virtue. 'There is in the French revolution,' he concluded, 'a *satanic* character which distinguishes it from everything we have seen and, perhaps from everything we will ever see.'[8]

Like those of Burke, which sold in great quantities and were translated into the principal European languages, the writings of Maistre echoed and gave form to the feelings of many who had viewed the progress of the Enlightenment with suspicion. As they watched events unfold during the 1790s they were confirmed in all their earlier objections to the writings of Voltaire, Rousseau and other eighteenth-century philosophers. With the benefit of hindsight, they could chart how the spread of their teachings had led to the catastrophe which had shattered their world.

While some saw it as an unfortunate process fostered by impious or misguided intellectuals, others saw it all in terms of a conspiracy against not only the established political order but against the very bases of European society and civilisation. Voltaire had waged a life-long war which verged on the pathological against the Catholic Church, which he referred to as '*l'Infâme*' (the infamous one). His influence was clearly discernible in the virulently anti-Christian tenor of the Revolution. Some related this not just to his writings and the secularising influences of the Enlightenment: Louis de Bonald saw everything that had happened since the first breaths of the Reformation in the fifteenth century as a gradual decline into the abyss. Others reached further back, tracing the rot to Jan Hus, John Wycliffe and the Lollards.[9]

There were those who pointed out that the date of the storming of the Bastille, 14 July, was the same as that on which Jerusalem fell to the First Crusade in 1099, suggesting some kind of revenge of the Infidel. To the more fanciful, the fall of the French monarchy was the outcome of 'the curse of the Templars', who had been destroyed by it nearly five centuries earlier. The Templars no longer existed, but there was a theory that while awaiting execution in the Bastille in 1314, the last Grand Master of the Order had founded four Masonic lodges to avenge its dissolution and his death on the French royal family.

Freemasonry had originated in Scotland at the beginning of the eighteenth century, spread to every country in Europe, and grew rapidly. As the movement attracted the intellectual elites, its membership was overwhelmingly secularist and freethinking, a loose brotherhood vaguely dedicated to the betterment of humanity through the spreading of reason, education and humanist values. Its members were grouped in lodges which met to listen to lectures and discuss anything from social problems to the latest fashions in the arts. Some came together for purposes of social networking, others in order to pursue more sensual interests such as drinking or sex. There was ritual involved, much of it extremely silly, purporting to have medieval or even Biblical origins. Freemasons often met in temples, crypts or artificial grottos, which added a whiff of the occult, and initiation rites involved blindfolding novices who were made to swear solemn oaths amid a panoply of gothick props, including cloaks, daggers, axes, burning braziers and cups of red wine symbolising blood – although real blood was sometimes drawn too.

As the lodges were founded by groups of individuals rather than by any organised system of delegation or procuracy, they evolved markedly different styles. In France, Freemasonry was generally social and often frivolous. In countries such as Poland and Russia it had more to do with aping French fashions than anything else. But in Germany it was taken very seriously. It reflected and partially overlapped religious trends seeking a return to a 'purer' form of Christianity and genuinely aspired to some kind of spirituality.

In 1776 Adam Weishaupt, Professor of Canon Law at the University of Ingolstadt in Bavaria, started a student society, the Order of Perfectibles. There was nothing remarkable in this, as German universities pullulated with such confraternities. In 1778 he changed its name to the Order of the Illuminati, and introduced grades, along with an elaborate system of signs and passwords. There were also synonyms for people and places: Bavaria was 'Greece', Munich 'Athens' and Weishaupt himself 'Spartacus'.

In 1780 a new recruit, Baron Adolf Franz von Knigge, alias 'Philo', began to transform the Order, imposing on it his own doctrine that all political states were unnatural and perverse creations which should be swept away. They should be replaced by a miasma of mutual respect and love which would bring about universal happiness. This supposed panacea to the world's ills attracted large numbers of supporters, and seeped into the Masonic network of Germany, and thence into those of Austria, Bohemia, Hungary, northern Italy and even France. Adepts included Goethe, Schiller, Mozart, Herder and many other notables.

In 1785 the Elector of Bavaria suppressed the Order, thereby according it a notoriety and validation it hardly deserved. Spine-chilling tales began to circulate as to its occult aims. An anonymous book entitled *Essai sur la secte des Illuminés*, published in Paris on the eve of the Revolution, traced the origins of the sect to the Freemasons and dwelt with evident glee on its induction rituals and ordeals, describing how occult symbols were painted on the body of the novice in his own blood, and so on. It revealed that the Illuminati had a castle outside Paris with underground *oubliettes* into which those who had betrayed its secrets were thrown and forgotten. The author affirmed that the sect 'has conceived the plan of taking over minds, and of conquering not kingdoms, not provinces, but the human spirit', with the ultimate aim of destroying all thrones and governments, and then society itself. It operated through a network of circles in every country, each controlling a cluster of subsidiary circles, which he listed meticulously, giving the impression that the whole of Europe was comprehensively covered.[10]

This chimed with a fashion for the occult and a fascination with ancient Orphic and Egyptian cults, with Eleusinian and Rosicrucian 'mysteries', and with secret societies of every kind, whose most famous expression is Mozart's *Magic Flute*. In Germany it gave rise to a literary genre, the *Bundesroman*, to which Schiller, Jean-Paul Richter and Goethe contributed works. Its most commercially successful product was Carl Grosse's novel *Der Genius* (1791–95), whose aristocratic young protagonist's picaresque adventures include not only much curious sexual activity but also involvement in an order which compels him to assassinate the King of Spain. Such books helped to propagate a belief in the ubiquity and omnipotence of the secret societies allegedly operating in the shadows, and a shelf of supposedly more factual publications established a connection between them and politics, confirmed in the minds of many by the fact that a majority of the prime movers of the French Revolution had been Freemasons. Some asserted that the ideological powerhouse of the Revolution, the *Club des Jacobins*, named after the former Dominican convent they met in, was actually an offshoot of Freemasonry. 'The political committees that gave rise to the Jacobin Club had their origins in Illuminism which started in Germany, and, far from having been snuffed out, they are operating underground and have become all the more dangerous,' wrote Leopold Alois Hoffmann. He pointed out that one of the leading Illuminati, Johann Christoph Bode, had visited Paris two years before the outbreak of the Revolution to confer with French Freemasons, and that the prominent revolutionary the marquis de Mirabeau had visited Berlin shortly before the fall of the Bastille.[11]

When, on 16 March 1792, King Gustavus III of Sweden was shot at a masked ball, it was evident to many all over Europe who was behind it. Later that year, when the Duke of Brunswick, a former Freemason who commanded the royalist forces invading France to crush the Revolution, drew back after the inconclusive Battle of Valmy, leaving the revolutionary army triumphant, it was again obvious that he had followed an occult order from above. A spate of sensationalist 'revelation' literature spoke of dark arts, secrets, spells and poison, and of their involvement in the unexpected deaths of various kings. The writers defended themselves against the charge of vagueness by hinting that their own lives were at risk, fuelling the growing myth of the 'sect's' omnipresence and omnipotence. While many of the books and pamphlets convinced only the converted, a wider readership was persuaded by an authoritative and seminal work by the former Jesuit Abbé Augustin Barruel.[12]

Barruel had been combating the Enlightenment in print since 1781, and kept up his critique in the first years of the Revolution, which he saw as God's punishment on the French for having tolerated and embraced its false philosophy. In 1792 he fled to England, where he published his two-volume *Mémoires pour servir à l'histoire du Jacobinisme*. It was reprinted six times in the space of a year and translated into all the major European languages, and continued in print for decades. Barruel's writing has a tone of authority that brooks no argument, and his assertions, extravagant and improbable as they might appear, carried conviction.

In the opening sentence, he declares that the French Revolution was the fruit of a vast conspiracy carried out by a sect which had latterly taken the name of Jacobins, whose aim was to overthrow all existing thrones and altars and unleash anarchy. According to him, it consisted of 300,000 active leaders manipulating a further two million. 'In this French Revolution, everything, including its most frightful crimes, was foreseen, premeditated, calculated, resolved, decreed,' he affirmed, 'everything was the consequence of the most profound perfidy, since everything was prepared and brought about by men who alone had knowledge of the conspiracy long planned in the secret societies, and who knew how to choose and bring on circumstances favourable to their plans.'[13]

Barruel believed it all began in the late 1720s, with Voltaire, who enlisted the support of Frederick II of Prussia and recruited D'Alembert and Diderot, who compiled the *Encyclopédie*, which under the guise of scientific knowledge and reason undermined religion, social hierarchy and most human institutions. The next step was the dissolution of the Jesuits, brought about by the manipulation of public opinion and statesmen. According to Barruel, the benign Freemasons interested in human welfare were the 'useful idiots' who helped destabilise society by creating spurious hierarchies and undermining existing institutions, above all the Church, with their pseudo-religious foolery. The Illuminati were more focused, and Weishaupt's philosophy more dangerous. Barruel defined it thus: 'Equality and liberty are the essential rights which man, in his original and primitive state, received from nature; the first blow to equality was dealt by property; the first attack on liberty by political society and governments; the only bases for both property and governments are the religious and civil laws; thus in order to re-establish man in his primitive rights of equality and liberty, one has to begin by destroying religion and civil society, and finish by abolishing property.'[14]

According to Barruel, the Illuminati were well organised and intelligent. In the interests of making useful converts to their cause they would gather information on persons of influence, meticulously recording their likes and dislikes, dietary preferences, sexual habits and so on, so as to be able to approach them in the most appropriate way, to manipulate them, and even blackmail them. They also meant to introduce women into their order, in two separate categories: one of virtuous high-born ladies who would help to make converts and raise money, the other of dissolute women and prostitutes who would pander to the needs of the members.

Barruel's book was not meant as history: it was a clarion call demanding action. He warned that 'the French Revolution is still no more than a trial of strength for the sect; its conspiracy covers the entire universe'. It was already preparing the subversion of other states, sending out envoys and using Masonic networks in countries the French were intending to invade – he claimed there were five hundred adepts in London waiting for the signal to act. 'It is still possible to crush this sect which has sworn to destroy your God, your motherland, your families and the whole edifice of your communities,' he warned his readers, but time was running out and they must face up to the threat. 'The danger is certain, it is continuous, it is terrible, and it menaces each and every one of you,' he hectored.[15]

The Anglican minister and distinguished astronomer Francis Wollaston, Fellow of the Royal Society, wholeheartedly agreed. 'To the liberty and equality of original Freemasonry; to the fierce rancour of Voltaire and his self-called philosophers against Jesus Christ and his religion; to the democratic principles of Rousseau, and his visionary schemes about the origin of all government', the Jacobins had added 'the rage of Weishaupt and his pretended more enlightened followers, against all kings, or rather against all who under any title bear any rule among men.'[16]

If educated people could view what was taking place in such wildly conflicting ways, it is hardly surprising that the ignorant and those living in rural areas adopted even more extreme positions. While some embraced the new shibboleths of freedom and the sovereignty of the people as though they were a new religion, others saw them in terms of Satanic wickedness threatening everything they held dear. Rumour and imagination conjured dread of what one historian has recently described as 'the eighteenth-century equivalent of a Martian invasion'. The word 'Jacobin' joined those of 'Freemason' and 'Illuminato' in the conservative canon of horrors, and came to stand for any member of what was increasingly referred to as the 'sect'. Blind fear set the seal of veracity on untested assumptions, and in the prevailing psychological climate every coincidence had the power of proof: there is a point at which fear becomes a social pathology that floats entirely free of evidence. A powerful conviction took root in conservative thought that a vast conspiracy was afoot. The concept of an occult association working for the overthrow of the social order entered the imagination, never to leave it.[17]

Having alerted society to the danger, Barruel suggested how it should be met. As the Jacobins were waging 'a secret war of delusion, error and darkness' against the mind, people should respond with 'wisdom, truth and light'. As they were unleashing 'impiousness and corruption' against the faith, the faithful should respond with morality and virtue, and strive to convert the enemy. 'The Jacobins are waging on Princes and the Governments of nations a war of hatred of the law and society, a war of rage and destruction, I want you to oppose them with society, humanity and conservatism,' Barruel wrote.[18]

Princes and governments did not heed his advice. Their response to the events unfolding in France was dictated almost entirely by fear, and fear breeds irrationality and aggression. It thrives on the notion that aside from identifiable threats there are others lurking in the shadows. The need to uncover these unknown dangers and to identify them becomes compulsive. This, and the compulsion to strike back at the source of their fears, was to dominate their policies over much of the next half-century, and was to play a decisive role in transforming the way European societies ordered themselves.

3

Contagion

No European state was remotely prepared to meet the challenge posed by the French Revolution, let alone that suggested by Barruel and other conspiracy theorists. Rulers and ministers interfered minimally in the lives of the majority of their subjects: cities administered themselves, outside them a semblance of order was maintained by a combination of local nobles, parochial institutions, religious constraint and custom. Central organs of control barely existed. The French monarchy had introduced a force dedicated to maintaining order when, in 1544, it set up the *Maréchaussée* (marshalcy), a body of mounted men whose task was to keep roads safe and an eye on who was using them. Paris acquired police in 1667 to contain the plague then ravaging the country. Police commissioners were appointed in St Petersburg in 1718, Berlin in 1742, and Vienna in 1751. But the word 'police' is misleading.

In his monumental four-volume *Traité de la police*, published in Paris between 1705 and 1738, Nicolas de La Mare explained that 'police' meant the ordering of public space for the benefit of all who occupy it. The word encompassed the regulation of the width, length and layout of streets, the way they should be signposted, lit, repaired, swept and sprayed with water on hot days; how houses should be built and how they should be lived in so they did not present a danger to anyone (people should not place flowerpots on their window ledges lest they fall and cause injury). It stood for laying down precise instructions as to how food was to be produced, transported, processed and sold; how livestock was to be slaughtered and dressed; how and where fish could be caught, with what tackle, and how they were to be salted and preserved; how gardens were to be cultivated and what was to be grown in them; how firewood and coal were to be procured and stored; what precautions were to be taken against flooding; how industry was to be carried on in the urban space; how wine shops and eating houses were to be run; how standards of hygiene were to be maintained in brothels and prostitutes checked for disease – in other words, everything necessary to keep the citizens fed, healthy and safe.[1]

In the course of the eighteenth century the Paris police extended their brief, building and supervising markets, a stock exchange, a fire service, a veterinary school and a hospital. They regulated every trade, and obliged practitioners to wear their identifying *plaque*. They set up the Mont de Piété, a nationwide network of pawn shops that would not cheat the poor. They intervened in family disputes and put away troublemakers and brutal husbands. In the interests of containing the spread of venereal disease, they classified prostitutes – according to age; who had recruited them, how, when and where; by their state of health; their specialities and their clients – and expended much energy on catching unlicensed ones.[2]

Only rarely did governments extend the concept of 'police' to embrace the political. In the reign of Elizabeth I, Sir Francis Walsingham used 'intelligencers' to detect plots against her. Cardinals Richelieu and later Mazarin operated similar networks to deal with the dissident nobility of the *Fronde*. The Russian monarchy introduced laws to make its subjects denounce each other. The Habsburgs set up a regular secret police service in 1713. But what these bodies focused on was the detection of conspiracies by leagues of nobles against the ruler, not information on what his subjects thought. The established Churches were more concerned with such things, but as the state gradually took over from these as the guardian of morality and conscience, so the police began to take on a more sacerdotal role. It was only in the second half of the eighteenth century, when debate about the way the world was constituted and organised began to involve more than a tiny educated elite and the opinions of greater numbers of people began to matter, that the authorities applied themselves to the task of finding out what these might be.

In the interests of controlling the spread of undesirable attitudes, the Paris police confiscated unauthorised literature. Books which undermined the orthodox view on religion, the law, the monarchy, history, philosophy, science and morality might be banned, and were liable to seizure and burning. Their authors and publishers might be gaoled, but few were, most of those under threat preferring to spend a few months abroad, and enforcement of this legislation being among the police's least favourite tasks.[3]

The Paris police prided themselves on keeping abreast of what was going on in the capital. The routine inspection of inns, wine shops, eating houses and brothels yielded information on what was said and done within these establishments, while a network of spies, called *mouches* (flies) and later *mouchards*, provided additional information. One eighteenth-century lieutenant general of police allegedly boasted that when three people came together for a conversation, one of them was sure to be one of his agents. These showed a pronounced appetite for catching amorous priests or prominent noblemen *in flagrante*, and describing in graphic detail exactly what they did with their partners. Antoine de Sartine, lieutenant general of police during the reign of Louis XV, was particularly active in this respect, 'spying on the shameful secrets' of his subjects 'to amuse a king even more libertine than himself, with all the nudities of vice', in the words of a later commissioner of police who had immersed himself (with evident relish) in the reports.[4]

Both the lieutenant general of the police of Paris, who by the end of the century commanded some 1,200 men armed like soldiers, and the four *inspecteurs*, who marshalled the *mouches*, bought their posts from the crown, and their principal concern was to recoup that investment and make a fortune by accepting bribes. In the words of the historian Richard Cobb, whose knowledge of the subject was unmatched, the *inspecteur* 'was out for a quiet life, and asked only to be left alone with his pregnant girls, his drunks, his dead horses and run-over errand boys, his *filles de joie*, his runaway children, and his everlasting *plaques*'. The police were an administrative corporate concern rather than an instrument of state control. And if the capital was being more and more regulated and invigilated, this was not true of other towns, and rural areas never saw more than the occasional troop of *Maréchaussée* trotting down the road.[5]

The only other major state to have a police force was Austria, or rather the Habsburg monarchy. Following her defeat at the hands of Prussia in the mid-eighteenth century, the Empress Maria Theresa had felt an urgent need to modernise the administration of her dominions, which involved an extension of state control. She too felt a need to know what was being thought and said. While her police relied on spies, known as 'bluebottles', she had issued a direct appeal to her subjects to assist them by sending in anonymous information on anything they believed might be of interest, and the response was enthusiastic. Her successor Joseph II carried on in this vein, and created a police force unlike any other in Europe.[6]

It owed its structure to Johann Anton, Count von Pergen, who believed that the state could not function properly unless the government controlled every aspect of the lives of the emperor's subjects. They were therefore required to register by place of residence, and householders were made responsible for their lodgers and guests. Pergen wished to know everything they were doing, and his spies lurked in shops, coffee houses, gardens, theatres and any other place where people might meet. They were recruited from every class of society, and included members of the nobility as well as priests, doctors, shopkeepers, prostitutes and servants of all kinds. In addition, ordinary citizens were encouraged to report on their peers, and this practice became a vital element in the police's information-gathering work.[7]

The Emperor Joseph believed in shielding his subjects from what he saw as the false philosophy and 'fanaticism' of the Enlightenment. He circumscribed the educational system and in 1782 abolished the University of Graz. He strengthened an already strict censorship, which came naturally to him in view of his loathing for 'scribblers'. As well as covering the usual subjects such as religion and the monarchy, it was focused on promoting 'the right way of thinking'. He was wary of 'sects', as he referred to almost any association, from Masonic lodges to reading clubs, in the conviction that they spread 'errors'. Foreigners were the subject of intense suspicion, and they were watched assiduously, as were the clergy.[8]

Elsewhere in Europe, what police supervision there was tended to be restricted to towns and was in the hands of guilds and magistrates. In Italy, the only force fighting crime were *sbirri* employed by the senate of a city or regional potentates. They were variously described as 'infamous', 'profligate' and 'corrupt'; and their behaviour differed little from that of the brigands they were supposed to combat. Any need to impose order by force was met with troops, usually the ruler's guards stationed in the capital, or by some kind of more or less volunteer parish or corporate watch.[9]

In England, nothing much had changed in this field since the Middle Ages. According to the principle set down in the Statute of Winchester of 1285, every parish and city was responsible for policing itself. Magistrates, or Justices of the Peace, drawn from the propertied classes and often clergymen, appointed constables who were ordinary citizens serving yearly terms of office in rotation. The magistrates had the power to enrol additional constables and to issue warrants for the arrest of individuals. They could also order the dispersal of mobs by reading the Riot Act of 1714, and call on the country yeomanry, the militia or regular troops if they did not do so within the hour. The other regional authority was the lord lieutenant, a Tudor creation. Usually the foremost landowner in the county, he represented the crown and presided over the meetings of the county's magistrates.

The administration of law and order in towns was on a similarly archaic basis, and only in London, the most populous city in Europe, had it been modernised, by Sir John Fielding, half-brother of the novelist Henry, a Justice of the Peace who in 1748 took over as chief magistrate, sitting at Bow Street. He persuaded retiring constables to stay on, and built up a force of some 150 experienced and salaried 'runners', as they were known, supplemented by over eight hundred volunteers. The inadequacy of these forces was exposed by the Gordon Riots of 1780, when a mob went on the rampage. It was only after several days and the intervention of troops that order was restored: 210 rioters were killed and 245 wounded, of whom seventy-five subsequently died. The physical damage caused to the capital was, according to a recent study, not surpassed until the Blitz in the 1940s. In 1785 the government introduced a Bill to establish a regular police force, but this was thrown out by Parliament: there was a deep-seated feeling that such a body would be an affront to English liberties.[10]

The ease with which the Revolution had taken place in France demonstrated that for all the boasting about knowing everything that went on in Paris, the authorities had been taken entirely unawares. (This was grist to the mill of those who believed in the Illuminati conspiracy, who argued that the Revolution could only have been carried out without the police knowing what was brewing by an efficient and ramified secret organisation.) Those who had seized power were made uncomfortably aware of their own vulnerability. Two days after the Bastille was stormed, the lieutenant general of police resigned, and the task of keeping order was entrusted to the armed civilians of the newly formed National Guard.

Less than ten days after the fall of the Bastille, the National Assembly decreed the crime of *lèse-nation*, high treason against the new sovereignty. This introduced a novel twist into Europe's political culture: as the nation was embodied by the government of the day, that government automatically assumed the status of sovereign, and with it some of the numinous qualities associated with it. Any attack on the government was an attack on the nation, and its critics were by definition guilty of high treason. That the nation itself was not under any identifiable threat was a strength: hidden danger might lurk anywhere, and it was the sacred duty of the government to seek out and destroy any dark forces that might be scheming in the shadows. This allowed it to create a climate of fear in which nobody felt safe and the masses could be galvanised into aggressive action. It also transformed the police into a political tool dedicated to hounding anyone who might be out of sympathy with the government. On 28 July the National Assembly set up a *Comité de recherches*, which took over the intelligence-gathering network and personnel of the former lieutenant general of police with the brief of regaining control of the turbulent political situation in the capital. This would in time become the *Comité du salut public* (Committee of Public Safety). After the fall of Robespierre in July 1794, the functions of the *Comité* were gradually brought under central control, and in January 1796 the Directory established a ministry of police. But this did not denote a return to traditional modes of policing. The minister's principal duty was to foil plots against the government: henceforth, 'police' in France would be more about political than venereal contagion.

The form of contagion feared most by France's neighbours was the example set by the French – news of what had taken place was embellished and distorted as it passed from ear to ear, with the result that within a few months of the fall of the Bastille, peasants in lower Austria were refusing to carry out their feudal obligations and slaves in the Spanish colonies of South America were stirring. States bordering France struggled to impose a general quarantine. The Spanish government prohibited the wearing of 'foreign outfits and caps', and a royal decree of August 1790 forbade 'the importation into these dominions or the export to America of waistcoats with the word "*liberté*", or any other effects with pictures alluding to the disturbances in France'. The King of Sardinia took similar measures, as did various reigning princes in Germany. Bavaria banned books which so much as mentioned the French Revolution, and in so doing relegated Burke's *Reflections* to the forbidden list. Further afield, Catherine II of Russia put in hand measures to prevent the spread of what she termed the 'epidemic' of new ideas. But none took the threat as seriously as the Habsburg monarchy.[11]

The political edifice over which the Habsburg dynasty reigned consisted of the largely titular Holy Roman Empire, an assemblage of hundreds of duchies, principalities, margravates, counties, baronies, bishoprics, abbeys, free cities and other political units dating from the Middle Ages. It also ruled the Habsburg family possessions, a basket of fiefdoms acquired over the centuries by conquest, marriage, treaty or exchange, scattered from what is now Belgium through Austria and Hungary down to Italy and Croatia. It reigned over Germans, Flemings, Walloons, Poles, Czechs, Slovaks, Croats, Italians and Magyars. The status of the monarch was different in each province, which had its own language and constitution, and often very little connection to any of the other provinces.

This edifice was the embodiment of everything the French Revolution challenged, and the implied threat made Joseph II halt his programme of administrative reform and partially reverse it. On his death in February 1790, his successor, Leopold II, concentrated on the preservation of the existing order. In one of his first decrees, on 2 May 1790, he ordered that 'all suspicious or dangerous persons must be removed from the country', and that foreigners, particularly French subjects, should not be allowed in.[12]

Resident foreigners, who included French and Italian actors and musicians, were placed under close surveillance and in some cases deported. Among those told to pack their bags was Mozart's librettist Lorenzo da Ponte, director of the Italian theatre in Vienna. Those, such as the young composer Ludwig van Beethoven, who came into contact with them, and therefore with the 'French way of thinking', were treated as political contaminees who might pass on the pestilence. Another to be expelled, even though he was an Austrian subject, was the celebrated hypnotist Dr Franz Anton Mesmer.

Matters were complicated by the influx into Germany and central Europe of large numbers of aristocratic fugitives from revolutionary

France. While those who had fled at the first sign of trouble were presumed sound on the political count, subsequent waves included many who had gone along with or played a part in the initial stages of the Revolution. However aristocratic their origins, such people were seen as a danger to the Habsburg monarchy and could not be tolerated. The marquis de Lafayette, who had played a prominent part in the revolutionary Assembly and served in its armed forces before making his escape from the rough justice of the Jacobins, was considered to be so virulently contagious that he was clapped in irons and kept in solitary confinement, hermetically isolated underground in the fortress of Olmütz.

Even among the first wave lurked danger. In June 1790 the imperial commissioner Count Metternich reported from Koblenz, where the French king's brothers had rallied an army of noblemen to reconquer France, that there were revolutionary agents concealed among them. A similar report was received not long after from the Austrian minister in Turin. These agents were, the reports assured, being sent out by a '*club de propagande*' in Paris with the aim of spreading revolution to the rest of Europe. From Strasbourg, the Austrian police chief Count von Pergen received reports that French agents were subverting the lower orders. 'All the methods used by Europeans to seduce the inhabitants of the Coast of Angola are deployed to intoxicate the senses of the inhabitants of the countryside,' one of them wrote. 'Trinkets, ribbons, cockades, feathers of every hue, ridiculously tall plumes, uniforms with golden epaulettes are given out to those peasants chosen to command in the villages.' The population on the west bank of the Rhine appeared to be accepting French rule, and there were indications that it would be popular elsewhere, with disturbances breaking out in other parts of Germany.[13]

In Austria itself, bands of peasants marched on manors and demanded or simply took and destroyed the documents in which their feudal dues were set down. The troops called out to disperse them were sympathetic and reluctant to use force. Pergen resigned as Leopold adopted a fresh approach, based on looking to the welfare of his subjects and protecting them from evil influences. Mozart's opera *La Clemenza di Tito*, written for his coronation, was meant to convey the message that people were better off placing their confidence in a good monarch than in a democratic rabble.

In a decree of 1 September of the same year, Leopold struck the keynotes which were to resonate through the thousands of directives issued by the Austrian authorities over the next fifty years: the whole Enlightenment and its spawn in the shape of the French Revolution were a malevolent manipulation on a gigantic scale by evil forces intent on destroying the European social order by tricking people into believing that this would lead to their liberation and happiness. It was termed the 'Freedom Swindle', *Schwindelgeist*, and since upheaval of any kind provided fertile ground for its propagation, all available measures must be taken against anything that might 'disturb the peace'.[14]

Leopold died unexpectedly on 1 March 1792, and was succeeded by his twenty-four-year-old son Francis, the product of a rigorous and not particularly happy upbringing at the hands of his uncle the Emperor Joseph II. This had left him with a deep sense of his own significance as the linchpin of the whole enterprise that was the Austrian monarchy. It had also left him with a very strong sense of duty, which he fulfilled by working hard, often at quite pointless tasks, sometimes ones his ministers were performing already. This made him a difficult man to work with, particularly as he was slow-witted, meticulous, pedantic and strong-willed, not to say stubborn.

To those who did not have to deal with him he appeared a kindly, paternalistic figure, a devoted husband and father, nowhere happier than in the bosom of his family. But he was by nature joyless, humourless and impervious. Described by one diplomat as being 'without vices, without qualities, without notable passions', he possessed all the middle-class virtues in the most damning sense of the phrase.[15]

Francis honestly believed that the Enlightenment was a swindle and that his benighted subjects had to be protected from it. He saw education as inherently dangerous, and viewed all private philanthropic activity with deep suspicion. In his scheme of things, the people should remain in the care of their God-given monarch and nobody else. A few days after mounting the throne, he ordered the police to maintain a constant and thorough watch for the spread of 'the fanatical pseudo-enlightenment' and any other ideas that might threaten public order, the maintenance of which he identified as the prime duty of the state.[16]

Before resigning, Pergen had presented Leopold with a memorandum alerting him to the possibility that a major conspiracy was brewing. Intelligence he had gleaned connected Freemasons and members of other secret societies in various countries with every civil disturbance since the American Revolution, and there were suggestions that they were now set on world revolution. French Freemasons were allegedly using their brethren in other countries as a kind of fifth column to prepare the ground for French military invasion by demoralising and subverting their populations and their armies. Leopold had not responded to this memorandum, but Francis was greatly taken with its contents.[17]

One of his advisers, Count Sauer, had been warning him that 'there can be no doubt about the presence of several French emissaries here, who conceal their activities in such a way that only prolonged and close observation can lead to their discovery'. This kind of logic – according to which a supposition, once put forward, was deemed to be true; that it was unverifiable only served to confirm its truth, and indeed its significance – was to become a hallmark of Austrian police thinking over the next half-century.[18]

Francis was duly alarmed, and on 3 January 1793 Pergen was back as minister of police in charge of a new department, the *Polizeihofstelle*, with a large budget for the employment of undercover agents. He was to operate independently of the normal organs of state, and answer only to the emperor. On 1 April he appointed as his deputy Count Franz Joseph Saurau, and put him in charge of investigating all associations and societies. Feeling the chill, the Austrian Freemasons stopped holding meetings. Not the least discouraged, Saurau infiltrated their homes with his spies.[19]

Pergen's assessment was that most of the emperor's subjects were well-intentioned (*Gutgesinnte*) and desired the same as their master, a state of undisturbed order. However, they could be turned away from this, and that order could be disturbed, by nefarious outside influences, such as the *Schwindelgeist* of the Enlightenment or various nebulous fantasies (*Schwärmerei*). They therefore needed to be protected from these at all costs.

Censorship was tightened and extended, with particular stress laid on the protection of 'morality'. This necessitated censorship not only of the printed word, which was relatively easy, but also the more complex area of words spoken out loud in a theatre or sung in an opera. These could assume or be given all sorts of significance by the mere fact of being uttered before a large gathering, and the censor, Court Councillor Hägerlin, came up against formidable problems. Nothing that could be thought to constitute a bad example was allowable, which ruled out plays and operas whose plots involved rebellion against authority (paternal, religious or political), murder, adultery, incest, and any other vice unless it was fittingly punished or the criminal repented in the last act. Only in the court theatre was it possible for a character to exclaim 'Oh, God!'; in the public theatres, it had to be 'Oh, Heavens!' The line 'Long live liberty!' in Schiller's *Don Juan* was changed to 'Long live joy!' Relationships between dramatis personae were altered in order to avoid placing them in morally unacceptable positions. The villain of Schiller's *The Robbers*, Franz, could not be called a blackguard as the emperor bore the same name. Schiller's *Faust* was deemed potentially heretical, since Mephistopheles is cleverer than the angel. Almost every play of his contained an alarming theme: political revolt in *Fiesco*, the execution of a monarch in *Mary Stuart*. Lessing's *Nathan* could not be performed at all, on account of its discussion of different religions.[20]

Religious instruction, which had been banished from it by Joseph II, was brought back into the school curriculum. The imperial resolution of 10 March 1796 established a school police, whose job it was to invigilate 'the moral and orderly behaviour' of pupils at primary and secondary schools, and to keep watch over the morals as well as the political attitudes of their teachers. Just as actors were forbidden to ad-lib, teachers were forbidden to 'improvise'. They were to use only approved textbooks, and avoid touching on political subjects even if they took an orthodox line, since they might inadvertently give their pupils the wrong idea. The Court Decree of 17 December 1794 stipulated that the text of any proposed lecture must be shown to the authorities not less than four weeks before it was to be delivered. Saurau pointed out that the state 'pays public teachers to teach that which is agreeable to the Church and the government of the state, and it is a dangerous fallacy for a teacher to believe that he can teach the youth which has been entrusted to him along the lines of his own convictions and his own views'.[21]

The surveillance of foreigners was taken over by the *Fremdenpolizei* or foreigners police. Embassies were infiltrated by agents in the guise of servants, who were to report the most banal goings-on, scour the wastepaper baskets and fireplaces for '*chiffons*', scraps of paper that might prove of interest, and purloin letters and other documents, which were passed to what was popularly known as the *Schwarze Kabinette*, the Black Cabinet. Here, letters would be expertly opened, copied and resealed in a matter of minutes so they could be replaced before anyone noticed their disappearance. The *Fremdenpolizei* was also to make use of informers belonging to every social sphere, who could be rewarded with money, but were preferably motivated by the conviction that they were working for the good of the empire.[22]

This was now under serious threat, and not only from the 'errors' of the Enlightenment and the 'poison' being manufactured in France. During a meeting in the magnificent baroque palace of Pillnitz in Saxony in August 1791, Francis's father Leopold and Frederick William II of Prussia had issued a joint declaration in which they warned the French not to allow any harm to come to Louis XVI and his family. They also agreed to make common cause if either were to be attacked by France. Taken together, these amounted to a challenge, and it was taken up. Within the year France had issued a defensive declaration of war on Francis.

There was little enthusiasm in Austria for this war, still less when it led to the loss of the Austrian Netherlands, present-day Belgium. Rather than provoking a desire for revenge, the French successes were accepted with resignation, and officers as well as soldiers discussed the Revolution in a way that suggested Francis's prophylactic measures had been of little use in keeping the 'poison' out. There were instances of his troops fraternising with French prisoners, and when these were marched across Habsburg dominions they aroused the sympathy of the population. They would give away their brass buttons, stamped with the slogan '*Liberté, Egalité, Fraternité*', which were accepted with reverence by the emperor's subjects. The police carried out frantic searches for these unholy relics and confiscated them as though they were dangerous weapons.[23]

Baron Johann Amadeus Thugut, who took over the direction of Austria's foreign policy in 1793, quickly realised that this was no conventional war. He had spent some time in Paris in 1791, and understood that the Revolution represented a powerful new force and a menace unlike any other. The French had, in the words of one of his advisers, 'made a discovery more menacing to human existence than powder'. 'If they had invented some new war machine, we could have made one just like it,' but by galvanising citizen-soldiers fighting for their own cause, not that of some crusty ruler, they had done something that 'no one dares copy'.[24]

The slogan of Liberty, Equality and Fraternity proclaimed by the French appealed to those living under oppressive regimes, and paved the road to victory for their armies, which seemed to be inspired by an entirely novel zeal. '[The French generals] Custine and Dumouriez, at the head of troops that know the value of victory, seem to be inflamed with a kind of zeal like that of Omar, and hitherto they have preached this new species of Mahometanism with a degree of success equal to that of the Arabian,' wrote William Augustus Miles, the British minister in Frankfurt. 'If the fury of these modern Caliphs is not successfully & speedily checked, every sceptre in Europe will be broken before the close of the present century, and the Jacobins be everywhere triumphant.' The analogy was not misplaced. While conservatives shuddered at the implications of the various conspiracy theories, the paladins of revolution, far from being ordered about by occult sects, were fired by a message which some referred to as their 'Khoran'.[25]

4

War on Terror

'It cannot be denied that the intoxication of the French in these unfortunate times is a real fanaticism, and that those who are styled patriots really do form a sect,' noted the young duc de Richelieu, who was in Germany at the time. But he did not join the other aristocrats forming a royalist army at Koblenz. 'It will be with this one as it has been with all those which have agitated the world. If it is left to itself it will die and vanish into the void from which it should never have emerged; if, on the contrary, it is persecuted, it will have its martyrs, and its lifespan will be prolonged far beyond its natural term.' Thugut took a less relaxed view. As far as he could see, Austria now faced 'a nation which has not only become utterly fanatical but which tries to drag along with it other people and which has prepared its current efforts for a long time in all of Europe through the voices of its prophets'. The Habsburg monarchy ruled a great many 'other people', and some were highly receptive to the message ringing out from France.[1]

That message had already taken effect in neighbouring Poland, which had, in May 1791, passed a new constitution embodying many of the ideas of the Enlightenment. It was in no way revolutionary, having been drawn up by the king and voted in by the nobility, led by the greatest aristocrats in the land. It enshrined Catholicism as the religion of state, and the king asked the pope to bless it, which he did.

It had been praised by Edmund Burke, the most stalwart defender of the monarchical order in Europe.

This did not satisfy the Empress Catherine II of Russia. She concluded that Warsaw was 'a brazier of Jacobinism' and sent in her armies, which quickly overwhelmed the small Polish forces. She then set about rooting out all traces of 'Jacobinism': those involved in passing the constitution had their estates confiscated and were stripped of their rank, houses of prominent figures were searched and their private papers scrutinised for dangerous material, and everyone had to sign a declaration abjuring the ideals enshrined in the constitution and giving thanks for her intervention. The principal Polish constitutionalists had taken refuge in Dresden, where, through the good offices of the King of Saxony, they tried to negotiate a compromise, to no avail.[2]

Catherine's intransigence had the effect of leaving them with nowhere to go but France, where they began to plot a real revolution in Poland. This broke out in March 1794 when the veteran of the American War of Independence Tadeusz Kościuszko proclaimed an act of insurrection in Kraków's market square. If his intentions were no more radical than those of the American colonists with whom he had fought in the 1770s, those of the Warsaw mob which rose in support went a great deal further. After two days' fighting it expelled the Russian troops from the city, set up a Jacobin Club and began lynching assorted aristocrats, labelled as 'traitors' to the nation.

'The whole business in Poland is the same as the French Revolution,' reported the Austrian minister at Warsaw, Benedikt de Caché, adding that there were French advisers, French officers and French money involved. An Austrian spy code-named 'Cézar' reported from Warsaw that the Poles were receiving arms and money as well as military advisers, particularly artillerymen, from France (there is no evidence of this). Thugut and Francis ignored the fact that far from being molested or harmed in any way the King of Poland had associated himself with the national cause, and even donated his jewels and plate to it. They were greatly relieved when Catherine sent in her troops, which prevailed over the Polish army and retook Warsaw, putting an end to the insurrection.[3]

Pergen had been more preoccupied with some Hungarian Jacobins who in the early summer of 1794 hatched a plot to overthrow the Habsburg dynasty, led by the former secret police operative and one-time Franciscan friar Ignác Martinovics. Martinovics may or may not have been working for the police, but one of his accomplices, Joseph Degen, certainly was. The conspiracy, such as it was, was nipped in the bud, and ended in seventy-five arrests and seven executions. Whether it had been initiated by his agents or not, it vindicated Pergen's policies, and the prestige of his police system was enhanced. 'Our Police safeguard our physical health,' the minister of justice Count Clary wrote to Francis, 'and I do not think that I am taking excessive liberties if I lay at Your Majesty's feet my humble suggestion that the Secret Police, this essential pillar of the Throne and our general security, should be entrusted with the task of looking after the spiritual and moral welfare of our citizens too.'[4]

Pergen and his deputy had identified a number of 'suspects' in Vienna itself, but had no case against them. In June 1794 Saurau's agents began spreading the rumour that there was a plot to set various buildings alight and in the ensuing confusion assassinate the imperial family and selected notables. *Agents provocateurs* were set in motion to elicit less than loyal responses, and the first suspects were arrested. Pergen urged the emperor to bypass legal process and have them tried by a special tribunal, in effect by the prosecution, but several highly placed persons, led by the eminent jurist Karl Anton von Martini, protested vigorously. The ensuing trial fell apart. All that could be proved against the 'Jacobins' was that one of them had written a bad poem in which there was a phrase about all men being equal, and others had made inflammatory statements of one sort or another.[5]

A new offence of 'impudent criticism' was put on the statute books to facilitate future prosecutions, and the censors were instructed to make more imaginative use of their powers. The press was to be encouraged to 'highlight the disorders provoked by the democratic system and demonstrate the beneficence of a monarchical system of government, to show up in all its sharpness the contrast between a good prince and a few hundred despots risen from the common people.'[6]

Beethoven, himself under police surveillance as a potential revolutionary, wrote to a friend in Bonn that there was much talk of revolution in Vienna, but concluded that 'as long as the Austrians have brown beer and sausages, they'll never revolt.' Nonetheless, the struggle against 'wild democratic aspirations' and 'revolutionary leanings' did not let up – and brought ideology into every sphere. In Pergen's view, economic development represented a danger, since it disrupted the desired calm and often involved contact with foreigners. He therefore imposed restrictions on trade and brought in legislation inhibiting the building of factories, in order to prevent the expansion of the urban working class. The numbers of journeymen allowed to become masters and thereby acquire the right to settle in the larger towns were also restricted, for the same reason.[7]

By the end of 1794, most European powers had accepted that the Revolution in France could not be crushed by military means and that, after the fall of Robespierre, it no longer posed an immediate threat. They were therefore prepared to recognise the French Republic and make peace with it. Austria was not. 'The Directory in Paris pursues with an unheard-of energy the consummation of its projects to destroy Europe,' Thugut explained. He stressed the sophistication of the 'secret manoeuvres that they employ to seduce and to corrupt the multitude' and warned that 'a deplorable catastrophe will inevitably envelop all the thrones' unless it was crushed. Austria would fight on. Saurau commissioned the words for a national anthem from Lorenz Leopold Haschka, a former Jesuit and member of the Illuminati, now a police informer. The music, composed by Joseph Haydn, is today better known as that of '*Deutschland, Deutschland über Alles*'.[8]

The only other power which had not come to terms with the French Republic was Britain. It was the only European state to have, in the shape of the Channel, a clear line of defence against 'contagion', which should not in any case have posed the same problem as it did for the others. Systems of government such as the Austrian denied not just the mass of the people and the middle classes, but most of the nobility any say in how things were run. They were predicated on the principle that the monarch and his chosen advisers knew best, and the rest of society should not trouble their heads with anything other than their private concerns. Such systems had everything to fear from the French example.

Britain had been inoculated by its long tradition of representative government, imperfect as it was. The right to think, question and publish views on the governance of the country had been practised by significant sections of the population for decades. The calling of the French Assembly of Notables in 1787 and of the Estates General in 1789 had been followed with interest, largely because the system of representation at Westminster, with its restricted franchise and 'rotten boroughs' at the disposal of major landowners, was crying out for an overhaul. Many felt that the Glorious Revolution of 1688 which had brought William of Orange to the British throne needed to be built upon: the Society for Constitutional Information, founded in 1780, and the London Revolution Society hoped to mark the upcoming centenary by reforming the constitution. The prime minister himself, William Pitt the Younger, made two attempts at improving the system, without success. The calling of the Estates General in France, followed by the fall of the Bastille, had as a result been welcomed by the majority of the articulate population of the British Isles. Political tourists trooped off to Paris to breathe the air of liberty and returned discussing constitutional issues. In March 1790 a group of Whigs brought a moderate Bill for reform before the House of Commons.

While they may have taken heart from what was happening in Paris, the advocates for reform in England were firmly rooted in a home-grown political tradition defined by the Glorious Revolution, Magna Carta and mythical rights supposedly enjoyed by their Anglo-

Saxon forebears. Several of the founders of the Norwich Revolution Society had witnessed the fall of the Bastille and the first days of the Revolution, but while they applauded the ends, they baulked at the very un-English means, and were disgusted by the sight of heads being paraded on pikestaffs. Over the past century Englishmen of all classes had defined themselves in contrast to the French, who were viewed with a rich mixture of mistrust, contempt and fear.

Some did have more radical designs. Thomas Spence, a Newcastle schoolmaster who had moved to London, voiced the view that all land should be held in common. William Godwin advocated the abolition of property and government, which placed him in the same camp as the Illuminati. Thomas Paine, the first part of whose *Rights of Man* was published in March 1791, was a republican, and some members of the various constitutional societies wanted to see monarchy 'ripped up by the roots'. Others, such as the Welsh minister Richard Price, while stopping short of republicanism, derided the notion of Divine Right and saw the king as little more than the highest civil servant. Implicit in the thinking of many of these was the notion of a right to resistance to the abuse of power by the king, in effect the right to revolt, but, as many pointed out, this was well within the spirit of 1688. Most of the would-be reformers wanted to see only a rationalisation of parliamentary procedure and an extension of the franchise.[9]

The parliamentary elections in the summer of 1790 went off peacefully. In May 1791, only three months before the Austro-Prussian declaration of Pillnitz, Pitt, who felt that the events in France were the internal affair of that country and adopted a policy of guarded neutrality, told the Commons that he saw 'no danger' in the large number of pamphlets calling for reform of one kind or another, and that 'he could not think the French Revolution or any of the new constitutions, could be deemed an object fit for imitation in this country by any set of men'.[10]

This did not reassure Burke. In his *Reflections* he set out to convince those who had given way to what he called 'a juvenile warmth' in welcoming the Revolution in France. Chiming with the Emperor Francis's view of the great 'swindle', he argued that they had fallen for the 'delusive plausibilities' of the arguments of the 'sophisters, oeconomists and calculators' aimed at the established Church, the monarchy and 'the manners of gentlemen'. He challenged those agitating for reform, disputing their contention that they were acting in the spirit of 1688, and fiercely attacked the likes of Price. He maintained that the English constitution was perfect in all essentials, and praised the 'sullen resistance to innovation' and the 'cold sluggishness of our national character' which he saw as both its inspiration and its safeguard. There was certainly nothing cold, sluggish or traditionally English about his own attitude. As the novelist Fanny Burney remarked, whenever the subject of reform came up, his face would assume 'the expression of a man who is going to defend himself from murderers'. He also liked to equate the desire for change with the 'ferocious dissoluteness in manners' he saw in France, making a connection between reform and immorality.[11]

Dissenters of every kind, be they Methodists, Wesleyans, Catholics or Jews, were generally associated with reform, as they had been campaigning throughout the 1780s for the repeal of the Test Act which placed civil disabilities on all those outside the Anglican Church. In one impassioned diatribe the Birmingham scientist and Unitarian theologian Dr Joseph Priestley had used an unfortunate metaphor, of laying gunpowder under the old edifice of error and superstition, and this was fastened on, leading to his being accused of plotting to blow up Anglican churches. Burke denounced Priestley and his ilk as revolutionaries whose real aim was not the repeal of the Test Act, but the overthrow of the English constitution.

Priestley and a number of prominent citizens, many of them Dissenters, used to meet at Birmingham's city library to discuss anything from science to theology. In July 1791, on the second anniversary of the fall of the Bastille, they held a celebratory dinner. And although they dined under a portrait of the king, toasting him and the English constitution, they also drank to 'the Majesty of the People' and to the French Assembly. After they had retired, a crowd gathered and went through the town destroying Unitarian meeting houses and the homes of Dissenters. The crowd then set off for Priestley's house, Fair Hill, which it sacked, destroying in the process one of the most important laboratories and collections of scientific instruments and specimens in Europe. In the morning the crowd forced open the city's gaols and rampaged for a further two days under the slogan of 'Church and King', meting out rough justice to Dissenters and suspected reformers with the tacit approval if not the active encouragement of the city's magistrates. This pattern was replicated in similar riots elsewhere. While the role of conservative magistrates was evident in some cases, the frenzy of the mobs was partly fuelled, as it was in similar explosions on the Continent, by undefined fears that the Revolution in Paris and its effects somehow threatened the traditional certainties of life.[12]

These disturbances alarmed Pitt and his cabinet, and in March 1792 he installed seven additional stipendiary magistrates in London, along with a complement of constables. He nevertheless persisted in his confidence that neither France nor the reformist agitation at home constituted a threat. In his budget speech of 17 February 1792 he prophesied that the country could expect at least fifteen years of peace. The outbreak of war in April 1792 between France and Austria, and the French invasion of the Austrian Netherlands, did not alter this view.[13]

A Corresponding Society for the encouragement of discussion on the constitution was founded in January 1792 by Thomas Hardy, a London shoemaker, and it soon put out branches in Manchester, Sheffield, Norwich, Birmingham, Derby, Stockport and Leicester. In April, a group of noblemen founded an Association of Friends of the People, and societies of various kinds up and down the country discussed reform, published pamphlets and formulated appeals to Parliament. By the middle of 1792 the Norwich Revolution Society had scores of branches in surrounding towns and villages. In April, the prominent Whig Charles Grey launched a campaign for parliamentary reform in the House of Commons, which was vigorously supported by the various societies.

But the Whigs themselves were split, with Burke thundering his warnings against 'the new and grievous malady' sweeping Europe. He felt 'great dread and apprehension from the contagious nature of these abominable principles, and vile manners, which threaten the worst and most degrading barbarism to every adjacent Country'. He was convinced that 'no Monarchy limited or unlimited, nor any of the old Republics, can possibly be safe as long as this strange, nameless, wild, enthusiastic thing is established in the Center [sic] of Europe'. He equated the desire for change of any sort with revolutionary purpose, warning that the Dissenters were 'preparing to renew 14 of July' and that if they had their way Christianity would be 'extirpated'. He bracketed anyone who did not hold the same views as himself as a 'terrorist', and accused English journalists of being in the pay of the Paris Jacobin Club. He contrasted sentimental notions of good old England with lurid references to the disgusting 'French Pestilence'.[14]

Many were beginning to think like him. On 10 August the Paris mob attacked the Tuileries Palace, massacring the Swiss Guards in a wanton display of savagery, and Louis XVI was imprisoned along with his family. In the first week of September the Paris prisons in which priests and nobles were being held were stormed, and thousands of men, women and children were slaughtered. Many of those who had welcomed the Revolution began to recant. 'How could we ever be so deceived in the character of the French nation as to think them capable of liberty?' wrote Sir Samuel Romilly, who had previously believed the Revolution to be 'the most glorious event, and the happiest for mankind, that has ever taken place since human affairs have been recorded'. Their horror turned to alarm in October, when news of the French victory over the invading army of the Duke of Brunswick at Valmy reached England.[15]

Public opinion polarised. Many welcomed the victory, holding public demonstrations in celebration. The London Corresponding Society and other reformist bodies sent congratulations and messages of support to the French Convention. But they were increasingly branded as 'Jacobins' and ostracised. Landowners threatened tenants with eviction if they held radical views, employers sacked workers, tradesmen and shopkeepers who belonged to reform societies were boycotted by their customers, and in some parts of the country house-to-house enquiries were conducted to check the loyalty of individuals. Landlords of public houses refused to rent their premises to reform societies for their meetings. The Cambridge University Court expelled one of its dons for having published a pamphlet approving of the French Revolution. A Regius Chair of Chemistry was deferred because the only candidate was a supporter of reform. In London, booksellers, authors and even ministers of religion whose sermons were considered seditious were sent to the pillory or to gaol. Flurries of pamphlets appeared denouncing 'French liberty'. Booksellers who sold radical literature saw their shops torched, and effigies of Paine, often clutching a copy of *Rights of Man*, were burned – almost as many of him as of Guy Fawkes on the night of 5 November 1792.[16]

Periodicals sprang up to combat the reformist tendency, first the *British Critic*, and later the *Anti-Jacobin* and the *Anti-Jacobin Review*. George Canning, founder of the *Anti-Jacobin*, commissioned the cartoonist James Gillray to produce images suggesting connections between the London Corresponding Society and the French revolutionaries. Other cartoonists joined in, taking considerable liberties with the truth and giving loose rein to their fancy, representing reformist Whigs such as Charles James Fox manning a guillotine or lynching members of the cabinet.

As conservatives closed ranks, even abolitionists were denounced: the slave rebellion which had erupted in the French colony of Saint-Domingue appeared an evil omen. Although the only property to have been destroyed so far in England was that of reformists and Dissenters, it was conservatives who on 20 November formed an Association for the Preservation of Liberty and Property Against Republicans and Levellers, which rapidly grew into the largest political organisation in the country.

In the general panic, the Home Office and the Treasury Solicitor's Office had begun employing spies to infiltrate reform societies and lurk in public places to report anything suspicious and gauge the mood of the public. In the second half of 1792 these began to send in reports of seditious talk, of expressions of discontent with the government and outbursts against the king, and even of people arming. One informer stated that bands of Frenchmen armed with daggers were disembarking at various ports and marching on London, and that 'within two months there would be a great riot and there would be no king and it would be worse than in France'. A French royalist émigré, Dubois de Longchamp, warned the government that there were large numbers of Frenchmen in London, some of them soldiers, planning an insurrection. One of their alleged contacts, a Piccadilly hatter by the name of Charco, was arrested and found to possess three daggers and some firearms. An Italian was said to be suborning soldiers in their barracks, and a 'dangerous' man by the name of Cervantes was keeping suspicious contacts, along with an Irishman who was 'the most dangerous of any'. The insurrection was allegedly to break out on 1 December.[17]

Pitt found 'nothing to agree with' in any of Burke's writings, and was dismissive of the threat of popular revolt. 'Tho there has lately been a disposition to a great deal of Alarm,' he wrote to home secretary Henry Dundas in mid-November, 'I believe the Bulk of the People here, and certainly the higher and middling classes, are still sensible of their Happiness and eager to preserve it.' But he could not afford to be complacent. With the French occupation of the Austrian Netherlands, which would have been perceived, Revolution or no Revolution, as a direct strategic threat to British interests, the situation at home assumed a new significance. As a result, in the second half of November 1792 Pitt drew up plans for mobilisation, and on 1 December embodied the militia in several counties. This was accompanied by a Royal Proclamation stating that extreme measures were necessary in the face of the imminent threat of revolution.[18]

Pitt was attacked in the House of Commons, with Charles James Fox pouring scorn on his fears and the playwright and Whig politician Richard Brinsley Sheridan jeering that the danger existed only in his 'foul imagination'. Replying to Fox, Burke pulled out a dagger and threw it to the floor of the House in a histrionic gesture that provoked hoots of laughter. 'It is my object to keep the French infection from this country; their principles from our minds, and their daggers from our hearts,' he bravely went on amid the guffaws. Pitt admitted that most of the evidence before him was 'uncertain hearsay', but argued that with levels of fear as high as they were around the country, prudence was justified.[19]

This was true enough, but the fear was largely the work of the government itself, which was spending some £5,000 a year in subsidies to newspapers and helped start the *Sun* and the *True Briton*, which fanned fears of French subversion. Its use of spies also contributed to spreading mistrust and fear: the notion of revolutionary France sending out agents to subvert enemy states before attacking them was gaining ground. An under-secretary at the Home Office, Evan Nepean, had already put together a system of surveillance of foreign undesirables who might be planning an insurrection.[20]

Seemingly alarmed at this possibility, Pitt introduced a Bill to deal with the threat. In the event, the Aliens Act of January 1793 was to prove anything but a defensive measure, and the Aliens Office to which it gave rise was soon paying more attention to infiltrating the London Corresponding Society than to foreigners living in London. Under the Whitechapel magistrate William Wickham, appointed 'Superintendent of Aliens' in 1794, it would go on to mount a number of attempts to overthrow the French government.[21]

Whether or not Pitt and his colleagues believed in the threat of revolution and French subversion, there can be no doubt it did provide them with a golden opportunity to split the opposition, by forcing the less radical to support him out of a fear of appearing to harbour revolutionary intentions. The Foxite Whigs who stuck to their guns were not only isolated, but made to look unpatriotic. It was also a heaven-sent opportunity to increase the powers of the government.

In December 1792 the Scots Association of Friends of the People held a Convention in Edinburgh. The delegates kept their speeches moderate and made frequent declarations of loyalty to the crown, but the very word 'Convention' was tainted by association with its French model, and the Home Office's informer in their midst reported a number of seditious off-the-record utterances. Several of the more radical delegates were arrested in January 1793.[22]

The execution of Louis XVI on 21 January profoundly shocked Pitt and most of British public opinion, and provided the excuse for the expulsion of the French diplomatic representative in London. France's subsequent declaration of war on Britain and the Dutch Republic on 1 February meant that enthusiasts of the Revolution and any kind of reform could now be represented as traitors. In Nottingham, encouraged by the mayor, crowds reinforced by navvies digging the Trent Canal attacked the houses of those thought to harbour revolutionary sympathies, on the pretext that they might be hoarding arms. Dissenters, be they Catholics or Quakers, were suspect, and despite repeated declarations of loyalty by John Wesley himself, Methodists were the object of particular suspicion and antagonism, as ignorance of what they actually stood for raised fears that they might be Levellers in disguise.[23]

The trial of the Edinburgh radicals was slow to get under way, and it was not until August 1793 that they were sentenced. The Vice-President of the Association of Friends of the People, Thomas Muir, was sentenced to fourteen years' transportation, and the others to shorter terms. The trial had been a travesty, and provoked numerous protest meetings. A new Convention met in Edinburgh in October, bringing together delegates of reform societies from across the whole kingdom. On the basis of reports that some members were talking of drilling and arming, and that quantities of arms were being manufactured in Sheffield, the government closed it down and arrested a number of the delegates, provoking yet more protests.

Since there were few restrictions to membership of the London Corresponding Society and the other associations, it was easy for government informers to be admitted as members, and all the pro-reform societies in the capital and the major cities had been infiltrated, with some informers holding high office. The founder of the Corresponding Society, Thomas Hardy, believed that secrecy was both counter-productive and might lead to their undoing. 'We conceive that the permanency of a reform must be founded on the acquiescence of the public, who, after maturely deliberating on everything proposed, shall have found the plan the most useful and the best that could possibly have been laid down,' he wrote. Generally, the reformists displayed a concern for due process and were profoundly offended by the government's bending of rules and shocked by its use of spies.[24]

Hardy's colleague John Thelwall could be more radical in his speeches, and drafted a resolution for one meeting in Chalk Farm to the effect that the compact between rulers and subjects was automatically dissolved if the laws securing the liberties of those subjects were violated. But he was opposed to violence. 'True reason ought to be the only weapon of the friends of liberty,' he declared. 'The pen is the only artillery, and the ink the only ammunition, that the London Corresponding Society must ever use.' Candidates for membership were in some cases obliged to make a declaration disavowing conspiracy and violence, and when some of the societies began to make more radical declarations, many members tendered their resignations, complaining that they had 'deviated from the Pursuit of their original proposed object, viz. to obtain Parliamentary Reform.'[25]

Even if a significant number of radicals had intended to bring about a revolution, it is difficult to see where they would have found the means. There was much misery both in the countryside and in the manufacturing towns. Events in France had given encouragement to the nascent working men's associations, and there was an increase in strikes, particularly around 1792. But these were almost entirely about wages and conditions, and restricted to a particular trade. They were conducted with a degree of ponderous legality, their aims set out in formally drafted petitions. Although the press occasionally pictured the strikes as being motivated by 'Jacobinical' ideas, the only one in 1792 with what might be construed as a political edge to it was that by Liverpool ships' carpenters who threatened violence if the slave trade were abolished, as it would reduce demand for their work. The government on the other hand had over 2,500 troops at its disposal in London alone, and plenty more, as well as militia, stationed around the country.[26]

Yet reports kept reaching the Home Office from magistrates and its own agents that preparations were being made for insurrection. Magistrates were unreliable, as some reported every minor incident while others failed to inform the home secretary of actual riots. Some of the Home Office's agents were capable and responsible, but they were outnumbered by opportunistic informers who were paid according to the importance and bulk of the intelligence they supplied, a recipe for exaggeration and invention, and sometimes provocation. Mostly they came up with no more than baseless gossip. Typically, Edward Gosling, a government spy who was a member of the London Corresponding Society, reported that John Baxter, a Shoreditch silversmith and chairman of the London Corresponding Society, had told him where he could obtain a gun and declared that a revolution could be effected in a few hours and blood would have to be spilt, particularly that of Pitt, Dundas and, unaccountably, Fox. Another report alleged that a Sheffield journeyman printer by the name of Davison bade a cutler make him 'about a hundred' pike-heads which were stored at the house of the secretary of the local Constitutional Society. One source revealed the existence of the 'Lambeth Loyal Association', an eighty-strong military force, but the only evidence further investigation yielded was that of a potential recruit, Frederick Polydore Nodder, 'botanic painter to His Majesty', who came to join them and found three men performing military drill with 'an old rusty musket and a broomstick or two'.[27]

Dundas and his colleagues were on the whole critical of the reports they received, and took them with a pinch of salt. It seems unlikely that Pitt and his cabinet could really have believed that a revolution could be carried out by a few hundred steamed-up pike-waving radicals. In Paris, as was well known at the time, the fall of the Bastille had only come about because regiments of the regular army such as the Gardes Françaises had been involved, and behind the events leading up to it stood not some group of would-be reformers or foreign undesirables, but a large section of the middle class and the nobility, with members of the royal family such as the duc d'Orléans at their head. In Britain, there was no comparable leadership, and the mob had repeatedly shown that it was more interested in roughing up radicals and Dissenters than overthrowing the government. Yet the government acted as though it believed the threat to be real.

It made out that the self-important declarations of congratulation and solidarity addressed by the various reform societies, and particularly the London Corresponding Society, to French revolutionary clubs were evidence that the English radicals were under the influence, if not the control, of the French Convention. From papers seized, it was clear that there was a certain amount of correspondence between the various societies, both among themselves and with similar bodies in France and Ireland. While the actual correspondence had not been found (as it was scrupulously burned by the recipients), Pitt and his ministers assumed that its purpose must have been to coordinate action, from which they extrapolated that 'a detestable conspiracy against our happy constitution' was being hatched. The government's informers were warning that violence 'will be used very soon', and in April 1794 a report compiled by Wickham convinced Pitt that what he called 'a new era in the history of insurrection' had dawned, and that he had enough evidence to act. In order to ensure greater support in Parliament he made an alliance with a segment of the Whig Party led by the Duke of Portland, who became home secretary.[28]

At 6.30 on the morning of 12 May 1794 a group of King's Messengers and Bow Street Runners entered the house in Piccadilly of Thomas Hardy, founder of the London Corresponding Society. Without allowing him or his wife to dress in private, they ransacked the lodgings and carted away everything they could lay their hands on in the way of papers, as well as a large number of legally published books. Hardy himself was conducted to the Tower of London. The society's secretary, Daniel Adams, was also hauled out of bed and arrested, and his home similarly searched.

The documents found were passed by the Home Office and the Treasury Solicitor's Office, along with reports they had received from their informers, to a Committee of Secrecy specially convened by the House of Commons to assess the level of threat. After studying the material, this reached the conclusion that the London Corresponding Society and the Constitutional Information Society were dedicated to the subversion of the British constitution.[29]

In a second, more detailed report, the committee sought to justify this conclusion. It insisted that the Edinburgh Convention had been modelled on the French, and that since the model had brought about the fall of the monarchy, confiscated Church property and judicially murdered the king and thousands of others, that must also have been the intention of its Scottish emulators. The committee picked out of the Convention's recorded proceedings words such as 'struggle' as proof of violent intent. The phrase 'it would appear that' recurs with numbing frequency throughout the report, and much of the evidence consists of 'certain persons' having overheard statements or had sight of documents of a seditious nature, attributed to people who were members of one of the societies, or had attended their meetings, or knew people who had. The report quotes as evidence a letter from Dundas to Pitt reporting that 'Paisley is in particular alluded to as being in a state of great readiness [for revolution]; and there has been positive information received through other channels, that within these three weeks persons of that description have assembled themselves to a very considerable number in the night-time, for the purpose of practising the use of arms.' No corroboration of this assertion is provided in the report, and there is none to be found among the papers delivered to the committee.[30]

'From what has been stated it appears, that the design of arming, as far as it has yet proceeded, has been conducted with great secrecy and caution, and, at the same time, with a remarkable degree of uniformity and concert in parts of the kingdom remote from each other,' the report asserted. 'The weapons principally provided seem to have been peculiarly calculated for the purposes of sudden violence, and to have been chosen in conformity to the example of what has recently passed in France. The actual progress made in the execution of the design, during the short period of a few weeks, sufficiently shows what might have been expected, if the societies had proceeded, without interruption, in increasing the number of their members, and the fund for providing arms.' No arms were actually listed, and nowhere in the papers seized was there any mention of them, but such details were not allowed to stand in the way of the committee's convictions. 'It also appears to your Committee,' its report pronounced, 'that subscriptions had been opened for the purpose of providing musquets.' Needless to say, neither muskets nor money were found.[31]

The committee covered itself against accusations of failing to provide evidence for its assertions with the excuse of confidentiality. 'Your Committee have, for obvious reasons, omitted to annex to their Report the evidence of particular witnesses, by whom the facts above stated are supported; and, for the same reasons, they have studiously forborne to mention the names of persons and places in all cases in which they could be omitted,' it concluded.[32]

Faced with this 'traitorous conspiracy' to overthrow the government and introduce French anarchy, Pitt proposed the suspension of the Habeas Corpus Act, which was done on 17 May. Although he as good as admitted that the government was overreacting, he justified this by the argument that it was better to err on the side of caution and by the need to appease opinion throughout the country, which was now in a state of near-panic. Further arrests were made, and John

Thelwall, his fellow radical John Horne Tooke and others were committed to Newgate or joined Hardy in the Tower. In a celebration of the Glorious First of June naval victory against the French, a mob attacked Hardy's house and ill-treated his pregnant wife, who later died in childbirth.[33]

In the space of less than two years, Pitt's government had radically changed its position, and by the summer of 1794 it was at war with subversion at home and with France abroad. At home, it sought to root out the supposed conspiracy and decapitate its leadership. Abroad, it hoped, by landing troops in France, to assist royalist rebels in overthrowing the French government. It justified both policies with the alleged threat of revolution, and almost any evidence was used to support this. Riots against the press gangs were represented as being politically motivated; reports from spies that military drilling was taking place on the outskirts of London and that the prisoners in the Tower were in communication with accomplices outside were made much of. In Edinburgh, while searching the house of a bankrupt, officers of the law found weapons apparently made to the order of a secret committee of the radical 'Ways and Means' society. Further investigation revealed that this had drawn up a plan of insurrection, supposedly at the instigation of the London Corresponding Society. The trial of the two ringleaders opened with eighteen pike-heads and four battle-axes laid out as the evidence for the prosecution. One of the accused, Robert Watt, turned out to have been the government's principal informer in Scotland, and it remains unclear whether he had turned radical or had had the weapons made in order to fabricate evidence for the government, as he was hanged on 16 October.[34]

In September, the Home Office was informed by a Thomas Upton of a plot to kill the king by firing a poisoned dart at him from a brass tube disguised as a walking stick while he was in his box at the theatre. Two members of the London Corresponding Society were hauled in for questioning. One of them was James Parkinson, a surgeon of Hoxton Square who had published a pamphlet entitled *Revolutions without Bloodshed*, and who would later identify a form of 'shaking palsy' as a disease which would in time bear his name. The questioning yielded no evidence, and it subsequently transpired that Upton had invented the whole story. A long-standing member of the London Corresponding Society, he had been asked to resign when it was discovered that he had defrauded its funds, and sought to avenge himself.[35]

On 28 October, the state trial of Hardy and twelve others on charges of high treason opened in London. Looking through the available evidence, the Treasury solicitor had advised the government that there were no grounds for believing that the accused were intending to use violence, bring down the government or kill the king. There were inflammatory statements in the papers seized referring to the cabinet as 'Placemen', 'Plunderers' and 'Neros', and even calls for the overthrow of the monarchy, but that hardly amounted to high treason. Nor did the correspondence with French political clubs and revolutionary leaders. But the government went ahead regardless.[36]

Hardy was the first to be brought to the bar, and after nine days in the course of which the case for the prosecution fell apart for lack of evidence, the jury threw out the charge of treason, arguing that there had been no attempt on the life of the king, and that whatever plots might have been laid were aimed at Pitt's ministry. Hardy was taken back to his lodgings in a coach drawn by an enthusiastic crowd. After three more of his colleagues had been similarly acquitted, the rest were discharged. It was a terrible loss of face for the government. But it was the state that had suffered most.

While the government battled to protect the country against the revolutionary bacillus supposedly threatening society, it succumbed to a far more serious infection itself. During these first five years of the French Revolution, almost every state in Europe built up intelligence-gathering networks and the surveillance of individuals to unheard-of levels, introduced or expanded the use of informers, spies and even *agents provocateurs*, encouraged denunciation, made use of dishonest propaganda, branded those it did not like as 'enemies of the state', tarred them with the brush of 'immorality', and repeatedly tried to use legal processes for political means. Since all of these had been either initiated or elaborated by the government of revolutionary France, it could be said that contagion was far greater at government level than among the ordinary people of whom they were so scared. While the virus of revolutionary upheaval had proved only moderately contagious, those of state control over the individual and the politicisation of the legal process had made serious ravages.

5

Government by Alarm

The war with France dragged on, with little to show in return for the expenditure in men and money. Most people had forgotten, or never understood, what it was about, and by the summer of 1794 its growing unpopularity was compounded by food shortages which threatened to become acute as an unpromising harvest drew near. In July, as the government deliberated on measures of relief, an angry crowd invaded Downing Street clamouring for cheaper bread.

The suspension of habeas corpus had expired in June, and the London Corresponding Society exploited the situation by holding a meeting at St George's Fields in London which brought together a crowd estimated variously (and probably with considerable exaggeration) at 50,000 to 100,000. Another meeting, at Copenhagen House Fields outside Islington on 26 October, brought together an even greater crowd than the first, possibly as many as 150,000. This emboldened the discontented, and three days later a mob assailed the king's coach as he was being driven to the state opening of Parliament.[1]

The government responded with a speed that suggests it had only been waiting for an excuse to act. On 6 November Lord Grenville introduced a Treasonable and Seditious Practices Bill in the House of Lords. This redefined the law on high treason, introducing the notion of 'constructive treason' and thereby extending it to cover the intention of bringing about a situation in which the king's life might be placed in danger, the direct or indirect intimidation of the monarch, and by extension of his ministry. Seditious practices were broadened to include composing or distributing material, printed or spoken, inciting hatred of the king, the constitution or the government. In the Commons four days later, Pitt introduced the Seditious Meetings Bill, which prohibited more than fifty people assembling without a magistrate's licence (and reclassified halls in which they took place alongside brothels as 'disorderly houses'). This ruled out the Corresponding Society's principal activity and ensured that nobody would allow it to use their premises. The Two Acts, as they became known, effectively closed the only legal means of advocating constitutional reform.

William Wilberforce, who had helped to draft the first of the Bills, insisted that it was no more than 'a temporary sacrifice, by which the blessing of liberty may be transmitted to our children unimpaired', but there was nothing temporary about it, and it was widely seen as a shameful abuse and extension of the government's powers. Meetings in defence of free speech were held all over the kingdom, with the Dukes of Norfolk and Bedford turning out alongside John Thelwall and other working-class radicals. The government did not in fact make much use of these powers, but its actions did outrage large bodies of public opinion and widen the gulf between defenders of the status quo and would-be reformers of every hue, who now began to complain of Pitt's 'reign of terror'.[2]

The government had reason to feel embattled. The war with France, unpopular as it was, was not the principal cause of concern. The foreign secretary Lord Grenville believed that despite their early victories, the French were now 'a People languid and exhausted'. Pitt too had a low opinion of France's military potential. But he was alive to the threat of a French invasion prepared by a revolutionary fifth column. He possessed a copy of Barruel's book, and while it may not have convinced him that there was a worldwide conspiracy at work, as he was himself involved in plots to overthrow the government in

France, with the bankers Coutts providing funds through their agents in Paris, he might naturally have assumed that the French were planning something similar for London. And there were two, interconnected, areas in which Britain was vulnerable.[3]

In April 1797 a mutiny broke out in the fleet at Spithead. The sailors demanded higher wages (these had not been increased since the 1660s), better victuals and the abolition of harsh punishments. The new practice of lining ship's bottoms with copper, which meant they did not need such frequent careening and extended the time they spent at sea, was another cause of discontent. The government granted most of their demands, but the mutiny then spread to the ships at the Nore, at the mouth of the Thames, whose crews took a more political line, although they too were principally concerned with pay and conditions (and demanded a higher share of prize-money). While they did fire salutes on the king's birthday, they put pressure on the government by blockading the Thames, leading to a logjam of over a hundred merchantmen. They also threatened to take their ships over to France, which, they suggested, would know how to treat free men fairly. The mutiny then spread to Admiral Duncan's squadron at Yarmouth, and it was not until June that it was pacified.[4]

The proclamations and addresses of the sailors abounded in words and phrases they would not have known the meaning of ten years before, suggesting that they were aware of what had been happening in France. But the likelihood of their sailing off to join the French was minimal, given that they had been fighting them with jingoistic enthusiasm for the past four years. In December a great Naval Thanksgiving, with thousands of sailors marching past the king in a frenzy of patriotic feeling, seemed to bear this out. Although investigators sent down to the Nore reported 'with great confidence that no such connections or correspondence ever did exist', the government could be forgiven for suspecting that the mutinies had been abetted, if not inspired, by London radicals. A more serious cause for anxiety was the possible connections with their homeland of Irish sailors, who made up well over 10 per cent of the total.[5]

The underlying political problem in Ireland was the divide between the small landowning Ascendancy, made up principally of originally English Anglicans, and the overwhelming majority of the indigenous population, almost entirely Catholic, which suffered a litany of disabilities and discrimination. This was aggravated by less than sensitive rule from London, which alienated not only the Catholics. Reforms had been introduced in the 1780s, giving more power to the Irish Parliament in Dublin. The outbreak of revolution in France encouraged many to consider further devolution, and while even the most radical continued to toast the king, the questions of reform and self-rule became entangled with notions emanating from Paris.

In October 1791 a group of young radicals, both Catholic and Presbyterian, including Lord Edward Fitzgerald, Hamilton Rowan and Theobald Wolfe Tone, set up the Society of United Irishmen in Belfast. Although, or perhaps because, its motives were confused and its membership inconsistent, it grew rapidly, with branches springing up in Dublin and many other places. The organisation was not sectarian in character, and the one sentiment common to the whole membership was resentment of the government at Westminster and its perceived arrogance. When that government took Britain to war against France at the beginning of 1793, it strained the island's already weak sense of loyalty, and some began to see France as a more sympathetic partner than England.

Although Catholics were granted some additional rights in 1793, the sectarian gap widened, as a consequence of often entirely local factors. In Armagh, Protestants formed bands known as the Peep o'Day Boys to harass Catholics considered to be getting above themselves economically. The Catholics responded by founding the Defender movement, and the violence spread, with varying motivations and inspirations attendant on regional gripes. The situation was not improved by the irresolute and often panicky behaviour of the lord lieutenant, the effective viceroy of the island, ruling from Dublin Castle. France, which saw Ireland as a convenient place in which to make trouble for the British government and a potential back door through which to invade the United Kingdom, began to meddle.

The London government took the step of suppressing the Dublin United Irishmen and arresting their leaders, and sent out a new lord lieutenant, Earl Fitzwilliam, to resolve the crisis. Burke had been calling for the sweeping away of penal laws against Catholics, arguing that the one thing which could prevent the Jacobin pestilence spreading to the island and turning it against England was the Catholic Church. Fitzwilliam agreed, and moved energetically to bring in Catholic emancipation, but when he heard of this Pitt grew alarmed and promptly withdrew him. The disappointment felt by Catholics turned to anger, and sectarian animosities flared. Protestants who felt under threat founded the Orange Order, while United Irishmen reorganised along paramilitary lines and, under the leadership of Fitzgerald, began to seek French assistance to break away from English rule. Other United Irishmen, such as Wolfe Tone, had fled to Paris, where they began plotting a French invasion for the liberation of the island.[6]

The Irish Insurrection Act, passed in 1796, which gave magistrates sweeping powers and provided for the mobilisation of the militia, only led to further polarisation. A countrywide search for weapons resulted in the houses of Catholics being burned down and their owners arrested and flogged. At the same time, it was not at all clear where the loyalties of the militia and the yeomanry being raised by the Protestant landowners really lay. The situation was nevertheless under control, if the twenty-seven-year-old MP and colonel of the Londonderry militia, Robert Stewart, is to be believed. 'Indeed I have no apprehension that the mischief existent within can ever be productive of any serious calamity, unless the enemy should pay us a visit,' he wrote to Pitt on 17 October 1796.[7]

As it happened, the enemy were planning a visit, and two months later a force of 14,500 French troops under the command of General Lazare Hoche set sail from the port of Brest bound for the south-west of Ireland. Had they been able to land there the island might well have been lost to the British crown. Although there was a large standing army in Ireland, it was poorly commanded and equipped, and was scattered around the country. As it was, the French expedition was cursed from the outset. One vessel went down with its full complement of crew and troops in sight of the French coast, and over half of the others were blown out into the Atlantic by violent gales. Only a few reached Bantry Bay, with 6,500 men on board, and rode at anchor there for a week in fierce blizzards vainly waiting for the rest to join them before abandoning the enterprise and sailing back to France.

No armed bands of United Irishmen appeared on shore to support the French in the course of that week, but the British government could not be sure that they would not come out on some future occasion. The French actually landed some troops in the south of Wales in February 1797, but they re-embarked after a couple of hours, once they had realised that there was no wish by the local population to have anything to do with them. The Edinburgh radical Thomas Muir, transported to New South Wales in 1793, had escaped and was in Paris agitating for a landing in Scotland. There were reports of activity there by a secret association of United Scotsmen, and of the existence of some thousand United Englishmen in Manchester mobilising in sympathy with their Irish counterparts. There were certainly some among the English radicals who were 'for putting an end to government by any means, foreign or domestic'.[8]

Another French invasion was planned for July 1797, this time with the use of the Dutch fleet. Although it was cancelled, the threat lingered. In March 1798 the government imposed martial law in Ireland, and magistrates took suspects into custody and impounded arms. Sympathisers of gaoled individuals would gather together to dig up their potato crops so they should not be lost. The authorities saw such activities as intended 'to terrify the peaceable and well-disposed', and as part of a pattern of meeting 'under various pretences, such as funerals, foot-ball meetings, &c. with a view of displaying their strength, giving the people the habit of assembling from great distances upon an order being issued, and making them more accustomed to shew themselves openly in support of the cause'. The cause did not benefit much.[9]

In May, one faction of the United Irishmen started a rebellion near Dublin which spread rapidly, generating a rash of savage skirmishes of terrible intensity which cost some 30,000 lives before it was put down at Vinegar Hill in County Wexford on 21 June. A 'Turn out' in Antrim that same month proved hardly more effectual: after two days of random and mostly criminal violence, the insurgents melted away at the sight of small detachments of regular troops.[10]

In August, a French force of a thousand commanded by General Humbert did manage to land, at Killala. It marched inland, joined by a rabble of locals brandishing banners with inscriptions such as 'France and the Virgin Mary', but surrendered when confronted by a force of regulars. Another landing was made on the coast of Donegal in September, but for all his bluster, its Irish leader, Napper Tandy, was unable to muster support on the ground, and sailed away having achieved nothing. A third force, under the command of General Hardy and Wolfe Tone, was intercepted at sea and headed off. With plenty of regulars and some 50,000 yeomanry to defend the island from the French and their potato-digging allies, the only thing British rule needed to fear in Ireland was its own incompetence: unnecessarily bloody reprisals for the rising, followed by the imposition of a less than sensible Act of Union and the failure to emancipate the Catholics, would lead to further rebellion.[11]

That was not how the authorities viewed the situation. 'Upon a review of all the circumstances which have come under the consideration of your Committee,' ran the concluding paragraphs of the Report of the Committee of Secrecy of the House of Commons in 1799, 'they are deeply impressed with the conviction – that the safety and tranquillity of these kingdoms have, at different periods from the year 1791 to the present time, been brought into imminent hazard, by the traitorous plans and practices of societies, acting upon the principle, and devoted to the views, of our inveterate foreign enemy.' It went on to declare that although only the United Irishmen had actually risen, 'the societies instituted on similar principles in this country had all an undoubted tendency to produce similar effects ...'[12]

There was certainly some anti-government agitation, with Whigs and radicals holding meetings calling for reform and an end to the war. Charles Grey tabled a motion for parliamentary reform in the House of Commons, and in their speeches both he and Fox praised aspects of the French Revolution. On 18 May 1798, at a dinner for a thousand people at the Crown and Anchor in the Strand to celebrate Fox's birthday, the Duke of Norfolk proposed a number of subversive toasts. In June, the Whig Club ostentatiously presented the Polish revolutionary Tadeusz Kościuszko, who had just been released from Russian captivity and was passing through London, with a sword of honour. In July the Corresponding Society, whose membership had reached a low of four hundred, held a rally in St Pancras Fields.[13]

The Home Office's intelligence-gathering network had become more efficient by this time, and Wickham could claim that it possessed 'without bustle, noise or anything that can attract the Public attention ... the most powerful means of observation and information, as far as their objects go, that ever was placed in the Hands of a Free Government' – which leads one to wonder about the government's motives for the crackdown that followed these provocative but hardly menacing activites.[14]

It implemented what one of the Corresponding Society's members, Francis Place, a London leather-breeches maker who had fallen foul of the authorities following a strike in 1793, called a 'Reign of Terror', arresting all those who had spoken at the St Pancras Fields meeting and hounding its critics. 'A disloyal word was enough to bring down punishment upon any man's head,' according to Place; 'laughing at the awkwardness of a volunteer corps was criminal, people were apprehended and sent on board a man of war for this breach of decorum, which was punished as a terrible crime'. A man in Gosport was sent to prison for having damned Pitt and the ministry. A bookbinder was given five years with hard labour for shouting 'No George, no war!' Innocuous debating clubs were investigated and their members placed under surveillance. The net of suspicion was cast wide. In August, the Home Office investigated reports of a French advance party which had holed up in a house at Nether Stowey near Bridgwater in Somerset, and who were walking around the countryside with portfolios under their arms, making plans of the area, often going out at night. An agent despatched from London ascertained that they were not French, but confirmed that the tenant of the house, a Mr Wordsworth, and his friends, who included a Mr Coleridge, were disaffected, dangerous, and needed to be watched.[15]

Heterodox views were punished in extra-judicial ways, with writers and journalists being harassed, beaten and detained for long periods. They were gagged in various ways, by having their works seized and destroyed, their plays shouted off the stage by organised claques, or their writings damned with slanderous accusations of immorality or sexual deviancy by a host of government-funded hacks given generous amounts of space in the pages of the *Anti-Jacobin* and the *True Briton*. Writers such as Amelia Alderson Opie and Mary Wollstonecraft were represented as unnatural, and therefore immoral. Their arguments were dismissed as 'weak' and 'womanish', they were criticised for being intellectually out of their depth, labelled as promiscuous, shameless and immodest, the implication being that their literary urge was no more than a manifestation of their lust. Wollstonecraft's husband William Godwin was ridiculed as a henpecked joke, the author of 'obscene' and 'nauseous' publications. Thomas De Quincey recalled that he was regarded 'with the same alienation and horror as of a ghoul, or a bloodless vampire'.[16]

The government introduced further repressive measures, including effective censorship through the registration of printing presses and forbidding the printing of material originating abroad. It banned all associations and trade unions, outlawing the London Corresponding Society, whose leaders were already either in Newgate or in Coldbath Fields house of correction – the 'English Bastille' to the Whigs. The Unlawful Societies Act had originally been phrased so as to ban all societies which demanded an oath of their members, but the Freemasons, for whom the oath was crucial, intervened. On 30 April 1799 the Earl of Moira, Grand Master of the Grand Lodge of England, and the Duke of Atholl, his Scottish counterpart, went to Downing Street and persuaded Pitt to insert a clause which would permit them to keep their secret oaths.[17]

In the House, Lord Holland denounced the government's use of the war and the threat of revolution in order to browbeat the people into submission, and challenged it 'to produce substantial documents, rather than the suggestions of ministers, or the vague suspicions of individuals' to justify its repressive measures. He accused it of employing 'a system of government by alarm', obtaining extensions to its power year after year 'on the score of allegations, which subsequent events have disproved'.[18]

In his *Letters on a Regicide Peace*, written in 1796 and arguing the case for a war to the death with revolutionary France, Burke claimed that the war was not over a particular issue, but was a war on 'evil', and assured his readers that it was a life-and-death struggle, as the system of government adopted by France '*must* be destroyed, or it will destroy all Europe'. According to him, the French 'system of manners' was 'at war with all orderly and moral society', and he invoked the 'Law of Neighbourhood', the law of civil vicinity which gives a householder the right to protest at a nuisance put up by a neighbour, likening the state of revolution in France to someone opening up an 'infamous brothel' next door. 'What in civil society is a ground of action, in politick society is a ground of war,' he argued.[19]

Burke calculated that there were some 400,000 active 'political citizens' in England. 'I look upon one fifth, or about eighty thousand, to be pure Jacobins; utterly incapable of amendment,' he wrote. 'On these, no reason, no argument, no example, no venerable authority, can have the slightest influence.' They represented a 'great and formidable' force, quite adequate to overthrow the government. He lamented that 'our constitution is not made for this kind of warfare'. 'It provides greatly for our happiness, it furnishes few means for our defence,' he wrote, revealing a surprising lack of faith in democracy's ability to defend itself by standing by its own values.[20]

He voiced the fear that if peace were signed, young Englishmen would travel to France, 'to be initiated in all the infernal discipline of the place' and 'to be corrupted by every means of cabal and corruption', and, having imbibed the pollution of atheism and Jacobinism, would return to gradually corrupt all aspects of English life by contagion, beginning with Parliament, followed by the courts, where criminals would end up becoming judges, then the press, then the army, and so on until the whole fabric of the nation was rotten.[21]

Burke's fears seem curiously overstated, given that the overwhelming majority of even the most radical advocates of reform were firm believers in the fundamental merits of the English constitution. There undoubtedly were revolutionaries conspiring underground, but the very fact that we know little or nothing of them is eloquent testimony to their significance. And for all the agitation by the Corresponding and other societies, the lower orders were politically indifferent. A recent study of nearly five hundred documented riots and disturbances between 1790 and 1810 reveals that 39 per cent concerned food, 7.2 per cent labour conditions, 21.6 per cent recruiting methods, and only 10 per cent had any political or ideological basis. It is true that the percentage of politically motivated disturbances was higher in London. It is also true that as the participants were driven by a variety of often hazy grievances, any crowd could be manipulated into a revolutionary frenzy. But none were. As for the supposed threat of contagion, there is overwhelming evidence that even at moments of war-weariness and discontent, hatred and contempt for France and all things French persisted in every class of society.[22]

To be fair to Burke and those who shared his fears, it is worth remembering that similar alarms agitated the United States, which one might have thought more immune, if only on account of its geographical position. While Jefferson and the Republicans made light of the excesses of the Revolution in France, the Federalists were horrified to see America's sister-republic and erstwhile ally descend into lawlessness. On the one hand, Louis XVI was guillotined in effigy and democratic societies were formed to protect the United States from counter-revolution. On the other, the September massacres in Paris were represented as a vision from hell, and some warned that if Jacobin ideas took hold in America bloody violence would sweep away the political and social edifice. Anti-Jacobin texts proliferated, feeding the fear that one of the many heads of the revolutionary hydra might appear on the American side of the Atlantic. William Cobbett, writing under the pseudonym of Peter Porcupine, labelled the Whiskey Rebellion of 1794 'American Sans-cullotism' and made out that the Illuminati were planning to subvert America. In his *Detection of a Conspiracy, formed by the United Irishmen, with the evident intention of Aiding the Tyrants of France in Subverting the Government of the United States of America*, he identified the 'Parisian Propagande' as the prime mover. 'Like Lucifer, they carry a hell about with them in their own minds; and thus they prowl from country to country,' he warned. George Washington himself feared the French influence. This fear culminated in the passing of the Alien and Seditious Acts in 1798, which provoked the Republicans into talk of a 'Reign of Terror' and much beating of the drum of English liberties. On the other side of the argument, fears aroused by the tales of revolutionary violence in France entered the political discourse and public discussion, fusing with the nightmarish trope of Red Indian savages scalping or roasting alive settler families, and their echoes have even been picked up in the early campaigns of the anti-slavery movement.[23]

An interesting aspect of Burke's apprehensions is that of the potential moral pollution of the English by contagion from France. This chimes with less sophisticated expressions of the view that a French invasion, or even the example emanating from France, was bound to unleash social and moral mayhem. 'The French rulers, while they despair of making any impression on us by force of arms, attempt a more subtle and alarming warfare, by endeavouring to enforce the influence of their example in order to taint and undermine the morals of our ingenuous youth,' warned the Bishop of Durham in a speech to the House of Lords in 1798. 'They have sent amongst us a number of female dancers, who, by the allurement of the most indecent attitudes, and most wanton theatrical exhibitions, succeed but too effectually in loosening and corrupting the moral feelings of the people.'[24]

Much of the population of Britain was living in conditions of the utmost squalor, both physical and moral. London had for decades shocked foreign visitors by its poverty, dirt and immorality, and other cities were fast catching up, particularly the busy ports and the growing industrial centres, which drew in people from the countryside, tearing them away from the constraints and supports of village life, brutalising them with gruelling working conditions and leaving them defenceless in the face of urban disease and depravity.

This 'national decadence' in the physical as well as the moral health of the lower orders aroused fears that it might undermine the fabric of society. People such as the economist Thomas Malthus felt it might lead to the degradation of the whole nation, since there was much mixing of middle-class and even aristocratic youth with the low life of the larger cities. The consequent erosion of deference, greatly assisted by the example across the Channel, alarmed the government and the propertied classes alike.[25]

Religious observance had declined among Anglicans in the course of the eighteenth century, and a lukewarm Christianity verging on deism or even humanism prevailed in the higher echelons of society. This tendency was associated in the eyes of not just the Bishop of Durham with reformist views and a generally unsound attitude, both moral and political. Many advocates of reform regarded religion and 'priestcraft' with hostility, seeing in it an obstacle, since it kept the poor docile and blind to the 'truth'. On the other hand, religious commitment of the wrong sort also aroused fears, and the Methodists in particular were viewed as dangerously fanatical. They preached millenarian prophecies which were inherently revolutionary, as the new Jerusalem of these mostly plebeian prophets had no room for king or aristocracy, or private property. The susceptibility of some Methodists to Antinomian concepts which liberated them from the moral law tainted the whole movement by association with licentiousness and immorality, and lurid tales circulated of their wild orgies. The prominent Methodist Robert Wedderburn, the illegitimate offspring of a Jamaican planter and a slave-girl, who stole, blasphemed, worked for a publisher of pornography and opened a bawdy house, only enhanced such an image in the public imagination.[26]

William Wilberforce was spearheading an evangelical revival with his writings, most notably *A Practical View of Christianity*, published in 1797. Hannah More had for some time been arguing that moral not constitutional reform was what the country needed, leading a kind of Christian mission against Jacobinism. A Society for the Suppression of Vice was founded in 1802. This was followed by the Bible Society, which sought to cure the evil through the evangelisation of the poor, by the Religious Tract Society and the Church Tract Society, by Sunday schools, and later by a surge in church-building in expanding cities. Others felt that the best way of thwarting the spread of revolution was by bringing assistance to the needy, and set up various relief organisations, such as the 1796 Society for Bettering the Condition and Increasing the Comforts of the Poor. The followers of Jeremy Bentham expounded the virtues of the utilitarian approach and called for the reform of prisons and lunatic asylums; those of Thomas Spence propounded a vague form of communism. A group known as the Westminster Radicals saw education as the main motor of social and constitutional transformation, and promoted the system of free schools for the poor pioneered by the Quaker schoolmaster Joseph Lancaster.

But many preferred to see the situation in terms of good and evil, and this is much in evidence in the popular anti-Jacobin novels, large numbers of which were published in the late 1790s. These revelled in lurid descriptions of revolutionary Paris, where innocent beauty was the stock victim of coarse and lewd revolutionaries, and everything was 'wild and licentious', in the words of one author. 'Order and subordination were trampled beneath the footsteps of anarchy,' he wrote, 'the streets were filled with terrifying *spectacles*; and the people seemed to be nearly frantic with the plenitude of dominion; while the excess of horror was strongly and strikingly contrasted by the vaunted display of boundless sensuality.' In his novel *The Vagabond*, George Walker painted a picture of how a revolution might look in London, with 'the rage of lust' let loose on young 'beauties' more used to genteel courtship, and aristocrats floundering in their own blood 'amidst the uproar the thunder of cannons, the whistling of bullets, the clashing of swords, the tumbling of houses, the groans of the wounded, the cries of the conquerors ...'[27]

At the root of all this wickedness lay 'the new philosophy', or even just 'philosophy', denounced as a mess of 'pernicious scepticisms and sophistical delusions', pestilential doctrines combining atheism, levelling (this was titillatingly terrifying to the property-owning middle-class readership), undermining conventions, and leading women towards independence and depravity. In these novels this philosophy is propounded either by idiots or by wicked charlatans with names such as Edward d'Oyley and Judas McSerpent, usually with the purpose of getting innocent young women into bed. Even the paid or self-appointed agents of the French Revolution, whose aim is the overthrow of the English constitution, have a sideline in the seduction of virtuous women by preaching to them the new philosophy of equality and free love. 'Can a priest muttering a few words, supersede the call of passion or give a higher zest to the affection of the heart?' cajoles one such character. 'In the heart are the issues of love, and where that leads, what institution of the church, what act of man, shall impede its progress? The time is passed for such superstitious restraints, and we revel in the full freedom of love, free in that as in all other respects.'[28]

The sense that society was somehow being attacked by a malignant disease of the mind or even of the moral sense was certainly not limited to bigots or the readers of popular novels. Thomas De Quincey remembered Barruel's book being discussed everywhere. The papers of the Treasury solicitor include a pamphlet entitled *Notes on the chief causes of the late revolutions of Europe*, which delivers a critique of the

Enlightenment and belabours the 'Encyclopaedists', lumping them together with Irish rebels, Freemasons and Illuminati. It explains the facility with which the French armies triumphed over their enemies by the fact that 'the principles of the conquerors had been implanted in the countries which they overran long before their armies arrived there', citing as evidence the publication of works by Paine, Campe, Paulus, Knigge and Gorani in their respective countries before hostilities commenced. It also asserts that the Grand Orient Masonic Lodge of Paris had issued a manifesto calling on their brethren all over Europe to facilitate French victory, which had also been assisted by the Illuminati. The London Corresponding Society and the other English reform movements were naturally involved too.[29]

In his *Reflections on the Political and Moral State of Society at the Close of the Eighteenth Century*, published in 1800, John Bowles asserted that modern philosophy was 'corrupting the heart of Europe', a view shared by many. Not far behind lurked the notion that this disease was being spread by a conspiracy. Burke admitted that people of intelligence and talent were naturally drawn towards what he termed 'the *Cloacâ Maximâ* of Jacobinism'. But most preferred the metaphor of seduction, and in otherwise serious arguments about the evils of the Revolution writers would effortlessly fall into the imagery of French wolves preying on innocent sheep, of corrupt conspirators ensnaring the pure. The publication of Barruel's book was followed by that of a number of others, most of them précis or derivations of it, which confirmed the existence of a 'diabolical' conspiracy. The Jacobins were fearsome, according to Bowles, as 'the cultivation of their talents, the extent of their knowledge, their advancements in science, only enable them the better to pursue their projects of destruction, more effectually to attack Religion, Government, and Social Order, and to establish more firmly their horrid sway of impiety and vice'. More terrifying still, the Jacobins were not merely a group of people, they were a monstrous entity. Jacobinism, according to another tract, 'is not merely a political, but an anti-social monster, which, in pursuit of its prey, alternately employs fraud and force. It first seduces by its arts, then subdues by its arms. For the accomplishment of its object it leaves no means unemployed which the deep malevolence of its naïve sagacity can devise. It pervades every department of literature and insinuates itself into every branch of science. Corruption is its food, profligacy its recreation, and demolition the motive of its actions, and the business of its life.' In consequence, anyone who raised in some circles the subject of prison reform, abolition of the slave trade or the regulation of child vagrancy could expect to be accused of peddling 'French philosophies'.

Like the politicians, the authors of these novels and tracts display what seems to have been a common instinct to avoid confronting the phenomenon of the French Revolution in the spirit of analysis. They prefer the parable of a mass explosion of every kind of wickedness, caused by the breakdown of the mesh of moral and social structures brought about by 'philosophy' concocted by the Illuminati and disseminated by Jacobins. It was a simpler explanation, and, implausible as it might appear, it was comfortingly understandable.

It also confirmed the necessity of pursuing the war and slaying the dragon. 'It is not the Cause of Nation against nation, but as you well observe, the cause of mankind,' explained Edmund Burke. 'We are at war with a principle. And an example, which there is no shutting out by Fortresses or excluding by Territorial Limits. No lines of demarcation can bound the Jacobin Empire. It must be extirpated in the place of its origin, or it will not be confined to that place.' There had, in his opinion, never been a war like it, and other conflicts had been 'the games of Children in comparison to it.'[30]

One of the worst things about the war as far as Burke was concerned was that it was in effect a civil war, since there was a home front. And even when, in 1802, the Treaty of Amiens brought an end to hostilities with France, the war at home continued. Food riots and disturbances in Lancashire and Yorkshire in 1801–02 were rumoured to be the fruit of a conspiracy by a society calling itself 'the Black Lamp'. On 16 November 1802 Colonel Edward Despard, an Irish landowner and British officer of some distinction, who had been a member of the

London Corresponding Society and been gaoled without charge for three years in the 1790s, was arrested in a public house in Lambeth along with a handful of soldiers and labourers. According to government informers, he believed that by seizing the Tower of London and the Bank of England he could bring about revolution, but it is not clear that he actually had any intention of doing so. He was also supposedly linked with the Black Lamp conspiracy. There is considerable disagreement among historians as to whether the Despard plot had any real substance, and whether the Black Lamp was an organised working-class movement or just the figment of an informant's imagination. The government was taking no chances. Despard and six others were found guilty of treason and executed. Although there was little evidence as to his designs and connections, the government's fears are well attested by the presence in the crowd at his execution of agents armed with rockets which they were to fire, should the need arise, to summon troops concentrated nearby in large numbers.[31]

War was declared against France once more in 1803. The threat of invasion galvanised patriotic fervour as Napoleon Bonaparte massed a large force in a camp outside Boulogne and set about building a fleet of barges in which to convey it across the Channel. That of moral contamination appeared slight, given that in 1803 the British government raised 85,000 men in the Militia, and over 400,000 volunteers. In the southern counties, about 50 per cent of all men aged seventeen to fifty-five came forward in what was an extraordinary social movement and demonstration of political will. In order to protect his flotilla of ungainly transports Napoleon needed the main French battle fleet. But this was disastrously defeated off Cape Trafalgar on 21 October 1805, a victory that removed the threat of armed invasion. Yet this did nothing to alter what seems to have become a convenient paradigm for the government.[32]

6

Order

While Trafalgar saved Britain from the threat of invasion, it also led to Napoleon's domination of Europe. Denied the opportunity to get to grips with his English enemy on land, he struck the camp at Boulogne and marched off to deal with Britain's Austrian and Russian allies. He forced half of the Austrian forces to surrender at Ulm, and defeated the rest, along with a large Russian army, at Austerlitz. He then turned on their new Prussian ally, whose forces he destroyed at Jena and Auerstadt, and crushed the last, Russian, army of the coalition on the fields of Eylau and Friedland.

Between 1805 and 1807 the triumphant Emperor of the French redrew the map of Europe and imposed his will on the Continent. He dismantled the Holy Roman Empire, turning its Emperor Francis II into Francis I of Austria. He reduced Prussia to the status of a second-rank power and garrisoned Berlin with French troops. And he forced Alexander I of Russia into an alliance which effectively set up a common security system dominated by France. In 1809 Austria tried to take advantage of Napoleon's involvement in Spain by attacking his forces and allies in Germany, only to be defeated at Wagram. The future of the monarchy hung in the balance, and was only bought by the sacrificial offering of the emperor's daughter Marie-Louise, who became Napoleon's consort. This amounted to official sanction of his imperial status: their son was given the title of King of Rome, which proclaimed him as the next Emperor of Europe and heir to Charlemagne. If Old Europe did not like it, it had at least to concede one thing – Napoleon had put the evil genie of the Revolution back in the bottle and sealed it.

When he became First Consul and effective dictator of France in 1799, Napoleon had been faced by indescribable chaos, resulting from ten years of revolution and counter-revolution, internecine political struggle, random political terror, class war and open civil war in some parts of the country. The authority of the state had been undermined by the rapid succession of governments, each of which overturned the legitimacy of its predecessor. The law had been turned into a tool by rival political factions and justice had been politicised. Napoleon may have been a product of the Enlightenment and what conservatives saw as its depraved values, but he was a pragmatist. If he did not believe in Divine Right, he certainly had no time for Jacobin ideology, Illuminati, or dreamers of any kind. He believed in order, and he knew how to impose it.

The key to restoring the rule of law, stability and public confidence was efficient policing. Yet the police he inherited had for a decade been used almost exclusively for factional political ends. Their intelligence-gathering was geared to monitoring the attitude of the population to the incumbent government and looking out for sources of potential opposition. Unlike the detection of crime, this activity was not subject to the disciplines imposed by physical evidence. It was in the interests of police officials and informers to report as much and as frequently as they could, and to make sure that their information was as sensational as possible. It was also in their interests to report what they assumed their superiors would wish to hear. Hence a limitless supply of stories of plots, treachery and cowardice on the part of enemies of the people on the one hand, and of touching tales of devotion to the motherland, revolutionary virtue and bravery on the other. In a sense, the police were not so much reporting on as painting a version of events which suited what they believed to be the views and intentions of the rulers.

The informers, whether they were regular police employees or *mouchards*, were on the whole neither intelligent nor educated. Their brief was to be on the lookout for anything out of the ordinary, and since both their experience and their understanding were limited, a great deal of what they saw and heard did strike them as such. When they eavesdropped on a conversation between two educated people they were likely to understand nothing, or to misunderstand, and in either case it would appear to them potentially seditious. The volume of information thus generated grew massively, as did the appetite for more, and as the British historian Richard Cobb, who trawled through the relevant archives in depth, explains, a brief report was 'clear proof of utter incompetence or of deliberate covering-up', and if there was nothing to report, something had to be invented.[1]

The more theatrically such information was presented, the better it was likely to be received. Cobb illustrates this with a case from 1793, when two agents eavesdropped on the same conversation on the terrace of a Paris café. One of them, who knew what he was about, began with a detailed description of the suspect's appearance and how he was dressed. He went on to say that the individual in question had uttered obscene propositions unworthy of a republican, that he had vilified the national representative body, berated the Convention, insulted national sovereignty, mocked the champions of the people, undermined the revolutionary government, mouthed overtly counter-revolutionary sentiments, expressed the desire to bring down the republican regime, revealed himself to be an agent of *Pitécobourg* (prime minister William Pitt and the commander of the Imperial Army operating against France, Prince Frederick of Saxe-Coburg), and so on. The other, either a novice or a man of singular candour, merely reported that the man in question had said: '*Merde à la Convention*.' He would not have been congratulated on his brevity.[2]

All of this tended to the production of reams of intelligence which was virtually fictitious and therefore valueless. Although his desk groaned with voluminous reports, the prefect of police in Paris had, at the very best, a highly distorted idea of what was going on in the capital, only a hazy one of what was happening in other cities, and none at all on the state of affairs in vast areas of the country. And he had as little control.

While all but the most privileged had welcomed the overthrow of the old regime and the abolition of feudalism, few appreciated the imposition of the new revolutionary order. States are as greedy as feudal lords when it comes to taxes, and the officials of the new regime rapidly overtook the former masters in unpopularity. In rural areas, their attempts to impose the authority of the state were met with mulish cunning. Such resistance was made all the easier as the revolutionary climate allowed the private and the public, the criminal and the political spheres to become gradually confused, and more inextricably with every new development in the political process.

The Revolution had been unpopular from the very beginning in the Midi, for a variety of regional, religious and other idiosyncratic reasons, and throughout the 1790s the government in Paris had great difficulty in affirming the authority of the state and collecting taxes there. Much the same was true of the west and north-west of France, where dumb resistance gradually flared up into full-scale civil war with the royalist rising of the Vendée. Despite ruthless military action, bordering on genocide, by the revolutionary government, the region was never entirely subdued, and the authority of the state remained frail. In addition, many coastal areas and port cities retained their own ways of doing things, and flouted the government's attempts to control their activities. They evaded tax through smuggling, and traded with the enemy on a regular basis. Many inland cities also displayed an independent spirit, which, in the case of Lyon, proved indomitable.

A major manufacturing centre at the confluence of the Saône and the Rhône, a vital centre of communication linking Switzerland, Piedmont and the valley of the Rhône, and between areas chronically resistant to control such as Burgundy, the Massif Central and the Midi, Lyon had a long tradition of rivalry with and opposition to Paris. The topography and architecture of the city itself defied control.

The density of many-storeyed houses along narrow, winding alleyways leading up the Grande Côte provided ideal conditions in which political or criminal fugitives could go to ground (it would be an important centre of resistance activity between 1940 and 1945). The rivers provided ideal means of disposing of evidence, as bodies would only be plucked from the swirling waters as far away as Avignon, if at all. In addition, Lyon was uncharacteristic of French cities in that its houses did not have concierges, the prime sources of information for the police. Nor, because of its steep, narrow streets, did it have many horse-drawn cabs, and therefore no *cochers de fiacre*, cab drivers. The *cocher de fiacre* was by the nature of things a party to criminals getting away from the scene of a crime, transporting stolen property, smuggling people in or out of town, abducting girls, and many other forms of illegal activity. As he had to be licensed by the police he was, even if he tried to play for the other side, an essential source of intelligence.[3]

There were swathes of rural France where bands of brigands roamed unchecked. In the Ardèche no road was safe, even for heavily escorted army pay convoys. The Revolution had led to an increase in the numbers of people living outside the law, and the wars swelled these through a steady flow of deserters. The introduction of conscription in 1798 only compounded the problem. Conscription was conceived both as a duty and a right, with the citizen not only serving the state but also participating in its workings, a notion based on Rousseau's ideal of the citizen-soldier. It was a useful tool for the imposition of the new order, inculcating in the conscript deference to military hierarchy and the state it served. But it also taught the docile how to fight and emboldened the timorous, and it forced those who did not wish to serve to go into hiding, where they could only survive through banditry.

The government's attempts to impose its will encountered formidable obstacles. These began with the near impossibility in remote rural areas and the overpopulated slums of larger cities of establishing a person's identity. Political fugitives, criminals, deserters or people on the run for any number of reasons changed names, of which they might have a variety, or were known only by sobriquets or nicknames, often derived from their region of origin, physical attributes or alleged intellectual, physical or sexual prowess. In May 1792 the Convention had introduced passports, which had to be carried by anyone travelling outside their commune. Many people had more than one passport, sometimes a pocketful, stolen or forged. It was not unknown for men to dress up as women in order to go through with a marriage to another man which would provide them with a new legal identity.[4]

The police strove to pin people down by filling their passports with descriptions of their physical appearance, listing colour of hair and eyes, height, weight and distinguishing marks such as missing limbs, fingers, toes, ears, noses and eyes, traces of smallpox and other diseases. Deformities were noted, along with possible causes – a broken leg badly set might connect with an escape from prison. Every blemish and scar was scrupulously noted, along with their supposed origin (pistol, gun or knife wound, sabre cut, agricultural accident, maiming by a wild beast, fire, scalding, etc.). Tattoos and brandings were deemed helpful, often denoting a spell in the army or navy, or past criminal conviction. Tics, accents, deportment, way of walking, even the expression of the eyes or face – suspicious, frank, shifty, timid, soft, provocative, and so on – were all meticulously listed.

This approach proved counter-productive in the long run. Those picked up by the police were predominantly vagabonds, beggars, pickpockets, harlots, fences and other petty criminals. Such people tended to be malnourished, crippled, maimed and diseased, their bodies covered with the testimony of a lifetime of marginal living in a dangerous and callous world. As a result the police ended up with detailed descriptions of legions of people with so many distinguishing features as to make none of them remarkable.[5]

On taking power, Napoleon adopted a form of administrative terror. He began by sending out military commissions backed by troops to dispense summary justice as they roved around the country, collecting unpaid taxes and recalcitrant conscripts. Once a semblance of order had been established these were replaced by special tribunals, which fulfilled the same purpose, but with due legal process and without the use of troops. They were nevertheless backed by force, in the shape of the *Gendarmerie*, the new name of the royal *Maréchaussée*.

The gendarme was the visible symbol of the state, and people took every opportunity to jeer at him, to jostle and impede him in his duties, and would often assist in the escape of those he had apprehended. Women, who resented their menfolk being taken away, were in the forefront of confrontations with gendarmes escorting conscripts and deserters, even if they were not from their own communities, and regularly caused affrays in which these were able to make their escape. But the efficiency of the *Gendarmerie* discouraged actual riots. The number of confrontations with the *Maréchaussée* thought worthy of being brought to the attention of higher authorities between 1771 and 1790 was 338, an average of about 1.4 per month. This dropped to virtually nothing under the Consulate and the Empire, but would begin to rise again when imperial authority started to disintegrate (the monthly average for 1813–17 would be 5.3, and it would remain at similar levels until 1850, a clear indication of the impact of the ruthlessness with which state security was enforced under Napoleon).[6]

Napoleon was the target of over thirty assassination attempts, but he knew better than to let this be known. 'I do not like to have conspirators judged,' he said to Pierre-François Réal, one of his senior police officials. 'In such situations governments always lose out: it is so easy for a man to become a hero!' He preferred would-be assassins to be thrown into gaol for a few months to cool off and then released. It was only when the conspirators could be successfully demonised that he would allow a public trial to go ahead. Assassination attempts were 'mere diseases of the skin,' he said after one failed attempt on his life, while 'terrorism' was 'an illness of the gut.' By 'terrorism' he meant those forces bent on undermining the state, and in this respect he saw the Jacobins as an altogether greater threat than the royalists conspiring against him, even if they did have the support and funding of the British government. The man who kept these terrorists at bay, his police chief Joseph Fouché, was as ruthless as himself, a cold, calculating individual whose instinct for survival was epic.[7]

Born in 1759 to humble parents in a small village outside the port city of Nantes in Brittany, Fouché was educated by the Oratorian Fathers and later taught in their colleges around the country. In 1792 he was elected to the National Convention in Paris, where he established a formidable reputation and was among those who called most insistently for the death of Louis XVI. He was then sent to root out counter-revolution in the Vendée, where, as well as purging large numbers of people, he stripped churches and eradicated every vestige of Christianity, which he identified as the Revolution's prime enemy: back in Paris he busied himself with establishing the new Cult of Reason which was to replace it. In October 1793 he was despatched to crush opposition in Lyon, where he staged mass executions in which hundreds of people were chained together, blasted with grapeshot and allowed to die in bloody heaps. He was expelled from the Jacobin Club by Robespierre two weeks before the latter's fall in July 1794, in which he played a part, thus saving his own neck. Over the next five years he sided alternately with royalists and Jacobins, and, by virtue of deft positioning, managed to get himself appointed minister of police on 20 July 1799. One of the first things he did on setting up shop at his headquarters on the quai Voltaire was to clamp down ruthlessly on his former Jacobin colleagues and silence protest by imposing strict censorship on theatres, publishing houses and the press. To show he meant business, transgressors were shot.

Fouché delegated criminal investigation to the *Sûreté*, headed by Commissaire Henry. The latter took into his employ a petty thief, François Vidocq, whom he set up in a small, dark old house on the rue Sainte-Anne, between the quai des Orfèvres and the Sainte-Chapelle. From there Vidocq ran a network of agents, all of them criminals, who shamelessly preyed on their own kin. That took care of the basics of law and order.

Fouché himself concentrated on what he called *la haute police* – state security. He created a new information-gathering network, which he financed 'by making vice, inherent in any great city, contribute to the security of the state', that is to say by imposing heavy taxes on gaming houses and brothels. He used these funds to employ as informers people of every class and milieu, so as to have eyes and ears in every rank in the army, in every salon and every household of note. He paid well, according to status and value of services rendered, and soon built up a remarkable matrix – it is believed that even Napoleon's wife Josephine was in his employ.[8]

Additional information was provided through the scrutiny of mail, which had long been carried out under the *ancien régime* for the purpose of spying on foreign embassies (and providing the king with salacious gossip about the amorous doings of his subjects). The practice was deemed offensive to the dignity of man by the idealistic revolutionaries, and on 26 August 1790 the National Assembly decreed that every postal official must swear not to violate the privacy of personal correspondence. But on 9 May 1793 the letters of émigrés were excluded from this on grounds of national security. *Comités de Surveillance de Lettres* were established in provincial towns, and by the time Napoleon came to power all correspondence was regularly pried into.[9]

The work was carried out by the '*cabinet noir*', in a nondescript house in the rue du Coq-Héron which backed on to the postal sorting office. Most of its personnel had followed their fathers and sometimes grandfathers into the job, and they were carefully prepared to take on the task. They not only received a thorough education with a heavy stress on mathematics; they were sent abroad, attached to a diplomat, financier or merchant, so that they might pick up not merely foreign languages, which they had been taught in Paris, but also dialects, popular expressions, slang and the most commonly used abbreviations, and to familiarise themselves with the handwriting styles of different countries. Once they took up their work this was camouflaged by another, official, post with an equivalent salary and standing.

They would hover in the sorting office, pick out anything that aroused their interest and take it through a small door into a laboratory situated in the adjacent house. To unseal the packet, scan its contents, copy relevant passages and reseal it was the work of a moment, and it would be back in the sorting office before any delay could occur. 'It was in vain that the arts of envelopes, seals and ciphers struggled to escape such intrusion,' wrote Agathon Fain, a lifelong civil servant and director of Napoleon's private secretariat. 'The school of the rue du Coq-Héron knew how to circumvent every ruse. It was familiar with all the chemical possibilities; the science of mathematical probabilities and grammatical analysis provided it with proven methods of decryption; it was as skilled in taking impressions, softening wax and hardening it again under the replicated seal as it was in penetrating, with time and study, the most inaccessible ciphers.'[10]

'I admit that there never has been a police as absolute as the one which I commanded,' Fouché later wrote, but he justified it with the argument that intelligent policing protected people from what in its absence would be random state terror. He believed surveillance to be more effective than imprisonment, as, knowing or even suspecting that they were being watched, people behaved themselves. It was terror in kid gloves. 'Surveillance was a policing method which was very light, and I had devised it precisely in order to protect the numerous victims of [Napoleon's suspicion] from arbitrary detention,' he insisted.[11]

Between them, Napoleon and Fouché succeeded in restoring a degree of order in France, and in making people fear if not respect the organs of the state. Their system gradually spread through Europe, as Napoleon imposed French patterns on most of Germany, the Netherlands, Italy, parts of Poland and, briefly, Spain. The concurrent introduction of French methods into the armed forces of various states in Germany and Italy created a new class of military servants of the state, while the need felt by all sides to gather information and impose order expanded the numbers of those engaged on police work in every region. The consequence was a dramatic growth in state organs of control all over Europe.

Britain remained aloof from changes taking place on the Continent, but if French methods of state control had not affected it, the tendency to politicise questions of law and order had. And although the repressive measures of the late 1790s had extirpated every germ of subversion and Trafalgar had removed the threat of invasion, the British government continued to act as though it were under threat from the French pestilence, and from revolution in general. At the same time, it acquired some of the bad habits wafting across the Channel. The practice of prying into private correspondence was illegal in Britain, and was only permitted in exceptional cases of national emergency, requiring a specific warrant from the home secretary in each case. While no more than six warrants had been issued allowing the inspection of mail between 1788 and 1798, the number for the period 1799–1815 was 139.[12]

William Pitt died in January 1806, and was succeeded in office by Lord Grenville's 'Ministry of All the Talents', which achieved little beyond the abolition of the slave trade. In March 1807 Pitt's supporters returned to power under the Duke of Portland, who was succeeded two years later by Spencer Perceval, a much-liked man but an unpopular prime minister. Diminutive but determined, a clean-living, devoted father of twelve, a relentlessly cheerful evangelical fervently opposed to Catholic emancipation, hunting, gambling and the slave trade, Perceval was utterly convinced of the rightness of his views. To Britain's isolation from the rest of Europe he brought a smug conviction that it was her Protestant destiny to resist the corruption that had laid all others low.

The war with France had turned into a trade war, which played havoc with grain prices and devastated the cotton industry. Perceval's Orders in Council, which gave the Royal Navy draconian rights over the shipping of neutral countries, imposed in 1807 ostensibly as a response to Napoleon's Continental System but also as a means to hound slavers, led to conflict with the United States and a sharp downturn in the economy. This was compounded by the failure of the harvests of 1809, 1810, 1811 and 1812, by which time an estimated one in five people in Lancashire towns was entirely dependent on relief. There were strikes in Yorkshire and Lancashire in 1808 and 1810, some violent. Economic depression in 1810 was followed by bank failures as a result of a shortage of specie. Unemployment generated by the introduction of machinery was intensified by the outbreak of war with the United States in 1812, which closed an important market. The weekly wage of handloom weavers in Bolton fell steadily from twenty-five shillings in 1805 to fourteen in 1812.[13]

The misery was only slightly palliated by the opening up of European markets in the course of 1812 and 1813 as Napoleon's stranglehold on the Continent loosened following his disastrous defeat in Russia. The harvest of 1813 was unusually abundant, and cheap grain flowed in from the Baltic ports, hitherto under French control. The price of grain fell from 120 shillings to fifty-six, which alleviated the suffering of the poor but ruined many farmers. And the winter of 1813–14 was unusually severe, with the Thames freezing over in February.[14]

The government's problems were exacerbated by a revival in the movement for parliamentary reform. A particularly irritating thorn in its side was the Wiltshire baronet Sir Francis Burdett, who having married the banking heiress Sophia Coutts could afford to carry on a running battle against the establishment, denouncing its corruption, humbug and despotic ways. Elected to Parliament in 1802, only to be excluded on a point of order, he was returned again in 1807 as a Member for Westminster. He continued to make trouble for the government until 1810, when he was sent to the Tower for contempt by the Speaker. At the news of his arrest, a mob gathered and clashed with the military escort conducting him to the Tower, and then roamed London breaking prominent ministers' windows. He was released after three months.

Burdett had befriended other would-be reformers such as William Cobbett, Francis Place and Major John Cartwright. Cobbett, originally a supporter of the government, now campaigned on behalf of the poor workers of the north, and would move on to champion reform of Parliament. Cartwright was a long-standing campaigner for universal male suffrage, secret ballots and annual parliaments. Born in 1740 into an old Nottinghamshire landed family, he had served as a naval officer, filled an administrative post in the colonies and then commanded his county militia, settling down as a farmer in Lincolnshire. But in 1803 he had moved to Enfield so as to be closer to London.

In 1811 he helped set up a club named after the seventeenth-century parliamentarian John Hampden, who had defied Charles I. Burdett was chairman. Its original purpose was to create a lobby of influential people for electoral reform, but lack of interest made Cartwright look elsewhere. He set off on a tour of manufacturing towns, travelling on horseback despite his seventy-two years, setting up Hampden Clubs wherever he could, and there were soon flourishing branches in Royston, Oldham, Rochdale, Ashton-under-Lyme, Middleton and Stockport. Their purpose was entirely constitutional and their methods legal. That did not stop Cartwright from being arrested.

The authorities were in a state of alarm at the rising tide of popular discontent. Unemployment, falling wages and the high price of bread gave rise to despair as well as anger at technological innovation and new practices being brought into areas such as the stocking-weaving industry.

Confrontations between workers and factory owners were sometimes violent, but more commonly took the form of collective bargaining, and the aggrieved workers were on the whole deferential. In Arnold, a small town outside Nottingham, knitters broke into workshops, removed jack-wires from the knitting frames to immobilise them, and deposited them in the local church, meaning to negotiate from a position of strength. The owners held firm, so public meetings were held to enlist the support of the wider population, but these were dispersed by troops. It was only then that the workers resorted to violence, against the hated machines which in their imagination stood for unemployment and downward pressure on wages.[15]

The machine-wreckers were known as 'Luddites', after a legendary figure, Ned Ludd, who probably never existed. Their attacks grew in frequency and ferocity in the second half of 1811, and by February 1812 about a thousand stocking-making frames had been destroyed. These were rented from the owners by the craftsmen who worked at them in their own homes, and were thus widely dispersed and vulnerable. A band of Luddites could sweep into a village at night, wreck several dozen frames and be gone in the space of an hour. As they grew bolder, they also destroyed machinery in factories and mills, sometimes burning these down in the process. The government reacted by strengthening an Act dating from 1721 to make frame-breaking a capital offence. Lord Byron made his only, highly impassioned, speech in the House of Lords against this.

Militia and troops were mobilised against the Luddites, which prompted some of them to arm, by raiding private houses at night or, in one case, the arms depot of the Sheffield militia. In this case they only took a few weapons, and concentrated on destroying the rest so they could not be used against them. But as detachments of regular troops patrolled at night, they heard, or fancied they heard, the occasional gunshot. This was taken as evidence of secret nocturnal drilling, although a more likely explanation would be poaching, a national pastime and an essential resource in hard times.[16]

On 11 May 1812 the prime minister, Spencer Perceval, was shot at close range and killed in the lobby of the House of Commons. The news brought jubilant crowds onto the streets, and troops had to be called out to restore order and conduct the assassin to prison at Newgate. This unlikely hero was a merchant from Liverpool by the name of John Bellingham who bore paranoid grudges against various members of the establishment, and may have been put up to the act by some commercial interest. But his trial was conducted with such haste that the investigation did not cover all possible avenues, and, aside from his personal sense of injustice, his motivation must remain a mystery. The event was nevertheless connected in the minds of many with the concurrent disorders. 'The country is no doubt in a most alarming situation,' William Wordsworth wrote from London to his wife Mary, 'and if much firmness be not displayed by the government confusion & havoc & murder will break out & spread terribly.'[17]

A new ministry was formed by Robert Banks Jenkinson, Earl of Liverpool. He had held government office since 1795, under Pitt, Addison and Portland, been secretary of state for war in Perceval's cabinet, and would go on to serve as prime minister for fifteen years. A modest and undemonstrative man, he had proved himself a good administrator with a tough streak. He was intelligent and only forty-two years old when he assumed office, but although his mother was half Indian and he himself had travelled widely on the Continent, he took an insular and defensive view of the world. He had been at the storming of the Bastille, but does not seem to have derived from the experience any deep understanding of how revolutions are made.

His home secretary was Henry Addington, created Viscount Sidmouth in 1805, a capable if mediocre man who had proved an undistinguished prime minister from 1801 to 1804. The son of a physician and a parson's daughter, he had grown up in the shadow of his school friend William Pitt, whom he admired enormously and who assisted his ascent in politics. He was an honest man, but dull, pompous and set in his views. Although he was fifty-five years old when he became home secretary in 1812, he had never been abroad or north of Oxfordshire.

One of the most notable members of Liverpool's cabinet, and in some ways the most controversial, was the foreign secretary, Viscount Castlereagh. Born plain Robert Stewart in 1769, the same year as Napoleon and Wellington, his father was a politically ambitious Ulster landowner of Scots Presbyterian descent, while his mother was the daughter of the Marquess of Hertford, a man of immense fortune who was close to the king. This connection helped his father advance rapidly, to become Baron Londonderry in 1789, progressing within seven years via a viscountcy to an earldom and a marquisate of his own.

Castlereagh, to which title Robert acceded in 1796 when his father vaulted into his earldom, was educated at Armagh and Cambridge. He was swept up in the general euphoria attendant on the Revolution in France, and toasted the Sovereignty of the People with gusto. But when he made his grand tour at the beginning of the 1790s he had occasion to see the disorders and licence this involved. His Ulster soul was repelled, and his growing interest in a promising political career made him recoil. He had fallen under the spell of Pitt, who rewarded his devotion in 1798 by nominating him chief secretary for Ireland. Castlereagh played an active part in suppressing the Irish rebellion of that year and in pushing through the Act of Union, for both of which he was widely reviled, not just in Ireland. The poet Shelley famously labelled him a murderer, while Byron called him a cruel despot.

A reserved, sensitive man who loved flowers and animals and was never happier than when tending them at his modest country retreat in Kent, Castlereagh was also devoted to his wife. Their unfashionably homely ménage was the butt of jokes, yet he was close to the dissolute prince regent. A poor speaker, Castlereagh was nevertheless a good manager of his party in Parliament and a competent administrator, proving his worth during spells at the Colonial and then the War Office during the crucial years of 1806–09. As foreign secretary he would frame British policy single-handedly over a decade, exerting a decisive influence in Europe and playing a significant part in the defeat of Napoleon. He was trusted by Liverpool, and assumed a dominant role in the cabinet. This had inherited some of Perceval's sense of evangelical destiny, which goes some way to explain why its members did not waver in moments of adversity or pause to ask themselves whether their opponents might not have a point.

The Luddite disturbances had diminished in frequency by the time Lord Sidmouth took over at the Home Office in June 1812, but chilling reports kept coming in from all quarters. Major Seale, commander of the South Devon militia, reported on 30 June that an informer had told him there was a huge conspiracy, stretching from Glasgow to London: delegates were travelling around the country holding meetings with local committees and planning diversionary risings in the provinces to draw troops away from London before they struck in the capital. The conspirators were allegedly armed to the teeth. The theme of a plot to lure troops away from London by staging diversionary disturbances recurs in other letters received by Sidmouth, and spies sent in information that appeared to confirm that 'a general insurrection' was being planned by 'secret committees'. A 'Mr. S' in Bolton had been overheard telling the town's machine-breakers that great personages in London such as Burdett were only waiting for them to make a move that would bring down the government, and encouraging them to give the signal by burning down a factory at West Houghton.[18]

In July both Houses set up committees of secrecy to report on the disturbances. The reports bristle with the stock phrases 'it appears', 'there is reason to believe' and 'evidence suggests', and paint an ominous picture of dark goings-on, based on presuppositions and unsupported inference. According to the Commons committee, the disturbances had nothing spontaneous about them, and were the result of 'organised systems of unlawful violence'; 'language of the most mischievous nature' had been employed by the rioters, who demonstrated 'a sort of military training and discipline'. It makes much of reports of the bands being marshalled by leaders with 'signals' and of the fact that 'rockets and blue lights have been seen by night'. Both reports dwell on the degree of organisation and coordination displayed, on the stockpiling of arms, on the existence of regional 'committees', on the 'signs and countersigns' used to guard against infiltrators. They quote an oath allegedly sworn by all adepts not to disclose the identity of members of the supreme 'Secret Committee' which was supposedly 'the great mover of the whole machine'. The unstated conclusion is that there was a far-ranging conspiracy to overthrow the government by force. On 23 July Sidmouth laid before Parliament a Bill giving magistrates wider powers. Soldiers were quartered in every inn throughout the affected localities, and camps were set up in Sherwood Forest and on Kersal Moor. By the end of the year some 12,000 regular troops had been deployed in the area, as many as Wellington had in the Peninsula.[19]

The Home Office received a steady stream of demands for military protection from factory owners and magistrates, while private individuals took their own precautions. The Reverend Patrick Brontë fired a pistol out of his bedroom window at Haworth Parsonage every morning. At Keswick in the Lake District the poet Robert Southey got hold of 'a rusty old gun' and kept it loaded against the revolutionaries. An ardent republican in the 1790s, he now smelled sedition 'even among these mountains', and warned Lord Liverpool that if the troops were withdrawn from London 'four and twenty hours would not elapse before the tricoloured flag would be planted upon Carlton House'.[20]

General Maitland, commanding the regular forces in the north of the country, did not believe in the likelihood of revolution. Earl Fitzwilliam, now lord lieutenant of the West Riding of Yorkshire, one of the worst-affected areas, maintained that the disturbances were no more than 'the offspring of distress and want of employment'. Such confrontations as did occur between rioters and troops or militia were usually non-violent, and crowds dispersed peacefully. In Sheffield, women had gone around in a mob, but rather than loot, they forced shopkeepers to sell them flour at a price they thought fair: a strong belief in the 'rights of free Englishmen' lay at the root of many of the incidents and shaped their course. In July, the same month that Sidmouth sent out the soldiers, Fitzwilliam reported that the incidents had ceased and the country was quiet. The knitters continued to gather, and there were sporadic outbreaks of machine-breaking, but the crisis was over. In February 1813 the prince regent issued a proclamation calling on 'all His Majesty's subjects to exert themselves in preventing the recurrence of these atrocious crimes, and to warn those who may be exposed to the machinations of secret directors of the danger and wickedness of such advice'. By then Fitzwilliam was able to report 'that the country is fast subsiding into a state of temper which promises that no further outrage will disturb the public tranquillity', and that it was safe to withdraw the troops.[21]

The authorities' tendency to view food riots and Luddite disturbances in political terms is difficult to understand. There was certainly some subversive activity by the detritus of the radical groups of the 1790s and the United Irishmen, those of Despard's associates who had not been hanged, Spenceans and others. They were joined by returning transportees of 1793 and 1794 whose sentences had expired, many of whom were eager to resume the struggle where they had left off. But the authorities knew who they were, and had spies in every cell, so they would have been aware that there was no connection between them and the Luddites, and that they did not even try to exploit the disturbances. The only reformist activity and political opposition to the government in the past decade had been carried on at Westminster by the likes of Burdett, and in the open by Cartwright and others. The Revolution in France had been shackled by Napoleon, and now Napoleon himself no longer represented a threat to Britain. In October he suffered a crushing defeat at Leipzig that put his own future in question.

The bumper harvest of 1813 and the influx of cheap grain from the liberated Continent ensured that there would be no food riots, and without the spur of hunger the lower orders were generally docile. 'I defy you to agitate a fellow with a full stomache,' Cobbett famously complained. Not only had they failed to be stirred by slogans crossing the Channel from France, they stolidly clung to their own cherished shibboleths. The Royal Jubilee held in 1809 to mark the fiftieth year of the reign of George III had unleashed a quite unexpected effusion of patriotism and attachment to the monarchy in all classes. As the end of the war and the prospect of peace drew near, people of conservative bent all over the United Kingdom could congratulate themselves that the storm had been weathered. In June 1815 the final act of Waterloo would only serve to place a gilded full stop at the end of the story. Yet the fear would not subside.[22]

'The revolutionary ideas of France have already made but too great a progress in the hearts of men in all countries, and even in the very centre of every capital,' warned a leading article in *The Times* a couple of weeks before the momentous battle. 'It is not Bonaparte that at present forms the danger of Europe: he is unmasked. It is the new opinions; it is the disorganisation of men's minds; it is the making revolt a calculation of private interest; it is the most deadly of all contagions, the contagion of immorality, of false philanthropy, of a perfidious self-styled philosophy; from all of which the world requires to be protected. This is the true hydra which must be destroyed, or it will destroy all Europe. The cause of morality is the cause of God; it is the cause of all men, of all nations, of all thrones!'[23]

Such a cause could not be defeated in the field, and, spectacular as it was, the victory of Waterloo did not alter the attitude of the cabinet, which refused to abandon its fable of a seething mass of revolutionaries bent on overthrowing the British constitution and murdering the king and most of the aristocracy.

7

Peace

The wars that came to an end in 1815 had been no ordinary wars. For the best part of a quarter of a century, military operations had swept across Europe, from Lisbon to Moscow, from the Baltic to the toe of Italy: if Sweden, Norway, England, Sardinia and Sicily had been spared invasion, Finland, Wales, Ireland, Malta, Egypt and Palestine had not, and the entire population of the Continent had been affected in material terms. The fighting took in almost all of Europe's colonies, from Florida in the west to Java in the east, and much of it took place at sea. It lasted six times as long as would the First World War, and four times as long as the Second. Battlefield casualties were not as great, but deaths among soldiers and civilians from wounds, disease, famine and exposure were comparable in relative terms, and certainly unprecedented.

The end of hostilities brought a change for the worse in material terms for the majority of the population of Europe, particularly of the poor. Markets closed by war reopened; others, created by the need for armament and military supplies, collapsed, giving rise to economic dislocation on a vast scale. War had been waged at the economic level, with both sides imposing blockades designed to ruin the other. While Britain did everything to starve France of its colonial trade, Napoleon had excluded British trade from mainland Europe. Items traditionally imported from Britain or the colonies had to be produced at home, and the absence of British competition brought prosperity to parts of Saxony, Austria, Switzerland and Catalonia, to the wool, iron and steel industries of Prussia. Belgium went through an industrial revolution caused by the demand for military goods. Rural areas benefited as the lack of colonial trade gave a boost to the sugar beet industry. The length of the wars lent these provisional developments an element of permanence.

The coming of peace removed trade barriers and flooded hitherto protected areas of Europe with colonial goods and cheap English imports, wreaking havoc with local economies. Yet it did little to alleviate hardship in England. While European markets opened up to English goods such as textiles and steel, it was stocks piled up during the blockade that were exported, and there was therefore no corresponding boost in production or reduction in unemployment. Meanwhile, imports of cheap European corn threatened to ruin British farmers.

The wars had coincided with the introduction of labour-saving machinery and of significant increases in population, and the resulting downward pressure on wages was increased by the influx of disbanded soldiers. The burdens placed on poor households were added to by the return of maimed men unable to work but needing to be fed. Dramatic fluctuations in the currency supply over the period and the introduction of paper money by revolutionary France and then Britain added to the instability and sapped confidence. Every government in Europe taxed whatever it could to pay off wartime borrowing. Britain had spent more in real terms than it would on the First World War, and its national debt was astronomical. Russia's had multiplied by twenty times between 1801 and 1809, and would more than double again by 1822. Austria was technically bankrupt: over the next three decades an average of 30 per cent of state revenue would be siphoned off to service its debt.[1]

The social consequences, both of the wars and of the peace, were far-reaching. Young men, and the women who often followed them, were plucked out of their families and communities, away from their restraints and taboos. They were often obliged to serve not the interests of their own ruler, but those of his ally, with the result that Portuguese peasants would find themselves fighting in Russia, and Poles in Spain. Their experiences both emancipated and brutalised them. Those who avoided conscription by running away from home and going into hiding lived by banditry, and would never again be susceptible to control by traditional means such as the influence of the Church or deference to local hierarchies and institutions. The same went for deserters, who were forced into a life of crime in order to survive. When peace came, such people drifted back not to their villages but to large towns, where they could lose themselves and hope to satisfy some of the aspirations encouraged by the slogans of the revolutionary and Napoleonic eras, and the mood of the times.

The urban population was also swelled by economic migration from the countryside, which not only lowered the standard of living of the poorer sections by creating downward pressure on wages and severe overcrowding leading to disease, but also had some unexpected consequences. The move from country to town usually severed or at least weakened not only family ties but also links to traditional forms of religious observance. Established Churches had either been abolished, as in revolutionary France, or seen their property and status dramatically reduced, as well as their social role as providers of education and health care; their influence had shrunk as a result. They had lost control of the poorest sections of the population in large towns, leaving these prone to a variety of new religious movements and political philosophies.

The wars had been preceded by the outbreak of the French Revolution, and were in many ways a continuation of it. They brought in their wake colossal disruption of all social and political relations throughout the Continent and its dependencies overseas: rulers were humbled or toppled, established religion undermined or abolished, hierarchies of every sort weakened or dismantled; individuals, classes, minorities and nations were liberated in one sense or another. This not only aroused dormant disputes and hatreds, it opened to question every aspect of social, political and spiritual practice, introducing an ideological dimension and intensity of a kind that had been absent from most European conflicts since the religious wars of the seventeenth century. Confronted by the revolutionary ardour of the French, the Bourbon kings of Naples had created an 'Army of the Holy Faith' to combat it, the Spanish launched a semi-religious *guerrilla* of great ferocity, Austria roused the passions of the Tyrolese in 1809, Russia used peasant militias to harry the French in 1812, and Prussia mobilised the population of Germany in 1813 for the *Freiheitskrieg*, or war of liberation.

As though all this were not enough, Nature contributed the greatest volcanic eruption in recorded history, more than four times greater than Krakatoa's in 1883. On 10 April 1815, as Napoleon was mustering the army that would be undone at Waterloo, Mount Tambora on the island of Sumbawa in the Indonesian archipelago exploded into what contemporaries described as a mass of liquid fire and sent volcanic ash twenty miles into the atmosphere. The eruption was heard more than 1,600 miles away, and the whole area within a radius of some four hundred miles was plunged into pitch darkness for two days. The death toll was somewhere between 70,000 and 90,000. Winds sent the particles of ash around the globe, and Londoners were astonished by brilliantly coloured sunsets at the end of July. But the real effects would only make themselves felt later.

There would be no summer in Europe in 1816. Constant rain and persistent cold would destroy harvests across the Continent, causing famine in parts of Ireland, Wales and northern Italy, where people were reduced to eating grass, berries, boiled vegetable peelings and animal manure. In Germany they made bread from the bark of trees. This would precipitate a mass migration of people to less affected parts of Europe, to Russia and to America. Weather patterns would return to normal in the course of 1819. But nothing else did. 'The volcano is not burnt out,' the British home secretary Lord Sidmouth wrote to a friend on 13 August 1815, and he was not referring to Mount Tambora.[2]

There were many at every level of society and in every region to whom peace was unwelcome, and who would take every opportunity to stir up old passions. Some out of ideological conviction, others out of loyalty to a defeated cause, others out of a desire to reverse a situation which had cost them wealth and or rank, others still because peace had no use for their talents. All over Europe, young men who craved adventure, glory and status faced a bleak and boring future. At the same time, the nature of the wars had transformed armies from the eighteenth-century model of pressed or indentured soldiers and mercenaries into citizens-in-arms and champions of the nation. The army had acquired a distinctive place in every European society, and would become a factor in the internal politics of every state in Europe. In recognition of this, almost every European monarch henceforth appeared in uniform.

Long periods of war, with their hardship and suffering, invariably raise expectations of the longed-for peace, often giving rise to dreams of a fresh start or a better world which might make up for and to some extent justify some of that hardship and suffering. In 1815 this phenomenon was magnified by concurrent spiritual awakenings which had been taking place over the past two decades, in Germany and other parts of central Europe, in England and in North America. Such dreams are almost as invariably dashed. But in this instance, it was not only the millenarian dreamers who were disappointed.

The peace settlement reached at the Congress of Vienna in 1815 had been the work of some of the most distinguished statesmen of the day, achieved at the cost of nearly two years of laborious negotiations. The peacemakers had set out with respectable, if not the best, intentions. These had been overtaken by the priority of creating a balance between the major mainland states, Russia, Prussia and Austria, henceforth designated as the great powers, and of making it strategically impossible for France to threaten them again. The final settlement failed to fulfil the expectations and longings of large numbers of people, and it injured cultural and religious sensibilities. It also offended the sense of justice of people at every level of society all over

Europe: while many who had prospered from the Revolution and military aggression were dispossessed and criminalised, others were rewarded, and few of the victims obtained satisfaction. Not surprisingly, the peace was widely denounced as unjust and immoral. The complaints of those left out in the cold were, as far as the peacemakers were concerned, irrelevant. But in ignoring them, they were creating causes dedicated to the overthrow of the system they had put in place.

Among the unsatisfied longings torturing various parts of Europe was the aspiration to independent nationhood. Many Italians, Poles, Hungarians, Irishmen, Belgians and above all Germans were unhappy to see their homelands divided or ruled by foreigners, and longed to give them life as independent nations.

Another longing strongly felt in various parts of the Continent, under different guises in every country, was for a return to a simpler and spiritually purer way of life. This had surfaced in the German Enlightenment and the Pietist movement in German religious life, and been taken up in the writings of the Russian journalist Nikolai Ivanovich Novikov, the mystic Louis-Claude de Saint-Martin, the German poet Novalis, the mining engineer Franz von Baader and Tsar Alexander's spiritual mentor Baroness von Krüdener. Underlying this trend was the belief not only that the Christian faith should be practised more in spirit than in traditional ritual, but also that love should transcend laws, and that the rights of rulers must be earned through the application of virtue. Some went so far as to see in the French Revolution a punishment for Europe's abandonment of Christian values, and therefore a salutary lesson which the supposedly Christian monarchs had failed to learn. Such views coincided with a strain in German Romanticism which had identified the Middle Ages as a time of purity and heroism. Writers such as Adam Müller called for a return not to the *ancien régime* obtaining before 1789, but to an imagined age of chivalry, untainted by the evils of the Reformation and the Enlightenment. In his *Advice to Young Noblemen*, Tsar Alexander's friend the duc de Richelieu propounded that the Revolution had been in large measure the consequence of the shortcomings of the French nobility, and enjoined their descendants to forget the 'false grandeur' of the eighteenth century and to reach back to the 'age of chivalry' for models.[3]

Inchoate as such ideas might have been, they drifted through sections of European society demanding attention and action. The frustrated emotions expressed by French poets such as Vigny and Musset, and later Lamartine and Hugo, came to be known as '*le mal du siècle*'. Those of their Russian counterparts Pushkin and Lermontov gave rise to the notion of the '*lichnii chelovek*', the superfluous man for whom there was no role in the ugly realities of the existing world order.

'A reputedly invincible revolution has just been vanquished,' wrote the conservative historian and former émigré soldier François Dominique de Montlosier as he considered the state of France in 1815. But this had solved nothing, since the victors were beset by 'both the old vices which produced the revolution and the new ones which the revolution produced' as they tried to rebuild the state. 'What plan is to be followed? The wisdom of past times is no longer applicable to the present; it is foreign to it: the wisdom of modern times is even less applicable; it is depraved.'[4]

The problem is well illustrated by what happened when, on recovering his temporal dominion, Pope Leo XII tried to turn the clock back. When the French occupied the Papal States in 1809 they reorganised the administration, lifted the disabilities on various groups, abolished the privileges of others and modernised the infrastructure. The pope sacked all those who had worked in the administration under the French, brought back the Inquisition and the Jesuits, and sent the Jews back to the ghetto. Other casualties included unholy revolutionary novelties such as street lighting and vaccination.

King Victor Emmanuel I of Sardinia took a similar line. He had been forced to flee his mainland capital Turin at the approach of the French in 1798. When he returned, he expelled all French nationals from his realm, even those married to Sardinian subjects, and closed down the botanical gardens created under the French, uprooting and burning plants as though they carried seeds of corruption. He too sacked officials wholesale. Clutching the court almanac of 1798 and muttering '*Novant'Ott!*' (ninety-eight), he reinstated people in the posts and ranks they had held then, with the result that grandfathers became pages once more. To the joy of breeches- and wig-makers he revived the fashions of the past, and the arch-conservative Sardinian minister in St Petersburg, Joseph de Maistre, had to stop on his way back to Turin in order to have a new wardrobe made (he admitted to a correspondent that 'at the risk of sounding ridiculous, I am not sure I will know how to walk in our *ci-devant* dress, having spent more than twenty years in tail-coat or uniform').[5]

Victor Emmanuel did, in one case at least, close down a textile factory operating in a former convent and, having traced a dozen former members of its Capuchin community, restore it. But neither he nor the pope returned much religious property confiscated by the state under the French. Nor did they abolish the efficient fiscal systems introduced by them. Victor Emmanuel also retained the French peace-keeping *Gendarmerie*, under the new name of *Carabinieri*. Principles crumbled before convenience.

The Congress of Vienna made many casualties of convenience – sovereign rulers, aristocrats, bishops, monasteries and other institutions which had been dispossessed by a revolution or Napoleonic regime saw their property handed over to third parties. Invoking the principle of legitimacy in order to reinstate some offensive aspects of the old order and trampling it for the sake of expediency, the new order set up by the congress alienated large sections of the very nobility and aristocracy that should have been its greatest support. By riding roughshod over the rights of these and other, more humble individuals, the settlement placed the state in opposition to the individual to a greater extent than ever before, and in so doing profoundly contradicted the spirit of the age, which elevated the individual and deified the collective in the shape of the nation. Such sentiments transcended the parochial gripes of wronged minorities, and would unite wildly disparate elements in protest. The philosopher La Harpe went so far as to venture that the peace settlement contained 'the germs of the disintegration of Europe'. The Italian statesman Camillo di Cavour termed it 'a political edifice without any moral foundation'. Maistre also denied it legitimacy. 'Justice, by its very nature, leads to peace,' he wrote. 'Injustice, by its very nature, leads to war.' He would be proved correct, but it would be a very different kind of war from that he imagined.[6]

The 'depraved' wisdom Montlosier referred to was a new liberalism based on considerations of utility and practicality which had left behind the utopianism of the Enlightenment and the idealism of the Revolution, and set aside such grandiloquent concepts as the Rights of Man in favour of a more pragmatic approach intended to achieve the greatest good for the greatest number. It took for granted that much of what had been done in terms of political enfranchisement, social emancipation, secularisation, disestablishment and extension of the protection of the law in France and wherever French influence had penetrated represented a huge step forward on the march of human progress.

'God has clearly indicated that He does not wish the order of royal generations to be interrupted,' argued one of Tsar Alexander's advisers, Sergei Semionovich Uvarov. But he believed the people had acquired 'a right to the gratitude of the Sovereigns whom they so valiantly defended'. He suggested that kings and people should make 'the mutual sacrifice of despotism and popular anarchy' on 'the tomb of Buonaparte'. Talleyrand took a similar line when he argued that legitimacy could no longer be based on Divine Right, but on the monarch's ability to ensure the happiness of his people. 'The general opinion today, and it would be pointless to try to change it, is that governments exist solely for the people,' he explained, 'and the consequence of this view is that legitimate power is that which can best assure their happiness and their peace.'[7]

History could not be rolled back. 'Without despising or wishing to denigrate the *ancien régime*, I regarded as puerile any attempt to reinstate it,' wrote the duc de Broglie, a twenty-nine-year-old aristocrat who had served as a minor diplomat under Napoleon. 'In heart and mind I belonged to the new society, I believed fervently in its boundless progress; and while detesting the process of revolution, with all the violence that it gives rise to and the crimes that sully it, I regarded the French Revolution *in globo* as an inevitable and salutary affliction.'[8]

To the conservatively minded, this was heresy. The principal reason why the Treaty of Vienna was so flawed was, according to Maistre, that the monarchs and ministers 'clearly allowed themselves to be penetrated by the philosophical and political ideas of the age', which he saw as an opportunistic pragmatism. 'The spirit of revolution *is dressed up* as the spirit of *reason*, and under this disguise it is very alluring,' he warned in August 1815. For people such as him, the threat of a return to 1793 exerted the same compulsive fear as did to all reasonable people in the decades following the Second World War the possibility of a return of fascism: the slightest reference to the episode tended to be pounced on as evidence of 'Jacobinism', just as post-war *bien-pensants* tended to brand anyone with right-wing sympathies a 'fascist'. The ultra-conservative politician Jean-Baptiste de Villèle referred to all liberals as '*la Révolution*', a word that epitomised for him a living force, a giant conspiracy on the move.[9]

'As long as the absurd and fatal (and also at first sight very plausible) dogma of the *sovereignty of the people* is more or less publicly recognised,' warned Maistre in March 1817, 'I do not think that a sensible man can rest easy.' Those who shared his views saw the Revolution not so much as a past event, but as the beginning of a new era in the struggle between good and evil. If the Revolution which had had such a devastating impact on people all over the world had indeed been brought about by a conspiracy, the danger was by no means past. The conspiracy could not have merely petered out, and its spirit could not have been extinguished by the military victory over Napoleon. The Revolution had not been the culmination, but an explosion, and, whether or not Mount Tambora had a subliminal effect, the prevailing imagery was volcanic.[10]

'The French volcano erupted,' in the words of Tsar Alexander's adviser Count Alexander Sturdza. 'Out came and rose up the spirit of evil. Its path was frayed and widened by religious deviance, excess of luxury, dissolution of morals, abuse of power and perversion of reason.' The conservative writer Louis de Bonald agreed, and warned that 'even if the eruption has ceased, the volcano is still alight and rumbling.'[11]

'It is not only peace that Europe needs,' reflected Bonald at the end of 1815, 'it is first and foremost *order* that she is in need of ...' But what kind of order? European society had been split along ideological lines to an extent not seen since the Reformation. One man's order was another man's prison. If the progressive forces in European society were split between liberals who believed in the gradual evolution of democracy by means of constitutional monarchy and the vociferous minority who called for violent revolution, the forces of conservatism were equally split between the constitutional monarchists and a strident faction which saw only revolution, murder and mayhem everywhere. And while some looked for spiritual solutions, those in power sought comfort in a dubious legitimacy and the security of bayonets. In the circumstances, the pursuit of 'order' was to become a self-defeating quest that would transform European societies and help to mould the modern state.[12]

8

A Hundred Days

What usually happened at the close of a war was that the defeated party ceded territory to the victors and undertook to pay them reparations in one form or another. The deal was often sealed by a marriage which made it difficult for the vanquished ruler to seek to take his revenge. It was not usual practice to overthrow a defeated monarch – at most, he might be forced to abdicate in favour of a less aggressive or capable son – which is what Napoleon proposed in 1814. But Napoleon was a highly unusual monarch. The British did not recognise him as one at all. Others did so only reluctantly, and while he had been crowned by the pope and had married the Emperor of Austria's daughter, they could not quite bring themselves to accept him. It was not merely a question of his lineage. While some saw him only as its infamous spawn, for others he was the Revolution incarnate. They referred to him as 'the Usurper', 'the Monster' or 'the Ogre'. The English prime minister Spencer Perceval likened him to the woman in the Book of Revelations, 'the mother of harlots and abominations of the earth', who rides upon the Beast and visits destruction on the world. If the revolutionary legacy was to be stamped out and its ghosts exorcised, it followed that Napoleon would have to go.[1]

They had not yet decided what to do with him when Tsar Alexander, who was first on the scene in Paris in 1814, took the matter into his own hands. In an access of misjudged chivalry, he signed a treaty with

Napoleon at Fontainebleau, giving him the Mediterranean island of Elba to rule, with a generous pension to be provided by the future ruler of France. The question of who was to replace him was settled in similarly arbitrary manner, largely by the arguments put forward by the French statesman (and formerly Napoleon's foreign minister) Charles-Maurice de Talleyrand. He insisted that whoever replaced Napoleon must, in contrast to the usurper, enjoy the full sanction of legitimacy. His accession should also mark the end of the epoch that had opened with the outbreak of the Revolution. Talleyrand convinced the victorious monarchs and their ministers that the only person who satisfied these criteria was Louis Stanislas Xavier, younger brother of Louis XVI, the last king of France under the *ancien régime*, who had been guillotined in 1793.

There could be no question of restoring the *ancien régime* as such. What had taken place in France between 1789 and 1814 could not simply be written out of history. Talleyrand had himself taken part in the opening stages of the Revolution, and had later been a pillar of the Napoleonic empire. During those twenty-five years France and French society had been transformed beyond recognition, for the better in most cases, and this needed to be taken into account. The allies duly foisted on the new king a constitution, in the shape of the *Charte*. The legislature was to be a bicameral parliament, the higher chamber made up of peers nominated by the king, the lower of deputies elected on a suffrage based on property ownership: a more liberal and rational version of the English constitutional model. Although it aroused little enthusiasm, the restoration of the Bourbon dynasty was carried out without trouble: the majority of the population of France, exhausted by two decades of war, was politically indifferent – most people could not remember the Republic, let alone the *ancien régime*, so they saw no reason to resist it. There was nothing about the new king to get heated over.

Born in 1755, the younger brother of the heir to the throne, he had been carefully brought up and well educated, but found no outlet for his ambitions. Deeply religious and conscientious, he stood, or rather sat, on the sidelines, devoting his energies to the study of his favourite subject, the classics. He also gave free rein to his love of food, and, being averse to exercise in any form, grew corpulent. His marriage to a repellent princess of Savoy remained childless, despite valiant efforts on his part, and he distracted himself with a mistress. When the Revolution came, he stood by the king as long as he could, but fled abroad in June 1791. He went to Koblenz, where his younger brother the comte d'Artois and a large number of émigré nobles were forming an army with the intention of marching back into France to reinstate the king. When this hope evaporated, he resigned himself to exile, first at Verona, then Brunswick, Mittau (Jelgava), Warsaw and finally Hartwell House in Buckinghamshire, struggling pathetically to maintain the decorum and trappings of royalty on the not always lavish generosity of others, latterly that of the prince regent.

King Louis was immensely fat, but he had good features and many found him handsome. Exuding benevolence, with a dignified bearing, he had the requisite regal presence. He was intelligent and aware that he must make some concession to the times, but he was out of touch with the people he was to rule. The costume he adopted, a combination of eighteenth-century court dress and nineteenth-century military uniform, was designed to marry the two epochs, and instead fell clumsily between them. Too heavy to mount a horse and too gout-ridden to wear leather ones, he invented top-boots made of velvet which, along with the sword he always wore, were meant to stress his adherence to the military traditions of his royal predecessors, but they compared unfavourably with the dashing uniforms of the Napoleonic era.

He took the name of Louis XVIII in deference to the son of Louis XVI, who had survived his father and therefore become titular King of France as Louis XVII before dying in a revolutionary gaol in 1795. Sticking fast to the principle of legitimacy, the new monarch considered himself to have been rightful king from the moment of his nephew's death, and on arriving in France on 3 May 1814 dated his official pronouncements as being made in the nineteenth year of his reign –

which was tantamount to a negation of everything that had happened since 1795. After doing all he could to wriggle out of having to accept the constitution forced on him by the allies, he insisted on 'granting' the *Charte* as a regal gesture. This was an insult to the notion of the sovereignty of the people, which had become the bedrock of French political life. More to the point, it presupposed that as he had granted the *Charte*, he could take it back if he pleased. Just in case there should be any doubt in the matter, he re-established the notion of Divine Right in official documents and in the oath of allegiance.

What could be forgiven in the king was less tolerable in the large number of émigré nobles who returned in his wake. Most had left France in the early stages of the Revolution, out of ideological conviction and loyalty to the monarchy or fear for their lives. Some had rallied to the princes at Koblenz, and later many had taken service with other monarchs, particularly in Russia. Others had just sat it out. As the Revolution turned into the Napoleonic empire many of the original émigrés returned to France and took service under its new ruler. Those who had held firm looked down on these, and when they in turn came back in 1814, they exhibited a bitter aloofness with regard to everything that had taken place in France over the past quarter of a century.

The revolutionary regime had confiscated the property of émigrés and sold these *biens nationaux* (national assets) to raise income. Many had since been sold on to new owners, yet the returning émigrés clamoured for their return. The Church, which had also been dispossessed, was in similarly assertive mood, and priests refused to give communion to current owners of former Church property. This kind of thing aroused strong passions in otherwise quiescent rural areas, where politics were of little interest but property rights all-important.

Supported by a large number of nobles who had formed associations with names such as *la Congrégation de la Vierge* (the Congregation of the Virgin) and *les Chevaliers de la Foi* (the Knights of the Faith), the Church also tried to recover its spiritual ascendancy. It organised missions to recapture the soul of France, holding mass baptisms in the army and provocatively ostentatious services to commemorate 'martyrs' of the Revolution and to 'expiate' its 'crimes', often at the spot where a liberty tree had been planted in place of a cross or where a guillotine had stood. It was tireless in sniffing out the revolutionary past of government officials and denouncing them, which often ended in them losing their posts and being ostracised. Many who had served the government of the day, often without conviction, during the Revolution, the Directory, the Consulate and the Empire, found themselves penalised and unable to pursue their careers.

Not surprisingly, the army suffered the most in this respect. Napoleon's Imperial Guard was disbanded and replaced by the *Maison du Roi*, officered entirely by nobles, mostly émigrés with little or no military experience. As with his own dress, the king had designed for them a uniform which made them a laughing stock. The army was reduced in number, and officers surplus to requirements were put on half-pay. Distinguished generals were replaced by émigrés who had been lieutenants in 1789 and had not borne arms since. The tricolour which had fluttered over victory across Europe was banned in favour of a white flag, the banner of the royalist insurgents of the Vendée. The colour of the uniforms was changed, regiments were disbanded and those that were left lost their identity, and their battle-honours with it. As a final insult, the despised General Dupont, who had capitulated to the Spanish at Bailén in 1808, was appointed minister of war. In wine shops, cafés and guardrooms up and down the country, veterans of Napoleon's campaigns, those who remained in the ranks and those who had been cashiered or retired on half-pay, the so-called *demi-soldes*, voiced their contempt for the new regime and talked of bringing back their beloved general.

Napoleon himself soon realised he was not going to be allowed to live out his days as sovereign of the island of Elba. Reports reaching him from Vienna confirmed that the powers assembled there in congress were planning to remove him to somewhere more remote, fearing that while he remained a free man he would be a magnet for discontent and opposition to the restored Bourbon monarchy. He was also aware of a number of plots being hatched to assassinate him. There is some evidence that as well as colluding in such plots, the Bourbon regime was trying to goad him, amongst other means by withholding payment of his allowance, into making a move that would force the allies to deal with him conclusively.[2]

Louis XVIII cannot therefore have been greatly surprised when, at the beginning of March 1815, less than a year since he ascended the throne, he was informed that Napoleon had landed on the south coast of France. He ordered units in the area to bar the road to Paris and sent his brother, the comte d'Artois, to take command, before despatching a strong force under the former Napoleonic Marshal Ney to defeat and capture his erstwhile master. He summoned the foreign ambassadors to the Tuileries and told them to instruct their courts that he felt 'no anxiety whatsoever with regard to this event'. 'I hope that it will not trouble the repose of Europe or my own,' he added. With similar self-assurance he declared to the Chamber of Deputies and that of Peers that he would die fighting rather than abandon Paris.[3]

Napoleon had landed on 1 March at Golfe Juan with just over a thousand men. He was obliged to bypass Cannes and Grasse on account of the hostility of the local population, and during the first days of his march he met with little more than morose curiosity on the part of the locals. But the mood changed as he moved north, and at Laffrey on 7 March a regiment of infantry sent to bar his way rallied to him. That night he entered Grenoble in triumph, and on 10 March he was in Lyon, where he was greeted with enthusiasm. Artois, who had set up his headquarters there, had fled at his approach. Troops sent out by Louis XVIII to stop him could not be counted on, and their commanders wavered. Some remained loyal to the king and fell back on Paris, others took their men over to Napoleon. At Avallon General Girard brought two regiments over to his side; at Auxerre Marshal Ney, who had with characteristic bravado promised Louis XVIII that he would bring the usurper back in a cage, rallied to his former master and took his troops with him.

In the early hours of 20 March, with Napoleon approaching fast, Louis XVIII furtively slipped out of the Tuileries and, gradually deserted by most of the *Maison du Roi*, fled the country. Late that afternoon, Napoleon was carried in triumph up the main staircase of the palace on the shoulders of his generals and former ministers. But he had few illusions. 'They have let me in just as they let the others out,' he commented to his treasury minister Nicolas Mollien. There was something distinctly haphazard about the whole business. Yet the events of March 1815 were to have huge significance. The 'Hundred Days' that followed did more than briefly disturb the repose of Europe and inconvenience Louis XVIII. The episode fundamentally altered the political situation inside France, and would have serious repercussions for the whole Continent.[4]

In 1814 the defeated Napoleon could call on not much more than the loyalty of his soldiers, and even many of those were weary. The rest of the population had come to see him as a tyrant and to associate him with oppression, taxation, conscription and deteriorating living standards. As far as they were concerned, there was little to choose between Napoleon and Louis XVIII, and the latter would at least bring peace and a relaxation of conscription.

Unlike the Bourbons, Napoleon had learned his lesson, and the man who landed at Golfe Juan on 1 March was no longer the imperious ruler of 1814. At Lyon, where he paused briefly before advancing on Paris, he issued edicts and hostile declarations concerning priests and aristocrats, threatening to string them up from lamp-posts. When he reached Paris he set out to galvanise the masses by holding a great ceremony of national federation, in emulation of the coming together of the *Fête de la Fédération* of 14 July 1790, the first anniversary of the fall of the Bastille. He did everything he could to revive the spirit of 1792, when to the strains of the '*Marseillaise*' the nation had flocked to repel the invading allied armies. The very ease with which he had toppled the Bourbon regime gave radicals of every hue new hope, and all the political issues of the past decades resurfaced.

He succeeded in rousing old revolutionaries and rallied them in defence of what he made out was a common cause. In Toulouse, Marc-Guillaume Vadier, a former Jacobin and friend of Marat and Robespierre, an enthusiastic regicide who had retired from political life in disgust in the mid-1790s, now came forward to lead his community in welcoming Napoleon's return. At Avignon, Agricole Morea, another rabid Jacobin and henchman of Robespierre, also sprang into action, seeing in the return of Napoleon the only hope of saving at least some of the legacy of the Revolution. Napoleon engaged the respected liberal Benjamin Constant to frame a new constitution, which appeased many enemies and critics. He abolished censorship. In an attempt to appeal to English public opinion he outlawed the slave trade. But the English were not impressed, and nor were the other powers to which he made conciliatory overtures, and whose delegates were still in congress at Vienna, finalising the new arrangement of Europe.[5]

News of Napoleon's landing in France put the French delegate at the congress, Talleyrand, in an unenviable position. If Napoleon were to reach Paris, recover his throne and accept all the treaties binding France and the allies, they would have no legitimate grounds to make war on him. That would leave Louis XVIII, and Talleyrand himself, out in the cold. In order to pre-empt such a situation, he persuaded the delegates of all the powers at Vienna to issue a proclamation he had drafted, which declared Napoleon to have placed himself 'outside the law' and indeed 'outside the human race' by returning to France; he was to be treated as a dangerous criminal, an enemy of mankind. It followed that those who supported him were also outlaws. 'The declaration is certainly the harshest measure ever taken against an individual,' Talleyrand commented with satisfaction.[6]

It was much more than that. It was an entirely new departure in the history of European diplomacy and politics: a political excommunication by a group of powers of not just an individual, but of all he stood for and all those who supported it. It set the scene for a struggle between the self-appointed forces of good against the implied forces of evil, a struggle that would, in time, draw in the whole of Europe, as governments stood by the Vienna settlement as though it had been Holy Scripture and peoples tried to pursue the course of human progress. In the first instance, it drew a battle line across French society which made France very difficult to govern. The Hundred Days had profoundly altered the political landscape in other ways too.

The abdication of Napoleon in the previous year had ingloriously concluded a narrative of which the majority of the people of France had grown tired. Contemporary sources overwhelmingly report an indifference to his fall born of war-weariness and despondency, and even much hostility to his person. His spectacular reconquest of France, followed by the monumental battle and the shattering defeat of Waterloo, was, on the other hand, the stuff of legend. Waterloo instantly became a symbol – of heroism, grandeur, tragedy, and much more besides, a focus for pride as well as sorrow, a sacred memory which the Bourbon king and his regime insulted and defiled by their very existence.

To others, Napoleon's return had been clear proof that the forces of revolution were still rampant, and that those who had supported him must be extirpated. As soon as news of the allied victory reached Marseille, a mob massacred retired Mamelouks of the Imperial Guard along with their wives and children. Marshal Brune was savagely murdered and mutilated at Avignon, General Ramel in Toulouse. A White Terror swept through the country, with random arrests, house searches, looting of property, beatings and occasionally murder. Owners of *biens nationaux* were molested and made to pay blood money to get royalist zealots off their backs. In Nîmes, it was the local Protestants, whose disabilities had been lifted by the Revolution and their rights safeguarded by Napoleon, who were the principal targets. All over France senior officers and functionaries were arrested and charged, and some condemned to death in legally dubious manner.[7]

In Paris, events took a less bloody course, but those who had fled in panic returned in a spirit of vengeance, clamouring for the execution of Napoleon and of dozens of his marshals and officials. Society ladies joined in the clamour for blood and, in the words of Marshal Marmont, 'It was the height of fashion to be without mercy.' Marmont was himself told he should be shot, despite his having remained loyal to the king.[8]

The more conciliatory Louis XVIII reportedly hoped that Ney would make his escape abroad, and was dismayed when he was apprehended. The marshal was to be tried by a tribunal of the Chamber of Peers, but its most distinguished members refused to sit in judgement over a man widely regarded as a national hero. Those who stepped in turned the trial into a mockery of justice, which only deepened the fault lines running through French society. While members of the highest aristocracy insisted on replacing the prison guards and donning their uniforms in order to stand guard over Ney between his condemnation and his execution, many others began to see him as a martyr.[9]

Napoleon's postmaster Lavalette was also condemned to death. While he awaited the guillotine, the king's entourage did everything they could to prevent his wife addressing a plea for mercy to him. When Marshal Marmont did manage to smuggle her into his presence he dismissed her petition, saying there was nothing he could do. '*Vive le Roi!*' his entourage roared; Marmont records that the ferocious sound 'reeked of cannibalism'. With remarkable devotion (considering that Lavalette was by no means young and had a mistress far fresher than her) she devised a plot to spring her husband from gaol dressed in her clothes, while she remained in his cell. With the help of friends, and the British general Sir Robert Wilson, he was then whisked off to England.[10]

An amnesty was declared, but it did not put a stop to the witch-hunts, and many were either banished or obliged to take shelter abroad. The army was further reduced and combed through for unreliable elements, resulting in the dismissal, disgrace, banishment or imprisonment of thousands. Anyone who had taken a seat in a legislative chamber under Napoleon was automatically disqualified from holding public office.

All the political passions of the past quarter-century had been stirred up. The humiliated army dreamed of revenge, Bonapartists of bringing back Napoleon or his son, revolutionaries of 1789 pined for a limited monarchy, others for the Republic of 1792, Jacobins for more extreme measures, and returned émigrés wanted the restoration of the *ancien régime*. Some monarchists felt that the lacklustre Louis XVIII, who had, as the saying went, forgotten nothing and learned nothing, should have been passed over in favour of the duc d'Orléans, head of a junior line, an intelligent man who had fought under the revolutionary tricolour in 1792, been a Jacobin and learned a great deal since. More reactionary elements favoured replacing him with a prince from the Spanish line of Bourbons, whose medieval mindset was more to their taste. Another candidate was the Prince of Orange, son of the newly created King of Holland, backed by deluded revolutionary French émigrés in Belgium who apparently believed that they would thereby succeed in adding the territory of Belgium to France.[11]

If Waterloo had convincingly demonstrated the strength of the forces of repression and the pointlessness of challenging them, Napoleon's sensationally successful seizure of power suggested that with a will anything was possible. Sensible people took note of the former and resigned themselves to reality; hotheads were inspired by the latter, and were inclined to believe that any '*coup de main*' might succeed. This meant that no serious group of would-be revolutionaries even considered the feasibility of action, while dreamers and adventurers were prepared to try their hand. If the probability of a well-organised conspiracy was negligible, that of sporadic isolated rebellion was not, particularly in Paris.

The city contained a vast number of manual labourers living on the breadline or beneath it as a result of the early stages of industrialisation, a drift from the countryside and the disbandment of the army. Between 1800 and 1817 the density of the population went up by 30.8 per cent. A volatile new element was the *jeunesse des écoles*, students of the *grandes écoles* established by Napoleon, who were filled with the spirit of individualism, philanthropy and rebellion against all authority fostered by the culture of the Romantic movement. The city also attracted restless spirits, including a group of English liberals, the most prominent of whom were Byron's friend Kinnaird and General Sir Robert Wilson, a flamboyant cavalryman who had fought his way to fame in the colonies, the Peninsula, Russia and Germany, and whose sense of chivalry was outraged at what was going on. Referred to by the Russian ambassador as 'the English Jacobins' and 'the English revolutionaries', they were, according to him, on a 'mission' to 'excite everywhere civil war'. The French prime minister referred to them as 'a turbulent sect which is seeking to stir up revolutionary ferment wherever it can find the means'.[12]

The ambassador was Charles André Pozzo di Borgo, a Corsican by birth and a one-time friend of Napoleon who had participated in the early stages of the Revolution, but then helped the British capture his native island in 1794. He was rescued from it by Nelson when the French reoccupied it two years later, and after spending some time in England had taken service in Russia. Alexander gave him the rank of general and employed him on various missions before posting him to Paris. There, Pozzo di Borgo played a leading role in the permanent conference of the ambassadors of Russia, Prussia, Austria, Britain and the Duke of Wellington, commander-in-chief of their joint army of occupation. This conference had been put in place by the allies to monitor the situation and coordinate their policy on France. It also edited the king's speeches, new legislation and other important documents, which were submitted to it beforehand by the French cabinet for approval. Pozzo di Borgo was a brilliant conversationalist, with a wit likened to a fireworks display. With his strong Corsican accent, his agility, his flexibility alternating with outbursts of feeling, he was very much a man of the south, and was described by one French statesman as 'a political Figaro'.[13]

The prime minister was Armand-Émmanuel du Plessis, duc de Richelieu. At the age of forty-nine, Richelieu had had an eventful life. Born into the highest aristocracy, he had been a gentleman of the bedchamber to Louis XVI. At sixteen he was married by his genealogically minded family to a hunchback dwarf of impeccable lineage and such ugliness that he fainted when he first saw her. He never did again: he left France in the early stages of the Revolution and took service in Russia, distinguishing himself at the capture of Ismail. He was befriended by Alexander, who in 1803 appointed him governor of Odessa, a city he developed and beautified over the next decade. In the autumn of 1815 Alexander persuaded Louis XVIII to appoint him prime minister, hoping that this would ensure that France would be governed in accordance with his views. Richelieu was a capable administrator, with frugal tastes and great integrity. 'No man had a finer face, a more elegant figure, more seductive manners,' noted a contemporary. 'In the midst of the most polite and elegant circles he stood out by his elegance and his politeness, like a grand seigneur among bourgeois.' He was not temperamentally suited to politics, but took up the challenge gamely.[14]

'The interior of the country is perfectly tranquil,' Richelieu wrote to Alexander in January 1816, 'taxes are being paid on time, the public funds are rising, and outside the provinces occupied by the allied armies, and particularly the Prussians, which are still suffering greatly, the rest of France is getting back on its feet, recovering some confidence, and looking forward to a happier future ...' His principal cause for anxiety was what he called the 'counter-revolution', which obstructed him at every step and threatened to upset the fragile political balance he was trying to maintain. He was referring to the ultra-royalists, known as *les Ultras*. They coalesced around Louis XVIII's sibling Charles Philippe, comte d'Artois, also known as *Monsieur*, the traditional style of the king's younger brother.[15]

Endowed with wit and charm, he had been the darling of the court prior to 1789, a constant companion to Marie-Antoinette in her frivolous diversions, noted for his amorous adventures. Foreseeing the worst, he had left France two days after the fall of the Bastille, and in 1791, after the failure of Louis XVI's attempt to escape, gathered a number of émigré nobles at Koblenz in Germany who hoped to march back into France to reinstate him. Nothing came of this plan and he moved to England, whence he launched an expedition to support the Vendée rebellion in 1795. He failed to bring his force and a shipment of supplies ashore to the aid of the royalists gathered there to support him, and sailed back to England, leaving them to be massacred by revolutionary forces. This does not seem to have damaged his reputation with the Ultras. They rallied around him because of his intransigent condemnation of the Enlightenment and its legacy, and his determination not to yield, as he felt his brother had done, to the temper of the times. As Louis had no progeny, Monsieur was heir to the throne. And as the obese and far from healthy king was not expected to live long, he was also a conduit to future preferment.

In Monsieur's apartments in a wing of the Tuileries known as the pavillon de Marsan (after his erstwhile governess Madame de Marsan, who had resided there under the *ancien régime*), the Ultras formed a political lobby both at court and in the capital. Their agenda was entirely at odds with that of the king, and they undermined him at every step. They wanted draconian reprisals against people who had served the Revolution or Napoleon, the return of the *biens nationaux*, the re-establishment of the Catholic Church and a litany of other reactionary measures, some of which, such as the abolition of divorce, they managed to push through the Chambers. Believing that the 'cursed race' of Jacobins, now operating 'under the title of *liberals*', were the heirs of Hus, Wycliffe, Luther, and Louis XVI's finance minister Jacques Necker, whom they held responsible for provoking the Revolution, they meant to carry out a 'counter-revolution' (a word coined at the time). This required an *épuration*, a cleansing, of the whole of French society. Anyone who was not with them was a declared enemy, and, as one contemporary observed, 'even in the salons there was a kind of civil war in which the harshest words and the most violent altercations were by no means rare'. The king quipped to Pozzo di Borgo that they would end up cleansing him. They would certainly make it as difficult as possible for him to bring tranquillity to France.[16]

9

Intelligence

'The multitude will always remain calm if one honestly takes care of its interests, if one avoids everything that might undermine its confidence, unnecessarily wound its prejudices, corrupt its habits of thought and action, or manipulate its ignorance and credulity,' Napoleon's former police chief Fouché explained in a memorandum written for the Duke of Wellington shortly after Waterloo. 'Everything has changed in our civilisation; it has made much fortunate progress, but it has also left us some new vices,' he went on, pointing out that the 'old deference' had gone. 'It is no longer possible to govern men in the same manner,' he concluded.[1]

Wellington had taken advantage of his paramount position in the weeks following the victory to pressure the returning Louis XVIII to appoint Fouché as his minister of police, arguing that only he had the ability to stabilise the situation. Louis acquiesced with the utmost revulsion: Fouché embodied everything that was most objectionable about the Revolution, and had been one of those most determined to send his brother to the guillotine. And his revulsion was reinforced by a fundamental divergence of views on how to restore order and stability. The king and his entourage could not admit that the ease with which Napoleon had recovered his throne might have had something to do with their own mistakes. They were, as Fouché explained, 'obsessed with the idea that the throne had been toppled as a result of a vast conspiracy'. This was, he believed, a 'fatal misconception', but conspiracy was in the air, and the publication of a book on the subject by Charles Nodier revived all the old fears of people working in the shadows for nefarious ends of one kind or another.[2]

As soon as he felt it was safe to do so, Louis XVIII dismissed Fouché and replaced him with a man of far less ability, Élie Decazes, a thirty-five-year-old lawyer who had been a minor official under Napoleon. Handsome and personable, he managed to charm Louis, whom he entertained with salacious gossip during their daily meetings. Their relationship quickly grew into a real friendship, and the childless king began to treat him as a surrogate son, addressing him in letters as '*mon enfant*' or '*mon fils*', and signing off as '*Ton père*'. Although he was only minister of police, Decazes gradually took over the direction of all internal affairs, leaving Richelieu to deal with foreign policy.[3]

Decazes did not have the benefit of Fouché's experience, and he had certainly not read his memorandum, in which he warned against the indiscriminate use of informers and advised treating all intelligence with a pinch of salt. 'Every day, the agent of the police has to furnish a report in order to earn his pay and prove his zeal,' Fouché wrote. 'If he knows nothing, he invents. If, by chance, he discovers something, he thinks he must enhance his own importance by inflating his discovery.' On the other hand, the manufacture of conspiracies did, he admitted, have its uses, as the government could 'seize the opportunity of a danger which it has conjured up, either to strengthen or to extend its power', adding that 'it is enough for it to survive a conspiracy to acquire greater strength and power'. But in the less than capable hands of Decazes, the opposite was to prove the case for the Bourbon regime.[4]

Decazes set to the task of tracking down subversives, making generous use of *mouchards* and paid informants such as chambermaids, hairdressers and dressmakers, as well as 'spies of *bon ton* who frequented the most distinguished salons of the capital, dined at the best tables, were only seen at the Opera in a box', in the words of one contemporary. The majority of them were women. 'At their head figured a lady of consummate ability,' he goes on. She was apparently 'neither pretty nor ugly', and could easily pass unnoticed, while being invited everywhere. By way of contrast, the same observer cites the example of another lady. 'She is without contradiction the most charming creature my eyes have ever seen; nature has never formed a more perfect work of art,' he writes. 'Her figure is ravishing, her movements graceful, her voice gentle and ingratiating ... She was in the full bloom of her beauty, being only about twenty-six years of age. Her life had been, so it was said, very adventurous. Nothing was known of her family or of the place of her birth. She had left for Russia three years before, with a gentleman said to be her father, from there she went to England, whence she returned with another gentleman said to be her husband.' The couple gave sumptuous dinners and dances, probably paid for by the police, which the most distinguished and influential members of Paris society would attend. The hostess 'moved around the rooms, mixed in every circle, spoke to all the men, listened to this one, asked questions of that one, and thus she fulfilled her role of observer'.[5]

The idea that any information was better than none led the police's informers down increasingly frivolous avenues of investigation. Those spying on supposed Bonapartists in London turned their attention to the duc d'Orléans. He had left Paris at Napoleon's approach in 1815 and gone to England, settling with his family at Twickenham. His house was placed under surveillance. The fact that the Neapolitan ambassador called regularly was deemed suspicious, even though the King of Naples was the duchess's father. So were his visits to members of the British cabinet and royal family. One report concerned Orléans' frequent contacts with the Duke of Kent, pointing out that most of the duke's servants were French, including three former Polish lancers of Napoleon's Guard, and that, when engaged in conversation by the spies, they expressed negative views about the Bourbons.[6]

The daughter of France's ambassador in London could barely believe the nonsense the spies passed on to the embassy as information of the highest importance. In one instance, they reported that

Orléans had a secret printing press producing anti-Bourbon pamphlets. When she drove down to Twickenham with her father one Sunday evening, they found the family sitting around a large table, with the children printing out a fable composed by one of them on a toy press.[7]

Orléans was not the only member of the French royal family under surveillance. Throughout 1816 and 1817 the police kept a close watch on the sexagenarian duc de Bourbon. Being the father of the duc d'Enghien, who had been judicially murdered by Napoleon, he was unlikely to harbour Bonapartist or revolutionary views even if he had shown any interest in politics. As it was, his attention was focused exclusively on his new teenage mistress.[8]

In the absence of real subversion, Decaze's police conducted an obsessive pursuit of the trivial. People were arrested for shouting '*Vive l'Empereur!*' or '*À bas les Bourbons!*', even though these were more likely to be incoherent outbursts of anger at losing a job or a mistress, indignation at the rate of taxation or the price of bread, or just frustration and dissatisfaction, than indications of intent to overthrow the regime. They were arrested for making statements insulting to the royal family in a public place (usually a wine shop), for calling royalists 'scoundrels', for making '*de mauvais propos*' (which can only be translated as 'saying bad things'), for being a '*mauvais sujet*', a 'rotten fellow' '*signalé comme un homme dangereux sous tous les rapports*' (said to be a dangerous man all round), for frequenting a tavern where 'suspect individuals' gathered, for having just arrived from Berlin, from London, from New York, for failing to doff their hat to the king's carriage, for not displaying a white cockade on it, for wearing a hat too red or multicoloured ribbons and trimmings which happened to include the colours of the tricolour (one jeweller's apprentice was arrested for wearing a mixture of pink, white and violet), for using old military buttons with the imperial eagle on them, and so on.[9]

The Paris fire brigade fell under suspicion because they did not present arms when the king's Gardes du Corps marched past. In

Besançon, a *mouchard* launched an investigation into 'a vast organisation of agitators' by reporting that he had noticed people apparently communicating with each other surreptitiously in the street by tugging at their moustaches in various ways. At Saint-Romain-de-Popey in the Rhône on 21 July 1816, during a votive holiday for which ancient custom dictated that the men wear white-braided tricorn hats with red and green feathers, the gendarmes presumed these to be an allusion to the republican tricolour and began tearing the plumes from the hats, precipitating a riot which only ended after serious casualties had been inflicted on both sides.[10]

According to the drivers of the *diligences*, or mail coaches, part of whose job it was to render a detailed report of the public mood in the towns they had come from and passed through, people around the country were far more preoccupied with bread-and-butter issues than with politics. Of 704 outbreaks of violence against the authorities recorded between January 1818 and June 1830, only forty-three (6 per cent) had any political undertone, and even then it was usually no more than general disaffection. The riots of 1816–17 were almost exclusively about the food shortages following the Tambora eruption, and those in Lyon in 1819 were Luddite protests against the introduction of the Jacquard loom. Yet almost all were reported as having a political motive.[11]

François Vidocq, the petty criminal turned police official, describes how *mouchards* would set up 'a sort of political mousetrap' in a wine shop: 'drinking with the labourers, they *worked* them, in order to enmesh them in faked conspiracies' before arresting them. They would teach the workers songs full of the crudest insults to the royal family, 'composed by the same authors as the hymns for the holidays of St Louis and St Charles', for, as Vidocq adds, the police had 'its laureates, its minstrels, and its troubadours'.[12]

The police agent Pierre Blanc was actually prosecuted for 'working to create a nucleus of malcontents in order to then denounce them to the authorities who employed him'. But his was an isolated case, and on the whole *provocateurs* were free to practise their art unmolested.

The Ultra mayor of Toulouse, Joseph de Villèle, discovered that the police in the town were orchestrating grain-price rises and printing inflammatory pamphlets denouncing the Bourbons.[13]

The obsession with acquiring intelligence was not limited to the organs of the state. The ambassadors of the four allied powers had their own intelligence service, based at 15, rue de l'Université, organised by the erstwhile Prussian police chief Justus Grüner. Shortly after appointing Fouché, Louis XVIII had instructed one of his former agents, Brivazac-Beaumont, to create a network of spies to keep an eye on the minister. Fouché himself had set up under the chevalier de Bordes a parallel force to his own official police in the rue de Jérusalem, operating from offices in the rue du Dragon. Given the climate of suspicion and distrust at every level, various ministers had their own intelligence-gathering networks. According to Jacques Peuchet, archivist of the Préfecture de Police, there were four discrete networks operating within the Tuileries itself. One, headed by the duc d'Aumont, first gentleman of the bedchamber, was confined to the palace and the king's person, and was made up of old émigrés and devoted noblemen, along with two duchesses, a marquise and six countesses. Monsieur had his own, run from the pavillon de Marsan and directed by Antoine de Terrier de Monciel, whose main purpose seems to have been to gather evidence to fuel Monsieur's conviction that the country was 'in a state of general conflagration'. Monsieur's elder son the duc d'Angoulême had his own network, covering the army. 'In every regiment there were three accredited spies,' explains Peuchet, 'one with the rank of captain, a second among the lieutenants, and the third, also a volunteer, kept an eye on the under-officers and the soldiers. There were aides-de-camp, generals and even a marshal of France in this odious militia.' The duke's wife, the dauphine, had her own '*police mignonne*' which kept her informed of all the amorous goings-on, something it was well qualified to do as it consisted of young ladies of the court and clerics who thought nothing of betraying the secrets of the confessional. The police of Monsieur's younger son the duc de Berry were less efficient. On one occasion he asked them to investigate his mistress in the hope of finding something in her behaviour that might provide him with an excuse to jilt her, as he wished to be free to conduct another affair with an actress he had just taken up with. But they confused the two names and investigated the actress instead: he was presented with evidence of her infidelities to him.[14]

Each of these networks employed its own stable of spies, both male and female, all acting on the assumption that any snippet of information was of value, however and wherever obtained, and that facts which did not add up to a narrative of some sort were unlikely to arouse interest; disparate and sometimes untrue gobbets were therefore mixed together to produce one. 'It was a curious spectacle to observe all these police networks going about their work on the same stage, trying to remain concealed from each other and to penetrate the actions of the others,' Peuchet concludes. 'There were occasionally highly amusing conflicts and some very bizarre encounters.'[15]

The motives behind them could be recondite. One evening in 1819, a man called on Decazes and informed him that he had learned that a lady in the entourage of the duchesse de Berry was to meet an agent of Napoleon at a certain address at nine o'clock the following night. He expressed the hope that his services would not go unrewarded, and Decazes duly gave him two thousand-franc notes. To head the operation of catching the agent, Decazes picked a general keen to show his royalist credentials and aspiring to the rank of marshal of France. The general duly gathered together a strong body of police and staked out the house in question by four the following afternoon.

At eight, a carriage drove into the courtyard and a lady alighted, followed by a maid. The general, who had set up his headquarters nearby, was duly informed. The two women went up to the second floor, and instantly the windows were lit up by a multitude of candles. Then a chef from a nearby restaurant arrived accompanied by a swarm of turnspits, and the policemen watched as 'a refined dinner, a sumptuous dessert, ices, wine' were carried up to the apartment. Nine o'clock came and went, and by half-past the general was growing anxious, but then a cabriolet appeared, preceded by a liveried outrider. A man got down and bounded upstairs, attended by the outrider.

The general waited a while and then went into action, at the head of forty policemen. 'The house was attacked, they mounted the stairs with precipitation, they entered an antechamber, the lackey on duty there cried out and ordered them to leave, and, seeing that they would not, threw a large cream cheese at the general leading the assault force,' in the words of Peuchet. 'But worse followed! Hardly had they managed to open the door to the salon when they saw … Guess who? First, Countess M …, wife of the aspiring marshal of France, lying on a divan, faint with fear. As to her cavalier, the emissary of Buonaparte, it was none other than H.R.H. the duc de Berry himself.' Incandescent with rage, the duke seized some fire irons and went for the general, threw him and his escort out of the apartment and sent them scuttling down the stairs. Since neither he nor his lady had recognised her husband, who had dressed in plain clothes for the operation and whose face was masked by the cream cheese, they sat down once again, did justice to the dinner and 'made love with added zest'. Decazes was furious, particularly as the whole of Paris was talking about nothing else by the next morning, and two days later he received a note from the Grand Almoner of France, thanking him for the gift of 2,000 francs to the fund for indigent priests.[16]

Gullible he might well have shown himself to be in this instance, but it was unwise to ignore even the most far-fetched intelligence, as people at both extremes of the political spectrum were prepared to embark on ventures of barely believable rashness; almost anything could sound plausible in the prevailing climate, with the phantom of Napoleon hovering in the popular imagination and the fear of 'Jacobinism' gripping people's minds.

Marooned as he was in the middle of the Atlantic on the island of St Helena, Napoleon continued to haunt the nightmares of his conquerors. Their fears combined with the vague longings of others to generate an extraordinary incidence of rumour. In the prevailing climate, official announcements were greeted with suspicion, which encouraged second-guessing and speculation, and this developed a life of its own, giving rise to new conjectures that turned into certainties with surprising rapidity. News also travelled at very irregular speeds. Reports of a riot in one place might take ten days to reach a neighbouring town but only three to reach Paris, from which it might come back to the second town first, giving rise to the impression that there was a revolution in Paris rather than nearby.

Many rumours were the consequence of discontent over the price of bread or of deep-rooted if inchoate anxieties, foremost among which were that the government might be planning to raise taxes, impose conscription, bring back the servitudes of the *ancien régime*, return the *biens nationaux*, and abolish the freedoms won during the Revolution. Whenever such anxieties were aroused, the poor would long for a guardian angel, a protective deity, and would fix on the one figure whose power they believed in – Napoleon. Wishful thinking would do the rest, and give rise to rumours that he was about to return, or had done so.

In the summer of 1814, shortly after he had reached Elba, rumours began to circulate that Napoleon had landed in France at the head of a Turkish army. At the end of 1815, before he had set foot on St Helena, talk of his imminent return alternated with reports that he had already landed, and even sightings of him. Rumours of this sort reached a peak in 1816 and 1817, when the effects of the Tambora eruption raised the price of bread to new heights. They continued over the next years, and would not cease with Napoleon's death in 1821, news of which would be widely disbelieved.[17]

The rumours had occurred most frequently in March 1815, the month he escaped from Elba. That miraculous return and the birth of his son the King of Rome, on 20 March 1811, were the two events on which his followers based their hopes for the future, and violets, which flower in March, became associated with those hopes. The cities of Lyon and Grenoble also featured as the focus for many rumours, as they had welcomed him enthusiastically in 1815. Each March between 1816 and 1825 there were reports of his return, some of them specific as to where he had landed, where he had been sighted and the number of troops he had with him. These troops were variously Turkish, Moorish, Polish, German, Persian, Chinese, 'barbarians' or 'two million Indians marching across the Ganges'. In one instance, Napoleon had landed first in the United States and recruited an army of Americans; in another, he was rescued from St Helena by 'the Emperor of Morocco'. The more sensational the image, the more easily it captured the imagination.[18]

These rumours had a destabilising effect in rural communities and led to a reluctance to show loyalty or even pay taxes to a regime which might be swept away at any moment. In late 1816 a rumour spread that the former Empress Marie-Louise was forming an army in Austria to liberate France, as a result of which thirty soldiers deserted and set off to enlist. In March 1817 a reported sighting of Napoleon spread paranoia through Lyon, with some barricading their doors and windows, and others fleeing the city. Parish priests who assured their flocks that the ogre would never escape from St Helena only made people wonder whether perhaps he already had. There were also impersonators of Napoleon or his marshals, who travelled around the country swindling people of food and money as they dispensed more or less fantastic pieces of information. In the Lyon area, highway robbers attacked in the name of Napoleon, leading to news spreading that he was advancing on Paris. Just as damaging were rumours that he had been murdered by the allies, which caused explosions of anger and rioting.[19]

In their reports, police agents, landowners, prefects, mayors and other officials often inflated the degree of support for Napoleon in their localities, either voicing their own worst fears or because they did not wish to appear lacking in zeal, thus magnifying the threat and causing alarm in Paris. This could lead to overreaction, which merely had the effect of making people believe that Napoleon really had landed. Such was the case in March 1816, when 6,000 National Guards were deployed in Lyon on the strength of baseless gossip. In 1821, a rumour that Napoleon had disembarked travelled so fast that a couple of days later a hundred communes sent in reports which mentioned sightings in almost as many places. Instead of suggesting the evident fallacy of the original rumour, this threw the authorities in Paris into a panic, the police came out in force everywhere, and the declaration of a state of emergency added credence to it.[20]

After Waterloo, the Bourbon authorities had seized all pro-Napoleonic literature they could lay their hands on, and the Chamber passed a law criminalising any endorsement of the emperor and his doings. Another extended criminal law to include incitement, direct or indirect, to change the line of succession to the throne of France. Symbols of Napoleonic rule were removed and representations of events or subjects connected with the Empire were banned. In 1816 two artisans from Beauvais were arrested for announcing the intention of naming their sons Paul-Joseph-Bonaparte and Louis-Henri-Napoléon. A doctor in Albi was arrested for naming his daughter Marie-Louise-Néapoldine, another for naming his Marie-Louise-Napoléonide. People were not infrequently arrested for wearing a violet in their buttonhole.[21]

In spite of this, millions of prints, statuettes and busts of Napoleon, as well as images illustrating the glorious episodes of his life, were clandestinely produced and disseminated all over the country by travelling salesmen. After his death, coins appeared on the market bearing the inscription 'Napoleon II'. The police were powerless to stop this illicit industry and trade, despite frequent arrests and severe penalties for possession.

A high priority for the French police was to keep a close watch on members of Napoleon's family, most of which had wound up in Italy. His mother had settled in Rome, along with his uncle Cardinal Fesch, his brothers Lucien and Louis, and his sister Pauline, whose beautiful villa was suspected of being a hub for all manner of dangerous conspiracy. Decazes despatched an agent to coordinate surveillance over them, and persuaded the Austrian and other police forces operating in the peninsula to tail him, in order to lend him credibility with other subversives. The only fruits of this surveillance are thick files of reports of numbing futility in the archives of Paris.[22]

Napoleon's brother Joseph had managed to escape to Switzerland after Waterloo, whence he made his way discreetly to an Atlantic port and sailed to the United States, which he reached in September 1815. Unaware of this, but finding that the trail they had picked up had gone cold, the French police began to suspect the worst – if he was not to be found, he must be in hiding, and if he was in hiding, he must be plotting. The prefect of the department of the Ain reported a sighting, and various houses were watched around the clock; on 20 October the minister of police received a report that he was in the Jura, conspiring with a group of Bonapartist sympathisers; the prefect of the Jura then reported that he had crossed Lake Geneva and was hiding in the village of Chablais. 'We have identified ten houses he has stayed in, but we can never find the one he is in at the time,' complained one agent. Other sightings, one of them of him disguised in women's clothing, kept the agents on full alert for months after Joseph had reached America.[23]

Another of Napoleon's brothers, Jérôme, was also a source of worry. His father-in-law the King of Württemberg had done everything to persuade his daughter to divorce him, and when she refused he locked them both in the gilded cage of the castle of Ellwangen. Jérôme was treated as a prisoner of state, with a commandant of the castle, a police commissioner and an agent of the postal service keeping watch over his every move. All the entrances to the castle were heavily guarded, he had to ask permission to go out of doors, and could only do so under cavalry escort. In spite of this, the French police sent agents into the area to observe and obtain information on his activities.[24]

The former wife of Louis Bonaparte and erstwhile Queen of Holland, Hortense, had been banished from France after Waterloo and, at the insistence of the French government, denied permission to settle in Switzerland (too full of plotters), so she went to Austria, where a close watch was kept on her. Surveillance was extended to people corresponding with members of the Bonaparte family, and to former servants, even cooks and footmen.[25]

What underlay Richelieu's anxiety was the fear that Napoleon might escape from St Helena. He believed that while the former emperor would find few supporters in France his very existence as a free man in any part of the world would be 'an interminable cause of disturbances' there. 'It is certain that the agitators and the malcontents of every country look to St Helena, certainly not out of love for the man who is incarcerated there, but because they would regard his appearance on the scene as a means of disturbing and destroying the present state of affairs,' he wrote to his ambassador in London, the marquis d'Osmond. 'The island of St Helena is a point on which our telescopes must be unceasingly trained,' he warned.[26]

He saw a potential threat in every ship fitting out in an American port if former Napoleonic officers had been spotted there. Although he did not credit all the reports he received warning of some plan to free him, he admitted that 'it is difficult to believe that there is not a project prepared for the overthrow of the established order in France and to bring back Bonaparte'. When he heard that a ship from America had docked at Civita Vecchia, he assumed it was connected with Joseph Bonaparte, whom he still believed to be in Europe, and with a sighting in Italy of Napoleon's faithful Marshal Poniatowski (who had been killed at Leipzig in 1813). Every rumour fed his anxieties, and at one point he believed that the former emperor might be liberated by slavers, who regularly crossed the Atlantic. When four ships sailed from England with volunteers intending to fight under Simón Bolívar for the liberty of Spain's American colonies, he feared that they might liberate Napoleon along the way.[27]

In the spring of 1818, General Gourgaud, who had accompanied Napoleon to St Helena, decided he could stand the exile no longer and returned. In London, on his way back, he had a long conversation with the French ambassador, who sent a record of it to Richelieu, who was appalled. Inflating his own importance, Gourgaud implied that

Napoleon had had ten opportunities to escape to America, and could do so at any moment.[28]

Richelieu was worried that the British authorities were not taking the threat seriously enough, and not checking on his presence every day, or that Napoleon might somehow manage to seduce his guardians. He was also afraid that a change of ministry in Britain might bring into government liberal sympathisers of the fallen emperor who would set him free, and he was not above suspecting the British of considering allowing Napoleon to escape, in order to destabilise France.

Accounts by British and French witnesses of Napoleon's incarceration on St Helena, whether they were sympathisers or denigrators, casual observers or those dedicated to his captivity, confirm that he never showed the slightest interest in escaping. If anything, he appeared to relish what he saw as his martyrdom. Even if they had been able to dodge the Royal Navy ships circling the island, any would-be rescuers would have had difficulty in approaching Napoleon, let alone freeing him. He was guarded by six hundred men of the 53rd Regiment of Foot and four companies of artillery. There were pickets posted all over the island day and night, severe restrictions on his and his party's movements, and a curfew after the evening gun. No unauthorised ship was allowed into the anchorage, and any vessel that stopped to take water had a guard posted on it. Napoleon's British gaoler, Sir Hudson Lowe, was as strict as he could be, and certainly nourished no feelings of sympathy towards his charge.[29]

After the Bonaparte family, the police prioritised former Napoleonic officers, particularly the 15,000 or so *demi-soldes*, most of whom had been banished to provincial towns. They were poor conspiracy material. For one thing, they affected an easily identifiable form of dress: a Bolívar hat, long blue frock-coat buttoned up to the chin in military fashion, black necktie, riding boots and spurs. They usually sported a moustache and wore the red ribbon of the *Légion d'honneur* in their buttonhole, or, failing that, a violet. As if that were not enough, they met in the same cafés and were as easily traceable as they were identifiable. All recent research has shown that the overwhelming majority of *demi-soldes* may have entertained a jaundiced view of the Bourbon regime and remembered with fondness their glorious general, but remained politically passive.[30]

That did not stop the police. According to General Berton, the *mouchards* swarmed round the *demi-soldes*, and 'if three people paused in a public place for a word and one of them was a military man, within the instant one or sometimes several of these minions of denunciation would creep up and place themselves at a small distance from the little group, staring in a distracted way at the stars or the tops of the trees, bending their ears to catch a few words which they half hear, but which, guessing the rest, they pass on in their fashion, according to the instructions they have received'. They would hang about the concierges and servants of former Napoleonic officers, asking questions, or call on them pretending to be officers who had fallen on hard times, offering to sell forbidden Napoleonic mementos.[31]

These tactics often led to ludicrous outcomes, as in the case of one former general turned police agent drawing into conversation an erstwhile member of the imperial administration who had been made a baron by the emperor. He made a number of provocative statements, with which the baron agreed, and then suggested they meet again in order to plan ways of staging a coup with the aim of bringing Napoleon back to power. The next morning a proud inspector handed his chief a lengthy report from the general incriminating the baron, only to have Decazes hand him the baron's report incriminating the general. Both were *agents provocateurs*.[32]

Some informed observers and many policemen believed that most if not all of the 'conspiracies' the police uncovered during this period were of its own creation. A typical example is that of two police agents, named Chignard and Vauversin, who accosted a former Napoleonic soldier in the street and invited him to join them for a drink. As the wine flowed, they began to mutter about past glories and to make toasts to the good old days. When the veteran was suitably liquored up, they suggested forming a brotherhood, and all three signed an oath 'to die for each other and for real liberty without monarchy'. He was then arrested, charged with plotting to overthrow the government and sentenced to a long term in gaol. Dozens of naïve ex-soldiers and *demi-soldes* were entrapped in this way.[33]

Richelieu himself dismissed as a fabrication the 'evidence' the police presented at the end of January 1816 of a conspiracy in Lyon. The same may have been true of the first actual insurrection against the Bourbons on the night of 4 May 1816, when some three or four hundred men led by a lawyer named Jean-Paul Didier attempted to take the city of Grenoble. It was put down within hours by the commander of the garrison, General Donnadieu, who had prior knowledge of Didier's plans. Six conspirators lost their lives during a brief shoot-out, fourteen more were shot by the general out of hand, and a further eleven were later condemned and executed. Richelieu was one of many who believed that Donnadieu had probably masterminded the rising so that he could show his zeal and obtain promotion.[34]

In May of the same year, the police arrested a number of people whom they suspected of conspiring to put either the Prince of Orange or the Duke of Kent on the throne. Later the same month, they were on to a plot by a group calling themselves '*Les Patriotes de 1816*', which seems to have involved little more than people distributing triangular pieces of paper printed with the words *Union, Honneur, Patrie* and an incoherent phrase about decapitation. They found some other texts to the effect that the sufferings of the people would soon be at an end. However, most of those arrested maintained under interrogation that they had never heard of *Les Patriotes de 1816*. They were equally ignorant of the other secret groups, such as the *Vautours de Bonaparte*, the *Patriotes Européens* and *Régéneration Universelle*, whose existence informers had reported to the police. The files on the case, which consist principally of the reports of agents and *mouchards* snooping and checking up on various suspects, tell us more about the eating and sleeping habits and sexual mores of Parisians of the day than about potential subversion.[35]

Later the same month, the police arrested an NCO by the name of Monnier, who had been making plans of the fortress of Vincennes; in his lodgings they found various papers, including an oath, a barely coherent diatribe calling on Frenchmen to free their motherland of the occupying foreign forces and overthrow the Bourbon monarchy in favour of Napoleon. He was tried and sentenced to death, but on the scaffold he implicated several others, the most senior of whom was a *demi-solde* captain by the name of Contremoulin. They apparently belonged to an association styling themselves *Chevaliers de l'Épingle Noire*, and wore a black tie-pin as a badge. But the charge that they had been plotting to seize the fortress, or possibly eliminate its garrison by pouring poison into its water tanks, did not hold up in court, and the case fell apart. They were lucky. In July, another group accused of plotting a Napoleonic restoration were executed. They had issued a stirring proclamation which, it turned out, had been composed by one Scheltein, a police agent.[36]

There was no more trouble for some time, and by the autumn Richelieu was more concerned with the failed harvest than with supposed plots. There was not enough food to feed the population of France, let alone the foreign armies of occupation, as he explained to Tsar Alexander, begging him to persuade his allies to withdraw some of them. He feared that the hunger might produce real political unrest. By the beginning of the following year, the situation had become catastrophic. 'At least half of France is in a terrifying state of distress, and with the spring announcing another bad year, I fear that the people might give in to despair,' Richelieu wrote in April 1817.[37]

In May 1817, twenty-eight men were put on trial in Bordeaux on charges of trying to overthrow the government. The alleged ringleader was one Randon, who had been a member of Fouché's police and subsequently served under Decazes. He had taken on the identity of a former lieutenant of Mamelouks of the Imperial Guard, Ali-Bey, and went around the Bordeaux area distributing cards with the letters VN for '*Vive Napoléon!*' and other cryptic texts. Three men were executed as a result. The same fate met a soldier who had been overheard talking about the possible return of Napoleon.[38]

In June, an uprising was stage-managed by the military governor of Lyon, General Canuel. He had served in the revolutionary army and committed atrocities while putting down the royalist rising in the Vendée in the 1790s, but had rallied to the Bourbons in 1814, and now felt a need to atone for past sins, and for promotion. Canuel enticed a number of former Napoleonic officers to Lyon and persuaded them to organise an insurrection, assuring them that a Captain Ledoux would call out the city's garrison in support, and that he himself would then take command. They duly went to work, recruiting former soldiers and other malcontents, which was not difficult given the food shortages, which had already given rise to multiple riots. The date set for the outbreak was 8 June. On the night, Captain Ledoux failed to show up, and the conspirators' suspicious were aroused, so they called off the rising. Those who were already on the march from the surrounding countryside were dispersed by waiting *gendarmes* without a shot being fired. Canuel promptly announced that he had foiled a dangerous conspiracy and set about ruthless retribution, meting out a hundred sentences, twenty-eight of them capital. There was uproar, and Marshal Marmont was sent from Paris to investigate. 'It soon became clear to me that the disturbance had been manufactured,' he noted. 'General Canuel and his agents had intended it to take place and to spread so as to have the glory of repressing it to receive rewards.' This resulted in Canuel's dismissal – but he did get a barony.[39]

Neither the food riots nor the events in Lyon had any deeper impact on the political situation. 'Even in the state she finds herself in, France is disposed to tranquillity,' Pozzo di Borgo reported in October 1817, 'the calm which reigned throughout the elections, contrary to everyone's predictions, provides the most convincing proof of this.' He was among those who were convinced that most of the so-called conspiracies had been engineered by Ultras bent on preventing the allies from withdrawing their troops from France, fearing that this would encourage revolutionaries and liberals to reach for power. They were certainly involved in an absurd incident which took place in February 1818, when a shot was fired at the carriage of the Duke of Wellington, commander of those troops. The perpetrator was eventually identified as a former sergeant of the Imperial Guard, but the conspiracy which the police extrapolated stretched as far as Brussels and included Lord Kinnaird as well as various Ultras, who were behind a number of plots meant to create a climate of fear.[40]

In April, a sergeant major of the 2nd Royal Guards stationed at Versailles informed his superior officer that three of his men intended to kill Monsieur during a parade. The colonel made light of the matter, and the parade went ahead without incident. As the sergeant major persisted in his claims, the three men he named were court-martialled, and two of them were shot. That summer, the Ultras cooked up a plot to raise some of the regiments stationed in Paris, arrest Richelieu, Decazes and other ministers, depose the king and replace him with Monsieur. The authorities only got wind of it because of the defection of some of the plotters. Neither Decazes nor any of the ministers took the affair seriously, Wellington thought it a joke, and Pozzo di Borgo felt it merited 'more pity than indignation'.[41]

Peuchet and other senior police officials confirm that all the 'conspiracies' it unmasked were in fact fabricated by the police, and that they never discovered a single one that had not been invented by themselves. If this implies that the state was not under any real threat from conspiracy, it also reveals that it was being severely damaged by its own security organs. As Louis-Matthieu Molé, former minister of justice, points out, 'the conviction spread that there could be no plots other than those invented by the police', and as a result 'conspirators were pitied as victims, and those who uncovered their designs as the most vile government stooges'. Every time a conspiracy, real, fabricated or imagined, came to light, public opinion divided, and those at the extremes would seize on the event and turn it to their own purpose. The Ultras would use it as evidence that the police were lax and the government was abetting revolutionary activity in order to bring down the monarchy. The liberals would accuse the Ultras of using *provocateurs* in order to create a crisis that would justify the imposition of arbitrary rule. There was usually just enough evidence of the nefarious activities of the people at each end of the political spectrum to allow their rivals to construe a scenario that suggested foul intent. This would spawn violent political debate which might rage for months, with moderates being denounced by both sides as lackeys of the other. In the aftermath of the Lyon revolt of June 1817 and General Canuel's draconian reprisals, the argument raged in open letters and pamphlets. The police and the army both despatched investigators, who sent back violently discordant reports. Unpleasant truths began to emerge about the past of most of those involved, and it all ended in court cases between the principal actors.[42]

'I consider this country as in a fair way to being lost,' a despairing Wellington wrote in March that year. The political divide had become so deep that people made the wildest allegations to discredit their political enemies – one Ultra pamphlet accused Decazes of having engineered the famine of 1816 in order to prepare the ground for Didier's rising in favour of bringing back Napoleon. It seemed to Wellington that, as he put it in a letter to a friend, 'The descendants of Louis XV will not reign in France ...'[43]

10

British Bogies

Britain suffered from none of the political problems afflicting France. As the kingdom had not been touched by revolution, there was no need to turn the clock back – or, as far as the dominant classes were concerned, to move it forward. It is true that with the war over, jingoistic feelings about the French and fear of 'Boney', which had united all classes, evaporated. The bonds of wartime solidarity binding the nation unravelled, leaving behind a sense of dissatisfaction and anticlimax, rendered more dangerous by the presence of increasing numbers of disbanded soldiers and sailors, often harbouring a grudge at the apparent ingratitude of the king and country they had fought for. Over the next two years more than 200,000 of these would join the ranks of the unemployed and the destitute.

The transition from war to peace did, as elsewhere, entail economic dislocation and hardship. A fall in the price of wheat consequent on the end of the wartime blockade and a bumper harvest in 1814 alleviated the suffering of the poor, but in order to protect the interests of landowners Parliament brought in legislation known as the Corn Laws, allowing foreign corn onto the market only at a price which was 'fair' for British producers. This raised the price of bread by 50 per cent in the space of a year. There were food riots in East Anglia, Devon and Cornwall, put down by the yeomanry and troops, and five of the rioters at Ely were hanged. Colliers and iron workers in South Wales who began a hunger march on London under the slogan 'Willing to Work, but None of Us to Beg' were turned back by troops. As the post-Tambora rain deluged the land, making it plain that there would be no harvest in 1816, the predicament of the lower classes worsened. In July Luddites struck in Loughborough and Nottingham. In October there was rioting in Birmingham over the price of bread, again quelled by troops.

The government and country magistrates alike refused to see these disturbances as anything other than manifestations of revolutionary intent. The Duke of Wellington thought their roots lay in unemployment, 'principally in the idleness, dissipation, and improvidence of all the middling and lower classes in England, produced by a long course of prosperity and of flattery of their vices by the higher orders and the government'. Castlereagh and others in the cabinet saw a connection between the disturbances and a drop in church attendance, and the government made a grant of £1 million to build new churches in manufacturing districts. His faith was not shared in the country at large.[1]

Fear of revolutionary upheaval began to grip country squires and mill-owners, and spread to some of the middle class. Robert Southey was convinced that 'all imaginable causes that produce revolutions are at work among us', and by September that 'The whole fabric of social order in this country is in great danger; the Revolution, should it be effected, will not be less bloody than it was in France. It *will* be effected unless vigorous measures be taken to arrest its progress.'[2]

'Those who are old enough to have a distinct recollection of those times are astonished now to think how great was the panic which could exist without any evidence at all: how prodigious were the radical forces which were always heard of but never seen,' the historian Harriet Martineau would write in 1849, 'how country gentlemen, well-armed, scoured the fields and lanes and met on heaths to fight the enemy who never came: how, even in the midst of towns, young ladies carried heavy planks and ironing-boards, to barricade windows, in preparation for sieges from thousands of rebels whose footfall was long listened for in vain through the darkness of the night.'[3]

What bothered the home secretary, Viscount Sidmouth, and his fellow ministers more than the possibility of revolution was the recent revival of the movement for parliamentary reform, particularly as this appeared to have been partially successful in harnessing the discontents of the lower classes to its cause. Hampden Clubs burgeoned. Delegates were travelling around the country collecting signatures on a petition appealing for the reform of Parliament through the introduction of universal male suffrage, annual parliaments, and voting by secret ballot. On 15 November 1816 Henry Hunt, who had become one of the most prominent reformists, held an open-air meeting at Spa Fields in London.[4]

Hunt, the son of a Wiltshire farmer, had pretensions to a higher station and behaved as he thought a gentleman should. This had landed him in gaol for assault, where he met Cartwright, Horne Tooke and Burdett. These contacts do not appear to have had much effect on him, as he continued to lead a rackety life, including ditching his wife and moving in with another's. In 1803 he raised a troop of militia to resist the French invaders, but soon lost interest in soldiering and reverted to his usual pursuits, which led to a second incarceration in 1810, again for assault. This time he shared a cell with Cobbett, whose attacks on the government had landed him in Newgate. This proved a turning point. From now on, the vain, self-serving and arrogant Hunt would devote himself to the cause of the people. Tall, well-built and something of a dandy, he quickly became a favourite at political meetings, sporting a white hat as a sign of the purity of his intentions.

At the meeting on 15 November, he harangued the 10,000-strong crowd from the window of a public house, waving the French tricolour and a cap of liberty, but while his oratory was characteristically flamboyant and vituperative, his purpose was hardly revolutionary. It was to obtain the endorsement of the assembled crowd to carry a petition for parliamentary reform to the prince regent. As he was refused admission into the prince's presence, he called a second meeting in the same place for 2 December to protest against this insult to the people. But on his way to it, Hunt was waylaid by a Mr Castle (or Castles), who delayed him. Hunt arrived late, to find a wagon decorated with banners from which Dr James Watson, a Radical follower of Spence, had just finished making a speech, flanked by his son James and Arthur Thistlewood, another follower of Spence. The younger Watson took over, calling on the assembled multitude to seize by force what was being denied to the people, and, French flag in hand, set off to capture the Tower of London, followed by some of the crowd and a group of sailors. They broke into a gunsmith's shop on the way and killed a passer-by in their advance on the City. At the Royal Exchange they were confronted by Alderman Shaw and five constables, who arrested three of the leaders and called out troops to clear the streets. The only one of the group to reach the Tower was Watson's associate Thomas Preston, and he summoned the guards to surrender, without success. The principal actors of this farce were charged with high treason.[5]

By January 1817 Sidmouth saw 'a great crisis' looming. He was receiving letters from magistrates, landowners and mill-owners in various parts of the country warning of unrest, alleging that the lower orders were conspiring, that the Hampden Clubs were plotting revolution and that the delegates travelling around collecting signatures for their petition were actually promoting 'a general union of the lower orders throughout the kingdom' intended to bring about a revolution which would break out simultaneously all over the country at a signal given from London. The prime minister, Lord Liverpool, believed in remaining calm, but he was nevertheless playing it safe: there were 25,000 regular troops under arms in England to back up the county militias and yeomanry, and another 25,000 in Ireland.[6]

It was against this background that the Lancashire weaver and Middleton Hampden Club's delegate Samuel Bamford arrived in the capital along with other 'country cousins' of the London reformists, bearing their petition. They were mostly hard-working artisans convinced of the justice of their cause, trusting in goodwill and common sense. They met Hunt, Burdett, Cobbett and the intrepid but recently cashiered admiral and Radical MP Thomas Cochrane, only to discover that not all of the London reformers shared their convictions.

Burdett, Member of Parliament for Westminster and chairman of the London Hampden Club, stayed away from the joint conference, held at the Crown and Anchor tavern in the Strand on 22 January. In his absence, Cartwright took the chair and proposed that they drop the demand for universal suffrage, and limit the franchise to householders. This came as a shock to the provincial delegates, few of whom were householders, who had collected over half a million signatures on the petition for universal suffrage. Hunt took up their cause, and the petition was borne by the swashbuckling Admiral Cochrane, carried to loud huzzas on the shoulders of the country cousins, to St Stephen's Hall. Mass meetings and petitions to the king were legitimate means of constitutional action, so this could in no sense have been seen as anything else.

But that same morning, as the prince regent was driving to Westminster to open the new session of Parliament, something hit and shattered the glass of his coach window. The authorities assumed that it had been a bullet. Hunt though it was more likely to have been 'some gravel or a potatoe [sic]'. Both Houses addressed bombastic loyal messages to the prince, and adjourned. A few days later, after documents relative to 'the dangerously disordered state of the country' had been presented to them, they set up committees of secrecy to investigate. The reports of these were presented to the respective Houses on 18 and 19 February.[7]

The House of Lords committee reported that they found 'such evidence as leaves no doubt in their minds that a traitorous conspiracy has been formed in the metropolis for the purpose of overthrowing, by means of a general insurrection, the established government, laws, and constitution of this kingdom, and of effecting a general plunder and division of property'. This was to have taken the shape of simultaneous attacks on the Tower, the Bank, various military barracks and prisons, whose inmates were to be armed and let loose on the city. It was supposed to have been sparked off by the first Spa Fields meeting, and 'Pikes and arms to a certain extent were actually provided', but was, according to the committee, called off as the necessary preparations had not been made. 'Even after the failure of this attempt, the same plans appear not to have been abandoned,' the report continued. 'Had it even partially succeeded, there seems much reason to believe that it would have been the signal for a more general rising in other parts of the kingdom.' That the danger was real it had no doubt: 'It appears that, in some parts of the country, arms have been lately procured by the individual members of these societies in considerable quantities, which can only have been done with a view to the use of force.' All this activity was being carefully orchestrated by a 'managing committee' which communicated with subsidiary committees through 'delegates and missionaries'. These committees were manipulating the innocent, claimed the report, and many of those involved were forced to swear oaths of secrecy on being admitted, without being fully informed as to what was being planned. The real aims of the leaders were apparent from the speeches they made at the mass meetings, the report continued, rather contradicting its previous assertion, and these 'tend towards the destruction of the social order, recommending a general equalisation of property, and at the same time endeavouring to corrupt the morals of the hearers, and to destroy all reverence for religion'. The meetings were 'frequently terminated, particularly in London, by profane and seditious songs and parodies of parts of the liturgy', all part of a process meant to prepare the people for 'the most outrageous scenes of outrage and violence'.[8]

The report of the House of Commons committee painted a slightly different, but complementary, picture. It had identified a concerted attempt by the Hampden Clubs to take advantage of the distress of the lower classes, 'to induce them to look for immediate relief, not only in reform of Parliament on the plan of universal suffrage and annual election, but in a total overthrow of all existing establishments, and in a division of the landed, and extinction of the funded property of the country'. It was in no doubt that churches would be demolished. It reproduced the following text of a flyer headed 'Britons to Arms!': 'The whole country waits the signal from London to fly to arms! Haste, break open gunsmiths and other likely places to find arms! Run all constables who touch a man of us; no rise of bread; no Regent; no Castlereagh, off with their heads; no placemen, tythes or enclosures; no taxes; no bishops, only useless lumber! stand true, or be slaves for ever.' The original of this, and the flyer allegedly handed out to the guards at the Tower, is not to be found among the papers, now in the National Archives, on which the report was based.

The Commons committee had also uncovered 'traces of a secret committee which directs everything'. 'It has been proved, to the entire satisfaction of your committee,' it assured the House, 'that some members of these societies, acting by an assumed or delegated authority, as an executive committee of the whole, conceived the project, and endeavoured to prepare the means of raising an insurrection, so formidable from numbers, as by dint of physical strength to overpower all resistance.' There was, apparently, a Committee of Public Safety of twenty-four members in existence. Those unwilling to join the ranks of the insurgents had their names entered in a 'Black Book', and would be dealt with after the revolution. There were reports that gunsmiths were doing excellent business, and people had been overheard calculating how much land they would receive from the redistribution. Again, no documents among the papers support this.

In the Commons committee's scenario, the insurrection was to have started at night, with the torching of barracks, from which artillery and arms would be taken, the seizure of the bridges over the Thames, and the securing of the Tower and the Bank. 'In furtherance of this design, a machine was projected for clearing the streets of cavalry,' an 'authenticated' diagram of which had greatly alarmed the committee. The conspirators had 'reconnoitred' the buildings to be stormed, drawing plans of them, had visited gun shops in order to see what might be stolen, and hung around with soldiers at barracks and ale houses in order to subvert. This original plan had been abandoned, and the conspirators had decided to make the second Spa Fields meeting, on 2 December 1816, the flashpoint for the insurrection.[9]

Both reports covered the members of the committees against charges of exaggeration, with the Lords committee remarking that any lack of actual evidence there might be was explained by the fact that the intentions and activities of the conspirators were 'seldom reduced to writing; they pass and are communicated by word of mouth'. The Commons committee insisted that they had presented 'what they conceive to be a fair, and not exaggerated statement of the result of their investigation', and explained that they did not append some of the more important pieces of evidence as these might compromise their informers. They went on to admit that there were in fact very few people involved in the conspiracy, hardly any of the middle classes, no agricultural workers and only some from a handful of manufacturing towns, and that most of the poor had been bearing their hardships with loyal stoicism. Nevertheless, the conspiracy had represented a very real threat of 'general confusion, plunder and bloodshed'.[10]

In this context, the actual papers on which the committees based their reports make interesting reading. It is only necessary to look through the list of items found at Dr Watson's lodgings in Bloomsbury to appreciate the flimsiness of the evidence. Each item is described in a manner designed to load it with the utmost significance. Much is made of a 'design of a flag', assumed to be a tricolour, which, on examination, has three horizontal bands of unspecified colour, bearing the hardly bloodcurdling inscription: 'Nature, to Feed the Hungry; Truth, to Protect the Oppressed; Justice, to Punish Crimes'. The 'plan of the Tower' found among the papers is a rough sketch of what appears to be the gate. The 'Supposed Calculation of military force in Cypher with Key and Explanation' might just as well be a laundry list. And the 'authenticated' design of the anti-cavalry machine is a doodle of something that looks like a mechanised cockroach, which only a frenzied imagination could have identified as a weapon.[11]

The Commons committee's report contains the assertion that 'Plans for the seduction of the soldiers were now adopted and pursued with unremitting activity,' with visits made to barracks to 'excite their sympathy'. The only document in the sealed papers on which this could be based contains statements taken from half a dozen soldiers at the Tower, who confirmed that a John Hooper had visited them, spent a shilling treating them to porter, given one of them a roll of handbills and taken a 'bunch of different coloured ribbon' from under his hat and waved it about saying he hoped they would all be wearing something like it one day. Some of the soldiers questioned had drunk Hooper's porter, but claimed nothing much had been said; others had not even noticed his presence. Not a shilling well-spent in the cause of revolution. According to one government spy, Thistlewood and others discussed 'offering the soldiers double pay for life or 100 guin. down'. How they were to procure a hundred guineas for every guard at the Tower is not explained.[12]

The assertion in the report that 'a large quantity of pike heads' had been ordered, paid for and delivered seems to have been based on indistinct and contradictory records of two conversations in the course of which Thistlewood, Preston and the Watsons agreed to order first 250 and then five hundred pikes, and the testimony of two government agents that they found 199 pike heads hidden in Watson's privy, though this assertion is not supported by any kind of inventory. Nor, given that they declared themselves 'ready to prove that the pike heads were not thrown into the privy by them or with their knowledge', is it certain that they did not plant them there.[13]

In his speech on 24 February 1817 introducing a Bill for the suspension of habeas corpus, Sidmouth assured Parliament that 'a malignant spirit' born of the French Revolution was manipulating the distressed lower orders by 'circulating the most irreligious and inflammatory publications'. He made much of alleged connections between the English Radicals and the revolutionary ferment on the Continent, and concluded that all the evidence he had seen 'left no doubt of the existence of an extensive plan of insurrection'.[14]

In the debate that followed, the Whig Lord Grey countered that the evidence was footling and the threat non-existent. He pointed out that every single offence referred to in the reports was punishable by existing laws, and that there was no need to bring in additional legislation, let alone suspend habeas corpus. In a petition to the House of Commons disputing the report, Hunt declared that he had kept the home secretary informed of all his intentions, and that there had been nothing revolutionary about the meeting and 'no such dangerous projects had ever entered the minds of those who constituted almost the entire mass of that most numerous meeting'. In the Lords, the king's brother the Duke of Sussex rebuked the cabinet, saying that there had never been any conspiracy and that they had made 'molehills into mountains'. Several speakers went on to blame the government for having failed to pluck the fruits of peace and allowed the 'disgraceful' settlement of the Congress of Vienna.

Sidmouth responded with a lurid picture of the conspiracy, insisting that 'These seditions had been spread over the country with a profusion scarcely credible, and with an industry without example,' and that 'scarcely a cottage had escaped the perseverance of the agents of mischief'. He warned that the Radicals 'had parliamentary reform in their mouths, but rebellion and revolution in their hearts'. Liverpool backed him up by saying that 'from information which he knew to be authentic, that in some parts of the country, the caution and secrecy of the conspirators were so great, that even though it was known that conspiracies did exist, yet the nature of the evidence that could be procured was such as would not be sufficient to send them into a court of justice'. He accompanied his intention of suspending habeas corpus with much hand-wringing and professions of how pained he was at having to resort to such a measure.[15]

Habeas corpus was suspended on 4 March, and ten days later the Seditious Meetings Act and other repressive pieces of legislation from 1795 were reintroduced. Attempts on the life of the prince regent were decreed as treasonable as those on the life of the king, and the seduction of soldiers was brought into the ambit of high treason. Arrests followed. On 27 March Sidmouth sent out a circular to all lords lieutenant informing them that they had the power to seize 'blasphemous and seditious' literature and take into custody publishers and vendors without the necessity of a court ruling. Cobbett and others fled to the United States in order to avoid arrest.

At the beginning of April, after a meeting at St Peter's Fields outside Manchester, a large number of destitute weavers set off for London in groups of ten with blankets to sleep in rolled on their backs and petitions to the prince regent begging him to do something about their plight. The Manchester magistrates read the Riot Act and took two of the leaders into custody, but the remaining six or seven hundred set off, in heavy rain, only to be harassed and arrested by companies of regular dragoons, yeomanry and special constables along the way. Only one of the 'Blanketeers' reached London.

At the end of April, the trial on a charge of high treason of Dr James Watson, Arthur Thistlewood, Thomas Preston and John Hooper opened at the Old Bailey. It soon degenerated into farce as the prosecution clutched at straws to prove that the accused had tried to 'put the king to Death' and 'Levy War on the king'. They were acquitted, to the discomfiture of the government and the delight of its opponents. Sir Samuel Romilly pointed out that if they had been charged with aggravated riot, they would have been convicted, and castigated the ministry, 'whose object it has been to give an extraordinary degree of importance to every appearance of disaffection or tumult which has manifested itself in any part of the kingdom'.[16]

On 9 June 1817, a couple of hundred men gathered in the Derbyshire village of Pentrich and set off under a redundant stocking-maker by the name of Jeremiah Brandreth, expecting to meet up with other groups on the way to Nottingham. Their aims were various and incoherent, ranging from free beef and rum to the abolition of all taxes and the liberation of great figures allegedly imprisoned in the Tower. The march was a shambles, and people began to peel off as soon as it started. The remainder scattered at the sight of two officers and eighteen troopers of the 15th Hussars, who gave chase, arrested twenty-eight men and picked up seventeen firearms and forty-five pikes. Brandreth and three others were hanged and posthumously beheaded, and a number of others were sentenced to transportation. The revolutionary nature of the threat they represented might be gauged by the fact that during the interrogations it transpired that some of the marchers believed the 'provisional government' with which they intended to replace the current one was of a kind that would supply them with provisions.[17]

There followed a marked fall-off in radical activity of any kind. This had something to do with the numerous arrests not only of ringleaders but also of ordinary weavers, often at night when they were torn from their beds with troops in attendance. This tactic of intimidation put off many peaceful activists and their followers. But there may have been other reasons for the decline in incidents of one kind or another, related to the authorities' handling of the supposed crisis.

William Cobbett for one was convinced that throughout 1816 the government had been looking for an excuse for a clampdown, probably in order to derail the movement for parliamentary reform. 'They are absolutely pining and dying for a plot!' as he put it. Following the Spa Fields disorders and the attack on the prince regent, the government appeared to be doing everything it could to spread fear. 'The ministerial newspapers were indefatigable in magnifying every movement into treason and sedition,' according to the London Radical Francis Place. '[They] took advantage of the general distress and partial discontent of the people, and employed spies to excite tumults, to form plots, to foment sedition, and to produce treason … Every plot, real or imaginary, every movement of the populace which could be instigated, every paltry penny publication (some of which were their own) which could be made to talk seditiously, as the nonsense they contained was called, were magnified into serious, seditious, outrageous tumults, horrid and widely extended treasons, shaking the very foundations of the Government and threatening its overthrow.'[18]

There was a growing suspicion that *agents provocateurs* were being used, and some believed that the disorders at the Spa Fields meeting had been provoked by the government spy Castle. He was the chief witness in the trial of Watson, Thistlewood and the others, and his evidence incriminated him and his puppet-masters more than it did the men in the dock. It was revealed that he had employed the old trick of trying to get them to agree, in front of carefully chosen witnesses, to his provocative statements, such as the French revolutionary slogan 'May the last of the kings be strangled with the guts of the last Priest!' The press began to pry. What emerged was that Castle, a maker of paper dolls for children, was also a forger and a thief as well as being a bigamist and a pimp. He lived in what he referred to as a boarding house run by a Mrs Thomas, which turned out to be a brothel, something he denied being aware of. He had a long history as an 'approver' – one who helped set up a crime in order to turn king's evidence and denounce his accomplices. In one instance, he had supplied with forged banknotes a gang of criminals who, once he had denounced them, were arrested, tried on his evidence and hanged. When his connection with the Home Office came out there was widespread revulsion, and the government came under attack in the Commons. Castlereagh's defence, which rested on the premise that the security of the state was an object of paramount importance which justified any measure, and which attempted to portray Castle as a doughty soldier in the battle against subversion, was ridiculed by William Hazlitt. 'According to his Lordship's comprehensive and liberal views, the liberty and independence of nations are best supported abroad by the point of the bayonet; and morality, religion, and social order, are best defended at home by spies and informers,' he wrote. 'It is a pretty system, and worthy of itself from first to last.'[19]

Evidence of the activity of other *agents provocateurs* began to emerge. In Lancashire, an unidentified man had attempted to persuade people to rise up, torch the factories and make 'a Moscow out of Manchester'. Samuel Bamford opened the door one night to a stranger, who told him that there were hundreds of people gathering to march on London with daggers fashioned from kitchen knives which they intended to plunge into the breasts of the cabinet, and urged him to join them. Bamford was convinced that the man was not himself an *agent provocateur* but an innocent dupe. 'Any administration which is base enough may in times of severe distress have as many plots and conspiracies as it pleases,' noted Francis Place. 'There are always reckless, desperate men eager to listen to tales from spies set on to impose upon them.' In London, the ingenuous 'country cousins' had been beset by agents, and when they left for home one of them was accompanied by a certain Mr Richards, a failed builder, a bigamist and a convicted fraud, but a born actor, who would play a significant role under the name Oliver. He travelled around Yorkshire telling all who cared to listen that London was on the brink of revolution and only awaiting a signal from the North; evidence that emerged at the trials of the Pentrich rebels suggested that the rebellion had been instigated by him.[20]

Sidmouth admitted to using informers, but evaded the charges of sending out *agents provocateurs*, and tried to bury any further enquiry by invoking the terrible dangers which the country faced, of which only he had knowledge. 'These men, besides confessing their own guilt,' he said of the executed rebels, 'gave certain information that an insurrection much more formidable than the one in which they had engaged was contemplated, and would infallibly have taken place had not the Habeas Corpus Act been suspended.' The government nevertheless stopped using *agents provocateurs* and reined in its spies for a time; according to Romilly, 'from the time when they ceased to be employed, all the signs of disaffection which had manifested themselves in different parts of the country had ceased'.[21]

This raises the question of whether there actually was or had ever been any real threat of upheaval. General Sir John Byng, commander of the troops in the Midlands and the North, a veteran of the Peninsula and Waterloo, took a relaxed view of the events throughout. There is no doubt that many of the old plotters of the 1790s were still active, and had grown more radical in their views with the passage of time. But they were hopelessly split. The likes of Watson and Thistlewood did want to see violent upheaval, but it is not at all clear what form they thought it should take, if they had ever thought that far ahead. There is reason to believe that most Radicals saw it in terms of a kind of mass demonstration, perhaps accompanied by peripheral bloodshed but primarily aimed at making the authorities back down rather than overthrowing the system. The Spenceans, generally regarded as 'harmless fanatics', were opposed to violence and boycotted the Spa Fields meeting. Following Spence's death in 1814 they had grown more religious, fusing their political desires with millenarian visions.[22]

There were those who thought the Spa Fields meeting had been orchestrated by French revolutionaries in the hope of sparking off a revolution in England which would lead to similar upheavals in France and Belgium. A witness at the trial of Watson and the others testified that he had seen Castle with a 'Genteel'-looking man in a 'French Great Coat' who 'talked about Paris'. Castlereagh was being warned by Lord Clancarty, the British ambassador in the Netherlands, that the 'machinations' taking place in England were 'intimately connected' with the activities of the French émigrés in Belgium, which had become 'the seat of intrigues and a nest for traitors and libellers to hatch their treasons, and thence spread them over the world'. He believed that there was a risk of the entire Vienna settlement being overturned by this revolutionary international.[23]

Hunt was no Danton, and Watson no Robespierre. The younger Watson, a twenty-year-old described by one informer as of a 'shabby genteel' appearance, had been drunk when he led the assault on the Tower (he had previously been treated for insanity). And it is doubtful whether even a Danton could have stirred the English masses into revolt. While there was much anger, it was not focused, certainly not against the monarchy. When the prince regent's daughter, Charlotte Augusta, died in November 1817 there was a truly nationwide outpouring of grief, with houses draped in black and shops shut for up to two weeks.[24]

Castlereagh for one had some experience of revolution and rebellion. He had once agitated for self-rule and drunk republican toasts before becoming a government loyalist. He had seen the amateurish enthusiasms of the would-be reformers, their weakness and lack of purpose. He had also seen, in 1798, how easy it was to crush such rebels with militia, let alone regular troops, and to restore order even in extreme revolutionary situations, as he had done it himself, with chilling efficiency. It seems unlikely that he or any other member of the cabinet should have been panicked by a handful of mountebanks such as Watson and Thistlewood. Sidmouth did remark that nobody should become a politician if they were not prepared to meet a violent death, and at one point Castlereagh made a provision in his will permitting his wife to sell her jewellery in the event of a revolution. But, as the Marquess of Wellesley mockingly pointed out in the Lords, if they really had been fearful of revolution breaking out, they would have recalled Parliament immediately, rather than wait for the shooting season to end before doing so. In May 1817 a House of Commons committee produced a report on the desirability of creating a police force, and the government came out firmly against the idea. When Bamford and the other 'country cousins' were arrested and interrogated by the Privy Council, they sat around a table with Liverpool, Sidmouth, Castlereagh and the others, being politely questioned about their activities. The atmosphere was so light-hearted that at one point they all shared a joke and 'tittered'. Perhaps the most charitable explanation is that the cabinet had fallen for their own lies, as politicians so often do, and succeeded in frightening themselves. A greater man than any of them was fast succumbing to the same syndrome across the Channel.[25]

11

Moral Order

Klemens Wenzel Lothar von Metternich-Winneburg-Beilstein was born at Koblenz in 1773, the son of an imperial count from an ancient family of the Rhineland. In 1788, aged fifteen, he was sent to university at Strasbourg. While he applied himself assiduously to his studies, he also displayed a marked devotion to elegance, taste, pleasure and the art of living well. He cut a dashing figure, and was viewed by his fellow students as something of a fop. To one, the rather severe Freiherr vom Stein, he seemed '*fin, faux, fanfaron*' (clever, sly and boastful). Unlike so many of his contemporaries, he did not greet the French Revolution as a new dawn. He was no bigot, and he was well versed in the political culture of the Enlightenment. That change and reform must come he did not doubt. But he believed in the orderly conduct of public affairs. He was shaken and disgusted by the spectacle of what he called 'a drunken rabble' storming Strasbourg's Hôtel de Ville in emulation of the Paris mob's assault on the Bastille. His conviction that the world was being turned upside down was confirmed when he watched the university's director of religious studies publicly burn the symbols of office of the bishops of Strasbourg. By contrast, the coronation in Frankfurt on 6 October 1790 of Leopold II as Holy Roman Emperor, at which he assisted, a ceremony as empty of practical significance as it was brimming with symbolic meaning, struck him as the embodiment of everything he believed in. The emperor and the electors made their ceremonial entry into the city in a hundred carriages, surrounded by outriders on richly caparisoned horses, to a three-hundred-gun salute. Metternich imbibed the subliminal message of divinely ordained hierarchy implicit in the elaborate rituals that followed, and was captivated. The young duc de Richelieu, who was also present, was more struck by the 'dazzling' array of diamonds with which the ladies of the court were bedecked, and indeed by the sumptuous liveries of crimson velvet dripping with gold of the young Count Metternich's servants.[1]

Less than two years later, in July 1792, Metternich witnessed the coronation of Leopold's successor, Francis II, which was to be the last such ceremony ever to take place. After brief travels which took him to London, Brussels and finally Vienna, in 1795, aged twenty-two, he entered the emperor's service. His first appointment was as diplomatic minister to Dresden, his second posting was to Berlin. There, in 1805, he negotiated the treaty which brought Prussia into the Third Coalition against Napoleon, and to disaster on the fields of Jena and Auerstadt. After the defeat of the allies, in 1806, Napoleon abolished the Holy Roman Empire, and Metternich's master Francis II became Francis I of Austria. At the request of Napoleon, Metternich was posted to Paris as Austrian ambassador.

Handsome and distinguished, graceful in his bearing, delightful in conversation, effortlessly charming, he was a natural diplomat. Flush with Napoleon's recognition of his talents, and eager to widen his acquaintance and his influence, he bedded nearly every lady of note in Paris, including the French emperor's sister Caroline. It was largely thanks to Metternich that after its disastrous attack on France in 1809 Austria and its monarchy were saved from extinction, and Francis did not, as some wags had foretold, become Francis 0. Having negotiated the Treaty of Vienna, which turned Francis into Napoleon's ally, Metternich was appointed Austria's foreign minister, a post he was to keep for the next thirty-nine years.

Metternich despised Napoleon as the product of the French Revolution and for being the upstart and bully he was, but he also admired him. He acknowledged his intelligence and ability to achieve his ends, and recognised that he had suppressed the Revolution and turned France into an efficient state. In this respect, Metternich would have liked to emulate him with regard to the Habsburg realm. But since the Austrian state was founded on medieval principles, and was only held together by the glue of hierarchy and tradition, he came to the conclusion that only strict adhesion to existing forms could safeguard the continued existence of the monarchy. This conviction became his guiding principle as he navigated the perilous international situation over the next years. He kept Austria in Napoleon's camp as long as this was necessary, while preparing for it a prime position in that of his enemies. After the Battle of Leipzig in 1813, which sealed the triumph of this policy, he was elevated to the dignity of prince (for his new arms he took the motto *Kraft im Recht*, Strength in Law). He went on to dominate the Congress of Vienna, providing Austria with what he believed were firm bases for its survival as an autocratic paternalist monarchy. The preservation of the settlement agreed there in 1815 was for him a matter of principle as well as a priority.[2]

The greatest threat to it would be the outbreak of war or revolution in Europe. But back at the beginning of 1814, when it had become certain that Napoleon would be defeated, Metternich and Castlereagh had set up a structure for avoiding the first and dealing with the second. In a treaty signed at Chaumont on 9 March 1814, Britain, Austria, Russia and Prussia had committed themselves to a long-term alliance aimed at containing France. It had stood the test of Napoleon's return from Elba, and mobilised the forces which defeated him at Waterloo. On his arrival in Paris on the tail of Wellington's army, Castlereagh suggested transforming the alliance into a permanent coalition. In consequence, on 20 November 1815 the plenipotentiaries of the four great powers, as they now styled themselves, signed the Quadruple Alliance. Though primarily directed against France, this engaged them jointly to defend all the arrangements they had made at the Congress of Vienna. They further agreed to hold regular congresses to review the situation and consider measures necessary for the preservation of peace. It was a pan-European security system intended to guarantee the existing territorial and constitutional arrangements. In the minds of Metternich and most of the rulers of the Continent, it was also there to preserve what they saw as the moral order those arrangements supposedly rested on.

Metternich was a curious amalgam of child of the Enlightenment and product of the *ancien régime*. He was not religious, and did not believe in the Divine Right of rulers, yet he worshipped an order based on autocratic monarchy underpinned by established religion. He regarded any change with suspicion, as it must perforce disturb this order. He viewed the professional and middle classes with antagonism, as it was in their nature to advance their interests, which could only be achieved by displacing existing hierarchies and altering the political structure, both of which threatened the system he stood by. It had been lawyers who had dominated the French Revolution, he never ceased reminding people.

There was a fundamental flaw in the logic of Metternich's position. He rejected liberalism and modern notions of progress in favour of an imagined *pax Christiana* resting on the twin pillars of throne and Church which had supposedly existed before the French Revolution, a time when the laws of God were observed and legitimacy reigned. A time when, in the words of the German philosopher Friedrich Schleiermacher, 'more outward religiosity dominated the people' and 'people lived in a more secluded and decorous manner', 'worked more cheaply and more untiringly', 'showed themselves more submissive' and did not 'allow themselves all kinds of opinions or even aspirations for a better life'.[3]

Such a state had never existed. Certainly not in the eighteenth century, which had been one of secularisation, of astonishing upward mobility as well as social degradation, when there had been an explosion of opinion on every conceivable subject, and when nakedly illegitimate wars raged, with the King of France abetting the rebellious American subjects of his Britannic brother-monarch, and the rulers of Russia, Prussia and Austria ganging up against the anointed King of Poland to dethrone and despoil him, to name but two. Every Catholic ruler in Europe, whose descendants now posed as defenders of the Church as a means of shoring up their authority, had abolished religious institutions, curtailed the prerogatives of the clergy, and closed down monasteries and convents, shamelessly helping themselves to their riches. Francis's uncle Joseph II had not only been one of the first to dissolve religious orders and pillage Church property, but had encouraged anticlericalism and made irreligion fashionable.

When Napoleon had taken over Francis's palace of Schönbrunn after his defeat of Austria in 1809, he had two immense obelisks surmounted by imperial eagles erected on either side of the gates, to emphasise his imperial status. Instead of demolishing what others might have seen as a reminder of his humiliation, Francis kept them. They were not the only Napoleonic legacy Francis and Metternich hung on to, and they accepted the abolition of ancient privileges and the structural changes brought about in Germany and Italy. They quietly relished the erosion of the prerogatives of the nobility and other bodies, and copied the French state in its intrusion into the private sphere. And while they professed ardent devotion to the Catholic faith, they subjected the Church to the state and used it as an instrument of social control.[4]

In 1815, the Austrian monarchy faced no threat: there was no social unrest or political opposition to speak of, as the system generally benefited those who craved nothing beyond the comforts of life and the rewards of honest work, which meant the overwhelming majority of the population. The only elements not happy with the state of affairs were certain conservative milieus in Austrian society fired by a Romantic vision of a return to the spirit of an imagined past; a faction of the Hungarian nobility aspiring to greater autonomy; a residue of patriotic nobles in Galicia dreaming of a resurrection of the Polish state; and a mixture of redundant aristocrats and disappointed Napoleonic administrators and officers in the Italian provinces. None of these elements was in any position to upset the tranquillity of the state, and all could safely be ignored. Some 75 per cent of the population still lived off the land, and since there was little industry and no populous cities, there was no industrial proletariat to contend with.

Metternich had accepted Pergen's credo that only a state of absolute 'calm' guaranteed the preservation of 'order', which had become gospel to the Habsburg monarchy. At the heart of that credo was the conviction, expressed by Pergen, that the task of the Austrian police was to invigilate not only the provinces of the monarchy itself, but 'the spirit reigning throughout Europe'. In consequence, the state chancellery over which Metternich presided outgrew the mere function of an office of foreign affairs, and became an extension of the police. It grew into a huge machine, with ten departments run by minutely graded civil servants, and auxiliary branches dealing with specific areas such as encryption and decryption, translation, printing of propaganda, the archives, the treasury, the postal service, and so on. While he was a devotee of strict censorship and regarded press freedom as 'a heresy', he used newspapers, most notably the *Österreichische Beobachter*, and a stable of writers, including Friedrich Schlegel and Adam Müller, to propound his own views and manipulate public opinion. He financed a number of papers and periodicals, and paid to have articles included in foreign papers such as the Parisian *Journal des débats* and the London *Morning Chronicle*.

Metternich and Count Josef Sedlnitzky, who became chief of police in 1816, identified control of the postal service as a key element in the invigilation of Europe. In the course of the eighteenth century Vienna had, by providing the most efficient postal service throughout the Holy Roman Empire, gained access to the correspondence passing through central Europe. Although the Empire had been abolished, much of the post carried around its former territory still passed through Austrian sorting offices. Metternich managed to extend this to cover Switzerland, a natural crossroads as well as a meeting place for subversives of every sort. All Swiss post passed through Berne, whose postal service was in the hands of the conservative patrician de Fischer family, with the result that all mail between France, Germany and Italy was accessible to the Austrian authorities. Most of the mail going in and out of Italy passed through Lombardy, where it came under Austrian police scrutiny. The rest went through the kingdom of Sardinia or port cities such as Naples and Ostia. In July 1815 Metternich sent his postal expert, Baron von Lilien, to Rome to negotiate a convention with the Papal States whereby all mail leaving them would pass through Lombardy. The papacy was in conflict with Austria over religious issues deriving from the anti-clerical reforms of Joseph II, and the secretary of state, Cardinal Ercole Consalvi, was in no mood to cooperate. Metternich then tried to create a barrier across northern Italy by signing conventions with Parma, Modena and Tuscany, through which mail from Rome had to pass – 'we cut Italy in two and become its masters', he anticipated. But Tuscany, despite being ruled by an Austrian archduke, demurred, under discreet diplomatic pressure from Rome, Sardinia and France. This was a setback for Metternich, as it was the monarchy's Italian provinces that were the most vulnerable.[5]

For centuries, Italy had been the arena in which an extended struggle for supremacy had been played out between the rulers of Austria and France. That struggle had continued after the Revolution, and it was in Italy that Napoleon had forged his reputation. After assuming the title of Emperor of the French he had taken that of King of Italy, bestowed on his son the title of King of Rome, and given the Bourbon kingdom of Naples to his brother-in-law Joachim Murat. The Congress of Vienna reversed this. The territory of the defunct republic of Venice was added to Austria's recovered Italian province of Lombardy. This was protected from France in the west by the kingdom of Sardinia, which regained its mainland provinces of Piedmont and Savoy, and was strengthened with the heritage of the abolished republic of Genoa. The Austrian emperor's brother was reinstated in Florence as Grand Duke of Tuscany, one of his grandsons became Duke of Modena, while Napoleon's consort (and Francis's daughter) Marie-Louise was given the former Bourbon duchy of Parma to reign over. The pope was restored to Rome and recovered his fiefdoms of the Legations and Le Marche. The Bourbons of Naples returned from Sicily and repossessed their former mainland kingdom.

Lombardy-Venetia was ruled directly from Vienna; Tuscany, Parma and Modena were under Austrian protection; and the pope was entirely dependent on Austrian support. The King of Naples, or of the Two Sicilies as his title now rang, was pressured by Metternich into signing a secret treaty which forbade any constitutional change to take place in his kingdom without the permission of Austria. Metternich would have liked to impose similar arrangements on the other Italian states, thereby binding them into a kind of federation dominated by Austria, but neither Sardinia nor the papacy would oblige. Metternich had nevertheless managed to exclude France entirely, and turned Austria into the policeman of Italy. In so doing, he had unwittingly set the scene for the unification of the peninsula – by giving all Italian patriots of whatever stamp a common enemy. And he had set himself an almost impossible task, for Italy was not liable to the kind of order he envisaged.

Before 1789, much of Italy had been a lawless place barely policed by its various rulers, most of whom knew better than to try to impose their will on intricate, centuries-old patterns of social interdependence and parochial loyalties. Remote areas were governed by a form of outlawry which has been termed 'social banditry' by some historians. Its practitioners were impossible to apprehend, as they were shielded by the poorer sections of the population, which they protected from oppression by landlords and taxation by the state, and subsidised in times of hardship from the proceeds of their robberies. Rulers, landowners and the Church had learned to accommodate themselves to such realities.

French incursions into Italy in the 1790s had a dramatic effect on this state of affairs. Rulers were toppled, feudalism was abolished, existing political and administrative structures were dismantled and replaced with French models, the Church was restricted and property confiscated. The whole peninsula was first subjected to republican forms of government, then incorporated into the French empire or turned into kingdoms. The imposition of French order on hitherto lawless areas had unintended consequences: resistance to the execution of the law, collection of taxes and conscription of young men grew in proportion to the energy with which these were carried out, and the latent banditry became more organised.

French rule had nevertheless achieved a great deal, much of it what former rulers would have liked to bring about themselves but did not dare or know how to, such as curbing the power of the nobility and the Church, enforcing the law and providing for the efficient collection of taxes. The rulers reinstated in 1815 were not about to reverse this, which put them at odds with those, such as the nobility and the clergy, who should have been the natural pillars of their thrones. Much of what the French had done had also upset the rural masses, by trampling on local interests and sensibilities, and the failure to reverse it alienated them.

French revolutionary influences had radicalised the educated nobility and middle class, making them more hostile to authority of any stamp, and awakening an aspiration to unite the whole peninsula in one Italian state. French rule had created a new administrative class, while Napoleon's exploitation of Italian manpower had created parallel military cadres. Not only did these two categories feel threatened by the return of former monarchs or the imposition of Austrian rule, they constituted a natural leadership and the skeleton of an alternative.

The vacuum created by the end of Napoleonic rule in northern Italy in 1813 and 1814 had quickly filled with aspirations for an independent Italian state. Some hoped to preserve the existing kingdom of Italy with Napoleon's viceroy, Prince Eugène de Beauharnais, as king. Others, encouraged by the British minister at Palermo, Lord William Bentinck, a dashing general and former governor of Madras who was enamoured of Italy, wanted the whole peninsula united under Napoleon's brother-in-law Joachim Murat, who was then still King of Naples. In 1815, when Austria was distracted by Napoleon's return from Elba, Murat sallied forth at the head of his army and called on all Italians to support him in creating a united independent Italy. His call was answered by no more than a few hundred, and his enterprise foundered.

When the Austrians reoccupied Venetia and Lombardy following the withdrawal of the French, the military commander, Field Marshal Heinrich von Bellegarde, provisionally confirmed existing French law and kept on the administration and the police. He and the new police chief in Venice reported that there was no resistance to the Austrians and no cause for alarm. But in 1815 the new civil authorities began the wholesale dismissal of Napoleonic civil servants and officers. Not only did this produce a marked decline in efficiency, a body of ambitious and articulate Italians had been deprived of their livings and their prospects. But the Austrian administration was not out to make friends. Heraldic commissions were established to tidy up the hierarchy after the various changes of regime, and these succeeded in alienating further sections of Italian society. Titles of nobility granted under Napoleon were abolished. Ancient Venetian titles were downgraded, on the grounds that they had been granted by a republic. A Venetian duke was reduced to the level of a German count, a Venetian count became the equivalent of a German baron, and the process of having to produce documents and plead with Austrian civil servants was as humiliating as the degradation itself. Metternich was entitled to his opinion of the Venetian and Lombard nobility as a 'bastard race of fallen aristocracy', but it was questionable policy to insult the class whose natural interest was to support the existing order.[6]

The Emperor Francis was no more tactful. Ignoring the advice of his men on the spot, he set about imposing his own standards of propriety on the administration of his Italian provinces. Interpreted by local police officials, these translated into a bizarre set of precepts, whereby people were denied appointments on grounds ranging from 'suspect relationship with a chambermaid' to being interested in financial speculation or simply too talkative. This involved the police intimately in the lives of people to the extent that according to one

Austrian commentator, 'It may be said that in Italy no social relationship exists that is not subject to its direct interference.'[7]

Francis, whose obsession with the Masonic/Illuminist conspiracy had not abated, banned all secret societies. Government officials, teachers and even candidates for doctoral degrees had to swear an oath that they did not belong to one. He ordered lists to be drawn up of everyone who had ever belonged to a Masonic lodge, and the results terrified him. Freemasonry had been fashionable in Italy since the last decades of the eighteenth century (it had only been banned by Napoleon, who feared its potential as a force of opposition, in 1812). The lists included most of the aristocracy and almost all government officials and army officers, prompting Francis to conclude that his Italian provinces were a hotbed of subversion.[8]

Metternich established the *Beobachtungs Anstalt* in Milan to gather information on Masonic and other secret societies operating on the peninsula, and tried to persuade the other rulers to do likewise. As they failed to cooperate, he set up his own agencies to gather information on the west and south of Italy, run by his diplomatic envoys in Florence and Rome. Their usefulness was open to question. Many of those coming forward to give information and those arrested had something to hide, and the best way of doing this was to point the finger elsewhere. Most informers had worked for many masters and turned their coats inside out several times over the past two decades, and were practised at telling the new authorities what they wished to hear. They would conceal the existence and activities of a sect they might have belonged to, and invent spurious ones to throw the authorities off their own trail. They would regale their masters with the fearsome-sounding names of non-existent secret societies, their rituals and occult aims. As a result, all the Austrians were able to gather were lists of names and unfounded allegations.[9]

Their search for trouble was rewarded when they were alerted to a conspiracy being hatched in Milan. The information came from one Saint-Agnan, who had it from a Count Comelli, who had informed him of a plan being prepared there for a rising to establish an Italian state based on Rome, with the support of thousands of Italian exiles who were to land at strategic points from British ships. While this information on its own did not sound convincing, it did coincide with other intelligence Metternich had received, from the governor of Tyrol. He took the precaution of transferring Austrian army units composed of Italians to other Habsburg provinces and replacing them with Austrian and Hungarian troops, and despatched Saint-Agnan to Milan to find out more. There, Saint-Agnan met a man named Marshal, who told him that the plan was backed by Louis XVIII of France, who meant to establish a kingdom of Italy with his nephew the duc de Berry as king. Saint-Agnan was introduced to some of the conspirators, from whom he managed to obtain a batch of papers, which he sold to the Austrian authorities for 2,800 francs. He then disappeared.

He reappeared in Turin, where he offered his services to the King of Sardinia, volunteering to infiltrate the Sardinian émigrés in Paris who were supposedly plotting against him. Having failed to extract any money from Victor Emmanuel, he went to Switzerland, from where he wrote to Bellegarde saying he had evidence of a plot by Lord William Bentinck and the Duke of Buckingham to start a revolution in Italy, and to Metternich himself claiming that he was in possession of important documents which he would only show him in person (on receipt of 12,000 francs, and possibly some land and a title). Metternich paid him 4,000 francs on condition he never set foot in Italy again. The conspirators identified by Saint-Agnan were arrested and their interrogation was conducted under the supervision of the emperor himself. The case against them was of the flimsiest, which was reflected in its outcome: a few were imprisoned on short sentences, others were exiled, some were set free – having spent twenty months in gaol during the investigation and trial.[10]

It is impossible to assess the extent of the threat posed by the conspiratorial networks which troubled Metternich and others so much, as very little is known about them. They had mostly originated in France. What was probably the first was founded by an Italian,

Filippo Antonio Buonarroti of Pisa, believed to be a descendant of the artist Michelangelo. Early reading of Rousseau's works had inspired in him dreams of an egalitarian society, and with the outbreak of the French Revolution he was drawn to Paris, where he collaborated with Saint Just and Robespierre. He followed the French army when it invaded Italy, and began building up a network of like-minded people covering the entire peninsula. On his return to Paris after the fall of Robespierre he was arrested, and in prison he encountered the socialist revolutionary François (alias Gracchus) Babeuf, with whom he wrote the *Plebeian Manifesto*, published on their release in 1795, which among other things called for the abolition of private property. Babeuf and Buonarroti then began plotting a *coup d'état*, to be carried out by small cells taking over the controls of power – they despised the idea of popular revolution, and meant to impose their order from above. The conspiracy unravelled, so, following Napoleon's invasion of Italy, Buonarroti returned there and recreated his network as a secret society which he called the Adelphi, all of whose members assumed the name of Emilio, in honour of Rousseau's *Émile*.

He may have taken the name Adelphi from a group of disgruntled officers in the French army calling themselves the *Philadelphes*, founded around 1803 in opposition to the rising power of Napoleon. In the wake of French incursions, secret societies sprang up all over Italy, some of them revolutionary, some pro-French, some anti-French, some in defence of the Catholic faith, others with no identifiable agendas. Some took over or overlapped with existing Masonic lodges. They sported a bizarre litany of names, based on astrology, religious symbolism drawn from Egyptian, Greek and Roman mythology, from Judaism and the Catholic canon, and their structures and rites were strongly marked by Masonry and Illuminism. To be precise about their numbers, or even to be certain of their existence, is impossible, as they would occasionally merge or change their names; because of the need for secrecy, members were often unaware of these changes, and so defunct societies lived on in the imaginations of members and their existence was reported by informers, and recorded by the police. Among these were not only the *Centri*, the *Raggi*, the *dei Cinque*, the *Silencio dei Greci*, the *Cattolica* and the *Apostolica Romana*, but also some whose names suggest that someone was having a joke at the expense of the Austrian police – the *Pancie Nere* (Black Bellies), the *Vampiri* and the *Scamiciati* (Shirtless Ones). They were joined in 1809 by a new society created by Buonarroti whose members were titled *Sublimi Maestri Perfetti*, and whose ruling body, the Grand Firmament, based in Switzerland, supposedly controlled a ramified organisation, of whose actual activities nothing specific is known.[11]

Less nebulous were the *Carbonari*. There are many theories as to the origins of the movement, placing them alternatively in Switzerland, France, Germany, Scotland, England and ancient Egypt, where they were allegedly founded by the goddess Isis, but others name the founder variously as Philomel of Thebes, the Roman god Mithras, the eleventh-century St Theobald, the Knights Templar, King Francis I of France, or just the German guild of charcoal-burners. The most likely explanation is that it was originally an offshoot of Freemasonry which drew inspiration from this guild and from its French equivalent, the *Compagnonnage de la Charbonnerie*, both of them loose but resilient networks based on the nature of their trade and their peripatetic way of life. Just as the basic unit of Masonry was the lodge, for the Carbonari it was the *vèndita*, and where Masons were 'brothers', the Carbonari were 'good cousins'. The first evidence of their existence in Italy dates from 1808, and by the end of Napoleonic rule the movement was supposedly huge: estimates of its membership (all of which need to be taken with a large pinch of salt) vary from 4,000 to 80,000, and one would place it as high as 642,000.[12]

The nature of this movement can best be deduced from its rites and ceremonies. Initiation took place in a *baracca*, a hut in the middle of a wood or, failing that, of an urban garden. It began with a moment of reflection, after which the postulant would declare that he had come to the good cousins in search of truth and in order to learn to conquer his passions. He was then blindfolded and led around an obstacle course of tree trunks, confronted with blazing flames which symbolised the spirit of charity that must always burn in his breast, and made to kneel, axe in hand, while he swore to keep the secret and never deny assistance to any cousin. The axe was there to remind him that were he to fail in this he would be killed, and his body would be chopped up and burned, and his ashes scattered to the winds. The entire process took some time, and was accompanied by inordinate quantities of bloodcurdling verbiage, dramatic promises and oaths. Surviving Carbonarist 'catechisms' contain violent language, asserting for instance that property is 'an outrage against the rights of the human race', but they are essentially series of banal precepts based on the Catholic catechism, proclaiming the principal virtues to be faith, hope and charity, with some vaguely Rousseauist notions of 'natural virtue' thrown in. Initiation into higher grades could take the form of a simulacrum of the passion and crucifixion of Christ, with the postulant playing the role of Jesus, and his oppressors and killers dressed as Austrians. After his supposed death on the Cross, he would be taken down and resurrected into a new life.

The paraphernalia involved included daggers, cloaks, axes, fire, wine, chalices and blood, while the printed matter bristled with crosses, crowns of thorns, suns, moons, cocks, fasces, ladders, representations of St Theobald, skulls, crossed bones, geometrical dividers, triangles, pentangles and the odd papal tiara being struck by lightning. More than any desperate urge to rise up and overthrow the existing order, all this nonsense suggests a desire to escape an unfriendly world, to come together in a confraternity of like-minded equals, and to assuage a religious urge that the established Church could no longer satisfy. Many travellers, such as Byron and Heine, noted a profound sense of disappointment and alienation among young Italians, which is nowhere better captured than by Stendhal in the hero of his novel *La Chartreuse de Parme*.

Metternich did not concern himself with such reflections as he travelled around northern Italy, where he spent the first months of 1816. The following year he set off on a longer tour. He was delighted not only by the weather, the sights and the monuments; everywhere he went he encountered people who appeared to think like him and who expressed their loyalty to the Austrian emperor. 'The Jacobins are hiding from me, as they see me as a whip hanging over them,' he wrote home cheerfully. 'The kind of European police which we have organised, on a scale far greater than any that has ever existed, has not failed us,' he bragged to his ambassador in St Petersburg. 'I am confident that no project against the existing order could ever be prepared without us being informed of the first moves on the part of the subversives.' He was even more sure of himself in a letter to the French minister at Turin. 'You see in me the great minister of police of Europe, I am overseeing everything,' he wrote. 'My contacts are such that nothing escapes me.' Others were not convinced.[13]

The British ambassador in Vienna, Lord Charles Stewart, had complained in a letter to his half-brother Lord Castlereagh of Metternich's 'Inordinate Taste for Spies and Police', which in his view 'put the Employer more oftener [sic] on the *wrong*, rather than the *right* scent'. The British diplomat Sir Robert Gordon, who accompanied Metternich and Francis to Italy two years later, took much the same view. 'Nothing can surpass Prince Metternich's activities in collecting facts and information upon the inward feelings of the people: with a habit of making these researches he has acquired a taste for them, which gives no repose, until he finds himself ignorant of nothing that was intended to be concealed,' he wrote. 'But it may be feared that the secrecy with which this taste is necessarily indulged leads him to attach too great importance to his discoveries. Phantoms are conjured up and magnified in the dark, which probably, if exposed to light, would sink into insignificance; and his informers naturally exaggerate their reports, aware that their profit is to be commensurate with the display of their phantasmagoria.'[14]

Metternich was confident that while the many 'sects' were indeed giving rise to 'a spirit of fermentation, discontent and resistance', they did not represent a threat. 'An active surveillance, which has not let up over the period of the past two years, has demonstrated to me that

Tsar Alexander I, who hoped that government guided by Christian principles would defeat the forces of evil unleashed by the French Revolution. Portrait by George Dawe.

The Holy Roman Emperor Francis II, who believed the Enlightenment was a Masonic plot to undermine religion and overthrow the social order. Portrait by Johann Baptist Lampi, 1816.

William Pitt the Younger, who led a crusade against revolutionary France abroad and a ruthless campaign of repression against dissidents at home in the name of preserving order. Portrait by John Hoppner.

An explosion in the rue Saint-Nicaise in Paris on 24 December 1800, the work of French royalists and Pitt's agents bent on assassinating Napoleon Bonaparte, who had defeated the Revolution and brought order to France. Contemporary engraving.

Joseph Fouché, the prototype of the modern secret policeman, who traced the plotters by forensic use of a horseshoe. Engraving by Philippe Velyn, c.1810.

The murder of the German writer August von Kotzebue at Mannheim on 23 March 1819 by Karl Sand, a suicide terrorist. Contemporary engraving.

A Prussian guardsman's corset was among the items cast into the flames by students at the Wartburg Festival, on 18 October 1817, to celebrate the tercentenary of the Reformation and the fourth anniversary of the Battle of Leipzig. The event caused panic in the courts of Europe. Contemporary woodcut.

Prince Klemens Wenzel von Metternich, chancellor of Austria, who welcomed such acts of 'terrorism', as they bore out his theory of a vast, worldwide conspiracy to overthrow thrones and altars throughout the world, a conspiracy he was determined to fight to the death. Portrait by Josef Danhauser.

Two Men Contemplating the Moon, by Caspar David Friedrich, 1819. This and similar images exercised the Prussian police, as the two men are wearing the banned 'Old German' costume and might be plotting.

This caricature by George Cruikshank typically associates the 'Radicals', who agitated for parliamentary reform by constitutional means, with murder, revolution, atheism, debauchery and every other sin known to man.

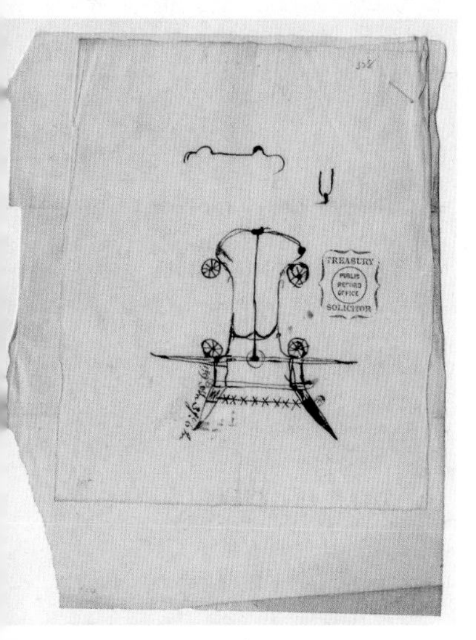

The 'authenticated' drawing of an 'anti-cavalry machine', which, so the Report of the House of Commons Committee of Secrecy claimed, proved that the Radicals were about to start an armed insurrection.

The Duke of Wellington, arch-reactionary and apologist for the 'Peterloo Massacre', in which one of his peacefully demonstrating veterans, a survivor of Waterloo, was mortally wounded by the forces of law and order. Attributed to Thomas Lawrence.

On 16 August 1819 the Manchester magistrates broke the law by using troops against a peaceful meeting in favour of parliamentary reform without first reading the Riot Act. Fifteen people were killed and hundreds wounded, some of whom died of their wounds. Coloured etching by George Cruikshank.

while the very real existence of these sects cannot be denied, and while they are nefarious and opposed in spirit to the Government, it is no less certain that they lack leaders of distinction capable of inspiring confidence, and that they have neither an overall directorship nor any of the other means required to effectively provoke revolutionary movements,' he wrote in a memorandum to the Emperor Francis on 3 November 1817 at the end of his travels in Italy. In his view, nationalist aspirations could be countered by the delivery of order and sound administration, which would convince Italians of the benefits of Austrian rule.[15]

This did not mean that vigilance should be relaxed. Count Saurau, the governor of Lombardy-Venetia who directed the Habsburg police's fight against subversion in Italy, developed an extensive network of agents, to cover not only the Austrian provinces but also places such as Rome, where he recruited a papal chamberlain in financial straits. Vast quantities of paper poured into Saurau's office, most of it utterly without significance. Typical is a report from Venice dated 11 January 1816. It goes on at some length about how everything was calm and people were concerned only with the economy, living standards and fashions. 'Nevertheless,' it continues, 'it being always prudent, in those who oversee public security, not to lose from sight the smallest political thing, even the most distant, I will not here omit to mention that in Italy there still exists an insidious faction which tends to promote the endlessly repeated and indulged mirage of national independence, in order to try to propel certain elements of this divided nation into the chaos of political confusion, from which to draw those advantages which the anarchists seem to always have as a project in their criminal machinations.' Such a report tells the recipient nothing, and can only serve to alarm, particularly as the author throws in, for good measure, that he has heard that in Naples a group of Jacobins is trying to manipulate the king's younger son against his father with the aim of starting a civil war.[16]

Another agent reported that he had been told 'in the greatest confidence' by a friend, 'a man of great probity and trustworthiness', that in

Trieste, whither she had retired, Napoleon's sister and former Grand Duchess of Tuscany, Countess Bacciochi, had been joined by her brother Jérôme and the former police chief Fouché, and that they were scheming with Joseph Bonaparte in the United States. She had been placed under the strictest possible surveillance by the Austrian police, but, the informant asserted, this was not sufficient. The consequence was reams of pointless tittle-tattle concerning the living arrangements and daily habits of every member of the households of the various Bonapartes, none of whom was remotely interested in political action, but all of whom were pathetically grateful to be allowed to live out their days in relative comfort.[17]

A nice example of the futility of this kind of intelligence-gathering is the disclosure to the Austrian authorities by a certain 'Duke of Brindisi' (who also traded under the names of Filipetti and Ancirotta) of the existence of a secret society, the *Guelfi*, allegedly set up in 1813 by British agents with the backing of Bentinck and Lord Holland to promote a rising which would bring into being an independent Italian state. He produced the society's constitution, cipher codes and other papers, all of them forgeries. It was only after intercepting his correspondence with accomplices that the Austrian police recognised the hoax, which led them to dismiss the *Guelfi* as an invention, although the society did actually exist, and was active in various parts of Italy.[18]

Not only was this method of combating the perceived terrorist threat inefficient, it was also counter-productive. Lord Burghersh, the British minister at Florence, assured Castlereagh that 'I am neither a Radical, nor that I have so far forgotten the principles which I have been brought up in, not to view with disgust the spirit of subversion and Jacobinism which is abroad; but I must at the same time declare that the system pursued by the Austrians in Italy, the ungenerous treatment of the Italians subjected to their government, will, as long as it is persisted in ... not add one jot to their security.'[19]

Not that the other rulers were much more sensitive. The pope, Pius VII, had suffered at the hands of revolutionary and Napoleonic France, and lived in constant fear of upheaval. One moment he was convinced of the existence of a conspiracy in Paris to involve Spain and Italy in 'a general revolution', the next that Turkey was planning to land a force in Italy while Hungarian patriots attacked Austria and revolutionaries in France toppled the Bourbon regime. He was even suspicious of his secretary of state Cardinal Consalvi, whom the arch-reactionary cardinals known as *zelanti* undermined at every opportunity, at one point even reporting that he had been seen to give a British diplomat a '*baccio di fra-massoni*', a 'Masonic embrace'.[20]

Consalvi was no liberal. Yet he had managed to maintain some of the administrative structures introduced by the French, and founded a force of *Carabinieri Pontifici*, modelled on the *Gendarmerie*. On 23 October 1816 he issued an edict on the organisation of the police, giving the governor of Rome a free hand, making it clear that 'he need not suffer any judiciary inhibition' in the execution of his duties. He was to be given a large sum of money with which to pay 'secret explorers', who were to build up a bank of information on each family, district by district, giving the name, date of birth, origins, profession, financial circumstances, mode of life, moral profile and other details of every member. The file on the household of ex-King Charles IV of Spain, who had retired to Rome, is illuminating, classing his entire household, from old courtiers to lackeys and kitchen maids, as *ottimo soggetto*, *equivoco soggetto*, *galantuomo* (a damaging epithet in this context) or outright *sospetto*.[21]

Local police chiefs were instructed to produce a *Rapporto Politico* every week, on everything from the adequacy of the food supply, the regulation of markets and the efficiency of the administration to suspect persons, foreigners, standards of public decency, offensive books and pamphlets, and the attitude of the people to religion and the government. In the Papal States, opposition to the government was deemed not just criminal, but heretical as well. Those assessed by the local police as being deviant in this respect were placed under a kind of injunction, the *precetto morale*: they were forbidden to leave the city without police permission, or to be away from home between dusk and dawn; and they had to attend the Easter services and a three-day religious retreat in a monastery, and present themselves to the police once a month with an attestation from a priest that they had been to confession and received absolution. Usually applied to educated young men of the nobility or middle class, this was deeply humiliating.[22]

Such measures were also ineffectual when it came to social control. The police were entirely taken aback when, in June 1817, a revolt broke out in the small city of Macerata in the papal province of Le Marche. It was a pitiful business, involving a couple of dozen conspirators who attempted to seize control of the place. After a certain amount of shooting in the dark they were rounded up. Eleven were condemned to death, eleven to life imprisonment, seven to ten years on the galleys and two to shorter terms. The severity of the sentences reflects the degree to which the authorities had been rattled.[23]

One thing that particularly worried all the rulers was travellers, particularly if they were foreign. In order to inhibit them, an onerous system of visas and rigorous frontier checks was put in place. 'Those who place purgatory in the other world would find it far more surely in the police offices and customs posts which have been set up in this one since the deliverance of Europe,' the tsar's erstwhile tutor La Harpe wrote to Alexander from Italy in August 1817. 'In order to go to Naples, one is searched and interrogated fourteen times ...!' Stendhal echoes his exasperation. 'The author's trunk has been searched twenty-one or twenty-two times,' he wrote at the beginning of January 1817. 'The sight of a book irritates the customs official, who is supposed to know how to read.' Mary Shelley records how, crossing from France into the kingdom of Sardinia in March 1818, one Milanese was sent back to Paris to have his passport countersigned by yet another official, and she nearly had to do the same, but was 'suffered to pass' (her books were not). Tiresome as they could be, these border controls were also highly inefficient, as the bored and poorly educated, and often illiterate, police or customs employees often let things through out of laziness or ignorance. One traveller was asked his name and other details by a police *brigadiere* to whom he had just handed his passport, and replied that all the information was contained in the document. The *brigadiere* then asked him to read them out, to which the traveller replied that the regulations required him to show his passport, not to read it out. The illiterate functionary had no option but to hand back the document and wave the traveller through.[24]

English tourists, who flooded Italy after two decades of privation, were treated with particular suspicion, being regarded as liberals by nature. None aroused more suspicion than Byron, who spent several years in Italy, leading a peripatetic existence, drawn hither and thither by the exigencies of his complicated love life. There was good reason for the authorities to be suspicious, as he naturally came into contact with the most disaffected elements in the country, such as aristocrats and writers. He understood their frustrations and sense of alienation, and joined their secret societies. Wherever he went, he was closely watched both by the local police and by Austrian agents. As a result, the archives of Venice, Lucca, Ravenna, Florence, Bologna, Pisa and the Vatican are full of reports on his daily doings – mostly dull, semi-literate, inaccurate and slapdash – detailing when he rose, when he went to bed, who visited him, at what time, how long they stayed, and so on.[25]

'The constant watch kept by the police upon Lord Byron has led to two discoveries,' reported the Austrian *agent provocateur* Giuseppe Valtancoli on 4 October 1819. 'The first is that his Lordship wears on his watch-chain a triangular (or rather pyramidal) seal, on the face of which are engraved three small stars; on the seal are cut the letters F.S.Y. This is the new signal adopted some months ago by the Guelph Society.' The second discovery was that a letter in the hand of Byron's secretary addressed to someone in Milan contained an extract from an English publication on 'Jesuitical Masonry'. Valtancoli's research also elicited the revelation from an apparently impeccable source that Byron was 'libidinous and immoral to excess', but in politics he was 'an Englishman in the fullest meaning of the term', bent on 'ruin and bloodshed'. Another spy reported that his secretary spent much time writing despatches in cipher, which were never seen by anyone or posted, suggesting to him that they were carried by the many English people passing through. One of the amusing aspects of the surveillance of Byron is that there are plenty of sightings of him, often accompanied by copious detail of his activities, in two places at once.[26]

The foreigners in Italy who particularly worried Metternich were not the English, or even the French. His diplomats and informers had identified Russian agents in Genoa, Turin, Bologna, Rome, Naples and elsewhere who were actively stoking up resentment of Austria and encouraging nationalist dreamers to believe that Tsar Alexander would support them in their endeavours for the liberation of Italy. To what purpose, Metternich could not be sure, as it was not easy to divine that monarch's thoughts.

12

Mysticism

When he came to the throne in 1801, Alexander had been determined to reform Russia according to the principles instilled in him by his tutor La Harpe. With the support of a small group of friends, he initiated a complete overhaul of the state, setting up ministries and implementing reforms. He soon came up against a stumbling block which impeded any further progress, institutional, economic or social: nine out of ten of his subjects were effectively slaves, belonging either to the state, the Church or noble landowners, and to free them would arouse violent protest, or worse, from the entire nobility. This had been growing increasingly hostile to his reforms, and in 1812, with Napoleon marching on Moscow, Alexander had been obliged to abandon them as the price for its support. He never forgave the nobility, which he despised for its backwardness and feared for other reasons – his father and grandfather had both been murdered by nobles.[1]

Once Napoleon had been defeated, Alexander turned his thoughts to Russia once more, and made no secret of his intention to reform the country and free the serfs. 'The peace of the world and the civilising of Russia, these are my ambitions, these are the goals of my policy, and let lightning strike me if I ever renege on these holy principles!' he declared. The generation of Russian nobility born in the last decade of the eighteenth century was the first to come into close contact with

European civilisation, as a consequence of the Napoleonic wars and the occupation of France, and this made them acutely aware of the backwardness of Russia. Visiting England in 1814, Colonel Aleksandr Benckendorff marvelled at 'the plenty, the wealth, refinement, freedom, which seemed to me the height of human happiness', and reflected gloomily on the fact that 'many generations would have to pass' before anything of the sort could be achieved in Russia. As they returned to their homeland, many young officers dreamed of supporting their monarch in his work of transforming it.[2]

Their more conservative parents, the clergy and ideologues such as the historian Nikolai Mikhailovich Karamzin, felt that the tsar's intentions went against the grain of Russia's traditions, its essence as a political and social entity, its spiritual base, and its destiny. Many had seen the French march on Moscow of 1812 not just as a military invasion but also as a spiritual assault. Admiral Shishkov believed that French influences should be extirpated and all Frenchmen exterminated, while the former governor of Moscow Count Rostopchin argued that young Russians who had fallen for the charms of French culture and thought should be 'destroyed'.[3]

Alexander was caught in an impasse, and lost heart. But while he could do little to bring about change at home, he pursued his dream of a better world. On Christmas Day 1815 he had published the text of the Holy Alliance, much to the annoyance of the other signatories, who considered it silly at best and potentially subversive. On 1 January 1816 he issued a proclamation thanking his army and his people for their contribution to the victory over what he represented as the Devil's latest attempt to take over the world, a victory which could only be safeguarded if all rulers took to heart the principles embodied in the Holy Alliance. In March he wrote to Castlereagh proposing a process of multilateral disarmament, arguing that the maintenance of large standing armies did not accord with the spirit of the peace they had made (Castlereagh suggested he make the first move).[4]

Metternich had always viewed the tsar's liberal enthusiasms with distaste, and his tendency to bring religion into public affairs with misgiving. 'Since 1815, he has left behind Jacobinism, only to throw himself into mysticism,' Metternich wrote to Francis at the end of August 1817. 'And since his proclivities are fundamentally revolutionary, his religious feelings are as well.' Later that year, Alexander bore this out by granting a constitution, the most liberal in Europe, to the kingdom of Poland, a semi-autonomous province of his crown. In his closing address to the first session of the Polish parliament, the Sejm, delivered on 15 March 1818, he announced that Poland was a testing-ground, and that he intended to extend the same constitution to all his dominions, urging the Poles to demonstrate the validity of the model. 'Prove to your contemporaries that liberal institutions, whose eternally sacred principles are being confused with the subversive doctrines which have in our time threatened the social order with dreadful catastrophe, are not dangerous,' he exhorted them. He commissioned Nikolai Nikolaievich Novosiltsev and Prince Petr Andreevich Viazemsky to prepare a draft constitution for the Russian empire, and announced his intention of reuniting with Poland the western provinces of Russia, taken from it in the 1770s, thereby extending the Polish constitution to a large part of his realm.[5]

The tsar's address, delivered in French and published in that language and in Russian, caused a stir throughout Europe, nowhere more than in Germany: according to resolutions reached at the Congress of Vienna, the rulers of the various German states, Prussia included, were to introduce constitutions, but most of them were dragging their feet. The address aroused even greater alarm in Vienna. Both Francis and Metternich viewed constitutions as the first step on the road to revolution. To them, Alexander's assertion that, 'applied in good faith and, most importantly, directed with purity of intention towards a conservative goal useful to humanity, they are perfectly compatible with order, and produce with common accord the true prosperity of nations' was little short of heresy.[6]

Metternich was greatly preoccupied by heresy: in June 1817 he noted with concern 'the progression of certain maladies of the mind, which show all the symptoms of veritable epidemics', in which he included Methodism. He feared this might find fertile ground in central Europe and particularly Germany, where increasing numbers of people were falling prey to mysticism. In Württemberg and Baden large numbers of people were, according to him, 'fanaticised to the point of abandoning all the things of this world to seek an existence and salvation in holy places'. It is unclear whether he made the connection between this rejection of the material and the famine sweeping Germany as a consequence of the apocalyptic harvest failure in 1816, when the Rhine and Neckar valleys had been washed out by rain. But he was convinced that there was a political threat lurking behind it. 'Some of these sectarians do have a purely and exclusively moral and religious motive; yet in others one can distinguish strong nuances of a political malady,' he went on. He was much exercised by Baroness Krüdener, who had sold her jewels and mortgaged her estate in order to distribute alms to the famine victims and was wandering through Germany and Switzerland preaching a primitive Christian message of love which, he claimed, was aimed at 'inciting the indigent classes against property-owners'. She also issued an appeal to all the monarchs of Europe to make a public confession and proclaim 'The Rights of God' as a riposte to the doctrine of the Rights of Man. The idea that he and his master the emperor should submit to some kind of spiritual scrutiny struck Metternich as not only preposterous but insidiously subversive. In his view, 'the repose of society and the tranquillity of States' was at stake, and 'the major Courts should waste no time in considering the means of hindering the plans of these mongers of a new kind of revolution'. He urged the rulers of Germany to move the baroness on, which most of them did, with unnecessary brutality.[7]

A wave of religious revivalism of one sort or another was also sweeping through the higher echelons of Russian society, with many conversions to Catholicism and other faiths. Alexander was ecumenical in attitude, and in March 1817 he relaxed restrictions, opening the door to a flood of refugees from famine and religious persecution in Germany. Metternich warned him that that the instincts which drove such people towards extreme religious beliefs would end up turning them into Jacobins.[8]

Alexander's 'mysticism' annoyed Metternich only marginally less than his interest in foreign affairs. Not only would he not demobilise his huge army, his agents were active in several parts of Italy, Corfu and Montenegro, and Russian diplomats at various courts were promoting the idea of intervention by the European powers in Central and South America to assist Spain in recovering her colonies there. These had taken advantage of Napoleon's invasion of Spain in 1807 to break free, and many feared that the emergence of independent republics in their place would spread republicanism from the New to the Old World. Metternich also suspected that underlying this Russian diplomatic activity was a strategy to build an alliance between Russia and the Bourbon courts of France, Naples and Spain. Alexander's ambassador in Madrid, Dmitri Pavlovich Tatishchev, was negotiating the sale of redundant Russian warships to replace those lost by Spain at Trafalgar, to be paid for by the cession of the island of Minorca – Russia had for decades been seeking a naval base in the Mediterranean. This worried the British cabinet even more than it did Metternich.[9]

Britain had been Spain's chief ally in 1807 when Napoleon invaded and installed his brother Joseph as king. When Ferdinand VII recovered his throne in 1814, he asked for British military assistance in bringing to order his South American colonies. Britain refused to get involved, but did sign a treaty promising to remain neutral, not to assist the rebels in any way, and not to permit the shipment of arms to them. Many disbanded British soldiers did nevertheless go to South America to fight for Bolívar and other rebels. Their cause was glorified by the Romantic *zeitgeist*, their leaders depicted as heroes. More to the point, the end of Spanish dominion had opened its former colonies to British trade. At Spain's request, in 1817 Castlereagh proclaimed Britain's opposition to armed intervention in South America by any power other than Spain, and eventually, in 1819, passed the Foreign Enlistment Act, which forbade the rebels recruiting in Britain. But Britain continued to trade with them.

In August 1816 Metternich sent a new ambassador to St Petersburg. For this mission he chose Baron Louis-Joseph Lebzeltern, the Lisbon-born son of an Austrian diplomat, who had followed Metternich to Paris in 1809. Lebzeltern was an amiable, joyful individual who livened up a party, fond of money and the luxuries it could buy, but hard-working and thorough. A curious combination of cynicism and candour, he was a devout Catholic, and it may have been this spiritual side that had helped him win the trust and affection of Alexander when he was sent to St Petersburg back in 1810. He had accompanied Alexander on the march to Paris, and then been posted to Rome. In his instructions, Metternich enjoined Lebzeltern to 'put a leash on the ambitious projects' of the Russian ruler, who was showing a tendency 'to interfere in every business in Europe' and 'to assume the role of arbiter in all discussions between various states'. Lebzeltern made a good start – received on arrival literally with open arms by the tsar, who embraced him and called him an old friend. Alexander denied any involvement in Italy, and explained that he had not demobilised out of fear of Prussia, which he felt was on the brink of revolution.[10]

He was also concerned at the profoundly 'gangrened' condition of France, and alarming developments in the neighbouring Belgian province of the kingdom of Holland. He had reason to believe that French and other exiles congregated in Brussels were planning an insurrection in France. In this he was not alone. According to the British minister at The Hague, Lord Clancarty, Brussels had become a magnet for 'jacobinical refugees', coordinating subversion in various countries. In a letter written in February 1817 congratulating the British cabinet on their robust reaction to 'the scenes of Spafields', Metternich warned Wellington that 'the kingdom of the Netherlands is today one of the centres, and perhaps the most active centre of disorder of every kind'. Lord Kinnaird had been heard 'taking extreme pleasure in speaking about a universal republic' there. In a memorandum he circulated to the allied courts in March 1817, Alexander called on them to prevent the wanderings of political refugees, who were 'the representatives, the organs of the revolutionary spirit which hovers over Europe, and perhaps over the two hemispheres of the globe'. Brussels was too close for comfort to France, which was still the focus of the allies' concern.[11]

After Waterloo, they had decided to leave an army of occupation consisting of 150,000 men in France, at her expense, for a period of five years. The arrangement was to be reviewed after three, and as this term drew near it seemed clear that the troops were serving no useful purpose. Their presence was tainting the Bourbon regime with their unpopularity, and the expense of keeping them there was crippling the country economically. 'The resentment of the people and the difficulty of paying for [the occupation forces] make the evacuation of foreign troops from the country essential,' Pozzo di Borgo wrote to the Russian foreign minister Count Nesselrode in December 1817. He argued that France was by now quite stable, and that an early withdrawal would assist a return to normality.[12]

Alexander feared that his ambassador had allowed himself to get too close to see clearly. Britain and Austria also had their doubts: both Metternich and Wellington found themselves wondering whether the Russian's advocacy of an allied withdrawal was not part of a rapprochement between his country and France, something each viewed with suspicion, for reasons of his own. Metternich mistrusted Pozzo di Borgo, and through the Austrian ambassador in Paris, Baron Nicolas Charles de Vincent, kept a suspicious eye on him. He was not convinced that France could be trusted to govern itself. He did not think much of the French minister of the interior Decazes, whose lowly origins probably irked him less than his evident lack of competence, and his contempt shines through the curled-lip prose of his letters to the Frenchman. He thought his attempts at intelligence-gathering 'utterly ridiculous', and when Napoleon's ex-police chief Savary assured him during a secret rendezvous in Trieste that Decazes was deliberately destabilising the situation in France in order to bring down the Bourbon dynasty, Metternich no longer knew what to believe. 'Is M. Decazes safe?' he asked Wellington on 19 February 1818. The question weighed heavily in the light of the proposed troop withdrawals, which were to be discussed at a meeting at the end of September that year. As the date drew near, the Ultras in France stepped up their efforts to persuade and frighten the allies into keeping the troops there.[13]

The conference was originally meant to involve only the principal ministers of the great powers, but Alexander, to the annoyance of Castlereagh and Metternich, had insisted on being present, which turned it into a full-blown congress. The venue was Aix-la-Chapelle (Aachen), chosen because it was conveniently close to but not in France, a spa town with plenty of good accommodation and the facilities necessary to receive a large influx of people. These would include the tsar, the Emperor Francis and King Frederick William of Prussia, with their foreign ministers and attendants, and the less showy British delegation of Lord Castlereagh, supported by his secretary Lord Clanwilliam and his ambassadors in the allied capitals, as well as the Duke of Wellington. They also included ambassadors of the various courts, a number of journalists and other interested parties, and a bevy of bankers. These were needed to provide loans to France so that it could pay off the remaining indemnities to the allies. One of them, Baron Trenck, was sent there by Sedlnitzky to spy rather than to lend: Aix was crawling with Prussian and Austrian spies.[14]

In the months running up to the congress Alexander had revived his South American plans. Through a special envoy to Vienna, Count Golovkin, he put the case that as the revolts in the Spanish colonies were part of the same evil they were fighting on the European Continent, the Alliance must help the Spanish monarchy reassert its rule. But Metternich and Castlereagh would not allow the matter to be placed on the agenda, and Britain's opposition was significant given its dominance of the seas. When Alexander arrived on 16 September, he found that Metternich and Castlereagh had already set the agenda.[15]

Metternich had been the first to arrive at Aix-la-Chapelle. He was in cheerful mood, which only improved as he drove into the little town with his carriages, attendants and servants: he was mistaken for the Emperor Francis, and cheered wildly. 'The position of Aix, of which I only had a vague memory dating from twenty-six years ago, is very picturesque,' he wrote to his wife. 'The countryside is rolling and the vegetation very abundant. The weather is magnificent and perfect for walking. We are all comfortably accommodated, and the measures to prevent the mass of diplomats from getting to us mean that we are quite apart.' It all began convivially enough, with Metternich accompanying Alexander and the King of Prussia on a visit to the cathedral, where they were shown the relics deposited there by Charlemagne, including the sheet in which Herodias carried away the head of St John the Baptist, a dress belonging to the Virgin Mary, Jesus Christ's childhood tunic and the loincloth He wore on the Cross. The congress attracted renowned musicians and players, and Goethe put in an appearance when one of his plays was staged. The painter Thomas Lawrence arrived with a commission from the prince regent to paint the monarchs and foremost ministers present at the congress for the Long Gallery at Windsor Castle. A specially designed wooden house with a studio was being shipped from England, but it arrived too late, and Lawrence had to set up his studio in the town hall.[16]

Alexander appeared to be in a good mood, and all seemed to be going well, so much so that Metternich reported to his wife that it was promising to be '*un joli petit Congrès*'. The delegates soon settled down to a relaxed routine, spending their evenings at informal gatherings. The uxorious Castlereagh was the only one of the major figures to have brought along his wife, who had already been the butt of much ridicule for her lack of savoir-faire at the Congress of Vienna. 'At first we would congregate at Lady Castlereagh's, but I do not know what inconceivable atmosphere of boredom has come over that house,' wrote Metternich. 'By common accord, we renounced the charms of milady and moved to my drawing room.'[17]

Lady Castlereagh's *soirées* were, it appears, not always dull, as Lord Clanwilliam reported after having had a difference of opinion with Lord Charles Stewart, Castlereagh's half-brother and the British ambassador in Vienna. 'He and I had a "jaw" one night at Lady C.'s supper-table, ladies present,' recalled Clanwilliam. 'In a sort of angry joke, he shied a large potato at me, which splashed against the wall. I lost my temper, and when he took up another potato, in horse-play, I lifted a bottle by the neck, and threatened to break his head. He saw I was dangerous and stopped.'[18]

The tsar had not abandoned his dream of bringing about a new age in international affairs: in a handwritten note he set out the main aims of the congress to be first the evacuation of France, and second a reconfiguration of the relationship between the powers. Further points covered means of containing the 'gangrenous' moral 'contagion' spreading from France. His suspicions were confirmed when he surveyed the condition of the regiments he had left there: a number of parades were held during the congress to review the allied troops about to be withdrawn, and the bearing of the Russian units struck him unfavourably. On 8 October he produced a memorandum urging the powers to pass a resolution that the existing territorial arrangements should be regarded as immovable, and binding themselves not only to intervene militarily in order to preserve them, but also to intervene against revolt in any country. He made repeated appeals to his brother monarchs to embrace the principles set out in the Holy Alliance, and renewed his attempts to bring South America onto the agenda.[19]

Castlereagh challenged Alexander on all these points, with the support of Metternich and the more discreet back-up of the Prussian prime minister Prince Hardenberg, whose master, Frederick William, was in thrall to the tsar. The British foreign secretary pointed out that Alexander's suggestion that the Alliance guarantee the status quo in every existing state would mean that no country could ever bring about any change in its form of government without fear of invasion by others. He went on to argue that until 'a system of administering Europe by a general Alliance of all its States can be reduced to some practical form, all notions of general and unqualified guarantee must be abandoned, and States must be left to rely for their security upon the justice and wisdom of their respective systems'. He even opposed Alexander's suggestion that they at least agree that a revolution in France should automatically provoke an allied intervention.[20]

Metternich and Castlereagh expressed unease about the size of the Russian army. Alexander assured them that he had as much territory as he craved and more than he could manage, and that his only ambition was to make his people happy. 'I consider my Army as the Army of Europe and as such alone shall it be employed,' he told Castlereagh. This was little comfort. Hardenberg floated the idea of a European army to be based in Brussels to prevent France from attacking Prussia's Rhenish provinces. But the others would not countenance the idea: such a force would almost certainly end up being made up predominantly of Russian troops. One of the few things all did agree to was that their security organs should keep a vigilant eye on all members of the Bonaparte family.[21]

Whatever their differences, as far as the public was concerned the allies did agree on essentials, and the congress had reaffirmed their commitment to the joint preservation of the status quo in Europe, which was a matter of grave importance, as Metternich's right-hand man and secretary of the congress Friedrich von Gentz explained. 'The domestic scene in every European country, without exception, is prey to a burning fever, companion or precursor of the most violent convulsions the civilised world has experienced since the fall of the Roman Empire,' he wrote. 'It is the struggle, the war of life or death between the old and the new principles, between the old and the new social order ... All classes are in a state of fermentation, all the powers are threatened with the loss of equilibrium; the most solid institutions are shaken to their very foundations, like the buildings of a city attacked by the first tremors of an earthquake which in a few moments will destroy everything.' The European sovereigns could, in his view, only survive by standing shoulder to shoulder, and if one of them were to break ranks they would all be swept away by the torrent.[22]

Gentz was a remarkable man. He had lived his epoch to the full, studying under Kant in Königsberg, indulging in both sentimental and highly sensual affairs, often concurrently, leading the life of the classic eighteenth-century rake while discussing utopias with the philosopher Wilhelm von Humboldt, experiencing the enthusiasms of the French Revolution, being acclaimed as a writer, fathering bastards and spying for Britain before settling into his role as amanuensis and foil to Metternich. During the Congress of Vienna, to which he had acted as secretary, he had built up a unique position on the European diplomatic scene, and he had used his influence to the full at Aix. 'I can view this congress as the high point of my life,' he wrote to one friend. 'Never have the laurels been heaped on my head as this time,' he wrote to another. More to the point, he had made a huge amount of money. It was customary on such occasions for the various monarchs and ministers to give the secretary a handsome tip, in the shape of a bejewelled snuffbox, a high decoration studded with diamonds and sometimes some cash, but on this occasion he had managed to milk all the bankers as well. They included Labouchère and Baring from London, Hope from Amsterdam, David Rothschild from Paris, and Solomon and Carl Rothschild, whom Gentz referred to as 'vulgar, ignorant Jews', but whose judgement he trusted.[23]

Aleksandr Ivanovich Mikhailovsky-Danilevsky, one of Alexander's aides-de-camp, noted that the functioning of the congress had been much smoother and more efficient than had been the case at Vienna, and he ascribed this to the absence of women, who had played such an insidious role in the events there. This was true up to a point, but while there were no balls and nothing like the amorous madness of Vienna, a number of Parisian ladies had gravitated to Aix, including the celebrated literary hostess Madame Récamier, who had been rolled out to entertain the sovereigns to tea. And one of the ladies present did manage to make a stir, and to cause havoc with Metternich's feelings.[24]

Alexander had summoned his ambassador to London, Count Kristof Andreevich Lieven, to join him at the congress, and the ambassador had brought his wife. Dorothea Lieven was an extraordinary woman: neither beautiful nor particularly intelligent, she captivated some of the greatest figures of her age, and positioned herself at the centre of political affairs wherever she went. A couple of months short of her thirty-third birthday when she came to Aix, she was looking forward to her first opportunity to play a role on the international stage.

Born Dorothea Kristoforovna Benckendorff, the daughter of a Russian infantry general and a lady-in-waiting to the Empress Catherine, both of them of German Baltic nobility, she was herself placed as lady-in-waiting to Alexander's mother the Empress Maria Feodorovna; in 1800, aged fourteen, she married General Lieven, another German Baltic nobleman. In 1810 he was appointed Russian ambassador in Berlin, and in 1812 posted to London. Her reception there was not favourable at first: she made the mistake of flirting with prominent Whigs and antagonising the prince regent. But within a couple of years she had made a position for herself in English society quite independent of her status as the wife of the Russian ambassador. She used this position to act as an informant for the Russian foreign minister Karl von Nesselrode, and to lobby for Russian policies, trying to persuade influential people to support Alexander's suggested intervention in Spanish America.

Metternich was smitten at their first meeting, at Nesselrode's lodgings on 22 October. As was usual with him, he let himself go with all the abandon of a teenager experiencing first love, spilling out in letters the feelings he did not have time to describe to her in their necessarily brief encounters, during which speech was sacrificed to passion. On 26 October the whole party went to Spa, and although Metternich had the pleasure of sitting next to her in the carriage, they were not alone. But the next day he spent an hour 'at her feet'. A couple of days later she came to his box at the opera and, as he put it, 'belonged to' him. She was a busy woman, as, apart from her affair with Metternich, she 'renewed' what she called her 'tender passages' with Alexander's younger brother the Grand Duke Constantine, with whom she had had a protracted liaison in 1805–07 while her husband was on campaign.[25]

Metternich was devastated when, in mid-November, Lieven's presence no longer being needed, the couple left Aix. Letters followed her in a gushing torrent, telling her how much he missed her and how he would frequently walk down the street where she had lodged and remember their moments of bliss. He complained that his was 'the most abominable of professions', and that only by loving as deeply as he loved her could he gain some solace from harsh reality.[26]

In the second half of November, with the business of the congress over and Lawrence's portraits completed, the monarchs and ministers went to Brussels, as Wellington was to give them a tour of the battlefield of Waterloo. Metternich was delighted, as the Lievens had stopped in Brussels on their way to London, and when he arrived on 23 November he looked forward to continuing his affair.

Alexander's staff received intelligence that a group of former Napoleonic officers were intending to kidnap him as he left Aix, take him to France and force him to sign a proclamation to the effect that the allied powers had decided to bring Napoleon back from St Helena and make his son emperor. The tsar's journey from Aix to Brussels was therefore meticulously prepared. All Dutch troops, many of whom had served under Napoleon, were to be kept well away, and he was to be guarded by Swiss mercenaries while hundreds of police were positioned along the way, some in plain clothes.[27]

In Brussels, Metternich did have a few intimate moments with Dorothea – she would send him a note every time her husband went out – but his one chance of a long tryst, when Wellington took the rest of the party off to Waterloo, was dashed when the duke insisted on his coming too. When she left, on 27 November, he sat down to write to her, but his tears smudged the ink. 'My only happiness today is *you*,' he wrote. 'My heart, my soul, everything that is worth anything in me belongs to you.' Two days later, after a particularly tedious meeting with Hardenberg, he wrote that public affairs no longer interested him.[28]

From Brussels, Alexander went back to Aix, and then via Frankfurt to Karlsruhe to see his wife. From there he travelled to Vienna. The proceedings at Aix had not made him happy, and his aide Prince Petr Mikhailovich Volkonsky recorded that he was impossible to deal with, suddenly flying into rages and insulting his attendants without apparent reason. He had been outmanoeuvred by Metternich on every subject close to his heart, and had not been allowed to enhance Russia's prestige on the international scene. His sister Catherine had been warning him that Metternich and Castlereagh were active members of the 'sect' which was striving for 'the overthrow of all thrones'. It is doubtful whether Alexander really believed her, but he certainly mistrusted Metternich – and he knew where to take his revenge.[29]

Alexander was the natural patron of those in Germany who resented the influence of Austria. His Warsaw address had marked him out as the champion of liberals, and, by extension, of German nationalists. He was closely related to the royal houses of Württemberg, Bavaria and Baden, which were often at odds with Metternich, and was seen by many as the natural leader and defender of the smaller states against 'Austrian Tyranny'. He would not need to try hard to get his own back on 'the Dalai Lama of Vienna', as his ambassador to Austria referred to Metternich.[30]

13

Teutomania

Although he considered Aix to have been a success, credit for which he generously awarded himself, Metternich ended the year 1818 on a world-weary note. From Koblenz, which he reached at the beginning of December, he wrote to Dorothea Lieven, telling her the story of his life and assuring her that while he had many defects presumption was not one of them, that he was ill-suited to being a statesman, and that the only thing that kept him going was the thought that he was doing good. From his castle at Johannisberg, he wrote that he wanted to drown himself in the Rhine, which he could see from his window. A couple of days later he was staying at Amrobach with the Duchess of Kent, who was pregnant (with the future Queen Victoria), and he reached Vienna on 11 December. 'The next day I was engulfed by all the horrors of my life,' he wrote to Dorothea. 'Court, the arrival of the Emperor Alexander, fifty people to dinner, three hundred at the soirée. My darling, I felt very lonely in my drawing room surrounded by them all!' Every day was spent attending Alexander as he reviewed troops, inspected barracks, took tea with old flames from the days of the Congress of Vienna and spent evenings in conversation of excruciating boredom. Metternich concluded that 'there are in the world no two people more fundamentally different than him and me'. He took advantage of the tsar's presence to try to persuade him to have Lieven posted as ambassador to

Vienna, so he might be able to pursue his affair, but without success. 'You know how much I detest the Court and everything that pertains to it,' he wrote, complaining that 'a minister's life is a terrible one'. The new year brought with it challenges which were to rouse him from his depression.[1]

Not long after the last allied troops had evacuated French territory, at the end of November 1818, the discouraged Richelieu had handed in his resignation as prime minister. This had been prompted by his inability to bridge the widening gap between the warring parties in the Chamber. The electoral reform of 1817, which favoured the middle classes, had brought in a liberal majority which was opposed at every step by the increasingly hysterical Ultras. Much of the political argument was over trivial issues, but it was conducted in extraordinarily vicious manner, as beneath it lurked visceral hatreds. 'I belong to those who are guillotined, you to those who are hanged,' one woman told Decazes, summing up both the triviality and the ferocity. The king was unable to rein in his brother and the Ultras, and Richelieu could not restrain the liberals. His departure was followed by the formation on 18 December 1818 of a new ministry under the marquis Dessolles. It soon became evident that the real head of the government was the minister of the interior, Decazes. This caused uproar among the Ultras, who regarded him as little better than a revolutionary and detested him for his influence over Louis XVIII.[2]

Decazes's assumption of power caused a mild panic in conservative circles around Europe. Alexander heard the news while he was still in Vienna, and promptly urged the Emperor Francis to begin mobilising his troops. The situation seemed all the more alarming as the King of France's health was giving grounds for concern. Wellington believed his death would lead to the fall of the French monarchy, and Metternich went so far as to consult with the other courts as to what action should be taken when the moment came. Louis, having got wind of this, drily informed him that he was quite well, and that when he did come to die, he would be succeeded by his rightful heir.[3]

Metternich was far from reassured. He charged Lebzeltern, who had been given leave to travel to Lisbon to wind up family affairs following his father's death, with a mission to deliver a letter to Decazes on his way through Paris, and to sound him out. Following a long talk with the French minister on 28 January 1819, Lebzeltern reported back that 'the revolution … is now advancing by leaps and bounds, without any restraint or opposition'. In almost hysterical tones he explained that regicides had been brought to power, along with men who had proved their disloyalty during the Hundred Days. Louis XVIII was, according to Lebzeltern, besotted by Decazes, whom he described as a misguided liberal who was being dragged helplessly towards the abyss.[4]

In February, the Ultras who dominated the upper Chamber voted in a new law reforming the electoral system, narrowing the suffrage in such a manner as to exclude most of the liberal deputies. In order to give Decazes the necessary majority in the upper Chamber, the king created sixty new peers. In Metternich's eyes, this was 'a catastrophe'. 'Louis XVIII is himself at the head of the revolutionary movement which is shaking his throne,' he wrote to his ambassador baron Vincent.[5]

Nesselrode's wife, who was in Paris and moving in Ultra circles, warned her husband that the situation was so bad that Russia and the other powers would be obliged to intervene militarily. 'There can be no more doubt about it, by the summer you will be on the march,' she wrote on 18 March. 'I cannot think without sadness of all the desolation that will follow, of the revolution which will spread even to the border of Asia … I cannot express to you the terror and the horror which reign here among decent people.' If he could take his wife's alarms with a pinch of salt, Nesselrode could not ignore Gentz, who warned him that 'All over Germany minds are being whipped up into a state of fermentation by the ever-increasing temerity of the incendiary papers,' that France was 'severely agitated' and England 'in a highly alarming condition'.[6]

In Metternich's view, it was Prussia that gave the greatest cause for concern. The country was on the verge of bankruptcy, and rocked by violent argument over whether a constitution should or should not be introduced. In January 1819 the king called on Wilhelm von Humboldt to take office and bring in a constitution. Humboldt declined, anticipating that in the prevailing hysteria he would not be allowed a free hand. Metternich's assessment was that the country was ripe for revolution.[7]

Napoleon's humiliation of Prussia following his victories at Jena and Auerstadt in 1806 had inspired a rapid administrative, legal, economic, educational and social transformation of the country, a 'revolution from above' in the words of Freiherr vom Stein, one of its principal motors. It was also perceived as a challenge, and the deep resentment it stirred up fired nationalist feeling all over Germany. This was a Romantic nationalism based on the 'rediscovery' of supposedly ancient traditions and values, and involved a semi-religious view of the 'genius' of the German people, *Volkstum*, and its destiny. In 1808 a League of Virtue, *Tugendbund*, was founded at Königsberg. The predominantly young men it brought together sought self-perfection with the aim of regenerating their country. A more middle-class version, the *Deutsche Bund*, was founded in Berlin the following year by Ludwig Jahn, who would subsequently also set up a network of *Turnvereine*, athletic associations meant to develop the physical and spiritual powers of the young. Jahn was an eccentric Teutomaniac, sporting a spectacular beard and advocating, amongst other things, the resurrection of an 'Old German' language which existed principally in his own imagination, and the substitution of saints' days in the calendar with those of victorious German generals. His gymnastic associations had been formed with the aim of reviving the spirit of young Germans. His followers wore a coarse linen tunic with a dagger in the belt, used supposedly medieval forms of address and sang a great deal when they were not holding contests to test their mettle and keep themselves fit for Germany.[8]

These associations had inspired men from various parts of Germany to take part in the *Freiheitskrieg*, the 'war of liberation' against France in 1813, and the events of that year took on huge significance as a historic moment when the German nation came together to throw off its shackles. The prime emblem of this was the Free Corps of idealistic volunteers formed by the aristocratic firebrand Major Adolf von Lützow, which adopted a supposedly old German uniform consisting of a long tunic, baggy pants and a large black beret, and drew to its ranks the young poet Theodor Körner, who immortalised it in verse before being killed in action.

The hopes raised in 1813 were dashed by the Congress of Vienna. The settlement disappointed both traditionalists hoping for a restoration of something on the lines of the old Holy Roman Empire, and radicals dreaming of a new unitary state that would give shape and expression to the German nation. Germany was left divided into thirty-nine political units, ruled in the main by those who had been the most agile in positioning themselves and the most servile to Napoleon. They were bound by the terms of the Vienna settlement to introduce constitutions, but only a few, such as Württemberg, Bavaria, Baden, Saxe-Weimar and Naussau, did, and even then the suffrage was severely restricted and the prerogatives of the rulers entrenched. They were tied into a federation under the presidency of Austria, the Bund, with its own diet, the Bundersversammlung or Bundestag, whose procedures, prerogatives and powers were to be fixed in due course. The Bundestag which met at Frankfurt in 1816, under the auspices of Metternich, showed no sign of growing into anything more than an obedient talking shop. Joseph Görres, who founded the *Rhenische Merkur* in 1814 to fight the liberal and national cause, branded the settlement 'a gigantic fraud'.[9]

None of this bothered more than a small portion of the population, which was for the most part politically supine, but while they did not represent anything resembling a political force, those who felt like Görres made enough noise and struck attitudes calculated to frighten those wishing to be. The dissatisfaction was particularly strong in the army. There had been more than a whiff of revolutionary ardour about the patriotic surge of 1813, and many of those who took up arms to expel the French took the Spanish *guerrilla* against Napoleon as their inspiration, adopting some of its brutal tactics, such as the murder of prisoners. The whole episode had had a radicalising and decivilising influence on those involved. In January 1816, the British envoy in Berlin reported that the Prussian army was 'infected with revolutionary stirrings', and his superior, Castlereagh, feared that it was 'by no means subordinate to the civil authorities'. Commanded by figures such as the ardently patriotic General Gneisenau, identified by some as the 'generalissimo' of what they regarded as a dangerous 'sect', the Prussian army did appear to pose a threat, and this was one reason Tsar Alexander gave for not standing down his own forces after 1815.[10]

What worried the Prussian authorities more than the state of the army were the various patriotic associations and the presumed existence of secret societies of one sort or another. The *Tugendbund* had dissolved in 1810, but its spirit survived. Young men had taken to wearing some version of 'Old German' wear, the *Altdeutsch Tracht*, or Jahn's white equivalent, visiting the battlefields of 1813 and cultivating the memory of that year of hope, giving the impression of an organised movement. Caspar David Friedrich's haunting paintings of such wanderers in their black costumes, lost in contemplation in some mythical landscape, were interpreted in many ways, and suggested to the suspicious and fearful an occult understanding. The student associations at the German universities, *Burschenschaften*, inspired little short of dread in conservative quarters. Their members, many of whom affected the *Altdeutsch Tracht*, were referred to as 'Teutomaniacs' and 'Teutomagogues'. Gentz was one who could barely contain his dislike of these 'grotesque and repulsive figures in filthy ancient German costumes, their books under their arms, abominations before God and man, on their way to absorb the false wisdom of their infamous professors'. As they were dedicated to the unification of Germany, they were 'consummate Jacobins', since that unification could, according to Gentz, not be achieved 'without the most violent revolutions, without the overthrow of Europe'.[11]

It did look as though unification could only come in republican form. The behaviour of the various German rulers during the

Napoleonic wars had forfeited them the respect of the patriots, and their determined efforts at the Congress of Vienna to hang on to titles and territory they had acquired through alliance with Napoleon only compounded this. German nationalists swung towards republicanism by default.

Prussia was particularly vulnerable. Over the previous half-century it had successively quadrupled in size, been reduced by over two-thirds, narrowly avoided being wiped off the map altogether, and then vastly expanded again. Some of its provinces were landlocked islands surrounded by other states, with no cultural or religious affinity with the core, awarded to Prussia in 1815 principally because Britain wished to see a strong German buffer on France's border to stop it expanding into Belgium or Germany. The result was a large but loosely-knit kingdom whose very existence raised many questions.

It had been at the forefront of the war to expel Napoleonic rule from Germany in 1813. Its army had distinguished itself during the final campaigns against Napoleon and had clinched the outcome at Waterloo. Prussia therefore appeared as the natural focus for the ambitions of nationalists who longed for the unification of all Germans into one political unit. But its ruler feared that his throne might not survive the process. King Frederick William III was a kindly and well-meaning character dominated by a sense of personal failure. Painfully shy, the most unmartial of all Prussian kings, he had been defeated, forced to give up half of his kingdom and thoroughly humiliated by Napoleon. He had enjoyed a happy marriage to his queen, Luise, and when she died in 1810 he was utterly bereft. A member of the 'Order of the Gold and Rosy Cross', he believed unquestioningly in the Bible, and considered alchemy and astrology to be sciences.

Frederick William had been open to the idea of reform when it could save what was left of his kingdom from disintegration, but once peace had settled he feared it could only serve to limit his power. He surrounded himself with a circle of courtiers, including his son's tutor the Huguenot preacher Johann Peter Ancillon, his privy councillor

Daniel Ludwig Albrecht, the nonagenarian lady of the court Countess Voss, a devoted companion of the last three kings, and Prince Wilhelm Ludwig Georg von Sayn-Wittgenstein, who became minister of police. This camarilla of diehard conservatives undermined the prime minister, Hardenberg, and fed the worst phobias of the king. These were also being nourished, and voiced, by Anton Heinrich Schmalz, professor of law at Berlin University, who made out that German nationalism was essentially republican and inimical to the Prussian state.

In May 1815, Frederick William had vowed to bring in a constitution for Prussia, but he showed little enthusiasm to fulfil this promise, and the process stalled. Conservative opinion rallied behind Schmalz, who published a pamphlet arguing that constitutions were mere tools to undermine all the dynasties in Germany, and the king made his preference clear by awarding him a decoration. Schmalz contended that the *Tugendbund* was still in existence, and that together with the *Burschenschaften* and other associations it was secretly propagating republican values under the guise of national sentiment. A witch-hunt was duly launched to root out this supposed threat. 'I suspect that those who have made it their business to spread this notion, with the exception of one or two, do not believe in such a secret society themselves but have merely been trying to arouse alarm as a tool for their persecutions,' commented General Gneisenau.[12]

Prussia had never had much in the way of police structures before 1806, when the kingdom became a virtual vassal of France. New measures were called for by the need to keep an eye on what the French were doing and to monitor their collaborators, and at the same time to prevent anti-French feeling from turning into anti-government action. The privy councillor Karl von Nagler was put in charge of the small police networks of the ministries of the interior and foreign affairs, and given control of the postal service. He found himself in competition with a rival police network, set up by the French, which paid spies better than he could and intercepted letters with greater finesse. In 1809 he was joined by Justus Grüner as

Polizeipräsident of Berlin, technically his junior but effectively in control of operations.[13]

Grüner was a thirty-two-year-old Prussian civil servant with a keen interest in the law who had published a number of works on jurisprudence. A brave and ardent patriot, nourishing a profound hatred of Napoleon and his treatment of Germany, he repressed his idealism in the national interest, and since one of his principal tasks was to counteract the French police he soon began employing the same methods as Fouché. 'It is necessary to observe clubs, coffee houses, gaming houses, where foreigners meet along with people who speak ill, equivocal writers, grumblers,' he explained, specifying that every government official should be an informant, and that liberal use should be made of spies in the 'observation of suspects'.[14]

In 1811 Grüner was promoted to head the state police, and he expanded his field of activity considerably. His *Fremdenpolizei* monitored every foreigner passing through Prussian territory, he had agents in every foreign embassy in Berlin, in every gambling den and brothel, and spies in foreign capitals and major cities. He intercepted mail and placed disinformation in the post for the French to read. He developed a discreet way of dealing with suspects, arranging for them to be lured, by women or the promise of a good card game, to an isolated spot, where they would be picked up and bundled away into the fortress of Spandau. Special commissions were set up so that their cases could be kept outside the judicial system.[15]

The struggle between Prussian patriots and the French faction intersected with one between the conservatives grouped in the court party and the reformers bent on regenerating Prussia. Grüner thus found himself navigating in murky waters. Society was divided, with wives and mistresses in some cases working for a different interest than their husbands and lovers in what was becoming an underground struggle for the soul of Prussia. The French viewed the reformers and members of the *Tugendbund* as Jacobins threatening the European *pax Gallica*. Grüner allied with the patriotic elements, working closely with the *Tugendbund* in the common cause against the French. In the same cause, he collaborated with the Austrian ambassador in Berlin, passing intelligence through him to Metternich. The French quickly recognised Grüner as 'a leading member of the sect' and concluded that his dismissal was essential. With the signature in 1812 of a military alliance between Prussia and France prior to Napoleon's invasion of Russia, Grüner was forced to resign.[16]

He was provided with funds by the Russian and British governments and went to Prague, from where he began to organise pan-German resistance to the French, creating an intelligence-gathering network which provided information on French troop numbers and movements to Russia, and at the behest of the Russian minister of police General Balashov laid plans for armed insurrections in the rear of the French armies. In August 1812 he was denounced by the Prussian police he had created, arrested on Metternich's orders and incarcerated in the fortress of Peterwardein.[17]

When Napoleon's fortunes waned, Grüner was released and re-employed by the Prussians in various administrative capacities, then as head of the military police, and in 1815 he set up a police network for the allies in Paris. Once he had achieved this, and reaction had set in in Berlin, he was sidelined in various minor posts. But he continued to play an undercover role on behalf of Hardenberg, putting together a pan-German network with the aim of promoting the idea of unification under Prussian rule.[18]

The man who had taken over from Grüner as head of Prussia's police was of a very different stamp. Prince Wilhelm Ludwig von Sayn-Wittgenstein was seven years older than Grüner. Although he bore a sonorous title, he came from an impoverished line of the family. The French Revolution broke out just as he finished his studies at the University of Marburg, and while his brother set off for Russia, where he would have a distinguished military career, Wilhelm went to join the counter-revolutionary army of the Bourbon princes at Koblenz. This turned out not to have been a good choice.

He never got the chance to march into France and fight at Valmy, as he was arrested on the orders of the Austrian and Prussian police authorities for his contacts with French émigrés. 'Escorted on foot, by soldiers, like a common criminal, and thrown into gaol', he was stripped of his possessions and not allowed to write letters. He was kept in solitary confinement for nine weeks, without an inkling of the reason, since he was never interrogated and was released without explanation.[19]

His fortunes picked up when Hardenberg, who had noted his pleasant manner and discreet ways, started using him for various errands, and most notably as a '*postillion d'amour*' in his communications with his mistress. He also drew close to the court, which proved to be his natural element. 'Prince Wittgenstein had all the qualities to obtain a good position for himself,' according to Stein, 'clever, cold, calculating, tenacious and pliable to the point of utter sliminess ...' He was indeed the perfect courtier, emollient with superiors, contemptuous of those out of favour, self-serving and mean, yet careful and scrupulous in his calculations, a master of intrigue and of what Stein called 'the influence of the wardrobe'. The king trusted him implicitly, and Wittgenstein soon supplanted Hardenberg, becoming, in the words of the war minister Hermann von Boyen, 'the prime minister behind the curtain'. In 1812 he was appointed to succeed Grüner.[20]

Wittgenstein took over the structures created by Grüner, and merely redirected them from acting against the French to assisting them in their persecution of Prussian patriots. He continued in the same vein even when, the following year, Prussia changed sides, as by then he had come to the conclusion that the patriots were Jacobins in disguise. He was deeply suspicious of the patriotic surge of 1813, and saw the newly created *Landsturm*, or volunteer army, as a revolutionary force dedicated to 'Anarchy and the overthrow of thrones', so he dissolved it.[21]

In 1816 Hardenberg decreed that the secret police should be abolished, its personnel sacked and its archives destroyed, arguing that it had only been called into being out of wartime necessity. Wittgenstein responded by declaring that there was no secret police as such, only the bare essential of surveillance of foreigners. Nobody was taken in by this. Far from scaling back its activity once the threat of French-inspired Jacobinism had been seen off, the Prussian police continued to extend their sphere of interest in the years following 1815 under the energetic direction of Wittgenstein's deputy, the jurist Karl Albert von Kamptz.

The number of police spies increased noticeably, and when people went for a walk they would look around and see men following them, taking notes. Mail was intercepted wholesale. 'I do not write to you how things are here, because this is quite impossible for me,' the biographer and diplomat Karl August Varnhagen von Ense wrote from Berlin to his publisher; 'give my regards to all my friends, but tell them not to write to me, for it would be critical under present circumstances when every word can be interpreted in a bad sense; paper is nowadays an evil treasure, at any moment it may become a red-hot coal.'[22]

The climate of repression provoked mounting anger among young people in particular. A greater proportion of the population attended university in Germany than elsewhere in Europe, creating a pool of educated young men with aspirations. Outlets for these were limited in the pre-industrial conditions in which most of the country stagnated. The German states and their capitals were both small (the dozen largest cities in Germany could have fitted comfortably into Paris in terms of population) and provincial. The lack of prospects for educated young men naturally made them long for a larger state with a proper capital that could accommodate their talents, and this could only be achieved through the unification of Germany. The absence of functioning political structures and the fitful application of the law in many of the states also offended their sense of justice, hence their calls for constitutions. One group, led by the twenty-two-year-old lawyer Karl Follen, known as the Giessen 'blacks' on account of the old German costume they wore, alternately as the *Unbedingten*, Unconditionals, petitioned the Grand Duke of Hesse, their ruler, to bring in a constitution and improve the administration of his realm.

On 18 October 1817 a group of students from twelve universities came together at the castle on the Wartburg in Thuringia to mark the fourth anniversary of the Battle of Leipzig and the tercentenary of Martin Luther's revolt against the Church of Rome. The castle was where Luther had translated the Bible into German, but it was not the religious aspect of his rebellion that enthralled the students: what resonated with them was his call for the spiritual purification and regeneration of the German nation, and for a restoration of the German realm to greatness.

They gathered at the foot of the hill, dressed in the *Altdeutsch Tracht*, and lit a bonfire, on which they proceeded to immolate a number of objects that stood for institutions which, they felt, prevented Germany from recovering its true greatness. These included some bizarre symbols, such as a Hessian soldier's wig and a Prussian guardsman's corset, as well as copies of the *Code Napoléon*, the text of the 1815 Treaty of Vienna, the Prussian *Codex der Gendarmerie*, and a variety of books which offended their sensibilities. After listening to rousing speeches and singing patriotic hymns, they marched up the hill to the castle, where the festivities continued in gothick mode.

This incident, which involved fewer than five hundred people, caused a grossly disproportionate stir. 'The mischief of the Wartburg assaults all sovereigns, great and small, promotes terrorism, intolerance, and demagogic despotism,' wrote Duke Charles of Mecklemburg, a relative and courtier of the King of Prussia; 'from there it is only a few steps to outright revolutionary actions'. Wittgenstein exploited the episode to stoke up fears of revolution (which he did not take seriously himself).[23]

The tsar urged Austria and Prussia to unite in forcing the Grand Duke of Weimar to punish the authors of the 'excesses' which had taken place in his realm. But things were not that simple, as Metternich pointed out. 'We foresee, and receive daily confirmation of our opinion, that the centre of German Jacobinism is to be found in Prussia and particularly in Berlin,' he wrote to his ambassador there, Count Zichy, on 28 January 1818; 'the revolution is, it is true, being openly organised only in Weimar, but the men who are working this vein are to be found in Berlin'. The Austrian police chief Sedlnitzky was convinced that the associations at universities throughout Germany were following 'a deep and carefully laid plan to kindle and encourage, not only among students but also among most teachers, a political and religious fanaticism which evidently has as its end the revolutionary overthrow of all monarchical institutions in favour of a demagogic, representative freedom and unity of the German people', which was all part of the *Schwindelgeist*.[24]

Tsar Alexander's adviser Aleksandr Sturdza published a pamphlet attacking the Prussian universities, which he claimed encouraged young people to 'plunge into the excesses that derive from the rebellion of the mind and the corruption of the heart'. He suggested abolishing academic privileges and placing students under police supervision. Germany, 'where all the calamities are concentrating', was, according to him, 'about to be swallowed up by the abyss of revolution', and the salvation of Europe and the whole universe demanded drastic action.[25]

The publication of this pamphlet came as a shock to German liberals and patriots, who, feeling betrayed by their own rulers, looked on Alexander, the liberator of Germany in 1813, as a kindred spirit, and fondly imagined him to be their champion. For all the alarmist nonsense written about them, their associations were small and weak, and they were defenceless in the face of the growing power of state organs of repression. Let down on all sides, they felt a growing desperation – which was to express itself in a way that played into the hands of their enemies.[26]

14

Suicide Terrorists

At about eleven o'clock on the morning of 23 March 1819, a man in his early twenties presented himself at the door of the writer August von Kotzebue in the small town of Mannheim in the grand duchy of Baden. He told the maid who opened it that he wished to pay his respects to the great man. She told him her master was out, but would be available in the afternoon. The young man went for a walk and had lunch at the Weinberg Inn, during which he discussed the Reformation with a couple of clergymen.

The fifty-seven-year-old Kotzebue was the author of over two hundred plays, which had been performed as far and wide as Moscow and New York, more frequently in Germany even than those of Goethe and Schiller, and of numerous stories and novellas, which had been translated into over a dozen languages. In the 1780s he had gone to Russia, where he had been given a senior legal post, married a Russian general's daughter and been ennobled. He had subsequently spent time as a theatre director in Vienna before returning to Germany in 1816 and settling in Mannheim. He received pensions from the Emperor of Austria, the King of Prussia and Tsar Alexander, for whom he acted as a foreign correspondent, sending him reports on what was going on in the literary and artistic world of Germany.

Kotzebue epitomised everything most German students and patriots despised. Born of the Enlightenment and steeped in eighteenth-century sentimentality, his work doted on themes such as the fall and redemption of female virtue, which accorded ill with the patriots' pseudo-medieval asceticism and concomitant view of women as a corrupting influence; he was accused of being 'the archservant of the false female era'. His conservatism grated on their liberalism. His derogatory views on the universities and the Teutonic antics of the students insulted them. He had already had his windows smashed, and his history of Germany had been one of the books burned at the Wartburg festival.[1]

The young man who had called on him that morning, Karl Ludwig Sand, was the son of a minor Prussian official. He had studied theology at the University of Erlangen in Bavaria, where he had joined the local *Burschenschaft*. Dissatisfied with its narrow aims, he formed a splinter group with the name of *Teutonia* and conducted moonlight ceremonies at an ancient German burial site. His efforts to persuade his colleagues to become more assertive and create a pan-German student body came to nothing, so in 1817 he left Erlangen for Jena, whose university was the centre of the *Burschenschaft* movement. He attended the Wartburg festival, where he produced a manifesto, a mash of Lutheran and nationalist slogans calling for a spiritual liberation of Germany to be achieved through chivalric self-denial. Sand was a weak and ineffectual character, acutely aware of these defects and determined to conquer them through some act of will and courage (he had enlisted in 1814, but the war was over before he saw battle). Under the influence of the professor of theoretical philosophy Jakob Friedrich Fries, a fanatical German chauvinist and notorious anti-Semite, Sand hardened his will and looked for an opportunity to prove himself.

When he returned to Kotzebue's house at around five o'clock in the afternoon he was shown upstairs and into the drawing room, where he was received by the writer. After exchanging a few words with him, Sand reached into his sleeve and drew out a dagger, with which he proceeded to stab him several times, calling him a 'traitor to the fatherland'. As Kotzebue's horrified family and servants rushed into the room, the assassin stabbed himself in the stomach and stumbled downstairs and out of the house. In the street outside he fell to his knees and, loudly thanking God for the success of his enterprise, stabbed himself twice in the chest. Kotzebue died, but Sand survived.

He was bandaged and searched. A proclamation was found in which he declared that he had been preparing his act for a long time, and called on the German people to rise up and continue the work of the Reformation, unite Church and state, and follow his example of self-sacrifice. He was also apparently in possession of a death warrant passed on Kotzebue by the *Burschenschaft* of his university.[2]

Metternich, who was in Rome with his emperor as a guest of the pope when he heard the news, struck brave attitudes as Francis warned him to be on his guard, retorting that he was not afraid of meeting his fate. 'We will both be assassinated,' the emperor concluded gloomily. Metternich was 'absolutely certain' that the murder had been decreed by a secret tribunal of students at the University of Jena which had passed the order for Kotzebue's execution to their comrades at Erlangen, and that the man who had carried it out should be regarded as 'a veritable *Haschischin*', a drug-crazed religious fanatic. 'What can one do against men who kill themselves?' he asked rhetorically.[3]

His question was immediately answered by Gentz. 'The most violent catastrophes both in the moral sphere and in the physical can be useful and even salutary,' he argued, 'if not for the victims they have already claimed, at least for those whom they have spared, on condition that they give birth to resolutions and provoke measures which it would be impossible to implement in other circumstances.' The event was 'an unmistakable symptom of the degree of malignity that the pestilential fever of our times has attained in Germany', which was 'incomparably more diseased' than France. The enemy was in their midst, he warned, and there was no time to lose. As the murder had profoundly shocked public opinion throughout Germany, confirmed all the conspiracy theorists in their beliefs, and even made large numbers of converts, it provided the perfect opportunity to act and an excellent excuse to clamp down on the universities. Metternich agreed. The students themselves were not the problem, and their societies no more than 'a puerile game which has no practical effect'; it was the teachers who were dangerous – 'they can produce a whole generation of revolutionaries if one does not manage to check the evil'.[4]

The evil was by no means imaginary. Wilhelm de Wette, professor of theology at the University of Berlin, wrote Sand's mother a letter, copies of which were widely circulated, in which he consoled her by stating that while her son's act had been 'unlawful and punishable by the worldly magistrate', he was redeemed by his personal conviction: 'he believed it was right to do what he did, and so he was right'. He assured her that the murderer would be rewarded in heaven and that his deed was 'a beautiful sign of the times'. Wittgenstein had de Wette dismissed from his post, but the damage had been done. All over Germany, students abandoned the subjects they were studying and opted for theology. When Sand was executed, by beheading with a sword, onlookers dipped handkerchiefs in his blood and distributed shreds of them as relics.[5]

News of the assassination of Kotzebue reverberated across Europe, arousing fear and outrage and giving rise to multiple theories as to what lay behind it. These were enriched by the attempted assassination on 1 July of the head of the government of the duchy of Nassau, Karl Friedrich von Ibell, by another student, Karl Löning, who told the interrogators that he had meant to kill Ibell because he was an 'oppressor of his Fatherland'. He then committed suicide. Löning had been an associate of Follen and a member of his group of Unconditionals, about which sinister stories circulated. Speculation about the events developed a life of its own, fed by the publication of a book entitled *Des Sociétés secrètes en Allemagne et en d'autres contrées*, by a former revolutionary, Lombard de Langres. 'Europe is experiencing a unique crisis,' he warned. 'Its condition, both moral and political, utterly at odds with nature, prophesies inevitable catastrophe … I must reveal terrifying conspiracies, perverted principles, plans worthy of hell. And let no one think that Germany is the only source of the fire; it is burning in Spain, in France, in Italy, in Poland; it is gaining ground in Russia; England itself has not escaped it.' He was putting his life at risk by revealing these secrets, he said, and claimed to be living in fear of the conspirators' special poison, *acqua tofana*, which was alleged to have done for the Emperors Joseph II and Leopold II, both of whom had died unexpectedly.[6]

The book, which regurgitated Barruel's theme of a permanently evolving conspiracy, linked the *Burschenschaft* to the *Tugendbund*, to Cromwell, the Levellers, the magician Cagliostro, turncoat Jesuits and the Illuminati, and explained in bloodcurdling language how a congregation of thousands of 'new men who know each other without having met, who understand each other without having spoken, who serve each other without friendship' had issued from 'the depth of the darkest shadows'. Their goal was to take power and govern the world. It was 'a conspiracy of a sect against the human race'. They operated in circles which instructed whole areas: that of Frankfurt am Main instructed Mainz, Darmstadt, Nieuwied and Cologne; Weimar directed Cassel, Göttingen, Wetzlar, Brunswick and Gotha; Dessau directed Torgau, Wittemberg, Magdeburg, Mecklemburg and Berlin; and so on, reaching all over Germany and beyond. These circles sent out emissaries, usually literary figures, to collect information on targeted individuals, whose names were written down in a 'blood-book', so that this 'infernal inquisition' should know the weaknesses of every person of power and influence, in order to be able to manipulate and destroy them. Their ultimate weapon, *acqua tofana*, was a colourless, odourless, tasteless liquid, based on opium and cantharide flies, whose very emanations could kill instantly, leaving no trace.[7]

The readers of this best-selling nonsense were treated to a description of the conspirators' rites of induction. The adept was first taken into a cave draped in black cloth, scattered with red flowers and slithering with snakes. The décor included three dim lamps, assorted skeletons and dusty books of curses. He would spend eight hours meditating there, visited by several ghosts which would vanish, leaving behind a bad smell. Then two men would appear, present him with three cups containing a greenish potion and bind his forehead with a blood-soaked bandanna adorned with hieroglyphs. He would be given a crucifix to hold. He would be stripped, patterns would be drawn on his flesh with blood, and amulets placed about his neck. His testicles would be bound with pink ribbon. Then five men would come and prostrate themselves. His clothes would be burned, and out of the fire would step another man, whereupon the five would be seized by convulsions. Then a booming voice from nowhere would tell him to abjure all his earthly ties, to his father, mother, family and friends. After swearing a terrible oath, he would be bathed in blood. The whole process took twenty-four hours. If he disobeyed or betrayed the sect he would be cast into the underground dungeon of a castle outside Paris and left to die slowly.[8]

Paris naturally drew to itself the thoughts of those who believed in conspiracy. Many, including Wellington, saw it as the fount of the evil, and the Austrian ambassador there, Vincent, agreed that it was where 'the centre of a sect which wants to substitute a new order of things' must be sought. The Ultras encouraged this notion, depicting Decazes as the instrument of the revolutionaries and the king as his puppet. 'Everything is falling apart here,' Countess Nesselrode wrote to her husband from Paris on 9 April. 'The first Jacobin is the king; he will end up with the red cap on his head.' She felt that only Russia could save the situation. 'Oh! If only the Emperor could grow disgusted with liberty, that word which is destroying Europe!' she wrote three days later. More letters followed, urging Nesselrode to act and predicting catastrophe. 'The assassination of Kotzebue makes one shudder and proves that these men will stop at nothing,' she wrote on 7 May. 'Count Stackelberg, who called on me just now told me that they have uncovered at Montorio the sect of Carbonari which was planning to poison the Emperor of Austria and, generally, to make attempts on the lives of all the sovereigns. I believe that all this merits serious attention, as none of this is exaggerated; people are overexcited to the point of being capable of anything ...'[9]

Alexander and Metternich were particularly concerned about the French army, which Decazes had transformed. Believing that the *demi-soldes* and former Napoleonic officers constituted a greater threat when left idle on the outside, he had nominated the former Napoleonic marshal Laurent de Gouvion Saint-Cyr to head it. Gouvion Saint-Cyr had got rid of many of the royalist placemen, brought back capable Napoleonic officers and made the army more professional. This alarmed Wellington, who pointed out that the French army was not like other armies, being by its very nature a political force. Lebzeltern warned that it had become 'bonapartist, or rather, revolutionary'. Pozzo di Borgo assured Nesselrode that 'the army of Waterloo is being recreated in its entirety'. By September he had convinced himself that the war ministry was 'in the hands of the secret military committee', a branch of the central organ of the grand revolutionary conspiracy.[10]

Metternich briefly considered Alexander's suggestion of concerting with the other three powers to demand the removal of Gouvion Saint-Cyr, and entertained the idea of reinstating the conference of ambassadors, discontinued by mutual agreement at Aix. But he feared such measures would be seen in France as an affront and would provoke more trouble than they could prevent. He was, in any case, more interested in exploiting the opportunities that had opened up in Germany.[11]

He played on the awesome threat of the suicidal terrorist, and without a shred of evidence warned that 'today in Germany one can count hundreds of men ready to sacrifice their property and their lives to the cause they espouse'. Evidence was unnecessary in the current mood of panic; Gentz himself, after receiving an anonymous letter which stated that he was to be assassinated, alerted the police and took to his bed, where he cowered for eight days. Metternich meant to extract the greatest possible advantage from the situation, and deal with what he saw as the German problem once and for all. But he also realised that he must act quickly, while the panic still gripped the public, and force the Bundestag, which was to meet in Frankfurt in

September, to pass a package of repressive legislation. To prepare the ground he convoked the delegates of the principal German states to a conference at the spa town of Karlsbad (Karlovy Vary) in August. He was confident that he would be able to manipulate this, and could not wait to reach 'the battlefield', as he referred to it.[12]

'I think that before long, even quite soon, you will hear a great clamour against me, but it will be the *canaille* which will be doing the shouting, and I regard such invective as so much praise,' he wrote to Dorothea Lieven from Munich on 18 July. 'As the rascals have begun murdering in Germany in the name of virtue and the motherland, I may be assassinated myself, and you may yet weep for me, along with a great many of those decent people who have not yet been gripped by madness.' He reached Karlsbad on 21 July in belligerent mood. 'With the help of God, I hope to destroy the German revolution, just as I vanquished the conqueror of the world [Napoleon],' he wrote to his wife five days later.[13]

The next day he met Frederick William and Hardenberg at Töplitz (Teplice) to assure himself of their cooperation beforehand. The king felt helpless. 'Six years ago, we faced an enemy in open country; now he is hovering around us in disguise,' he complained. Metternich took advantage of this to undermine the king's confidence in those Prussian ministers who did not see eye to eye with him, suggesting that if they had not actually been suborned by the conspiracy themselves, they were harbouring revolutionaries who were plotting to bring about the collapse of the Prussian monarchy. The following morning he reported to the Emperor Francis that he felt he had convinced Frederick William. On 6 August representatives of the nine major German states assembled at Karlsbad held their first meeting. They convened almost every day for the next two weeks. The Prussian foreign minister, Christian von Bernstorff, and some of the others were not convinced by Metternich's arguments, but he and Gentz had orchestrated the proceedings so well that he carried them all with him. In this he was greatly assisted by the arrival of shocking news from England.[14]

Perhaps inspired by the Wartburg festival, a group of English Radicals, including Henry Hunt, had held a grand dinner in London in January 1818 to mark the tercentenary of the Reformation. Vibrant speeches were made and lofty toasts drunk, but they could not obscure the fact that the movement for parliamentary reform had run out of steam, and particularly of support among the working classes. In the June elections a number of Radicals and fighting Whigs were returned to Parliament, including General Wilson, but this did not produce much in the way of results.

The summer of 1818 had seen numerous strikes, particularly in Lancashire, where spinners' wages had fallen in the past three years from twenty-four shillings per week to eighteen, and by July there were 20,000 people, nearly one-fifth of the city's entire population, on strike in Manchester. The suspension of habeas corpus had expired, which facilitated the preparation of demonstrations and strikes, and in some cases drilling exercises were held on heaths and areas of open country to ensure their orderly conduct. The workers were thus able to make an impressive show of force behind their banners, whose slogans grew more desperate as the poor harvest of that year and the glut in the textile industry made themselves felt. George Canning expressed the fear that the dangers were 'greater than in 1793'.[15]

The French tricolour and the cap of liberty may have been favourite props, but it was bread-and-butter issues that dominated, and would continue to do so the following year. When 40,000 weavers met outside Glasgow on 16 June 1819, it was to support a petition to the prince regent for passage money to Canada for the unemployed, and it was only as a result of lobbying by some Radicals that an amendment was added demanding parliamentary reform. Five days later a meeting was held at Manchester's St Peter's Fields by distressed weavers also asking for passage money. In London the most revolutionary group, the Spenceans, restricted their energy to a 'chapel' in a hayloft in Soho, where they let off steam to the loud applause of the assembly, many of whom had come for the entertainment. They ranted on about Magna Carta and the Bill of Rights, threatened nobles, clergy and mean shopkeepers, and, while spouting republican slogans, stuck to the traditional trope of the prince regent being deceived by corrupt ministers.[16]

Although it was receiving regular reports from magistrates and informers of subversive talk, drilling, and pikes and other weapons being stockpiled, often concluding with assessments such as 'some alarming insurrection is in contemplation', and although it made much of these threats and issued statements which suggested it took them seriously, the government implemented no commensurate measures. The French *chargé* in London, Latour-Maubourg, reported on 20 July that the government 'would not be sorry to see some kind of disturbance that would allow it to make use of the means of repression which the constitution places in its hands'.[17]

As the Radicals who had been returned to Westminster were making little impact there, Hunt, Cartwright and others took to agitating at open-air meetings, which could be well-attended. They provided a more gratifying platform, and demonstrated the support they enjoyed around the country. They were usually followed, once the starving unemployed audience had gone home, by hearty dinners for the speakers and organisers at some large inn, such as the Spread Eagle in Manchester, at which toasts were drunk to 1688, to Hampden, Cobbett, the poor weavers, Tom Paine, the Rights of Man, the people and various imprisoned colleagues, in a spirit of self-righteous jamboree. Instead of drawing up petitions to be sent to Parliament, they took to staging mock elections of their own 'members of parliament' or 'legislatorial attorneys' to plead their cause to Parliament in person. At a meeting due to be held in St Peter's Fields on 22 July, Henry Hunt was billed to be elected to represent Manchester.

Manchester, the second-largest city in England, stood on land belonging to the Mosley family, and it was Sir Oswald Mosley who appointed the magistrates – all of them High Tory landowners or clergymen. These had whipped themselves up into such a state of anxiety that they formed a Committee in Aid of Civil Powers consisting of worthy citizens, in order to give themselves courage. In the event, this only meant that they had a group of jittery local worthies and insurrection-obsessives breathing down their necks. They were particularly alarmed by the drilling exercises being held by the workers, and could not accept that these were motivated by a sense of self-respect and the wish to present an orderly body rather than a disorganised rabble. On 5 August Mr Norris, the resident magistrate in Manchester, reported to Sidmouth that the practice of drilling was creating 'the most formidable engine of rebellion'. 'They affect to say, that it is for the purpose of appearing at Manchester in better order, &c. on Monday next,' he continued, 'but military discipline is not requisite for this purpose, and a more alarming object is so palpable, that it is impossible not to feel a moral conviction that insurrection and rebellion is their ulterior object.'[18]

The 'Monday next' he was referring to was the open-air meeting planned by Hunt at St Peter's Fields for 16 August 1819. It had originally been announced in the following terms: 'The public are respectfully informed, that a MEETING will be held here on MONDAY the 9th August, 1819, on the Area near ST PETER'S CHURCH, to take into consideration, the most speedy and effectual mode of obtaining Radical Reform in the Commons House of Parliament ...' The magistrates responded by branding the meeting illegal. The organisers consulted lawyers, as did Sidmouth, and they all agreed that it was legal. The meeting was rescheduled for the following week, and provocative words such as 'Radical' dropped from the billing.[19]

On the day, an estimated 50,000 to 60,000 people turned up, including families with small children, many of them dressed in their Sunday clothes. They marched in order behind banners, the most violent of which read 'Equal Representation or Death' – but even this was adorned by a heart, clasped hands and the word 'Love'. The Oldham contingent included two hundred women dressed in white following a banner with the inscription 'Universal Suffrage, Annual Parliaments, Election by Ballot, No Combination Acts'. Hunt rolled up in his barouche, attended by an escort of Manchester Female Reformers dressed in white. In his usual boastful manner, he noted that 'ten or twelve bands struck up the same tune, "See the conquering hero comes"'. After he had mounted the podium everyone doffed their caps as the band played 'God Save the King'.[20]

The magistrates had prepared for rebellion: their contingent of special constables was supported by the Manchester and Salford Yeomanry; out of sight were six troops of the 15th Hussars, the 31st Regiment of Foot, several companies of the 88th, and a troop of horse artillery. Without any preamble and in contravention of the law, the magistrates ordered Hunt's arrest. The chief constable present said that he would not be able to do this without support, so the yeomanry were ordered to back him up. This force, consisting of an assortment of shopkeepers, merchants, manufacturers, lawyers, a couple of watchmakers, an insurance agent and a dancing master, had been breakfasting heartily, and many had drunk so much they had difficulty in mounting and controlling their horses. As they careered down the street making for St Peter's Fields, one of them struck a woman holding a baby, which was killed as it fell to the ground. When the yeomanry appeared on the scene, Hunt called on the crowd to cheer them, which they did, little expecting what would happen next.[21]

The amateur soldiers waded unsteadily into the crowd and soon got stuck fast, unable to go forward or back. The magistrates later claimed that they read the Riot Act, but nobody heard them, and they did not wait for the statutory hour to elapse before sending in the hussars to assist the yeomanry. The hussars tried to clear their way with the flats of their sabres, but wounds were inflicted and a panicked rush for safety ensued. By the end of the day fifteen people had lost their lives and hundreds had been injured, some of whom, like John Lees, a survivor of Waterloo, would die of their wounds. The incident was immediately branded 'the Peterloo massacre'.[22]

Far from giving the magistrates pause for thought, the events seem to have acted like a tonic, and that night troops patrolled the city looking for trouble. The following day the senior constable of Manchester informed the authorities that up to 50,000 men armed with pikes were marching on the city from Middleton and Oldham.

The Exchange was closed down, as were most shops, and people were told to stay indoors while troops patrolled the silent town. The rumour had been entirely unfounded, and nothing happened.[23]

There was outrage around the country over the number of women and children among the dead and wounded, and the conduct of the Manchester magistrates and the yeomanry was widely denounced. The lord mayor, aldermen and Common Council of London were among the many bodies and individuals petitioning the prince regent to hold a public inquiry. But the government dug in its heels. The cabinet felt they had to stand by the forces of law and order, and sent an open letter to the Manchester magistrates congratulating them on their firmness and resolution. When asked about it over dinner by Lady Shelley, Wellington replied that 'unless the magistrates had been supported in this instance, other magistrates on future occasions would not act at all; and then what a state the country would be in!' The home secretary now declared that the meeting had been illegal and the magistrates had acted properly. He took the view that, in the words of one his correspondents, 'every meeting for radical reform was not merely a seditious attempt to undermine the existing constitution of government, by bringing it into hatred and contempt, but it was an overt act of treasonable conspiracy against the constitution of government, including the king as its head.'[24]

Those calling for an inquiry were accused of sedition, and Earl Fitzwilliam was relieved of his lieutenancy for having attended a meeting in favour. The government held fast to its declared conviction that revolution was brewing, and did everything to encourage the sense of crisis. Sidmouth resorted to every argument and open falsehood to blacken the Radicals, and when challenged by Lord Grey in Parliament, declared that the demonstrators at St Peter's Fields had been 'carrying caps of liberty, bearing pikes apparently dipped in blood.'[25]

Wellington, who had been warned by Liverpool in September that 'the state of Lancashire and its immediate neighbourhood is very alarming', notified Major General Sir John Byng, commanding the troops stationed in the north, that 'the proceedings of the Radicals in different parts of the country tend to prove that we are not far removed from a general and simultaneous rising in different parts and at different places'. He further informed him that 'their business ... will be neither more nor less than the Radical plunder of the rich towns and houses which will fall in their way', and that as long as the general kept his nerve and managed to avoid allowing a single unit to be defeated, 'the mischief will be confined to plunder and a little *murder*, and will not be irretrievable'.[26]

The sense of fear generated by this kind of talk affected even the Whig grandee Earl Grey, who wrote to a fellow supporter of parliamentary reform that 'the Mob' wanted 'not Reform but Revolution', and that if they continued to agitate for reform they themselves might well end up 'on the scaffold'. Many felt, like Robert Southey, that 'there is an infernal spirit abroad', and Francis Place, at the other end of the spectrum, thought the country was on the brink of civil war. Samuel Bamford thought that if anyone had wanted to start a revolution, they could not have hoped for a more propitious moment.[27]

When another meeting was scheduled by the Radicals, the Manchester constables warned that 'open violence' would break out and took appropriate measures: the New Bailey prison was turned into a fortress, with trenches and earthworks, and the barracks fortified. But the doom-sayers were disappointed. The numerous meetings of protest after Peterloo passed off peacefully wherever troops did not interfere. Thousands did manifest their anger, but they did so by joining the Union Societies for parliamentary reform set up the previous year by a Methodist clergyman. The government and its supporters were not prepared to accept that the instincts of the people were essentially law-abiding. In a self-congratulatory letter to Pozzo di Borgo in Paris, Wellington announced that they had weathered the storm and set a good example of how to deal with 'the universal revolution which seems to menace us all'.[28]

Alleging the inadequacy of existing legislation for dealing with such a threat, the cabinet brought forward Bills in December which became known as the Six Acts. The Training Prevention Bill made any kind of drilling punishable by transportation for seven years; the Seizure of Arms Bill limited the right to bear arms and gave magistrates wide powers of search; the Misdemeanours Bill streamlined the administration of punishment; the Seditious Meetings Bill imposed restrictions on the right to hold public meetings of more than fifty people, outlawed marching and banners, and reduced the dispersal time from one hour to fifteen minutes; the Blasphemous and Seditious Libels Bill and the Stamp Duties Bill imposed censorship by the back door.

Speaking against the proposed legislation in the House of Lords, Lord Holland argued that the new legislation would 'exasperate discontent and hostility' and would do nothing 'to defeat the designs of turbulent men, or to reclaim the alienated affections of a mistaken multitude'. 'Large meetings, in periods of political ferment, furnish the means of ascertaining the designs, and measuring the strength of the malcontents,' he argued; 'they tend to disunite and discredit the rash and mischievous agitators of a mistaken multitude; and they not infrequently serve as a vent, comparatively innoxious, of that ill-humour and discontent which, if suppressed, might seek refuge in secret cabals and conspiracies, dangerous to the safety of individuals in authority, and subversive of the peace and happiness of Society.'[29]

In the event, the measures proved superfluous. An improvement in the economic climate sapped the Lancashire textile workers' interest in agitating, and in politics altogether. Their colleagues further north continued to plan meetings and demonstrations, and in April attempted to stage a general strike in Glasgow and the surrounding country, which may have been the work of government *agents provocateurs*. About five hundred people paraded with weapons, and twenty of them tried to start a revolution but fled once they realised there was no appetite for one among the population. Another forty men set out under Andrew Hardie to enlist the support of the ironworkers, but were rounded up by a troop of cavalry. The ease with which these and other such attempts were put down corroborates other evidence that while there was a hard core bent on violence, the overwhelming majority were, however bloodthirsty their slogans, indulging in little more than mass protest. The London mob's manner of demonstrating its discontent was breaking the windows of ministers' houses – a mark of aimless frustration if ever there was one, and hardly a prelude to revolution. As the future judge and Whig minister James Abercrombie wrote to a friend at the beginning of January 1820, 'No rational person ever thought the deluded Radicals could overturn the state'. But overreaction and unnecessary legislation were the order of the day, nowhere more so than in Germany, where the actions of Sand and Löning had provoked reactions bordering on the hysterical.[30]

Metternich had managed to exploit Kotzebue's murder to the full. 'I am now, thanks to God, delivered of my task,' he announced to his wife from Karlsbad on 1 September. 'The confinement passed off successfully, and the child will be presented to the world.' At a final meeting on 31 August, the delegates of the leading states of the German Confederation had agreed to all the repressive measures he had put forward. It was, Gentz noted approvingly, 'the greatest retrograde step since 1789'. The official closing conference on 1 September was but a formality. The same could be said of the vote by the Bundestag in Frankfurt on 20 September, which endorsed what would come to be known as the Karlsbad Decrees.[31]

These imposed strict limits on the press, the censorship of books and restrictions on the import of printed matter. Public addresses, including lectures and church sermons, were to be invigilated, with police agents sitting in on them so as to note down exactly what was said. Each of the German states was to appoint a commissioner to supervise teachers and what they taught, as well as those whom they taught. Student associations were banned, and any student who had belonged to one was barred from holding public office. The universities were to be gradually transformed from places of inquisitive study to training schools for civil servants.[32]

In order to get to the bottom of the 'vast association' with its 'numerous ramifications', working 'without pause not only to spread fanatical, subversive and unashamedly revolutionary doctrines, but also to encourage and prepare the most criminal enterprises', a Central Commission of Investigation, the *Zentral Untersuchungs Kommission*, was established in Mainz. It was to coordinate and complement investigations being conducted by the various German states, to research and analyse the character of 'the revolutionary machination and assess its nature, roots and extent'. Metternich wanted it to act 'like a thunderbolt', and it tried its best.[33]

Without waiting for the Karlsbad meeting or the subsequent legislation, he had initiated a clampdown on all educational establishments in Habsburg dominions. Other German rulers had followed suit. In Prussia, Wittgenstein and Kamptz had swung into action with a vengeance, launching an all-out war on 'demagogues', the *Demagogenverfolgung*: the wearing of the *Altdeutsch Tracht* was forbidden, along with the outfits of Jahn's gymnastics societies, which were closed down.[34]

In July, the Prussian government set up a commission of inquiry with powers to seize documents and interrogate at will. Jahn was arrested, sent in chains to Spandau prison and sentenced to a long term in the fortresses of Küstrin and Kolberg (the most serious charge against him was that one of his gymnasts had expressed the desire to assassinate Kamptz). The home of the professor of history at the University of Berlin, Ernst Moritz Arndt, was raided by police who carried off armfuls of papers. 'Regicides and *sans culottes* do not suddenly appear,' argued Kamptz. 'In France there were first Encyclopaedists, then Constitutionalists, next Republicans, and finally regicides and high traitors. In order not to have the last types one must prevent Encyclopaedists and Constitutionalists from appearing and becoming established.' This logic placed every educated person under suspicion. Among those charged with having 'even unintentionally' 'caused, encouraged or promoted revolutionary efforts' were most of Prussia's leading intellectuals, including Stein, Schleiermacher and Fichte, and the military elite, with Generals Yorck and Gneisenau to the fore.[35]

Wittgenstein complained that the investigations were conducted 'under the most difficult conditions' due to 'the very high level of opposition and a universal outcry from highly respected people'. This did not deter him or the commission's chief interrogator, *Regierungsassessor* Tzschoppe, who turned the hunting down of demagogues into a private passion, and was known to plant forged evidence among the papers of suspects (he would later develop a persecution mania, believing himself to be the object of a witch-hunt by his victims). The police hauled in whomever they chose. They encouraged denunciations and blackmailed people to implicate others. Lodgings were searched, papers removed by the bundle, correspondence intercepted. Words were taken out of context and woven into a different sense. Making wild allegations that he had discovered a vast movement dedicated to the unification of Germany even at the cost of provoking civil war, Kamptz leaned heavily on judges to rule that treason could be extended to embrace hypothetical action, and used the criminal courts to judge people on their attitude to the state, effectively turning the Prussian legal system from an organ upholding the law to one dedicated to the conduct of political war on behalf of the state. People could be convicted for lack of deference and an impudent attitude to civil authority.[36]

Draconian sentences were the order of the day. In Prussia, seventeen students were sentenced to twelve years' imprisonment in a fortress for belonging to an unauthorised club. Another eight who were deemed sympathetic received sentences totalling sixty-one years. In Bavaria, forty-two doctors, professors, clergymen and students would be tried and given long terms of imprisonment. At Wiesbaden, the high court sentenced a teacher, C.R. Hildebrandt, to nineteen years' confinement in a fortress.[37]

In its relentless pursuit of 'revolutionary intrigues and demagogic connections', neither of which was defined, the Mainz commission interrogated hundreds of people and pored over mountains of papers. It did not need to justify its intrusions, and picked up people on the slimmest of evidence, or even on a whim. Kaspar David Friedrich was interrogated about the significance of those of his paintings which showed young men in *Altdeutsch Tracht* lost in contemplation in a landscape – the inference being that they must be plotting.

Stein thought this 'inquisitorial apparatus' absurd and unnecessary as well as outrageous. Gneisenau agreed. 'Neither an actual conspiracy nor a society with oaths and mysteries has been discovered so far, merely a lot of silly twaddle in letters and articles, all sorts of opinions about various forms of government, a desire for a constitution and for a common Germany,' he wrote to a friend that summer. An impartial observer, the English traveller William Jacob, also saw those calling for a united Germany as harmless. 'No two that I converse with, could agree even on the preliminary step to what they all clamoured to obtain,' he remarked. Plenty of others were astonished at the exaggerated reactions of the authorities. 'The disorders which have taken place in the universities have almost always been the result of inept, arbitrary and completely unnecessary interventions of ministers who, without motive and without restraint, have taken pleasure in humiliating studious youth accustomed to respect,' La Harpe wrote to the tsar. As far as he could see, the supposed revolutionary movement in Germany was little more than a 'ministerial conjuring trick'.[38]

Others began to view what was going on in a more sinister light, as a calculated counter-revolution cynically fabricating evidence and exploiting people's fears in order to put back the clock and curtail such civil rights as the inhabitants of Germany enjoyed. The increasingly hysterical declarations by Metternich and Gentz to the effect that Germany was in the throes of 'one of the most horrible of European revolutions', and that only 'heroic means' could stave off catastrophe, would seem to support this. Many believed that Metternich and Wittgenstein were bent not so much on crushing actual revolutionaries as on denying the middle classes and the liberals any say in public affairs. Their efforts were to be crowned with success, as the clampdown was accompanied by an exodus of educated professionals to Switzerland, France, Britain and America. But it also nurtured real revolutionary instincts, for, as Heinrich von Gagern, observing the events from the safety of Switzerland, pointed out, revolution was 'the only recourse of nations against the violation of the law by their sovereigns'.[39]

The Karlsbad Decrees earned Metternich the approval of many in Europe, including Castlereagh and his colleagues in the British cabinet. 'No one is more anti-revolutionist than [the prince regent],' reported the secretary of the Austrian embassy in London, Philipp von Neumann, adding that recent events in Britain 'have not been such as to inspire any liking for such ideas'. But he was disappointed by the British cabinet's 'feebleness' in not making a public statement endorsing the decrees. 'The proclamation of principles in the midst of the storm is a strong measure,' Metternich wrote to Decazes on 7 October. Decazes seems to have taken the point.[40]

A couple of weeks earlier, as Metternich was preparing the Bundestag to endorse his decrees, Abbé Grégoire, an erstwhile deputy to the revolutionary Convention who had voted for the death of Louis XVI, was elected to the French Chamber. The news sent waves of horror through conservative society. The Dessolles ministry fell, and in November Decazes became prime minister. He promptly introduced changes to the electoral law, and managed to have Grégoire excluded from the Chamber. He had also, to the great relief of Wellington and others, replaced Gouvion Saint-Cyr with General de Latour-Maubourg.

Metternich was indeed bent on more than just the repression of revolutionary students, and intended to close all avenues to the liberals and the middle classes. In his view, the existence of constitutions in some of the states of Germany, and the stipulation of the Congress of Vienna that the others should also introduce them, was bound to lead eventually to the triumph of those Gentz referred to as 'the innovators and partisans of revolution, numerous in all classes of society and even in the vicinity of thrones'. This would, in his view, spell disaster for the Austrian monarchy. He therefore set out to stop and, if possible, reverse the trend.[41]

He had managed to persuade the German states to send delegates to a conference in Vienna at which he hoped to repeat his triumph of Karlsbad with regard to the question of constitutions. Most of the rulers and their chief ministers were so rattled by the events of that year, and so terrified of being assassinated by some suicidal terrorist, that they could be expected to rubber-stamp anything he proposed. But the King of Württemberg did not take the threat as seriously as Metternich, and, being closely related to the tsar, was not as easily swayed as some of the other rulers, and Alexander himself was proving a problem.

Following a conversation with the tsar in October, Lebzeltern reported that Alexander understood the gravity of the situation in Germany, and had expressed himself in violent terms on the necessity of taking repressive measures against 'the spirit of corruption and immorality which menaced public order'. He had been incensed that young Germans in 'their absurd costume' had entered the kingdom of Poland to fraternise with Polish students. They had been expelled, after having had their long *Altdeutsch* locks snipped off and their heads shaved in the manner of Russian footsoldiers. The tsar now saw that much of Germany, and particularly Prussia, was 'gangrened', and he had fallen out of love with the Poles, who were not showing due gratitude for the benefits he had bestowed on them. He was nevertheless proving less than dependable. He put paid to Metternich's plan to revoke all the constitutions in Germany by encouraging Württemberg to protest, a move motivated, according to Lebzeltern, entirely by a wish for revenge for not getting his way at Aix-la-Chapelle over the Spanish colonies. He covertly backed the southern German states at the Vienna conference in resisting all Metternich's proposals for changes to the Federal Act.[42]

The conference, which opened on 25 November 1819, did not close until the following May. In its Final Act, which passed into law at the Frankfurt Bundestag on 8 June 1820, it stopped short of abolishing constitutions or forbidding the introduction of new ones. But it did stipulate that any constitution that was brought in must be founded on the sovereignty of the monarch, and not that of the people. It also regulated relations between the various states of the confederation in ways that severely circumscribed the freedom of action of individual states, thus closing the door to creeping liberalisation. But by then Metternich and everyone else had far weightier matters on their minds.

15

Corrosion

Only a few days into the new year, alarming news arrived from Spain. Outside Cádiz on 1 January 1820, Major Rafael del Riego and Colonel Antonio Quiroga had led out the troops under their command and staged a *pronunciamiento*. This was a comparatively new form of action. It was not primarily a rebellion, more of a political demonstration, a declaration of political protest or intent. In a country in which all normal channels of political expression had been abolished, it could only be carried out by the army, which was the sole institution in existence (aside from the Church). If it did not gain the support of most of the army and other sections of the population, the regiments involved would go back to barracks and the leaders would face retribution or emigrate. There had been at least three such actions since 1814, when the returning Ferdinand VII had abolished the constitution brought in by the national assembly, the Cortes, in 1812, and they had all failed to gain wider support. Riego's *pronunciamiento* would prove more successful.

Ferdinand had been massing a large force at Cádiz to send across the Atlantic and restore his authority in the former Spanish colonies, not a cause most of the officers and men were keen to fight for. Nor were they happy at the prospect of an open-ended sojourn on the other side of the world. They were also underpaid, bored and disaffected. In their *grito*, the manifesto announcing the aim of the *pronun-*

ciamiento, they demanded the reinstatement of the constitution of 1812 and the summoning of the Cortes. Riego and Quiroga nevertheless failed initially to enlist the support of the other units in Cádiz.

Wellington dismissed the affair as being of little consequence, and expected the troops to return to barracks soon. Metternich too made light of the matter, as it did not appear to threaten the stability of the rest of Europe. The French foreign minister, Étienne-Denis Pasquier, a former prefect of police under Napoleon, knew better than most how tempting it was for army officers to try anything that might create the opportunity of promotion. He also felt the event should give pause for thought to monarchs who kept large armies on which they relied heavily, and which in some cases were the only pillar of the throne. But events in Spain were soon overshadowed by a more dreadful occurrence, in Paris.[1]

At 11 p.m. on 13 February 1820, as he was re-entering the opera, having escorted his wife to her carriage after the first act, the duc de Berry was approached by a man and stabbed. He fell to the ground and was carried back into the antechamber of his box, still clutching the dagger he had himself pulled from his side. He was laid on a sofa and medical help was summoned. When it became evident that he was mortally wounded, a priest was called. As nobody wished to start a panic the show was allowed to go on, and the prelate administered the last rites to the strains of an opera set in the Venice carnival. The duke's wife returned, and Louis XVIII soon arrived on the scene, staying with his nephew until he died several hours later.

Berry was not the heir to the throne, as he was the younger son of Monsieur, but in him had resided all the hopes of the monarchists. His elder brother, the duc d'Angoulême, was married to the daughter of Louis XVI, who was heavily marked by the five years she had spent in a revolutionary prison, and was barren. Berry was not particularly clever, but he was brave and generous, and his liberal instincts had made him popular. Although he had no male heir, his twenty-one-year-old wife had in the previous year been delivered of a daughter, and was expecting another child. His death caused dismay and sadness among all classes. It also had serious political consequences.[2]

Polarisation in the Chamber over the past months had led to increasingly acrid debates, accompanied by more and more aggressive outbursts at both ends of the political spectrum outside it: dark threats were bandied about, and suppressed fears aired. When news of the assassination broke, people jumped to conclusions suggested by their worst fears and prejudices. As it spread it assumed a life of its own and became unrecognisable, with some affirming that a vast conspiracy had hatched, others that the Tuileries had been stormed, that there was fighting in the streets, that a St Bartholomew's Day massacre of the royal family and its supporters was in progress, and so on. Where local prefects delayed making official announcements before receiving the full story, tales spread by travellers, embellished by speculation, led to wild inventions. Stories circulated that the assassin, a saddler named Louis Pierre Louvel, was a heroic former Napoleonic officer, that Berry had insulted him, that he had spat in his face, that he had torn the *Légion d'honneur* off his chest, that he had seduced his wife, or daughter, or sister. In a curious leap of the imagination, Louvel was linked to Napoleon, and rumours began to circulate that the emperor had landed in France, in Spain, in America.[3]

Louvel did have Napoleonic sympathies, but his only ascertainable motive was the desire to extinguish the Bourbon dynasty, and he had acted on his own. This did not stop people from seeing accomplices everywhere, and Ultras were quick to spot their chance. The police were deluged by anonymous letters pointing the finger at Decazes. A spate of books and pamphlets related Louvel's act to a long succession of assassinations and attempts stretching back to the eighteenth century, taking in the kings of Portugal and Poland, committed by members of 'an impious sect' that merely changed its name, from Masons to Illuminati to Jacobins, and currently called themselves Liberals. Decazes himself was accused of complicity at best, and of having personally ordered the assassination at worst; one publication suggested an accomplice in the shape of a sinister Jew.[4]

'I have this moment heard of the assassination of the duc de Berry,' Metternich wrote to his family on 20 February. Like Pozzo di Borgo, who had written to Wellington that 'Jacobinism and Bonapartism are marching together, head held high, not only with audacity, but with rage,' Metternich immediately jumped to the conclusion that 'Liberalism is on the march,' and anticipated 'a deluge of assassins'. To Lebzeltern he pointed out triumphantly that the assassination provided proof that there was, as he had always believed, a Europe-wide conspiracy. Alexander thought likewise. 'The daggers of Sand and Louvel are forged in the same fire,' he said to the French ambassador, Pierre Louis de La Ferronnays, during a ball in St Petersburg. 'Are you quite sure that this latest assassin does not have accomplices deranged like himself, determined like him to brave the scaffold in order to strike at other august victims?' In London, the prince regent assumed that he himself was personally threatened. Wellington, in a letter to his Spanish former comrade-in-arms General Álava, dismissed the idea that Louvel could have been a lone wolf. 'It seems fairly certain that it was a conspiracy; and we shall see whether the French have the courage to unmask this conspiracy,' he wrote, likening the state of France to that in 1793. 'God knows where all this will end, but for my part, I believe we need a rain of fire to put things in order.' Two days after he wrote that letter, an event took place in London which appeared to vindicate his worst fears.[5]

According to the *Annual Register*, only four months after Peterloo 'The situation of the country at the commencement of the year 1820 was more tranquil, than the violent popular agitation of the preceding months would have given reason to expect.' This tranquillity was disturbed by Arthur Thistlewood, aka 'Marcus Brutus'. He was the natural son of a Lincolnshire farmer, who had served as an officer in the army in the West Indies, then travelled in America and France, where he joined the French army for a time. On his return to England he indulged his taste for gambling and his revolutionary instincts by becoming a Spencean and conspiring to assassinate the king in 1802. He had been one of those who attempted to hijack Hunt's 1816 Spa

Fields meeting, and had been arrested along with Watson and Preston, charged with high treason and acquitted. He now proposed to murder the entire cabinet over dinner at Lord Harrowby's house in Grosvenor Square on 23 February. He intended to burst in through the servants' entrance with a gang of men recruited for the purpose, cut off the heads of Sidmouth and Castlereagh and bear them on pikes to the Mansion House, where he would proclaim himself president of the Britannic Republic. In pursuance of this plan he rented a stable in Cato Street off the Edgware Road, and began to fill the hayloft above it with guns, swords, daggers and bombs.[6]

Thistlewood had never been strong on discretion. He had made the acquaintance of one George Edwards, a maker of casts for plaster figurines (his best-selling piece was a bust of the headmaster of Eton, which the school's pupils would purchase in order to throw things at). During the Napoleonic wars Edwards devised a lucrative scam of extracting money from French prisoners on the promise of getting them out of the country, and then denouncing them and pocketing a reward. After the end of the war he became a Home Office spy. He was, in the words of his contemporary biographer, 'a diabolical wretch, who created the treason he disclosed; who went about – a fiend in human form – inflaming distressed and desperate wretches into crimes, in order that he might betray them to justice, and make a profit of their blood'. Thistlewood welcomed Edwards into his gang, another member of which may also have been a spy, and the plot was leaked to the government. As a result, the ministers did not go to the dinner, and most of the conspirators were arrested by a group of constables as they were buckling on their arms in the hayloft. Those who got away in the scuffle were apprehended the following day. Thistlewood and four others were hanged, the rest had their sentences commuted to transportation. Edwards lived on, well-rewarded, to judge by his lavish lifestyle.[7]

The discovery of the conspiracy was highly convenient for the government, as it silenced the continuing criticism of its handling of the Peterloo affair. 'I do not know whether we shall ever be able to publish everything we know about this business,' Wellington crowed in a letter to Richelieu, but he could confide that it had been planned with chilling deliberation, and greater lust for blood than the September massacres of 1792. There is some reason to believe that the whole enterprise had been set up by Edwards, possibly with the assistance of other Home Office agents, with or without the knowledge of members of the cabinet. They certainly played up the danger. At a dinner given by Castlereagh in his house in St James's Square in London on 28 February, Countess Lieven asked him whether he was taking any precautions, 'whereupon he produced two small pistols which he carries everywhere, even at his own dinner table', according to one of the guests. Whether this was a sign of genuine apprehension or a theatrical display is impossible to tell. Either way, following hard on the assassination of the duc de Berry, the affair reinforced the government's case that the country was threatened with revolution. While awaiting their sentence, the conspirators had been visited by a clergyman, who concluded that they 'had cast off the fear of God', which explained how they could conceive such evil plans. This chimed with a notion being propagated of a connection between irreligion and the various 'blasphemous' Churches springing up and revolutionary proclivities. Public opinion remained unconvinced and, significantly, condemned Thistlewood and his accomplices for their 'folly' and 'wickedness', rather than as dangerous assassins who had nearly brought down the government. In other respects too, public opinion was at odds with government policy.[8]

On his release from Lancaster gaol, where he had been sent after Peterloo, Hunt set off for London. His horse died along the way, near Preston, and its burial, under a headstone inscribed 'Alas! Poor Bob!!!', was attended by thousands. As he entered London he was greeted by a crowd estimated at 300,000 people. On 2 March, at a dinner held at the Crown and Anchor in honour of the Radical politician and friend of Byron John Cam Hobhouse, just released from Newgate, the first toast drunk by the 450 guests was to the Sovereign People. Revolutionary graffiti was not uncommon, with texts such as 'Civil war – Liberty-Death or no George the Fourth – Hunt for ever – No tyrant, no damned royal crown – No damned king – No George the 4th – No churches'. There were reports of drilling and even of people arming, which may have been true: following Peterloo, those who attended meetings expected to be set upon by troops. Passive as much of this activity was, the authorities kept up the alarm, and Sidmouth made a connection between the 'diabolical' Cato Street conspiracy and Manchester, and with 'men of similar Principles in other parts of the World'.[9]

The situation on the Continent appeared to have stabilised. Louis XVIII had done everything to keep Decazes in office, but the Ultras played on the feelings of horror inspired by the assassination of the duc de Berry, orchestrating more anti-royal plots. Not long after the event, two former Napoleonic officers and a police agent hatched a plan to induce the duchess to miscarry by setting off explosives in her apartment in the Tuileries. They managed to plant one charge and set it off on 29 April, to no apparent effect on the duchess. Disheartened, the two officers gave up, but they were worked on by the police agent, who accused them of cowardice, so they planted a second charge to be set off on the night of 6 May. They were caught, tried and sentenced to death, but reprieved at the request of the duchess herself. Some time later, she handed Monsieur a note she purportedly found on her dressing table warning of a plot to assassinate the entire royal family. Monsieur passed it to Richelieu, and strict security measures were implemented. Various suspects were brought in and questioned before, a few days later, the duchess's confessor called on the magistrate in charge of the case and informed him that she had confessed to writing the note herself. The king was finally obliged to give way and let Decazes go. A new ministry was formed under Richelieu with the support of the Ultras, which brought in a raft of repressive measures and moved legislation restricting the suffrage. This would bear fruit the following year in a new electoral law which shifted power from the urban middle class back to the landed nobility. France, it seemed, was under control.[10]

But now Wellington was having second thoughts about the situation in Spain. In late February, units in Galicia and Aragon had come out in support of Riego and Quiroga, and by the beginning of March the mutiny had spread to Madrid. 'What makes the revolt of these troops alarming is that in Spain the government has nothing in common with the people of the country, nor any other authority over them except by means of these troops,' Wellington wrote to Richelieu. On 6 March the king agreed to summon the Cortes. The following day, with the royal palace in Madrid surrounded by troops, he agreed to reintroduce the constitution of 1812. 'It is a terrible example for those states in Germany which have armies based on the same model,' Wellington wrote to Richelieu on 24 March, adding that what was happening in Spain was 'pure evil'. The events there had prompted him to 'serious reflections on the dangers menacing the social order'. Metternich too was anxious about the effect the example being set by the Spanish rebels might have elsewhere, with good reason. From St Petersburg, La Ferronnays reported to Pasquier that there was more revolutionary talk among the officers of the imperial guard than among their Parisian counterparts. Pozzo di Borgo on the other hand believed the bad example was coming from England, which was 'vomiting missionaries of revolt on all the corners of the globe'.[11]

Metternich was beginning to despair of Europe. To his ambassador in London, Prince Esterházy, he wrote on 7 April 1820 that he felt like a physician standing by the bedside of a sick man of whose survival he had given up hope. In a letter to Lebzeltern, he likened Europe to 'a sea whipped up by the storm'. He did not know what to make of events in Spain. 'I have for so long made it a habit not to allow myself to try to comprehend what goes on in Spain, since I understand nothing of it, nor of what those people want or say,' he wrote. Of one thing he was certain, namely that there could be no such thing as 'a revolution steeped in rose-water', and as far as he was concerned, a constitutional Spain was a nonsense. The Spanish constitution of 1812, which had been closely modelled on the French one of 1791, was based on the principle of the sovereignty of the people, and reserved for the monarch an essentially executive role. Such 'false doctrines', if allowed to take root, would undermine the foundations of other states. Gentz echoed this view of the danger posed by 'poisonous' and 'corrosive' principles emanating from Spain, although he believed that it was not Spain, but France, that would precipitate 'the fall of the existing social order in all civilised countries'.[12]

Alexander was for military intervention. According to him, the Spanish nation owed the world an act of 'expiation' for the evil it had perpetrated. This did not suit Metternich at all. In a deft attempt to satisfy his lust as well as reasons of state, he instructed Lebzeltern to persuade Alexander that a conference of ambassadors should be called to discuss the matter, and to suggest to the tsar that he replace the existing ambassador in Vienna with Count Lieven, who had a better grasp of the situation. Castlereagh was also worried by talk of intervention. At the beginning of May he drew up a State Paper in which he stressed that the purpose of the Quadruple Alliance was the maintenance of the territorial settlement created in 1815; only a clear threat to this or to world peace could sanction military intervention in another country's internal affairs. Wellington contributed a memorandum, citing first-hand experience. 'There is no country in Europe in the affairs of which foreigners can interfere with so little advantage as Spain,' he wrote.[13]

Such arguments were lost on the Continent, where porous borders provided no protection from the ever more fearsome threat: the vocabulary of occult conspiracy was now enriched with a more scientific and medical lexicon, as people spoke of 'corrosion', 'inflammation', 'consumption', 'gangrene' and similar processes. 'The world is in the grip of fever,' Metternich wrote to Vincent in June 1820; 'it will not kill everyone, as even the plague spares some individuals. The most important thing now is to live in the midst of the epidemic without being infected and to bring assistance to those who are sick.'[14]

Vigilance was of the essence, and the faintest rash had to be treated as a possible symptom of the creeping malady. Metternich duly noted every detail, and his police anticipated. Reports that Napoleon's former police chief Savary was plotting something with Napoleon's stepson Prince Eugène de Beauharnais, and was allegedly travelling around Switzerland meeting 'persons unknown', were meticulously noted by Metternich and by Pozzo di Borgo in Paris, where an outbreak of violence had set alarm bells ringing.[15]

Ultra guards officers in plain clothes had taken to roughing up liberal deputies as they left the Chamber, and forcing people in the street, particularly students, to shout '*Vive le Roi!*' At the beginning of June they beat Nicolas Lallemand, a law student, so badly that he died. His funeral became the focus for a demonstration which turned into a riot. There followed several days of violence which some saw as the prelude to revolution, and it was not brought under control by troops until the end of the second week of June. Many believed, with some reason, that the episode had been a provocation by the Ultras and the police.[16]

The director general of police, baron Claude Mounier, the son of a prominent revolutionary of 1789 and a former Napoleonic civil servant, insisted that the whole thing had been carefully planned by a '*comité general d'insurréction*'. The idea was taken up by those who did not wish to contemplate the possibility that the unrest might have had natural causes, and rumours began to spread of money having been paid out to bring people onto the street. Gradually, a conviction grew in conservative quarters that there was some kind of sinister body controlling events, and people began to talk of a '*comité directeur*'. On 24 June Pozzo di Borgo reported to Nesselrode on a 'vast conspiracy' which had failed to materialise: the plotters had apparently hoped to gain the army, but having failed, decided to blacken its reputation and goad the people into attacking it by paying teachers to release schoolchildren and instruct them to jeer and throw stones at soldiers and provoke a 'massacre of the innocents'. There is no evidence to suggest that any of these events, aside from the provocations of the Ultras and their agents, had been planned. But conspiracy and revolution were in the air.[17]

In response to anxious enquiries from Nesselrode, Countess Lieven reported from London that the only revolution occupying people's minds there was a 'boudoir revolution' precipitated by the king taking a new mistress. But the streets of London were by no means quiet, as public opinion was highly frothed up over the treatment of Queen Caroline, and many prominent Whigs and Radicals such as William Cobbett had taken up her cause in order to enlist the support of the masses for reform.[18]

From the moment she arrived in England in 1795 to marry the prince regent, Princess Caroline of Brunswick had declared her intention of making herself loved by 'the people'. She largely succeeded, because she was seen as the victim of her much-disliked husband. Rejected by him, she had spent the past six years abroad, at the centre of an indecorous circus of shady characters, giving rise to tales of unbridled debauchery. On the news of the death of George III at the end of January 1820, she hastened to England in order to take her place at the coronation of her husband as George IV. He attempted to bribe her to stay away, and, failing that, to divorce her. When she arrived in London she became the natural focus for all the ill-feeling against him and the government.

As this prepared his case against her, she consorted with leading figures in the opposition and made public appearances, admirably playing the role of the wronged wife. She engaged feminist opinion, and her peccadilloes were forgotten in a surge of sympathy as a sense of chivalry was awakened in the masses. Public demonstrations of support for her easily turned into anti-government riots, and in June Sidmouth's house was attacked on three consecutive nights. The carriage in which he and the Duke of Wellington were travelling was mobbed and had its windows shattered. Sidmouth and Castlereagh received death threats, as did the king himself. There were cries of 'No Queen, no King!', and on 15 June the 3rd Guards Regiment mutinied, refusing to give up their cartridges when coming off duty. They were brought back into line by force and marched out of the capital the following day, but that night a mob assembled outside their vacated barracks and the Life Guards had to be called out to disperse it. 'I feel the greatest anxiety respecting the state of the military in London,' wrote Wellington in something of a panic; 'in one of the most critical moments that ever occurred in this country, we and the public have reason to doubt in the fidelity of the troops, the only security we have, not only against revolution but for the property and life of every individual in the country who has anything to lose.' Recent events in Spain could not be ignored, and he advised against using troops to restore order. Soldiers could be seen drinking the queen's health and making ugly jibes about the king. It was reported that even the whores were refusing to service soldiers who would not side with the queen. According to the Austrian *chargé* in London, Caroline's presence was like 'a contagious illness' undermining all existing institutions, and he prophesied that if she were to be found guilty of the charges being levelled against her there would be a revolution.[19]

With alarmist reports of brewing discontent coming in from all parts of the country, it was with a sense of foreboding that the government prepared for the start of the divorce proceedings in August. Barriers were erected around the Houses of Parliament, and troops and even field guns were deployed at strategic points, although nobody could be sure how they would behave in an emergency. As its anniversary drew near, meetings and processions were held to commemorate the victims of the 'Peterloo massacre.' The queen made inflammatory statements suggesting her husband should be dethroned, and the Sunday papers poured oil on the flames by spreading scandal about the royal family in general. The Home Office informer John Shegog alerted his masters that the Radicals were preparing to act in alliance and cooperation 'with all the Republicans all over the world' – there were, by that time, a growing number of these.[20]

At the beginning of July Metternich had gone to Baden, to the bedside of his favourite daughter Marie, who was dying, and it was there that, on 15 July, news reached him that revolution had broken out in Naples. He was so shocked that even his daughter's death three days later could not distract him from it. Gentz had never seen him in such a state of disarray. Metternich had visited Naples no more than a year ago, and had written that he could see 'no possibility of *any kind* of movement' anywhere in Italy. 'In the region of Naples in particular the population is *positively* contented,' he had written. 'If it were not for all those Russian agents who are travelling around Italy in every direction and who seek to inflame the hopes of various groups by telling them of the liberal tendencies of the Emperor Alexander, there would be no *permanent* agitation in people's minds. There have always been malcontents in Italy. The Italian shouts a great deal, but he does not act.'[21]

He was not the only one to have been taken by surprise. 'The quiet and prosperous state of these Kingdoms afford but few subjects worthy of being brought to your Lordship's notice,' the British minister at Naples, Sir William A'Court, had reported to Castlereagh only three months earlier. Austria's ambassador in Naples, Prince Jabłonowski, admitted that 'news of a revolution on the moon would have seemed more likely'. The events were not only unexpected, but confusing as well.[22]

On 1 July, the feast of St Theobald, patron of the Carbonari, a priest by the name of Luigi Minichini, who was the grand master of the *vèndita* in the small town of Nola, had slung an old musket over his shoulder, mounted a horse and led his fellow Carbonari off towards the nearby town of Avellino. He had persuaded Lieutenant Michele Morelli and his troop of cavalry, who were unpaid and disaffected, to join him. The peasants they expected to rouse along the way were either indifferent or hostile. On arrival at Avellino, Morelli proclaimed his loyalty to 'Ferdinand the constitutional king', which was something of a joke.

King Ferdinand IV had been chased from the mainland part of his realm by the French in the 1790s, and had taken refuge in Sicily. Under pressure from the British, who were guarding him there, in 1812 he granted the island a constitution, modelled on the Spanish one of the same year. It was said that the very word 'constitution' gave him 'nervous spasms', and as soon as his supplanter, King Joachim Murat, had been expelled from Naples and he was back on his throne there (as Ferdinand I of the Two Sicilies), he had revoked it. A story had nevertheless been put about by some Neapolitan Carbonari that on regaining his mainland kingdom, Ferdinand had declared: 'The People will be sovereign, and the monarch will only be the depository of the laws which shall be decreed by a constitution ...'[23]

Not knowing what to do about the loyal subjects of the king who had appeared on his patch, the commander at Avellino sent for instructions. Troops were sent from Naples to restore order, but they fell in with the loyal subjects. The Neapolitan army was officered mostly by men who had served in the Napoleonic wars and fondly remembered their flamboyant general and king Joachim Murat. Typical was General Guglielmo Pepe, who had served with distinction and attained the rank of marshal. He had been well treated by Ferdinand, but he was out of sympathy with the Bourbon regime, and bored.

Faced with rebellion and the apathy of his army, King Ferdinand decreed on 6 July that he would bring in the constitution of 1812, at the same time announcing his retirement from political life and proclaiming his son Francesco, Duke of Calabria, vicar general of the kingdom. Two days later, in a grandiose ceremony, the king and his sons solemnly swore to uphold the constitution. On 9 July Lieutenant Morelli made his entrance into Naples at the head of his troopers and other units which had joined him along the way, followed by Father Minichini and some 6,000 barely armed men marching under the Carbonarist tricolour of red for the fire of charity, blue for the smoke of hope, and black for the charcoal that represented their name. The vicar general of the kingdom saluted them, and there followed wild feasting and celebrations throughout the city, accompanied by some random violence.

What worried Metternich was that as the whole thing had passed off bloodlessly and the king had accepted the constitution, Britain might take the view that it should be allowed to stand. He need not have worried. A'Court was an arch-conservative, and painted a very dark picture in his reports to his chief. Castlereagh was so alarmed as he contemplated the state of affairs that his usually measured prose was now overcome with torrential and volcanic imagery. From Milan, Lieutenant Colonel Browne reported on 29 July that the 'infection from Naples' had reached that city, the coffee rooms were crowded with people discussing politics in terms 'more assuming and desperate', and that 'Constitution and insurrection are in every one's mouth'. 'The Liberales here are loud in their celebration of the Spaniards and Neapolitans,' he continued. 'They are ripe for anything.' Byron, who was in Ravenna in the Papal States, could feel the excitement too. 'Here there are as yet but the sparks of the volcano,' he wrote, 'but the ground is hot, and the air sultry.' Castlereagh told Decazes, now France's ambassador in London, that if they did not act promptly, 'the fire will take hold, spread and soon engulf everything'. Both Castlereagh and Wellington, who thought it was 'time to set an example', believed Austria should act immediately, possibly with the support of France.[24]

Austria could not tolerate what had taken place, if only because its treaty with Naples stipulated that no change could be introduced into its form of government without its sanction. More important, Metternich was convinced that what had happened in Naples was an offshoot of the revolution in Spain. 'The calmness and the kind of order which has characterised the doings of the Neapolitan revolutionaries can leave no doubt that the events of 1 to 8 July had been planned beforehand and are only the development of a conspiracy hatched in the dark, conceived and decided by men highly placed in society,' he wrote to Esterházy in London on 17 July. He went on to make out that the fate of the Austrian monarchy was at stake.[25]

The threat posed by the events in Naples was in fact negligible. There was no revolutionary urge among the population, merely a tradition of lawlessness which, not being in a position to curb, the kingdom's rulers had accepted. At the end of the eighteenth century and during the Napoleonic wars they had either formed or encouraged corps such as the *Santa Fede* to combat the French and their influence under the guise of defending the Catholic faith. In 1816 they created the *Calderari* as a foil to the Carbonari. This unholy alliance of throne and popular posse worked against the middle class and the nobility. The French-style administration of the kingdom under Murat had favoured the aspirations of these by introducing a more workable system along with opportunities for economic development and social advancement. Most of this was reversed on the return of Ferdinand, who propped up his throne with the lower orders in order to check the ambitions of the propertied classes and the army, which had also infiltrated the Carbonari. The elections held after the revolution returned a majority of moderate nobles. The new government's actions were placatory. The status of the papal enclaves of Pontecorvo and Benevento was scrupulously respected. A paper which criticised Austria in unseemly terms was suppressed. A popular revolt in Palermo was successfully put down. The foreign minister, the Duke of Campochiaro, did everything he could to reassure all the courts of Europe that his government had the situation under control.

The Austrian *chargé d'affaires*, Count de Menz, took a positive view of what had taken place. 'One has to admit,' he reported to Metternich, 'that constitutional ideas do dominate and have taken root in the nation. The clergy, the nobility, the military, the bourgeoisie, and, above all, the judicial order are imbued with them.' He went on to say that the revolt had not been aimed at the monarchy but at the incompetent, corrupt and despotic ministry, which had been incapable of providing order and had stifled economic activity. Menz took the view that the new regime could bring stability to the region, and reported that it was willing to introduce changes into the 1812 constitution, which was such a red rag to conservative bulls, by including an upper chamber of peers and a royal power of veto. Even the reactionary A'Court admitted that the previous state of affairs had been indefensible.[26]

The Russian and Prussian representatives broadly reinforced this analysis, while the Bavarian minister strongly contradicted the alarmist assertions that had been printed in Metternich's press mouthpiece. 'Up to the present, nothing which has taken place in the kingdom since 1 July justifies the declamations of the *Österreichische Beobachter*,' he wrote to his superior, Count Rechberg, on 26 September. 'Everything leads one to assume here that if foreign armies do not intervene the new institutions will establish themselves without resistance.'[27]

Such views undermined the very bases of Metternich's policy. His war on demagogues in Germany had recently come under criticism, and the press had begun to question whether there had ever been any threat of a kind to justify the Karlsbad Decrees. The justification for the Mainz commission was beginning to look threadbare as it thrashed about in an increasingly futile but desperate quest for evidence of subversion. In January it had tracked down Justus Grüner, who was undergoing a forlorn hope of a cure at Wiesbaden, and subjected him to interrogation on his deathbed. At the end of February the Bavarian minister Baron von Zentner complained that this kind of thing reflected badly on the rulers of the German states, who were finding it hard 'to maintain the trust of their people'. Metternich's response was to place even more pressure on the commission to produce some credible evidence that there really had been a conspiracy. In the words of Matthias Edler von Rath, one of its members, they were instructed no longer to look for the perpetrators but to find the crime.[28]

In the case of Naples, there was a crime – there had been a revolution. Since it was demonstrably the work of the Carbonari, there was also a conspiracy. Metternich was not going to let anyone rob him of it by suggesting it was some kind of justifiable plebiscite which had righted wrongs and should therefore be acknowledged. The challenge now facing Europe, he declared, came from 'the *secret societies*', which constituted 'a real power, and all the more dangerous for working in the shadows, undermining every part of the social structure, and leaving everywhere the germs of a moral gangrene which will rapidly develop and bear fruit'. Behind the Carbonari and other secret societies stood the middle classes with their 'immeasurable ambition', which could most easily be satisfied through social upheaval. What strengthened his case was the fact that the conspiracy was potentially immense, on the Barruel scale. Suddenly, everyone was talking and writing about the Carbonari, their power and their reach. The Neapolitan ambassador in St Petersburg told Alexander that there were 700,000 of them in Naples alone. Cardinal Consalvi's informer in Naples assured him that there were over 1,200,000. The political police of various countries gathered documentation and compiled memoranda in a race to prove that they had known about them all along.[29]

Metternich had other, more weighty reasons for refusing to accept what had happened in Naples. If the kingdom of the Two Sicilies were to stabilise as a constitutional monarchy with the attendant freedoms of speech and press, Austria would have lost control of the southern part of the Italian peninsula. Moreover, such a kingdom was bound to develop cordial relations with its sister constitutional Bourbon kingdom of France, thus providing that power with a conduit for exerting influence on the peninsula. It would also provide a base for all malcontents and nationalist enemies of Austrian rule in Italy.

Others were more worried by the military aspect: following so soon after the Spanish *pronunciamiento*, the role of the army in the events in Naples suggested a pattern. 'These two latest mutinies, in Spain and Naples, should make rulers think of the future, because the fall of thrones is now ... carried out by the first support of royal authority – the armed forces,' Count Rostopchin, the former governor and incinerator of Moscow, who was in Paris having his haemorrhoids treated, wrote to a friend on 1 August. 'I am of the opinion that if strong measures are not adopted now to bring back the former order of things, over the next twenty years the greater part of European thrones will undergo the most terrible convulsions and fall under the dictatorship of the military, and that will be the real fruit of the Enlightenment.'[30]

Alexander was keen on military intervention against the Neapolitan revolutionaries. His generals less so. General Vassilchikov, commander of the Guard Corps, believed the Russian army was not up to the job. 'The state of mind is not good,' he wrote to Prince Volkonsky. 'Universal discontent and no desire to endure the sacrifices demanded by the conduct of a war the necessity of which is not clear to ordinary mortals ...' The officers had no wish to fight the Neapolitans, and even sympathised with them. Metternich would have been delighted to hear this, as the last thing he wanted was Alexander interfering in what he considered to be his own back yard.[31]

On 1 August Metternich sent a memorandum to all the courts of Italy, giving his view of the situation. He traced the origins of the problems facing Europe to the French Revolution, which, he asserted, derived from the influence of England, which had been 'imbued ... for nearly a century with the errors of a false philosophy'. Recent events in Germany and Italy had been the natural and foreseeable consequence of the French Revolution. What had taken place in Spain was of a different order, the result of 'ineptitude on the part of the government on a scale that few examples in the past can be found to compare with'. The Neapolitan revolution was more sinister in character, since it was not the army itself which had carried it out: 'it was a sect, to which the army belonged more than it belonged to the king'. 'It was the orders of its real superiors, of an invisible though universally felt power, that the army followed,' he concluded. He warned that the Carbonari, 'a secret sect, founded on criminal statutes', had attained a 'degree of perfection' in the 'art' of carrying out revolutions that made it impossible to predict when any government might be toppled. 'The revolution which has just broken out in Naples is therefore of a very particular character, one that is without doubt the most menacing for any government; since *a sect* conceived and prepared this catastrophe *in the shadows*; since it *made use* of a gangrened portion of the *armed forces* to consummate it.'

In the second part of the memorandum he prepared the ground for Austria's intervention, and tried to allay any fears that it might have ulterior motives. He argued that the status quo fixed in 1815 was perfect and immutable, but that the middle classes in every society, 'those classes always ready, at any time and in every place, to embrace a career of ambition which offers them a chance to reach for the rudder of government', had goaded the people to try to subvert it. This meant that all legitimate governments were under threat. 'If the revolution in Naples establishes itself, if the reign of the Carbonari is recognised as a legitimate institution, no government in Italy can rest easy.' He went on to explain the particular position in which Austria found itself as guarantor of the King of Naples's monarchical rights, which left it with no option but to declare its opposition to the new state of affairs.[32]

But he was determined that Austria, and Austria alone, should act. It needed the sanction of its allies, not their assistance. The active support of France, for instance, might lead to an increase in French influence in the peninsula. But while Metternich was wary of the intentions of France, even suspecting it of trying to use the crisis in order to take control of the duchy of Lucca, the French were alarmed that Austria might use it to enlarge its own holdings in Italy, and some of their informers were hinting that the Austrian chancellor was actually using the Carbonari to that purpose. They were also not beyond suspecting Britain of using it to turn Sicily into a British protectorate. And nobody could be sure of Russia's intentions: Alexander's longstanding interest in Italy was a source of universal apprehension.[33]

16

The Empire of Evil

The tsar was in Warsaw for the opening of the Polish Sejm. Ironically, given the anti-constitutional mania of the day, he was now presented by Novosiltsev with the final text of the constitution for Russia which he had asked him and Viazemsky to draw up two years before. He looked at it, put it aside, and never mentioned it again. Nobody beyond the tsar, Novosiltsev, Viazemsky and Novosiltsev's secretary was to know of the existence of the document for many decades.

In his opening address to the Sejm, Alexander had said that while a vigorous loyal opposition inspired by the desire to serve the public good was praiseworthy (which annoyed Metternich, who complained that it was an invitation for all the malcontents of Europe to start voicing their grievances), he warned that 'the spirit of evil is once more trying to extend its harmful empire; it is already hovering over Europe'. His worst fears were confirmed when the deputies rejected a number of measures put forward by the ministry and demonstrated an unwelcome spirit of independence. Grand Duke Constantine, commander-in-chief of the Polish army, was convinced that there were 'missionaries' being sent out from Paris to spread revolution, and warned his brother that trouble was brewing in Poland. It was in Warsaw that Alexander received news of a military conspiracy in Paris, which seemed to confirm his worst fears.[1]

While the French director general of police, Claude Mounier, was developing his concept of a *comité directeur*, a real conspiracy was afoot which, characteristically, entirely escaped the police's attention. Mounier had been given warning of it, but having recently received so many reports of impending plots from his various agents, he ignored it. The conspiracy centred on the Bazar Français, a shopping mall in the rue Cadet run mainly by former Napoleonic officers, whose comrades would frequently congregate there. Gradually a plot to overthrow the Bourbons in favour of Napoleon's son germinated. A former captain, Léon Nantil, and Colonel Charles Fabvier made contact with men of the various units stationed in Paris, but most of the senior officers they approached were either non-committal or sceptical, and some would only support the replacement of the Bourbons with either the duc d'Orléans or a republic. The plotters also made contact with soldiers in two regiments of infantry and one of cavalry, stationed at Cambrai, which they hoped would march on Douai, engage the support of three more regiments stationed there, then move on Valenciennes, raise the troops there, and reach the Belgian frontier, on the other side of which some 4,000 émigrés would supposedly have gathered. The combined force, which should by then have numbered at least 12,000, was to advance through all the garrison towns of the departments of the Nord, the Pas-de-Calais and the Somme on its way to Paris. A mutiny by troops in Paris was to provide a distraction.[2]

The coup was to have taken place on 10 August, but was put back by nine days. During that time several soldiers defected, and Marshal Marmont, commanding the troops in Paris, acted swiftly. Thirty-six officers and NCOs were arrested, and a further fifty-three questioned. This failed to produce any firm evidence on the alleged conspiracy. The police files reveal pathetic attempts to construct some by piecing together unconnected snippets of information. The fact that a sergeant major of the 1st Legion of the Seine Inférieure had deserted on 19 June, taking with him 'a sabre and a pair of braces', is deemed noteworthy.[3]

The court which judged the conspirators acted as though it had no wish to get to the bottom of the affair, and there is some evidence that highly placed persons might have been aware of the conspiracy, if not actually involved. Some of the conspirators on trial also appear to have been *agents provocateurs*. Three men were sentenced to death, and a handful received prison sentences. The atmosphere in the courtroom was relaxed, not to say light-hearted. Having interrogated all the officers of one regiment and received the same alibi, that they had been visiting their mistresses, the chief investigator, General Rapp, could not help complimenting the regiment on its '*galanterie*'.[4]

It was also in Warsaw that Alexander heard alarming news from Portugal. On 24 August a military insurrection had broken out in the city of Porto, and rapidly spread across the country. A bloodless affair, aimed principally against the British presence and at bringing the royal family back from Brazil, where they had taken refuge from Napoleon, it was controlled by liberal constitutionalists, and threatened nobody. But the fact that it had originated with the army classed it with those that had taken place in Spain and Naples.

News from Spain was not encouraging either. The moderates who had originally been in a majority in the Cortes were losing ground. The hostility of every other European government denied them credibility and encouraged extremists. In August Riego had appeared in Madrid, fêted by crowds, and demanded to be nominated dictator. Although he failed to get his way, he raised the temperature with his populist antics.

Alexander could not but be shaken by such news. His aide-de-camp Arsenii Andreevich Zakrevsky wrote to General Vassilchikov in St Petersburg urging him to keep a close watch on all 'hotheads', but common sense no less than his liberal instincts inclined the tsar to consider a new approach. In a long letter to Francis, he suggested that if they had agreed to negotiate with the Spanish revolutionaries, and thereby encouraged the moderates, there might never have been a revolution in Naples. 'Perhaps the only way of paralysing this terrible enemy is to take away from it the power it uses to stir the masses,' he mused. 'By anticipating the desires or the needs of the people, and by offering them in advance a part of that liberty which they seek to seize with violence.' He was beginning to think that the best way of resolving the crisis in Naples was to involve Louis XVIII, as head of the house of Bourbon and a constitutional monarch, and to replace the unacceptable 1812 constitution with one modelled on the French *Charte*.[5]

Metternich was horrified, and thought he could smell the influence of Alexander's adjunct minister for foreign affairs, Count Ioannis Capodistrias. Capodistrias was a Corfiote nobleman who had entered the service of Russia when the Ionian islands had been overrun by the French in 1807. He was on Alexander's staff from 1813 to 1815, when he was made secretary of state, and played a significant part in the negotiations at the Congress of Vienna. Gentz summed him up as 'a man of honour, of the utmost integrity, a true friend of all that is fine and good in human nature, a noble and disinterested soul, a lofty spirit – but, unfortunately, occasionally of poor judgement'. By that, he meant that he had liberal instincts and did not always agree with him and Metternich.[6]

Metternich was convinced that Capodistrias was Alexander's evil genius, and he had been trying to undermine his influence ever since the Congress of Vienna. He had Capodistrias tailed, and collected every shred of evidence that might suggest he was in league with subversive elements. He regularly intercepted Capodistrias's letters in the hope of discovering something that might link him to them, and was delighted when he found some correspondence with the apocryphal Duke of Brindisi. He promptly informed Alexander that his minister was in league with Italian revolutionaries. The Austrian chancellor's continuous insinuations were so obviously venomous that Capodistrias's colleague Nesselrode actually refused to show Alexander some of the information passed to him by Metternich. Metternich urged Dorothea Lieven to use her influence to have Capodistrias removed from office. (When a delighted Decazes, whose police regularly intercepted Metternich's most private correspondence, showed Capodistrias some of the letters in question while he was passing through Paris in 1819, the latter was so shocked he assumed it was a French forgery designed to make mischief between Russia and Austria.)[7]

Capodistrias shared his master's conflicting sympathies, being himself dedicated to Russia's state interests and at the same time sympathising with liberals and nationalists who were in conflict with them, and tried to help him square the circle between his liberal instincts and his fear of revolution. He also shared some of Alexander's spiritual and religious enthusiasms. He was a very personable young man, and it was not difficult for him to encourage or restrain, occasionally to influence; but it is doubtful that he could have manipulated anyone as unstable yet as headstrong as Alexander.

By the end of the summer of 1820, Alexander had drifted back to a more reactionary position. According to Capodistrias, the events of the past few months 'inclined the Emperor to see and to suspect in everything the action of a certain directing committee, which supposedly exerted its influence from Paris over the whole of Europe, with the aim of overthrowing established governments in order to introduce in their stead the methods and despotism of revolution'. He had become convinced that Paris was the 'active and permanent source' of the revolution, and claimed to have in his possession 'evidence whose authenticity it would be difficult to call into question', as he wrote to Richelieu from Warsaw on 3 September. The 'evidence', which he did not actually produce and which has so far eluded the searches of historians, 'proved' that 'the clubs of Paris' had been behind the Spanish revolt and 'the clubs of Madrid' behind that in Naples. This may have been the same 'evidence' which the British ambassador in St Petersburg, Sir Charles Bagot, was shown by his Portuguese colleague, from which it was clear that 'the object of [the secret societies in Spain] is to establish republics in every country in Europe; and that, for this end, they have agents in every quarter, but that the principal central societies are established at Paris, Venice, Genoa, Leghorn, in Prussia, and in Poland', as he reported to Castlereagh on 16 September.[8]

'Men formed in the school of populist despotism during the French Revolution and perfected in the art of upheaval by the despotism of Buonaparte are working with a deadly perseverance to repossess the power which was taken from them by the re-establishment of order in Europe,' Alexander asserted. 'The pernicious influence of these enemies of society has penetrated everywhere, and everywhere it is propagating with a fatal intensity.' Lebzeltern, whom Metternich had sent to Warsaw to meet the tsar, reported back that Alexander was ranting about English Radicals, Irish ribbon-men, Neapolitan Carbonari, Spanish rebels, and seeing subversion everywhere, even in Russia, all of it orchestrated from Paris. The by now familiar imagery of corrosion and gangrene was being enriched in the letters of the day with a more geographical lexicon of 'deluge', 'torrents', 'cascades', 'tidal waves', 'earthquakes', 'volcanoes' and 'eruptions'.[9]

The otherwise welcome conversion of Alexander to the ranks of the defenders of the status quo nevertheless posed problems for his allies. Metternich wanted to convene a congress of foreign ministers in Vienna which would sanction Austrian military action against the Neapolitan revolutionary government. He also hoped to persuade the other powers to set up a joint police 'information centre' on the model of the Mainz commission, a pan-European counter-revolutionary agency with extensive powers directed by envoys of each of the powers to act without referring back to their courts. But Alexander insisted on a congress of monarchs, one that would commit all the members of the Alliance, including France, to a joint strategy of uncompromising opposition to not only revolutionary upheaval but even constitutional change anywhere in Europe.

France, which did not wish to see Austria given a free hand in Italy, proposed making an offer to mediate. But it needed Britain's support for this initiative, and, keen as he was on resolving European problems through high-level meetings, Castlereagh had indicated that Britain would not be taking part in a congress that looked as though it would turn into a counter-revolutionary alliance. Liverpool's cabinet was in an uncomfortable position. The king's divorce proceedings had brought the monarchy into disrepute, and there was an ugly mood in the country. 'I cannot describe to you how grievously I suffer and have suffered, on account of the dangerous and deplorable situation in which our country, the king's government, and indeed all of us, have been so long placed,' Sidmouth wrote to a friend in September 1820 as the queen's trial was about to start, 'a situation out of which, I profess, I see no satisfactory, indeed no safe, deliverance.' The last thing the government could afford was to embark on a line of foreign policy that would cast it in the same image as the absolutist monarchies bent on repressing popular constitutionalist movements. As Castlereagh pointed out to Britain's ambassador in Vienna, Lord Charles Stewart, a British government could not make pledges which it might not be able to redeem, as it would always have to seek the approval of Parliament for any action. Britain could therefore not take part in the forthcoming congress.[10]

Pasquier and Richelieu were disappointed by his stance; they, and others, felt that Britain's failure to support vigorous action over Naples would give revolutionaries all over Europe the impression that it was on their side. Metternich and Alexander were desperate to have Britain's support, or at least participation, and they tried hard to persuade the British cabinet to change its stance. In London, Lieven, and particularly his countess, lobbied assiduously to persuade all and sundry that Britain should take part, arguing that by taking a strong line on Naples and Spain the government would teach the Radicals at home a lesson.[11]

At Alexander's insistence, the congress was held not in Vienna, whose social whirl he feared might be a distraction, but in the small town of Troppau (Opava) in what was then Austrian Silesia, situated conveniently close to the borders of Prussia and the Russian kingdom of Poland. It convened on 20 October. The only monarchs present were Alexander and Francis, as Frederick William of Prussia had delegated his son the crown prince. They were accompanied by their respective plenipotentiaries, Capodistrias, Metternich and Hardenberg. The Russian ambassador in Vienna, Count Golovkin, and the Prussian foreign minister Bernstorff were also present. The conference was to be presided over by Metternich, with Gentz acting as secretary. Britain was only present in the person of Lord Charles Stewart, in the capacity of an observer. France had taken a similar line, ordering its ambassadors at St Petersburg and Vienna, La Ferronnays and the marquis de Caraman, to attend in the same capacity. The Alliance had divided, with the two constitutional powers standing aside while the three absolutist monarchies clubbed together.[12]

'The little town of Troppau has an extraordinary number of beautiful and comfortable houses, so the members of the congress are comfortably accommodated,' Metternich wrote to his family on arrival. The 7,000 inhabitants had cleaned up the streets, painted their houses, and erected a triumphal arch and other decorations to welcome their august visitors. Their enthusiasm is not surprising, considering that some four hundred people descended on the town, and 1,200 more would join them for shorter periods, quite a fillip for the local economy. But incessant rain soon turned the streets into a sea of mud. The town council laid down planks to create walkways, but these posed problems of protocol as ministers, ambassadors, generals, dukes, princes and counts came face to face going in different directions and had to assess each other's credentials, political, diplomatic, military, aristocratic or otherwise, before one stepped aside into the mud to let the other pass.[13]

The morning after his arrival in Troppau, Alexander had a three-hour conference with Metternich. 'He greeted me like an old companion-in-arms,' Metternich noted with satisfaction. He was delighted with what he heard, and felt that Alexander had come to see reason. Metternich spent the following morning in conference with Capodistrias, who, to his surprise, was thoroughly 'reasonable'. He could not believe the change that had come over them. 'All this is too wonderful, and if I did not pinch myself, I would think I was dreaming.'[14]

Alexander collared Stewart in a last attempt to involve Britain, explaining to the sceptical ambassador that there was a vast conspiracy operating from Paris, in which Sir Robert Wilson was a prime mover. They should all unite to combat the 'fatal spirit' and 'settle upon some principle of common action and conduct with regard to it, so that military revolution and the machinations of occult sects and incendiaries should be arrested and paralysed'. This was precisely what Castlereagh and his cabinet opposed.[15]

At the opening session, on 23 October, Metternich set out his agenda. He wanted the powers to declare that there existed an illicit state of revolution in the kingdom of the Two Sicilies which they condemned, that they would never recognise any government brought into being by it, and that it was their duty to 'liberate' the king, which would entail military intervention to suppress the revolution. Bernstorff lent Prussia's support, but a few days later the Russian position was defined in a memorandum composed by Capodistrias. While not ruling out military intervention if it proved necessary, it suggested that this should be followed by a joint allied reconstruction of the kingdom of the Two Sicilies in a form acceptable to its people. The memorandum also proposed that the allied powers accept a doctrine of intervention against any state which changed its constitution in a manner which might pose a threat to others, or even present a bad example. Metternich was not pleased. 'The clouds here begin to lower, and the placid aspect of the first week has given way to dark and thoughtful countenances,' Stewart reported to Castlereagh on 3 November. The mood would only grow more sombre.[16]

On 9 November Alexander received news from St Petersburg that the Semeonovsky Guards regiment had mutinied. The Semeonovsky was Alexander's favourite. He had served in it himself, and had been its honorary colonel when still a grand duke. Most of his aides-de-camp were drawn from its ranks. It had fought with distinction throughout the war with Napoleon and had returned to Russia covered in glory. But it had also developed some of the dash and swagger of a victorious fighting unit, which displeased Alexander's brother Grand Duke Nicholas, who had appointed a new commander, Colonel Schwarz, to smarten it up.

On 16 October, Schwarz had ordered the flogging of some soldiers decorated with the St George Cross, the highest Russian military decoration, whose bearers were traditionally exempt from this humiliating punishment. The unit to which they belonged registered a complaint, which the outraged Schwarz treated as mutiny. He had the men locked up in the Peter and Paul fortress, whereupon the remainder of the regiment came out in sympathy. Since Schwarz had made himself scarce, they broke the windows of his quarters and took their complaint to the corps commander, General Vassilchikov. He ordered them to go and join their comrades in gaol, which they meekly did. Vassilchikov and the governor of St Petersburg, General Mikhail Andreevich Miloradovich, both wrote to Alexander, assuring him that everything was under control, that the episode was of little consequence, that it had been caused only by Schwarz's lack of judgement.[17]

Alexander would not accept this. He viewed the episode not just as mutiny, but as yet another piece of evidence confirming the existence of a devilishly efficient grand conspiracy. It was, as he put it in a letter to Princess Sophie Meshcherskaia, a manifestation of 'the *empire of evil* which is rapidly gaining ground through all the *occult means* used by the *Satanic spirit* which directs it'. There was no arguing with him. 'Nobody on earth can persuade me that these events were the work of the soldiers or that it was merely the consequence, as they say, of the cruel treatment meted out to them by Colonel Schwarz,' he wrote to General Arakcheev. 'I am convinced that other motives are hidden here ... I blame it on the secret societies.' As he told his youngest brother, the Grand Duke Michael, he had not the slightest doubt 'that a foreign influence had been exerted on the regiment'. He had the Spanish ambassador in St Petersburg put under strict surveillance and followed everywhere (the police duly noted his frequent and regular visits to the best whores in town). Alexander would later tell Wellington that 'the late Spanish minister in Russia laid out large sums of money to corrupt my officers and troops'. Grand Duke Nicholas was also convinced that the Spanish ambassador in St Petersburg had had a hand in the mutiny.[18]

Extrapolating from the available evidence and anticipating the motives of the 'satanic spirit', Alexander leapt to the conclusion that the mutiny had been ordered from Paris with the aim of forcing him to return to St Petersburg, which would have crippled the Troppau congress and thereby saved the revolutionaries in Naples. On 22 November he wrote to Vassilchikov that he would not return before he had finished the business in hand, 'Because all these radicals and Carbonari scattered all over Europe want to force me to leave the unfinished work; we have more than one document in hand to prove this; they are furious seeing the work we are occupied with here.'[19]

'We are on a crater, there is no doubt of it and I do not exaggerate anything, nothing short of the presence of the Emperor can save us,' a frantic Countess Nesselrode wrote to her husband from St Petersburg on 24 November, adding that the whole of St Petersburg society was terrified, and feared that the garrison might revolt in the absence of the emperor, who should look to his own country rather than sitting around at Troppau. 'Do not think I am exaggerating,' she went on; 'if I were to relate to you everything that is being said, of the spirit that reigns in this army, you would shudder.'[20]

That such a degree of paranoia should have taken hold in some quarters is astonishing, given that Vassilchikov and Miloradovich were so relaxed. The French *chargé* in St Petersburg, the comte de Gabriac, devoted two lengthy reports to the events, and dismissed them as being of no consequence. He pointed out that keeping large numbers of troops with nothing to do, albeit relentlessly exercised with punishing parades, which entailed severe penalties over footling derelictions, was a recipe for discontent, and blamed 'that fatal military mania which consumes the whole imperial family'. He was adamant that no societies, Masonic or otherwise, were involved. The young officers were obsessed with supposedly liberal principles, but in his view they had no idea what these really meant, and treated their soldiers and servants like dirt while talking high-minded nonsense about liberty and equality. Metternich's envoy in St Petersburg concurred, and assured him that the mutiny 'has nothing of the character of the military revolts of our day', adding that the officers were incompetent as well as cruel.[21]

Metternich did not see the mutiny as posing any threat to the rest of Europe, and welcomed the fact that it would make Alexander easier to deal with and less likely to insist on sending Russian troops anywhere. Underneath all the volcanic talk of revolutionary upheaval threatening the fabric of Christian society lurked straightforward *realpolitik*, and Austrian interests of state could not countenance a Russian presence in Italy any more than they could a French.[22]

But Alexander was not so easily deflected from his purpose. On 6 November, Capodistrias once again put forward a proposal to solve the Neapolitan problem peacefully, through the granting of a *Charte* along the lines of that of France. He argued that this would steal some of the fire of the revolutionaries around Europe. He was backed up by Nesselrode, who also suggested involving France. 'It was after all France that gave birth to the calamities which have desolated Europe over the past twenty-five years, and it may be from France that even now secrets and instructions which are orchestrating the victory of crime are coming,' he wrote on 9 November; 'it therefore behoves France to take first place in a system which such disasters call for when they threaten to once more smother the civilised world in blood and mourning.'[23]

Castlereagh was also being unhelpful, arguing that no association of states should arrogate the right to decide the internal affairs of others, and that 'no man can see without a certain feeling of fear the lot of every nation submitted to the decisions and to the will of such a tribunal'. He pointed out that the revolutions that had taken place in Spain and Naples did not threaten anyone, but that if they were to be attacked by the Alliance, they would become defensive, belligerent and possibly as aggressive and victorious as the French Revolution.[24]

Those in power in Naples were open to every reasonable proposal, as A'Court explained. 'The moderate constitutionalists (amongst whom we may class all the nobility, the superior officers of the army and most of those who compose the present administrations) are cast down and alarmed in the same proportion [as the radicals were encouraged], for their hopes rest upon the arrival of some firm and energetick declaration on the part of the greater powers, dictating those conditions which may, at the same time, offer a sufficient guarantee to Europe, and secure this country the enjoyment of a constitution in which property may be admitted as the basis of representation, and the Royal Prerogative be allowed that just latitude which is denied to it by the Constitution of the Cortes,' he reported from Naples. 'I have every reason to believe that the nation, generally speaking, is prepared for and would agree to accept conditions of this nature, if proposed by the united voice of the Congress.'[25]

Metternich was not going to be put off his determined course by the arguments of Castlereagh or anyone else. He had already made his own plans for the reconstruction of Ferdinand's kingdom following its occupation by Austrian troops. In the first place, there would be severe reprisals against all those involved in the revolution (in stark contrast to the revolutionaries' scrupulously lenient treatment of the tyrants they had toppled). The government, administration, army and police would be reorganised along lines set out in a long document which took as its point of departure that, due to 'the hot temper of the people and the vivacity of their hatreds', representative institutions were not suitable for Italians.[26]

All Metternich needed in order to proceed was the sanction of Russia and Prussia, which was not difficult to obtain. 'The Emperor of Russia is now convinced of the dangerous influence of the political or mystical secret societies,' Metternich wrote to Consalvi. 'His fiery imagination helps him overstep the limits imposed by strict reasoning. In consequence, he ascribes to them not only all that they are responsible for but also much that they are not.' The Prussian crown prince was also easily swayed.

On 19 November Metternich published a preliminary protocol signed by the plenipotentiaries of Russia, Prussia and Austria. It began by justifying their concern on the grounds that an allied court had been attacked, that all countries of Europe were threatened by 'the contagion of crime', and that they wished to 'ensure the happy and peaceful development of civilisation, the reign of justice and the law under the auspices of Christian morality'. The protocol stipulated that the three allies would not recognise any political changes achieved by illegal means, and would strive to bring things back to normal first by 'amicable approaches' and, if that failed, by 'coercive force'. They were determined to 'give back their liberty to the king and the nation' of the kingdom of the Two Sicilies with the support of an Austrian army of occupation. While it was only signed by the representatives of the three courts, it implied that Britain and France had approved it.[27]

Stewart and Caraman were incensed at not having been informed, and protested vigorously against the implication that their governments were parties to the document. Castlereagh was so angry that he insisted it be withdrawn, which it was. Metternich nevertheless pursued his course. He wrote to Ferdinand, inviting him to meet the three monarchs and their ministers in order to discuss the future of his kingdom, and to appeal to them for assistance.

Still looking for a peaceful solution, Alexander suggested they ask the pope to act as mediator with the government in Naples. Metternich went along with the tsar's proposal, and sent Lebzeltern off to Rome bearing letters from himself to Consalvi and from Francis to the pope. Instead of asking the pope to mediate, Lebzeltern was to negotiate the passage of Austrian troops through his dominions and persuade him to join in the crusade against the 'sacrilegious' Neapolitan regime. Neither Consalvi nor the pope wanted to get involved, fearing it might expose them to attack from Naples, with which the Papal States shared a long frontier.[28]

While they awaited Ferdinand's answer to their invitation, Metternich and Gentz took up the idea put forward by Alexander at

Aix and got down to work on the formulation of a universal principle of intervention, to be embodied by an Act of Guarantee. The idea was to insure all existing governments with a guarantee of military assistance. Any change in any state – even if introduced by its ruler – which might, if only by example, incite the peoples of other states to subversion would trigger automatic military intervention by the Alliance. Although these principles were never translated into a formal Act, they reveal the width and depth of the gap that had opened between the three courts and the British cabinet. Metternich would have liked to have had the support of Castlereagh, but when it came to what he saw as Austrian reasons of state, he was prepared to forge ahead on his own.

It was nevertheless essential for the sake of appearances before the outside world to keep up the pretence that the Alliance was still intact. Gentz affected to blame the apparent discordance on what he described as the less than constructive part being played by the British observer. 'A year ago, Lord Stewart married one of the richest heiresses of the Three Kingdoms,' Gentz commented on 31 December 1820. 'This woman, whom he loves to distraction, has so far enslaved him that he hardly dares come to Troppau. Receiving every day more imperious summonses to return to Vienna, he has never stayed at Troppau for more than five or six days, and for the greater part of the month of December he has been absent.' Stewart had concluded that there was little point in his hanging around, since, as he put it to Castlereagh, 'policy here was framing more upon alarm of future visionary evils, aided by the spectre of Buonaparte raised into *reality by a breath*'; and anyway, conditions in Troppau were hardly enticing.[29]

The mud precluded going for walks or riding, it grew extremely cold with the onset of winter, and there were no distractions. 'We are all bored to death,' wrote Alexander's aide-de-camp Prince Volkonsky. Most of the important figures would gather in the evenings at Metternich's lodgings. 'It is the most agreeable moment of the day, particularly when he leads the conversation himself,' La Ferronnays wrote to his wife on 20 December. 'He really does have all the wit he is credited with, he speaks well, tells a story beautifully and knows how to add interest to details which might seem the least likely to have any.'[30]

The less exalted did what they could for entertainment. One of the Russians in Alexander's suite held a ball, decorating his quarters with silver paper and making lemonade for the ladies out of some crystalline concoction he obtained from a local chemist. They danced until two in the morning and, according to another of Alexander's aides-de-camp, 'the ball was extremely merry, but towards the end, there was an awful smell of sweat, because the local ladies are not very clean and apparently wash very little.'[31]

Having issued their invitation to Ferdinand, all the monarchs and their ministers could do was wait. Metternich complained that his *chargé d'affaires* in Naples and the envoys of the other courts could supply them with no information as to whether Ferdinand would come or not. 'Without a little Jew who is there because he is everywhere, we would know absolutely nothing,' he wrote to his family on 23 December. 'From the little that we can learn from this Jew, we assume the king will come.' He had suggested that they all adjourn to the greater comforts of Vienna, but Alexander would not hear of it, as it would involve him in the court and social life of the capital. He spent his free time with his sister Maria and his younger brother Nicholas. 'I am living in complete isolation,' he wrote to Aleksandr Galitzine in December. 'My sister is my only distraction at mealtimes or when we have an opportunity to go out and take the air together.' Christmas was therefore spent in Troppau, without much in the way of celebration. Metternich did receive one present, in the shape of the news that Ferdinand had accepted their invitation.[32]

In the end, the Emperor Francis could stand it no longer and left for Vienna, precipitating a general move there. The congress was adjourned, to reconvene in January at Laibach (Ljubljana), which was closer to Italy and, it was hoped, a little warmer. Everyone was relieved to leave Troppau except for Alexander, whose forebodings about Vienna proved prophetic when he had a coach accident as he was driving into the city which nearly proved fatal.[33]

17

Synagogues of Satan

King Ferdinand of the Two Sicilies reached Laibach on 8 January 1821. Metternich had arrived four days earlier and, as usual, provided himself with 'a pleasant office, a good bedroom and an enfilade of drawing rooms', as he informed Dorothea Lieven. The Emperor Francis arrived two days later, and the King of Prussia two days after that, followed by Tsar Alexander. Lord Charles Stewart was to act as Britain's observer, and the comte de Blacas represented France in a similarly passive role. Alexander had wanted to invite Ferdinand VII of Spain in order to reinforce his case for military intervention there, but Metternich, who saw no Austrian interests at stake in the Iberian peninsula, managed to persuade him that it would impede the other business of the congress. He had also put off a request for participation from King John of Portugal, by suggesting that he turn to his British ally for support.[1]

The congress, which opened on 11 January, was no more than window-dressing. Ferdinand was to publicly disown his adherence to the revolution and the oaths he had sworn to stand by the constitution, to denounce everything that had taken place in Naples the previous summer, and to appeal for help to his brother monarchs. But dealing with Ferdinand was not easy, as Gentz pointed out. 'He has never had the slightest taste for work, and he has so far lost the habit of it that it is difficult to make him read a despatch if it is more than a page long. Although he is physically extremely well preserved, age and misfortune have contributed to dulling his spirit, and since he remarried three years ago Madame Parthana, who now bears the title of Duchess of Floridia (and who is expected here at any moment), he has lapsed into complete idleness.'[2]

The problem was resolved by appointing as Ferdinand's plenipotentiary his ambassador to Vienna, Prince Alvaro Ruffo, a devoted admirer of Metternich. Metternich and Gentz provided Ruffo with the texts of the letters the king was to send to his son the vicar general and the government in Naples, along with that of his appeal to the allies. Gentz was then to compose a manifesto from the three allied courts to the effect that Austria was, with the full support of its allies, sending an army into the kingdom of the Two Sicilies to assist its king in recovering his throne. The document, which was made public before the representatives of either of those powers had had sight of it, slyly implied that Austria, Russia and Prussia had the approval of Britain and France.

Stewart protested, and Castlereagh was so indignant that on 19 January he issued a public circular in which he distanced Britain from the other powers, stressing that while Austria did, through its treaty with the King of the Two Sicilies, have a right to intervene, the Alliance did not. The circular recalled that Britain had already, in 1815, in 1818 and in 1820, protested against the tendency of the Alliance to act as the policeman of Europe. This caused dismay at Laibach. 'England is dead so far as the Continent is concerned,' Metternich lamented.[3]

Castlereagh's circular may have delighted liberals in Italy and elsewhere, but it did not shield Liverpool's ministry from strong criticism in the British press and attack in Parliament for associating itself with what were seen as the despotic actions of Austria and Russia. The reports of the debates frightened Gentz 'more than all the revolutions in Italy', and he concluded that Britain had 'adhered to an entirely different political and moral order'. 'Revolution must be fought with flesh and blood,' he had come to believe. 'Moral weapons are manifestly powerless ... With cannons and Cossacks on the one side, and firebrands and volunteers on the other, both systems must in the end fight a life-and-death struggle, and to him who remains standing belongs the world.' Those who disagreed were 'dogs'. He had come a long way since his euphoric praise for the French Revolution in 1789. Although Castlereagh vigorously defended in the House of Commons Austria's right to intervene in Naples, there was no disguising the discord at the heart of the Alliance. Richelieu believed Metternich was making a mistake, and that his policy would lead, sooner or later, to a 'terrible reaction' which would undermine Austria's already weakening influence in Italy. He also warned that the allies' declarations and protocols, which were intended to demonstrate their unity, by lumping together everything they did not like had the unwanted effect of creating the illusion of unity among very disparate and disunited enemies. Doctrinaire statements produced doctrinaire reactions and forced the lukewarm into extreme positions, he warned.[4]

On 6 February an Austrian army of 60,000 crossed the river Po to enter the Papal States and begin its march on Naples, 'in peaceful and amicable intent'. Metternich then settled down to dictate to Ruffo his blueprint for the reorganisation of the government of Naples. On 20 February Ruffo duly presented these proposals to the allied sovereigns, who graciously approved them. Metternich asked the envoys of the other states of Italy, whom he had invited to Laibach for the purpose, to consider adopting them as well. He also lectured them on the desirability of establishing a 'centre of information' at Milan, which would serve the same purpose for Italy as the commission in Mainz did for Germany, and provide the basis for 'moral action' against the forces of the Parisian *comité directeur*.[5]

The congress closed on 25 February, with the resolution to meet again in eighteen months, in September 1822, in order to review the situation in Italy and deal with any other matters demanding attention. Alexander made one last attempt to raise the question of Spain, where the situation had deteriorated further and the prospect of civil war loomed. But Richelieu ruled out French intervention, believing it would do for Louis XVIII what it had done for Napoleon, and nobody wanted to see Russian troops march across Europe.[6]

With the Austrian army on the march towards Naples, the monarchs stayed on at Laibach in case of unexpected developments. There was nothing for them to do. Alexander's aide-de-camp Zakrevsky took advantage of an improvement in the weather to go hunting, and bagged two mountain goats, but the distraction was fleeting. 'The boredom is so dreadful that in the evenings everyone falls into despair,' he wrote to a friend. Metternich held a ball, but as there was only one lady present it was not much of a success, and with the weather continuing cold there was nothing to allay the tedium.[7]

This was dispelled by the arrival from Paris of the sensational news that there had been an explosion in the Tuileries. As the news travelled, it was embellished to include multiple royal casualties and ascribed variously to the Illuminati and the *comité directeur*. In effect, the 'bomb', hidden behind a laundry basket on a servants' staircase and detonated at four o'clock on the afternoon of 27 January, had been little more than a firework, almost certainly planted by some Ultras. Richelieu did what he could to reassure all and sundry that there was nothing to worry about, but he could not shake the general conviction that it had been an attempt to bring down the monarchy. 'That the ramifications of this sect are spreading and consolidating every day is demonstrated by only too real evidence,' Nesselrode wrote to Richelieu, enclosing a note intercepted by the police in St Petersburg which he believed had been sent by one of the conspirators to an associate in Russia, and urging him to heighten his vigilance. In reply, Richelieu remarked that the police were generally a blunt tool. Even Napoleon's supposedly efficient police had failed to prevent assassination attempts, he reminded Nesselrode, and there had been no fewer than thirteen against the most popular of French monarchs, Henri IV. He assured Nesselrode that 'neither the life of the king nor that of any other member of the royal family had been at any risk from this explosion'. That reassured neither Nesselrode nor Alexander, who was in apocalyptic mood.[8]

'Are we not bound by our duty as Christians to struggle against this enemy and its infernal works with all our strength and by every means that Divine providence has placed in our hands?' the tsar wrote to Aleksandr Galitzine from Laibach on 15 February. After alluding liberally to Judith and Holofernes, Nebuchadnezzar and other biblical monsters, he went on: 'For, make no mistake about it, there is a general conspiracy of all these societies: they communicate and co-ordinate, I have in my possession certain proof of this.' He argued that since the Christian faith had become 'the fundamental basis of the principles' which the Alliance stood by, 'all these sects, which are anti-Christian and which are founded on the principle of the so-called philosophy of Voltaire and others similar, have vowed the most determined vengeance on all governments. We have seen attempts in France, in England, in Prussia, while in Spain, Naples and Portugal they have already succeeded in overthrowing governments. Their motto is to kill the Inf ... [*l'Infame*: Voltaire's shorthand for the Catholic Church] I do not even dare to write out this horrible blasphemy ...' The letter, which was written intermittently over the space of a week, reveals the extent of the paranoia gripping Alexander, who was feeling let down and betrayed, believing that 'hell is let loose against us', and quoting liberally from St Paul and the Book of Revelations. Only a couple of weeks later news would reach Laibach that confirmed him not just in his conviction of the existence of the international conspiracy, but of its devilish efficiency and perfidy.[9]

On 10 March came tidings of the first successes achieved by the Austrian army. As soon as it had become known in Naples that it was on the march, the heroics died down, people began to shed their uniforms and make excuses. General Pepe marched out to meet the advancing Austrians with an hourly dwindling army which was duly routed at Rieti on 7 March. But on the morning of 14 March Metternich was woken by a courier with the news that revolution had broken out in Piedmont. He immediately went into conference with Francis and Alexander, and they agreed that the *comité directeur* must have ordered the Piedmontese rebels to create a diversion in the rear of the

Austrian army marching on Naples. It was also clear to them that with two kingdoms on either side of France in a state of revolution, there were ideal conditions for one to break out in Paris – where the news from Turin had caused panic: 'The bourse was obstructed with the carriages of the nobility of the court who were coming in person to sell their government stocks at any price,' noted Richelieu.[10]

What had actually happened in Piedmont was a good deal less dramatic than was reported. A group of noblemen and artists in Turin, dissatisfied with the reactionary regime of the ageing King Victor Emmanuel I, wanted to force him to abdicate in favour of the heir to the throne, his brother's son, the twenty-two-year-old Charles Albert, Prince of Carignano, in the belief that he held similar views to theirs. These were a muddle of poetic visions of a united Italy and Romantic notions of 'liberty', shared by a number of bored and disgruntled army officers. While the nobles in Turin worked on Charles Albert, on the night of 9 March a group of officers raised the garrison of nearby Alessandria, hoisted the green, white and red tricolour Napoleon had designed for Italy back in the 1790s, and proclaimed the Spanish constitution of 1812. This had become a shibboleth standing for ill-defined freedoms in the eyes of politically illiterate liberals and for equally ill-defined subversion in those of conservatives. On 12 March the garrison of Turin came out in solidarity with their comrades in Alessandria, not only demanding the adoption of the constitution but also a declaration of war on Austria. Taken aback, the king abdicated in favour of his brother, Charles Felix. As the latter was out of the country, his son Charles Albert took on the role of regent and adopted the constitution.

After considering the options, Metternich, Alexander and Francis decided that the Austrian troops marching on Naples should carry on, while another force of 60,000 Austrians would be assembled to strike at Piedmont from Lombardy, to be joined if necessary by 90,000 Russians. 'Piedmont has just been revolutionised after the model of Spain, Naples and Portugal, and by the same *comité directeur* of Paris which produced all the earlier upheavals ...' Alexander wrote to Galitzine. 'I now understand why the Lord has kept me here until this moment!' It was thanks to the Almighty that he was still with his allies and able to put in hand the necessary measures. It was at times like these that congresses of monarchs were invaluable, he argued. 'At this moment we are fighting the kingdom of Satan; no ambassador can suffice: only those whom the Lord had placed at the head of Nations can, *if He so wills*, persevere in this struggle and not bow to this satanic power, growing ever greater and shedding its mask more and more.' As he was writing these lines, the mask in this imagined scenario slipped off entirely.[11]

Back in 1814 a group of Greek residents of Odessa had founded an association, the *Philiki Hetairia*, which brought together like-minded compatriots scattered around Europe. It had a Masonic structure and a hazy goal of bringing about the 'purification' of the 'Greek nation', and, in the long term, the liberation of Greece from Turkish rule. It had fewer than a thousand members, most of them intellectuals or merchants operating from far-flung emporiums. Some of them had, on a number of occasions, approached Capodistrias and other Greeks in Russian service with a view to enlisting the support of Alexander in their cause. Capodistrias had consistently brushed them off; however much the tsar would have liked to lead a crusade for the liberation of his co-religionists, and expand his empire southwards – he and his brother had not been named Alexander and Constantine for nothing – he realised that it would have serious diplomatic consequences. He could not afford to be seen to promote any subversive cause against a recognised power, even the Porte.

In 1820 the *Hetairia* elected a new president in the person of Count Alexandros Ypsilantis, a former Russian officer and aide-de-camp to Alexander. After leaving Russian service he began to lay plans for a war for the liberation of Greece, assuming that once it had started the tsar would have no option but to come to the aid of the Greeks. That same year, Ali Pasha, the Turkish governor of the Greek province of Janina, hitherto a loyal vassal of the sultan, announced that he was a friend of the Greeks, joined the *Hetairia*, and declared his independence from Turkey. A Turkish army was despatched to bring him back to heel, and while it was occupied with this task Ypsilantis struck. On 6 March 1821 he led a motley force of some 4,500 expatriate Greeks into Turkish territory and called on his compatriots to rise up against their oppressors. This rag-tag army was effortlessly dispersed by the Turks, and Ypsilantis fled for the shelter of Austrian territory, where he hoped to find asylum; instead, he encountered the Austrian police and began a seven-year spell in gaol.

The tsar took the news personally, convinced as he was that the *comité directeur* in Paris had engineered the whole thing, in the knowledge that his every instinct would drive him to support the Greek cause, and thereby betray his allies and his principles. He admitted to his brother Constantine that 'never before had a trap been set for him with more cunning, more skill and more perfidy'. It had been done, as he told the new British ambassador in St Petersburg Sir Charles Bagot, 'with the sole object of distracting the attention of Russia from the affairs of the rest of Europe, and of placing him, as they unquestionably had done, in a very difficult position'. That it had been the work of the *comité directeur* was doubted by nobody. Even Castlereagh was convinced. '[The Greeks] form a branch of that organised spirit of insurrection which is systematically propagating itself throughout Europe,' he wrote to Bagot, 'and which explodes wherever the hand of the governing Power from whatever cause is enfeebled.'[12]

There could, in Alexander's view, 'be no doubt that the impulse for this insurrectionary movement was given by that same *comité central directeur* of Paris, in the hope of making a diversion in favour of Naples and preventing us from destroying one of those synagogues of Satan, established solely in order to defend and propagate his anti-Christian doctrine'. At moments such as these, they must all unite in defence of 'the Faith of Our Saviour'. Greece was but a distraction. 'The revolutionary *comité central* resides in Paris,' he explained. 'After having ignited all the fires it could outside the country, it is more than probable that it will try to set alight France itself, and in that way to link up with the revolutionaries of Spain and those of Piedmont.' He was in the process of reading the Book of Job, and in the first four chapters found 'an analogy with my own personal situation'.[13]

On 20 March an armistice was signed between the Austrian and Neapolitan commanders. 'The world is on the eve of its salvation or at the threshold of the abyss which will engulf it,' Metternich wrote to Austria's finance minister Count Stadion, who had been complaining about the cost of his military intervention. A week later he received the news that his troops had made their triumphal entry into Naples, cheered as warmly as the Carbonari had been. 'The hour of resurrection has struck!' he exclaimed to one French diplomat. To his wife, he wrote that 'the whole business will blow away like smoke, because it was, in fact, nothing but smoke'.[14]

On 12 April 1821 Francis once again wrote to the pope, asking him to excommunicate the Carbonari, or at least to issue a declaration of support, arguing that temporal power on its own could not accomplish the 'salutary work', and that 'the source of the evil is in the domain of morality and religion'. Cardinal Consalvi was not to be rushed. The Carbonari in the Papal States had not risen in support of their Neapolitan good cousins or tried to prevent the Austrian troops from marching on Naples. But they were numerous enough to cause serious trouble, and since they made frequent protestations of support for the Church and the Catholic faith, there were no grounds for excommunicating them.[15]

By the beginning of April Metternich had so far regained his composure as to declare that 'revolutions are rather out of date ... I am not saying that there will be no more revolutions, but they will be without *substance*'. The latest one, in Piedmont, certainly appeared to have borne this out. No sooner had the hapless Prince of Carignano accepted the constitution than his father repudiated it. He found himself in a difficult position: moderates bickered with radicals in his entourage as he himself wavered. The Russian ambassador in Turin warned him of dire consequences if he did not quickly bow to the inevitable. The confused prince laid down his regency and left. The remaining rebels were defeated by loyal Piedmontese troops and Austrians at Novara on 18 April.[16]

On his return from Laibach at the end of May, Francis nominated Metternich chancellor, a post he had effectively been filling since 1809. This set the seal on what had, for Metternich, been a triumph. He had stamped out liberalism in the two largest Italian states, and cowed the others with his demonstration of military power. On 13 September 1821 the pope at last issued, in his breve *Ecclesiam a Jesu Christo*, the desired condemnation of the Carbonari, for 'giving everyone the licence to create at will his own religion according to his own convictions', because they 'parody sacred rituals by their sacrilegious ceremonies', and finally because 'they plot to ruin the Apostolic See against which … they have a special hatred'. Having obtained this, Metternich put pressure on all the other Italian states to pass legislation outlawing members of the sect. By November 1821 he was boasting that he had destroyed the Carbonari. Perhaps most important, he had managed to 'turn the Emperor Alexander away from the territory of liberalism', as he put it to Esterházy.[17]

In Metternich's view, it was time to take stock and prepare for the future. 'It has been revealed that a vast and dangerous conspiracy has since 1814 acquired enough force and means of action to have taken control of a great many branches of the administration in many countries,' he summed up. 'I saw the revolution, with its inevitable consequences, disorder, anarchy and death, where many others only saw enlightenment grappling with prejudice.' The revolution had been able to grow because people had failed to heed his warnings. 'The clear and precise goal of the seditious elements is *one and uniform*. It is that of the *overthrow* of all legally existing things … The principle with which the monarchs must oppose this plan of universal destruction is that of the *conservation of all legally existing things*. The only way of achieving this is that of *no innovation* … It has been proved that the seditious elements of all countries and of all hues have established a centre of information and of action … *To this centre of information*, we must oppose another.'[18]

People were still not listening to him. His proposal to create a pan-European intelligence-gathering and police centre was brushed aside even by Alexander. Richelieu even poured cold water on the theory of a *comité directeur* in Paris. 'It is perhaps more convenient to attribute to an invisible power whose lever is in France and whose effects can be felt everywhere catastrophes whose real cause could more simply be found in the weakness and incompetence of those governments which a mere breath has been enough to overthrow,' he wrote to Capodistrias on 9 May. Particularly disappointing for Metternich was the fact that he could no longer count on the support of Britain and France. He was beginning to write off Britain as an ally, baffled as he increasingly was by its seeming inability to maintain the kind of decorous 'calm' that was the mainstay of his own domestic policy. The country was now being convulsed with a further bout of trouble caused by Queen Caroline, this time from beyond the grave.[19]

Despite her extraordinary popularity in the previous year, her attempt to force admission to the coronation of her husband as George IV on 19 July 1821 ended in humiliating failure, and she was jeered as she drove away by the same crowds that had cheered her twelve months before. But following her unexpected death a few weeks later, they swung back to her side in the most spectacular way. Her funeral on 14 August 1821 became the focus for resentment against the government, just as the divorce proceedings had in the previous year. She had died in Hammersmith and had expressed the wish to be buried in Brunswick. As the authorities considered it dangerous to allow the funeral cortège to pass through central London on its way to embarkation at Harwich, a circuitous route was devised in secret. This inflamed those who had come out to pay their final respects or just watch, to such an extent that they confronted the considerable numbers of troops deployed and obliged the procession to pass through the centre of the city. The resulting battle between the crowd and the Guards cost a number of lives.[20]

In October, when George IV visited Hanover, accompanied by Castlereagh, Metternich went there to greet the king and took the opportunity to confer with the British foreign secretary. They were able to reaffirm their support for each other and to agree on common ground, principally on the need to prevent Alexander from marching his armies into Spain. Another opportunity provided by the trip to Hanover was that of seeing Dorothea Lieven, whose husband had accompanied the king. It was therefore as a happy man that Metternich contemplated the world in the autumn of 1821.

The tsar was in a very different frame of mind. He had gone to Troppau and Laibach meaning to redefine the Alliance, by laying down principles on the right of intervention in the internal affairs of other countries, and to bring peace to Spain by force of arms and to Naples by constitutional means. This would have extended Russia's influence in the three Bourbon monarchies and outmanoeuvred Austria. In the event, it was he who had been outmanoeuvred. His constitutional schemes had been ignored, and Spain had been side-stepped. He had been obliged to repress all his instincts over the Greek rising, but had not reaped any benefit from it.

The issue loomed large when he returned to Russia. Although Ypsilantis's foolhardy enterprise had been defeated by Turkish forces, a popular rising had broken out in the Morea, initiating a protracted war of unspeakable savagery on both sides. Russian society was traditionally Turkophobe, the Russians were Orthodox Christians like the Greeks, the Russian diplomatic and military services were liberally staffed with Greeks, and the army had built its reputation over the past half-century on a series of wars against the Porte. The stories filtering out of Greece of Turkish atrocities being carried out against their Orthodox Christian brothers were causing outrage in Russia, and people were seething with impatience to support their co-religionists and punish the Turks. The army, bored by inaction, was keen to show its mettle.

People could not understand why the tsar refused to do the obvious thing and go to the aid of the Greeks. But Alexander felt powerless. 'If we answer the Turks with war, the *comité directeur* in Paris will have triumphed,' he explained to Capodistrias one evening at Tsarskoe

Selo that August. He assured the French ambassador that he had firm evidence that Ypsilantis had been put up to it by the *comité directeur*, which had forced him to act in order to assist the Italian revolutionaries. The aim had been not only to place Alexander in the position of having to betray his principles, but also to divide Russia and Austria, thereby breaking up the Alliance. Any Russian military action against the Turks would have to take place in the Danubian principalities of Moldavia and Wallachia, along the south-eastern border of the Austrian empire, in an area of such strategic sensitivity that any Russian move there threatened Austria.[21]

Alexander wrote to Metternich and Castlereagh, and appealed to Francis and George IV in an attempt to find a solution. He drew parallels between Austria's need to intervene in Naples and Piedmont and the necessity of Russian action on behalf of the Greeks. Metternich was not having it, not only because the Greek insurgents were revolutionaries, and one could not support one kind of revolutionary while crushing others. Military intervention by Russia would inevitably lead to Russian territorial gains in an area of vital interest to Austria. Britain did not wish to see any expansion of Russia or its influence in that area, both because it lay in its interests to protect the Porte and because it brought one step closer a Russian foothold in the Aegean, which would lead to a naval presence in the Mediterranean. France was traditionally an ally of the Porte, and did not contemplate the possibility of a Russian navy operating off its southern shores with any greater relish than did Britain. Prussia remained passive, as Bernstorff did not wish to see it embroiled in any new international complications.[22]

Much to the embarrassment of the various governments, the Greek cause had caught the imagination of the public, and people all over the Continent were clamouring on behalf of the Greek rebels, who were represented, in paint and in print, as the ultimate Romantic freedom-fighters, wild but worthy descendants of the ancient Greeks. The rising elicited almost fanatical declarations of support from poets, intellectuals, artists and dreamers of every class and both sexes of every country in Europe, nowhere more than in its German heartland. As it did not challenge any aspect of the social structure in any of them, it also attracted the support of the most conservative elements of the aristocracy and the bourgeoisie.

Never slow to spot an opportunity, Metternich accused Capodistrias and Russian diplomats all over Europe of stoking up this enthusiasm and disseminating pro-Greek propaganda. Capodistrias denied these charges, but he was tainted by association, and soon found himself in an impossible situation. In order to avoid giving the impression that he was encouraging the Greeks in any way, the tsar distanced himself from his minister, who eventually had no option but to ask for extended leave, supposedly to take the waters in Germany. He then retired to Switzerland, while formally retaining his title in the Russian service, until 1827 (when he would be elected president of the newly founded Greek Republic, only to be assassinated by a compatriot in 1831). Metternich was delighted to have seen off a man he had all along regarded as a thorn in his side.

Metternich might have triumphed, but by forcing his own will upon it he had succeeded in splitting the Alliance. The two constitutional monarchies of Britain and France could not march in step with the three absolutist ones along the course he had mapped for them. He had also fatally undermined the Alliance's moral credibility. The use of military force against the reasonable aspirations of the more enlightened sections of the Neapolitan nobility and middle class had made it clear to all but the most bigoted that it was not defending civilisation from barbarism. To many, the opposite seemed to be true.

'The intellectual forces of nations are striving for the perfection of the social order,' wrote baron Bignon, an experienced French diplomat and official, and a deputy of the French Chamber since 1817. 'In opposition to this tendency, the cabinets have deployed all the means at their disposal, both intellectual and material, to halt this march of the nations, and even to make them turn back.' He pointed out that the Holy Alliance now stood in the imagination of most thinking Europeans for an unholy cartel devoted to combating everything that frightened it or threatened its privileges. 'Born of barbarism, and only to serve it, absolute power is now the master and judge of institutions intended for enlightened nations.'[23]

18

Comité Directeur

'Here, there is plenty of talking, shouting and intrigues, but actually everything is very calm,' the French prime minister Richelieu wrote to a friend in June 1821. 'Confidence is growing ... a multitude of bridges are being built, canals dug, insurance companies founded, savings banks established, along with other institutions which prove that the spirit of association has made rapid progress. Everywhere industry is in motion and commotion, factories are prospering as never before, the causes of which I admit I cannot explain.' The report of the police commissioner for the notoriously unruly manufacturing centre of Lyon in March of the same year confirms Richelieu's assessment. 'All is quiet, all is peaceful,' it read; 'the only source of agitation is the imagination.'[1]

News of the death of Napoleon, on 5 May, caused surprisingly little stir. Many of his worshippers simply refused to believe it and went on dreaming of a third coming. Others transferred their political hopes to his son, who was with his grandfather in Vienna. But most active Bonapartists realised that their cause was dead, and transferred their support to the mainstream liberal opposition, which consisted of Benjamin Constant, the marquis de Lafayette, the liberal deputies Marc-René Voyer d'Argenson and Jacques-Antoine Manuel, the lawyer Joseph Merilhou, the banker and deputy Jacques Lafitte and a handful of generals. Many were members of a Masonic lodge, *Les*

Amis de la Verité, which brought together many students of the *grandes écoles*.[2]

The director general of police, Claude Mounier, did not drop his guard. 'Various symptoms lead us to believe that the revolutionary faction is preparing something,' he noted on 22 January that year. 'Perfect unity and extremely active communications exist among the liberals of Paris, Madrid, Naples, Lisbon, Turin, and London.' General Donnadieu, who knew a thing or two about provocation and exaggeration, ridiculed this and publicly accused the police of fomenting disturbances through *agents provocateurs*. The contemporary historian and politician François Guizot was convinced that whatever conspiracies did exist arose from a symbiosis of a disordered society and incompetent government. 'Plots become necessary to it, both in order to legitimise its fears, and to provide it, through punishment, with the strength which its incompetence has forfeited.' According to him, whenever a conspiracy was needed, it could be provided 'by the self-interested ardour of unworthy agents'. In this case, however, Mounier seems to have been on to something.

Following the failure of the Bazar Français plot of August 1820, those of its leaders who were able to fled the country, many seeking sanctuary in revolutionary Naples. In the spring of 1821 one of these, Pierre Dugied, returned to France and began setting up cells based on the Carbonarist model of *vèndite* he had seen in Naples, which he called '*ventes*'. The first, established in Paris in May 1821, brought together a large number of students and shopkeepers, along with Lafayette and a handful of deputies.[3]

The example was followed by disaffected groups all over the country; as Carbonarism had no principles and no specific programme, it could happily accommodate Bonapartists, Orléanists, liberals, revolutionaries, bored soldiers, and all those nursing a grudge, against wealth and privilege, a political faction, the clergy, the police or nothing in particular. In the army, where it made rapid inroads, particularly among non-commissioned officers, Carbonarism was little more than a club for men nostalgic for the days of Napoleonic glory. 'To be honest, the revolutionary party was a confused assemblage of patriots of every hue and of malcontents,' recalled Francisque de Corcelle, the lawyer son of a liberal deputy. People like him were more interested in orderly progress, but this was impeded by the repressive measures introduced under the second Richelieu government. 'From then on, a large part of the thinkers and politicians, despairing of achieving anything through legal means, began playing at revolution.' In the course of 1821 Carbonarist *ventes* fanned out all over France, with possibly as many as 50,000 members. Whether many of them were active is doubtful, and few had any specific aims. According to Alexandre Dumas *père*, who knew some of them, Lafayette and his son George, Voyer d'Argenson, Jacques Charles Dupont de l'Eure, Claude Tirguy de Corcelle, Jacques Koechlin, Merilhou and others made up a '*comité directeur*', and this is confirmed by the socialist historian and politician Louis Blanc. Although he was only ten years old at the time, one must credit him with insight and access to extensive first-hand sources. But if they did constitute a committee, it signally failed to direct anything.[4]

The only conspiracy which has been tangibly linked with this group took place late in 1821. Its aim was to raise the garrison of the fortress of Belfort in eastern France, to coincide with revolts by that of Marseille and the cavalry school at Saumur. The risings were to take place on the night of 29–30 December, but the Saumur conspiracy was betrayed a few days before, and the rising at Belfort was put back to 1 January 1822. The conspirators there were slow to act, inadvertently raised the alarm, and displayed remarkable incompetence. They were rounded up without much trouble within a couple of hours. Their associates in Marseille did not even get that far, and their supposed directors in Paris washed their hands of them. A repeat attempt at Saumur in February 1822 lasted longer and even achieved some success, but its head, General Berton, wasted time on parleys and lunch, letting the initiative slip from his hands, and was eventually caught by an *agent provocateur* and executed. The captured conspirators of Belfort were used as bait in a provocation which netted another officer, Lieutenant Colonel Caron. In September, four sergeants of the 45th Infantry Regiment stationed at La Rochelle staged another ill-starred mutiny, and paid for it with their lives.[5]

None of these conspiracies managed to raise a whole regiment, and none of the estimated tens of thousands of Carbonari came out in support. Nor did they evoke an echo in the people. While always ready to shout '*Vive l'Empereur!* or '*À bas les Bourbons!*', the population remained politically supine, as even the socialist historians of the period were forced to admit. But this in no way affected the authorities' perceived need for stricter and more pervasive police.[6]

In December 1821, Richelieu's second ministry was brought down by the Ultras, who accused it of being too liberal, and replaced by that of Jean-Baptiste de Villèle, one of their most active deputies in the Chamber. Within a week of taking power Villèle had appointed a new prefect of police for Paris, Guy Delaveau. This choice was dictated less by Delaveau's questionable talents as a lawyer than by his devotion to the Bourbon dynasty and the Church, and particularly his connections with the *Congrégation*. This had originated as a movement founded by Jesuits with the aim of promoting a more devout lifestyle among aristocratic Catholics, and had spawned other bodies such as the *Société des Bonnes Études*, which encouraged the reading of 'good' books and denounced subversive ideas. As many of its members had also become active in the *Chevaliers de la Foi* and other militant Ultra associations, the *Congrégation* had grown increasingly political in nature. Delaveau was given a new director general of police, Franchet d'Esperey, installed in January 1822, a man of limited intelligence and little competence who was close to the *Chevaliers de la Foi*. Over the next seven years these two would do everything in their power to carry out a counter-revolution.

Delaveau forced strict religious observance on his employees, demanding that they show him certificates from a priest confirming that they had been to confession. The '*certificat de confession*' was the equivalent of the English Test Act, which excluded anyone from holding public office unless they took communion in the established

Church. Given the extent to which France had become secularised over the past half-century, this was a shocking innovation. At the same time, Delaveau turned a blind eye to his subordinates' actual conduct, with the result, according to one of them, that the Préfecture de Police 'presented the most upsetting spectacle, the most odious mixture of asceticism and debauchery'. 'Never,' he claimed, 'have hypocrisy, false zeal, the love of gain under the mask of a grand show of royalism and devotion to the family of Louis XVIII, presented a more repellent, more detestable, more hideous spectacle.'[7]

Delaveau trusted nobody, and he set up a network of spies within the secret police to watch them too. He placed his own agents in the offices of all the commissaires and chiefs of department, with orders to report directly to him. 'It is not difficult to understand how, with such wheels within wheels, the prefecture rapidly turned into a hub of intrigues, cabals, hatreds and passions, where the provocations and the vengeance of the congregation against the supposed enemies of altar and throne were hatched,' wrote Paul Louis Canler, chief of the *Sûreté*. 'As the attention of the administration was concentrated on political matters, the result was that the police as such were relegated to second place and totally neglected.' Funds destined for them were diverted to pay political agents, and criminality flourished in consequence.[8]

Anyone of note who did not fit Delaveau's and Franchet's idea of a faithful subject was placed under surveillance, and a huge amount of police time was spent simply watching people, often for no very good reason. Groups of friends who met for dinner more than once in private rooms of restaurants were eavesdropped on. People might be placed under surveillance because they were, as in one man's case, 'well known for a long time as one of the most exalted supporters of the revolutionary system, and no less ill-famed for his morals'. A Swiss national running a studio for artists was watched because he corrupted young men with 'obscene and seditious' talk and the reading of 'detestable works'. A former clerk fell under suspicion because he had abandoned his family in Nantes and brought a young girl to Paris 'to give himself over to idleness and a shameful life' – and because he had been heard talking of 'the Glory of Bonaparte'. The duc de Broglie had to dismiss two servants after discovering that they were copying his correspondence and diary for the police. The *cabinet noir* was hyperactive, and, to add insult to injury, some of its employees not only opened and copied letters, but also stole any enclosed money. Venality was common: George Ticknor, an American studying in Paris, was visited one day by a commissaire and a judge, who announced that they must search his lodgings, which they proceeded to do at very great length, pausing to talk to him several times. A complaint through the American minister in Paris yielded only a denial that any such search had taken place – the two men had evidently only visited him in the hope of eliciting a bribe to make them go away.[9]

A request for a passport to travel in France exposed the applicant to 'being an agent of the liberal faction charged with carrying into the provinces orders from the *comité directeur*, which never existed except in the heads of those congregationists with their extended ears', in the words of one contemporary. 'If one requested a passport for abroad, it was something else, one was considered a conspirator who wanted to overthrow everything.' When one of Fouché's erstwhile chiefs of department, Pierre-Marie Desmarest, now long retired, went off to spend two weeks of the summer with an old friend, the mayor of a little country town, he gave rise to a mountain of paperwork and a hilarious correspondence involving his own former deputy, two ministers, two prefects, a mayor and several police officials on the subject of his movements, when and by whom he had been issued with a passport, where it had been stamped, who he was staying with and with whom he dined every day.[10]

One day the poet Pierre-Jean de Béranger requested a passport in order to go to Breteuil, and since the liberal deputy Manuel had also requested one for the same place, the police concluded there was something brewing, and both had to be watched. As far as they could ascertain, the two never met at Breteuil, but the police nevertheless decided to probe Béranger on his return to Paris, without success. 'It is impossible to speak to him if one is not *well known to him*,' complained one agent. 'The defiance in his house is such that neither we nor our inspectors can obtain admittance, as we are suspected, if not actually known, to be from the police. *Latterly, one of our agents who was sent there only saved himself by prompt flight, having been set upon by the porter*.'[11]

The agents were a mixed bag, drawn from both sexes, usually abandoned women with no other source of income or men with a gambling or drug habit to feed, but sometimes fantasists or political zealots. But they all shared the characteristics of amateurishness and incompetence. Police agents often recruited their own stables of informers and pools of petty criminals with various skills, usually by means of blackmail. They would post themselves in brothels, gambling dens or other establishments of disrepute to catch out people who could then be manipulated to provide information and even sent out on missions to spy or to purloin documents. Petty criminals and unlicensed prostitutes could be let off a charge for the price of favours, and each fresh crime they were put up to would implicate them further and make them more malleable tools of the agent, who could then order them to entrap, break in, steal, set up, or otherwise help in the extraction of intelligence.[12]

As Canler explains, since there was only one way for an agent to gain the approval of his or her superiors, 'by uncovering some conspiracy, or, if after lengthy searches he could find nothing, to adroitly invent some foul machination, incriminate in a supposed plot some honest husband and father who in his life had never thought of conspiring, invent a few accomplices, choosing for these roles other innocents, and, finally, to deliver the whole lot to the police.'[13]

Police agents regularly disguised themselves as workers, went to bars and plied men with drink before prompting them to complain about conditions, about the government and the monarchy, or to sing Napoleonic songs, before arresting them. Many an innocent labourer who had gone to have a drink after work woke up in gaol. Posing as merchants, police agents entrapped craftsmen, printers and traders into manufacturing, printing or supplying forbidden goods, banned literature, tricolour cockades or busts of Napoleon. One agent befriended a group of workmen, one of whom was a joiner, whom he commissioned to make a box with steel pipes according to a drawing he supplied, and when this was ready, reported them all as members of a secret society, producing as evidence the box, which he affirmed was an 'infernal machine' designed to wipe out the royal family. The joiner hanged himself in his cell on the night of his arrest, ostensibly confirming his guilt.[14]

The prime motive for all the investigation was the search for the elusive *comité directeur*, and former officers were under relentless surveillance, as they were thought to be its most likely messengers. The prefects of every department received regular circulars and special admonishments reminding them to check that everyone passing through their area must have their passports checked, and specifying where they should be stamped and by whom. They were enjoined to check that postmasters did not give fresh horses to anyone without a correctly endorsed passport. They were upbraided for allegedly letting people slip through their department without having their passport checked, yet retailed travellers' complaints to them about being disturbed by over-zealous gendarmes barging into their hotel bedrooms in the middle of the night to check their papers. From the extant archives it is clear that the ministry in Paris received alarmist letters from busybodies in the country about travellers, accusing the local authorities of being dilatory. And for all the passports, visas, hotel and inn registers, *feuilles de route* of the stagecoaches and other red tape, it seems the police were continually losing track of people supposedly under close surveillance.[15]

In the autumn of 1822 the police were keen to find out how many former Napoleonic officers and revolutionaries of one kind or another were crossing into Spain to join the liberals, so a police agent assumed the identity of a former officer, and presented himself at the Spanish embassy in Paris to offer his services to the constitutional government. He was well received, assured that he would obtain a rank commensurate with his status, and encouraged to call again. More interviews followed, to discuss practical matters such as how and by which route he should travel, what papers he should carry, where and when he would be given money, a cipher and other necessary means. The agent's frustration mounted as the matter dragged on, assuming an almost surreal aspect, and it was only after several weeks that he realised that the Spanish ambassador, the Duke of San Lorenzo, was in fact playing him along, trying to find out what the French police knew about the means by which he was despatching genuine volunteers across the border. Another agent, who had made contact with and apparently been befriended by a former Napoleonic officer in touch with the Spanish revolutionaries, was fed fantastic information about how all French liberals would at a given signal from the *comité directeur* congregate at Bayonne on the French border, where they would meet up with a Spanish force and march on Paris, while he himself was going to assassinate Louis XVIII with a poisoned arrow, assisted by the supposedly subverted Gardes du Corps.[16]

The system was not merely inefficient and pointless, it also often ended in farce. One evening in Paris two agents, one working for the director general of police, the other employed by the military police, and both looking to uncover some plot, met up in a tavern and began standing each other drinks, pretending to be former Napoleonic officers nostalgic for the old days. They agreed to meet the next day in the Tuileries gardens to discuss means of bringing them back. More meetings followed, in various cafés and eventually private rooms, to which each introduced colleagues who also assumed the guises of disaffected Bonapartists. The discussions, vague at first, became more specific as to ways of overthrowing the Bourbons in favour of Napoleon's son, until one day the police raided one of their meetings and arrested the agent working for the military police and his colleagues. They were thrown into the prison of La Force, and it was a full month before they could get a message out to their chief at the military police headquarters to secure their release.[17]

In September 1823 Delaveau urgently wanted to know the whereabouts of the sons of Marshal Ney, and instituted a search which involved the whole country and lasted for weeks, only to reveal that they were living quite openly in Paris. When the police heard that Hippolyte Carnot, son of the exiled regicide minister of war under the Directory, had come up to Paris but could find no trace of his trip in the passport office or on the *feuilles de route* of the stagecoaches, or of his residence in any of the capital's *hôtels garnis*, they deemed this suspicious and put in hand an investigation. They eventually tracked him down to lodgings at 18, rue des Quatre-Fils, 'in an apartment in which everything bespeaks opulence', and where he was living with a 'physically pleasing' lady. Two agents called on him, claiming that they were the employees of a bank anxious to trace another Napoleonic notable in order to make a payment to him. They kept a close watch on his lodgings and his lady, and noted that he received a visit from Antoine Boulay de la Meurthe, a magistrate who had held high office under Napoleon. They then called on Boulay de la Meurthe, again posing as bankers (a favourite ploy), and asked him whether by any chance he knew the whereabouts of Carnot. He denied any knowledge, probably because he suspected them of being police agents, which placed him under suspicion, and therefore under surveillance. Further attempts to gain admittance to Carnot, under various guises, came to nothing, as 'whoever asks for M. Carnot is immediately ejected by his servants, with the epithet "*mouchard*"'.[18]

The ploy of pretending to be bank employees seeking to contact someone in order to pass on a legacy or a significant sum of money fooled nobody, and the gauche manner in which the agents put their questions usually identified them as what they were, whereupon servants would amuse themselves by giving misleading answers. The phrase 'we enquired *in an appropriate manner*' is used, frequently, in agents' reports to cover what was clearly a clumsy question, and the lack of a satisfactory answer would be attenuated by passages such as: 'he responded negatively, but with *a contraction of the face, gestures of surprise and anxiety which clearly proclaimed that he had strong reasons for betraying truth in this instance*'. When there was no evidence to cite against a suspect, the report would throw in that he 'combines the most profound immorality with the worst political principles', as though a taste for loose women or young girls had any bearing on the case.[19]

The majority of the police archives relating to this period went up in flames at the time of the Paris Commune, but there is no reason to suppose that what perished was of a superior quality to what remains. Judging by the information to be found in the surviving files, the time expended on intelligence-gathering was mostly wasted. Those concerning subversive activity of one sort or another contain no firm evidence, only mountains of suggestive irrelevance and reams of documents relating to supposed secret societies, most of them transparently bogus.

They did, however, provide the chief archivist, Simon Duplay, with material for an authoritative-sounding memorandum on the subject of the great conspiracy, which he compiled in the autumn of 1822. Duplay had been Robespierre's secretary and, narrowly surviving his fall, had subsequently been employed by Fouché in a department dedicated to 'the search for all plots and projects against the constitution, the government and the person of the first magistrate, as well as the tracking down of the agitators, authors and accomplices of such enterprises ...'[20]

Duplay's memorandum bears all the marks of having been commissioned by a believer in the grand conspiracy. 'It has been established that all the conspiracies which have taken place since 1816 have been the work of secret societies and resulted from the same impulse, and that the source of all these machinations was to be found in the Capital,' it boldly asserted. 'While the authorities have not been able to obtain judicial proofs with respect to the prime movers, that *comité directeur* which has revealed its existence by so many multiple acts on so many different occasions, they have at least gathered together enough facts to be able to designate with certainty its principal members.' He went on to list Lafayette, Constant, Voyer d'Argenson, the deputies Jacques Koechlin and Auguste de Kératry, and General Foy. The only 'fact' Duplay adduces is that some of them gave financial assistance on their release from prison to various persons who had been implicated in conspiracies.[21]

According to him, the grand conspiracy originated in Germany where, following the defeat of Jena, the student societies turned their attention from mutual rivalry to the aim of assassinating Napoleon and subsequently toppling all the German monarchs. Their influence penetrated France in the 'literary cortège' of Madame de Staël, who was popular among French liberals. In 1815 there were, according to Duplay, two secret societies operating in France, one of them the *Chevaliers de l'Épingle Noire*, on whom he admits 'there exists in the archives of the Police Générale no specific piece of information'. The other, the *Société du Lion Dormant*, a Masonic order founded by French captives in England with Napoleon as Grand Master, supposedly had lodges all over France. Yet the only information Duplay had on it derived from the testimony of one adept who had been inducted without really knowing what he was letting himself in for, but thought they meant to kidnap the royal family and threaten to murder them if the allies should invade.[22]

'Thus, at the end of 1815 or the beginning of 1816, a *comité directeur* existed in the capital,' writes Duplay in a total non-sequitur. He goes on to affirm that under the name *L'Indépendance Nationale*, this set up regional committees in every department of France. According to him, it orchestrated Didier's rising of 1816 and had a hand in the *Épingle Noire*'s attempt to seize Vincennes (although Duplay had earlier confessed that he had no information on the existence of that organisation). The proof he adduces of a connection between some disturbance or alleged conspiracy and the Parisian *comité directeur* is in some cases no more than a deposition by some individual that he had seen someone receiving a letter from someone the police suspected of having contacts with one or other of the liberals in Paris. 'The points of contact with the capital are no less evident, although there is no information which could reveal the *comité directeur* which was directing the conspirators of 1817 from Paris,' Duplay writes with regard to the Lyon revolt. 'It appears that the house of Madame de Lavalette provided the point of contact.' The surviving police files containing the reports of the spies watching her house support no such likelihood.[23]

According to Duplay, following the failure of the Lyon revolt the *comité directeur* concentrated on parliamentary means, canvassing for petitions and organising election campaigns, and influencing deputies. It nevertheless kept in touch with all the secret societies around the country. These presented quite a challenge to Duplay. Informers reported the existence of groups with a baffling variety of names, such as *L'Ordre de l'Amitié*, *Les Admirateurs de la Valeur Française*, *Trois Cents Laboureurs du Champ de la Veuve*, *L'Ordre du Soleil*, *La République*, *Marie-Louise et son Fils*, and so on. Upon investigation it would sometimes turn out that some had already ceased to exist or had changed their name. Duplay was confused by the connections between societies such as *Les Chevaliers de la Liberté* and the *Société des Réformateurs*, which he thought might be another name for the *comité directeur*.

Surprisingly, Duplay does not dwell on the papers concerning the Grand Firmament that found their way into his archive. These include induction rites which involved abjuring the Christian faith and burning crowns and sceptres, several bloodcurdling decrees and oaths, some in dog Latin, and the statutes of the organisation. An informer had supposedly been admitted to a session of its 'synod' in Turin, and discovered that the *Adelphi* were in close contact with a *comité directeur* in Paris which included Benjamin Constant, Jacques-Antoine Manuel, Pierre Paul Royer Collard and Auguste de Kératry.[24]

Duplay was puzzled by the discovery of a seemingly Masonic society calling itself *Misraïm*, which appeared to have ramifications in the most unlikely places. Its existence was reported in towns such as Montpellier, Nîmes and Mâcon, in Switzerland and Italy, and as far afield as Russia. It also allegedly had branches in Scotland, headed by the Duke of Atholl, and in England, where the membership was reported to include the king's brother the Duke of Sussex. The archives contain the society's catechism (an unreadable skein of mumbo-jumbo), its hierarchy of seventy-nine grades, various papers issued 'under the Equator', impressions of Masonic-looking seals seized at Calais, and the information that members wore a black rosette with a black cross on it, with an inscription that could not be deciphered.

Duplay came to the conclusion that all these names were red herrings planted by the conspirators to put the police off the scent of the real one. In his view of things, everything was intricately linked, and above all orchestrated by the fabled *comité directeur*. In the case of Louvel's assassination of the duc de Berry, 'even if it has not been proved that the *comité directeur* itself directly ordered the assassination of 13 February, it is at least proved by the confessions of the assassin himself that his fanaticism had been fed and inflamed by the agitation reigning all around him'.

Ironically, Metternich, who had from the beginning taken a dim view of the French police, was now convinced that they had been thoroughly infiltrated by the *comité directeur*. Alexander was so concerned about their unreliability that he insisted they could only issue passports for travel to Russia to people who had produced a certificate of good morality.[25]

19

The Duke of Texas

Tsar Alexander was still fixated on Spain. 'He regarded Spain,' the British minister plenipotentiary in Vienna, Sir Robert Gordon, reported to Castlereagh in May 1821, 'as the *tribune* to which all the revolutionists of Europe have recourse, as to a vehicle from which they can disseminate their pernicious doctrine.' The fall of Richelieu's ministry in December 1821 had unsettled the tsar, and he feared that if the Spanish revolutionaries were permitted to continue, their 'insolent victory' might provoke revolution in France. Also, as he explained to Wellington, it was impossible for him, a monarch who relied so heavily on his army, to countenance anything that originated in military insubordination.[1]

He suggested marching a Russian army of 40,000 men through Austria and Italy into France, where it could be used to quell revolution if the need arose, or alternatively to invade Spain in order to restore King Ferdinand.

The hostility of the powers to the constitutional government in Spain, and the encouragement given to the king's supporters by Ultras in France, had undermined the moderates and strengthened the extremists, known as *exaltados*. In the elections of 1822 they gained a majority, and Riego was elected president of the Cortes. Civil war loomed as the government held the king a virtual captive in Madrid, and a group of royalists gathered in Catalonia and set up a regency in his name.[2]

Metternich now took the view that what was happening in Spain was 'one of the greatest plagues which have been reserved to our century'. The language in which his letters were couched was by now verging on the pathological: in June he had assured Lebzeltern that the conspiracy had penetrated 'every vein of the body of society'. 'This revolution is special in that it is the premeditated work of a faction spread across the whole of Europe,' he wrote to Vincent in Paris on 5 July 1822, with the Parisian *comité directeur* dispensing 'considerable funds' to finance revolutions wherever it chose. He had reached the conclusion that the Carbonari, the Teutomaniacs, Bonapartists, Neapolitan, Spanish and other rebels had 'consummated their fusion' into one organisation.[3]

Events in Spain could not be divorced from what was happening in its former colonies in the Americas, from Mexico to Peru. These had by now almost entirely broken free of Spain, and this confronted the European powers with the dilemma of whether to recognise them as independent states, thereby sanctioning revolution. 'There are already enough republican ideas in the world,' René de Chateaubriand, France's ambassador in London, said to Castlereagh during an interview on 10 April 1822; 'to increase the sum of these ideas is to compromise more and more the fate of monarchy in Europe.' Castlereagh, who had acceded to the title of Marquess of Londonderry on the death of his father the preceding year, assured him that the British cabinet was 'by no means disposed to recognise the revolutionary governments'. Chateaubriand suggested they direct their efforts 'to bringing monarchies into existence in the New World rather than these republics, which will send us their principles with the products of their soil'. Castlereagh agreed in principle, although he was wary of the French interest in Spain and its former colonies.[4]

The issue was complicated by a declaration on 8 March by the American president James Monroe to the effect that the new nations of South and Central America deserved recognition, the first of a number of utterances that would culminate in the United States warning the European powers off the Americas. Lebzeltern termed the declaration 'subversive of every legally constituted government of whatever form'. He had long suspected Monroe of 'Jacobin opinions', and in his view the United States government derived its authority from 'an impure source', since it had been born of revolution. He was also convinced that the move had been prepared in concert with the revolutionary leaders of the rebellious colonies. Metternich went further, asserting that the evidence 'does not allow of any doubt that these various moves derive from a common source and were orchestrated by the same body which is relentlessly occupied with the destruction of the old social order in both the old world and the new', and implying that President Monroe had been given his orders by the *comité directeur*. Alexander too saw the global threat, and suggested the formation of a combined European army which could put down the revolution in Spain, then cross the Atlantic and deal with the rebellious colonies. The idea was described by one British diplomat as 'bordering on madness'.[5]

Castlereagh took the same view, and was determined to distance Britain from the reactionary policy of the three absolutist monarchies. But, in the hope of being able to restrain them, he gave in to Metternich's entreaties that he should participate in the congress which was to convene in September 1822. He agreed to attend not the congress of monarchs in Florence, which would be concerned primarily with Italian affairs, but a conference of foreign ministers that was to take place beforehand in Vienna, where Greece and Spain were to be discussed. On his way to Vienna he meant to pause in Paris in order to dissuade Louis XVIII and his ministry from intervening in Spain. Metternich considered it a major coup to have obtained the attendance of the British foreign secretary, even if only for the one conference. 'The moment, my dear marquess, is immense,' he wrote to Castlereagh on 6 June 1822. 'I frankly regard it as the point of departure for a new era, and if the results were not to be such as I expect, the fault could only lie at the doors of the allied Cabinets.'[6]

Castlereagh was not well. He had been showing signs of mental strain, even muddling his words while speaking in the House. Liverpool and Wellington were concerned, and he was persuaded to go and rest at his beloved retreat at Cray in Kent. His secretary Hamilton Seymour visited him there, and was struck by the change that had taken place in him. They took a walk in the garden, and Seymour ventured that Castlereagh must be looking forward to the forthcoming trip, which would afford him the pleasure of renewing some old acquaintances. 'Lord Londonderry drew his hand across his forehead, and said, very slowly, "At any other time I should like it very much, *but I am quite worn out here*" (keeping his hand upon his forehead), "quite worn out; and this fresh responsibility is more than I can bear."' A couple of days later, the British foreign secretary committed suicide by cutting his throat.[7]

'This catastrophe is one of the most terrible that could have struck me,' Metternich wrote on hearing the news, with good reason. Castlereagh was succeeded at the Foreign Office by George Canning, who immediately imposed his view that Britain should have as little to do with Europe as possible. He nominated Wellington as Britain's observer at the congress, with a brief to do nothing beyond urging the powers to implement the ban on the slave trade and trying to discourage France or anyone else from intervening in Spain.[8]

By the time Wellington reached Vienna, the monarchs had arrived and there was no time to hold the preliminary conference of ministers. He was therefore obliged to attend the congress of monarchs, whose venue Metternich had changed to Verona. 'Florence is crowded with foreigners of every kind,' he explained to Lebzeltern, 'and there is no doubt that busybodies of every sort will aim to take themselves to that place for the conference, some to satisfy their idle curiosity, others with all manner of intrigue and espionage in mind.' Lying as it did within Austrian jurisdiction, Verona could be more easily isolated and covered by his own spies. He reached the city on 13 October 1822, which gave him a few days to conduct preparatory meetings and set the agenda for the congress, which he considered 'the most important to have been held since 1814.'[9]

The turnout was certainly impressive. As was the custom, the inhabitants hung tapestries, carpets, bedspreads and even clothes from their windows to decorate their houses in honour of the monarchs as they drove into the city. These included the tsar, the Emperor Francis, the King of Prussia with his two sons, the Kings of Sardinia and of the Two Sicilies, the Grand Duke of Tuscany, the Duke of Modena, the Duchess of Parma and lesser Italian rulers, ministers, ambassadors and aristocrats. When they gathered at the theatre for a play or an opera, performed by singers and actors imported for the occasion, it glittered as much from the decorations on the breasts of the men as from the diamonds on those of the ladies. Only Wellington usually appeared in civilian dress and without decorations. The guest book of the better of the city's two hotels, the Torre di Londra, looked to one bemused visitor like a court almanac, with its list of princes, dukes, counts and barons. Those who could not find a space there or at the other hotel were accommodated in the run-down palazzos of local nobles who dusted down and refreshed grand interiors that had grown shabby with the decline of their fortunes.[10]

The sessions of the congress were held irregularly, usually prompted by a note from one of the courts which needed to be discussed. While it had been called to review the security of Italy and take the necessary measures to defend the European order in the face of the revolutionary threat, it quickly became apparent that there was no unity of purpose, and that each of the powers had its own agenda. Individual state interests and great-power rivalry overrode any common policy on the supposed threat from the universal conspiracy. Austria needed to reinforce its hegemony over Italy, France yearned to invade Spain, Russia wanted to gain for France the permission to do so and for itself to intervene in Greece, Prussia wanted to avoid involvement and keep out of trouble, and Britain was principally interested in enforcing the ban on the slave trade. Metternich would ostentatiously doodle whenever such subjects, of no interest to him, were being discussed. The congress rapidly degenerated into a series of disjointed horse-trades. The clash of national interests intersected with personal prejudice and private animosity. 'A thousand little hatreds, envies and calumnies intersected,' in Chateaubriand's picturesque view; 'people loathed one another while professing their esteem; between four walls a man whose praises had been sung outside was torn to pieces ...'[11]

While Gentz held discreet meetings with Lord Strangford, the British ambassador in Constantinople, to work out a way of pandering to the philhellenic rage sweeping Europe without supporting the rebels, Chateaubriand discussed with Alexander how to organise an invasion of Spain behind the back of France's foreign minister, Montmorency. The tsar's conviction that the Spanish mutineers had to be punished went deep, but his desire to see the Alliance agree to armed intervention there was reinforced by the idea that this might give him some purchase to demand the right to intervene in Greece. Metternich was not having this, and kept reminding Alexander that the Greek rebels were no different from any of the others directed by the *comité directeur*. 'Conceived by the artifice of a sect, nourished and supported by it, the Greek people is no more than a tool in the hands of men who, under false pretences, have never had any other goal than to sow discord among the allied Powers, and particularly between the imperial Courts of Austria and Russia,' he reminded Nesselrode.[12]

Metternich's reason for inviting the rulers of the Italian states lay in the hope that he might be able to bully them into adopting a form of administration dictated by himself. He had not had much success so far: the overthrow of the Neapolitan revolution might have been a triumph, but what followed was less than glorious. Two months elapsed from the moment the Austrians marched into Naples before Ferdinand could be persuaded to return to his kingdom, and when he did he began a vicious purge of all those who had not sided with him during the revolution. The allied commissioners supposedly advising him were powerless to prevent this, and their advice was ignored. Ferdinand appointed a government even less competent than that which had provoked the revolution. The introduction of Metternich's new order was sluggish and the results disappointing. It failed to address the real evils, which, his *chargé* Menz reported, were not and never had been the Carbonari, but rather the 'buffoonery', the 'degradation of morals', and the lack of education of those in power. 'Instead of uniting the king and his nation,' Lord Burghersh reported, 'the Allies have widened the breach between them.'[13]

While he refused to accept advice even from Metternich, Ferdinand begged him to leave the Austrian army of occupation in Naples. Metternich had insisted that the costs of the campaign would be borne by the kingdom of the Two Sicilies, and since this had been in financial difficulties even before the revolution, he had brought in the banking house of Rothschild to provide it with a loan with which to discharge its obligations towards Austria. This was just as well, as the troops would remain in Naples until 1827, eating up some 75 per cent of the kingdom's revenues. Further north, in Piedmont, Charles Felix, who had ascended the Sardinian throne in the wake of the unsuccessful rebellion, wanted the Austrians who had assisted him to leave. Metternich on the other hand contrived to keep them there, as it suited him to have garrisons stationed in various parts of Italy at the hosts' expense. In other respects too, the situation in Piedmont was less than satisfactory, as the new king was not introducing the forms of government suggested by Metternich.[14]

Metternich lectured the rulers and ministers of the various Italian states on the subject of good governance, and encouraged them to agree a common programme. The result was the adoption of a set of principles according to which all the states were to frame their legislation and reorganise their administration. These were: 1. a close union of throne and altar, with the propagation of the faith to counteract subversive ideas; 2. the strengthening of the role of the nobility in government and society; 3. the reinforcement of paternal authority; 4. more rapid and severe punishment of the crime of *lèse-majesté*; 5. limiting the number of schools and universities; and 6. tighter censorship of the press.[15]

Metternich had hoped to obtain the support of the Italian states for his plan of setting up in Milan an investigating commission on the model of the one at Mainz, and for a postal convention that would give him power to inspect mail throughout the peninsula. Most of the

Italian states were amenable to the idea of the commission, but the best-ruled of them, Tuscany, saw no point in it and questioned the principle, while Rome was openly hostile to the idea, fearing that the spiritual independence of the papacy might be impaired. Cardinal Consalvi recruited the French ambassador at St Petersburg, La Ferronnays, and his minister Montmorency to his cause, and they had little difficulty in engaging the support of Alexander. Consalvi also resisted Metternich's attempts to route all mail services through the Austrian offices in Lombardy, in which he was likewise supported by Russia and France. Needing all the influence he could command over them to prevent armed intervention in Spain and Greece, Metternich could not force the issue.[16]

Alexander had brought with him not only Nesselrode but also his ambassadors in Madrid and London, Tatishchev and Lieven, and the latter had, to the delight of Metternich, brought his wife. She wasted no time in establishing her drawing room as the heart of the congress. Metternich, Wellington, the Neapolitan plenipotentiary Ruffo, the French plenipotentiary Caraman and the Prussian minister Bernstorff would spend their evenings there (Chateaubriand's presence was not encouraged, as he was inclined to bore everyone with tales of his recent travels in America). Much of the business of the congress was carried on there, often with her participation and encouragement. 'I am very glad to find myself here; my curiosity is altogether satisfied; it is perhaps a more interesting meeting than any of the previous [congresses],' she wrote to her brother in St Petersburg on 23 October. 'The feminine element is weak; there is not a single woman here ...'[17]

This is a curious remark, given that among those present was Napoleon's widow Marie-Louise – who shocked more than one person by her gaiety, as she would appear at the opera, covered in diamonds and make-up, squired by her one-eyed consort Count Neipperg. To Chateaubriand, who tried to draw her out on the subject of past glories, she retorted that she never thought about the old days. Another lady of note present in Verona was Madame Récamier, with whom Metternich is believed to have had an affair while he was Austria's ambassador in Paris. He did not renew his tender acquaintance with her but, as gossip related, in his spare time stalked new and younger women. In this he was outdone by Wellington, who, as Chateaubriand noted acidly, when not attending to exclusively British interests was looking for sex in the streets of Verona. The authorities had banned all the prostitutes from the city, and they had withdrawn to the country, but many would come into town with baskets of fruit or vegetables, posing as street vendors. Since they could not very well ply their trade in the street, those who craved their company had to move them into their quarters and employ them in some domestic capacity.[18]

Countess Lieven noted that the other Russians in Verona treated her with coolness. 'As I have spent ten years in England, they consider me English, and as I see Metternich every day, they think of me as an Austrian,' she wrote to her brother. This may have had something to do with the fact that the tsar was not paying her enough attention. He had been bowled over by the sight of the new Lady Londonderry, the former Lord Charles Stewart's young wife Frances, and he was following her around like a star-struck young lover. His feelings were, however, almost certainly platonic.[19]

The Quaker abolitionist William Allen, whom Alexander had met in London in 1814, had come to Verona expressly to see him. The books on the slave trade he was bringing the tsar had been confiscated by the Austrian police, but in the course of two long interviews he briefed him on that and various other subjects close to his heart, such as prison reform and education. They also talked about the Greek insurgents, and Allen noted that 'the Emperor seemed to feel deeply for them, and said, he had proofs that this rebellion against the Turks was organised at Paris, by the revolutionists'. At the end of their second meeting, Alexander suggested they pray together. 'We then had a precious tender time of silent waiting upon the Lord, and were favoured with a sweet holy feeling,' Allen recalled. Alexander's physician Dr Tarasov recorded that as a result of spending so much time on his knees, the tsar had a large area of hardened skin tissue around his kneecaps.[20]

Alexander was still set on military intervention in Spain. 'He said that he considered that country as the head-quarters of revolution and Jacobinism,' Wellington reported after a conversation with him on 21 October, 'that the king and the Royal Family were in the utmost danger; and that so long as the revolution in that country should be allowed to continue, every country in Europe, and France in particular, was unsafe.' Metternich hoped to block Alexander by suggesting the five powers make a 'moral stand' against the Spanish revolutionary government, in the form of a joint condemnation. But at the second full session of the congress Montmorency insisted that France would keep its options open with regard to Spanish affairs, as it alone was directly threatened by events there. Alexander backed Montmorency, pledging to support French military intervention if necessary. Wellington protested that Britain would not tolerate such action. The tsar persisted, and told him he wanted to march an army of 150,000 into Piedmont, with the aim of supporting France.[21]

In an attempt to paper over the rift that had opened in the Alliance, Metternich came up with a new idea. He suggested that the powers each address a note to the Spanish government and the Cortes, demanding that changes be made to the constitution, failing which they would withdraw their ambassadors. He managed to persuade Alexander and Frederick William to follow this course, but Montmorency reserved for France the right of addressing its own note independently. The three courts eventually agreed the text of a note, and pledged support and military assistance if necessary, should France come under attack or be obliged to go to war with Spain. They also, at Metternich's behest, sent a joint circular to all their respective ambassadors and ministers informing them of the official line regarding the Greek rising. 'At the very moment when the military insurrections which had broken out in Naples and Turin were faltering in the face of the approach of regular troops, the Revolution cast one of its firebrands on the Ottoman empire,' it ran. 'The coincidence of these facts can leave no room for doubt on the identity of the causes which produced them. The appearance of the evil at so many different places, the fact that everywhere it appeared under the same forms and spoke the same language, even if it did not always break out under the same pretexts, point only too clearly to the common fount from which it sprang.' With this reaffirmation of faith, the congress closed. The end was marked by a horse race and illuminations. Two days later, Metternich accompanied Francis and Alexander on a trip to Venice, which involved a visit to the opera and a meeting with Rossini – despite the warnings of the Austrian police that the composer was 'strongly infected with revolutionary principles'.[22]

On 25 December, the day Metternich left Venice to return to Vienna, Montmorency was replaced as foreign minister by Chateaubriand. He was set on military intervention in Spain, not so much because he wished to see the revolution crushed, more out of a desire to employ the French army in a manner that would take its mind off subversion, efface the shame of Waterloo and restore the prestige of France. Metternich did everything he could to discourage him, as he feared that, having defeated the revolution, the French might allow the Spaniards to keep a constitution on the model of the *Charte*. The last thing he wanted was to see Spain become a functioning constitutional monarchy, as that would pose the question why Naples had not been allowed to. He even came up with the bizarre suggestion that Ferdinand I of the Two Sicilies should be appointed regent during the reconstruction of Spain, to ensure that this would take place along legitimist lines. Canning was also desperate to prevent French intervention in Spain, for quite different reasons. He thought any extension of French influence in the Iberian peninsula would be a 'calamity', and wrote to the French government, Louis XVIII and Monsieur urging them to hold back. None of this made any impression on the French ministry, which prepared for war.[23]

On 6 April 1823 a French army 60,000 strong, supported by 35,000 Spanish volunteers, commanded by Monsieur's son the duc d'Angoulême, crossed the border into Spain. Notwithstanding his disappointment at Russia not being allowed to participate, Alexander was delighted at the news. So was public opinion in Vienna, to Metternich's annoyance.

Nobody could be certain how the troops would perform in military terms, or how they would be received by the population – Napoleon's invasion and the *guerrilla* it had inspired were still fresh in the memory of both sides. Another unknown was how the troops would react when confronted with Spanish constitutionalist forces, which might seek to subvert them politically: many Napoleonic officers had gone to Spain to fight for the constitutionalist cause. To complicate matters, there was an explosion of rumour, particularly rife in south-western France, that Napoleon was not dead and had landed in Spain. In March the *gendarmerie* of the Puy-de-Dôme region reported that most of the population was convinced that he had joined up with the Spanish revolutionary General Francisco Espoz y Mina and was preparing to march into France. In Toulouse it was rumoured that Mina was in fact none other than Napoleon in disguise.[24]

The fears proved groundless. When the French army crossed the Bidassoa river on 6 April it was confronted by a band of some five hundred men clad in a variety of Napoleonic uniforms drawn up under the French tricolour, singing the '*Marseillaise*' and urging the soldiers to join them. One artillery salvo was enough to disperse them. A later brush with a force of French ex-Napoleonic soldiers near Corunna, led this time by the British general Sir Robert Wilson, passed off without any hesitation on the part of the royal troops, let alone the feared defections. In contrast to 1808, the French were generally well received by the rural population of Spain, and sometimes greeted with joy. This time they were seen as liberators by the clergy, who were on the side of the throne. When they entered Madrid on 23 May the crowds burned an effigy of Riego in a show of enthusiasm.

The Spanish government had retreated to Cádiz, taking King Ferdinand with it, so Angoulême established a regency in his name in the capital. Metternich, still insisting that Ferdinand of the Two Sicilies should be made regent, refused to recognise it. The French ignored him, and their armies made good progress. At the end of September, Angoulême stormed the fortress of the Trocadero and delivered the king. A few days later, Ferdinand rescinded all the reforms introduced since 1820 and put in hand savage reprisals. On 7 November Riego was executed: he was dragged through the streets of Madrid in a basket attached to a donkey's tail, then hanged, and his body was cut into five pieces.[25]

The victorious invasion of Spain was a triumph for the French government and the Bourbon monarchy in more ways than one. The cloak of military glory in which they could wrap themselves did much to eclipse the previous image of obese indolence and unmerited privilege. Significantly, 2 December, the anniversary of Austerlitz and of Napoleon's coronation, was chosen for Angoulême's triumphal entry into Paris at the head of his victorious troops.

More important, a bored and frustrated army which had found no outlet for its energies other than conspiracy had been given something to do, and had enjoyed the experience. Its interest in subversion vanished overnight and, in the words of Francisque de Corcelle, 'the secret societies were left to die of feebleness and boredom'. Without the army, Carbonarism withered. It had, according to Corcelle, never been anything but 'a transaction between some bitter resentments and diverse principles, a kind of transitory coalition incapable of surviving the singular circumstances that produced it'. Ironically, the great alliance ranged against it withered concurrently, and for much the same reasons. While Alexander now considered duplicating the French triumph across the Atlantic, and King Ferdinand decided to honour Metternich with the title of Duke of Texas, in total disregard of his allies Canning appointed British consuls in all the successor states to the former Spanish colonies. On 3 December President Monroe declared both American continents, north and south, closed to European colonialism.[26]

20

The Apostolate

Metternich never used his transatlantic title, but modesty was not the reason. 'My life has become a kind of apostolate,' he confided to his wife in July 1824. 'Wherever I go I find a flock of the faithful waiting for their shepherd, and I cannot in all conscience leave them without having bestowed upon them spiritual consolation … a real *multitude* follows me, surrounds me, looks to me, stretches out its hands to me.' For years he had been 'preaching to the deaf', but now that people had seen how he had brought Germany back from 'the very brink of revolution', to which it had been driven by 'the most contemptible weakness' of its rulers and the influence of 'innovators and ideologues of every kind', they listened gratefully.[1]

Germany was certainly calm, but many cast doubt on whether there had ever been much of a storm in the first place. The King of Württemberg, for one, openly mocked Metternich and his crusade, accusing him of having mistaken 'the dreams and exaltations of youth for conspiracy'. The report of the Mainz commission in 1822 did little more than confirm that there had been conspiratorial contacts between the various student organisations, and that subversive sentiments were rife. The only group which did appear to have been party to Karl Sand's murder of Kotzebue were the Giessen 'blacks', but their leader, Karl Follen, had fled abroad in 1820, robbing the commission of the opportunity of interrogating him. He went to Paris, where he met French liberals such as Joseph Rey and Voyer d'Argenson, and then settled at Coire (Chur) in Switzerland, where he founded a Youth League, the *Junglingsbund*, which was to take over from the banned *Burschenschaften* and create a pan-German network. One of his associates, the Dane Johannes (sometimes Joachim) Witt von Dörring, had fled with him, but finding himself short of funds agreed to spy on Follen for the Austrian police. He was not, however, able to provide much in the way of information, as in 1824 Follen gave up on Europe and moved to America (where he obtained the post of Professor of German at Harvard, introduced gymnastics into the university and, it is claimed, the Christmas tree into American homes). In its report, the commission did make much of possible effects on the student bodies of what had been taking place in Spain and Italy, and particularly Greece, but it was obliged to admit that subversive political activity 'expresses itself less in actual performance than in enticement, preparation and preliminaries'.[2]

In September 1822 the Prussian educational reformer and minister Freiherr von Altenstein had further embarrassed Metternich by writing an open letter defending the students. In his view they were guilty only of naïvety and perfectly praiseworthy longings to see Germany great, and he denounced the state's treatment of them as dangerous delinquents. At the same time, the judicial authorities were beginning to complain at the disgraceful behaviour of the police and the random detention of people without charge, and to overturn convictions made in the heat of the first months after the assassination of Kotzebue.[3]

Pressed by Metternich to try harder, the commission redoubled its efforts. As so many German students had fled abroad, to Switzerland or Paris, the commission recruited spies; it would arrest a student and, by threatening him with a long sentence, blackmail him to go abroad and spy on his brethren. This sometimes led to his being unmasked and murdered by them, but yielded little in the way of evidence. The commission's 1824 report confirmed that there were secret societies in existence, but could provide no evidence on their activities.[4]

None of this could shake Metternich's conviction that there did exist in Germany a 'vast anti-social conspiracy'; he explained its lack of activity by the fact that it was powerless without a strong impulse from the revolutionary 'bases' in France. In April 1824 Franchet d'Esperey furnished him with an extensive report that confirmed the existence of a *comité directeur* in Paris which had 'no organisation, no statutes, no regular reunions'.

But France too was tranquil. The long-anticipated death of Louis XVIII on 16 September 1824 had not, as some had feared, been the signal for revolution, and the smooth succession of Monsieur to the throne as Charles X demonstrated that the restoration was secure. 'This calm transition, which has turned the Revolution into a historical episode, proves beyond doubt that the moral regeneration of France is progressing apace,' Metternich admitted.[5]

That did not mean the danger had passed, and Metternich harassed the Mainz commission to come up with more evidence. Mail was opened throughout Germany and every possible lead pursued, but the results were disappointing. In its final report, in 1828, the commission would come to the conclusion that revolutionary tendencies in Germany were almost entirely intellectual in nature, that there was no chance of them producing a revolution unless galvanised by foreign intervention, and that there was no evidence of anyone having given any serious thought to what kind of order might replace the existing one. It concluded by stating that what was happening in Germany was, as elsewhere in Europe, the inevitable consequence of the process of modernisation taking place throughout the Continent, and could not be tackled independently of it.[6]

Instead of reassuring him, lack of evidence of conspiracy tended to make Metternich more suspicious. His instinct was to pry further and delve deeper, regardless of past experience in this sphere. In order to be well-informed on every score, he had put in place for the peace congress at Vienna in 1814 a vast network of informers at every level; he knew what every single member of every delegation was doing, with whom, at every moment of the day and night. It had been a triumph of intelligence-gathering. The fact that it had helped him not one jot in the achievement of his diplomatic aims (and only provided generations of historians with amusement) did not dampen his lust for information. He had informers of every sort in all the capitals and courts of Europe, and devoted much time and effort to the police. Given the challenge as he perceived it, they would have to extend their search for potential subversion into new and ever-expanding areas, involving the most intimate invasion of everyday life, in a pursuit of the elusive that was both endlessly self-justificatory and self-defeating.

In Austria itself, the police were ubiquitous and prided themselves on knowing everything. They watched and pried without any sense of shame, and, as Martha Wilmot, the wife of the chaplain at the British embassy, wrote to her sister shortly after her arrival in the city, 'there is a sort of *Web* cast round you the very day you arrive'. This is echoed in the accounts of other travellers, who were struck by the brazen lack of discretion. It was well known that in every household there were servants on the police's payroll, but an American merchant travelling in Austria, Charles Sealsfield, was astonished by the lack of secrecy involved. One evening at a dinner given him by a Viennese merchant, his host mentioned a proposed new public loan, only to be summoned by the police the following morning and upbraided for discussing matters of state which were not his business. On coming home he dismissed his servants, and was summoned again, to give the reasons for which he had done so.[7]

'Every footman in a public house is a salaried spy,' Sealsfield wrote; 'there are spies paid to visit the taverns and hotels, who take their dinners at the table d'hôte. Others will be seen in the Imperial library for the same purpose, or in the bookseller's shop, to inquire into the purchases made by the different persons. Of course, letters sent and received by the post, if the least suspicious, are opened; and so little pains are taken to conceal this violation of public faith, that the seal of the post-office is not seldom added to that of the writer. These odious measures are not executed with the *finesse* which characterises the French, nor with the military rudeness of the Prussian, but in that silly and despicable way of the Austrian, who, as he is the most awkward personage for this most infamous of all commissions, takes, notwithstanding, a sort of pride in being an Imperial instrument and a person of importance.'[8]

Foreigners were prime objects of suspicion, and popular spas such as Töplitz and Karlsbad were stocked with Austrian noblemen with a command of foreign languages, who lived in the hotels, dined at the *table d'hôte*, took the waters, frequented the concerts and promenaded along with the visitors, reporting on them to the police. Homes in which travellers took rooms were under the constant surveillance of the master of the house.[9]

In 1817 a group of Swiss students at the University of Vienna formed 'the Swiss Society in Vienna', which met at a public eating house and discussed the situation in their homeland. They soon grew so alarmed at the obvious attentions of the police that they decided to dissolve it. They were nevertheless arrested and interrogated, and it was only after repeated diplomatic intervention by the Swiss authorities that they were released, on condition they leave Austria and never return. In 1819 a Prussian student who was sketching the Krimml waterfalls was surrounded by police who demanded to see his papers. He duly produced them and they went away, but that night he was snatched from his bed in a nearby country inn, clapped in irons like a dangerous criminal and taken to Innsbruck. He was released after a few days without charge or explanation, but given to understand that it would be best if he left the country as soon as possible.[10]

The *Polizeihofstelle* archives on the surveillance of foreigners which have survived to this day are not impressive. The files contain little more than skeins of bureaucratic verbiage, lists of names, often misspelled, of foreigners visiting spa towns and of those who have aroused suspicion, with little information to back this up. One man is said to be sympathetic to the Neapolitan rebels, another to have Carbonarist connections, a third has been seen reading the London *Morning Chronicle*. Meetings between two people are deemed suspicious because one of them is Italian, or Polish, or had served in the Napoleonic army. Fantastic conspiracies are hinted at, supported by gossip and even snippets copied from newspapers.[11]

Students continued to be the object of intense observation. They were subjected to repeated interrogations and searches. Every contact with a person from another town was grounds for suspicion, as was any mention of the events in Spain, Naples or Piedmont. The singing of songs such as '*Das Deutsche Vaterland*' could land a student in the guardhouse for forty-eight hours. The *Polizeihofstelle* compiled reports of secret 'machinations' by student societies, which were allegedly communicating with Jahn in gaol, with students in Switzerland, Paris and Warsaw, planning a revolution in France in league with Bonapartists which would lead to the unification of Germany, all of this being orchestrated by a body calling itself the *Classe Dirigeante des Hommes*. The societies that had sprung up in support of the Greek struggle for independence were represented as branches of the *comité directeur*. But suspicion fell on all sorts of other groups as well – Protestant communities in predominantly Catholic areas were identified as 'revolutionary', and even travelling salesmen's movements were tracked with infinite precision.[12]

This blanket surveillance was largely self-defeating. Back in 1804 the Viennese police had noted that the ubiquity of snoopers had made people avoid speaking to each other in public places, with the result that friends would meet in a coffee house and sit for a couple of hours in silence, breaking it only to say goodbye. The police inspector Anton Krametz-Lilienthal complained that the students at Grätz had been so terrified by blatant instances of informing that they would barely exchange a word with each other.[13]

The Austrian police were not on the whole brutal, but they did detain people, sometimes for a very long time. Karl Freiherr von Glave-Kobielski was incarcerated without charge from 26 March 1810 until his death in 1831. János Bacszany had been arrested in connection with the Jacobin conspiracy of 1794 but released two years later. He settled in Vienna, where, after his victory at Wagram in 1809,

Napoleon employed him to compose an appeal to the Hungarians urging them to rise up against Habsburg domination. He left Vienna with the French army and set up home in Paris, but in 1814 the Austrian police ferreted him out, took him back to Austria and put him in gaol, where he died in 1845.[14]

The Austrian police regime in Lombardy-Venetia had, by the mid-1820s, imposed what Stendhal described as 'a kind of reign of terror', with the province treated 'like a colony on the brink of revolt'. Conversation had become 'the most dangerous of pleasures'. An American traveller, George Bancroft, was unpleasantly surprised as he watched the sunset from a hill overlooking Brescia in October 1821. 'Just as I was giving way to feelings of rapture, two Austrian soldiers presented themselves not far from me, one armed with a gun and bayonet, and in the grossest and most absolute terms ordered me to descend, adding harshness to insolence and threats to contumely.'[15]

In 1826 the secret police of Lombardy-Venetia were reorganised and a new set of eighteen regulations issued to the supreme commissioner of police, setting out his duties in order of precedence. The first was 'to investigate and uncover all the schemes, conspiracies, plots, projects, attempts, machinations and enterprises against the safety of the most august ruling house and particularly of the sacred person of H.M. the Emperor himself, as well as the state; to investigate anything and everything that could compromise the public safety, internal or external, of the monarchy'. The second was 'to track down secret societies, corporations, fraternities, gangs and sects, whatever their nature', both inside and outside Austrian dominions. The third was 'to penetrate public opinion', 'to watch those who have a major influence on public opinion, those who invent or propagate false, inaccurate or alarming news', and 'to gather up all the observations, comments, remarks, propositions, desires and complaints of the population'. The fourth, to observe the effect produced by newspapers, periodicals and other publications, to use every possible means to detect those responsible for smuggling forbidden items, and to keep watch on bookshops and print sellers. The fifth, to invigilate the public and private conduct of state functionaries, and the religious practice and doctrinal beliefs of the clergy and people working in the field of education. Further duties were 'to watch all consuls, foreign diplomats, or other accredited agents, or secret emissaries, adventurers, libertines, explorers, etc.', to keep an eye on all travellers, their contacts and correspondence, to set up a network of espionage, and so on. The instructions recommend avoidance of 'any sort of provocation, seduction' or criminal means to obtain results, and warn that as 'the spirit of political faction, the fanaticism for secret sects, the vehemence of temperament and private considerations, no less than the almost universal habit of calumnying the reputation of others all too easily incite the passions into a spirit of vengeance and persecution', the police should be careful in their choice of informers, whose reports should be treated accordingly.[16]

The police of the Habsburg grand duchy of Tuscany were neither efficient nor discriminating in their choice of informers. They wasted huge resources on following Byron and his household when the poet moved to Pisa in 1822. His courtesy visits to the small English colony there were interpreted as briefings from a higher body. One spy, Luigi Torelli, was so imaginative in his interpretation of Byron's activities that an affray with an off-duty dragoon sergeant was described as a 'pitched battle', and the poet was reported as having artillery concealed in the palazzo he had rented. The police of the duchies of Parma and Modena, nominally ruled by Napoleon's widow Marie-Louise, exhibited similar levels of excessive zeal and incompetence. But Metternich had his own people on the spot. In 1822, the French minister in Florence complained that his Austrian counterpart was 'established here like a power within a power, with his spies and his police'.[17]

The Vatican was the most reluctant to cooperate, preferring to rely on its own organs. These were pervasive, invasive and largely ineffectual. Like their colleagues elsewhere, they were obsessed with the danger presented by travellers, who had to show their documents at every border, both state and provincial, in spot checks along the road, at city gates, at inns and even at livery stables. Anyone wishing to stay more than one night had to register with the local police, justifying their visit, and their words might carry less weight than the secret messages contained in their documents: the higher police authorities issuing these would use their own signals to warn any official examining them, and a double-crossed 't' or an undotted 'i' could condemn the traveller to constant surveillance or being moved on. At the same time, the constant movement to and from markets of peasants who failed to carry or had lost their documents, vagabonds and pilgrims on their way to Rome overwhelmed the police, and people were regularly waved through city gates without a check.[18]

Similar levels of ambition, activity, incompetence and laziness characterised the papal police's enforcement of political conformity, the so-called *alta polizia*. They snooped, eavesdropped, followed people and opened letters, but as they were so blatant about it people would keep their mouths shut in public, employ tricks to lose those following them, and consign nothing to the post except trivia. Rumour, hearsay and denunciation were often all the police had to go on, and their only guides to what people were thinking were the slogans scrawled in charcoal on the city walls and public buildings, which they would efface every morning. Every matter was treated with the same gravity. When a group of Bologna's wealthiest citizens established a club for their entertainment and applied for the necessary licence, an investigation was ordered which culminated a two-hundred-page report to Cardinal Consalvi.[19]

In the wake of the events of 1820, the Austrian police and their allies in various parts of Italy made a number of arrests, and the prisoners provided a mixed bag of information. The Illuminati were allegedly active in Tuscany, the Templars in Rome, and a dizzying array of other societies with absurd names in various other parts of the peninsula. One of those arrested, in 1821, shortly after the suppression of the Piedmontese coup, was Karl Follen's follower Johannes Witt von Dörring, who was believed by some to be one of Metternich's own secret agents. He had aroused the suspicion of the French police when he came to Paris in 1818 by staying in expensive hotels under different names and meeting a confusing variety of people. He had supplied the police with information on the secret societies in Germany, which were, according to him, preparing a massacre of ruling princes. Their password was 'INRI', standing not for *Iesus Nazarenus Rex Iudaeorum*, but *Iustum Necare Reges Iniustos* (It is right to kill unjust kings). Döring had moved on to Switzerland to join Follen, and subsequently to England, where he posed as a refugee from Prussian persecution, before travelling to Italy. He told the Austrian police that there was an international conspiracy, indicating links between Germany, Italy and Switzerland, from where the whole thing was being directed. He claimed that although he had been a Freemason, he was not himself a member of any secret society, yet he discoursed authoritatively on the subject of the Carbonari. According to him, they and the Illuminati were one and the same, and were dedicated to the destruction of the existing social order, to murder and mayhem.[20]

Towards the end of 1822, the police in Milan arrested a young Frenchman by the name of Alexandre Andryane. As a student in Geneva in the previous two years he had come across Buonarroti and fallen under his spell. Buonarroti had been working for years to bring all secret societies and conspirators together under the aegis of his *Sublimi Maestri Perfetti* with its Grand Firmament, a kind of areopagus whose membership remains a mystery. His ambition was not the overthrow of one monarchy or another, but universal social revolution. In 1818 he changed the name of the *Sublimi Maestri Perfetti* to *Il Mondo*, and according to some informants operated in Italy under the name of the *Adelfi*. Andryane (codename Plato) claimed to be on a mission to make contact with whatever revolutionary movements he could identify, to try to bring them together and give them renewed hope after the failures of the past two years. He contacted a number of conspirators and attended meetings of secret societies, and he was not impressed. The men he met regurgitated the bloodthirsty slogans and oaths of the Carbonari, but were actually passive liberals who merely longed for a slightly less oppressive system such as a constitutional monarchy. They grossly exaggerated their own numbers, influence and potential, and some of the more honest admitted to him that their societies were a sham. He decided to hand on the papers Buonarroti had entrusted to him and leave. Before he could do so he was arrested and the documents he was carrying seized. Among them was evidence of international conspiracy and the structures and rituals of the *Sublimi Maestri Perfetti*.[21]

Andryane was condemned to death, later commuted to life imprisonment, but after eight years in the Moravian fortress of Spielberg he was pardoned and returned to Paris. There he published memoirs which would give new life to the conspiracy theories. Dörring would also publish sensationalist memoirs on his release from gaol in 1830, in which he rolled out the usual nonsense, enriched by his time in captivity, about the grand conspiracy. On entering a cell he would scour the walls and, so he claimed, discover coded messages from previous incumbents, with instructions to be passed on. This kind of thing only fed the fears of the gullible.[22]

What is astonishing is that it was given any credence by the police. Andryane and Dörring told tales and produced documents which were, to put it mildly, incredible. That they tallied with supposed facts gleaned elsewhere made the police treat them seriously. What the police do not appear to have considered is that from their own files it would seem that where it is not made up this evidence echoes the grand conspiracy of Barruel and the occult secrets of Lombard de Langres. There had been so many books and pamphlets on the theme of the grand conspiracy of the Templars, Masons, Illuminati and the rest, scraps of which found their way into common parlance, that it had become a familiar theme. It inspired poseurs and fantasists, and frauds who would try to sell the police vitally important evidence on some plot or other. It also provided a means of diverting a charge, as in the case of one André Achard, arrested by the French police for highway robbery in July 1824, who attempted to get off by confessing to being part of a conspiracy by Piedmontese revolutionaries directed from Paris operating under the name of *l'Union Croisée* which meant to place Napoleon's son on the throne. He gave the names of officers involved which, when checked, turned out to be false, and the only elements in his 'confession' that were true were publicly known.[23]

Neither the French nor the Austrian police appear to have paused to consider the plausibility of the stories they were fed by the likes of Andryane. If those he identified had been serious conspirators, in touch with colleagues in France, Germany and Switzerland, it seems unlikely that a man like him could have turned up in Milan unannounced and been entrusted with important documents. The members of the secret societies would surely have been given notice that an emissary was due, and have insisted on passwords or other validation. Some of the documents in the French police archives are of an amateurish silliness that beggars belief. The induction rituals described all derive from one of the many books on the grand conspiracy, while the recipes for invisible ink are infantile (e.g. 'Take an oak gall, grate finely and dissolve in fresh water until the mixture is white but not too thick, write with a new pen on white paper').[24]

The other thing the police and their masters failed to do was to confront the claims made about the extent and power of the alleged secret societies with their failure to achieve results. This led them to exaggerate the threat and to impose grossly disproportionate punishments, which had the effect of creating martyrs. In October 1820 the journalist and poet Silvio Pellico was arrested in Venice, although it seems the '*vèndita*' he belonged to was actually a literary society. At the beginning of 1822, after a lengthy trial, Pellico was sentenced to death. This was commuted to fifteen years of *carcere duro*, and he was sent in chains to the Spielberg. He would be released in 1830, and two years later published the account of his sufferings in a small book entitled *Le mie Prigioni*, which became an international best-seller, turning a mediocre poet incapable of doing any harm to anyone into a martyr whose treatment blackened the reputation of the Habsburg monarchy around the world and inspired countless young men to take up arms against it.

Another who achieved the status of martyr was Count Federico Confalonieri, who had conspired with the Piedmontese constitutionalists, encouraging them to help their comrades in the liberation of Lombardy-Venetia in 1820. He was tracked down and arrested in 1822. Early in 1824, after a trial which also took an inordinately long time, he was sentenced to death, commuted to life of *carcere duro*, also in the Spielberg. But on his way there he was to have a curious, almost surreal experience. He was conveyed from Milan in a windowless carriage resembling a large black box, his hands and feet chained, sitting between two armed policemen. At the beginning of March 1824 his convoy stopped at Vienna. He was so emaciated after two years of incarceration and interrogation that he could barely walk, so he was carried upstairs to a tastefully furnished apartment. The following evening he was driven in an ordinary carriage across the city, whose palaces were illuminated and whose streets swirled with gaily attired people laughing and singing, as the carnival was in full swing. It drew up outside the Ballhausplatz chancellery and he was carried upstairs and into a small study, where he found himself face to face with Metternich.

During their interview, which lasted a full two hours, the Austrian chancellor questioned him with exquisite courtesy about his activities in Italy, repeatedly asking the baffled Confalonieri about the *comité directeur* in Paris. Metternich lectured him as he might a naughty child, reproaching him for having embraced 'false' ideas and ending up on the wrong, and the losing, side. 'Our cause is therefore not only the better one,' he blandly affirmed, 'it is the more successful.' Confalonieri was struck by the Austrian chancellor's certainties as he exposed for his benefit the Metternichian world-view, in which everything that did not entirely accord with his own opinions was *de facto* Jacobinical, a term with which he embraced philanthropists, liberals, constitutionalists, deists, agnostics and a multitude of others. Metternich for his part also learned something which astonished him, even though he had suspected it for some time. In a letter to Lebzeltern after his interview with Confalonieri on 7 March he wrote that he had heard 'some curious things concerning the dealings of the Russian embassy in Turin before the outbreak of the Piedmontese revolt'.[25]

21

Mutiny

The last vestiges of Alexander's liberalism had dissipated, and his 'mysticism' had grown decidedly reactionary. 'To maintain peace, to combat the revolutionaries and attack them everywhere, that is my ambition, and the only glory to which I aspire,' he declared to La Ferronnays in July 1824, and he had already achieved a great deal in the way of crushing the spirit of those whom he had encouraged to dream and to place such high hopes in him.[1]

Among his first acts on ascending the throne in 1801 had been to abolish the Secret Expedition, a sinister body which dealt with political subversion; to free some seven hundred political prisoners, most of whom had no idea why they had been locked up; and to forbid the use of torture in interrogation. 'In a well-ordered state all crimes should be embraced, tried and punished by ordinary law,' he explained in a manifesto issued on 2 April that year. Things did not work out that way. The Secret Expedition's functions were seamlessly taken over by the office of the governor of St Petersburg. In 1805, before setting off to war, Alexander was obliged to set up a body to deal with state security, and in 1807 a Committee of Public Safety (*Komitet Obshchei Bezopasnosti*). In 1810 he established a ministry of police, modelled on Napoleon's, under General Balashov, who adopted the worst aspects of the model. Alexander's friend the statesman Viktor Pavlovich Kochubey complained that St Petersburg had become 'infested with spies of every kind: there are foreign spies and Russian spies, salaried spies and voluntary spies; police officers have begun to adopt disguises; they even say that the minister himself has begun to disguise himself'. According to him, 'they did everything to provoke crime and suspicion … resorting to tricks of every sort' to entrap people. Alexander criticised Balashov's methods, arguing that surveillance was pointless and that all denunciations should be ignored. Yet he created a new Secret Chancellery run by Yakov Ivanovich Sanglen (a French émigré formerly named Saint-Glin) – whom he instructed to spy on Balashov. The governor of St Petersburg had his own independent secret police force, but it was not his spies who were feared most.[2]

While the tsar was occupied abroad with waging war and peacemaking, the man left in control back home was General Aleksey Andreevich Arakcheev, a brutal martinet commonly referred to as 'the vampire', whom Alexander had appointed to head the council of ministers. Although he scrupulously refrained from doing anything but carry out his master's commands, Arakcheev quickly extended his power into all areas of government. His presence was felt, and feared, everywhere. When he returned to Russia, Alexander left the running of the country to the general while he concentrated on his programme of reform.[3]

When this foundered, he turned his attention to what he saw as the more serious task of facing up to the forces of evil attacking his country. In 1817 he amalgamated the ministries of education and of religious affairs, and appointed Aleksandr Nikolaevich Galitzine minister. An old friend of the tsar, Galitzine had enjoyed a dissolute youth, but after being nominated procurator of the Holy Synod of the Orthodox Church he began reading the Bible, and gradually found his way to God. He had helped Alexander to spiritually weather the trials of 1812, and fed his ardour to save the world. One of the founders of the Russian Bible Society, he encouraged all faiths based on the Book: like Alexander, he was more of a reborn Christian than a conventional Orthodox believer; he nevertheless came to reject the Enlightenment, which he equated with immorality.

In 1819 Alexander instructed Mikhail Nikolaevich Magnitsky to cleanse the University of Kazan, reportedly a hotbed of atheism and immorality. After a cursory inspection, Magnitsky sacked more than half of the teaching staff. The library was purged of nefarious literature, beginning with Machiavelli and taking in all the philosophers of the Enlightenment and many contemporary German writers. Geology, deemed to be incompatible with the Bible, was removed from the curriculum, the teaching of mathematics and philosophy was curtailed, and priests were brought in to provide religious instruction. By way of justification, Magnitsky pointed out that the sole purpose of education was 'the formation of true sons of the Orthodox Church, true subjects of the tsar, and good and useful citizens of the fatherland', and to counteract 'the evil spirit of the times'.[4]

The universities of Kharkov, Dorpat, Vilna and Moscow were subjected to similar purges. The University of St Petersburg was vigorously defended by its founder, Sergei Semionovich Uvarov, who battled the concept that everything Western was tainted, and maintained that there could not be 'education without danger, that is, fire which does not burn'. He was forced to resign. His replacement, D.P. Runich, a close friend of Magnitsky, labelled all those who did not agree with him 'reptiles of revolution', and promptly sacked four professors. This provoked an exodus of students; within a few months the university only had forty left.[5]

In the first years of Alexander's rule press laws had either been abolished or fell into desuetude, and the number of periodicals grew, leading to a lively literary scene; but this changed in 1817. Admiral Aleksandr Semionovich Shishkov, president of the Russian Academy, set the tone, arguing that the eighteenth century had bred a 'spirit of godlessness and depravity' that had brought in its wake 'destruction and murder', which had drowned religion and civilisation in 'torrents of blood'. It was the French language that had spread the evil 'from country to country, from house to house, from school to school, from paper to paper, from theatre to theatre' like some corrupting plague.[6]

While such views might appear to go against the grain of everything he believed in, Alexander did not react against them. He was growing increasingly taciturn. The death of his sister Catherine in January 1819 deeply affected him, and he felt isolated as he struggled with his contradictory impulses, both spiritual and political. His search for inner peace seemed less and less compatible with his role as absolute monarch, and he expressed the desire to abdicate more than once. At the same time he saw the act of abdication as one of cowardice and failure in his duty to God, who had placed him on the throne. He was also developing alarming levels of paranoia. Whenever a name was mentioned, he would consult a little black book Metternich had given him listing all recorded political suspects. The paranoia was also personal. 'Not only did he fear for his security, but, if he heard someone laugh in the street or caught one of his courtiers smiling, he was convinced he was being laughed at,' his former mistress Maria Antonovna Naryshkina confided to the comtesse de Boigne. His worsening deafness meant that he thought people were mocking him in his presence, as well as making fun of him behind his back.[7]

In June 1822 he met the 'holy man' Photius, who lived only on bread and water, wore a hair shirt and an iron penitent's belt. The tsar quickly fell under his spell. Photius was determined to expel all 'heretics' from Russia, among whom he included members of the Bible Society. On 30 April 1824 he revealed to Alexander 'the plan of the revolution' and the 'secrets of the iniquitous aim towards which the secret society is working in Russia and everywhere else', and persuaded him to ban the Bible Society and dismiss Galitzine.[8]

On 1 August 1822, before leaving for Verona, Alexander had ordered the dissolution of all associations, including Masonic lodges. The measure was deeply unpopular. There was only one French-style café in St Petersburg, and that was closely watched by the police. There were no salons where free and easy social intercourse or intellectual discussion could take place. Masonic lodges and other societies provided a welcome social diversion. Idealistic young officers congregated in associations such as the Union of Welfare, dedicated, like the *Tugendbund*, to rebuilding the moral fabric of society. There were also literary societies such as the Free Society of Lovers of Russian Literature, the Green Lamp, and Arzamas, of which Pushkin was a leading light, whose members were concerned not only with literature, but also with its function – which many of them saw in political terms. They celebrated Karl Sand's assassination of Kotzebue as an act of heroism, idolised Bolívar and hailed Riego and Quiroga's *pronunciamiento*. They wrote and recited poems and essays criticising the state of affairs and calling for change. Pushkin's 'Ode to Freedom' suggested a constitutional monarchy, while in 'The Village' he expressed the hope that the oppression of the people would cease and liberty would reign in Russia.

There was nothing revolutionary about such bodies. When a young man by the name of Nikolai Turgenev joined the Union of Welfare, he was surprised to discover that all the members did was sit around bemoaning the state of Russia and formulating pious wishes for the future. When he freed two of his house-serfs and suggested others do likewise, he met with stunned silence. 'Among the many contradictions one finds here in the character of men and the state of affairs, one must include the *so-called liberal* ideas widespread among young men who serve with zeal a purely despotic government,' noted a French diplomat; 'armed with his knout, subject to an absolute Monarch, surrounded by his own slaves, a young Russian officer will lecture you on the rights of peoples and on liberty as though he were a citizen of the United States.'[9]

These societies provided comfort to a generation by fostering a sense of togetherness in an alienating world which appeared to have no place for them and their talents. There were many such, who fell into the category of the *Lichnii chelovek*, the superfluous man. In his poem *Eugene Onegin*, Pushkin describes how such young men would come together to discuss great things between the Veuve Cliquot and the Château Lafitte. Although the discussions led to nothing, they allowed the young men to indulge their enthusiasms in harmless ways.

While most of the societies obediently dissolved, others went underground, and their members discovered the thrill of conspiracy. The Union of Welfare grew more political, and divided into a Northern Society based in St Petersburg and a Southern in the military bases in Ukraine. The first was led by the twenty-four-year-old Guards captain Nikita Mikhailovich Muravev, who had joined up to fight the French at the age of seventeen and distinguished himself in battle. While he did draw up a list of the society's aims, embracing a constitutional monarchy and the emancipation of the serfs, he was typical of his generation in that he occasionally drifted to the left or the right of this position. Other members of the society fluctuated even more in their views, while many did not have any fixed ones at all. One, Aleksandr Ivanovich Yakubovich, bragged that he would kill the tsar, but was described by one of his own colleagues as 'a storm in a glass of water'.[10]

The Southern Society was more radical. Its leader, Pavel Ivanovich Pestel, was the son of the governor of Siberia. He had studied in St Petersburg and in Germany, been wounded at Borodino in 1812 and was, in 1821, a full colonel at the age of twenty-seven. He was a republican, but how many of his members shared his views is uncertain, as is how many of them there actually were: he confided to Nikolai Turgenev that there were only five or six he could rely on. The Northern and Southern Societies held talks aimed at achieving consensus, but never managed to agree a common programme, let alone a course of action.[11]

Being mostly military men, they saw Riego and Quiroga's *pronunciamiento* as the obvious model. 'Our revolution,' one of them explained, 'will be similar to the Spanish revolution of 1820; it will not cost a single drop of blood, for it will be executed by the army alone, without the assistance of the people.' The fact that the Spanish revolution had caused a great deal of bloodshed before being crushed does not seem to have been addressed. Nor do any of the plotters appear to have had any idea of what would follow their *pronunciamiento*. Pestel told one friend that after carrying out the coup he would retire, like Washington (to a monastery rather than Mount Vernon). He did not explain who would govern the country or how. The Northern Society actually designated a 'dictator', in the shape of Prince Sergei Petrovich Trubetskoy, a conservative who feared revolution and seems to have hoped the whole thing could be arranged amicably through some kind of deal with the tsar. Although they were plotting revolution, few of them were, in any real sense of the word, revolutionaries. Their impulse was idealistic, histrionic and thoroughly immature: they were, in effect, playing at revolution.[12]

The Russian imperial family had, over the past three generations, built up a cult of the military, partly as a means of control, partly as a form of self-validation. The tsar and his siblings had been playing at soldiers from the cradle. They never appeared out of military uniform. They relished parades, balletic rituals of domination which had no military value – quite the contrary, as their frequency irritated the troops and removed any hint of the sense of special occasion that a rare opportunity to parade before the sovereign might have held.

The Russian empire had, over the past half-century, expanded more rapidly and further than any other on the globe, yet as it did so it had developed an almost pathological fear of invasion. That it had in 1812 managed to repel the most formidable force ever assembled in Europe, led by one of the greatest generals in history, all without making much of a military effort, had done nothing to allay this fear, and Alexander would not stand down the huge army he had built up for the conquest of France. Its maintenance involved crippling expense, eating up half of the national budget (without including the navy), and kept hundreds of thousands of able-bodied men away from the plough and the factory, where they could be contributing to the economy. The officers should have been in politics, the arts, journalism, the law or other liberal professions. With no war to distract them or to offer a chance to shine, they were bored and frustrated, and offended by the brutal routines of military service. To make matters worse, they were so poorly paid that many subalterns, not being able to afford new ones, did not go out for fear of wearing out their uniforms, and wrapped themselves in blankets when in their quarters. Foreign diplomats regularly reported the disaffection, and in August 1822 the French acting minister in St Petersburg, Boislecomte, noted that everyone was commenting on the unrest in the army and the mood of discontent among the younger sections of the nobility. One general told him that the only thing preventing a revolution was the lack of a leader.[13]

The 'mutiny' of the Semeonovsky Guards came as a shock, yet instead of enquiring into its causes, Alexander laid it at the door of the *comité directeur*. He had the entire unit disciplined and the men dispersed among line regiments all around the country – a curious way of dealing with 'contagion'. He ordered the setting up of a spy network of soldiers and officers of each rank in every unit, who were paid to inform on their comrades. What he did not do was address any of the underlying problems.[14]

Only weeks after meting out these punishments, the tsar was handed by General Vassilchikov a list of officers who were planning to stage some kind of mutiny. After looking through it Alexander fell into a reverie. 'My dear Vassilchikov!' he said after a while. 'You who have been in my service since the beginning of my reign, you know that I have myself shared and encouraged these illusions and these errors.' After a pause, he added: 'It is not for me to inflict punishment.' Not long after, Alexander received a report from Colonel Benckendorff, chief of staff to the Guard Corps, which listed various nests of disaffection. Some of the stated objectives of the conspirators were alarming, but there was no danger to the state: they might be able to find some kindred spirits among foreign-educated individuals in Moscow and St Petersburg, but nowhere further afield. 'It can confidently be said that in the interior of Russia nobody has even thought about a constitution,' it pointed out, adding that the nobility had no wish to lose their privileges and the people were used to doing what they were told. Alexander did not react. 'I know that I am surrounded by assassins who have evil designs on my person,' he said to one general, but did nothing about it. He was showing less and less interest in what was happening around him, and had taken to travelling around Russia with no apparent purpose beyond that of getting away from the constraints of court life.[15]

In July 1824 Alexander was handed a report from an officer of English origin, Captain John Sherwood, stationed in Ukraine, which contained chapter and verse on the Southern Society. The tsar muttered something about the will of God, and left it at that. In 1825 General Diebitsch warned him of trouble brewing, and in October of that year Benckendorff produced another report, drawing attention to a near collapse of discipline in the officer corps; inactivity and scant prospect of promotion had, he explained, bred a profound sense of grievance among them. It was only on receipt of a further report that the tsar at last ordered an investigation.[16]

He then set off on another journey, leaving the governance of his empire in the hands of Arakcheev. While the tsar was away, Arakcheev's mistress was brutally murdered by the serfs on his estate of Gruzino, whereupon, mad with grief and rage, he dropped everything and left for the country, where he indulged both emotions to the full. He ignored urgent letters from Sherwood warning that the conspirators in the Second Army stationed in Ukraine were preparing to rise.[17]

On 19 November, after a brief illness following a chill, Alexander died at Taganrog, on the Sea of Azov. The news reached St Petersburg on 27 November, and the army and civil service duly began swearing allegiance to the new tsar, Alexander's younger brother Constantine. As it happened, Constantine was not in fact the heir to the throne. Back in 1819, Alexander had decided to pass him over, partly on account of his volatile and tempestuous temperament, partly because he was divorcing the German princess to whom he was married in order to wed a Polish lady whose rank was not commensurate with the exigencies of the Russian imperial family's code. Constantine had renounced his right of succession in favour of the next brother, Nicholas. But Alexander did not tell anyone about this except his mother, and consigned the relevant documents to the safekeeping of a Church dignitary, who was given no inkling of their significance.

When Constantine, who was in Warsaw, heard that he was being hailed as the new emperor, he wrote to Nicholas informing him that in fact he, not Constantine, was the new tsar. Nicholas did not at first believe him. After a multiple exchange of letters and much soul-searching, Nicholas accepted the succession, and the date of 14 December was set for the army and civil service to swear a new oath of allegiance to him. For reasons it is hard to understand, Constantine was popular with the army, and was believed to have liberal instincts. The Northern Society decided to take advantage of the confusion attendant on swearing the new oath to make its move. Neither aims nor consequences were uppermost in their minds, only the desire to act. At their last meeting, on the evening of 13 December, the leadership were in a state of Romantic delirium, making heady speeches and declaring their readiness to die. But no plan was made beyond that of making a *pronunciamiento* in favour of Constantine and constitutional government. Neither had it occurred to them to prepare their men to participate in a revolution: they would merely order them out, as their rank entitled them to do.[18]

Early on the morning of 14 December, the brothers Mikhail and Alexander Bestuzhev led a battalion of their regiment, the Moskovsky, out of its barracks in St Petersburg, having told the men that the rightful Emperor Constantine was in chains and they must help deliver him. They marched off to Senate Square, where they drew the battalion up in parade order. They were soon joined by units of the Marine Guards and the Grenadiers. As they waited, watched by a gathering crowd of bemused onlookers, various other plotters turned up, delivered themselves of florid declarations, and wandered off. Colonel Bulatov, aide to the Northern Society's 'dictator', Prince Trubetskoy, also put in an appearance, but then went off to swear allegiance to the new tsar. Of the dictator himself there was no sign. After driving around the city trying to explain to various authorities that he had never meant any disloyalty, Trubetskoy sought asylum in the house of the Austrian ambassador, Lebzeltern, who happened to be his brother-in-law.

The 3,000 troops drawn up on Senate Square were getting colder and increasingly bewildered. They obediently huzza'd when their officers shouted various slogans which they did not understand: not having the faintest idea what a constitution might be, they took 'Constantine and the Constitution' (*Konstantin i Konstitutsia* in Russian) to refer to Constantine and his wife.

Meanwhile, Nicholas had gathered other units, but before confronting the mutineers he sent General Miloradovich to parley with them. He was shot by one of the rebels as he rode up. Nicholas then sent another officer, then the Metropolitan Serafim, and finally his own younger brother, Grand Duke Michael, who was also shot at. He then ordered a unit of cavalry to disperse the mutineers, but the icy cobbles proved their undoing, and their charge turned into a chaotic withdrawal which caused much mirth among the by now sizeable crowd of onlookers. These were passive, although by early afternoon more and more shouts of support for the mutineers could be heard, mingled with calls for Nicholas to abdicate and the hurling of a few stones.

After sending one more emissary offering clemency, Nicholas brought his artillery into play and ordered them to open up with canister shot. The mutineers made no attempt to charge the guns or defend themselves. They began to fall back, but their ranks were broken by the civilians fleeing in panic, precipitating a general rout, peppered by the artillery, which changed to ball shot to break the ice on the river Neva when some of the fugitives tried to make their escape across that. Exact numbers of those shot and drowned have never been established.

Nine days passed before news of the Northern Society's plans reached their comrades in Ukraine. Pestel had been arrested, so leadership was taken over by Sergei Ivanovich Muravev-Apostol. He did not manage to muster his troops until 30 December, when he marched out of barracks at the head of some eight hundred men of the Chernigov Regiment. He had read out a declaration in which he explained that their ills stemmed from the fact that the tsar was not fulfilling the will of God. After a certain amount of marching about in an attempt to galvanise other units, he came up against loyal troops, and was defeated.

The rebels' action had been a gesture rather than an attempt to seize power, and did not constitute an attack on the monarchy itself, but while the episode smacked of farce rather than revolutionary terror, it placed Nicholas in an unenviable position, personally as well as politically. The shy twenty-nine-year-old had never been prepared to rule, and it cannot have been easy to suddenly find himself thrust forward into a role he did not particularly relish, and then to face the enmity of his subjects. Having to fight for his throne at the outset was less than dignified, and presented the new tsar to his people in aggressive guise: normally successions were accompanied by amnesties. This was reflected in the way Nicholas and his diplomats represented the revolt to the outside world, which swung between outrage at the enormity of the event and a calm assertion that it had been a minor incident of no significance. It was all, in the final analysis, horribly embarrassing.[19]

Nicholas was not only ill-prepared, but was also poorly endowed to deal with the challenge fate had dealt him. A tall, good-looking man with a commanding presence, he was not devoid of charm, and captivated many by his manner. According to one of his pages, he was 'a bizarre mixture of defects and qualities, of pettiness and grandeur: both brutal and chivalrous, courageous to the point of temerity and suspicious to the point of cowardice; equitable and tyrannical, generous and cruel, fond both of ostentation and simplicity'. Much of this was probably the consequence of a less than happy childhood.[20]

He had been his father's favourite, and losing him before his fifth birthday had come as a shock. From then on he was at the mercy of General Lamsdorff, who was in charge of his upbringing and that of his younger brother Michael. 'General Lamsdorff knew how to implant in us one emotion – fear,' Nicholas later wrote. The boy found comfort in the person of his English nanny, Jane Lyon, and he cried bitter tears when she left. He reacted against this harsh upbringing with defensive stubbornness which frequently turned to aggression, and his tutors noted that there was 'too much violence' in his behaviour, his games were noisy and disorderly, and that he always ended up hurting himself or others.[21]

Nicholas and his younger brother were given a broad, if superficial, education and the rudiments of religious instruction, but the main thrust of his upbringing was military, and he grew up to the sound of orders, bugles and cannon shot, which implanted in him a respect for hierarchy, and a strong sense of honour and duty. In the structures and routines of the military life he saw the surest code of conduct as well as a comforting refuge from the uncertainties and disorderliness of life.[22]

He regarded uniforms as a way of reminding people that they were not private individuals who could do as they pleased, but members of a structure which demanded service. A uniform immediately identified a person and his place within that state structure. That is why he introduced them into the civil service and even the universities, and why he imposed military structures on areas of the administration such as land surveying, forestry, mining, engineering and transport. The regimentation did not stop at uniforms: officers were obliged to wear a moustache, which had to be black whatever the colour of the man's hair, while civil servants had to be clean-shaven. Nicholas would issue dozens of decrees concerning the numbers of buttons on uniforms and the cut of jackets, trousers and breeches.[23]

In 1817 he had married Princess Charlotte of Prussia, the daughter of Frederick William III. The two loved each other dearly, and their home was a model of conjugal affection and propriety. On 12 December 1825, after reading the letter from his brother Constantine which finally convinced him that he had to accept the succession, Nicholas went to his wife and knelt before her, his empress, while she embraced her dear 'Nicks', as she called him.[24]

He admired Ivan the Terrible and particularly Peter the Great, who had drawn up the table of ranks which defined the hierarchy; he viewed the country as a pyramid with himself at the apex, performing his duty to God, with every person beneath him fulfilling theirs to those above them in the hierarchy, each bound by his obligations to his superiors and receiving those of their inferiors. Since he dismissed any alternative view of things and regarded unfamiliar ideas as 'abstractions', he saw no useful purpose in discussion.

The December mutiny had been so far from everything Nicholas regarded as proper that he was baffled as well as shocked by it. Returning home to his anxious wife after putting it down, he wasted no time setting up an interrogation room in the Hermitage Palace, to which he had the first prisoners conducted that very evening. They were brought in one after the other, with their hands bound behind their backs, and Nicholas questioned them himself. The following day he set up an Investigating Committee, but insisted on personally interrogating the principal mutineers. He treated them like wayward children, sometimes talking to them more in sorrow than in anger, like a disappointed father, trying to engage their sympathy, professing a desire to help them. At other times he would shout at them, stamp his feet and threaten harsh punishment, while they were forced to stare into a bank of candles. He would modify his approach with the same person on different days, and at the end of every session, when the prisoners were escorted back to their cells in the Peter and Paul fortress, he specified whether they were to be chained, manacled or left unfettered, granting and withdrawing minor privileges. But, try as he might, he still found the whole thing utterly incomprehensible.[25]

Following the investigation, five were hanged, a further 121 received various custodial sentences or were banished to Siberia, and three hundred others were disciplined, reduced in rank and transferred to other regiments, where they were kept under surveillance. A number who had been abroad at the time and did not return to face interrogation were condemned to death *in absentia*. The sentences were light by comparison with those handed out in England and France, where people were hanged, guillotined or transported on the flimsiest of evidence. But these 'Decembrists', as the participants of the revolt were known, quickly came to be seen as martyrs. The death penalty had not been applied in Russia for decades, and the rank of the condemned, all of whom were nobles, some from very aristocratic families, made punishments such as a lifetime in a peasant hovel in Siberia or service in the ranks of a line regiment in the Caucasus seem excessively harsh. Wives of common criminals exiled to Siberia were allowed to join their husbands and return home with them at the end of their sentence, but Nicholas decreed that the wives of the rebels would be stripped of their noble status, would forfeit the right to dispose of their property and could never return, even after the end of the sentence or the death of their husband, and any children they might bear were to be registered as state serfs.[26]

There was also much unfavourable comment on the manner in which the investigation had been carried out. In its report, the committee represented the Union of Welfare as a well-organised body with organs of government ready to take over the country, even though most of its members knew this to be untrue. One of them, Aleksandr Dmitrievich Borovkov, a minor literary figure who had been employed as a police informer for the past fifteen years, admitted that they had built up a dangerous conspiracy from the spoutings of nonentities. How could anyone, he pointed out, take seriously a man like Zavalishyn, a boastful fantasist who had, during a visit to England in 1822, declared that he was going to fight for the revolution in Spain, but failed to make a move, then gone to California, which, having been enchanted by the climate, he decided to conquer for Russia, and thence to Mexico, where he meant to play a glorious role, before returning to Russia and sounding off at meetings of the Northern Society. Maksim Yakovlevich von Vock, one of the most senior police officials in Russia, summed up the revolt as a desperate outburst against an intolerable state of affairs, a cry for help. While the enterprise had been criminal and reprehensible, he pointed out that 'everything had been done to provoke the discontent and nothing to smother it at birth'.[27]

Nicholas did not see it that way. 'Louis XVI failed in his duty and was punished for it,' he had written in a history essay as a child. 'A monarch has no right to pardon the enemies of the State.' Baffled and insulted by the whole episode, he took refuge in the conspiracy theory. In this he was not alone. Several members of the Investigating Committee assured the Dowager Empress Maria Feodorovna that in order to join the Southern Society a man had to swear his readiness to murder his father, his mother, his brother and his sister if ordered to by his superiors in the society. They had been deluged by denunciations and accusations against various generals and officials, against foreigners, Freemasons and secret societies of one kind or another. Wild allegations were made, the Illuminati resurfaced, and bizarre theories were constructed. The kind of nonsense being peddled is well illustrated by an entry in the diary of Philipp von Neumann, secretary to the Austrian embassy in London: 'the scheme of the conspirators was to assassinate the whole of the Imperial family at the grave of the Emperor Alexander on the day of his burial at St Petersburg …'[28]

For Nicholas, a grand conspiracy by foreign '*canaille*' was the only explanation. He commissioned the Prussian minister of justice Karl Albert von Kamptz to write an article in the *Allgemeine Litteratur-Zeitung* to the effect that the rebellion had been the work of a Europe-wide network of secret societies. In April 1826 he gave orders that everyone who had ever belonged to any association, secret or not, must be identified and obliged to make a full confession. He was haunted by the idea that the conspiracy might still be in existence, that some of the conspirators had got away and were rebuilding their forces, and even that those exiled to Siberia might be concerting with the numerous Polish prisoners and exiles there.[29]

22

Cleansing

On the day of the five Decembrists' executions, Nicholas issued a manifesto in which he announced the necessity of cleansing society of 'the consequences of the disease that had been incubating in its midst'. He went on to explain that this disease was an alien element in Russia, whose 'heart' was pure. He stressed the necessity of parents safeguarding their children from evil (foreign) influences and educating them to understand that 'love of the Monarch and devotion to the throne are rooted in the national character' of Russia.[1]

Nicholas meant to break with the past and adopt an entirely new approach to protecting the state. He did not want the kind of secret police that spied and repressed; he wanted an organ that would enable him to exercise his fatherly role of keeping his subjects out of harm's way and guiding them, with loving severity – and he meant to keep direct control of it. He transferred all police work concerned with law enforcement and criminal investigation to the ministry of the interior. Matters of a political nature were to be dealt with by his own chancellery, within which he created, by imperial *ukaz* on 3 July 1826, a dedicated section, the third. To head the Third Section of His Imperial Majesty's Chancellery and implement his concept he appointed the forty-four-year-old General Aleksandr Kristoforovich von Benckendorff.

Benckendorff was an unlikely candidate to run the secret police of an empire faced with revolutionary perils. A charming ladies' man, not particularly intelligent or energetic, vague, forgetful and absent-minded by the time he had reached middle age, he was seen by many as a bumbling nonentity, even as something of a joke. The scion of Baltic German barons and the son of an infantry general who had been close to Tsar Paul I, he had been sent to a school in Bavaria, followed by one in St Petersburg run by French Jesuits. In 1798 he became an officer in the Semeonovsky Guards, in whose ranks he fought at Eylau nine years later. In the same year he accompanied Petr Alexeevich Tolstoy on his embassy to Paris, which he enjoyed greatly. He met many interesting people, including Metternich, then Austrian ambassador in the French capital, whom he seems to have emulated in his numerous amorous conquests, to the extent of sharing some. In 1812 he was given command of a 'flying detachment' with orders to harry Napoleon's retreating army, which he did with success and with greater humanity than most of his colleagues, treating both French prisoners and the serfs who fought under his orders with consideration. The following year he commanded a brigade at the Battle of Leipzig, and went on to liberate Holland and Belgium and to take part in the French campaign of 1814.

In 1819 he became chief of staff of the Guard Corps, and quickly realised that all was not well. He was particularly alarmed by the young officers, who combined low morale and lax discipline with unorthodox political views, but his attempts to remedy this were thwarted by unit commanders. His conviction that the Semeonovsky mutiny of 1820 had nothing to do with any international conspiracy did not endear him to Alexander, and he was transferred to the command of a cavalry division.[2]

Benckendorff grew close to Grand Duke Nicholas, who liked and trusted him, and from the moment news of Alexander's death reached St Petersburg he was present at most of the confabulations concerning the succession. He was with Nicholas on the morning of 14 December, and was the first to call out his unit in support of the new tsar. Nicholas appointed him to the Investigating Committee, to which he contributed a voice of sanity and a note of humanity. During interrogations he was always polite and even solicitous towards the prisoners, many of whom noted his kindness.[3]

On his return from Paris in 1810, Benckendorff had submitted a memorandum to Alexander on the desirability of establishing a political police force along the lines of Fouché's, with the proviso that it should have a moral base and constitute a 'cohort of right-thinking people'. Alexander had never shown much interest in police. In the decade 1810–20, while the budget of the foreign ministry quadrupled, that of the ministry of police remained roughly the same, at under 3 per cent of state revenue. In 1819 he abolished the ministry, and the police continued to function as a law unto themselves, using bribery and intimidation to acquire evidence, which they used for various purposes unconnected with the enforcement of the law or state security. Staffed mostly by people of low calibre, uneducated and venal, this body epitomised the worst stereotypes of the snooping, sinister, corrupt secret police of legend, spying on harmless individuals while ignoring more serious matters. In February 1820 the Moscow police reported how many people gathered at the English Club, how many went to a masquerade and how many to the theatre on a given day (120, 136 and 769 respectively). But they did not report, as the French ambassador did in the very same month, and for months before and after, that people were bored, fed up with Alexander's obsession with religion and his growing taciturnity, and overwhelmingly wished he would try to enjoy life and let them do so too. They also failed to note what many ordinary people were commenting on, namely that the guards stationed in St Petersburg were on the verge of mutiny. The street police were also inefficient and corrupt, and brutal in the extreme, administering rough justice and beating people up in full view of passers-by.[4]

Following the Decembrist revolt, Benckendorff produced a new memorandum which painted a dismal picture of the existing state of affairs: 'our secret police is almost brainless', he wrote, and, what was worse, 'honourable people are afraid of it, while rascals manipulate it'. An efficient secret police ought to be centralised, he argued, with agents everywhere and a semi-military arm covering the whole country. Vigilant postmasters in St Petersburg, Moscow and all the provincial capitals ought to keep close watch on all private correspondence. But the most important element in ensuring the body's effectiveness was to make it honourable, beginning with its chief, so that decent people 'who might wish to warn the government about some conspiracy or to appraise him of interesting news' should feel inclined and confident enough to come forward. 'Evil-doers, intriguers and other such people who have repented of their faults or wish to redeem themselves by some denunciation will at least know where to turn.' There were contradictions in his argument: while denouncing the evils of 'a police which relies on denunciation and intrigue', he advocated extensive use of spies.[5]

The Third Section consisted of sixteen people, based in an office on Fontanka Street. They were marshalled by Benckendorff's director of chancellery, Maksim Yakovlevich von Vock, a likeable, educated man of progressive views, and rapidly built up a pool of some 5,000 informers, most of them strategically embedded in society. A letter from Vock to Benckendorff written in July 1826 provides a window on to the process of recruiting such agents. Vock had identified a minor noble by the name of Nefedev who, he believed, could render excellent service 'as a consequence of his connections in the middle and higher social circles of Moscow'. He would be 'a walking encyclopedia, to which I can always refer', and would be perfectly positioned to produce information on anyone in Moscow, which he had plausible reasons to visit frequently, and where he had a house in which he often entertained, which meant that he could invite the objects of the Third Section's interest rather than having to approach them at social gatherings. Nefedev was 'a state councillor with the Order of St Vladimir 3rd Class, vain and eager for honours', so there should be no trouble in recruiting him, and 'his usefulness is obvious'. Vock was surprised and offended whenever he met with a refusal. 'People who enjoy all the privileges of birth, wealth and intellect, and do not use these gifts for the general good, are guiltier than the plotters,' he wrote, mirroring Nicholas's view that every member of society should do his duty. Benckendorff was less censorious, and was prepared to pay spies and to use criminals who wished to 'redeem their crimes'.[6]

On 25 June, ten days before the creation of the Third Section, Benckendorff had been put in command of the *Gendarmerie*, originally founded in 1815 when a dragoon regiment had been renamed and given the task of providing a military police for the Russian units in France. It was now to be the executive arm of the Third Section. The military background of this force suited Benckendorff perfectly, as he wished to have at his disposal a body untainted by the corruption associated with the police. He reorganised it, giving it the name of the New Corps of Imperial Gendarmes, with sky-blue uniforms, to symbolise the clarity of the heavens, and white cross-belts and gloves to stand for purity; it was to be a moral force for good. The empire was divided into five, and subsequently eight, districts, each under the command of a general of gendarmes. As he was a direct representative of the Third Section of the emperor's chancellery, the chief of gendarmes in any given district, whatever his rank, could overrule even the governor of a province.

Legend has it that when Benckendorff asked the tsar for a directive defining the role of the Third Section, Nicholas, who was holding a handkerchief at the time, handed it to him with the words: 'Here is your directive. The more tears you wipe away with this handkerchief, the more faithfully you will serve my aims.' The gendarmes were supposed to mingle with society and make themselves liked and trusted. 'If they like you, you will easily achieve everything,' Benckendorff said to one newly-appointed gendarme. 'If a gendarme is not popular,' he said to another, 'he is of no use.' Operating on a higher moral plane than the notoriously corrupt administration, the gendarmes could exert a beneficial influence; they were to lead by example, shame corruption, protect the weak and offer help and advice wherever they were needed, even in family disputes.[7]

'In you, everyone will see an official who can, through my agency, bring the voice of suffering humanity to the Imperial Throne and immediately place the defenceless and voiceless Citizen under the protection of the Tsar,' Benckendorff told one new recruit. Being in a position to right wrongs and help the helpless, the gendarme would have the support and assistance of all who loved their country, the truth, virtue, and so on. He also warned that, being a champion of virtue, he would be confronted by evil, and must stand firm against it.[8]

Public opinion was sceptical at best. As spies in the drawing rooms of St Petersburg and Moscow reported, people believed the new police might just improve things if they were controlled by competent and upright people, otherwise 'the medicine will be worse than the disease, and instead of having one bad police force we will have two'.[9]

An unexpected problem was that the establishment of the Third Section was viewed as a threat by the other police forces in operation – the city police, the governor general's police and the military police. These now sprang into feverish activity in order to demonstrate their zeal and their superiority to the newly-founded organ. They began to gather information on everyone and anyone, and Moscow and St Petersburg swarmed with spies. People lived in fear of their own servants, and became guarded even in the best society, which was riddled with aristocratic informers. On 23 August, less than two months after the foundation of the Third Section, an indignant Vock complained to his chief that he was himself under surveillance by the city police, who were watching his house, noting the names of visitors, and following him wherever he went. He was outraged that 'surveillance itself is being made the object of surveillance, in defiance of all sense and propriety'. In the field, the agents of the rival organisations disrupted each other's operations, laying false trails and provoking disturbances which they then accused the others of having started by their clumsiness. The Third Section and its gendarmes soon adopted some of their tactics, and, rightly or wrongly, people believed they too took bribes.[10]

Nicholas was aware that his punishment of the Decembrists had turned him into a figure of hate in many quarters, in Russia and abroad, and was therefore keen to demonstrate that there really was a conspiracy threatening his throne. 'We arrest people not in search of victims,' he once said, 'but in order to let the truth be known to our accusers.' This dictated the true mission of the Third Section: to find plots against the tsar and his government. Whatever Benckendorff might have hoped, its priority was not assisting the downtrodden but the discovery of subversion. Ineluctably, it became an instrument of political manipulation and propaganda.[11]

The mood of the country, according to Benckendorff's overview for the year 1827, was not in the least revolutionary. The document assesses the attitudes of every social group, beginning with the court, which was entirely loyal and without influence outside its own circle. The aristocracy, top officials and others of note inhabiting the capital are described as 'contented', with the exception of those who are 'discontented' because they no longer enjoy the positions and influence they held under the previous tsar or because they would like to see a more liberal form of government. They did not, in his view, represent the slightest danger. The 'middle class', consisting of landowners living in the capital or larger towns, nobles not in government service, merchants, educated people and writers, was described as being 'contented' and supportive of the state. The civil servants and the whole administration were 'morally the most corrupt', but did not present a political threat. The army was passive. The serfs were unhappy and the clergy despondent on account of their poverty and low status, but these classes were of no consequence.

There was only one class which did provide cause for concern. 'Our youth, that is to say the young gentry between the ages of 17 and 25 constitute as a group the most gangrened element in the empire,' the report maintains. 'Among these madcaps we can see the germs of Jacobinism, a revolutionary reformist spirit,' it goes on, concluding that, unchecked, this would 'turn these young people into real Carbonari'. It all stemmed from their upbringing. This would have come as no surprise to Nicholas. During the investigation into the Decembrist revolt he too had become convinced that the educational system was spreading 'gangrene' through the nobility's youth. An inspection of the University of Kharkov in February 1826 yielded a report that 'the present generation is entirely infected with gangrene and there should be not a moment's delay in remedying a disease whose effects are already making themselves strongly felt'. Private education at home was no better. It was 'a plague which one must seek to extirpate'. 'In a word,' the inspectors concluded, 'we need an essentially monarchical and not a subversive education, without which the tranquillity of the empire is in jeopardy.'[12]

'Our infected youth needs vigilant and persistent surveillance,' Vock advised Benckendorff, and the Third Section concentrated on this area, pursuing every lead it could pick up. In 1826 one of its informers, actually an *agent provocateur*, came up with intelligence of a conspiracy among students led by three brothers by the name of Kritsky who supposedly intended to start a revolution and murder the tsar. The investigation did not uncover any real evidence, but the brothers were locked up for good measure in the Schlusselburg fortress, a favoured place of detention for political prisoners. Two years later, Ivan Ivanovich Sukhinov, who had taken part in the revolt of the Southern Society and been sentenced to death, commuted to life with hard labour in a mine in Nerchinsk, apparently tried to organise a rebellion in the mine with his fellow convicts, but was betrayed, condemned to be shot, and hanged himself. There were other reports of officers and young nobles associating and making subversive noises in various parts of the country. The scarcity of any actual subversion is demonstrated by the alacrity with which in the summer of 1826 Vock's agents, who had been alerted that a number of youths met frequently at the lodgings of a certain Mordvinov, set about infiltrating the group, only to report that 'Mordvinov and his associates are nothing more than rakes who gather together with the sole aim of holding orgies.' Matters were not allowed to rest there, and much further investigation went into observing which brothels Mordvinov scoured in order to find the right girls.[13]

In 1831 the Third Section received a report of a conspiracy being hatched in Irkutsk in Siberia by the exiled Decembrist A.N. Muravev. The source of the report was Roman Maddox, a cursory look at whose background might have given the Third Section pause for thought. The son of a theatre manager of English origin, he had revealed remarkable histrionic talent in 1812 when, aged seventeen, he had decided to raise a partisan unit of Circassian tribesmen. He forged documents which represented him as a lieutenant of horseguards and aide-de-camp to the minister of war, as well as powers of attorney from both him and the minister of finance. Armed with these he set off for the Caucasus, where he strutted about military bases and inspected installations, and unwisely wrote a critical report to the minister of police. He was locked up in the Peter and Paul fortress and then the Schlusselburg for thirteen years. Barely out of gaol, he enlisted as a gendarme. In 1829 he was posted to Irkutsk, where he busied himself with spying on Muravev by paying court to his wife's sister. He reported that Muravev was corresponding in code with other Decembrists, and that there were two secret societies operating, one in St Petersburg, the other in Moscow, under the name 'Union of the Great Cause', dedicated to overthrowing the state. The Third Section sent a senior gendarme out to assist Maddox, who had penetrated deeper into the conspiracy and acquired a 'coupon' which would gain him admission to the inner circles of the St Petersburg and Moscow societies. He was recalled to St Petersburg, where he showed Benckendorff a clutch of fantastic forgeries. The latter despatched him to Moscow, where he was to use his 'coupon' and penetrate the local Union of the Great Cause. A general of gendarmes was attached to him to provide liaison and duly passed back various scraps of information, accounts of secret meetings and random denunciations. In the course of his 'penetration' Maddox contrived to marry the daughter of a wealthy family and promptly vanished, taking her dowry but not her person with him. He succeeded in evading the police for some time, but eventually, having run out of money, returned to Moscow, where he was caught and thrown into the Schlusselburg once more.[14]

Another who played fast and loose with the gullibility of the Third Section was Captain Sherwood. He had proved his worth by his warnings about the conspiracy of the Southern Society, and been richly rewarded for it: he was promoted, ennobled and given the surname *Vernii* – 'Loyal'. He was also given a post in the Third Section. In 1827 he was sent south to check if there was any conspiratorial activity there. He travelled about, taking the waters in the Caucasus, lingering in Odessa and coming to rest in Kiev, where he set up a network of informers. Wherever he went, he adopted an enigmatic manner, hinting, winking and bluffing, playing on people's fears and encouraging them to denounce before they were themselves denounced – in a manner later parodied by Gogol in *The Government Inspector*. He found that the families of exiled or imprisoned Decembrists, if a hint or two was dropped that their beloved husband, brother or son might be released in return for services rendered, were prepared to denounce anyone they could think of.

Unfortunately for Sherwood, the local chief of gendarmes became anxious that his own authority was being undermined and that any intelligence, real or fabricated, that Sherwood might send to Benckendorff might reflect badly on him. He therefore had Sherwood watched, put together a file listing all his misdemeanours – professional, ethical and sexual – to which he added a number of well-documented insulting things he had said about Benckendorff, and sent it off to St Petersburg. Sherwood was duly recalled and cashiered. He resorted to criminal activities of one sort or another, and attempted to recover the confidence of the Third Section with fresh revelations. To no avail: he was exiled from St Petersburg for his pains. Not content to let matters rest there, Sherwood wrote to Grand Duke Michael, enclosing a report which castigated the Third Section for being ineffectual, affirming that it was failing to address the very real threat posed by exiled Decembrists and Polish revolutionaries, and accusing Vock's successor and Benckendorff's deputy Leontii Dubelt of inefficiency and corruption. He assured the grand duke that the whole of St Petersburg knew that in order to affect a judgement, send someone to prison or exile, or obtain a person's release, all that was necessary was a call on Dubelt's mistress, and accused him of having taken more than 100,000 roubles in bribes. The grand duke passed the report to Dubelt, who had Sherwood thrown into the Schlusselburg.[15]

Legislation dating back to the seventeenth century had made a virtue of denunciation, and failure to denounce someone who might be guilty of a crime against the state (which could include 'evil intent') was itself a crime, punishable by death. By the beginning of the eighteenth century the concept of passivity as a criminal act was well established, and suspicion had become an admissible element in judging a case. The reforms of Peter the Great effectively made anyone who fell under suspicion guilty by implication, and reinforced the obligation to denounce. Denunciation could earn rewards such as promotion, noble status, decorations, estates and pensions. It was therefore well worth a try. Given the prevalence of corruption among the civil service, a random denunciation might yield unexpected fruit when the official in question came to be investigated.[16]

An experienced provincial chief of gendarmes, Colonel Lomachevsky, claimed that he could tell at a glance which denunciations to disregard and which to investigate. But failing to look into an evidently spurious one might lay him open to denunciation himself, for either lack of zeal or corruption, on the assumption that he had taken a bribe not to pursue the matter. At the level of the Third Section in St Petersburg, under the eagle eye of Nicholas, nobody was willing to take such responsibility. Nicholas never entirely ceded control to Benckendorff, and kept looking over his shoulder. And his suspicions were as easy to arouse as they were difficult to allay.

A certain Lukovsky, probably a Pole, turned up from England in 1835 with the information that there was a Russo-Polish secret society in that country preparing to overthrow the Russian monarchy by means of a march from British India, through Persia, Georgia and Astrakhan. He did not produce a single name or fact to back this up, yet Nicholas, while thinking it a little 'unclear', believed that 'in our times nothing should be ignored', so the matter was pursued.

In January 1831, Yakov Ivanovich Sanglen, now aged sixty-four and retired, was summoned by the tsar. When he arrived he found Nicholas in a state of panic, having received a report which he asked Sanglen to study and assess. The report painted a lurid picture of a conspiracy by the Illuminati, who had apparently infiltrated the highest circles of Russian society, making converts among the late Tsar Alexander's closest advisers and even, it suggested, Alexander himself. It claimed that the entire civil administration, including the Third Section, had been infiltrated and that Nicholas was surrounded by traitors only waiting for an opportunity to assassinate him. The inclusion of the Third Section was something of a giveaway, and it is now known that Sherwood had a hand in the report, in an attempt to get his own back. Sanglen managed to convince the tsar that it was nonsense and restore his peace of mind – but not for long.[17]

A few days later he received a communication from Magnitsky, also in retirement, warning him that Europe was threatened by a vast plot by the Illuminati. Quoting a dizzying array of supposedly original sources, Magnitsky took Nicholas through the whole well-worn story, from the foundation of the Illuminati in the 1780s, their invention of *acqua tofana*, their possession of a sacred box in which their secrets and the counterfeit seals of thirty kings were kept, which was designed to explode if touched by a profane hand, to their involvement in the French Revolution and their defeat of the allied intervention against it in 1792 by the Duke of Brunswick, an adept, rigging the outcome of the battle at Valmy. From that point onwards, 'conspirators of whatever name against God and rulers, Masons of various degrees, Rosicrucians, Knights of the Sun, pupils of Voltaire and Rousseau, Templars, followers of Swedenborg, Saint-Martin and Weishaupt, all came together under the name of Jacobins'. They had infiltrated the whole of Europe and Russia, and the murders of

Kotzebue and the duc de Berry, and the Decembrist rising, had all been their work.[18]

In further letters, Magnitsky exposed the more insidious aspects of the conspiracy. 'Literature, all the sciences, and all the arts have already been geared to its aims by means of the most poisonous artifice, because from the most elementary children's books to the courses of higher education classic illuminism is inserted with such artfulness that on the one hand it is detectable only upon most experienced and minute examination, and on the other hand (and this is essential to the Illuminati) it is easily accessible to the most simple minds.' Liberals pressed for wider education only so they could spread their creed, and by branding anyone who opposed them as a 'Jesuit' or an obscurantist, they shamed and ridiculed right-thinking people. German scientific congresses were no more than staff meetings at which they discussed strategy, and the Churches, particularly the Anglicans and the Methodists, were controlled by the Illuminati, along with 'worshippers of fire and the Dalai Lama'. Most of the establishment of Europe had been infiltrated, and the French and English governments were little better than Lodges, with the Duke of Wellington a typical example of a man apparently supporting the throne, but actually bent on its overthrow.

Russia, by virtue of its moral strength, attracted the full fury of the sect. It would be attacked at the political level through revolts, wars and diplomatic means, and at the moral level through 'political demoralisation'. The sect's means for achieving this were literature and foreign travellers, particularly merchants and bankers, who were only pretending to do business but were in fact spreading the disease. Most of them were Jews, with the Rothschild brothers at their head, though the chief Illuminato in this sphere was the French banker Lafitte.[19]

The idea that Jews were involved in spreading dangerous disease fell on fertile ground, as Nicholas had long disliked them for their otherness and what he saw as their restlessness, itself essentially subversive. They did not fit naturally into the hierarchical order he believed in, and he would try to assimilate them forcibly. One of his first acts as ruler was to compel them to perform military service (which entailed infringing all their religious laws). He would go on either to subject their schools and institutions to Russian ones or dissolve them, and eventually even to ban their traditional dress.[20]

Literati and intellectuals were not among Nicholas's favourite kind either, and the notion that they were undermining society fitted his own suspicions. He tightened censorship with a new law designed to control what young people read, to ensure internal security by fashioning the mores of society, and to manipulate public opinion in favour of the existing system. The first was achieved by censorship of all new publications and the withdrawal from circulation of anything that might provoke speculation. 'Aside from logic and philosophy textbooks necessary for the education of young people, other works of this kind, filled with fruitless and destructive sophistry of our times *should not be printed at all*,' ran the instruction. The second aim, of safeguarding the moral tone of society, was more difficult to implement, and provided grey areas whose shade depended on the degree of prudery of the censor. The third, which ruled out criticism of the government and the administration or anything that weakened respect for the system in any way, degenerated into a nitpicking pursuit of any comment that some member of the civil service might perceive as casting an aspersion on his own work.[21]

As far as Nicholas was concerned, writers were there to write up the triumphs and greatness of the empire, provide a positive gloss on life and induce a mindset of consensus with the views of the ruler. The Third Section, which effectively took over the task of censorship, therefore kept an eye on what writers were thinking and doing, admonished them when their behaviour seemed politically or morally dubious, and even suggested appropriate subjects. Many writers were content to go along with this, grateful for the pensions and honours that followed. Those who did not were treated with a mixture of incomprehension and exasperation. Benckendorff would call in or write to authors whose works troubled him. His objection to one of Lermontov's works was not political, he politely informed the poet, it was that the protagonist, Arbenin, left his wife. To Nikolai Aleksandrovich Polevoi, editor of the *Moscow Telegraph*, he courteously expressed his dismay that 'such an intelligent man' as him had in an article on revolutions stated that some had had beneficial effects. He was surprised that such a great mind had descended to writing such 'nonsense'. 'A writer of your talents could bring great benefits to the state if he were to direct his pen in a right-thinking direction, calming passions rather than arousing them,' he cajoled, arguing that young people needed Polevoi's wise guidance.[22]

In his annual report on the year 1828, Benckendorff boasted that in the three years of its existence the Third Section had opened files on 'all those who have in one way or another stood out from the crowd', and that 'all liberals, enthusiasts and apostles of a Russian constitution' had been placed under surveillance. But the quality of his informants was so poor that, according to the Russian historian who enjoyed the widest access to its archives, the Third Section disposed of mountains of irrelevant information, such as the colour of the socks a person wore at a ball or how much they won or lost at cards on a particular day, giving the public the impression that it was omniscient, but no evidence of any substance. And 90 per cent of the information it received from unpaid informants was false.[23]

Information pouring in to the Third Section was not filtered in any way. A wild accusation or a report that proved to be entirely fictitious did not lead to the reprimanding, let alone punishment, of the agent concerned. Informers were not confronted with the accused, and their word carried greater weight. This lack of answerability was complemented by a disregard for judicial procedures: people could be arrested, sometimes in the middle of the night or in the street, imprisoned for varying lengths of time, and then released without ever being the wiser as to why. Foreigners, particularly if French, were liable to be arrested for no apparent reason and expelled from the county without explanation.[24]

At the same time, the elaborate mechanisms designed to keep tabs on everyone were hopelessly unreliable, as the correspondence between Benckendorff and Grand Duke Constantine in Warsaw reveals. While Constantine occasionally congratulates the chief gendarme for having 'directed this matter *with the hand of a master*', much of it concerns vain enquiries about the whereabouts of people who had been issued with a passport to go to one place and had either turned up in another or gone to ground altogether, or about suspects who had slipped through a supposedly close mesh of surveillance; the picture which emerges in one of serial incompetence.[25]

When Arsenii Andreevich Zakrevsky took over the ministry of internal affairs in 1828, he found a shambles. The personnel were lazy and unmotivated, ignored procedures and often took work home with them, with the result that there were papers scattered around lodgings all over St Petersburg. The worst offenders were those working in the department of police, where he found there were 797 important matters lying in the pending tray, some of them having spent up to twelve years there. In a drive to curb corruption, a number of officials at the ministry of finance were summarily sacked. This gave rise to a rumour that they had been dismissed for political reasons. The rumour was picked up by a different person at the Third Section from the one who had been investigating the corruption, and he launched an investigation into a supposed conspiracy at the ministry.[26]

It did not really matter that the administration was shambolic and the security services a joke. The pall of horror and gloom that overlay Russian society following the sentencing of the Decembrists smothered all desire to revolt and cowed people into a state of acceptance of the immutability of the system. Much the same could be said of most of Europe, and in particular France, which had ceased to brim with revolutionary effervescence.

23

Counter-Revolution

On succeeding to the French throne in September 1824, Charles X made clear what kind of king he intended to be, not least by having himself anointed and crowned according to the ancient rites of the French monarchy, in Reims Cathedral, which his predecessor had not dared to do. He felt strong enough to make gracious gestures to the duc d'Orléans, whom Louis XVIII had held at arm's length, and to various Napoleonic generals, and he pardoned a number of political prisoners. The success of the Spanish campaign had proved the reliability of the army, the Carbonarist movement had withered, and there was a marked drop in the number of secret societies reported by the police. The elections of that year had passed off quietly, with the police openly canvassing for the royalist candidates and discouraging those who intended to vote otherwise.[1]

In January 1826 a new Austrian ambassador, Count Apponyi, arrived in Paris. He would move into a fine building, the Hôtel d'Eckmühl, belonging to the widow of Marshal Davout, at the corner of the rue Saint Dominique and the esplanade des Invalides, where his wife would host one of the most brilliant musical salons of Paris until his recall in 1848. In his instructions, Metternich expressed the view that while the foul influence of France was still threatening Europe with the 'moral poison' being poured all over the Continent through the publications it daily spewed forth like deadly 'projectiles', and that it was still 'the great factory of revolutions', the country itself was no longer susceptible to revolution.[2]

He had visited Paris in March 1825, meeting prime minister Villèle, whom he rated highly, and the police prefect Delaveau, who gratifyingly shared Metternich's attitude and suspicions, and whose mind worked in much the same way when it came to seeing conspiracy everywhere – in May 1824 he had noted that wherever the Quakers Stephen Grellet and William Allen had been on their travels, insurrections had broken out, which in his opinion permitted no doubt that they had been involved. A cosy relationship sprang up between the French and Austrian police.[3]

Metternich was more worried by England than France, and took a dim view of the foreign secretary George Canning in particular. As far as he could see, the agitation against the Combination Acts was revolutionary, and their repeal in 1824 was a sign of the government's weakness. It was apparently blind to the creeping influence of 'the sect', clear evidence of which was the plan to establish a new secular university in London. 'I authorise you to say to His Majesty,' he instructed Esterházy in 1825, 'that I am certainly not mistaken when I say that if the plan were to be carried out, it would be the end of England.' With the foundation of University College London in 1826, the first university in Britain opened its doors to students of every race and religion.[4]

The accession of Nicholas to the Russian throne had done nothing to reassure Metternich. He had a poor opinion of the new tsar, and feared the influence of his wife, whom he regarded as dangerously liberal. Although Lebzeltern had persuaded his brother-in-law the 'dictator' Trubetskoy to leave the Austrian embassy in St Petersburg, where he had taken asylum, and hand himself in, Nicholas regarded the Austrian ambassador as a Jacobin and demanded he be recalled, so Metternich no longer had a good source of information and influence in the Russian capital. As he surveyed a peaceful and politically quiescent Europe, he felt far from reassured.

Towards the end of 1827 Metternich remarried. Marie-Antoinette de Leykam, a great beauty, thirty-three years his junior, filled his life with happiness. The catty Dorothea Lieven, now a princess, her husband having been promoted, remarked that, the young woman being not particularly well-born, Metternich had abandoned the Holy Alliance for a *mésalliance*. In January 1829, only fourteen months into their marriage, she died, leaving him disconsolate. It was in a grim mood that he watched a new storm gathering in France.[5]

The Villèle ministry had been gradually implementing the Ultra programme of counter-revolution. It not only righted wrongs by, for instance, passing legislation which indemnified those who had had their property confiscated in the 1790s, but introduced measures making the Catholic faith, and particularly the Church, central to public as well as private life. Various laws were brought in to protect it and shore up its position, and in 1825 sacrilege was made a capital offence. As often happens in such a climate, officials and functionaries who may or may not have been personally devout displayed an excess of zeal, as in the case of the prefect of the department of Haute-Normandie, who banned a scheduled performance of Molière's *Tartuffe* on the grounds that it insulted the Church. This caused such an outcry that he was overruled by the ministry in Paris, but that did nothing to allay a conviction growing in various quarters that the country was being surreptitiously clawed back by what Montlosier described as 'an ambitious and invasive faction, creeping in the shadows under the inspiration of the Jesuits, an anonymous and illegal congregation, infiltrating the whole secular administration, affiliating to itself magistrates, suborning ministers, gaining and distributing all the favours ...' – and he was a royalist who had defended religion in the Constituent Assembly before emigrating in 1792.[6]

The Jesuits, legally excluded from France, were running several religious schools while the government turned a blind eye. Sensible estimates put their number at anywhere between 108 and five hundred, but liberals believed there were many more; those perturbed by creeping conservatism focused on the image of the Jesuits as the agents of a subtle counter-revolution (mirroring the Illuminati scare on the right) and began to see them everywhere. Some claimed the

Jesuit house at Montrouge held as many as 50,000 priests – and there were even rumours that they were training in the use of firearms. While he was not counting on armed Jesuits to support him, the king was gradually positioning himself to carry out a real counter-revolution.[7]

On 12 April 1827 he insisted on attending a parade of the 50,000-strong Paris National Guard. This body represented the people of Paris in arms, with the units from the prosperous *quartiers* predictably conservative and those from the working-class ones decidedly less so, but all of them essentially interested in the orderly functioning of their city. The police had warned of discontent in their ranks, and even plots to assassinate the king during the parade, and his entourage advised him not to attend. In the event, the majority of the men cheered Charles warmly. A couple of the units also shouted: '*À bas les ministres! À bas Villèle! À bas les Jésuites!*' Only one showed any hostility to Charles himself. But he was incensed, and an even angrier Villèle had no trouble in persuading him to issue a decree disbanding the National Guard. As Marshal Marmont, military commander of Paris, commented, the king seemed to be looking for confrontation; the National Guard, originally created in 1789, was a symbol of citizen-power, and its dissolution was an affront to the principle of the sovereignty of the people. It also pushed a large armed force into opposition.[8]

The act raised the political temperature, and this was further stoked by the police. The police chief Franchet d'Esperey was warned that a conspiracy was being planned by liberals including Lafitte and Merilhou, and took seriously reports that the *comité directeur* was sending emissaries into the provinces, their secret talisman a small gold heart the size of a hazelnut hanging from their watch chains; that in Rouen one Adrien Barbet, who had ordered a couple of daggers from a goldsmith, had been arrested and interrogated; that the principal liberals of Paris and London were concerting. Lord Dudley Coutts Stuart was refused permission to pass through French territory on his way back from Switzerland, as he was married to the daughter of Lucien Bonaparte, one of Napoleon's brothers, which may or may not have been connected to another report, from earlier in the year, that Lucien had crossed into France from Switzerland disguised as a woman.[9]

The elections of November 1827 were accompanied by tumultuous demonstrations which, according to the testimony of one senior police official, groups of Ultras and police agents did everything in their power to provoke into violence. This failed to materialise, and, despite the greatly restricted electorate, a liberal majority was returned. Villèle was obliged to step down, and the king called on the moderate royalist vicomte de Martignac to form a new ministry. Martignac attempted to steer a middle course, bringing in legislation to relax censorship and to curtail the activities of the Jesuits, but he could not maintain power for long, and in April 1829 he was forced to resign. Reverting to his policy of confrontation, Charles replaced him with the prince de Polignac, the most extreme of the Ultras, who was said, rather unfairly, to believe that he had been entrusted by the Virgin Mary with the task of saving France. He did believe, as did the king, that the revolution, whose manifestations he saw everywhere, needed to be confronted head-on and royal authority re-established.[10]

The moment seemed propitious. The reports of departmental and police prefects over the previous three years speak of 'complete tranquillity' reigning throughout their regions and cities, and of widespread 'devotion to the monarchy'. The secret police also reported little interest in politics, except at the time of the elections, after which it quickly lapsed. The Paris police reports are full of brawls, robberies, suicides, drownings, infanticide and misbehaving prostitutes, but there is no mention of the 'seditious cries' of earlier times. A new prefect of police, the politically moderate lawyer Louis-Maurice Debelleyme, cashiered the *agents provocateurs* and shifted funds from the political police to the pursuit of criminals. He also created a new force in Paris, the *sergents de ville*, who, though uniformed in military manner, were less formidable than the disliked *Gendarmerie Royale*.[11]

The harvests of 1826 and 1827 had been poor. The following years saw food shortages, unemployment and poverty, with grain riots in Ireland, Wallonia and the Rhineland as well as France. The winter of 1829–30 was glacial, and food prices in France rose by as much as 75 per cent in some areas. None of this translated into anything more serious than the odd bread riot. According to the contemporary socialist historian Louis Blanc, the people were gripped by a paralysing docility. They felt 'a profound contempt for the Jesuits and the clergy', and despised the Bourbon dynasty, mainly on account of the manner in which they had recovered their throne, 'which [the people] associated with all the humiliations of the motherland', but they had no sense of their rights or their power, and no vision of a better world, so 'they were as incapable of wishing as they were of looking forward', and there was 'between the bourgeoisie and the people neither community of interests nor conformity of hatreds'. The dissolution of the National Guard had passed off without incident. The army was not giving cause for concern: a successful expedition to capture Algiers had given it something to do and had raised morale.[12]

On 2 March 1830, during the first session of the new, predominantly liberal, Chamber, a group of deputies addressed an appeal to the king, warning him that he was not listening to the voice of his people, and to adopt a more conciliatory approach. His reaction was to dissolve the Chamber and call a new election. This produced a landslide victory for the liberals. Given Charles's attitude, many expected something in the nature of a *coup d'état* as they dispersed to the country to wait for the new Chamber to reconvene on 1 August.

On 25 July Charles signed four ordinances, dissolving the Chamber, reducing the electorate by 75 per cent and subjecting all publications to a government licence. 'The king has thrown down the gauntlet to the liberals,' Metternich wrote to Francis. Yet neither Charles nor any of his ministers had made any preparations or contingency plans for the reaction that was bound to follow this challenge. The day after issuing the ordinances, 26 July, he drove off to the château of Rambouillet to go hunting. The military governor of Paris, Marshal

Marmont, who only learned of the ordinances from the newspapers, immediately sent to the king for orders. Having had no advance warning of them, he was not prepared, with not enough troops in easy reach, or victuals and ammunition for an emergency, while many officers were on leave.[13]

There was no immediate popular reaction. The report of the *Gendarmerie* of Paris for the night of 26–27 July reads much like those for any other day. It begins with the arrest of twelve men for illegal assembly and '*perturbation du repos public*' on the place du Palais-Royal, and of one for '*rébéllion*' at the barrière de Clichy. Otherwise, one has to look carefully among the reports of brawls and robberies, the drunks and the whores brought in for medical checks, a duel and a corpse fished out of the Seine to find out that there was also an '*atrouppement*' which required the intervention of a few mounted gendarmes. The calm could not last. Alarmed at the action of the king, the Paris banks withheld credit, and a number of workshops closed and laid off workers.[14]

The next day saw barricades go up in various parts of the city, and people spilled out onto the streets airing a multitude of grievances, political aspirations and emotional desires. Students, artists, writers and composers joined in the exuberant explosion, Dumas, Béranger, Ary Scheffer, Liszt and Berlioz among them. The cry of '*Vive la Liberté*' was accompanied by an astonishing variety of other slogans, including many connected with the running literary battle between the Romantics and the Classicists, which had erupted at the first night of Victor Hugo's groundbreaking play *Hernani* in January.

'Everything is still very quiet here,' the liberal deputy the duc de Broglie noted on the evening of 27 July; 'yesterday the police tried to provoke some riots, but failed miserably; people looked on and shrugged their shoulders. We are awaiting the peers and deputies who are still away, so we can deliberate and decide on a course of action.' Later that night the situation began to change. As Marmont had gathered his troops together around the Louvre, the streets were left free and groups of workers and petty shopkeepers began to congregate.

Members of the disbanded National Guard joined them, and the tricolour was hoisted here and there. By the morning of 28 July Paris was in a state of revolt. The situation was nevertheless salvageable, according to Marmont, who still could not obtain any orders from the king.[15]

This is the more surprising as Charles X and Polignac repeatedly claimed that a *comité directeur* had been planning an insurrection and distributing money to workers, manufacturing daggers and acquiring firearms. Yet, having decided on a confrontation, they omitted to prepare for it, and at the crucial moment the king's nerve failed him. The challenge he had thrown down with his ordinances had, as Broglie points out, 'encountered neither secret societies nor a *comité directeur*', only a handful of baffled deputies wondering how to react. It should therefore have been successful, and almost certainly would have been if it had been backed by adequately prepared military force. But, in the words of Louis Blanc, Charles lacked the courage of the tyrant he aspired to be.[16]

In the face of insurrection, delay in the use of troops rapidly undermines their reliability, and as Marmont waited for orders his men began to desert. He pressed the king to take action, as he was still confident the situation could be brought under control, and he was probably right. Normally, a body as unpopular as the *Gendarmerie Royale* vaporises at the first sign that its paymasters might fall; it is usually those who do a government's dirty work who are the first to be torn apart by insurgents. Yet its report for 28–29 July is more concerned with three women arrested for '*provocation à la prostitution*' than anything else.[17]

'I will, if necessary, mount a horse, but not a tumbril like my brother,' the king defiantly announced to the duc de Mortemart. But he did not place himself at the head of his troops, or even issue any sensible orders to Marmont. In order to avoid being caught in a trap, Marmont began to withdraw from the city. After a certain amount of hesitation Charles climbed into a carriage and drove off towards the coast, where he took ship for England. Perhaps he had fallen for his own propaganda, and had come to believe that an all-powerful *comité directeur* had taken control and would embark on the bloodthirsty rites he and others like him attributed to it. In fact, as Béranger remarked, 'the government of Charles X was alone in conspiring against itself at that moment'.[18]

The revolution had caught the leaders of the opposition unawares, and those, such as Lafayette and Lafitte, who had supposedly been plotting insurrection for years found themselves at a loss as to how to deal with the situation. If Metternich could have seen them, he would have laughed. But it was no laughing matter, as in his ineptitude the king had created a revolutionary situation, and power now had to be picked up out of the proverbial gutter where it was lying and order had to be restored.

Lafayette and other liberals hurried to appropriate this 'anonymous victory', as one of them called it. They were fortunate in that there were no other contenders: the more radical had also been taken by surprise, and the lower orders making up the revolutionary surge were leaderless. One observer noted that during the three days of the revolution, insurgent labourers deferentially asked middle-class men and students of the *grandes écoles* to lead them. Some believed that if Napoleon's son had appeared on the streets there would have been a restoration of the Empire. By the same token, if the republicans had seized the initiative France might well have become a republic.[19]

The confusion was well captured by Louis Blanc, who witnessed the storming of the Tuileries and noted that the mob displayed a bewilderingly incoherent variety of loyalties, viciously destroying some portraits and doffing their caps before others. In the event, skilful manoeuvring by Lafayette, Lafitte and others resulted in the duc d'Orléans being named lieutenant general of the kingdom while the possibility of preserving the Bourbon monarchy still hung in the air, and then king when it turned out that it was not to be salvaged. Louis-Philippe I, as he became, took the title of King of the French rather than King of France, and adopted the tricolour as the national flag, thereby acknowledging the legacy of the Revolution of 1789 and the Napoleonic empire, and with them the sovereignty of the people.[20]

While the 'July Days' did result in a change of regime, and although they were to be glorified as such in paint and print by the likes of Delacroix and Victor Hugo, they were hardly revolutionary: the motives and mood of those who came out into the streets could not have been further from those imagined by the likes of Metternich. 'I was present at nearly every event of our revolution [of 1789], and I can assure you that those of 27, 28 and 29 July had nothing whatever in common with them,' the former prime minister Louis-Mathieu Molé wrote to the Duke of Wellington on 18 August. 'During the revolution, the people were the aggressors, and this time they were defending themselves; then, they were violating the law, this time, they were standing up for the law.' He went on to point out that despite the high levels of exaltation and indignation, there had been little looting or criminal activity. 'It was carried out without conspiracy and without conspirators,' he explained; French society had been attacked, and it had defended itself. He was not the only one to note the great sense of fraternity between classes which united people in their enthusiasm.[21]

The only similarity between the July Days of 1830 and those of 1789 lay in the reactions they elicited. As then, news of the events in Paris was received like a clarion call by liberals and would-be revolutionaries throughout Europe, and like the distant rumbling of a dangerous volcano by the more conservative. To both, it revived memories of 1792, and with them either fear of or longing for the appearance of French armies exporting revolution or liberty on the tips of their bayonets.

The news from Paris was greeted with particular jubilation in Germany. A Prussian officer stationed in Mainz noted that 'Many young men in the city put on the French cockade and sang the "*Marseillaise*", and applauded in the theatre at every sentence expressing hatred of tyrants, and love of liberty.' The events could not fail to resonate in Belgium, the francophone former Austrian Netherlands which had been incorporated into the new kingdom of Holland by the Congress of Vienna. The unsympathetic government of the

Protestant Dutch King William I was deeply resented in these Catholic provinces. Two poor harvests and discrimination against the industries in the south of the country had caused serious hardship. Brussels was the home of many exiled French revolutionaries and former Napoleonic officers. Rather than start a revolution there, most of them rushed back to Paris, but the Dutch authorities nevertheless played safe and decided to cancel the celebrations of King William's birthday scheduled for 25 August. This act of perceived pusillanimity emboldened local patriots. At a performance of the French composer Auber's opera *La Muette de Portici* in Brussels that evening, the aria '*Amour sacré de la Patrie*' was met with wild applause, which spontaneously turned into a rendering of the '*Marseillaise*' by the audience. In a mood of exaltation, this spilled out of the theatre onto the streets, where the crowd developed into a mob which proceeded to riot, attacking government offices and tearing down royal insignia. The royal troops evacuated the city, leaving it to the civic guard to police, and the black, yellow and red colours of Brabant were hoisted.[22]

Barely two weeks later, on 8 September, in the wake of a bread riot in Brunswick, the palace of the reigning duke, Charles, was attacked by demonstrators calling for the reconvening of the local parliamentary body, the Estates. Charles, a petty despot known as the 'diamond duke' on account of his predilection for flashy jewellery, fled by a back door, and his guards stood idly by as the mob ransacked his palace. The duke's brother William stepped in to take his place, and everything returned to normal – perhaps not surprisingly, as there is some evidence that the aristocracy of Brunswick had been behind the whole business. Disturbances of a similar kind broke out in Saxony and Hanover. In Hesse-Kassel, where William II had failed to bring in the promised constitution or to reform the corrupt administration, there were riots over the price of bread and such issues as guild regulations and tolls. Further up the social scale, the resentment focused on the monarch's vulgar money-grabbing mistress, whom he wished to ennoble. The riots and confrontations which ensued forced William to call the representatives of the Estates. (When they did convene, in January 1831, they would insist on making his son co-regent, only aggravating the situation, as an unseemly squabble between their rival mistresses would eclipse more urgent political business and plague local politics for much of the next decade.)[23]

In Britain, the reverberations of the events in Paris were less sensational but more serious, and when he landed at Portsmouth as part of the exiled Charles X's entourage, Marshal Marmont was astonished to see the French tricolour being flown everywhere. 'The feeling at Portsmouth was entirely in harmony with that which had caused the revolution in France,' he noted. The Whig Earl Grey's reaction reflected the views of many. 'What could be done by legal resistance to a power which had overturned all law? Force was the only resource, and, thank God, it has triumphed,' he wrote to Princess Lieven on 3 August. 'The people of Paris seem to me to have shown no less moderation than courage, and are entitled to the thanks and admiration of everyone who feels that they have not only preserved the liberty of France, but have prevented the destruction of that of every country in Europe.' The Whig politician Henry Brougham sent Broglie his 'hearty congratulations on the greatest event for liberty in modern times.'[24]

The death of King George IV on 26 June, exactly a month before the revolution in Paris, and the subsequent dissolution of Parliament had once again raised the issue of parliamentary reform in Britain. The success of the revolution in bringing about constitutional change in France with a minimum of bloodshed made some consider the use of force in order to achieve it there. 'With the Parisian affair of July 1830 there arose here, amongst the bulk of the nation, a loud cry for changes of the most important nature,' in the words of the politician and landowner Edward Gibbon Wakefield. 'This new Revolution produced a very extraordinary effect on the middle classes, and sent a vast number of persons to me with all sorts of projects and propositions,' noted Francis Place in July. 'Everyone was glorified with the courage, the humanity, and the honesty of the Parisians, and the common people became eagerly desirous to prove that they too were brave and humane and honest. All soon seemed desirous to fight against the Government if it should attempt to control the French Government.' News of the subsequent relatively bloodless revolution in Belgium two months later only raised the expectations of the reformers and the levels of fear of the defenders of the status quo. These had been feeling under threat from another quarter.[25]

In the summer of 1830 a new kind of disturbance had broken out in rural areas of southern England, starting in Kent and gradually spreading westwards and then northwards as far as Leicestershire. Labelled the Swing riots, after a mythical 'Captain Swing', it was essentially a spontaneous labourers' revolt, driven by poverty and low wages attendant on the agricultural depression. But a mix of other gripes, including resentment against tithes, rents, game laws and the introduction of threshing machines, backed up by Radical agitation, sucked in tenant farmers, blacksmiths, carpenters and other country dwellers. The riots varied in form and ritual. In many cases the first call was to the vicarage, whose incumbent was asked in more or less threatening ways to reduce tithes. Others confronted were tithe collectors, overseers of the poor, bailiffs and wealthy farmers. The negotiations generally passed off civilly, with food and drink sometimes offered to the protesters, who claimed that they were acting within the law. It was only when they met with a refusal to negotiate that things would turn ugly; they would burn hayricks and threshing machines, and might manhandle the offending farmer as well, and perhaps duck him in his pond.[26]

The predominantly nocturnal and sporadic character of the attacks, with flames lighting up the night sky and the rioters, sometimes numbering a couple of hundred, melting away into the countryside to reappear no one knew where or when, could not fail to induce fear among the propertied classes. The government despatched units of cavalry to towns such as Tunbridge Wells, Cranbrook and Canterbury, more in an attempt to make a show of force than to quell the riots, which were too volatile. It left the rest up to local magistrates and landowners. England was still a long way behind the Continent when it came to policing.[27]

Despite the fiasco of Peterloo and the alarms connected with the Cato Street conspiracy, Queen Caroline's trial and her funeral procession, and despite the need to call on the military again and again to quell the food riots occasioned by the agricultural depression of 1822 and those attendant on the repeal of the Combination Acts in 1824, there had been stiff resistance to the idea of creating a force to keep order. Only in Ireland was the need for an efficient peacekeeping force generally recognised, and a rural police to cover the island had been established in 1822. The rest of the United Kingdom made do with traditional forms of policing, which were considered adequate, particularly as, after the political excitement of 1820, the attitude of the government to unrest had altered.

By 1820 the country had emerged from the post-1815 depression. There was an agricultural crisis in 1822 and a financial one in 1826 following the bursting of a bubble, largely caused by a rush to invest in the newly independent former Spanish colonies of South America. In November 1825 panic had spread in the money market and there was a run on the banks; sixty country banks and six London houses failed. This caused much distress and some rioting, put down by troops, but economic growth resumed and calm descended. Liverpool's government had softened its attitude, and no longer regarded every civil disturbance as incipient revolution. It was succeeded by a ministry under Canning, whose outlook was so little reactionary as to brand him a crypto-Jacobin in Metternich's eyes.

The second half of the 1820s saw the formation of trade unions and other organisations, and this was accompanied by a wide-ranging debate on economics, the principles of the organisation of capital and the problems of social adaptation to a changing and increasingly industrialised world, but it was a debate that was neither political nor revolutionary. The Radicals of the 1790s had been a mixed lot, drawn from many levels of society, and their political activities, which entailed some expense, the paying of fines, the need to move domicile, periods in gaol and frequent changes of wives or partners, had propelled even the more respectable of them into a downward spiral as they embraced any trade they could in order to survive, becoming printers, bookbinders, stone-cutters, breeches-makers, braces-makers, shoemakers, publicans, brothel-keepers, pimps, clerks, teachers, preachers, pickpockets, and so on. They had either died, fallen away or moved on. The old Spencean Radical underworld was dead. Most of the extremists of the previous decades had become respectable tradesmen 'in business'. There were now more prosecutions for pornography than sedition or blasphemy. The only truly revolutionary events of the decade were the repeal of the Test and Corporation Acts in 1828 and the passing of the Catholic Emancipation Act in the following year, but these did not produce a threat to law and order.[28]

On 15 April 1829 Robert Peel, home secretary in Wellington's Tory cabinet, put forward a Bill which became law as the Police Act on 19 June. This set up a statutory authority for the London metropolitan area in the person of the home secretary, who appointed two commissioners to exercise it on his behalf, in the first instance a colonel and a lawyer. The new force faced hostility from the Whigs, from magistrates and from parish councils, whose jurisdiction the Act appeared to infringe. It was widely denounced as an attack on civil liberties, an attempt by the government to establish a private army and introduce 'espionage' into the country, and as thoroughly un-English. When they first appeared on the streets in their blue uniforms and top hats (blue tailcoat and white ducks in summer), their only weapons a rattle and a truncheon, the members of the new force were either ridiculed with epithets such as 'Peelers', 'Bobbies', 'raw lobsters' and 'Jenny Darbies' (gendarmes), or vilified as oppressors and spies.

There was still no organised police force in rural areas, and the yeomanry regiments raised during the revolutionary and Napoleonic wars had mostly been disbanded – possibly a good thing: in Wiltshire, which had kept its yeomanry, the Swing riots developed a more bitter and violent edge than elsewhere. In other areas, landowners took matters into their own hands. The Duke of Richmond enrolled a private constabulary which patrolled his estates in Sussex, while others assembled bands of retainers, grooms and gamekeepers to hunt down the rioters. The troubles continued to spread, and in the light of events taking place on the Continent, Wellington grew uneasy. On 26 October 1830 he drew up a 'memorandum on the precautions to be taken to prevent any disaster to the troops in case of their being called out in the north of England', although he argued that the military should not be used unless 'their employment is not only legal, but necessary'.[29]

Those at the other end of the British political spectrum made light of his fears. 'The *manie des revolutions* would not be to be feared if Governments were wise and moderate,' Grey wrote to Princess Lieven in September. 'I have never yet known a popular revolution that might not be ascribed to provocation on the part of the Government, more or less remote. "*Ce n'est jamais par envie d'attaquer, mais par impatience de souffrir, que le peuple se soulève*," is an observation as old as Sully, which all history will verify. That the example of France will give encouragement to the people in different countries, who suffer from the same oppression, to wish for similar relief cannot be doubted. But the security against this is not to be found in armies and Holy Alliances.' He went on to point out that if the settlement reached at Vienna had been more equitable, there would have been no trouble in the first place. There was much truth in this, as the events of the next couple of years were to show.[30]

24

Jupiter Tonans

Metternich had been spending the summer at his country residence of Koenigswart (Kynzvart) in Bohemia when, on 3 August 1830, he heard of the first disturbances in Paris. News of the outcome reached him in the middle of the following night, and he immediately penned a letter to his emperor. 'The revolution, a revolution of the worst kind, has triumphed,' he wrote. 'This proves two things: one that the ministry made a mistake in the choice of its means; the other that I was right when, more than two years ago, I drew the attention of the cabinets to the dangers of the situation. Unfortunately, my voice was lost in the wilderness.' The next day he left for Vienna.[1]

On the way, he stopped at Karlsbad to consult with Nesselrode, who was taking the waters there. As was his wont, Metternich quickly saw the opportunities provided by the new state of affairs. Events in Paris were bound to act as an encouragement to revolutionaries in other countries, particularly Italy and Germany, and if they were to rise this might in turn lead to French armed intervention in support. This threat should help unite the powers and recreate the post-1815 concert, and, in his view, justified a new congress. Nesselrode could do nothing without consulting Nicholas, but he agreed that Russia and Austria must stand united in defence of the 1815 settlement. Once back in Vienna, Metternich put in hand the reinforcement of Austrian troops in Lombardy-Venetia, and ordered the call-up of more men. 'We are arming to the teeth,' he reassured Apponyi in Paris, but he was far from confident that Austria and its allies could raise enough troops to stand up to the numerically superior French. The Habsburg monarchy was almost bankrupt.[2]

By 1 September, he was growing despondent. 'My innermost feeling is that we have reached the beginning of the end of old Europe,' he wrote to Nesselrode. 'Being determined to perish along with it, I will continue in my duty, and that goes not just for me, but for the Emperor as well.' 'The *old* Europe has not existed for forty years,' Nesselrode replied; 'let us take it as it is today and try to preserve it; if it does not get any worse we will have already achieved a great good, for to wish to make it better would be to attempt the impossible. Charles X undid himself because he did not recognise this truth.'[3]

Metternich wanted the German states to come together in the Bundestag at Frankfurt in order to jointly confront 'the spectre of revolution'. But Bavaria, Baden and Württemberg, which felt exposed to possible attack by France, were inclined to remain neutral, arguing that it was all very well for Metternich to goad them into an anti-French and anti-revolutionary stance, but that having despatched the bulk of its troops to guard against trouble in Italy, Austria was in no position to come to their assistance if they were attacked. And there was no lack of evidence to suggest that, if provoked, France would attack. On 30 November, Armand Carrel, editor of the paper *Le National*, wrote: 'The revolution can only defend itself by attacking: that was the instinctive cry of the French in 1792 and once again there is no salvation for us unless we strike the first blows.'[4]

Prussia, which had been given territory on the Rhine at the Congress of Vienna for the very purpose of creating a buffer against possible French aggression, was the most exposed, particularly when revolution broke out in nearby Belgium. Metternich insisted that Frederick William stand firm and act jointly with Austria and Russia, but the Prussian king did not have the stomach and could only see that he was the most at risk from the revolutionary plague. In order to avoid provoking the French, he cancelled the manoeuvres of the Prussian army scheduled at Koblenz that autumn. Nor would Prussia be pushed into acting as policeman in Germany, as Metternich suggested. The Prussian foreign minister Bernstorff took the view that the troubles in Brunswick, Hanover and elsewhere in Germany had less to do with France or the revolutionary spirit than with poverty, hunger and 'the blundering and injudicious administrative practices of individual officials and leaders'. He refused to contemplate military intervention, if only because troops sent out to quell justifiable riots by poor people at the end of their tether might well become demoralised and, if there really were a revolutionary spirit abroad, contaminated. For this reason too, he opposed Metternich's attempts to put together a pan-German military force to ward off a possible French invasion and intervene in France should circumstances require it. The Prussian ambassador in Paris, Heinrich Wilhelm von Werther, advised recognising Louis-Philippe and supporting the new government in Paris in order to avoid worse developments.[5]

Metternich was against accepting the new status quo by recognising Louis-Philippe, in part because he did not believe he would maintain himself on the throne for more than a couple of months. The idea of a citizen-king caught between hostile legitimists on one side and republicans on the other struck him as absurd. But there was also a matter of principle involved. The regime the allies had put in place in France in 1814 was the bedrock of the settlement reached at the Congress of Vienna. If that could be overturned by three days of popular disorder, so, theoretically, could the constitutions of other states and all the territorial arrangements reached then. Nicholas agreed. Although he had repeatedly warned Charles X through his ambassador in St Petersburg to abide by the *Charte* and not to provoke the liberals, he saw Louis-Philippe as a living insult to the principle of legitimacy. 'That Orléans will never be anything but an infamous usurper,' he wrote to his brother Constantine. He insisted that the powers should make a moral stand against him, and even thought of launching military operations to dethrone him. In the interim, he ordered his ambassador in Paris to withdraw with his entire staff, and all Russians in France to leave the country immediately. Frenchmen were to be denied entry to Russian dominions, and ships flying the tricolour were to be turned away from Russian ports. He gave instructions to the censors to look sharp and not allow 'anything impious or Jacobin' to be printed.[6]

According to Benckendorff's reports, the majority of Russian society greeted the fall of Charles X with joy, if only because people viewed his regime as 'jesuitical'. Liberals hailed the accession of Louis-Philippe, the young toasted him, and his assumption of the title of 'King of the French' provoked discussion on possible changes to the nature of the Russian monarchy. The reports stressed that this was all only 'chatter', but that could change if France began supporting revolutionary movements in other parts of Europe. Field Marshal Diebitsch suggested massing Russia's army in Poland to counter a possible French invasion.[7]

Poland itself presented a major problem. The Congress of Vienna had set up a small kingdom of Poland attached to Russia by personal union, the tsar being also King of Poland. The Congress Kingdom, as it was called, had its own 40,000-strong army, under the command of the tsar's elder brother Grand Duke Constantine. The kingdom's administration was controlled by the Russian plenipotentiary Count Novosiltsev, whose attitude to due process did not accord with either the spirit or the letter of the constitution. The opposition in the Sejm grew in number and truculence, and by 1825 Alexander had become so exasperated that he dismissed it.

Young Poles were no less inclined than their Russian and German brothers to associate in pursuit of self-improvement and the regeneration of society. The *Philomaths* of Vilna University and the *Panta Koyna* of Warsaw had much in common with the German *Burschenschaften*. The Union of Free Poles and the Patriotic Society, on the other hand, set national independence as their goal. In 1822 a law was passed banning all such societies, and arrests were made. This had the effect, as it had in Russia, of encouraging conspiratorial activity. As the Patriotic Society and the Union of Free Poles both had members in the western provinces of Russia and in the Polish army, which was involved in manoeuvres with Russian forces, the plotters of both nations were in touch. The chaotic nature of the Decembrist revolt did not allow the Poles time to join in, but their contacts were revealed. Constantine erupted. 'Enraged at having been deceived, humiliated at not having uncovered plots which were hatching under his very eyes, he abandoned himself to the full fury of his nature,' in the words of his son's tutor, an old French émigré. 'Swarms of spies' were brought into play, 'their denunciations were granted the weight of truth' and the prisons filled up.[8]

Nicholas had put off for as long as he could his coronation as King of Poland, and when he came to Warsaw in April 1829, his visit was not a success. His coming had been anticipated with some optimism, as people hoped he would take matters in hand and sack the hated Novosiltsev, and on 28 May Benckendorff reported back to St Petersburg that the Poles loved their new king. But Nicholas feared and hated Poles, and could not hide it.[9]

He found the attitude of the Sejm insolent. Every speech he or his Polish subjects made seemed to raise uncomfortable questions from the bloody past dividing the two nations. There was also tension between Nicholas and Constantine, who felt that having left the imperial crown to his younger brother he should at least be allowed to rule Poland as he liked. He also felt that it was time that Alexander's wish to join the former Polish western provinces of the Russian empire to the Congress Kingdom was put into effect. The units of the Russian army raised in those provinces were already under his command, bore Polish names and wore uniforms with Polish crimson in place of Russian red on their collars and cuffs, an anomaly Nicholas wished to reverse. In the light of the Spanish and Neapolitan revolutions, the Semeonovsky mutiny and the Decembrist revolt, one might have expected them to have taken note of what was going on inside those uniforms.[10]

Like his brothers, Constantine had been brought up in what was effectively a military camp, and he lived for the army, which he treated as a voluptuary might his mistress. Military expenditure engulfed more than half of the budget of the kingdom, and a high proportion of it went on uniforms, which he never ceased redesigning. He held almost daily parades, regardless of the weather, which suited neither uniforms nor men. Sadistic punishment for any minor infraction, such as a missing or less than brightly polished button, was an integral part of his philosophy, and corporal punishment was inflicted even on officers, leading some to commit suicide rather than submit to the ignominy.[11]

Constantine was horrified when he heard of the July revolution in Paris. '*The comité directeur*, whose existence has been so strenuously denied, has at last dropped its mask, as we can see from the fact that the insurgents had been given and from the very beginning knew their posts and the roles they were to play,' he wrote to Nicholas, at the same time assuring him that there was no threat of trouble in Poland. 'I guarantee that you can count on the army and the majority of the population,' he wrote. Nicholas had already begun to mass troops so as to be in a position to march against France, and with the outbreak of revolution in Belgium he considered taking them to the aid of his brother-in-law King William of Holland.[12]

With the arrest of senior members of the Patriotic Society, the leadership was left in the hands of a small group of subalterns. They decided to rise and set a date in December, but with the police closing in, brought it forward to the night of 29 November. Like the Decembrists, they were under the illusion that once they rose up and waved the flag the nation would rally to their cause, and their enterprise was just as shambolic. The signal to begin was bungled, some of the conspirators lost their way, the group that was supposed to assassinate Constantine let him get away, some of the most capable Polish generals were murdered because they would not join the rebels, and the only outcome was that, with the raiding of the arsenal, an armed mob took over the streets.

'All my measures of surveillance proved useless,' a distraught Constantine wrote to his brother on 13 December. His trusted police network had showered him with information, most of it inaccurate, and while he had been aware that a conspiracy was afoot, he had been taken entirely by surprise. He complained that he was 'barefoot' and without clothes or cash, having had to flee his bedroom at night. Most of all, he was in despair at the fact that sixteen years of untiring work on his beloved army had gone to waste. He suggested withdrawing all Russian units from the kingdom and waiting for the Poles to sort things out, as he believed they would once they had let off some steam. As he predicted, senior figures in Poland quickly took control and reined in the revolutionaries, then sent an emissary to St Petersburg to negotiate an accommodation. But Nicholas demanded total submission before he would agree to speak to anyone. The issue divided Russian society into those, mainly young aristocrats, who supported the Poles, and those who thought it provided an excellent opportunity to crush them and stage a 'massacre' that would finally shut them up.[13]

The Russian empire was all but bankrupt, and to make matters worse, a virulent cholera epidemic had broken out. Dark rumours circulated as to its causes, and there were riots and attacks on hospitals. Nicholas had shown courage during one of these, driving into the crowd without an escort and telling the enraged populace to get to their knees and pray to God, which they did. Less easily put down was a mutiny in Novgorod, in which three generals and 160 officers and officials were massacred. In this instance Nicholas sent in troops to overpower the mutineers, 129 of whom died from the floggings he ordered. It was not a time to show hesitancy, and he ordered his troops into Poland.[14]

This came as a relief to his neighbours. With unrest in many parts of Germany, the last thing Prussia needed was revolution on its eastern frontier as well as on its western one. Frederick William also ruled over large Polish provinces, which might, if the Poles in the Congress Kingdom did manage to win their independence, wish to emulate them. The spirit of revolt appeared as contagious as the cholera relentlessly advancing towards Europe from the south and the east. 'The striking resemblance of this evil and its operations to an epidemic is visible both in the infection by which it is propagated, as well as in the feverish nature of its movements,' Bernstorff wrote to his king on 29 January 1831. Another Prussian official felt they were fighting 'an outright cholera of the spirit'.[15]

Metternich welcomed the Polish rising; he had no doubt that it would be put down by Russia, and it would distract Nicholas and keep him from interfering elsewhere in Europe. He needed a free hand in Italy, where news of the July revolution had caused panic in ruling circles and unwelcome enthusiasm elsewhere. There were attempted risings in Piedmont and Modena, and more were expected by the doom-sayers. The sense of uncertainty only grew worse when, on 30 November, Pope Pius VIII died. The conclave to choose his successor opened on 14 December, and Metternich went into action, pressuring all the cardinals he knew in order to obtain the election of a pope who shared his views. The conservative Cardinal Cappellari was elected on 2 February 1831, taking the name of Gregory XVI, but before the news had even travelled through the peninsula, on 3 February, risings took place in Parma, Modena and in the Papal States themselves, at Bologna and in the Legations. After inept attempts to reassert its authority, Rome called on Austria for help, and Metternich sent in troops.[16]

While his police minister Sedlnitzky had gone grey in the course of a month, Metternich managed to keep his composure, and even his sense of humour, such as it was. After a day of browbeating ministers and ambassadors, like *Jupiter Tonans* (as one lady put it) he would be charming the ladies in some salon and making jokes. But he was disappointed in his hopes of recreating the concert of the great powers: Russia was bogged down in Poland, Prussia wavered, and Britain remained aloof.[17]

Wellington did not wish to be associated with the forces of reaction on the Continent, and rejected Metternich's proposal for a conference, as he feared it would be seen as another Pillnitz (where the original coalition of Austria and Prussia issued their declaration against revolutionary France in 1791). Yet that summer and early autumn he, and many like him in Britain, felt that if the Belgian rising were not put down by the King of the Netherlands, subversive elements everywhere would be encouraged to 'set Europe in a blaze', and as Princess Lieven noted in a letter to her brother Aleksandr Benckendorff, 'this rich, free, happy, and prosperous England is not by any means free from the dangerous contagion which disturbs Europe'.[18]

Although Wellington's Tories had won the election in the summer of 1830, reform was in the air. Wellington had lost much of his erstwhile popularity as the hero of Waterloo, and his ministry was beleaguered by Radicals and Whigs who exploited the ill-feeling against the metropolitan police, established the previous summer. On 26 October they organised demonstrations at Covent Garden and Piccadilly under the slogan 'No New Police!', and two days later staged a confrontation at Hyde Park Corner. The Peelers, armed only with batons, managed to contain the mob.

At the opening of Parliament on 2 November, Wellington made it clear that there would be no parliamentary reform on his watch. Whigs and reformers expressed various degrees of shock and anger, while those lower down the social scale released all manner of grievance and pent-up rage. The Swing rioters were matched by urban mobs breaking windows, setting fires and breaking into houses in a week of sporadic violence. Wellington's confidante Mrs Harriet Arbuthnot noted that the king was 'very much frightened, the queen cries half the day with fright', Radicals such as Francis Place rubbed their hands in the belief that such a demonstration of popular feeling would force the government's hand, and Princess Lieven reported to her brother in St Petersburg that Britain was 'on the brink of revolution'. Wellington deployed 7,000 troops around London, and drew up detailed instructions for the military defence of his residence Apsley House, specifying how many armed men should be posted at the windows of the Piccadilly drawing room, Lord Douro's drawing room, the duchess's bathroom and so on, and at what point they should open fire.[19]

Matters reached a climax on 9 November, when the king was due to attend a banquet given by the lord mayor at the Guildhall. The extreme Radicals had organised a demonstration. One poster read:

> *Liberty or Death! Britons!! And Honest Men!!!*
>
> *The time has at last arrived. All London meets on Tuesday. We assure you from ocular demonstration that 6,000 cutlasses have been removed from the Tower for the use of Peel's Bloody Gang. Remember the cursed speech from the Throne!! These damned Police are now to be armed.*
>
> *Englishmen, will you put up with this?*

Another called on people to look to France, and argued that 'If a New Police be requisite, let it emanate from the People, and be under their entire controul [sic]', like the French National Guard.[20]

The king was persuaded not to attend the banquet, and the demonstrators, robbed of their prey, moved off in the direction of the West End, bent on causing trouble. The Peelers met them in the Strand and dispersed them without bloodshed by the use of a newly devised tactic, the baton charge. But the troubles did not cease. The opposition made hay, and the government was defeated in Parliament on 15 November, leading to the formation of a Whig ministry under Earl Grey.[21]

Among those in favour of reform expectations reached a new pitch. Henry Hunt, who had been elected to Parliament, caused a stir by tabling a motion in favour of female suffrage. The number of disturbances as well as meetings of one kind or another rose dramatically. 'The state of the country is dreadful,' noted the diarist Charles Greville on 21 November; 'every post brings fresh accounts of conflagrations, destruction of machinery, association of labourers, and compulsory rise of wages.' He was convinced that the disturbances had nothing to do with poverty, but were inspired by the inflammatory speeches of Cobbett and his like, and particularly by news from abroad. The new home secretary, Lord Melbourne, took a more vigor-

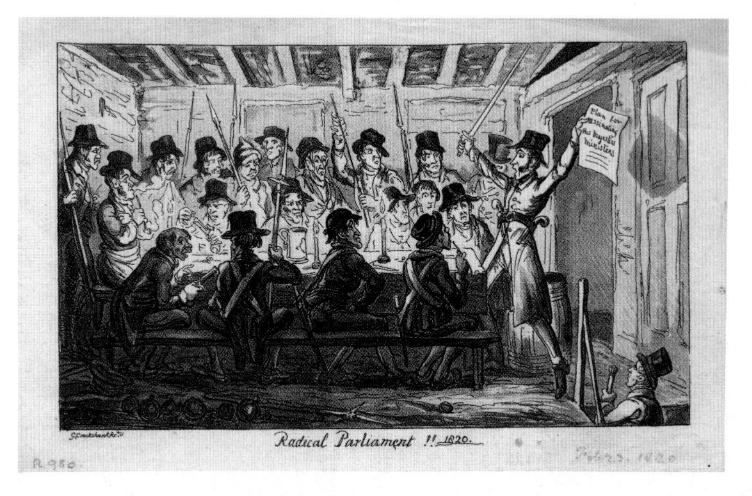

A cartoon aimed at associating the law-abiding agitators for constitutional reform with the Cato Street conspiracy to murder the prime minister and other members of the cabinet, which was partly fomented by Home Office agents.

The murder of the duc de Berry on 13 February 1820 by a lone anti-monarchist was assumed by most of the rulers of Europe to be the work of a centrally directed conspiracy. This contemporary engraving misrepresents the facts by having the duchess present, in order to maximise the emotional outrage.

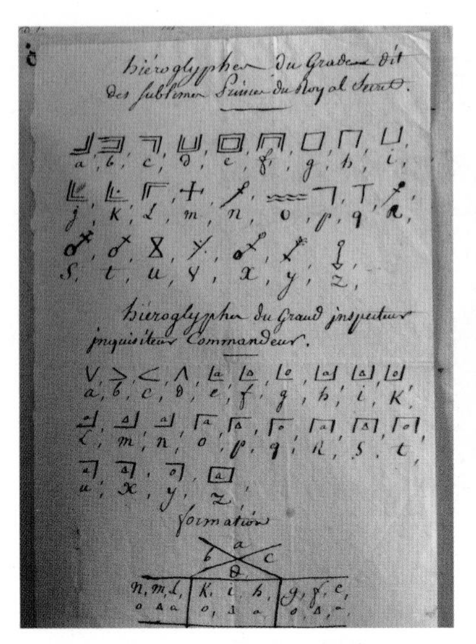

A document purporting to be a copy of the hieroglyphs used by a secret society. Such confections, usually produced by informers who were paid by bulk, litter the archives of the French police.

A meeting of the Carbonari, as imagined by a contemporary illustrator.

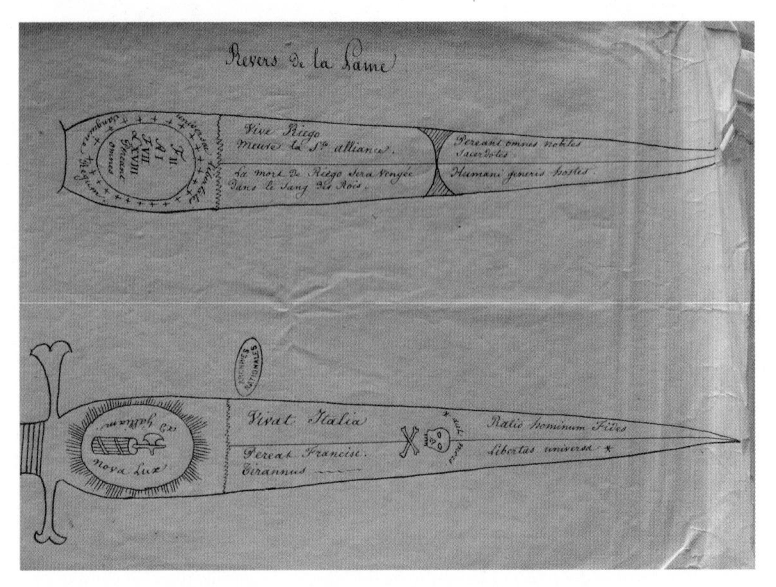

A drawing supplied to the French police by an informer, supposedly of daggers being forged by French and Italian secret societies for the murder of European monarchs.

General Alexei Arakcheev, who ran Russia while Alexander dreamed of a better world, by an anonymous artist.

Russian political prisoners in the dungeons of the notorious Schlusselburg fortress. A later engraving.

The Peter and Paul fortress in St Petersburg, a favoured place of detention for young men suspected of plotting the overthrow of the monarchy. Nineteenth-century photograph.

Count Alexander von Benckendorff, head of the notorious Third Section, whose gendarmes invigilated the private lives of Russian subjects. Portrait by Yegor Bottman.

Benckendorff's master, Tsar Nicholas I, whose fear of disorder bordered on the pathological. Portrait by Vassily Tropinin,1826.

Russian troops parade in a comforting display of how order should be enforced, following the suppression of the Polish insurrection of 1830. Painting by Nikanor Grigorievich,1837.

The remains of the *'machine infernale'* used by Giuseppe Fieschi in his attempt to murder King Louis-Philippe.

The French government's intelligence was supplied by bungling busybodies whose 'secret' agents reported revolution everywhere, yet failed to uncover a single plot that had not been fomented by the police themselves. This caricature of 1830 sums up the public's view of their qualities.

The folkloric and nationalist jamboree held at the castle of Hambach in May 1832 was interpreted by Metternich as part of the Europe-wide revolution being planned from Paris, and helped him tighten repression throughout Germany.

A cartoon satirising the Duke of Wellington's last-ditch resistance to parliamentary reform in 1832, which he regarded as heralding the end of the British monarchy, and ridiculing his posting of armed men at the windows of his London residence at Hyde Park Corner.

This contemporary print of a barricade in Sachsen-Altenburg in June 1848 shows the essentially middle-class nature of the protests which the likes of Metternich could only see as part of a worldwide conspiracy to destroy the social order.

This painting by Johann Velten of political prisoners in gaol at Trier following the suppression of the local revolt in 1848 accords ill with the image cherished by most of the rulers of Europe of a conspiracy directed by fanatical Jacobins bent on murder and mayhem.

Once Metternich had been forced to resign, the enforcement of order was taken over by a National Guard formed by the 'revolutionaries'. Anonymous contemporary lithograph.

This German cartoon of December 1848 satirises the rulers' view of the events of that year.

ous line than Peel with the Swing rioters, sending out senior military officers to the disturbed areas to take the situation in hand, but many still felt the country was sliding towards revolution.[22]

News of the revolution in Warsaw on 29 November, and of troubles in Piedmont, only darkened the picture. 'I never remember times like these, nor read of such – the terror and lively expectation which prevail, and the way in which people's minds are turned backwards and forwards from France to Ireland, then range excursively to Poland or Piedmont, and fix again on the burnings, riots, and executions here,' Greville noted on 30 December. Colonel Sir William Napier thought a revolution 'inevitable', while the poet Robert Southey told Greville that if he could find the money he would take himself and his family off to America.[23]

'I entertain no doubt that there exists a formidable conspiracy,' Wellington wrote to the Earl of Malmesbury on 6 December. 'But as yet I don't believe that we have got a trace of it.' He had been receiving reports of Irishmen in Paris preparing to raise the standard of revolt in the island. 'I am inclined to think that the operations of the conspirators in this country are conducted by Englishmen,' he wrote, but he felt that 'the original focus is at Paris ... I know that the *Société Propagande* at Paris had at its command very large means from subscriptions all over Europe, but particularly from the revolutionary bankers in France. A part of these means is, I think, now applied to the purpose of corrupting and disturbing this country.' He even considered the possibility of a French invasion. The term 'bankers' had now joined 'liberals' in the canon reaching back to the Templars.[24]

Metternich felt that his theory of universal conspiracy was being fully vindicated. 'There is not one event taking place these days whose origin and provenance cannot be easily identified, and the centre of the action can everywhere be traced,' he almost crowed in October. 'The revolution in Modena is no isolated event,' he wrote in February 1831, 'it is an episode of the vast conspiracy which embraces the whole of Italy; it is the signal for a conflagration which its authors would like to be universal. One could furnish a mass of proofs, but the simultaneous nature of the revolts which have just broken out in the Papal States renders all proofs unnecessary.' He claimed that French agents were roaming Italy dispensing large sums of money. He was not seriously worried by the Italians themselves. 'Italy is full of idlers and proletarians who make great expenditure of speech in cafés and other public places which are their habitual haunts,' he explained to Esterházy in April. But, as he assured Apponyi, 'there is nothing *Italian* about the measures which accompany the revolts: the form is entirely French; it is that prescribed by the *comité directeur* of Paris; it is that which was followed by the recent minor disturbances in Germany.' All the reports he was receiving from those places in Italy where there had been disturbances were 'unanimous in expressing the conviction that the whole revolution in Italy is nothing but the outcome of *the work of the committees of Paris* … agents of the *comité directeur* gave the signal for the rising'. 'In every village which has risen, one or several Frenchmen are at the head of the movement,' he affirmed, without a shred of supporting evidence. 'The intensity of the workings of the sects in Europe is beyond belief,' he wrote to Apponyi on 3 June, 'but its effect would be negligible if the *comité directeur* of Paris were not there to activate and regulate the Revolution.'[25]

'The most recent French revolution and the outbreaks bursting forth shortly thereafter at so many points make indubitable the truth previously simply suspected, which for years was evident to any thinking person, that the revolutionary movements of all lands arise from one focus and that this centre is in Paris,' he affirmed. 'The committee which directs those evidently strongly organised sects which seek to overthrow all legitimate monarchical constitutions scarcely bothers to hide its existence and its designs. Only its means and the agents which it uses are still a secret.'[26]

The only rising Metternich did not link to Paris was the Polish one, which he recognised as a specific case, essentially an inter-state war. The Polish Sejm had voted for the dethronement of Nicholas as King of Poland on the grounds that he had violated the constitution, and this dissolved Poland's union with Russia. The Poles had won a succession of battles with the invading Russian army, and Diebitsch and other senior Russian commanders were growing discouraged; cholera was devastating his forces. But Nicholas was determined to punish what he saw only as 'rebels'. The Polish leadership, headed by the eminently un-revolutionary Prince Czartoryski, knew they could not sustain the war indefinitely, and were desperate to negotiate a settlement. They attempted to engage the good offices of Austria and Britain, suggesting the creation of a neutral Polish state with an Austrian archduke or one of the late King George IV's brothers on the throne. But neither Britain nor Austria wished to get involved. Prussia was vehemently opposed to the emergence of an independent Poland, which, it feared, would ultimately result in the loss of its own Polish provinces, but had to step cautiously as public opinion throughout Germany was enthusiastically pro-Polish.[27]

This posed problems for Metternich, who was continuing his preparations for war on France. He had reinforced the Austrian army with the aim of creating a combined force including Prussian and Russian contingents, to be commanded by the Austrian Archduke Charles, victor of Aspern in 1809. But the archduke refused. On 7 March 1831 he produced a memorandum arguing that Austria's military and financial resources were inadequate for such a conflict, and that it would be a war against ideas, which, by definition, could not be won. He pointed out that left to its own devices, the French revolutionary spirit would burn itself out. Challenged, it would become dangerous. A victory over France would only plunge that country deeper into chaos, which would affect the allied armies operating against it, and inflame revolutionary tendencies in Germany, Poland and Italy. Metternich responded with the argument that they were engaged in a 'life and death struggle' against the forces of anarchy, and it was not admissible to stand idly by.[28]

Those forces of anarchy could in reality only be contained by Louis-Philippe, yet he was under siege from all sides. The republicans may have been slow to act in July 1830, but they were making up for lost time, meaning to take the revolution to what they saw as its logical conclusion. The same was true of others whose expectations had been raised, including many, both in the army and among the working classes, who felt the shame of 1815 should be wiped out by war against those who had inflicted it. Louis-Philippe had to repress the first and humour the second, and to reassure the great powers of his peaceful intentions, which they doubted. The revolution in Belgium only added to his troubles; it cried out for French military assistance. Every rising in Germany and Italy produced waves of sympathy in France and demands for armed intervention on its behalf. The rising in Poland, which had come to be seen in France as a sister victim of 1815, brought people out into the streets demanding immediate armed action on its behalf. Louis-Philippe had to navigate a tortuous course between loud statements of sympathy for Poland and quiet assurances to the powers.

In December 1830 he was nearly toppled by an attempted revolution concerted by the *Société des Amis du Peuple*, but while he managed to weather this crisis, there was continuing instability. 'Still the same madness,' Count Rodolphe Apponyi, cousin of the Austrian ambassador in Paris, noted in his diary in February 1831. 'There's dancing in the drawing rooms, fighting in the streets, the revolution is in full swing; everything seems to be falling apart, we are on a volcano, which rumbles and threatens, the new monarchy is shaken, as is the government, down to its very foundations.'[29]

The Emperor Francis would later admit that the only reason he had not gone to war with France in 1830 was that Austria could not afford to. There was a good deal of truth in this, and it permitted the much-maligned bankers to take a salutary hand in the proceedings. The five Rothschild brothers, and particularly James in Paris and Salomon in Vienna, had lent most of the governments of Europe, and particularly those of Austria and France, large sums of money in return for government bonds. James Rothschild let it be known that were war to be declared against France, the French bonds would go down from their current low of 73 per cent to under 45 per cent. Austrian and Prussian bonds would also fall in value, with attendant loss to all those who had invested in them. Louis-Philippe, who was a heavily invested businessman, did not need to be reminded of this, and nor did his ministers Lafitte and Casimir Perrier, both of them bankers. Metternich had close links with the Rothschilds, who had resolved many difficulties for him in the past and who now arranged for his mother-in-law's 400,000-franc debt to be written off. Gentz had an even closer connection to the banking brothers, and had received substantial rewards from them. He tried to persuade Metternich to go along with a planned conference on mutual disarmament suggested by Louis-Philippe and supported by the Rothschilds.[30]

The other place where the foundations of government were being shaken was Britain, where the prominent Whig Lord John Russell had introduced his Reform Bill on 1 March. This was anything but revolutionary: it would abolish a number of rotten boroughs and the more shocking electoral anomalies (one Member of Parliament represented Old Sarum, a field with a ring in it, while two were returned for Dunwich in Suffolk, most of which had long ago fallen into the North Sea) and enlarge the electorate by just over half. The Bill passed its second reading, by one vote, but a month later it was defeated by a spoiling motion. There was rioting in London and other cities. The Whig prime minister Earl Grey persuaded the king to grant a dissolution of Parliament at the end of April. The subsequent elections gave the Whigs an overwhelming majority, and the Bill was introduced once more. Grey warned that unless the enemies of reform did not back down, 'there will ensue troubles such as the world has never yet seen, and will in the end submerge everything'. By the end of May, Wellington believed that 'we are on the eve of a great revolution, or rather that we are already in a state of revolution'. He had convinced himself that the changes proposed by the Bill would fundamentally undermine the whole fabric of British society. 'I don't in general take a gloomy view of things,' he wrote to Lord Melville a few days later, 'but I confess that, knowing all that I do, I cannot see what is to save

Church, or property or colonies, or union with Ireland, or eventually monarchy, if the Reform Bill passes.'[31]

His fears were echoed by, amongst others, Nesselrode, who admitted in a letter to Princess Lieven that the Bill, a copy of which she had sent him, had 'inspired a real terror' in him. 'To entirely suppress the rotten boroughs would be to overthrow the government, and if the project were to pass, I will take my leave of England,' he wrote. The princess herself was appalled by the way the issue of Belgium was addressed in the King's Speech at the opening of Parliament in June 1831, which referred to 'the right of the people of Belgium to regulate their own internal affairs, and to establish their Government according to their own view of what may be most conducive to their future welfare and independence'. A conference had been convened in London to resolve the Belgian crisis and, reluctantly in the case of Austria and Russia, the powers had agreed that the country should become a neutral, independent kingdom, with Leopold of Saxe-Coburg as, significantly, King of the Belgians. The notion that a people should be allowed to secede and choose their own king was 'most unseemly' to someone who believed in the Russian empire, and it was fraught with danger, since it posed the question: if Belgium, why not Poland? It also spelled the end of any possible concert between the autocratic powers and the liberal ones. Princess Lieven warned Nesselrode that if the tsar were to support the King of Holland against the Belgians, it would drive the two liberal powers Britain and France into each other's arms, with the result that the whole of Europe would be revolutionised.[32]

Revolution did not break out in Britain, and for all its reformist zeal the government applied the necessary measures to suppress the disturbances. In June, militant miners at Merthyr Tydfil in Wales were dispersed by troops. The courts imposed savage sentences against the Swing rioters who had been apprehended: of 1,976 tried in thirty-four counties, 252 were sentenced to death (in the end only nineteen were executed), and the others were transported, sent to prison, fined or bound over. The superintendent of convicts who visited those about to be transported before they sailed said that he 'never saw a finer set of men', and noted that they had been motivated by outrage at injustice rather than by any revolutionary instincts.[33]

On the night of 6–7 July 1831 Russell's second Bill passed in the Commons by 136 votes, but this only served to stiffen the resolve of diehard Tories, who raised the spectre of a grand conspiracy embracing France, Belgium, Poland, Italy and Germany as well as Britain. Wellington did not make much of the reports received by the Home Office that there were '2000 French soldiers with officers about the town, that certain of them were seen standing at the corners of streets with maps in their hands, as if they were getting a knowledge of the town', and thought that perhaps the presence of a few tourists had given rise to them. He was putting on a brave face, boasting that he could put down a revolution with a single regiment, but in the event the Metropolitan Police had contained and dispersed many meetings without provoking the sort of rage that the appearance of troops was wont to do. On 15 October the home secretary, Lord Melbourne, introduced the Special Constables Act, which permitted the rapid enlistment of large numbers of these officers, and the very knowledge that 'specials' were being enlisted made the organisers cancel more than one meeting.[34]

When the Reform Bill came before the Lords on 7 October, it was thrown out by a majority of forty-one. This prompted a rash of rioting in London, Manchester, Derby, Nottingham – where the Duke of Newcastle's castle was burned – and other cities. Magistrates and Tories were insulted and assaulted in the street, and churchmen, particularly bishops, pelted with mud and stones – twenty-one of the twenty-three bishops in the Lords had voted against the Bill. Houses of known opponents of reform were sacked, and factories torched. In Bristol the rioting lasted three days, in the course of which the Mansion House, the Bishop's Palace, the Custom House, three prisons and countless other buildings were burned to the ground. Possibly as many as four hundred people lost their lives. Lord Melbourne was, in his own words, 'frightened to death'. The rejection of the Bill had altered the mood of large sections of the population, and the hitherto stalwart support for the monarchy as the basis of British national life was beginning to fray. King William IV's popularity waned, and republicans felt emboldened enough to question the point of keeping 'Fat Billy' at all, while there were plenty of voices raised in favour of doing away with the aristocracy.[35]

Wellington was by now convinced, as he put it in a letter to the Bishop of Exeter on 5 November, that there were 'strong indications of an expectation, if not of an actual plan, of insurrection against property among the lowest orders'. That Guy Fawkes Night, the effigies burned were not those of the Catholic plotter, but of the hero of Waterloo and assorted bishops. Tory landowners began to fortify their houses and arm their retainers, and the Duke of Rutland installed cannon at Belvoir Castle to repel the putative revolutionary mob. A casualty of all this alarm was John Henry North MP, whose epitaph in a Harrow church informs that he died, aged forty-four, as a result of 'a mind too great for his earthly frame in opposing the Revolutionary Invasion of the Religion and Constitution of England'.[36]

25

Scandals

One who might have been expected to go the same way was Metternich's closest collaborator and alter ego, Friedrich von Gentz, who had wanted to see 'revolution and counter-revolution drawn up against each other in battle array' and the spirit of the age 'vanquished with cannon'. He had called for the reintroduction of religion into everyday life, the shutting down of schools and the imposition of 'any feudalism', however inefficient, 'if only it delivers us from the power of the mob, of counterfeit scholars, of students, and of journalists especially'. Yet the events of 1830 had made him reconsider.[1]

None of the risings had in fact been about toppling thrones or overthrowing the social order; they had all been reactions against oppression, injustice, corruption and hypocrisy. Gentz urged Metternich to recognise Louis-Philippe, supported the Poles against Russia, and in a letter to James de Rothschild expressed the conviction that a contest between legitimism and the sovereignty of the people was a nonsense, since the sovereignty of the people was fast becoming the new legitimacy, and any war waged against it 'would only hasten the fall of all the thrones, even those of the victors'. He argued that Austrian policy had been fundamentally flawed in its resistance to the march of history. 'I shall stand or fall with Metternich,' he wrote on New Year's Day 1832, 'but nowadays he is a fool. If I were to write the history of the past fifteen years it would be one long indictment of Metternich.' To a friend he admitted that he now considered that the overthrow of Napoleon had proved a misfortune for Europe and the greatest blunder of Austrian policy.[2]

Metternich's attitude was closer to that of the Duke of Rutland. To him, the July Days were nothing short of a 'renewal' of 1789. 'The false and disastrous principle of the sovereignty of the people has declared itself triumphant,' he lamented. This triumph had been aided and abetted by the powers, particularly Britain and Prussia, which had shown weakness by recognising the change of dynasty in France and, what was worse, by their 'outrageous' resolution of the Belgian crisis by creating a new independent state – to which Austria had, with the utmost reluctance, given its assent. He considered this 'odious' because on the one hand it sanctioned rebellion, and on the other it undermined the 1815 settlement – it was no coincidence that many in France referred to the July Days as a riposte to Waterloo.[3]

Yet Metternich was almost elated by the disasters taking place all around. 'For many years those who had pointed to the existence of a *comité directeur* working secretly for universal revolution were met everywhere only by incredulity; today it has been shown that this infernal propaganda exists, that it has its centre in Paris, and that it is divided into as many sections as there are nations,' he maintained. 'Everything that refers to this great and dangerous plot cannot, therefore be observed and surveyed with too much attention.'[4]

He was focused on Germany, which was in a state of effervescence whipped up by the publication of hundreds of political pamphlets. A Patriotic Association was founded to support freedom of the press; liberals were calling for constitutions and cheering the Poles fighting against their Russian overlords; poems and songs hailing freedom fighters in Paris and Poland were sung in defiance of the authorities. The publication of Witt von Dörring's sensationalist memoirs and an eight-hundred-page book on the secret societies active in Germany, supposedly based on the Mainz commission's archives, suggested that there was more under the surface.[5]

Metternich warned Wittgenstein, who was by now effectively the prime minister of Prussia, that the revolution was approaching with 'mile-long steps', and must be confronted with 'fire and water'. He urged Prussia to arm in self-defence, for 'revolution leads to war as surely as a plague leads to famine'. In August 1831 he called on the major courts of Germany to delegate generals who could plan a joint armed response, and convoked a conference in Vienna in September of their foreign ministers. He dismissed Bernstorff's opinion that there was no real revolutionary threat in Germany as 'disgusting nonsense'. He went so far as to organise an intrigue, planting a letter from Emperor Francis to King Frederick William, with the seal broken, in Bernstorff's office and arranging for it to be discovered. Bernstorff was dismissed. But the German states still baulked at Metternich's exhortations to bring in a new version of the Karlsbad Decrees and to mobilise for war with France.[6]

The fall of Warsaw to the Russians on 8 September sparked off riots in Paris and demonstrations all over Germany. It was soon followed by the arrival of Polish soldiers fleeing Russian reprisals, who were fêted as they passed through the country. People drew them into beer houses or their own homes and plied them with food and drink. 'It seemed to be an affair of honour with the Mayence citizens not to suffer a sober Pole in their city,' recalled a Prussian officer stationed in Mainz. 'I, at least, never saw one.' The émigrés were particularly popular with the womenfolk, and the officer noted that 'Many a rascal put on a Polish uniform and spoke broken German, as it helped him better through the country than even a passport from the chief of police himself would have done.'[7]

Committees sprang up to provide assistance for the destitute exiles, and Metternich leapt to the conclusion that they were 'branches of the French *Propagande*'. 'It is absolutely clear that Germany is permanently being worked upon by the *Comité directeur* in Paris,' he assured the Bavarian minister Prince Wrede. The presence of the Poles emboldened young Germans to flaunt their nationalist and liberal feelings openly. 'The Polish enthusiasm was followed by the black-red-gold fever,' recalled the Prussian officer, who received orders to arrest anyone wearing a cockade in those colours, a measure which 'did much to increase the excitement instead of quelling it, as was intended'.[8]

By the spring of 1832, Metternich was feeling isolated and beleaguered by 'pedantic *sans-culottes*' in Germany who were arguing that there was no revolutionary threat. Abroad, he had become involved in confrontation with France over Italy. Austrian troops had evacuated Bologna, leaving the task of peacekeeping to the pope. But the papal troops behaved so badly that revolution broke out once again, and in January 1832 Metternich was obliged to send his own back in. At this point, France protested and landed a force at Ancona, supposedly to defend the pope against Austrian aggression. Metternich was furious, and declared the French action 'a political crime'. (The stand-off would last until 1838, when both forces were withdrawn.)[9]

He could not count on Nicholas or Frederick William and the other rulers of Germany. Britain seemed on the brink of giving way to reform: on 22 March 1832 the Reform Bill was brought before the Commons for a third reading, and was passed in the early hours of the following day. It was defeated in the Lords by nine votes, so Grey asked the king to create a number of new peers in order to give the Whigs a majority there. The king agreed, but subsequently changed his mind. When Grey was informed of this, on 9 May, he resigned. 'As things now stand in England,' Metternich wrote to Wrede, 'all roads towards the good are barred, and a mad revolution is in the offing.' The mood in the country was ugly, and references to Charles I abounded in political discussions.[10]

As Wellington attempted to form a new ministry, he was warned of plans to assassinate him. Mass meetings were held up and down the land, plans were made for resisting taxes, for barricading towns to turn them into fortresses, for mass demonstrations, and for outright armed resistance. In the City of London, men of trade and business confabulated on how to apply pressure, and came up with the threat of starting a run on the Bank of England, summed up in the slogan 'To Stop the Duke, Go for Gold'.[11]

There was by now greater coordination between the Radicals and the working classes. These had become more organised, and there were arms in considerable quantities available to them. Perhaps most important, large sections of the middle class were no longer prepared to accept the dominance of the landed aristocracy, resting on a system that was patently absurd as well as unjust. There was a growing feeling that if force was needed, it would have to be used, and even some regular army officers made it clear that they would side against the authorities if things were to come to that.[12]

At the same time, the middle classes and all but a handful of the most radical reformers were as fearful of social revolution as they were keen on carrying through reform. While they threatened violence, and in the case of the Birmingham Political Union actually laid plans for insurrection, they used the working classes as a dog on a lead, ready to be let loose but kept firmly in hand. There was an element of bluff in this brinkmanship, but the threat of revolution was nevertheless real. On 15 May Wellington came to the conclusion that he would not be able to form a government, and abandoned the struggle to hold back the tide. Metternich was appalled when he heard the news. 'England is facing disaster,' he wrote. A few days later he was faced by what he immediately recognised as a challenge closer to home, to which he must rise.[13]

On Sunday, 27 May 1832 people began to gather at Hambach, a village in the Rhenish Palatinate nestling beneath the picturesque ruins of the castle of Kästenburg. They were the first wave of a crowd which would grow to some 20,000. The original idea had been to hold a folkloric festival of a kind that had become popular, underpinned by the need to stimulate the local economy by staging what was sure to be a tourist attraction. As the crowds gathered it became clear that all sorts were keen to contribute. Cartloads of young men wearing ribbons in the black-red-gold colours of the national movement jostled with processions of maidens dressed in white with oak-leaf garlands in their hair singing folk songs. German exiles turned up from France singing the '*Marseillaise*' and airs from Rossini operas. There were also Polish émigrés in uniform, and the procession to the castle was led by women bearing the German tricolour and the Polish flag. The festival, which lasted until 1 June, included fairground attractions and the atmosphere was convivial, although there was some drunkenness and even criminality. Bombastic speeches were given on subjects ranging from the overthrow of tyrants and the liberation of nations to medieval customs and Old German morality. Slogans such as 'United States of Germany', 'Common German Fatherland' and 'Confederated Republic of European States' were liberally bandied about.

News of these revels was greeted by Metternich with a horror that barely masked his glee. He pointed out that on the same day, 27 May, German exiles in Paris had held a banquet with Lafayette as guest of honour, which proved that 'the scandals of Hambach' had been orchestrated from the French capital. 'Everything is connected and can be identified as *the attempt at a European* revolution,' he wrote to Wrede at the beginning of July. To Wittgenstein, he wrote that he did not actually care about what had happened, but welcomed the fact that they had something tangible with which they could frighten the rulers of Germany. Wittgenstein replied with even greater cynicism, complaining that the event had not been 'great enough', and wishing that the organisers of the festival had gone the whole way and deposed the King of Bavaria.[14]

'Western Germany has recently been the theatre of scandalous scenes hardly less shocking than those which England and France have for so long offered to the world,' Metternich wrote to his ambassador in Rome. 'These scenes do not yet amount to revolution, but they are its immediate precursors, and they contain all the elements.' Unity and firmness of action on the part of all the rulers of Germany were called for. 'The dangers menacing the States today are not limited to one or other of them; the risk is equal for all,' he asserted. The Illuminati were alive and well, in the guise of the *Burschenschaften*, he assured Neumann in London.[15]

The Hambach festival had the desired effect of sowing panic in governing circles in Berlin, and Frederick William was easily persuaded to back Metternich's proposal to put before the Bundestag for approval a document he had drawn up containing six articles restating the sovereignty of the monarch and reinforcing his rights to raise taxes at will and to rule without the assent of his estates. There was some opposition in the assembly, and outside. The British foreign secretary Lord Palmerston, who disliked Metternich as much as Metternich despised him, taunted him with a sarcastically ingenuous public note expressing the hope that he would use his wisdom and influence to curb the repressive zeal of the assembly.[16]

Metternich duly bullied it into passing the six articles on 28 June 1832, followed on 5 July by ten more articles, also drafted by himself, essentially reasserting the Karlsbad Decrees: forbidding the circulation of political material published outside Germany; banning all associations, assemblies and festivals; forbidding the wearing of ribbons, cockades or other insignia, the flying of flags and the planting of liberty trees; placing the universities under strict surveillance, along with foreigners; and providing for the extradition of fugitives and for mutual military assistance. The assembly then went on to decree that all protests and petitions addressed to it would be treated as acts of rebellion.

This touched off a wave of protest and passive resistance. Patriots and liberals sang the '*Marseillaise*' and the pro-Polish '*Varsovienne*', and when the authorities banned these, they took to singing traditional German songs laced with subversive messages. Popular folk songs were amended to vilify hate figures such as the Prussian police chief and minister of justice Kamptz and to praise Karl Sand, the Poles or the Greek freedom fighters. A subliminal contest was carried on through symbols. Instead of the banned black-red-gold ribbons and cockades, they would wear blue ones, and when the police caught on that this was a sly reference to the banned colours, and forbade the wearing of the blue ones, they would adopt green, then pink, and so on; the police would lumber on, one step behind, led into more and more absurd prohibitions, of certain styles of tie, hat or waistcoat, until the Bavarian authorities outlawed the wearing of any kind of moustache.[17]

Bavaria had set up a special department to deal with 'political machinations' under councillor Anton von Braunmühl, which, in cooperation with the Mainz commission, produced dossiers on every university lecturer and professor in the kingdom. Professor Behr of the University of Wurzburg was sentenced to fifteen years in gaol, Professor Jordan of Marburg to five, and then another five, for high treason, to be served in a fortress. Pastor Weidig, a schoolmaster, committed suicide after five years in detention without charge; his suicide note to his wife was not passed on, for political security reasons.[18]

On 3 April 1833, at about 9.30 in the evening, a group of young men, some of them armed, stormed the principal guardhouse in Frankfurt shouting revolutionary slogans and calling to arms the citizens, who stopped and stared in amazement. It was the climax of a conspiracy of astonishing silliness involving a motley assortment of students and young artisans, with a sprinkling of Polish émigrés. The would-be revolutionaries roamed the city for about an hour, trying to elicit a reaction from the citizens, before fleeing at the sight of the civic guard and regular troops, who succeeded in rounding up just over fifty of them.[19]

The police files on the investigation of these and others implicated provide little evidence of any coherent, let alone unified, motivation. Most of them come across as muddle-headed (in at least one case the police were convinced that the boy was mad), and seem to have been inspired by a morally rather than politically based revulsion at what they saw as the corruption of public life in Germany. They mostly hoped that by standing up and demonstrating their determination to do something, they could bring about change for the better, although they gave no idea of how this better world was supposed to look. The investigations dragged on, and it was not until 1836 that sentence was passed on 204 students, thirty-nine of whom received the death penalty. One of them, the poet Fritz Reuter, was sentenced to death by beheading for having attended meetings and offended the majesty of the King of Prussia. The sentence was commuted to thirty years of confinement in a fortress.[20]

Two months after the Frankfurt guardhouse incident, in June 1833, a pan-German police information exchange, the *Bundeszentralbehörde*, was set up, along with a ministerial commission headed by Prussia's notorious police chief and minister of justice Karl Albert von Kamptz, a man described by a colleague as being 'addicted to hunting down demagogues'. This organisation would sit until 1842, and would investigate alleged plots all over Germany, involving some 1,800 individuals. Its great achievement was to draw up the *Gesamtinkulpatentabelle*, popularly known as the Black Book, a meticulously documented list of everyone who had ever been involved in or interrogated in connection with subversive activity, which added up to 2,140 names.[21]

Metternich exploited the guardhouse incident to the full, urging the other German states to take action against 'the sickness of the times'. 'The enemy stands with his forces concentrated, ready to strike, and he has his headquarters, his army corps, his vanguard and his reserves,' he warned. He admitted to Wrede that he was not seriously worried by street revolts, which were easy to put down, more by what he called 'revolution ex-cathedra', the progress of liberalisation through courts of law. This chimes nicely with the frustration of the Russian minister at the court of the King of Württemberg, Baron Peter von Meyendorff, who in April 1833 complained to Nesselrode that almost all government employees in Germany, in the administration, the courts, the police and the post office, 'belong to the faction'. 'The police knows how to move on vagabonds and uncover burglaries, but it is rare for it to try to recognise the French and Polish agents who are carrying the orders from the *propaganda*,' he complained, adding that judges were letting dangerous subversives walk free. He was outraged by the attitude of the postal service. 'When, in order to find out more about the plots of a Pole who was living here in hiding and corresponding with Nakwasky in Carlsrouhe [sic], I asked for his correspondence to be watched, I received the reply that all postal employees had on the accession of the present King taken an oath to respect the secret of letters, and despite all my efforts, it has been impossible to have this correspondence impounded or examined.'[22]

Meyendorff saw conspiracy everywhere. On 8 June he reported to Nesselrode on a riot at Tübingen, where a group of students broke the windows of the university chancellor, a conservative deputy to the Württemberg assembly. Order had been restored by sixteen gendarmes, who arrested eight of the students. But in his view the riot revealed 'new symptoms of the revolutionary fever from which German youth is suffering so gravely', proved 'the existence of a vast revolutionary ramification throughout the German universities, particularly those in which the *Burschenschaften* have never ceased to exist', and clearly demonstrated that 'this youth has become fanaticised to the point of stopping at nothing'.[23]

Annoyingly for Metternich, not everyone thought like Meyendorff. The Austrian minister of the interior, Count Franz Anton von Kolowrat, was a particularly irritating dissenter. 'Your method is a forest of bayonets and the inflexible maintenance of everything that exists,' he wrote to Metternich in June. 'To my mind, that is the best way of bringing about revolution.' He went on to explain that this method was ruining the state financially and obliging it to impose onerous taxes, which turned people against the government, that his refusal to allow the middle classes to share in the running of the country filled them with hatred for the aristocracy, and that this would, sooner or later, inspire them to make use of the disgruntled masses to topple it. He suggested that they make concessions which would contribute to the well-being of the masses and allow the middle classes some influence. 'That is the only path which can save us; yours will lead us, perhaps not tomorrow or next year, but certainly soon enough, to total disaster.'[24]

Metternich ignored him. In August 1833 he met Frederick William at Töplitz, and persuaded him that it was time to muzzle the press more tightly, and to abolish all the constitutions brought in since 1815. This meeting was a prelude to a more important one, between the two emperors and their ministers, to take place at Munchengrätz (Mnichovo Hradiště) in Bohemia in September, with the object of agreeing an offensive–defensive alliance between Russia and Austria.

If Metternich is to be believed, on arrival at the picturesque town the tsar greeted him with the words: 'I have come here to place myself at the disposal of my leader; I am counting on you to correct any errors I have made.' Metternich responded by calling Nicholas the guardian angel of Austria. If Nicholas's consort is to be believed, the tsar regarded the Austrian chancellor with the deepest suspicion. 'Every time I see Metternich, I involuntarily make the sign of the Cross,' she recalls him saying. Be that as it may, on 3 September 1833 Russia and Austria signed a joint convention providing not only for close cooperation on tracking down and extraditing people suspected of subversive activity in either country, but also for the surveillance of suspects on request. Two weeks later the two emperors signed a convention which condemned, among other things, the 'false doctrine of non-intervention', as though it were an impious heresy.[25]

This once more raised the spectre of intervention in the Iberian peninsula, where, following the death of King Ferdinand VII in September 1833, civil war had broken out. The issue divided the powers, as the instinct of the conservatives was to back Ferdinand's younger brother, the Infante Don Carlos, against the legitimate heir, Ferdinand's daughter Isabella, since she was less than three years old, and her mother Queen Maria Christina governed in her name with the liberal minister Zea Bermudez. To complicate matters, a contest broke out in Portugal between the two pretenders Dom Pedro and Dom Miguel. Nicholas lent tacit support to Don Carlos, but could not afford to intervene against the principle of legitimacy.

At the beginning of 1834 Metternich held a conference in Vienna bringing together the ministers of the major German states with the aim of coordinating security policy. Once again he found them reluctant to follow his lead, and he was particularly irritated by the Bavarian foreign minister Baron August von Gise, whom he called an 'empty pumpkin'. His own side were not being supportive, with the Austrian state councillor Karl Friedrich von Kubeck echoing Kolowrat's line that reliance on bayonets was dangerous and that his policy would eventually push the middle classes into the path of revolution. Gentz too was by now openly critical, accusing Metternich of 'standing athwart the times'. Metternich and Austria were losing influence in Germany on two counts. One was that the monarchs and ministers of the various German states were growing tired of being bullied, even if they agreed with his policy. The other was that most were beginning to see Prussia as a more reliable champion than Austria in the event of war with France. The establishment of a customs union, the *Zollverein*, between Prussia and the other German states paved the way for closer cooperation. At the same time, Metternich's attention was being increasingly drawn to other areas as he pursued the phantom of revolution.[26]

In the previous year, while he was trying to rally the German ministers at Vienna, he had had to deal with a conspiracy in his own back yard. A couple of hundred Polish émigrés had left Paris, travelling in twos and threes to allay suspicion, aiming to start an insurrection in Austria's Polish province of Galicia. The inhabitants of the province had no intention of rising, and the conspirators were quickly rounded up. At the end of 1833, a band of some seven hundred Italians, Poles, Germans and Swiss had begun to gather in Switzerland with the plan of entering Savoy and starting an insurrection in Piedmont. They included veterans of the Spanish and Italian risings of the 1820s and the Polish one of 1830, and a fair number of free spirits of various nationalities. Some were patently mad, some were swept along by a Romantic desire for heroic deeds, while the Polish commander of one of the units was a drunk. They were commanded by the half-Italian bastard son of the Napoleonic Marshal Lannes, who had already proved his incompetence and cowardice in Poland in 1830. At the beginning of February 1834, one group numbering four hundred crossed Lake Geneva by boat meaning to enter Savoy that way, but found the shore well guarded, and after sailing up and down until they ran out of food and water, they sailed back and dispersed. Another marched into Savoy, planted a liberty tree at Annemasse, and then limped back whence they had come. The participants in these pathetic enterprises would have been gratified to learn how much significance Metternich attached to them. They were, in his opinion, the prelude to 'the universal explosion of a revolution which was meant to attack the very highest summits of government and inflame the lowest levels of society', as he explained to Apponyi. 'The universal revolution, which has been planned for a number of years in the committees of Paris, needed for its success an active and warlike force. It has found this in the Polish refugees greeted everywhere as heroes.' He went on to assure Apponyi that he was in possession of evidence that would 'open the eyes' of the most incredulous as to the magnitude of the conspiracy: every minor disturbance, when examined, turned out to be part of the universal revolution.[27]

The invasion of Savoy had no connection with Paris, and there was nothing revolutionary about it; it was the brainchild of an Italian, Giuseppe Mazzini. Mazzini was born in 1805 in Genoa, then under French rule, the son of a university professor of Jacobin convictions and a fervently religious mother. He studied law, but his literary leanings took the upper hand and he began to write. In the late 1820s he joined the Carbonari, but was denounced and imprisoned. On his release he went into exile in Geneva, from where he watched the various Italian revolts of 1830–34 fail. He concluded that they had been doomed because they pursued the ideal of constitutional government, which was the wrong goal and would never engage popular support: in the Legations, peasants fought on the side of the government against the Carbonarists; in Bologna, the population cheered the Austrian troops when they marched in to restore order.

After the failure of these risings, Italian liberals on the whole abandoned secret societies and concentrated on more constructive programmes, such as trying to improve economic and social conditions. The greatest problem in Italy was poverty, itself the result of chaotic economies, corruption and misrule – in the Papal States in 1829 there were over 400,000 beggars and vagrants out of a population of two and a half million. The dedicated revolutionaries went abroad, mainly to France and England, and were gradually rallied by Mazzini, who had come up with his own solution to the ills of Italy.[28]

In his view, the underlying problem was that the Italian nation was being denied its natural life because it was divided up between a number of states. 'The question of Italy is not one of more or less personal security or administrative improvement in one or another corner of our country,' he argued; 'it is a question of *nationality*; a question of independence, liberty, and unity for the *whole* of Italy; a question of a common bond, of a common flag, of a common life and law for the twenty-five millions of men belonging – between the Alps and the sea – to the same race, tradition, and aspiration.'[29]

The answer was to liberate the whole country and incorporate it into one state. Although he was no monarchist, Mazzini realised that this could only be achieved if one of the existing rulers were to gradually take over all the other states and unify the country under his rule. Some saw the pope as the obvious unifying figure, but with the accession in 1831 of the arch-reactionary Gregory XVI, whose encyclical of 1832 *Mirari vos* condemned the entire liberal movement, this ceased to be an option. Others favoured the liberal-minded Grand Duke of Tuscany, but his pathetic behaviour in 1831, when he encouraged the liberals only to disown them, put paid to that. Given the reactionary nature of the King of Naples, this left only the King of Sardinia, hardly an ideal choice. The man who acceded to the throne in Turin in 1831 was Charles Albert, formerly Prince of Carignano, a shifty, cowardly and unreliable individual who had let down the liberals in 1821 and had since become a convinced devotee of Metternich's vision of the universal conspiracy. Mazzini nevertheless greeted his accession to the throne with an open letter calling on him to take up arms in the sacred cause of liberating and uniting Italy.[30]

From his base in Marseille, Mazzini created a network of like-minded people all over the peninsula and in various places of exile outside it. In July 1831 he founded a new movement, *Giovine Italia*, Young Italy. In contrast to the Carbonari and other such societies, it dispensed with rituals, initiations and oaths, along with cloaks, daggers and cups of blood. He referred to it as an apostolate. This accorded with a gradually developing dogma: suffering Italy assumed a Christ-like victimhood with its promise of resurrection. In this scenario, the Austrians, widely regarded by Italian patriots as 'Huns', assumed the identity of the imperial Roman persecutors. The clumsy brutality of Austrian rule worked in Mazzini's favour, by creating martyrs for the sacred cause.

As Charles Albert had not responded to his call, Mazzini decided to prompt him by organising the invasion of Savoy, to coincide with a coup by officers in Turin and a mutiny in the Sardinian navy. The military coup in Turin misfired, the naval mutiny was a fiasco, and the invasion of Savoy a farce. Twelve people were executed in Turin, over a hundred imprisoned, and hundreds more fled abroad, adding further martyrs and fighters to the cause. In April 1834, along with seventeen representatives of other nations, Mazzini founded 'Young Europe'. Within a year it would include eighty-six clubs of Young Italy, 260 of Young Switzerland, fifty of Young Poland, and fourteen each of Young Germany and Young France; these would be joined in time by a Young Ukraine, a Young Tyrol, a Young Argentine, a Young Austria and a Young Bohemia. It was, in effect, a nationalist international, based on the growing secular cult of the nation.

Mazzini was obliged to move from Switzerland to Paris, and thence to London, from where he spun his plots like a spider at the centre of some enormous web. Over the next decade there would be eight attempts to raise a revolt either planned or inspired by him – two in 1837, one in 1841, three in 1843, one in 1844 and one in 1845 – all of them ending in fiasco. Four took place in the kingdom of the Two Sicilies, where the would-be liberators met with fierce resistance from the local peasantry, three in the Papal States, where they were greeted with hostility by the natives, and one in Tuscany. This did not deter Mazzini. Those hacked to pieces by loyalist Italian peasants as well as those shot by Austrian or Royal Neapolitan troops swelled the ranks of martyrs, to be revered in verse and cheap prints. But the numbers of the faithful remained pathetically small.

They sufficed for Metternich, who did not differentiate between Mazzini's movement and the Carbonari, and was concerned that the appeal of national sentiment might lead to the demoralisation of the Austrian army. Soldiers serving in Italy were instructed to be on the alert for this 'seduction', and warned that if they allowed themselves to fall for it, they would be tried by the revolutionaries' 'secret courts' and murdered. He created a special department within the police, consisting of eighty people, to monitor the activities of the Italian conspirators, and dedicated even more of the Austrian empire's revenues to the purpose.[31]

The failure of the various revolutions had produced a growing pool of political émigrés, who gathered principally in England and France, where there would be some 13,000 by 1837. The most numerous were the Poles, who posed a particular problem, as, having nothing to lose, they were ready to make common cause with any enemy of the status quo. 'The Poles play a major role in all conspiracies, because they have filled a gap which was not easy to fill – namely that of strong men who are always ready,' Metternich wrote to Wrede in April 1834. 'The activities of the Parisian *Propagande* have taken a very different and very much stronger character since the appearance of the Polish refugees.' It was nevertheless the Germans whom he feared most at this stage. Their number in Paris doubled every five years after 1831. They were mainly artisans, printers and professionals, and they were politically active. The most eminent was the poet Heinrich Heine, whom Metternich designated as part of a German '*comité*'. He detailed a bespoke spy, Professor Doktor Wilhelm Binder, to infiltrate himself into Heine's circle and befriend him, in order to 'discover the connection through which the German Party of Revolution was connected to the French propaganda'. The mission was not a success, as Heine saw through Binder at their first meeting, and fed him irrelevant gossip. Both Metternich and the Prussian minister Johann Peter Ancillon repeatedly demanded the extradition of Heine and other émigrés, but their demands were rejected by the French ministry. While the presence of the émigrés was a continuous irritant to the French authorities, as they were implicated in much subversive activity in France itself, they stood by the traditional practice of granting asylum. This had long been observed by France, various Swiss cantons and to a lesser degree Britain and other countries, out of a Christian tradition of hospitality, but after 1830 the concept of political asylum became entrenched in states like Britain, France and Belgium. The idea that demands for extradition should be resisted followed on logically. In Belgium legislation was passed to prevent any government extraditing a political refugee.[32]

In 1835 the Bundestag condemned the entire *oeuvre* of Heine, and along with it that of the liberal poet Ludwig Börne, the novelist Heinrich Laube and the journalist Karl Gutzkow. On 13 December that year Meyendorff explained to Nesselrode that Gutzkow had published an 'irreligious and immoral' novel. 'Having gathered about him a few young authors lacking conscience but not without talent, most of them Jews, Gutzkow had created the group Young Germany, whose name itself is not without significance,' he explained. Gutzkow was dangerous because he disseminated foreign literature, argued that 'all the nations should combine their enlightened views and desire for civilisation', and attacked 'as a superannuated nonsense the German hatred of France'. Meyendorff stressed 'the danger of these doctrines', which could 'most efficaciously pave the way for revolution'.[33]

In February 1834 Austria and Russia signed a convention on extradition which allowed for greater cooperation between the police of the two states, and prevented Russian émigrés or fugitives from passing through Habsburg dominions. Metternich and Benckendorff began exchanging information – mainly tip-offs about groups of Poles supposedly on their way to Vienna or St Petersburg to assassinate Francis or Nicholas or to some part of their respective empires to start a rebellion, most of them entirely spurious. In September 1835 the two met once more at Töplitz and agreed measures of further cooperation, which resulted in a senior gendarme being sent to Vienna to acquaint himself with Austrian police methods and provide liaison. They also agreed to coordinate propaganda, and a Russian, Baron de Schwietzer, was sent to Vienna, whence he exerted his influence over the German press in conjunction with Metternich. Metternich was delighted by the Töplitz meeting. The tsar, who was also present, had called him the 'key-stone' of the Alliance, which had greatly flattered the Austrian chancellor. The relationship between the two powers had been sealed, and that between Metternich and Benckendorff took on an almost comradely character.[34]

'I do not know, my dear Count, whether you have taken any measures for the observation of London: it has recently acquired an importance it did not have before,' Metternich wrote to Benckendorff in December 1836. 'Followed everywhere, even in France, the refugees of all nations have flowed towards England, and I have every reason to believe that the English propaganda is making common cause with them and that it is furnishing funds for revolutionary operations abroad.'[35]

Britain had, according to him, taken over as 'the propagator of the sickness'. 'France is an extinguished crater,' he wrote to Apponyi in Paris on 2 December 1835. 'France was *yesterday*, England will be *tomorrow*.' The Reform Bill had finally been passed on 4 June 1832. In a show of bad grace that led to comparisons with Charles I and Louis XVI, King William IV would not come to Parliament to give the royal assent in person. On 18 June, the anniversary of Waterloo, Wellington had been assailed by a mob as he rode back from the City, and nearly pulled off his horse. In Holborn he was pelted with stones and muck, and had to take refuge in a solicitor's chambers in Lincoln's Inn. The following day, at Ascot, the king was struck by a stone thrown from the crowd.[36]

'The whole question of the British monarchy now depends on the discipline and efficiency of the British army,' Wellington commented; the country could henceforth only be governed with 'the assistance and support of a military body'. There were plenty of other doomsayers, and even Wordsworth considered that the Reform Act had been 'a greater political crime than any committed in history'. By January 1833 Metternich was of the opinion that 'the true Devil is now enthroned in England'. The conditions for revolution were certainly there.[37]

Britain's cities had grown rapidly in the past decades, with Liverpool's population rising from 82,000 in 1801 to 202,000 in 1831, Manchester's from 75,000 to 194,000, and Leeds' from 53,000 to 123,000. During the agitation over the Reform Bill a meeting of the Birmingham Political Union drew a crowd of 150,000, and the Bristol riot of 1831 showed that a crowd could take control of a city and rampage unchecked. The only city to have a proper police force was London, and the past three years had seen the formation of several working men's associations, the largest of which, the National Political Union of the Working Classes, was particularly hostile to Peel's Metropolitan Police, with which it often clashed. There was much agitation for further parliamentary reform and the repeal of the Corn Laws. The introduction of a new Poor Law in 1834 aroused discontent and disturbances as it was implemented around the country.[38]

The Duchess of Dino, who played hostess to Talleyrand, Louis-Philippe's ambassador in London, noted in her diary on 19 July 1834 that 'everything going on here takes one back to the first stages of the French Revolution'. 'It is impossible not to feel fear as one thinks of the future of this great country, still so brilliant and proud only four years ago, when I arrived here, so tarnished today,' she wrote a month later. When, in October, back in France, she heard of the fire which destroyed the Houses of Parliament, she felt it was not fortuitous. 'It is a horrible catastrophe, and one whose character is altogether ominous; the physical edifice crumbling along with the political edifice!' she wrote. 'Those old walls did not wish to dishonour themselves by giving shelter to the profane doctrines of our times!' In November 1834 the poet Thomas Moore, a lifelong Whig, noted in his journal that the late Whig government had done more 'to unsettle, not merely institutions, but principles, than it will be in the power of many future generations to repair'. 'The country is now fairly in for revolution,' he concluded, 'and stop it who can.' That is certainly how it looked to Metternich.[39]

26

Sewers

On 1 April 1833 the French paddle steamer *Le Sphinx* left the Egyptian port of Alexandria towing a barge on which lay a 3,000-year-old obelisk from the site of the ancient city of Thebes. It was one of a pair which had been donated to the French government by Mehmet Ali Pasha, the Khedive of Egypt, in appreciation of the military support he had received from it. This inconvenient gift had necessitated the building of a special barge capable of navigating the Nile, crossing the Mediterranean, negotiating the Atlantic coast of Portugal, the Bay of Biscay and the Channel, and being towed up the Seine to Paris, where it arrived in 1834. The effort involved was such that the second obelisk was never collected (more than a century and a half later it would be given back to the people of Egypt by that most pharaonic of French presidents, François Mitterrand).

The question of what to do with the cumbersome object once it reached Paris was resolved by King Louis-Philippe. On 25 October 1836 he watched from behind a net curtain as it was erected in the place de la Concorde, with the help of ingenious machinery invented for the purpose. As the obelisk came to rest in perfect erection the breathless crowd exploded into jubilant applause, which he emerged on to a balcony to gather to himself.

The space it dominates was originally the place Royale, and it had at its centre an equestrian statue of Louis XV. In 1789 it was renamed the place de la Révolution, and the statue was replaced by a guillotine which cut off the head of, among hundreds of others, Louis XVI. In 1795 it was renamed after the goddess of Concord, but in 1814 it became the place Louis XV. Twelve years later the duchesse d'Angoulême persuaded Charles X to rename it after her father Louis XVI, and work began on a statue of him to adorn it. Following the revolution of 1830 it became the place de la Concorde once more, and Louis-Philippe was determined that it should remain so. By placing at its centre a politically neutral stump covered in hieroglyphs exalting the reign of the pharaoh Ramses II he had exorcised the space of its ideological charges and, at the cost of a few predictable ribaldries about its phallic significance, cleared a political minefield. This monument could have stood as a symbol of what he had achieved over the past six years.

If the July revolution really had been planned and carried out by a *comité directeur* it would certainly not have unfolded in the haphazard way it did. The '*trois glorieuses*', as the three days of mayhem came to be called, began with a few random affrays with the gendarmes, then developed into rioting which, unopposed by troops, created a festive sense of empowerment that manifested itself in the raising of the beloved tricolour and a state of anarchy. This was then successfully hijacked by a liberal elite which contained the upsurge by engineering the acclamation of Louis-Philippe as King of the French, a compromise between monarchy and republic which had the support of most liberals and many Bonapartists, as well as all realistically-minded monarchists. But to a hard core of those who had manned barricades it did not appear to be an outcome at all. As far as they were concerned the revolution had been aborted, and needed to be carried through to fruition in the form of a republic.

In many ways, the situation recalled 1789. Lafayette was given command of the restored National Guard, which took over control of the city from the disbanded *Gendarmerie Royale*. Clubs and societies sprang up, and a wide-ranging debate opened in a multitude of new periodicals as constitutional monarchists, republicans and socialists argued their respective cases. The new king and his ministers gradually curtailed this by circumscribing the freedom of the press through stamp duty and taxes on distribution, new regulations complicating the procedures of obtaining permissions, and multiplying the number of technicalities on which publications could be seized, publishers fined and authors brought to court.

Bringing order back to the streets proved more of a challenge, as the public mood remained volatile, and any minor event could easily cause it to flare into a riot. On 17 September 1831 a new prefect of police was appointed to deal with the situation. The thirty-nine-year-old banker and liberal activist Henri Gisquet was a surprising choice, but turned out to be a good one. 'It is almost unnecessary to explain that my mission was essentially a political one,' he later wrote. 'The heated passions by which the country was being swayed, which endangered the social order as well as the July monarchy, had to be the foremost object of my preoccupations and care; there lay the danger, and that was where I had to apply all the moral and material means at my disposal.' At the same time, he firmly believed that he was not dealing with an organised conspiracy, merely a number of identifiable interest groups which needed to be confronted and disabled by various means.[1]

The police functionary Lucien de La Hodde identified sven types of people who were always ready to cause trouble, in any cause. The first was the *jeunesse des Écoles*. 'It is in the nature of these gentlemen to be against the government; many of them would feel the sting of ridicule were they to hold the same opinions as their bourgeois neighbours,' he wrote, 'and then the *jeunesse des Écoles* likes noise, fights, excitement.' The second group he termed the impotent ones – 'lawyers without a brief, doctors without patients, writers without readers, shopkeepers without clients, and the herd of naïve people who, having studied politics in the newspapers, aspire to be statesmen.' The third were the bohemians, 'a class of fantasists who view an ordinary life with horror'. The fourth were 'the sovereign people, which is to say the working-class native of Paris or one who has settled in the *faubourgs*.

Brave by nature, a fighter by habit, he flourishes in any public disorder.' The fifth were the suckers. 'This is a class to pity rather than condemn. They are not bad people, but they have been told by M. Bareste, compiler of almanacs, that the country is appallingly governed; by M. Proudhon, detestable conjuror, that property is theft; by M. Ledru-Rollin, millionaire besieged by creditors, that the patriots are dying of hunger.' The sixth were the malcontents, embracing a wide spectrum of people of some ability who had been sidelined by one or other of the changes of regime. While they were too clever to commit to a cause until it had triumphed, they were always prepared to ride one out in case it succeeded, and as such, according to La Hodde, represented the greatest danger for the government. The seventh were the political refugees. Following the suppression of risings in Spain, Italy, Germany, Poland and elsewhere, thousands of these had obtained asylum in France. Having failed to carry out successful revolutions at home, they longed to revolutionise France so that it might repeat the 1790s and liberate their countries. 'This is a virus with which France has inoculated herself and which has aggravated her revolutionary sickness.'[2]

The numbers involved in any activity or riot were, according to La Hodde, never anywhere near as great as they appeared and as the ringleaders claimed. Nor was the extent of their support in the army. 'The troops supposedly gangrened by the democrats consisted of a handful of ignorant or drunken soldiers easily indoctrinated with a few fine phrases and some glasses of wine,' he asserted. This is borne out by another observer and participator in several riots: 'I have always noticed that the republicans never calculated their numbers correctly; they wanted to see a hundred thousand, they believed they were a hundred thousand,' he wrote. 'At the first shot, the onlookers melt away, and suddenly they are only a couple of hundred strong.' Motivation, too, was questionable.[3]

The only political organisations dedicated to the overthrow of the July monarchy were the *Amis du Peuple* and the *Droits de l'Homme*, which struggled valiantly to turn every incident into a confrontation and to exploit every riot, be it about food prices or sympathy for the Polish rebels – news of the fall of Warsaw to the Russians in September 1831 led to several days of rioting in Paris. Rioting had become something of a regular pastime. Following the discovery in January 1832 of a plot to start a revolt by setting fire to the towers of the cathedral of Notre Dame, when the judge enquired as to his profession, the ringleader, Considère, replied: 'Rioter.'[4]

'Every evening, people would gather on the boulevard, without any specific aim,' wrote Alexandre Dumas. 'The gathering would consist of no more than five or six people at first, but it would swell progressively; the *sergents de ville* would appear, and begin walking up and down the boulevard in provocative manner; urchins would start throwing cabbage stalks or stubs of carrots at them, and that was enough to turn it, after half an hour or an hour, into a nice little riot, which would start at five o'clock in the afternoon and end at midnight.'[5]

The funeral of General Lamarque on 5 June 1832 provided a perfect focus for the demonstration of discontent. Lamarque was a brave and principled soldier who had never wavered in his loyalty to Napoleon and made no compromises, and a great coiner of fine, if fatuous, patriotic phrases. Many passers-by joined his funeral cortège out of a variety of motives, none of them particularly urgent or considered, and the crowd swelled to the kind of volume which gives rise to violence simply because some people are bound to be swept forward in a surge and collide with the forces of law and order. For a day it looked as though the riot might turn into a revolution, as groups of demonstrators bent on confrontation, some of them brandishing red flags, clashed with the police and then troops. But things quietened down, for lack of leadership and serious motivation.[6]

The *Amis du Peuple* went into decline after the violent clashes of June 1832, and its active remnants joined the *Droits de l'Homme*, which operated openly, with a *comité directeur* presided over by the republican activist Éléonore-Louis Cavaignac, and could muster between 3,000 and 4,000 members in Paris and its suburbs. There were also possibly as many as three hundred clubs and organisations, some more philanthropic than political, scattered around the provinces. But none of these represented any kind of serious threat, and by the summer of 1832 the Paris prefect of police could confidently state that 'the republicans no longer make up a real party, they are isolated and while they stand by their political opinions they do not dare at this moment to rally the scattered members of their discouraged bands'.[7]

The political instability in France had been to some extent the result of a dire economic situation. A crisis which began in 1827 led to a severe slowdown, with factories falling idle all over the country and high levels of unemployment in 1830 and 1831. There were bread riots and outbreaks of machine-breaking in weaving centres such as Lyon, and while the economy began to pick up towards the end of 1832, the benefits did not immediately percolate down to the poorer classes. At the same time the cholera epidemic sweeping through Europe struck Paris, bringing not only suffering and death, but also social unrest. As often happens, people began to blame the authorities and supposed carriers of the disease, and there were instances of group violence which sometimes ended in murder, as well as a surge in petty crime. The year 1833 saw strikes and riots in Lyon, Saint-Étienne, Nantes, Avignon and Paris, but they were almost entirely concerned with working conditions and food.[8]

Most Bonapartists had rallied to the new regime, but the pacifism of Louis-Philippe disappointed many of the rank-and-file in the army, and even simple workers, who nourished vague hopes of wiping out the 'shame' of 1815. 'The workers are talking about the coming war and say there will be no real peace until the enemies of 1815 have been defeated,' reported the prefect of police in 1832. The death of Napoleon's son the Duke of Reichstadt on 22 July that year might have robbed the Bonapartists of their pretender, but it left the field open to a far more ambitious member of the Bonaparte family, the emperor's nephew Louis-Napoléon, who would stage a number of attempts to subvert the country, but these would cause little more than embarrassment to the new regime.[9]

The legitimists too were an irritant rather than a threat. At the end of 1830 there were some disturbances in the old Bourbon strongholds of the west and the Midi in connection with the trial of Polignac and other royalist ministers. From London, where she had taken refuge, the duchesse de Berry did her utmost to keep the Bourbon cause alive. In 1831 she arranged for a Mass to be said for her husband on 14 February, the anniversary of his assassination in 1820. A grand catafalque was installed in the church of Saint Germain l'Auxerrois, with a portrait of her son dressed in a royal mantle as Henri V much in evidence. This caused annoyance, and a crowd gathered. One thing led to another, the church was stormed and sacked, and after an orgy of pillage the mob went on to lay waste to the residence of the archbishop of Paris and to break into other churches, tearing down royal emblems and even crucifixes as they went. The following year the duchess landed in the west of France and attempted to raise a rebellion in the style of the Vendée revolt of the 1790s. It failed to get off the ground and she was arrested in November, to be quietly released and packed off abroad as a nuisance in June 1833. That same year, the police scotched a legitimist plot to infiltrate a ball at the Tuileries and murder Louis-Philippe and his family. Quite how this was to advance the legitimist cause is not clear, but it did not make life any easier for the new king and his ministers.

A greater cause for concern was the large number of foreigners who had found asylum in France. By 1832 there were some 6,000 Poles and 4,000 Germans, Italians, Spaniards and Portuguese milling around Paris with nothing to do and no means of subsistence. Some of them were not real political exiles, but criminals who had been liberated by the revolutions in their home countries, and some, according to Gisquet, were Russian, Austrian or Prussian spies posing as persecuted nationalists. The Poles, who were mostly soldiers, were treated as such. They were sent to depots and given a *feuille de route*, a kind of military passport, which fixed their identity and dictated their movements. Gradually all the exiles were given identity cards, a fixed place of abode and a pension. They were settled in groups of no more than twenty, typically in a medium-sized city such as Poitiers, Toulouse or Orléans, far from any border which they might cross to cause trouble in neighbouring states. It was expensive – by 1837 the French government had spent twenty million francs on the Poles alone – but it provided an effective means of invigilation. Anyone who strayed from his assigned place of residence could not collect his pension. But the system was not easy to administer, and was not always effectively enforced. The Poles in particular were apt to move about, and usually homed in on Paris, where every dissident group tried to enlist their support.[10]

Gisquet was an intelligent man who recognised the ineffectiveness of many favoured police methods. He saw no point in using *agents provocateurs*, or in sniffing around looking for non-existent conspiracies. He believed that genuine political activists were discreet and therefore difficult to trace, but at some stage they all needed to recruit footsoldiers among the lower orders, and these would eventually lead him to the leaders, if only through their indiscretions. Conspirators also often betrayed each other as a result of differences of opinion or internal infighting. 'The *Société des Droits de l'Homme* furnished me with many agents,' he wrote. 'I sometimes got the impression that people joined and rose to prominence in it for the sole purpose of rendering greater service to the prefect of police.' But he believed in close surveillance, and 25,000 dossiers on political suspects were created over the next decade and a half.[11]

Gisquet made use of house searches and interrogations to harass members of the various societies, and to encourage mistrust between them – anyone who had been hauled in for interrogation and subsequently released was likely to be suspected of having been turned by the police. He disrupted their plans by banning public banquets at the last minute, after all the tickets had been sold and the victuals bought. On one occasion, 27 September 1833, he posted forty policemen in uniform around an open-air banquet, which proceeded in a 'sad and silent' manner. On another, the police turned up mid-banquet and told everyone to drop their forks between mouthfuls and go home. In

1834 a law was passed forbidding the association of more than twenty people. This did have the effect of driving republicans underground, and led to the formation of secret societies based on small cells, but this only served to atomise them. The *Société des Familles*, founded in June 1834, operated in cells of eight to twelve people, each known as a family and provided with a code-name such as *bonbon* or *maman*. They did not write anything down, and only the father of each family could communicate with others. Their aim was 'the deliverance of the people and the human race' through the abolition of privilege and financial inequality, and to bring about a 'social revolution' through armed insurrection, but they never made any serious attempt to achieve it.[12]

Gisquet harassed the press in similar style. The police would subject the printers of anti-government material to endless searches and threats, to seizure of text just as it was about to go to print, and other vexations, until they eventually desisted from printing anything unfavourable to the government. Distributors were treated similarly, and papers and periodicals were hauled through the courts over every conceivable technicality – in a period of four years, *La Tribune* was taken to court 111 times, *Le National* fourteen, and *La Caricature* seven. This tactic did have one unintended consequence, which was that the court cases provided good propaganda for the republican cause, as the accused turned the courtroom into a platform from which to air their views and score political points. More dangerous was the fact that when journalists and publishers were sent to prison, they were able to proselytise and make useful recruits among those classes whose support they needed if they were ever to bring about revolution.[13]

'The fashion for riots is completely over,' Princess Lieven, now living in Paris, wrote to Lord Aberdeen in September 1835. 'That of assassinations persists and the government is still on the look-out, but that style will probably go the way of others.' The last serious disturbances had taken place in the summer of 1834, in Lyon, Bordeaux, Grenoble and Paris, but they were over wages, working practices and conditions, and hunger. They had lacked leadership and were easily contained. 'I do not share the alarm of many who fear the overthrow of the social order,' wrote the fervently legitimist duchesse de Maillé. 'The government encourages it because it is useful to it. Fear is a means which it exploits with much skill.' According to her, people wanted peace and quiet, and the government seemed best placed to provide it. 'People do not like it, they prefer it,' she concluded. Another resident of Paris, the Englishwoman Frances Trollope, had commented that 'in this city the business of getting up riots on the one hand, and putting them down on the other, is carried on in so easy and familiar a manner, that we daily look for an account of something of the kind as regularly as for our breakfast bread'. While the disturbances of the first years following the July revolution had been menacing, by 1835 they had become something of a joke, and had more to do with ritual police-baiting than political purpose.[14]

The extent to which people had learned to live with the riots is well illustrated by the behaviour of the heir to the throne, the duc d'Orléans, when he was caught up in one while on a mission of gallantry. He was busily engaged with a young lady in her humble lodgings in the rue Tiquetonne, situated in the poor Mouffetard quarter, when he heard distant sounds of riot, followed by the roll of drums and the crackle of gunfire. The sounds grew louder, and soon the street was filled with people tearing up cobblestones and overturning carts in order to build a barricade. He put on his clothes – he had dressed in a manner appropriate to the area he was visiting – kissed the young lady goodbye and went down into the street, where he lent a hand with the building of the barricade. Choosing a moment when nobody was looking to slip over it, he made his escape, and an hour later he was on horseback in full uniform directing the troops storming it.[15]

There had been a number of attempts on the life of the king, the most vicious of which took place on the boulevard du Temple on 28 July 1835, the fifth anniversary of the *trois glorieuses*. It was a sunny day, and large crowds of people had gathered in their holiday clothes to watch the king and his suite ride by on his way to pass the National Guard in review. Suddenly, an 'infernal machine' consisting of twenty-five gun-barrels spewed a volley of shot from a window, missing the king but killing his horse and those of his sons the duc de Nemours and the Prince de Joinville, and seriously wounding a number of his party, including Marshal Mortier, who died, and several bystanders.

The event shocked public opinion. The police, who had been tipped off, had blundered and searched the wrong house, but they were quick to catch the perpetrator, a Corsican petty criminal by the name of Giuseppe Maria Fieschi who had at one stage worked as a police agent. His unsavoury past emerged in the course of the trial, along with his callous manipulation of his mistress, Nina Lassave, a puny, callow, one-eyed girl whom he had raped while living as her mother's lover. He was described by the historian Louis Blanc as 'a kind of clever scoundrel, with a low, cruel and excessively audacious nature', who 'belonged to no party and combined a crude sense of exaltation with limitless greed'. His chief accomplice, Pierre Morey, was no more appealing a figure, having been a supporter of one of the false Louis XVII pretenders and subsequently planned to blow up the Chamber of Deputies on its opening day, just to vent his disgust with the world.[16]

Metternich was convinced that the Fieschi attempt was the work of Mazzini. 'I do not hesitate to lay the blame for this horrible crime on *Young Italy*, or rather *Young Europe*, into which have fused the representatives of all the republicans of every part of the continent,' he wrote. He explained that Mazzini had hoped to make France his base, but, having been expelled from there, had vowed revenge on Louis-Philippe. This had no basis in fact, any more than his assertion after another assassination attempt the following year by a young ex-soldier, Louis Alibaud, that it was the work of 'a well-organised secret society' operating in cells of no more than three. The French ambassador in Vienna noted that Metternich received news of attempts on the life of Louis-Philippe with a kind of glee, as they reinforced his belief in the existence of the grand conspiracy.[17]

The Fieschi attempt proved something of a turning point. Following Alibaud's attempt on the king's life in June 1836, Princess Lieven reported to Aberdeen that while Fieschi's had provoked fears of revolution, 'This time, nobody doubted for a moment that even in the event of its being successful, the duc d'Orléans, even if he were away at the time, would have been proclaimed king with universal support.' Six months later the writer Sophie Gay complained in blasé tones of the number of assassination attempts, adding that 'it is becoming rather monotonous'. Subsequent attempts would be made in December 1837, October 1840, and April and July 1846, but if they were a source of anxiety for many, particularly the queen, they were no more politically significant than most of those made on Queen Victoria across the Channel.[18]

With the threat of riot and revolution in recession, that of assassination assumed the character of a nuisance, as did the potential source of political instability represented by various rivals for the throne of France. The Bourbon pretender, the duc de Berry's son Henri, comte de Chambord, did not concern the police much. 'I credit him with the sentiments of a decent bourgeois who avoids trouble,' wrote the minister of the interior, Charles de Rémusat. 'Very fat for his twenty years, he has little more than the illusions and the prejudices of a pretender.' The legitimists had grown similarly quiescent.[19]

Much the same went for the Bonapartists. While the July revolution had not altered the balance of power in the country substantially, it had resulted in a significant comeback of Napoleonic military and administrative elites which had been marginalised between 1814 and 1830. Having ensconced themselves in comfortable posts and asserted their standing in society, they were not eager to overthrow it. The emperor was dead, his son was dead, and so were many of his soldiers. Those who were left had last seen service two decades before.

The duchesse de Saint-Leu, formerly Queen Hortense of Holland, came to Paris to settle her affairs in 1831, accompanied by her son Louis-Napoléon Bonaparte, the emperor's twenty-three-year-old nephew. Although the law of banishment still embraced all members of the Bonaparte family, Louis-Philippe allowed them in, provided they remained incognito. Five years later, on the morning of 30 October 1836, the same Louis-Napoléon attempted to raise the 4th Artillery Regiment (the one in which his uncle had distinguished himself at the siege of Toulon in 1793), stationed at Strasbourg, a city with strong Napoleonic sympathies. The attempt failed, and the young man was arrested. Not wishing to accord him the importance of a trial, Louis-Philippe packed him off to America with a warning, like a delinquent child. Four years later, Louis-Napoléon tried his luck once more, landing at Boulogne and attempting to start a rebellion, and once again he was arrested. This time a trial could not be avoided, and he tried to use it as a platform from which to promote the Bonapartist cause, but he elicited little interest, and far from being anxious, the prefect of police Gabriel Delessert dismissed him as 'this unfortunate young man'.[20]

Delessert had succeeded Gisquet on 10 September 1836, and this too was a sign of change. Gisquet, who had been appointed in 1830, had been obliged to deal with very real threats and had employed harsh methods. His efficiency had made him unpopular, and his dismissal was both a symptom of the fact that the political threat had receded and a signal that the police, who would now concentrate on crime, needed to engage the confidence of the public. Delessert, ascetic and respected, was to provide that new face. He cleaned up the police and sacked all *agents provocateurs*, focusing the force's attention on criminals. He only considered tracking specific political subversives and investigating credible threats of assassination. There would be no more talk of a vast conspiracy to overthrow the social order. The police budget, which had doubled in the previous decade, remained the same throughout the 1830s, and only began to rise again in the 1840s.[21]

Ironically, it was at this time that the police became an object of fascination and a literary topic, the prefect lurking in his rue de Jérusalem headquarters in the shadow of the Saint-Chapelle and later the rue de Grenelle likened to a spider whose web extended over the whole city. In his novel *Une Ténébreuse affaire*, written in 1841, Balzac, who had researched his subject with many policemen and agents, including the notorious Vidocq, paints a picture of a Mephistophelian nexus of espionage, counter-espionage and intrigue operating according to its own logic, mysterious, incomprehensible and frightening to ordinary people. One of his policemen is so cold and calculating that he is described as working for the sheer love of his 'art'. Policemen and *mouchards* are also lovingly described in *Splendeurs et misères des courtisanes* and other novels. In *Les Mohicans de Paris*, set in 1827, Alexandre Dumas *père* created the character of a brilliant policeman appropriately named Monsieur Jackal. Vidocq himself and others connected with the police cashed in by publishing memoirs, often spiced with pure fantasy.

Balzac, Dumas, Eugène Sue, Victor Hugo and many other writers reflected and fed a widespread preoccupation bordering on obsession with criminality as a social phenomenon and its intersection with politics. They regaled the upper and middle classes with horrific insights into the squalid and depraved underbelly of Paris, insights that were both titillating and terrifying. Novels such as Sue's *Les Mystères de Paris*, published serially in 1842–43, contrast the physical and moral filth of the low-life of the city with the transcendent virtue of some of its denizens with a sentimental indulgence that borders on pornography.

There was certainly much to write about. By the mid-1830s Paris had become the social and cultural capital of Europe, offering all that was best in music, literature and the arts, with more theatres and concert halls, greater galleries and museums than any other city. It was also a magnet for novelty of every kind, scientific as well as artistic, and drew in cultural as well as political exiles, the curious and the idle rich of other countries. But beneath the balls, the spectacles and the display of luxury lurked a huge class of labouring poor who were both the source of and a challenge to that wealth; and beneath that a parasitical underworld of people with nothing to live off and nowhere to go, who somehow managed to exist on the insalubrious emanations of this huge dunghill. Every poor harvest or harsh winter was followed by further influxes of desperate people from distant regions. The density of the city's population grew by 10.5 per cent between 1831 and 1836, by 7.5 per cent between 1836 and 1841, and by 12.9 per cent between 1841 and 1848. The new arrivals were often rootless and lost. They contributed to the break-up of an already fragile social cohesion, and to a rise in poor-on-poor crime. This and the lack of social structures had the effect of encouraging concubinage rather than marriage, and soaring rates of illegitimacy, often resulting in infanticide. Swarms of abandoned children swelled the criminal classes as they struggled to stay alive in an environment of endemic hunger and a population of thousands with no regular means of earning a living, and prostitution of every kind increased dramatically.[22]

The literati also wrote about the political underworld. In *Le Médecin de campagne*, Balzac describes the almost religious cult of Napoleon that survived in the countryside, where many still refused to believe the emperor was dead. Sue's *Le Juif errant*, published in 1844, took up an older theme, revived in 1833 by Charles Didier, whose *Rome souterraine* is a thriller based on the underground activities of the Carbonari. Sue's tale involves a secret sect with branches in every country devoted to the destruction of the monarchy, the clergy and society itself, whose members were prepared to assassinate anyone who stood in their way, and whose female adepts used every charm in pursuit of their terrifying goals. George Sand in *La Comtesse de Rudolstadt* created a world of pseudo-Egyptian mystery cults, subterranean rituals and dungeons in Bohemia, where a new socialist religion was being forged and the working masses prepared for violent revolution. Dumas titillated his readers with descriptions of political conspirators gathering for ghoulish meetings in the catacombs of Paris. Hugo frightened his with images of violent republican workers prepared to mount the barricades and fight for the sacred cause.[23]

That there was some conspiracy going on in Paris is beyond doubt: the debris of various dissolved organisations and erstwhile followers of Babeuf mingled with a *Société des Travailleurs* and with a number of sects, such as the Saint-Simonians, Fourrierists and the followers of Proudhon, who believed in the reorganisation of society into various 'systems' of a more or less utopian nature. But their leaders, and indeed most of the leading socialists such as Étienne Cabet and Louis Blanc, did not support violent means. Only Louis Auguste Blanqui and his followers wished to bring about a revolution, and even they took a long view, judging that the working classes were not ready to carry one through.

The legitimists might grumble about the upstart usurper Louis-Philippe and make jokes about his pear-like shape, but they were comfortable, and fearful of risking what they had. The middle classes were not in revolutionary mood, and while the anniversary of the July Days of 1830 was celebrated every year with fireworks and junkets, affluent republicans were, as Sophie Gay noted, furnishing their houses in the Louis XV style. As Princess Lieven put it in a letter to Aberdeen in November 1836, there was 'a desire and a very general need to preserve and to enjoy'; she summed up the mood as 'egoism'. She belonged to a category of people who saw revolution everywhere, and could not see the rough and tumble of politics as anything but an epic and potentially catastrophic struggle between an immutable order of things and a restless and violent revolutionary surge which took on various disguises, such as liberalism or, in the case of England, Whiggism: in July 1837 she was convinced that Britain was about to be engulfed by revolution; in France, she viewed Louis Adolphe Thiers, a pillar of Louis-Philippe's constitutional monarchy, as the revolution incarnate.[24]

Princess Lieven's future lover, François Guizot, believed that by 1840 France had become a solid constitutional monarchy with a stable parliamentary system. The memoirs of the then minister of the interior, Rémusat, would appear to bear this out. Under him and Delessert, the political police accounted for less than 1 per cent of the whole police budget. Letters were no longer intercepted. 'There was no espionage in what one calls society,' he affirms, explaining that in a free country opponents of the government make themselves known, and that it is only in despotisms that they have to remain hidden and therefore need to be rooted out. 'The press and the tribune told me all that the police can tell the minister of a despot.'[25]

The police did keep a close watch on the activities of the supporters of Louis-Napoléon Bonaparte, the Bourbon comte de Chambord and Don Carlos. They also tracked the socialists, and had to investigate every snippet of information they were given about possible assassination attempts, even though much of it was spurious. A man would call on the prefect of police or the minister of the interior saying that he had important information about a plot, and demand money. A game of cat-and-mouse would ensue, with the police trying to pay the absolute minimum in order to be able to take matters further and ascertain whether there might not be some substance to his story, while he tried to wheedle more money out of them before feeding them more information. Most of these informers were transparently fraudulent – one revealed that he was on to a plot by some anti-monarchists to foul up the succession by getting a commoner to seduce the wife of the heir to the throne and impregnate her. But each had to be investigated. As Rémusat explained, in such cases 'the police were stupid, because they had to be stupid'. They also had to take seriously the multitude of packages addressed to the king, usually with the superscription that the contents were top secret and for his eyes only. One, which they were tipped off might contain a bomb, was observed, sniffed at and prodded by a specially convened committee of chemists before Delessert resorted to the simpler method of immersing it in a bath and waiting until the water dissolved the packaging and soaked the contents. Around 1844 a package sent to the Tuileries and addressed to the king turned out, on being opened by Delessert, to contain four rattlesnakes.[26]

There was no room for complacency. 'At any given time, there were in Paris ten thousand scoundrels ready to overthrow the existing government and to shout: Long live the Republic, the Empire or the Monarchy, or whatever else, at the price for some of a week's anarchy to take advantage of, for others of some ambition, some hatred or some cupidity which they could satisfy,' in the words of one police agent. 'And all revolution, I have said it before, I repeat it now and will go on repeating it *ad nauseam*, comes from that murky legion. The mistakes of the rulers are the pretext, the leadership of the middle class is the motor, but the real force, the machine which catches governments good or bad in a horrific spiral and tears them to pieces, is the herd which swarms in the sewers of Paris.'[27]

27

The China of Europe

Metternich had long seen Paris as a sewer, from which nothing but filth could be expected to flow. But he had expected better of Britain, which, viewed from Vienna, now appeared to be well on the way to anarchy. In May 1838 Francis Place and the Radical William Lovett drew up a charter for the London Working Men's Association, listing their demands for further parliamentary reform, which were: universal male suffrage, secret ballots, annual elections, constituencies of equal size, the payment of Members of Parliament and the removal of the property qualification to stand for election. On 9 February 1839 a National Convention of the Industrious Classes opened in London, bringing together a motley assortment of traditional Radicals, anti-Poor Law agitators, Methodists, trades unionists, socialists and others. It reconvened in Birmingham in the summer in more bellicose mood. The city magistrates requested assistance from the Metropolitan Police, which sent ninety men, but this was seen as provocation, and there was a series of ugly confrontations in the Bull Ring, followed by riots which were only contained by the intervention of troops. A petition for reform bearing 1,280,000 signatures was presented to the House of Commons, which rejected it out of hand. This set off a rash of strikes and other disorders around the country.

The government appointed General Charles Napier to command the northern district, and he was in no doubt as to the danger of the situation. He realised that he must avoid a clash at all costs, and kept his troops concentrated in large bodies in order to discourage attacks. He invited Chartist leaders to watch demonstrations of artillery fire, and explained how much effort and organisation it would take them to keep together and feed a body of insurgents, and just how long his grapeshot would take to kill them. As he put it in a letter to one of his officers, if one small detachment were to be overwhelmed, it would lead to 'the total defeat of the troops', as the rioters smelled blood and success. But he had no doubt of the final outcome. 'Poor people! They will suffer,' he noted in his diary in August. 'They have set all England against them and their physical force: – fools! We have the physical force, not they ... Poor men! Poor men! How little they know of physical force.'[1]

Others took a different view, and *The Annual Register 1838* was damning on the subject of the associations of workers: 'Terror becomes the main foundation of their authority. Like all secret associations, they begin by the institution of certain mystic and superstitious rites, which not only impose upon the imagination of their neophytes, but give a dramatic interest to their proceedings, and a dignity to their lawless schemes. Thus it appears, that the apartments in which their nocturnal conclaves assemble, are often, on occasions of especial solemnity, decorated with battle-axes, drawn swords, skeletons, and other *insignia* of terror. The ceremony of inauguration itself, is said to partake of a religious character. The officials of the society are ranged on either side of the room, in white surplices; on the table is the open bible. The novice is introduced with his eyes bandaged – prayers and hymns are recited – and certain mystic rhymes pronounced ...' There follow bloodcurdling extracts of the alleged oath sworn by new members. 'The ordinances of these societies are usually enforced by violence, and too frequently assassination has been resorted to by their emissaries. When a "*strike*" has been determined upon in any factory, the avenues to the building are invested, and regular picquets, of men who are strangers to the neighbourhood, are stationed by night and day, to intercept the arrival of fresh workmen ...' The reader is alerted to the 'profound secrecy' surrounding the associations' operations and the 'very considerable' sums of money raised.[2]

Such disturbances as did take place were in fact sporadic and unrelated to any wider cause. Those that broke out in Wales in 1839 were a case in point. Known as the Rebecca riots, they were largely the result of the breakdown of rural structures and the progress of nonconformism, and hostility to English magistrates and stewards, though rents, tithes, rates and the Poor Laws also played a part. But the immediate motive was the imposition of new toll gates. These were destroyed at night by men with blackened faces dressed in women's clothes, supposedly in emulation of a mythical Rebecca, whose origins are as nebulous as those of Ned Ludd and Captain Swing. The only overtly revolutionary explosions were an armed march on Newport and an abortive rising in Sheffield and the West Riding of Yorkshire. The disturbances died down in the spring of 1840.[3]

In July 1840 the National Charter Association was launched in Manchester, and it quickly sprouted four hundred local branches which concentrated on proselytising rather than agitation. It also began collecting signatures under a new petition to Parliament. When this was presented, in 1842, it had over 3.3 million signatures, more than all the registered voters in the United Kingdom. Like the first, it was dismissed. This coincided with worsening conditions, unemployment and rising food prices. By the summer of 1842, almost 10 per cent of the entire population was on poor relief. Food riots were accompanied by the so-called 'Plug-Plot' events, where industrial workers pulled the plugs out of boilers in order to immobilise steam engines. The Chartists sought to exploit the unrest, which spread through Lancashire, Yorkshire, Staffordshire, Cheshire, Warwickshire and South Wales. The government reacted vigorously, and some 15,000 arrests were made.[4]

The repeal in 1826 of the Aliens Act of 1793 was a landmark; it demonstrated that the authorities were no longer afraid of infiltration and contagion by subversives. But they were taking a risk. It greatly facilitated the immigration of foreigners, and not a single political refugee was refused entry or expelled until the introduction of the Aliens Bill of 1905. And while France and Belgium also accepted political refugees, Britain was the only country in which they were allowed to carry on their political activities openly.

The first wave of political refugees was made up of Italians who had to leave their homeland following the abortive revolutions of 1820–21. They were mostly educated, and found employment of one kind or another. They were joined by Germans and some Spaniards, and, after 1831, by a significant number of Poles. More Spaniards and numbers of Frenchmen came in the course of the 1830s, followed by a large number of Germans. They mostly lived in rookeries in the dirty, narrow streets east of the Charing Cross Road around Seven Dials, behind Leicester Square, in Soho and Islington. Most eked out a living, if only by giving language lessons. This was not a resource for the Poles, for obvious reasons.

The Polish insurrection had aroused high levels of emotion and sympathy in England, among both the aristocracy and the politically conscious working classes. The refugees who settled in the early 1830s, who numbered just over five hundred, were granted a pension by Parliament based on their military rank. Apart from a handful associated with the aristocratic and constitutionalist Polish Party, which was embraced by the Whigs, most of the Poles were republicans, and the Radicals and the Chartists warmed to them. The Poles eagerly joined in the working-class agitation, and brought to it a more vigorous and revolutionary edge. They encouraged insurrection and were involved in most of the more violent disturbances, such as the march on Newport.

The Working Men's Association issued a proclamation declaring their solidarity with all the refugees and their cause:

> *Fellow producers of wealth! Seeing that our oppressors are thus united, why should not we too, have our bond of brotherhood and holy alliance? Seeing that they are powerful through your ignorance,*

why should we not unite to teach our brethren a knowledge of their rights and duties? Perceiving that their power is derived from our ranks, why should we not unite in holy zeal to show the injustice of war, the cruelty of despotism, and the misery it entails upon our species? ... Let us, therefore, brethren, cultivate feelings of fraternity among nations, and brotherly union in our respective countries. Let us not be so ignorant as to allow ourselves to be converted into soldiers, police, or any other of the infamous tools by which despotism is upheld, and our brethren enslaved. Let us be prepared to make any sacrifice in the dissemination of truth, and to cultivate feelings of toleration, between Jew, Catholic, Protestant or Dissenter!

In 1846 a group of Chartists came together with Polish and German émigrés to found the Fraternal Democrats, which was supposed to unite the like-minded all over Europe, but remained little more than a talking shop. The émigrés would attend each other's commemorations – Bastille Day on 14 July for the French, 29 November for the Poles – and deliver addresses ringing with grandiose visions of international solidarity, but that was where it stopped.[5]

Metternich believed otherwise. 'The underground activity which the political émigrés and the sects never tire of carrying on against legitimate governments obliges these to extend their surveillance far beyond their own borders if they wish to avoid the risk of being taken unawares,' he wrote to his new ambassador in Russia, Count Fiquelmont, in December 1837. 'I do not in truth accord more than a very restricted degree of credence to the reports of our paid informers abroad, for one should not entirely trust agents whose primary interest is money. But when people who do not know each other and watch from very different points send in the same alarm signals, it is very difficult not to believe them.' He was receiving reports of 'noticeable agitation in the propaganda', and above all among Polish émigrés, who had set up a 'Cosmopolitan Society' with its headquarters in London and branches in Paris and Brussels, which was actively planning revolutions in Poland, Germany and Italy. Research by historians has so far failed to find any trace of the existence of such a body, but its existence was real enough for Metternich.[6]

The Emperor Francis had died in March 1835, but his doctrine of maintaining 'calm' at all costs did not perish with him. He was succeeded by his son Ferdinand, who was mentally incapable of ruling the country, and Metternich continued in command of foreign policy and security, which in effect meant everything except finances. Whatever Gentz and Kolowrat may have said, he continued to place his trust in bayonets, and since he felt he could not count on the support of Prussia or any of the German states, let alone Britain, which was 'making great strides *towards a revolution*', his policy increasingly took on the characteristics of a siege mentality. As his erstwhile allies could not even be relied on to provide him with intelligence, he felt obliged to extend his tentacles and assume the role of policeman for the whole Continent.[7]

The effects verged on the surreal. The exchange of information between Metternich and Benckendorff, both through diplomatic channels and in direct correspondence, most of it concerning alleged plots by Poles, paints a picture which no historian of the movements in question would recognise. In 1838 Metternich supplied Benckendorff with information on a vast conspiracy prepared by 'anarchist parties' in France and Belgium, involving republicans in Paris, 'the Clubs of Belgian malcontents', English Chartists and 'partisans of the revolution in the Rhineland'. The following year he warned him that one of his best agents, operating in Belgium, had uncovered 'a vast conspiracy in Russia'. The information was corroborated by intelligence he had received from Naples. It was linked with a Polish conspiracy whose tentacles reached as far as Kiev, Odessa, Vilna, even Moscow and St Petersburg. The societies Alexander had banned and the Decembrists had revived, and the conspiracy was in contact with like-minded groups in Poland, Germany, France and Belgium. The agent in question, a Baron Forsting, was sent to St Petersburg to divulge the detail to Benckendorff, but failed to convince him. In the politest terms, Benckendorff reassured Metternich that a preliminary examination suggested that the whole thing was 'very minimal', and that a minute and far-reaching investigation would probably not turn up much more than 'some dreams, or, at the very most, some unconsidered conversations of young men'. Russia, he declared, was perfectly calm, no Russian would ever dream of collaborating with any Pole, and everyone mentioned by Forsting had been investigated and cleared.[8]

In the spring of 1841 Metternich warned Benckendorff that a Pole serving in the Austrian army who had attempted to overthrow the monarchy was in contact with a movement among Russian officers planning to found a Slav republic. Benckendorff replied that the allegations had 'not the slightest foundation', and that 'unless the Corps Commanders of our Army, the Governors of our provinces and myself are struck by some strange blindness, nothing of the sort exists in Russia'. But he did warn Metternich that his own spies in Paris had informed him that Polish émigrés had infiltrated the Lazarist Order and were sending agents into Habsburg dominions disguised as missionaries.[9]

The low quality of the intelligence supplied by police informants in general is staggering, but it is not altogether surprising. Judging by the information in their files, the French police never managed to recruit agents among the émigrés in their midst, or even to find spies with a command of the relevant languages, which seriously limited the amount of intelligence they could gather, while their agents' inability to spell foreign names rendered all their lists of suspects worthless. Even more astonishing, given that the Habsburg monarchy reigned over speakers of every language of its supposed revolutionary enemies, is that the Austrian police files are full of ludicrously misspelled Italian and Polish names.[10]

Spies reporting from the various spa towns regularly got the wrong end of the stick by piecing together whatever scraps of conversation they could understand, and sometimes misunderstand. They struggle to give weight to pointless reports, such as that a Pole, Count Czapski, on a cure in Karlsbad, is 'exalted and nourishes a prejudice against the

Russian government'; or that a Dr Kalitowsky working in a hospital in Pest is part of a plot to assassinate Metternich, as he is 'lugubrious' and 'extremely suspicious', and seems to be in contact with Poles in Paris. The wild allegations and the bureaucratic verbiage lend these reports a numbing quality that must presumably have had the opposite effect on Metternich, who lapped them up, and on one occasion asked rhetorically, 'Where would society be without surveillance?'[11]

When he first came to power, Metternich expanded the interception of mail, which yielded such a rich crop of interesting material that the Emperor Francis developed something akin to an addiction, awaiting with impatience each morning after hearing Mass his 7 a.m. delivery of intercepts. The mail was checked at all major post offices throughout the monarchy's dominions, at seaports and at fashionable spas frequented by foreigners, such as Karlsbad, Marienbad and Töplitz. Private mail was opened indiscriminately at the whim of local operatives, and neither high officials, members of the imperial family, the emperor, nor Metternich himself were immune.

To ensure that as much European mail as possible continued to pass through Austrian domains, Metternich saw to it that the Habsburg postal service was cheaper and faster than the alternatives. In 1822 the police minister Sedlnitzky complained that this placed a huge strain on his operatives, since it reduced the amount of time they had to turn the intercepted mail around. Letters arriving at Vienna were brought at 7 a.m. from the post office to the secret cipher chancellery, where one of the sub-directors would pick out those which might be of interest. These had to be opened, copied, resealed and returned to the post office by 10 a.m. An hour later, letters were brought in from provincial post offices, and the same procedure had to be gone through in quick time, so they could be back in the post by 2 p.m. Two hours after that, the first letters posted in Vienna that day would be brought in, and they had to be processed in time to catch the outgoing post at 7 p.m. (A letter posted in Vienna took ten or eleven days to reach Paris, one sent by special courier took seven, but Metternich often relied on the banking house of Rothschild, whose communications were mysteriously swifter.) The canny soon learned to post their letters at the last minute in order to leave as little time as possible before they left the city, which put further strain on the censors.[12]

These numbered no more than twenty-two, all of them housed rent-free, and well paid. But they were in effect prisoners, as they could never get away from the hectic activity. Metternich was extremely proud of their achievements, and once boasted that one of them, Eichenfeld, had single-handedly deciphered eighty-three codes. Another, Josef Schneid, spoke nineteen languages. One French ambassador admitted to a colleague that he had never been provided with a cipher that the Austrians were not able to decrypt within a month.

But Metternich's satisfaction was misplaced; he should have realised that if his personnel could be so proficient, so could those of other powers. If, as he prided himself, his men could 'borrow' the French cipher from the bedroom of France's ambassador, the same could be, and was, done by the other side. And if his experts were brilliant, those of the French *cabinet noir* were a match for them. As Austrian ambassador in Paris in 1806–09 Metternich became aware that his letters were being read, so he commissioned an engraver to make a barely perceptible modification to his seal. When he noticed that the letters he sent were being resealed with a copy that had been made of the original one, he wrote a note to the head of the French postal service, saying: 'I have the honour to inform you that my seal has, by misfortune, been slightly chipped. Please amend yours accordingly, so that I may continue to notice nothing.'[13]

If Metternich could be so clever, so could the French. In 1818 he had set up what he thought was a foolproof secret channel of communication for conducting his affair with Countess Lieven. He arranged for her letters to leave London in the British diplomatic bag, addressed to Baron Binder, the secretary at the Austrian embassy in Paris. On arrival at the British embassy the sealed package would be passed by hand to Binder. Inside he would find another, also addressed to himself. Inside that that was a further sealed envelope, with no address, which he knew to send through the Austrian diplomatic bag to one of Metternich's secretaries in Vienna. The secretary in question would open the envelope and find another unmarked, sealed envelope, which he would hand to Metternich, who would bask in the loving words it contained, ignorant of the fact that a copy of each of the letters was lying in the archives of the French police in Paris.[14]

If any letter could be intercepted, any code could be broken. As Joseph de Maistre pointed out to his superior when he was Sardinian minister in St Petersburg, diplomats had a tendency to over-encode, which made the code easier to crack. Encoding text also lent it an importance that could be harmful: if an ambassador reported the amorous goings-on at the court to which he was accredited, the other side would treat it as mere gossip, but when the information was encrypted it drew attention to itself, and even if, once decrypted, it appeared to be harmless, the snoopers of the other side would try to read hidden significance into it. In 1833 the head of the Russian cipher office came to the conclusion that 'the role of the decrypter is over', as everyone had become so good at breaking each other's codes.[15]

The surveillance of correspondence was of dubious value anyway. Those reading the letters were under subliminal pressure to discover something of importance, and as a result read significance into innocent text or distorted the sense of a passage, which nullified the whole point of the exercise. Once people realised that their letters were being read, they took various precautions, such as using their own codes and nicknames. Others resorted to various kinds of 'invisible ink', usually based on lemon juice – a pointless exercise, as the method of reading this (by warming it next to a candle flame) was widely known even among amateurs. Some actually inserted messages into their letters which they intended to be picked up by the police for a number of reasons, none of which was helpful to the forces of order. Many just stopped writing letters or using the postal service – in France, the resulting drop in postal revenues was so marked that it precipitated a debate in the Chamber.[16]

Metternich's desire to know everything that was going on was matched by the determination of the rulers of the Habsburg realm to protect their flock from the evils of the *Schwindelgeist*. The first step was to limit access to education, which was self-evidently a bad and dangerous thing. They could not prevent the aristocracy or wealthy people from acquiring it, but they were opposed to spreading it to the lower orders: in Mantua, a Lancaster school was closed down precisely because it provided free education, and Caroline Augusta, the Emperor Francis's fourth wife, was opposed even to kindergartens.[17]

'I want not scholars, but good citizens,' Francis told a group of teachers to whom he gave an audience at Laibach in 1821. 'It is your duty to educate youth in this direction. Whoever serves me must teach according to my orders. Whoever is not able to do so, or starts new ideas going, must go or I will eliminate him.' Teachers were not supposed to have any original thoughts, and an edict of 1820 stipulated that all lectures must be monitored by the police for signs of deviance. Applicants for teaching posts had their origins, their past, their ideas and their friends checked by the police. The information was passed to the emperor, who personally vetted each one. Those he approved were employed for a three-year probationary period, during which they had to demonstrate that they were not encouraging in their charges 'behaviour hostile to or threatening to public order'. In Lombardy-Venetia, where the need to engage the loyalty of the local population was recognised, the Austrian authorities did provide compulsory primary education, with higher rates of attendance than elsewhere in Europe. Based on the inculcation of civic duty, loyalty to the sovereign and obedience to the laws, it ensured that generations of Italians grew up into faithful subjects of the Austrian emperor.[18]

Francis viewed science, literature and history as inherently dangerous: the first because it was by definition in conflict with Holy Scripture, the second because it involved reading frivolous and corrupt books, and the third because it raised all sorts of political issues. In 1810 a set of regulations on the conduct of censors ruled that only serious scientific books were to be passed, while most novels should be banned out of hand, particularly if they contained anything that could be seen as disparaging to the throne, religion or the law.

Having no interest in education himself, Francis was suspicious of anyone who did wish to broaden their horizons, and those running his empire had been brought up to think like him. As a result, any activity dedicated to the acquisition or extension of knowledge was regarded by the authorities as suspect. The Austrian police in Italy viewed institutions of learning and literary academies with the utmost suspicion, and when these began corresponding with each other across the provincial and state boundaries criss-crossing the peninsula, they jumped to the conclusion that they were in fact a thinly disguised Carbonarist network. Metternich raged at 'the spirit of association which is in evidence everywhere', and did everything he could to prevent the formation of any kind of institution or society, even small-town reading clubs, for, as Sedlnitzky put it, 'people would read and read until they became murderers'.[19]

One of Metternich's most trusted weapons was censorship. He regarded the very concept of the freedom of the press as heresy, and strove throughout his life to limit it, not only in Austrian dominions but in every other country too. Where he could not muzzle it, he used the press to put forward his own arguments, making use of a stable of talented writers as well as his own pen. As with all attempts to manipulate news, this produced some curious effects, as people tried to deduce the truth from what was or was not reported and printed, second-guessing what they read. The inhabitant of Vienna could read about events in Paris or London in the local press, but rarely about what was going on in Vienna, for which he would have to read the London or Paris papers, if he could get hold of them – and, despite the multiple restrictions, this was not all that difficult. Censorship was a double-edged weapon, as in denying society a voice, it deprived the authorities of the knowledge of what society was thinking, and obliged them to pry into people's lives in order to find out – which made people suspicious and secretive.

Censorship was extended to cover every conceivable manner of expression that could be seen, heard or read by the public, including music, pictorial representations, even advertisements and epitaphs on tombstones. The dedication to Chopin on a piece of sheet music was banned on account of his association with the Poles' struggle for independence. The publication or exhibition of the likeness of any member of the Bonaparte family was strictly prohibited, including those of Napoleon's wife, even though she was the daughter of the Emperor of Austria. Images of Kościuszko, Poniatowski, Riego, Ypsilanti and other heroes of various wars of independence were banned, not only in engravings, but on buttons, rings and pipe bowls. Portraits of living figures had to be shown to the police before they could be exhibited, and the depiction of the emperor or any court official in civil attire was forbidden.[20]

Manuscripts destined for publication and books imported from abroad had to be submitted to the fourth department of the *Polizeihofstelle*. Authors would bring their manuscript to the Central Book Revision Office, which would pass it on to two readers, often eminent scholars, each of whom would make a report which would be handed in to the Court Police Office. Medical books were submitted to specialist censors at the university. If two censors arrived at differing conclusions, the manuscript would be sent to a third for assessment. The process could take anything between eight and twenty months, since various offices of state needed to be consulted on passages which might concern their purview. In theological matters, the emperor was the final arbiter.[21]

No criticism was allowed of the monarch, the imperial family or the administration. Unfavourable comment on monarchs and authority in general, even foreign or historical, was also prohibited. Religion was protected territory, and any reference to it was likely to cause trouble for the author. Anything that infringed morality, and all erotic literature, was scrutinised for lapses of 'taste'. The effects were often ludicrous. History books were banned because they described thrones being toppled, kings being killed and alternative forms of government. In 1816 Metternich forbade the production of a play by Caroline Pichler, *Ferdinand II*, which was set in the days of the seventeenth-century religious wars, on the grounds that the image of princes fighting amongst themselves undermined legitimacy and might give hope to revolutionaries. A history of ancient Greece was banned on the grounds that the models of Athens and Sparta might incite enthusiasm for democracy. For similar reasons, the press was not allowed to use the word 'constitution'. The censor's mind is naturally paranoid, and sees potential criticism everywhere. When one of his plays had been rejected, Grillparzer confronted the censor to ask which were the offending passages; the censor replied that there was nothing wrong with the play at all, but 'One never can tell!' When an essay was put forward for publication in the *Wiener Zeitung* advocating the establishment of houses for the improvement of criminals released from gaol, it was turned down on the grounds that 'the aforementioned suggestion could be used to blame the government for the fact that no such institutions exist'. In a rare moment of clarity, Francis himself reportedly admitted that 'our censorship is really stupid'.[22]

By the mid-1840s the number of censors employed by the police had doubled; they were dealing with 10,000 titles a year, most of them foreign publications, and they had to draw up lists of banned foreign books once a month, and from 1822 once a fortnight. But these lists were not published, and booksellers had to go to ingenious lengths to find out which titles were on them. This was no easy task, as the numbers of books banned went into the thousands, and every so often rulings on previously allowed books were reversed, which entailed the booksellers having to pulp their stock. In 1845, less than a quarter of the 10,000 titles published in Germany were approved for circulation in Austria, while one in five manuscripts submitted in the country itself were turned down. And although censorship was formally in the ambit of the ministry of police, the foreign ministry also took a keen interest, and operated its own office reviewing new books.[23]

A similar system obtained in Lombardy-Venetia, where manuscripts had to be submitted to a special office which passed them to the police ministry, which classified them under one of four categories. Those marked *Admittitur* could be published and sold freely. The classification *Transeat* meant they could be published, but only sold under certain conditions and not translated. *Erga Schedam* signified that while the book was dangerous in tendency, it could be printed and made available to certain persons of proven character. *Damnatur* meant it could not see the light of day. Here too, the system produced idiotic results. An essay on the art of tying cravats was banned because one fashionable knot was known as *à la Riego*. Lessing's play *Emilia Galotti* was banned because the villain was a duke, and the regulations stated that nobody above the rank of baron should be depicted unfavourably. Italian classics such as the works of Tasso and Ariosto were expurgated. Among all the foreign authors banned in Austria, the seafaring tales of Captain Marryat were prohibited, probably because he had once stood for Parliament as a Whig.[24]

In Italy, history was the object of particularly careful censorship, as the country's past offered a vast field for reflection and speculation as to where its tempestuous trajectory, from the greatness of Rome, through subjugation and division, might ultimately end. 'Those who devoted themselves to such a study,' noted Johann von Mailath, 'were seen as dangerous or mad, and in either case useless to society. The government, more especially the police, mistrusted history, from a fear that its teaching must encourage ideas of liberty and the spirit of rebellion … It was believed that in obliterating the past it would be easier to manipulate the present.'[25]

Expensive collected editions of banned works published abroad were sometimes allowed in, in the conviction that only the aristocracy could afford them, and they could be trusted to read them without being inspired to start a revolution. The purpose of censorship was, first and foremost, to keep the masses in docile ignorance of everything that was not necessary for their day-to-day work and existence. In this context the theatre was an area of deep concern for the authorities, since it attracted people from every class and could deliver a powerful message to the uneducated. This was particularly true of Italy.

The authorities throughout the peninsula patronised the most popular forms of entertainment, the theatre and the opera. Given the high rates of illiteracy, this was the only point of contact with culture for the majority of the population – and for some of the lazy and uncultured monarchs themselves. The theatre had the advantage of being a respectable and controllable space, a social *agora* in which the various classes could assemble, and the ruler could commune with his subjects in a pleasurable common pursuit, safely segregated in his royal box, with the aristocracy, middle and professional classes, artisans and others, each in their respective enclosures. More than six hundred new playhouses were built in Italy during the decades following 1815.[26]

But the theatre, and particularly the opera house, also became a pulpit for the expression of discontent and the spread not so much of ideas as of a mood, which posed problems for the censors, and as a result there was little logic to what was allowed and what was forbidden. Verdi's *Nabucco* got past the censors because of its biblical setting (and because nobody thought that anyone would wish to associate themselves with Jews). *Ernani* was potentially subversive, but the emperor was portrayed in a sympathetic way. In some parts of Italy his *Giovanna d'Arco* could only be performed in a version set in ancient Greece. Rossini's *Guillaume Tell* could only be performed in Italy after it had been reworked and set in Scotland, under the title *Rudolph of Stirling*.

But it was impossible for the censors to predict audience reaction at every given moment. The crowd responded with enthusiasm to any aria which called for war, and naturally identified with the embattled Druids in Bellini's *Norma* and the crusaders in Verdi's *I Lombardi*. In some cases, medleys of popular arias or choruses from various operas would be played in preference to the performance of a whole work, and this would excite the audience to a frenzy that could lead to rioting, and eventually to insurrection. Auber's *La Muette de Portici* had an extraordinary track record for starting revolutions.

The safest course was to ban as much as possible. The list of foreign books forbidden in Austria between 1815 and 1848 includes three historical novels by William Harrison Ainsworth, Bunyan's *Pilgrim's Progress*, four novels by James Fenimore Cooper, Disraeli's *Contarini Fleming*, Washington Irving's *History of New York*, nineteen works by Walter Scott, Mary Shelley's *Frankenstein*, Smollett's *Roderick Random*, Swift's *Gulliver's Travels*, several hundred French romantic novels, most of them set in medieval times or sixteenth-to-eighteenth-century France, over three dozen works by Balzac, *The Three Musketeers* and all the other novels of Alexandre Dumas, several works by Théophile Gauthier, Victor Hugo's complete works, three by Mérimée and most of those of Alfred de Musset, Abbé Prévost's *Manon Lescaut*, Rousseau's *Émile* and *La Nouvelle Héloïse*, everything by George Sand, Stendhal and Eugène Sue, much of Alfred de Vigny – but not, oddly enough, Laclos' *Les Liaisons Dangereuses*.[27]

There were only twenty booksellers in Vienna in 1800, and although this would rise to thirty by 1848, the number of printers declined in the same period. Some booksellers took considerable risks to stock and sell prohibited literature, but the police conducted snap inspections of their premises and penalties were stiff, with the result that most conformed. Publishers reprinted books without paying royalties, as it was considered immoral for an author to profit from the success of his book; the consequence was that most of them had to have other jobs, mostly in the civil service (two-thirds of them in 1822), which imposed a degree of self-censorship.[28]

Although it was always possible for the determined to obtain the books and press they craved, the majority of the educated classes were browbeaten by the pervasive surveillance and accepted the censorship with surprising passivity. As far back as 1809 the then police chief Baron Hager had warned the emperor that such a system endangered the future of the state itself, as those preparing for a career in public service made a point of avoiding broadening their minds through education and reading, fearing it might lay them open to suspicion and spoil their prospects. The consequence was that the administration was in the hands of uneducated men, and very little of the political thought of Western Europe penetrated Austrian society, which became atrophied and inward-looking. Hermetically sealed off behind a great wall of repression and censorship, by the 1840s the country had, as the saying went, become 'the China of Europe'.[29]

28

A Mistake

In a curious document he entitled *Ma Confession*, Tsar Nicholas spelled out his views on the situation created by the revolutions of 1830. Russia was, according to him, in the happy position of being unaffected by their spirit, and had held to the moral high ground. Prussia and Austria had turned away from it over the past decade, and this had weakened them. They had caved in one after the other and recognised the 'illegitimate' monarchy of Louis-Philippe. He, Nicholas, had fulfilled what he saw as his duty by standing up for the principle of legitimacy. Their recognition of Louis-Philippe had been a 'fatal' error, as it meant the acceptance of the principle of revolution and therefore of the sovereignty of the people, and had led to a string of disastrous consequences elsewhere in Europe.

While he was eventually persuaded by Metternich to recognise the King of the French, Nicholas would never use the received address of '*Monsieur mon frère*' in correspondence, only that of '*Sire*'. When Marshal Mortier arrived in St Petersburg (a questionable choice for an ambassador to Russia, since it was he who had blown up the Kremlin in 1812), Nicholas conversed at length with him about Napoleon, but refused to mention Louis-Philippe. Three years later, when Marshal Marmont met Nicholas at Töplitz, the tsar could still not bring himself to pronounce his name. When he visited London in 1844 he dreaded the possibility of running into the King of the French, who had also been invited by Queen Victoria. Similarly, he had recognised the independence of Belgium, but only because the King of Holland had done so, and he would not acknowledge Leopold as king. (It did not help that in creating an army for his new kingdom, Leopold had taken advantage of the large pool of Polish émigrés who had borne arms against Russia to fill its most senior ranks.)[1]

Unlike Austria and Prussia, Russia would remain true to itself and its duty. 'Let us conserve, I say, the sacred fire for the solemn moment, which no human power can avoid or delay, the moment when the contest between justice and the infernal principle must break out,' Nicholas wrote. 'That moment is near, and let us in preparation for it be the standard around which, of necessity and for their own salvation, those who tremble now will rally for a second time ... at the moment of danger we will be seen to be always ready to fly to the aid of those of our allies who will return to their old principles ... That is my confession, it is solemn and decisive; it places us in a new, isolated, but I dare to say honourable position, and one worthy of ourselves.'[2]

A crucial element in the tsar's strategy was to isolate his people from pernicious outside influence, particularly that of France. For decades the cultivated aristocracy had been entirely French in culture and outlook, which contrasted with the more German influences in the imperial family and much of the court, made up as it was in large part of German Baltic nobles. Nicholas was suspicious of all things French, particularly after the July revolution of 1830, and regarded Paris as a sink of moral as well as political depravity. His immediate reaction to the July Days had been to recall all Russians from France. Princess Lieven, by then estranged from her husband and enjoying a remarkable position in English and French society, failed to comply, as a result of which she was cast adrift by Nicholas, and her brother Benckendorff had to sever relations with her. Admiral Chichagov, a venerable commander with a distinguished war record (which had ended somewhat ingloriously when he failed to prevent Napoleon crossing the Berezina in 1812) had married a Surrey vicar's daughter, and spent his time between their home in Brighton and Paris, where he had many friends. He wrote to Nicholas pleading to be exempted from the new ruling; in response he was stripped of his estates in Russia, his honours, his rank and even his nationality.[3]

An *ukaz* of 1831 decreed that all Russian youths between the ages of ten and eighteen must be educated in Russia. After that they could study abroad, but only after passing a strict vetting process, and they might not go to France. As a result, Russian students who had traditionally attended French universities were now encouraged to study at German universities – with the unintended consequence that French influences were superseded by those of Hegel and Marx, which would in the long run prove far more dangerous for the Russian monarchy. At the same time, Russians in Germany had no trouble in acquiring French books and periodicals, which they would then either smuggle back or read and relate to their friends on their return home.[4]

In 1834 restrictions were introduced limiting the time Russian subjects could spend abroad to five years for nobles and three for all others. Non-observance or settling in other countries caused repercussions such as confiscation of property and possible repression of family members. In 1840 a tax was levied on passports to travel abroad, and a special committee which included the chancellor Nesselrode, Benckendorff and the interior minister Perovsky reviewed every application. Further impediments and restrictions followed. 'A couple of weeks ago a new decree was published against travel,' Countess Nesselrode wrote to her son in April 1844. 'It would be difficult to convey to you how it has enraged public opinion ... It inspires the most violent utterances from the most passive who see in it a new attack on the nobility.' The decree in question forbade foreign travel to anyone under the age of twenty-five, and the process of applying for a passport was complicated further, requiring a visit in person to offices in St Petersburg, and lengthened inordinately.[5]

'The Emperor's rage against Paris is stronger than ever, and I, who inhabit that evil city, am regarded as a rebel, and will probably be taken for a spy before long,' Princess Lieven wrote to her friend Lady

Cowper (the future Lady Palmerston) in October 1838. Two years later she reported that Paris was 'full of Russian ladies, all very distinguished', and two years after that she commented that 'this forbidden spot' had become 'a place of pilgrimage, though not a very holy one' for Russians; 'the whole of St Petersburg' had turned up there, and Paris was 'swarming with Russians'. This anomaly is explained by the fact that Russia's secret police organ, the Third Section, felt a pressing need to know what the Polish émigrés gathered in Paris were doing and thinking. It therefore began sending out spies in the shape of apparently innocent pleasure-seeking Russian aristocrats. Since these were not to be trusted themselves, and must therefore be watched, others were recruited to keep an eye on them. The system was extended to other countries where Russians might be travelling or Poles congregating. 'With its army of amphibian agents, political amazons, with their clever masculine minds and their feminine language, full of shrewdness, the Russian court gathers news, receives reports,' in the words of the marquis de Custine. The ladies were not, however, allowed to attend the court of the 'illegitimate' Louis-Philippe.[6]

Both Alexander and Nicholas had always shown a tendency not so much to control the society they ruled over through repression, as to mould it morally to the desired form. The fusion in 1817 of the ministries of education and religious affairs had initiated a process of aligning the educational system with the appropriate world view. This had not achieved the desired result, and reports reaching Nicholas bristled with complaints that schools and universities were 'gangrened' with immorality and incorrect political attitudes. Something more comprehensive was called for, and Nicholas turned to Sergei Semionovich Uvarov to come up with an educational programme that would, if not cure Russian society, at least ensure that future generations were *bien-pensant*.

Born in 1786 into a family of well-connected gentry, Uvarov started out as a young man of literary tastes and liberal views, writing lyrical poetry in French and German. He met and corresponded with such literary luminaries as Goethe and Madame de Staël, and played a lively part in the rich literary life of St Petersburg; he was one of the founders in 1815 of the literary society Arzamas. His career included a posting at the Russian embassy in Vienna in 1806, and in 1810, at the age of twenty-four, he had been appointed superintendent of the St Petersburg educational district. He was instrumental in the founding of the city's university, but was forced to resign in 1821 under pressure from Galitzine and Magnitsky. In 1826 Nicholas brought him back into education. In 1832 he was appointed deputy minister of education, and the following year minister, a post he was to hold until 1849.

Nicholas wished to see the educational system reformed in such a way that it would deliver solid citizens and servants of the state. Uvarov later confessed that he almost gave way to despair when confronted with this task, but understood that it was crucial to 'the very fate of the fatherland' in view of 'the social storm raging across Europe'. He saw his task as being 'to rebuild our fatherland on firm foundations, on which to establish the prosperity, strength and life of the nation', to identify the essential 'distinctive character of Russia', and 'to gather together into a single complete celebration the remains of her nationality in which to anchor our salvation'.[7]

Russian society had, he believed, fallen behind others in the human progression towards what he called 'maturity', and could not be left to itself but had to be 'brought up' as might a child. In establishing the principles on which that upbringing was to be based, his point of departure was the Orthodox faith, which was common to the overwhelming majority of the nation. The second defining element in Russia was, in his view, the supreme and boundless authority of the tsar. 'Autocracy constitutes the very condition for the political existence of Russia,' he argued. 'The Russian colossus rests on it as on the cornerstone of its greatness.' For a people at the stage of maturity of the Russians, the fatherly authority and protection of the tsar were the best guides towards a virtuous life. The third element he called '*narodnost*', meaning something like faith in the value of the distinctly national character.[8]

This trinity of Orthodoxy, autocracy and nationality was proclaimed in 1833 as the basis for not just the educational system but the whole social and cultural environment. It was supposed to create a new identity which would define both state and nation, and set Russia apart distinctively from other nations – and make it immune to the 'gangrene' devouring them. Elements of it, particularly the idea of the essential genius and virtues of Russianness, appealed to the Russian Romantics and inspired some interesting thought and literature, including works by Pushkin and particularly Tiutchev. Gogol lent his support with an astonishing justification of serfdom as being based on the will of God. But it quickly turned into a siege mentality resistant to 'dangerous' and 'destructive' influences flowing from the west, and indeed to any new development in these decades of discovery and invention.[9]

In both academic works and popular literature, Russian history was written in such a way as to present a process which derived from the particular genius of the Slavs and their unique communal patterns, and should not be viewed or judged by the same criteria as the histories of other nations. Ironically, this Romantic particularism owed a great deal to German thought.

It was not Uvarov's intention to repress. He wanted to encourage young men to study, but only what he felt would be good for them: the sum of human knowledge could not be safely passed on to them whole. He took pride in the fact that the number of titles published in Russian rose from seven hundred a year to nine hundred over the decade and a half of his ministry. He was, however, against the printing of cheap books, on the grounds that they might 'set the lower classes in motion.'[10]

The universities flourished under Uvarov; he reduced the social impediments to admission, and exercised minimal control. The young Aleksandr Herzen remembers his fellow students saying 'anything that came into their heads' without fear of being reported, prohibited poems circulating in manuscript and even officially banned books being readily available. After the University of Vilna was closed down as a consequence of the role it had played in fostering Polish patriotism, the new University of St Vladimir was intended to bring Poles, Belorussians, Lithuanians and Russians (Ukrainians did not officially exist) together in a spirit of Slavic brotherhood. While Kiev had been chosen because it was supposedly the cradle of Russian Orthodoxy and statehood, Benckendorff pointed out to Nicholas that it also happened to be the headquarters of the First Army, which could guarantee order.[11]

Things did not work out as Uvarov had hoped. Inspectors were introduced into the universities to keep an eye on what teachers and students were doing and an ear open to what they were saying. Schools too were watched for any departure from conformity. Nicholas himself would make surprise visits, looking for signs of subversion and even seeing it in the physiognomy of certain students, making disapproving comments on their looks. In 1834 inspectors were briefed to monitor the behaviour of students outside the classroom.

Private tutors were not exempt. They had to take exams and observe the same rules of behaviour and the same standards as civil servants. Even those employed by the most aristocratic households were subject to invigilation and assessment. They had to have certificates which to all intents and purposes reduced them to the status of state officials.[12]

By the mid-1840s Uvarov had grown disillusioned, and whatever enthusiasm his vision had inspired had evaporated, leaving only an increasingly soulless system grinding on under its own momentum. When a group of Ukrainian students founded the Society of Saints Cyril and Methodius (who had introduced Christianity to Russia), they were severely punished for what the head of the Third Section described as this act of 'delirium'. In 1838 four students of the new university were tried by a military court and sentenced to garrison duty at Orenburg, principally for the possession of banned books by the Polish poet Mickiewicz.

Ironically, foreign books were relatively easy to get hold of. The number imported rose from around 200,000 in 1832 to almost a million in 1847, and only 150 titles were actually banned. When, however, a group of Moscow booksellers requested a list of the banned books they were told this was impossible, as it 'might serve to direct special attention to the forbidden books'. This kind of reasoning did not serve the authorities well: the search of one St Petersburg bookshop turned up 2,581 forbidden books.[13]

It was not only foreign books that needed to be controlled: the Third Section applied strict censorship to all Russian publications. What made the censor's job difficult was that it was a censorship of spirit and tone as much as one of substance. He might pass an article as being harmless, only for it to provoke violent reaction from a dignitary or official who had read something quite different into it. Those who missed an implication that was later picked up by a senior official or the tsar himself were regularly sent to spend a few days or weeks in the guardhouse, along with the offending authors and editors. This was not a sentence, and did not qualify as incarceration; it was a paternal smack across the wrist and an encouragement to try harder. Although Benckendorff was never sent to the guardhouse, he too was occasionally reprimanded, as happened when he missed the political subtext of Lermontov's poem 'Death of the Poet', which represented Pushkin's death in a duel as murder. Others called the attention of the tsar to it, branding it 'a call to revolution', and Benckendorff had a great deal of explaining to do.[14]

Pushkin had always proved a headache to Benckendorff, who was obliged to read everything he wrote, hold lengthy talks with him and carry on an arcane correspondence which sometimes revolved around the possible meanings of a single word. There had therefore been considerable relief at the Third Section when Nicholas decided to personally take over the role of Pushkin's censor. To begin with, Pushkin welcomed the tsar's interest. His mood changed when Nicholas, having read the manuscript of his play *Boris Godunov*, addressed him as a great author might a fledgling, suggesting he rewrite it as a novel in the style of Walter Scott. It soon emerged that Nicholas was interested not only in Pushkin's work, but also in his attitude, as expressed in his behaviour and even his clothes. He was admonished regularly on the most personal matters, including the state of his marriage, was supposed to report regularly everything he did, and was generally treated as a perverse child.[15]

By the mid-1840s there were, according to one writer, more censors in Russia than books being printed. Another described the apparatus of censorship aimed at the press as 'a cannon aimed at a flea'. There was something in this: in 1840 the most popular periodical had a circulation of no more than 3,000, while the readership of the entire periodical press did not exceed 20,000. Yet editors were repeatedly reprimanded or sent to the guardhouse, often on pretexts which were recondite, to put it mildly.[16]

Faddei Venediktovich Bulgarin, co-founder and editor of the *Northern Bee*, himself a regular informer for the Third Section, was arrested for printing a poem entitled 'The Forced Marriage', about a loveless union in which the adulterous wife justifies herself by the fact of having been forced into it, in which Nicholas saw a reference to the relationship between Russia and Poland. The publication of Gogol's *Dead Souls* (1842) encountered the objection that the soul is immortal, and the title therefore constituted blasphemy. In one poem the censor crossed out a passage about a Roman emperor being killed, as the very notion was subversive. A love poem was returned with a litany of objections, beginning with the fact that a woman could not be described as divine, since only God was; that her looks could not be heavenly, because only that which emanates from God is; that 'one tender look' could not be 'worth more than the attention of the entire universe', because the universe contained the tsar and other 'lawful authorities' which would be insulted by the notion; and that the desire to retire from the world to be alone with the undivine lady suggested a wish to shirk duty to the state.[17]

In 1836, Piotr Yakovlevich Chaadayev published a piece in the form of a letter, which constituted a comprehensive attack on everything the Russian state stood for. He maintained that Russia had contributed nothing to civilisation except autocracy and serfdom, and chastised what he called 'the imbecilic contemplation of [Russia's] imaginary perfections'. Since there was no conceivable way to treat this matter in a rational way without opening to discussion the matters he raised, he was branded a lunatic, the censor who let the piece through was dismissed, the periodical in which it was published was closed down, and its editor was sent to Siberia.[18]

Censorship was by no means restricted to the printed, or even the written, word; it also encompassed attitude, and therefore behaviour. Nicholas banned smoking in the streets of St Petersburg, out of a conviction that it disrupted order. He also forbade the wearing of grey hats, which, for reasons unknown, reminded him of Jews, whom he loathed and suspected of being a subversive force. White hats were also outlawed, as he associated them with Poles. He had an almost pathological dislike and fear of the Poles, whom he described as 'a species of animal between man and beast'. He lived in fear of being assassinated by one, and whenever he travelled he took extreme precautions. In his Polish provinces, false itineraries were posted in order to confuse would-be assassins. Outside Russia he would travel incognito, and sometimes in disguise: when he went to London in 1844 his itinerary was such a closely guarded secret that the Russian ambassador there had no idea when he was coming, where he would cross the Channel and what route he would take.[19]

In 1834 Herzen, then a student at Moscow University, was arrested for attending a party at which, according to an informer, a scurrilous song was sung. He was able to prove that not only had he not attended the gathering, he had not even been invited. He was nevertheless subjected to a sermon by an avuncular general of gendarmes by the name of Lesovsky. 'Lesovsky, himself a Pole, was not a bad man, and was no fool: having wasted his property over cards and a French actress, he philosophically preferred the place of general of gendarmes in Moscow to a place in the debtors' prison of the same city,' Herzen wrote. Lesovsky counselled him to lie low and keep his mouth shut for a few months. The contrarian youth did not take his advice: he and his fellow students went about ostentatiously wearing berets *à la* Karl Sand, and once more fell foul of the Third Section.

Among Herzen's papers, which were gone through attentively, the gendarmes found a text written by him arguing against constitutional government, and he was asked for an explanation. He replied that the tsar himself was against constitutional government. The interrogating official agreed that this was so, but explained that one could attack constitutional government for the right reasons and the wrong reasons, and he suspected Herzen of the latter. The interview degenerated into an argument about semantics which left both of them exhausted and neither of them any the wiser. The Third Section came to the conclusion that the young man was 'not dangerous, but *could be* dangerous', and he was sentenced to ten months in prison, to be followed by five years' exile in Siberia. He was pardoned in 1840, but on his return committed the grave fault of not calling on the head of the Third Section to thank him. He was therefore hauled before him, and reprimanded for his lack of manners.[20]

There was an accepted etiquette. On the one hand, people were usually arrested at night, often in ways calculated to instil fear and to disorient, and might be driven round and round in a windowless black police *kibitka*, to give them the impression that they were being taken far away from home. On the other, the officials of the Third Section and the gendarmes were impeccably polite – 'the very flower of courtesy', according to Herzen; 'the impersonation of grace and urbanity', in the words of a French traveller – and made such show of hating what they had to do that it was not unknown for them to shed tears while interrogating someone. Benckendorff himself was, in Pushkin's words, a kindly man 'with a good sensitive heart', and was solicitous even with authors who caused him trouble – he obtained financial assistance for Gogol, and helped to lift the ban on *Dead Souls*. People arriving in or leaving St Petersburg, even generals off to take up a posting, were expected to pay him a courtesy visit.[21]

One official who stands out by his urbanity is Leontii Vassilievich Dubelt. Dubelt was an intelligent man with an unusual pedigree. While travelling through Spain in the early 1790s his father Vassily

Ivanovich had eloped with a young lady from the princely house of Medina Coeli, whom he married in Italy before bringing her back to Russia. Leontii Vassilievich, born in 1793, was brought up by his cultivated mother, and at the age of fourteen he joined the Pskov infantry regiment as an ensign. He was wounded in the leg at Borodino, but recovered and went on to serve throughout the campaigns of 1813 and 1814. He was then in sympathy with the spirit of the times, and a member of two Masonic lodges. By 1818, when he married, he was colonel of an infantry regiment, and he did not retire from the army until 1829, after a quarrel with his divisional commander. He thereupon decided to become a gendarme, to the dismay of his wife, who, like most of Russian society, regarded the police with the utmost distaste. Dubelt loved his wife and valued her judgement, but defended his decision vigorously. In joining the gendarmes, he argued, he would 'become the support of the poor, the defender of the unfortunate', and help 'obtain justice for the oppressed'. And he warned Benckendorff that he would not carry out orders he considered ignoble.[22]

He was given a staff post in Tver, but a few days after he left to take up his posting, one of Benckendorff's staff officers died, and Dubelt was recalled to replace him. Benckendorff was delighted to find a kindred spirit who believed in the mission of the gendarmes, and kept him by his side, promoting him to the rank of general and appointing him chief of staff, effectively commander, of the corps. In 1838 he became Benckendorff's deputy, and therefore effective head of the Third Section as well as of the gendarmes. With Benckendorff growing increasingly absent-minded (he was known to fumble for a visiting card to remind himself of his own name), it was Dubelt who ran the whole operation. He would carry on after his chief's death in 1844; Benckendorff's successor, Count Aleksei Fyodorovich Orlov, was more than happy to delegate all the work to him.[23]

Dubelt had a talent for appearing less intelligent than he was, and his kindly approach smoothed the path of many an interrogation. It was not uncommon for him to call personally on a man who had just been arrested, check whether he had all the comforts he needed, enquire as to whether he smoked a pipe or cigars, and provide him with his favourite brand. But his features reminded one of his victims of a wolf, and his manner of the 'cunning of predatory animals'. While he clung to his early ideals for a few years and refused to employ underhand methods, he gradually grew into the role of a circus-master operating a vast network of spies and manipulating the lives of thousands.[24]

The Third Section had turned into a huge operation. It received at least 10,000 – sometimes up to 15,000 – items every day, including denunciations, petitions to the tsar and appeals against court rulings, for tax exemptions, for scholarships, for advice on legal matters and for a range of other favours. It was also sent plans and projects of a scientific or administrative nature, suggested improvements and new inventions. But the bulk concerned more private matters, and the Third Section's archive bulged with the most intimate details of people's lives: accounts of family quarrels, local feuds, marital problems, changes of mistress, and financial difficulties.[25]

A landowner from the province of Penza, I.V. Selivanov, was surprised to be arrested (in the most courteous manner) by a gendarme and brought to St Petersburg, where he was shown into Dubelt's office. Lying on the desk was a half-finished letter he had thrown into his waste-paper basket in the country a few months before, describing the poor harvest and remarking that it was the moral responsibility of landowners such as himself to help see their serfs through the hard times. In the margin he could see the word 'liberalism' scrawled in Dubelt's hand. He was asked to respond to a number of questions regarding the institution of serfdom, and whenever he gave an answer that seemed to displease his interrogator, Dubelt would suggest the correct one, which he would duly write down. Having thus shown himself to be fundamentally sound, he was sentenced to only six months' exile in Siberia.[26]

Foreign travellers became intensely aware of the blanket of invigilation smothering them from the moment they crossed the frontier.

The future president of the United States, James Buchanan, then a diplomatic envoy, was astounded by what he encountered on his arrival in 1833. 'In Russia the police are long past any feelings of shame,' he wrote. 'We are continually surrounded by spies, both of high and low degree in life. You can scarcely hire a servant who is not an agent of the secret police.' They were so open about intercepting his mail that they hardly bothered to reseal his letters, or did so with a different-coloured wax. 'A Yankee, arriving on business in 1843, was told by the gendarmes that he had been to Russia once before, in 1820, on a trip of pleasure, and the details of that visit of twenty-three years earlier were recited to the traveller's great surprise. One felt in Russia as in a glass cage.'[27]

The various police forces, and particularly the Third Section, employed hordes of spies, many of whom played the tired game of leading conversation towards criticism of the government in order to obtain a response that could become the subject of a report. Barbers, laundresses and purveyors of any kind of service were expected to note anything and everything they considered suspicious. Servants were suborned to provide intelligence on what was going on in a household, and family members encouraged to spy on spouses, parents and children.

'The secret police of Russia has its ramifications both among the upper and the lower classes of society,' wrote one contemporary. 'Nay, many ladies notoriously act as spies, and are yet received in society and have company at home; even men who are stigmatised with the same reputation, are not the worse treated on that account, and bear their disgrace with a kind of haughty dignity. There is not a single regiment of the guard which has not several spies; in the theatres, and especially in the French theatre, there are often a larger number of spies than of mere spectators. In short, there are so many spies that people imagine they see them everywhere, an apprehension which admirably serves the turn of the Government.'[28]

This was true in one sense: once people were aware that there were eyes and ears everywhere, they assumed the authorities knew more than they did, and were inclined to avoid getting involved in anything questionable. But it also encouraged them to develop secretive habits. These in turn aroused the suspicion of the police and their informants, leading them to pursue futile avenues of investigation. This kind of self-censorship did not serve the police well, as people learned not only not to comment on various things, but to affect not to see them at all, and as a result the relationship between the intelligence received and reality lay in the realms of the surreal.

In this situation there was less and less for the security apparatus to do. As a result, the agents looked closer and closer for anything that might conceivably be worthy of note, and indulged in arcane arguments over what some word or phrase might be construed to mean. The police lurked and snooped, straining eyes and ears for a word, a hint, a laugh, a snort, a look, anything that might betray an incorrect attitude; a hat, a cloak, a necktie, a kerchief, a stick, or any other piece of apparel that could be seen as a manifestation of nonconformity. This turned the relationship between the citizen and the state into a game of cat and mouse which was both self-perpetuating and futile, and, with time, people stopped noticing the absurdities.

After his release, Herzen was given an administrative job in the provinces. He spent most of his time stamping passports, reviewing complaints and passing on the reports of various other officials. In this capacity he found himself countersigning and endorsing the local police report on himself. The prominent Decembrist A.N. Muravev was appointed mayor of Irkutsk after he finished serving his sentence there, but although he was a state official, his mail continued to be opened and scrutinised. When he complained, the head of the postal administration denied the accusation vehemently, but added: 'The opened seals are replaced so skilfully that it would in any case be impossible for you to prove.' A Pole exiled to hard labour in Siberia found it easy to avoid the work by doing favours for the guards and serving as tutor to the children of various officials. He progressed to petty trading, and lived quite well. When, after his release in the 1850s, he arrived in Berlin, he compared conditions there unfavourably with his life in Siberia.[29]

In St Petersburg, Countess Fiquelmont, wife of the Austrian ambassador, had a couple of copies of Silvio Pellico's violently anti-Austrian and inherently subversive *Le mie Prigioni*, which she was lending out to members of the Russian court as if it were the latest best-selling romantic novel. The tsar got to hear of it, and asked her to lend him one of them. He read it, and commented that it was well-written. But it does not appear to have made him reflect on the absurdity of the system it describes. The struggle against the many-headed hydra of revolution had become part of the mindset of the tsar, and his underlings.

Colonel Lomachevsky, head of gendarmes in Vilna province, returned to his post after a short absence in 1840 to find a commission nominated by the governor of the province torturing a student. When he pointed out that the evidence they were wringing from him was ridiculous as well as contradictory, they accused him of 'spoiling' their work. 'In order to convince yourself of the existence of a plot,' the chief interrogator said to him, 'you have only to observe the activities of Thiers and the Egyptian Pasha, to read through the journal of *The Third of May* [a Polish émigré periodical] issued in Paris, and the brochure "Young Poland", and then it will be clear to you that a plot has enmeshed not only Russia, but all Europe as well, and even Egypt …'[30]

This system may have inspired some remarkable literature, most notably the short stories and plays of Nikolai Gogol, whose masterpiece *Dead Souls* could never have been written in a saner one, but it did nothing to combat subversion, because there was none, and it did not create useful, loyal citizens. It succeeded only in stupefying people, stultifying society, arresting the development, economic and industrial as well as social and intellectual, of Russia, and inspiring a revolutionary tradition that was to bring it down decades later.

'As an honest man, if I had to choose under which kind of government to live, I would choose for myself and my family a republic,' Nicholas confided one day; 'to my mind this form of government provides the best guarantees of safety. But it does not suit every country; it is acceptable to some and dangerous to others.' At the beginning of his reign, he had convoked a committee to look through all Alexander's projects for reform, to identify those that might be implemented. Under the chairmanship of Viktor Kochubey, who had been one of Alexander's Secret Committee of 1801, they duly set to work, but their meetings grew less and less frequent, and the committee eventually withered as Nicholas's interest faded. The Third Section also addressed the question of reform, for reasons of its own. In an internal report of 1839 it assessed serfdom as 'a powder-keg buried under the state'. Another report, on illicit workers' associations in the province of Perm, noted that the root cause was the appalling standard of living. After looking into working conditions in St Petersburg in 1841, the Third Section had a hospital built for the workers. It later did the same in Moscow, and in 1845 introduced a ban on children working at night. 'There is no doubt that serfdom, as it exists at present in our land, is an evil, palpable and obvious to all,' Nicholas told the Council of State in 1842. 'But to touch it *now* would be a still more disastrous evil.' He feared that doing so would precipitate full-scale rebellion, and was afraid of how the landed nobility would react.[31]

By the mid-1840s Nicholas was going through some kind of mid-life crisis, aggravated by health problems. In 1841 he had begun an affair with one of his wife's ladies-in-waiting, which entailed bouts of guilt and self-loathing. He would often lock himself up in his study for hours. 'There are days when I look up to heaven and ask myself: why am I not there? I am so tired ...' he said to another of the empress's ladies-in-waiting in March 1845.

But if doubt ever entered his mind as to the way he was ruling his empire, he never showed it. 'It is with very real fear that one contemplates the future when one sees the Emperor becoming daily more bitter and authoritarian,' Countess Nesselrode wrote to her son. 'It is no longer possible for anyone to make him reconsider his views.'

Aleksandr Nikitenko, a professor of literature and himself a censor, delivered probably the most fitting verdict: 'The main failing of the reign of Nicholas consisted in the fact that it was all a mistake.'[32]

29

Polonism

By the end of the 1830s, Nicholas saw the Russian empire as an embattled state let down by its allies as it prepared to face the forces of evil. 'The bulwark constituted by Austria and Prussia will fall,' ran a note composed in 1838 by one of his diplomats, Baron Brunnow. 'The battle of ideas taking place on the banks of the Rhine will move to our own frontiers. In a word, Russia will once more, as in 1812, be obliged to take on France; but this struggle, one can safely say, will be more dangerous than the other one. We will not be fighting the enemy out in the open, but defending ourselves against a more terrible foe. We will come face to face with the spirit of revolution, undermining with determination the most powerful kingdoms.'[1]

The primary source of concern to Nicholas was Prussia. The less than reliable Frederick William III died in June 1840, and was succeeded by his son Frederick William IV, who presented, from the Russian point of view, an even greater problem. The new king, who was the brother of Nicholas's wife, was a complicated personality in which contradictory instincts vied with each other. Fat, balding and short-sighted, a poor horseman, he lacked all the attributes of the kind of monarch he wished to be. Inspired by the chivalric romances of the writer Friedrich de la Motte Fouqué, he had embraced a sentimental vision of the Prussian monarchy based on an emotional and ideological bond between throne and people. He loved the 'German' music of composers such as Weber, was thrown into raptures at the sight of the Rhine, and enthusiastically took upon himself the task of completing that great symbol of High German culture, Cologne Cathedral. He believed in the regeneration of Germany not just in political, but also in spiritual terms, and was affected by the current religious awakening sweeping the country.

He opened his reign by decreeing a wide-ranging amnesty and restoring to grace people such as the military reformer Hermann von Boyen, the *Turnvater* Ludwig Jahn, the historian Ernst Moritz Arndt and the liberal statesman Wilhelm von Humboldt, and welcomed the brothers Grimm, who had been persecuted for their nationalist leanings. He dismissed the hated Kamptz, who had had to admit in 1839 that there was no revolutionary threat, and that those young men who did commit subversive acts were simply lost souls inspired by nefarious literature who should be regarded as victims. The *Zentral Untersuchungs Kommission*, which had become redundant, was abolished in 1842. But the new king was no liberal, and he had no intention of granting the long-promised constitution. His vision of the future may have been able to accommodate the unification of Germany (under Prussian rule), but it assumed a spiritual bond between king and people to the exclusion of the middle class, and was bathed in the light of an archaic patriarchy. His close friend and political adviser Joseph von Radowitz would be described by Bismarck as 'a skilful keeper of the medieval wardrobe in which the king dressed up his fancies'.[2]

Nicholas's imagination did not stretch to grasping his brother-in-law's Romantic ideal, and all he could see was that he was dangerously liberal, far too close to the nationalists, weak and generally unsound. In the summer of 1842, in Cologne to celebrate the commencement of work on the cathedral, Frederick William tried to impart to Metternich, who was also present, his view of how the Prussian monarchy should be recast. He explained that he was laying the foundations of a new, counter-revolutionary political religion that would inspire and save Prussia. Metternich's world view could not accommodate this any more than could Nicholas's; he was appalled, describing the king's ideas as far too 'artistic'.[3]

As he was childless, Frederick William nominated his younger brother William 'Prince of Prussia' in anticipation of his succession to the throne. The two did not see eye to eye on fundamentals, and the prince would consistently undermine the king's programme of reform. In this he was supported by the next brother, Karl, who, as Frederick William admitted to his sister, Nicholas's wife, considered him 'a silly instrument in the hands of revolutionaries'. Nicholas wholeheartedly agreed, while Nesselrode and the Russian ambassador in Berlin, Baron Meyendorff, believed that the new king's intended reforms were the greatest threat since 1830.[4]

What particularly worried the Russians was the Prussian king's laxity with regard to the Poles. After putting down the Polish insurrection, Nicholas abolished the kingdom of Poland in 1832 and turned its territory into an integral part of the Russian empire. There followed confiscations of property of all those who had participated in the insurrection and of the Catholic Church, the closing down of institutions of higher education, the imposition of a Russian administration, and various sanctions against Polish language and culture. A number of activists had taken refuge in the less repressive Prussian part of Poland, the grand duchy of Posen (Posnań). They were joined every year by hundreds of Polish deserters from the Russian army, with the result that, in the words of Meyendorff, who visited Posen to assess the situation, 'the revolutionary spirit is spreading like an oil-stain'. In September 1840 he wrote to Benckendorff urging him to send a senior Russian agent to set up Russian police networks in cities such as Posen and Danzig, as the Prussians could not be relied upon to keep an eye on the doings of the Polish revolutionaries. In 1843 a shot was fired at Nicholas's carriage as he travelled through Posen, apparently confirming this – though it was widely thought in Berlin that the incident had been arranged by the Russian police.[5]

The Russians' lack of faith in the Prussian administration's ability to police the country was hardly justified. The reforms initiated in

1808 had by the mid-1820s created a professional state-wide bureaucracy dedicated to the preservation of 'the common good', which in the first instance meant order. 'All who were not in government employment or in the army, were submitted to the strictest surveillance, and to endless vexations by the police,' in the words of one Prussian officer, according to whom 'the passport nuisance' involved 'such varied and complicated regulations, that it required quite a study to avoid difficulties'. The police had a particular dislike for unattached individuals, be they vagrants, seasonal workers or pilgrims, and made life difficult for them. All overnight stays, even by close relatives, had to be reported to the authorities by the householder.[6]

It was accepted among Prussian officials that any protest, be it a demonstration over guild rights or a student disturbance, was a challenge to the established order, and that any degree of force was justifiable in dealing with it. As a class these officials were educated and propertied, and had a stake in the status quo. They were backed up by a police force which was not highly efficient but was omnipresent, a *gendarmerie* mainly recruited from the non-commissioned ranks in the army, and by the army itself. The army had been democratised and integrated with society between 1808 and 1815, but over the next years the old aristocratic officer class had reasserted its influence, and its contempt for the civilian. The commanding officer of the Prussian Guard Corps, General Duke Karl of Mecklemburg, argued that only brute force was capable of dealing with the wrong-headed 'theories' put forward by would-be reformers, who were 'like a predatory animal which having once tasted blood can never be tamed, only subdued'.[7]

Most fair-sized towns were garrisoned, with guardhouses or 'watches' at street corners whose bored but officious soldiers would stop passers-by to check their papers and admonish them on whatever might strike them as relevant. In citadel towns, of which there were twenty-six in Prussia, the watches were even thicker on the ground, and their occupants correspondingly more tiresome, particularly as the governor of a citadel was the ultimate authority and could imprison people or throw them out of town at will. There was a soldier to every five or six inhabitants, so these were in no position to confront the military.[8]

This predominantly bureaucratic approach to law and order did not eclipse the search for subversion, and even after the abolition of the *Zentral Untersuchungs Kommission* eyes and ears remained alert. The police were particularly concerned by a group of young wits who wrote in the Berlin press and published caricatures making such oblique references to the political realities of the day that they were never quite sure whether an article or a drawing was subversive or not. Arguing that it was better to be on the safe side, the minister of the interior, Count Adolf Heinrich von Arnim-Boitzenburg, assured the king in 1842 that supposedly humorous drawings 'corrupt general opinion on moral, religious, and political [matters] and prepare the way for the destructive influence of negative philosophies and democratic spokesmen and authors'.[9]

Neither Nicholas nor his ministers were reassured. By 1845 his ambassadors all over Germany were reporting alarming developments, such as the resurgence of Pietism and other religious movements, 'communist' activity among workers in Silesia and 'terror' in Posen, suggesting that the Prussian army could not be counted on; that the Prussian police were out of their depth; that the royal court was going through a religious phase, along with the king, who was intending to bring in a constitution; and that Prussia was on the brink of revolution.[10]

Frederick William's hopes of grounding his throne on the love of the people failed to be realised. In July 1844 a paranoid individual with no discernible political motive had fired shots at the king and queen as they sat in their carriage in the courtyard of the royal palace in Berlin. He was duly condemned to death, and although Frederick William had wanted to commute the sentence, he had been persuaded by his ministers that this would set a bad precedent, and the man was executed, which went down poorly with public opinion. An increasingly assertive middle class was calling for reform and liberalisation. Frederick William was by then prepared to go along with this, but his brother the Prince of Prussia strongly disapproved and opposed him, with the support of Nicholas and Metternich. By the mid-1840s the two brothers were in open conflict, and the king's programme of reform soon ran into the buffers.

By then there were graver problems facing Prussia. The first three decades following the coming of peace in 1815 had seen an improvement in living standards for all classes throughout Germany, with increased prosperity experienced even by workers. This had come at the cost of profound dislocation as the population, which grew in the same period by 38 per cent, from twenty-five to nearly thirty-five million, adapted to an entirely new set of economic patterns, resulting in part from the early stages of industrialisation and in part from the removal of guild and other restrictions and protections, and from the introduction of the *Zollverein*. The disruption of the pre-capitalistic organisation of labour and production, and of society itself, resulted in a drift to the cities by the poorest classes, who could not accommodate themselves to the new realities. By the beginning of the 1840s between half and two-thirds of the population of Berlin were classed as indigent.[11]

Economic growth in the industrial sector came to an abrupt end in 1845. Agricultural crises in 1842 and 1844–46 caused widespread misery and hunger riots, and emigration to America rose dramatically. The repeal of the Corn Laws in England in 1846 started an international bidding war for a dwindling supply of grain as poor harvests and potato blight began to affect one area of Europe after another. The average rise in the price of food throughout Germany between 1844 and 1847 was around 50 per cent, but that of the basic foodstuffs on which the lower classes depended was much sharper: the price of some grains and potatoes more than doubled. By the summer of 1847 the whole of Germany was undergoing a catastrophic crisis. In Berlin, troops had to be called out against crowds of women attacking potato-sellers, and cavalry clashed with hungry workers.[12]

Austria was also affected by the economic crisis, which, in its case, was aggravated by national grievances of one kind or another. The Italians, Poles, Hungarians, Czechs and now even the Germans saw the Habsburg monarchy as an obstacle to realising their various dreams of a national existence. Metternich had consistently blocked all the initiatives of the liberal aristocrats such as Count Sźechényi to create a cultural national space in Hungary, only with the utmost reluctance agreeing to allow Latin to be replaced by Hungarian as the official language in 1844. 'Hungary is on the verge of the abyss of Revolution,' he declared as he gave way. By opposing moderates such as Sźechényi he was only encouraging the more radical nationalists such as Lajos Kossuth, but neither here nor in Italy, where the Austrian police chief of Venice himself was advising him to make concessions, would he differentiate between the national and the revolutionary.[13]

Metternich was exasperated by the failure of the other powers to see, as he did, that 'the revolutionary propaganda is working without cease, with an ardour worthy of a better cause, to undermine by all the means at its disposal the present bases of the social and political order, and to prepare everywhere the ground for a universal upheaval'. The general acceptance by the other powers of the July monarchy in France and the growing popularity of Louis-Philippe represented 'an enormous danger for the preservation of the present state of affairs in Europe', he argued, as, if one accepted that a constitutional monarchy brought in by a revolution was a good thing, the logical next step was democratic elections of kings and, as far as he was concerned, anarchy. When Louis-Philippe sought to marry his eldest son, the duc d'Orléans, to an Austrian archduchess, Metternich persuaded the father of the girl in question, who was delighted with the proposal, to reject it, reminding him of what had happened to Marie-Antoinette.[14]

Next to France, the principal brazier of revolution was Switzerland, whose authorities were far too lenient. 'Switzerland has now turned into a fortified sewer,' Metternich wrote to Apponyi in Paris in March 1845. 'All that Europe contains in terms of lost souls, adventurers and engineers of social upheaval has found a refuge in that wretched country. All those men practise their craft there with impunity.' To make matters worse, a struggle had broken out between the liberal cantons, which were mostly Protestant, and the Catholic cantons of the Sonderbund. Metternich supported the latter, which put him at odds with France and most of public opinion in Germany, and found himself backing the losing side. 'In Switzerland, one has to expect to see the revolutionary lava overflow imminently,' he warned the King of Württemberg in June 1847.[15]

Switzerland's geographical position made it an uncomfortable neighbour for the Austrian provinces in Italy, and although Mazzini had moved from there to London, Metternich still saw it as a key strategic stepping-stone for subversion in the peninsula. The British government waved aside his repeated requests for the expulsion of Mazzini, or at least the curtailment of his activities. Metternich railed at the fact that the Italians were able to plot and fund-raise openly in London. He did have some success in 1844, when, following a particularly shambolic attempt by some of Mazzini's followers to start a rising in Calabria, he managed to persuade the British cabinet to intercept Mazzini's correspondence. But this victory blew up in his face.

Mazzini had begun to suspect something, and asked those writing to him to place poppy-seeds in the envelopes of their letters. When these reached him without the seeds, he made his suspicions public. They were taken up by the press, and the House of Commons was forced to set up a Secret Committee on the Post Office, which duly reported that the home secretary had indeed issued a warrant to the Post Office commanding it to pass Mazzini's correspondence to him. It also revealed that at the request of the Russian government, warrants had been issued with regard to two Polish émigrés in London, though nothing had been found in the correspondence 'to criminate the gentlemen.'[16]

The Italians and the Poles were by the mid-1840s the only ones still actively plotting insurrection. The Polish Democratic Society, based in Paris, had at last managed to foster activists on the ground in

Poland, and in 1845 one group in Posen, with another in the independent city-republic of Kraków set up by the Congress of Vienna, began to plot a revolt to break out simultaneously in the Prussian grand duchy of Posen and the Austrian province of Galicia. Having taken these over, they would then raise the standard of revolt in Russia's Polish provinces. Their associates in London urged Mazzini to organise diversionary risings in Italy to pin down Austrian troops there. The leaders of the planned risings, the thirty-one-year-old Ludwik Mierosławski and the twenty-three-year-old Edward Dembowski, were as benighted as their plans were fantastic and ill-starred.

The rising was to begin on 21 February 1846, but long before that the Prussian police arrested Mierosławski and the entire leadership of the Posen rising. As a result, some of the conspirators wanted to cancel the revolt, others to hasten it, and the ensuing rash of uncoordinated disturbances was quickly contained by police and troops. The Kraków conspirators decided to go ahead, and issued a proclamation to the peoples of Europe calling for solidarity and affirming the inevitability of their victory. Dembowski, dressed in peasant costume and clutching a crucifix, led a march through the countryside in an attempt to rally the population to the cause, but it was set upon by Austrian troops assisted by scythe-waving peasants professing loyalty to the emperor, and he was bludgeoned to death. Bands of peasants all over western Galicia attacked manor houses and any travellers they could lay their hands on, massacring some 2,000 Polish gentry, most of whom had no connection with the plotters, before the Austrian authorities got round to restoring order.

Metternich was in triumphant mood. According to him, the émigré Poles in Paris had distributed 'hundreds of thousands of catechisms and instructions on the organisation of free corps', and were 'preaching the division of property and forming in bands in order to attack landowners' as part of 'a vast communist conspiracy covering all the Polish territories'. But 'the people' had put down the revolution out of love for their emperor. 'It is the peasants who are acting as the police today,' he crowed. The Polish émigré plotters had been revealed as being 'like a general staff going to war without an army', and 'demagoguery itself was wrecked on the very element of democracy, that is to say the people'. It was not long, however, before he realised that the massacre had gone down rather differently with the overwhelming majority of European public opinion, which was horrified at the slaughter of landowners by bands of peasants out for blood. He suddenly became aware that he was celebrating something very like the *grande peur* of 1790.[17]

To make matters worse, stories began to circulate to the effect that the Galician peasants had been paid or otherwise incited by the Austrian authorities. There is some evidence that this may have been the case, but it is not conclusive. Some police officials had spread rumours that the Polish gentry had summoned French colonial troops and black cannibals were about to swarm into Galicia to murder and then eat the peasants. In the prevailing conditions, it did not take much to arouse class hatred among the most abject, and all the police needed to do was to tip a wink for violence to break out. The Austrian authorities had never been squeamish when it came to using the instruments of divide and rule, and in 1837 Metternich had considered bringing the Hungarian nobility to heel by giving their peasants just such a signal. Either way, Austria was gravely damaged by the events.[18]

Metternich set about repairing the damage, but only tied himself in knots. On the one hand, he concocted a version of events in which the Polish nobles had called on their peasants to join them in a massacre of all non-Poles, which the peasants had refused to do. The nobles had then tried to force them through 'harsh treatment', and when this had no effect, by shooting some of them, at which point the peasants had resisted and some nobles had been killed in the ensuing fighting. 'If fortune had not turned against the conspirators, thousands of innocent victims [Austrian soldiers, police and officials] would have been felled by the daggers and the murderous weapons that these self-proclaimed patriots had placed in the hands of the people.'

On the other hand, he insisted that it had all been planned in Paris. 'It is from there that the emissaries of upheaval go forth, and thither they return, only to issue forth once again.' These democratic emissaries were particularly dangerous when they operated in Poland, he argued. 'As democratic ideas are not applicable to a Slav population like that of Poland, these ideas, put forward by one faction of the emigration, they necessarily turn into communism, that is to say to the pillage of landed estates and the murder of the landowners.' In his eagerness to demonstrate that there was no such thing as legitimate Polish patriotism, he had turned his argument on its head.[19]

'The seat of the Revolution is not in Poland, but in France,' he argued in a memorandum on the Galician affair. 'Poland is only a staging post, a subsidiary of the great revolutionary society of which the Polish émigrés like those of other countries are no more than the instruments of French radicalism ... *Polonism* [a word invented by him] is only a label, a word behind which lurks revolution under its most brutal form; it is *the Revolution* itself, and not merely a part of it; that is clear from the demonstrations of the Polish emigration. Polonism does not declare war on the three powers which are in possession of the former Polish territories; it declares war on all existing institutions, it preaches the overthrow of all the bases on which society rests; to combat it is therefore not just the duty of the three powers, it is the duty of all.' This was why it was so reprehensible of countries such as Britain, France and Belgium to give shelter to émigrés and allow them to operate freely: these countries had become little better than 'base camps' of the revolution.[20]

It was clear that the republic of Kraków could not be allowed to remain as a potential outpost of revolution, and Nicholas urged Metternich to incorporate it into Austria. Metternich hesitated, as this would constitute an open breach of the arrangements made at Vienna in 1815. Nicholas made it clear that if Austria did not annex the republic, Russia would, and on 6 November 1846 Metternich went ahead. The republic, he argued in a justificatory memorandum, had consciously thrown itself into the revolution and turned itself into 'the provisional capital of the revolutionary government'. Palmerston remarked that if the Treaty of Vienna no longer obtained on the banks of the Vistula, it no longer had any validity on the banks of the Po or the Rhine.[21]

What happened on the banks of the Po was crucial to Metternich. According to him, the whole Polish affair had been merely a feint designed to tie down Austrian forces there while the real revolt was mounted in Italy. 'This plan is no secret; although it was elaborated in the mystery of the clubs, it had not been confined there; it has been conceived on a vast scale and its first stage was put into effect, but it failed,' he explained to his minister in Turin in May 1846. 'One fact on which it would be impossible to have any doubt is that if the rising in the Grand Duchy of Posen and in Galicia had been successful and had spread to the kingdom of Poland, an insurrection in Italy would have been the immediate result.' And although this attempt had been defeated, there were no grounds for complacency, as 'the Revolution is a Protean force which can skilfully change its nature to suit the circumstances'. 'The motto which it has inscribed on the standard around which it seeks to rally the masses is "nationality". It is in the name of the love of the motherland, in spreading this sentiment, so elevated and so legitimate in itself, and by exalting it in a direction which removes it from the existing state, that it drives the people to forget their most fundamental duties ...'[22]

Ironically, the best-ruled part of the Italian peninsula, and the only one where law and order was protected, was Austrian Lombardy-Venetia. It was more prosperous than any other Italian state, and industrially far in advance of the others. Austrian rule was more benevolent than the government of most of the Italian states, with lower taxes and, for instance, twice as many newspapers published as in neighbouring Piedmont. With its backward economies, the remainder of the peninsula was plagued by endemic poverty. The Papal States were bankrupt by 1832, and Metternich saved the pope by persuading the Viennese banking house of Rothschild to provide him with a loan. The various rulers' perceived need to keep large standing armies took hands away from the land and whatever industry there was: in Piedmont, conscripts were torn from their homes for a period of eight years to man an army 30,000 strong; in Naples the period of service was six years, and the army stood at 60,000 (Sicilians were not conscripted, as their loyalty was considered doubtful). And these armies were no more effective in keeping order than were the police forces of the various states.[23]

The kingdom of Sardinia had been the first to set up a corps of *Carabinieri* on the French model of the *Gendarmerie* in 1814, followed by the Papal States, which after the disturbances of 1830–32 supplemented it with a band of thugs graced with the name of 'Centurions' and two other corps. One was a force of 4,400 Swiss mercenaries under General de Salis, whose lack of familiarity with the language and local conditions resulted in an explosion of criminal activity. The other was a force of Pontifical Volunteers recruited from among the unemployed and criminal classes by Prince Capece Minutolo di Canosa, who had carried out the purges of liberals in Naples after 1821. He created a similar force for the Duke of Modena to cow the nobility and middle classes into submission. Petty crime and outright brigandage flourished, while the police concentrated on political surveillance and the investigation of supposed liberal opposition. This only served to create an underlying sympathy between political dissidents and the criminal classes, making detection of both more difficult.[24]

Sardinia was also the first to introduce greater control of the people, through the introduction of the *libretto di lavoro*, essentially an identity card. Other states gradually followed suit, and brought in passports and travel permits. The new fashion for regulation as a means of control led to state interference in traditionally sensitive matters of property rights, and into more personal spheres with the introduction of medical policing, at first of doctors and nurses, then of midwives, then prostitutes, and so on. This extension of state control was not a success. On the one hand it provoked riots by whole villages, often led by their priest, in defence of ancient wood- or other gathering rights.

On the other, it expanded the scope for corruption – regulations on the inspection of prostitutes resulted in the largest brothel in Palermo, staffed by four hundred girls, being run by the city's chief of police.[25]

Just as much as Metternich, the various Italian rulers weakened their own position by their fear of all innovation. Pope Gregory XVI refused to allow the building of railways. Sardinia's censorship, which banned the use of the words 'nation', 'Italy' and 'liberal', as well as 'constitution' and 'revolution', actually made it illegal to write about railways, even in scientific journals. The kingdom's first minister, Camillo di Cavour, admitted that after a short stay in London, returning to Turin was like entering 'a kind of intellectual hell'.[26]

The election of a new pope, Pius IX, in the summer of 1846 seemed to augur well. Metternich wrote to his ambassador in Rome that he was convinced it would 'contribute fundamentally to outmanoeuvre the sinister projects of the enemies of order and to greatly revive the courage and the hopes of those who have devoted themselves to the defence of the immutable principles by which Empires live and prosper'. It would not be long before he took back those words.[27]

Among the new pope's first acts was the release of political prisoners, and this was followed by a shoal of reforms. Liberals all over the peninsula cheered. King Charles-Albert of Sardinia emulated the pontiff, announcing reforms and striking attitudes which delighted liberals and nationalists. The Grand Duke of Tuscany followed his example, and both of them marked their adherence to the new order by signing a customs union with the Papal States. In order to prevent this new bloc from growing any larger, Metternich felt obliged to force treaties on Parma and Modena which stopped them from following suit.

The new pope's reforms were slow to take effect, and in 1847 the citizens of Bologna were so exasperated by the lack of effective law enforcement by the papal police that they formed a civic guard to maintain order in the city. Metternich saw this as a poorly-disguised attempt to replicate the French revolutionary model of setting up a National Guard, which not only symbolised the power of the citizens, but also effectively arrogated the powers of the legitimate government. He ordered Field Marshal Radetzky to reinforce the garrison of Ferrara, but this provoked the anger of the Bolognese and an outburst of patriotic feeling; a considerable influx of volunteers from all over Italy had the effect of turning the civic guard into a more militaristic and anti-Austrian formation than originally intended.

'The old year ended in scarcity, the new one opens with starvation,' the Prussian minister Count Galen wrote on 20 January 1847. 'Misery, spiritual and physical, traverses Europe in ghastly shapes – the one without God, the other without bread. Woe if they join hands!' The financial and agricultural depression touched bottom in Germany in the summer of 1847, and the price of food fell sharply. But while this brought an end to the food riots, it did nothing to alleviate Prussia's problems. In June, Metternich likened its condition to that of France in 1789, and for once he was right – but for the wrong reasons. 'The world is very sick; every day provides evidence that the moral gangrene is spreading,' he warned Apponyi, but the real problem lay elsewhere, in Prussia's fiscal condition. With the advent of the economic crisis in 1845 and the Europe-wide credit squeeze, the Prussian government found itself running out of cash and credit. It badly needed to raise more funds to carry on with the development of its railway network and other investments, and, just as Louis XVI had in 1788, was obliged to summon a Diet that would allow taxes to be raised. Frederick William duly called the Diet for 1847. Just as had happened in 1788–89, once convened to discuss the country's fiscal straits, the representatives quickly moved on to other topics, and the Diet turned into a forum for the airing of liberal views, which led on to debates on the subject of German unification.[28]

Hitherto, the forces for change had been made up principally of the aspiring classes – doctors, lawyers, merchants and industrialists. They wanted a less restricted social environment, but they were propertied and socially ambitious, lacked any radical instincts, and had remained hostile to the hungry rioters throughout most of the 1840s. But the financial crisis, which affected them too, changed their attitude and brought them into closer contact with those lower down the social scale. Gradually, their demands grew more radical and overtly political. In September 1847 the leaders of the Baden Radicals, Gustav von Struve and Friedrich Hecker, made a declaration demanding freedom of the press, assembly and conscience, and the repeal of the Karlsbad Decrees and other repressive legislation.

Austria was in exactly the same political–fiscal deadlock as Prussia. The Habsburg monarchy was run by a large, hard-working and honest but inefficient and unimaginative bureaucracy of some 140,000. It was reigned over by the incapable Ferdinand, but ruled by a Council of State presided over by Archduke Louis assisted by Metternich and Kolowrat, who loathed each other so profoundly that at one stage they communicated only in writing. Metternich stooped to spreading rumours that his rival's brain was affected by violent attacks of haemorrhoids. By the late 1840s, the whole machine was running on nothing but momentum. The Austrian state had been bankrupt in 1815, and over the next three decades it spent nearly a third of its revenues on servicing its debts. Throughout most of this period the military budget accounted for some 40 per cent of revenue. Every military intervention, in Italy or elsewhere, threatened the state's credit status. It also spent a huge proportion of its revenue on police – 1,131,000 florins by 1847, compared with only 37,000 on education. The state badly needed to raise money. The Hungarian assembly had been uncooperative in agreeing to raise taxes, voicing demands for ever-greater national autonomy every time finances were mentioned. Metternich's gloom intensified in the second half of 1847, with comparisons to 1789 cropping up in his correspondence with greater frequency.[29]

'If I am not mistaken, the year 1848 will shed light on many things which the vanished year shrouded in mist, and since, despite my reputation as a great friend of obscurantism, I am a friend of light, the new year cannot but be more agreeable to me than the last, of which I cannot keep a fond memory,' he wrote to Frederick William at the very end of 1847.[30]

30

Satan on the Loose

On 2 January 1848 an Austrian captain was walking down the street in Milan puffing at a cigar when, suddenly, it was knocked from his teeth. This meant war. In a burst of patriotism, the citizens of Milan had decided in November 1847 to stop smoking in order to deprive the Austrian treasury of the revenue from the excise duty on cigars. Anyone who broke the boycott was bullied into complying, but until now no representative of the Austrian authorities had been involved. They retaliated by issuing large quantities of cigars to their troops and sending them out to swagger about the streets in groups of three and puff defiantly at the natives. They were hissed and jeered, and then assaulted. Street urchins, fishwives and petty criminals joined in, and it was not long before casualties began piling up, with at least two dead and hundreds wounded; the soldiers withdrew to the safety of their barracks.

On 12 January, revolution broke out in Palermo. This had been sparked off by associates of Mazzini, but rapidly attracted the riff-raff of the city and the brigands of the surrounding countryside. The troubles spread to Naples, and soon the kingdom of the Two Sicilies was in turmoil. King Ferdinand pleaded for Austrian help, but this was not forthcoming. 'Europe is engulfed by a conspiracy of the party of subversion against the legally existing order, of which Austria is recognised as the only true defender, and as a result, the agitators have chosen her as the target for their attacks,' replied Metternich, who was still recovering from the shock of the cigar plot. Ferdinand was going to have to resign himself to granting a constitution. In order to forestall any eruptions in Piedmont, the King of Sardinia granted one as well. The Grand Duke of Tuscany would do so next, followed by the pope.[1]

The next attack on Austria was no less sneaky than the tobacco offensive. It was delivered by an internationally renowned dancer, a darling of the London and Paris stages, the Neapolitan-born Fanny Cerrito. She was currently performing the ballet *La Vivandière* at the La Fenice theatre in Venice. On 6 February she flew on to the stage to deliver her *pièce de résistance*, a 'Siciliana' in which she could show off her famously nimble footwork, wearing a dress trimmed with the Italian nationalists' colours of red, white and green, and rattling a similarly adorned tambourine. The audience went wild. The police intervened, arresting a number of people and closing down the theatre until further notice.

Perhaps thinking of the events in Palermo and Naples, of Etna and Vesuvius, Alexis de Tocqueville warned his colleagues in the French Chamber of Deputies on 24 January that they were sitting on a volcano. Three days later he conjured another metaphor. 'Can you not feel … how shall I put it? a revolutionary draught?' he asked rhetorically. 'This wind, I do not know where it was born or whence it comes, nor, believe me, whom it will sweep away …' There was certainly something in the air, and had been for some time.[2]

There was ill-feeling all over Europe, but particularly in Germany and Italy, against the progressive encroachment of the state into private life, against increasing regulation and taxation, and against the officials and police who enforced it. The Industrial Revolution had altered the economic, social and political landscape in most of Europe, creating inequalities on a scale hitherto unknown, and a huge underclass at the mercy of every dip in the economic cycle, threatened with starvation with every poor harvest. As a result of the economic crisis that began in the mid-1840s, waves of helpless people flooded into the larger cities, causing housing shortages which turned the centres of many of them into squalid anthills. At least a quarter of the population of Paris was indigent, living in filthy slums cheek-by-jowl with the *hôtels particuliers* of the rich. It was not just the poor who felt there was something wrong with this.[3]

There was, among young people and intellectuals, a sense of disillusion with a system which could produce such a state of affairs, and perhaps more important, of spiritual and cultural boredom. At the beginning of the 1840s, the heir to the French throne, Louis-Philippe's eldest son the duc d'Orléans, said in conversation with the painter Ary Scheffer that 'the present epoch is prosperous and peaceful, but it is too flat not to soon become stagnant and corrupt'. In 1847 the French poet Alphonse de Lamartine called for 'a revolution of contempt' against what he saw as a soulless and pharisaical political and social order. In February of that year, the socialist Louis Blanc and the historian Jules Michelet both published the first volumes of their respective histories of the French Revolution, which they depicted as poetic, patriotic and ultimately glorious. In March, Lamartine's own contribution to the subject, *Histoire des Girondins*, added yet more poetic lustre. People who had been used to view the episode with horror and loathing began to see it in a different light, as something heroic and magnificent. The current epoch shone by the absence of such qualities.[4]

Tocqueville's talk of volcanoes and revolutionary draughts may have been fanciful, but there was a sense of crisis. While some went as far as suggesting the king should abdicate in favour of his grandson the comte de Paris, most were agreed that he should at least sack his unpopular prime minister, François Guizot. The retired British officer Captain Rees Howell Gronow, who had settled in Paris, noted expressions of 'sullen defiance' as he strolled along the boulevards, and expected 'squalls'. On 18 February 1848 the queen, Marie-Amélie, noted that there was no more gold to be had anywhere in Paris, that people had stopped transacting business, and that many had left for the country. She was even thinking of sending her diamonds to Brussels for safekeeping.[5]

So far, the only noticeable thing that had wafted over from the events in Palermo and Naples had been a fashion for the 'Calabrian look', an outfit including a conical plumed hat, thigh-high boots and a cloak, which was how most theatre producers dressed the Italian bandits who turned up frequently in operas and plays of the time. Students all over northern Europe began to affect the style, often growing fierce moustaches to go with it. But the vagaries of history were about to make Tocqueville's warnings prophetic.

Beginning in July 1847, to obviate the ban on public meetings liberals had taken to holding political banquets in Paris to draw attention to the plight of the poor and to voice their grievances. These had proved ineffectual and were discontinued, but in the new year the 12th Legion of the National Guard, recruited from the poorest areas of the city, decided to hold one of its own. The government raised objections and on 21 February denied permission, so the event was cancelled. The following day a group of students staged a demonstration against this decision, marching through the slums on their way to protest in front of the seat of the Chambers at the Palais Bourbon. By the time they reached it, they were leading a huge and menacing crowd. The National Guard and troops were called out to disperse it and restore order, which they did, overpowering and dismantling a few barricades which had been erected. They then retired for the night.

The authorities had learned to live with this kind of disturbance over the past two decades, and the king was unruffled. He assured the painter Horace Vernet, who had called to discuss a portrait commission, that there was nothing to worry about, and that the 'straw blaze' would quickly burn itself out. The principal liberal agitators and the most active dissidents, such as Ledru-Rollin and Louis Blanc, had been notable by their absence from the scene, since they too believed the people of Paris were in no mood for insurrection.[6]

By the next morning, 23 February, more barricades had gone up and the National Guard was called out once more, but this time only units from the more well-to-do *quartiers* turned out. This unsettled Louis-Philippe, and he caved in to the general demand for the sacking of Guizot. This was well received, and the crisis was defused as public opinion rallied to the king. Those students and workers bent on further action were isolated and leaderless, so nobody thought of moving the troops in to clear the remaining barricades and mop up. The mood on the boulevards was jubilant as Captain Gronow sauntered off to dine at his club that afternoon. The general sense of relief was also noted by the police functionary La Hodde, and by the journalist Maxime du Camp, who had spent the day wandering around the city with his friends Louis Bouilhet and Gustave Flaubert. They detected an inchoate enthusiasm, with shouts of '*À bas Guizot!*' alternating with '*Vive le Roi!*', '*Vive la République!*', '*Vive la Garde Nationale!*' and '*Vive la Troupe!*' as rumour and rhetoric brushed the groups assembled on the streets. They and the overwhelming majority of eyewitnesses were convinced that the whole affair was over, and none of them expected any more trouble: former head of the *Sûreté* Paul Louis Canler judged that the *émeute* had blown itself out like a passing storm. But Captain Gronow's dinner was rudely interrupted.[7]

He and his fellow diners were disturbed by a commotion in the street outside. When they went to the window they beheld a lugubrious procession filing past, drawing a wagon piled with corpses and calling for revenge; he could hardly believe the change of mood that had taken place within the space of an hour or two.

While the government had made no further use of the troops called out earlier, it had not withdrawn them, and various units were left encamped in streets and squares all over the city. On his way to dinner Gronow had passed a company of the 14th Regiment of the Line, stationed at the corner of the boulevard des Capucines. The bored soldiers stood around improvised braziers trying to keep warm, while passing civilians alternately cheered and taunted them. At one point an altercation developed, drawing in a number of passers-by. A random shot fired by one of the civilians provoked the soldiers, who opened fire before retreating to the shelter of the courtyard of the ministry of foreign affairs. At this point the incident turned into tragicomedy, as the bandsman bearing the big drum got stuck in the *porte-cochère* of the ministry, and those behind him had to make a stand outside. This minor incident left at least three dozen dead and over seventy wounded (figures differ). The dead were loaded on to a wagon, and drawn around the city by a snowballing crowd demanding revenge and calling the people to arms.[8]

By the morning of 24 February the city was in a state of chaos, with armed mobs attacking military outposts. But the situation was by no means desperate. Marshal Gérard had long before drawn up a plan to deal with popular insurrection, and it was considered foolproof. It was not, however, Gérard who was in command in Paris, but the talentless General Tiburce Sebastiani. The National Guard was under General Jacqueminot, a good soldier but not the man to rally his forces in a crisis. The prefect of police was Gabriel Delessert, described by one French statesman as 'a very good man, but more fitted to preside over some philanthropic association than to directing the police of Paris'. Much the same could have been said of Louis-Philippe himself. While most of Paris waited for a vigorous reaction on the part of the government and a brisk restoration of order, the king dithered.[9]

Seventy-four years old and feeling his age, he had recently lost his dearest sister and closest adviser, Madame Adelaïde. He had been profoundly shocked by the unreliability of the National Guard, the citizenry-in-arms which he had considered to be the mainstay of his throne. He did not like the idea of using troops or shooting civilians. It was not until the early afternoon that he decided to hand over command to Marshal Bugeaud, with the brief of restoring order.

The younger son of an impoverished marquis from rural Périgord, Thomas Robert Bugeaud had won his corporal's stripes at Austerlitz and distinguished himself as a colonel during the Hundred Days, when he defeated a sixfold-greater Austrian force ten days after Waterloo. He was certainly up to the job in hand: in Algeria, he had capped some spectacular victories with ruthless pacification, and he had no time for what he called 'political prudery'. During the capture of Saragossa in the Peninsular war he had learned to deploy men hugging the walls on either side of the street, too close for the snipers on their own side but well placed to pick off those on the other, to take barricades and to enter houses by blowing holes in the walls with small infantry field-pieces.[10]

But, according to Bugeaud, the king's order reached him too late, by a few hours. He believed that 'every quarter of an hour which you abandon to the riot increases its physical and moral force'. The troops had been standing around in what he termed 'a shameful position with regard to the insurrection' for sixty hours, without adequate food, fodder or munitions. 'All I could do was to raise my eyes to heaven and profoundly bemoan the fall of this monarchy which had given France seventeen years of peace, freedom and progress in every field.'[11]

Louis-Philippe's eldest son, the duc d'Orléans, had been killed in a coaching accident four years earlier, leaving an infant son, the comte de Paris, in whose favour he abdicated. The king changed out of the uniform he habitually wore and put on a frock-coat, removed his toupee and covered his head with a black hat. Arm in arm with the queen and followed by a small retinue, he left the Tuileries by a side door and walked to the place de la Concorde, where the party climbed into two broughams and a cabriolet. The carriages rolled out of Paris in the direction of Saint Cloud, where they changed horses, and then made for the coast, via Versailles and Dreux. At Le Havre they took ship for England and landed at Newhaven. Throughout the flight, the disconsolate king kept muttering to himself, 'Worse than Charles X!', and the phrase came up again and again even after the royal party had settled into exile at Claremont House near Esher in Surrey, originally built for Clive of India and by 1848 the property of Louis-Philippe's son-in-law Leopold, King of the Belgians.[12]

A couple of years earlier, Louis-Philippe had chided the liberal statesman Hyacinthe Odilon Barrot, saying, 'You are too young, Monsieur Odilon Barrot … you never saw the Revolution!' To which the young man replied, 'For my part, Sire, I am beginning to fear that you are too old, and that you have contemplated it too much, this Revolution!' Barrot remembered this exchange now. 'Was it the phantom of the Terror and its scaffolds which clouded the natural wisdom of that otherwise sharp and open mind, was it that phantom which, at the crucial moment, robbed him of the courage which had not failed under the Prussian guns at Valmy, during the cruel trials of a long exile, or, later, the repeated attempts of the assassins: the king's moment of weakness on the morning of 24 February and above all his precipitate flight cannot be explained otherwise.'[13]

Shortly after the exit of the king, the mob had stormed into the Tuileries, which was sacked, along with the other Orléans family properties of the Palais-Royal and Neuilly. The duchesse d'Orléans had driven over to the Chamber with the comte de Paris in a last-ditch attempt to have his right to rule endorsed, to no avail. The poet Alphonse de Lamartine had gathered together all the oppositionists he could rally, and from the balcony of the Hôtel de Ville, where less than eighteen years before Lafayette had presented Louis-Philippe to the people, he declared the Republic.

'In this extraordinary manner, and almost I may say by chance, the Orleans dynasty ceased to reign over the French people,' commented Captain Gronow. He was not the only one to be astonished at the randomness of the developments, and people all over Paris, including some of those making up the rapidly-cobbled-together provisional government, were asking themselves what had actually happened and how it had happened. Nobody had planned any of the events of the past few days. The opposition leaders had not played a part. The majority of the workers who manned the barricades had wanted a living wage, not a republic. 'Paris had played at a bit of rioting and ended up with a revolution,' commented Maxime Du Camp; 'it had called for reform and proclaimed the Republic.' Tocqueville too, while he felt that the revolution had been in some sense inevitable, admitted that it had happened entirely by chance.[14]

The atmosphere seems to have been even more good-natured than in the July Days of 1830. 'All the dangers which surrounded us have disappeared,' noted Count Apponyi in his journal on 28 February. 'There is no safer town on earth at the moment than Paris,' wrote this arch-conservative who had trembled at every riot of the past decade. 'One could hardly be more polite than the people in the street: never, at any time, have I seen the lower classes more obliging towards everyone.' The only immediate demands the people made of the provisional government were the rights to work and to form trade unions, and for a ten-hour working day. There was very little in the way of aggression towards the rich, attacks on châteaux or calls for blood.[15]

News of the events in Paris began to reach Vienna on 29 February, provoking wild rumours, a violent rise in the price of food and a crash of government bonds. 'Well, my dear,' Metternich said to the Russian ambassador, 'all is lost!' He wrote to the tsar to coordinate their response. On hearing the news from Paris, Nicholas had flown into a panic. 'Act *firmly and promptly*, or, I am telling it to you, I am repeating it, *all is lost*,' he wrote to Frederick William of Prussia. The Prussian king did not need his brother-in-law to tell him things were looking bad. 'Satan is on the loose again,' he exclaimed. His first reaction had been to write to Queen Victoria, Nicholas and Metternich, suggesting they create a league of solidarity, his second to call for a congress of German states. But he was overtaken by events.[16]

Prompted by the news from Paris, every malcontent and body in Germany with an axe to grind began voicing demands. On 3 March a mass demonstration in Cologne had to be dispersed by troops. In Baden, violent demonstrations obliged the king to grant concessions, and two days after that in Stuttgart a petition was presented to the King of Württemberg demanding he convene a German assembly, abolish censorship, introduce trial by jury, grant freedom of assembly and religious worship, and reform the fiscal system. Similar demands were made in Hesse-Darmstadt and Nassau, and on 6 March the King of Saxony was obliged to call the Estates. In Bavaria, political discontent was reinforced by outrage at the king's recent scandalous affair with the dancer Lola Montez, and he was forced to abdicate in favour of his son. One after the other, governments caved in without the semblance of a fight.

In Berlin, crowds came out into the streets on 6 March calling for constitutional change, and more meetings and demonstrations took place over the next two days. The exceptionally fine spring weather and the carnival atmosphere swelled the crowds, which the city *gendarmerie* of 150 men was inadequate to control. The authorities felt obliged to fall back on the army, which was arrogant, brutal and greatly disliked, and on 13 March troops ordered to disperse demonstrators killed a number of civilians. There was uproar, and Frederick William could only placate it by promising to introduce reforms.

When news of this reached St Petersburg, the empress broke down. 'My poor brother, my poor William!' she wailed. 'Never mind your poltroon of a brother, when everything is crumbling in Europe, when everything is on fire, when Russia too could be turned upside down,' snapped an exasperated Nicholas, who felt no pity, having repeatedly warned Frederick William where his 'liberal' tendencies would lead. He then turned on his children's tutor, who had been in the process of reading Goethe's *Faust* to the empress, and berated him for propagating such 'godless' literature. While he was horrified by the revolutionary surge, the tsar could not repress a sense of satisfaction, even *Schadenfreude*, at the fact that Frederick William had fallen prey to demons he had himself nourished, and above all that the usurper Louis-Philippe had met his comeuppance. 'Louis-Philippe has only received his just deserts,' he wrote. 'He has gone out by same door by which he came in.' In contrast to 1830, Nicholas did not recall his ambassador in Paris.[17]

Metternich had also appealed to the British cabinet for moral if not military support in containing the spreading crisis, but this only earned him a pious snub from Palmerston. 'Your politics of oppression, which tolerates no resistance, is a fatal one and leads as surely to an explosion as a hermetically sealed cauldron which has no safety-valve,' the foreign secretary lectured the Austrian ambassador in London. The words were lost on the Austrian chancellor.[18]

Events taking place elsewhere had emboldened Metternich's critics at home, and while the Hungarian nationalist Lajos Kossuth made fiery speeches to the Magyar Diet at Pressburg (Bratislava) and Czech patriots held rallies in Prague, various individuals, groups and associations began to voice demands, many in the form of loyal addresses to the throne: booksellers asked for the abolition of censorship, lawyers changes to the legal system, professionals a revision of regulations, manufacturers fiscal reform, others the creation of proper ministries, the establishment of local assemblies, the limitation of the powers of the police, and so on. Metternich ignored them. He believed in standing firm in the storm, and he trusted his police to scotch all plots and conspiracies.

A rowdy demonstration in Vienna on 11 March was dispersed by police without recourse to the use of force, which seemed to bear out his confidence. But a demonstration by students two days later outside the building in which the Land Estates were meeting proved more difficult to handle. Attempts at communication broke down in misunderstanding, rumours spread by troublemakers raised the temperature, and in the early afternoon troops were called in to disperse the crowd. (This may have been done deliberately at the behest of Metternich's arch-enemy Count Kolowrat in order to precipitate a crisis which would unhorse the chancellor.)

Shots were fired, blood was spilled and barricades were erected as more and more people came out onto the streets voicing a litany of demands, all of them requiring Metternich's resignation. 'At last the malady has come to the surface,' he commented as he watched from the windows of his chancellery a Polish student haranguing the angry crowd outside, evident proof of the international conspiracy. By contrast, he was now utterly isolated, and faced the great hydra alone. Worse, all those who should have stood shoulder to shoulder behind him were putting pressure on him to resign. Without support from any quarter, at nine o'clock that evening Metternich bowed out. He left Vienna with his family and two faithful associates, travelling under an assumed name with nothing in his pocket beside the thousand ducats

Salomon Rothschild had lent him. Worst of all, he was obliged to take refuge from the storm engulfing the whole of Europe in that den of liberal iniquity, London.[19]

This time Nicholas did not feel any *Schadenfreude*. 'On Sunday, at 8 o'clock in the evening, we received by the Warsaw telegraph the first news of the worst political misfortune which could befall us in this terrible epoch for governments and peoples,' Nesselrode wrote to Meyendorff on 21 March. 'Words fail me to describe such a great catastrophe, human prediction cannot encompass the consequences which might flow from it.' The immediate consequences were not hard to predict.[20]

On 15 March, a crowd led by two poets had crossed over from Pest and stormed Buda Castle, releasing a solitary political prisoner from this pseudo-Bastille; Hungary was well on the way to declaring independence from Austria. The following day, as news of Metternich's resignation reached the city, Berlin began to stir. On 18 March a mass of people gathered in front of the royal palace to celebrate the king's abolition of censorship and promise to introduce a constitution, and the king came out onto a balcony to accept their thanks. He was cheered, but the size of the crowd frightened him. He ordered the area to be cleared, and his troops set about the task with predictable clumsiness. There was confusion in the crowd, which was too big to disperse easily, fights broke out, shots were fired, and by nightfall the city was in a state of insurrection.

That same day the Milanese revolted against Austrian rule, attacking the 12,000-strong Austrian garrison and expelling it from the city after five days of fierce fighting, which went down in history as the illustrious *Cinque Giornate*. Venice declared independence from Austria on 22 March. The rulers of Parma and Modena were forced to leave by revolts in their states and, in order to keep his throne, at the end of March Charles Albert was obliged to take Sardinia to war against Austria in support of the risings in Lombardy and Venetia. Tuscany and the Two Sicilies gave token support, as did the pope.

By then, events had moved on in Germany. On the morning following the violence in his capital, Frederick William issued a proclamation to his 'dear Berliners'. He assured all and sundry that the peaceful and joyful demonstration of the previous day had been taken over by anarchists, Freemasons, Jesuits, Jews, Poles, French convicts, democrats and Italians who had come to Berlin for the purpose and had been in hiding for a week, biding their time. He ordered the troops to withdraw, to the disgust of the Prince of Prussia, who called his brother a coward and threw his sword at his feet before going off to London in a state of dudgeon. Another who thought the king weak and ineffectual was Lady Burghersh, wife of the British ambassador in Berlin, who was in 'no doubt the whole affair was got up by paid emissaries, chiefly from France and Poland, assisted by the Jews of this country'. After a long conversation on the subject with Queen Victoria a couple of months later, she related that the queen 'was convinced the German people must have been long worked up by the French and Poles to have become so bad'.[21]

The defenceless Frederick William was obliged to nominate a liberal ministry. A newly formed Citizens' Guard, made up principally of students wearing a Teutonic version of the Calabrian look, took up sentry duty at the palace, and the king had to come out onto the balcony and doff his hat to the corpses of those killed by his troops, which were paraded around the city. Also paraded around the city were Mierosławski and the other Polish would-be insurgents of 1846, who had been freed by the mob and hailed as heroes. The king was obliged to promise autonomy to his Polish provinces, whither the liberated heroes set off to prepare a country-wide insurrection. Frederick William was being hailed as the leader of the German nation, and had to ride around Berlin behind the hated and hitherto banned German tricolour.

The black, red and gold colours had been officially adopted by the Bundestag at Frankfurt, which had already passed a number of laws permitting the individual states to repeal repressive legislation such as the Karlsbad Decrees. It also voted to summon a new all-German parliament. On 31 March, 574 delegates to the preliminary Vorparlament met in Frankfurt. The Baden delegates Friedrich Hecker and Gustav von Struve demanded the immediate proclamation of the German Republic. On 4 April the Vorparlament decreed that the partitions of Poland had been illegal and the duty of the German people was to restore the country's independence. A few weeks later the new Austrian government would declare that 'Free Austria will bring freedom to Poland, and with the support of Europe, will not hesitate to fight Russia in order to realise so high an ideal.' Obliged to give in to exorbitant demands, the Austrian imperial court abandoned Vienna and retreated to Innsbruck. The monarchy was effectively at war on two fronts in defence of its dominions in Italy and Hungary, and a third front was threatening to open in its Polish one. Metternich's beloved settlement of 1815 was being blown to bits.[22]

From Switzerland, Friedrich Hecker led a legion of volunteers into Baden, aiming to link up with one of émigrés enlisted in Paris by the poet Georg Herwegh in order to provide armed support for the nascent German republic. The length and breadth of Europe, poets, sectarians and demagogues ranted from balconies to crowds assembled in streets and squares below, waving an assortment of tricolour flags. Every week brought news of barricades going up, gaols being broken open, and concessions being granted by panicked rulers. Student 'legions' marched about in support of their own and other people's causes, dressed in fantastic editions of the Calabrian look. Émigrés of every nationality joined in, shouting slogans of solidarity. The excitement even appeared to have crossed the Channel, and on 10 April London braced itself for the worst as the Chartists marshalled their forces.

There had been a lull in activity by the various working men's associations, partly as a consequence of the harsh clampdown on the events of 1842. A number of towns had created bodies similar to the Metropolitan Police in 1835, and following the disturbances of 1838–42 some counties established their own constabularies. The fall-off in agitation was partially explained also by the improvement in living conditions during the 1840s: food prices fell, and the repeal of the Corn Laws in 1846 removed both one of the factors which had made them rise and one of the targets of the agitation. Some historians have identified a concomitant cultural explanation. The meetings and conventions of the first pro-reform societies, founded in the 1780s, had given rise to an associational culture which had gradually evolved into something which by the 1840s absorbed more and more of the energy of those involved. With their charters and constitutions, their often formalistic procedures, their agendas, motions, resolutions and minutes, the various unions and associations gave humble people a Pickwickian sense of their own dignity and worth. The attendant ceremonial of marching behind banners and hymn-singing, with addresses which were little short of sermons, added ritual which complemented or even replaced church attendance. There was an overlap between pro-reform and unionist activism and that of a growing number of other activities which also helped to divert energy, such as Sunday schools, oratorio societies, choirs, bands and sporting clubs, and a growing number of causes, such as pacifism and animal welfare. The propertied classes and civic authorities encouraged such trends among the working classes, with employers laying on dinners and outings, and with the provision of public amenities such as Preston's Moor Park, opened in 1844, with its bandstand, lake and public conveniences.

Conditions began to decline again in 1847, and this revived the Chartist cause in early 1848. While there were some food riots in Glasgow and Manchester, the protests were conducted in orderly manner, and revolved around presenting a petition to Parliament, supposedly signed by six million people. A mass meeting was held on Kennington Common in south London on 10 April to deliver it. Mindful of events taking place across the Channel, the government refused permission for the 150,000 or so Chartists to approach Westminster, and closed the bridges over the Thames. A vast number of special constables were enrolled, and a sizeable military force was assembled under the command of the Duke of Wellington. There was no violence, and the petition was delivered in three hansom cabs. Place's and Lovett's charter repeated in almost every detail what a Reform Committee in Westminster, of which Charles James Fox had been a member, had drafted fifty-eight years before, and once again it was ignored.[23]

On 18 May the new German National Assembly met at Frankfurt. Heinrich von Gagern, just old enough to have fought at Waterloo, a dedicated *Burschenschafter* and a moderate liberal, was elected president. The Assembly's composition bore out every one of Metternich's prejudices, including as it did more than a hundred university professors and two hundred lawyers, not to mention dozens of journalists and literati of one kind or another. There was a holiday atmosphere, and the members leapfrogged each other in making declarations of support for various causes and solidarity with other nations. The clamour for the liberation of Poland was accompanied by violent diatribes against 'barbaric' Russia and the need to push it back into Asia.

Nicholas responded with a manifesto. 'Following the sacred example of our Orthodox forefathers, after invoking the help of God the Almighty, we are ready to meet our enemies, wherever they may appear, and, without sparing ourselves, we shall, in indissoluble union with our Holy Russia, defend the honour of the Russian name and inviolability of the borders,' it ran. With its battle-cry 'for faith, Tsar, and fatherland', Russia would show the world. 'God is with us! Understand this, O nations, and submit, for God is with us!'[24]

He ordered all Russians travelling abroad to return home – which proved a headache for the Third Section, as some 90,000 flooded into the country, spreading news of events taking place abroad, and revolutionary ideas with it. Motivated by the need to recount sensational events, letters also poured in from abroad, some 400,000 to St Petersburg alone, all of which needed to be checked. Nicholas could see the danger. 'Gentlemen! I have no police, I do not like them,' he proclaimed in an address to the gentry. 'You are my police. Each one of you is my steward and must, for the sake of peace in the state, bring on his own to my knowledge every evil doing and transgression he has noticed.' 'God alone can save us from the general ruin,' he confided on 30 March, but he did not trust in God alone. He ordered Field Marshal Paskevich to bring all the fortresses along Russia's western frontier into a state of readiness and to mass his troops in Poland in order to repel invasion. Martial law was declared in border areas.[25]

He need not have troubled. In France, the revolution never evolved. Lamartine's provisional government was a random gathering of socialists and philanthropists rather than Jacobins bent on overturning the social order. The elections held in April returned three times as many Orléanists and legitimists as Jacobins, and more moderate liberals than those three categories put together. Disappointed by the results, those on the extreme left resorted to agitation in the streets, and on 15 May held a mass demonstration, ostensibly to force the government to support Polish national aspirations. They swamped the guards outside the Chamber and swarmed in, took over and appointed a new government, then marched on the Hôtel de Ville, but were dispersed by the National Guard. This kind of behaviour dissipated any goodwill the middle classes might have felt towards the workers, and paved the way for a swing to the right. When the workers attempted an insurrection in June, they were savagely crushed by the National Guard, assisted by newly-formed *Gardes Mobiles*, unemployed workers drafted in for the occasion (Karl Marx would refer to them as a 'despicable lumpenproletariat', 'the dregs of society'). Beyond the capital, armed peasants scoured the countryside in gangs looking for 'revolutionaries' to kill. 'The Republic is fortunate, it has the power to order troops to shoot at the people,' Louis-Philippe commented when he heard of the bloody repression of the insurrection. There had been nothing to stop him from doing the same, except his own compassion, and such feelings were out of date. Events in Paris were, with minor variations, replicated elsewhere.[26]

Once the original excitement of wringing a few concessions from helpless rulers had died away, profound cleavages appeared between the various elements which had contributed to the revolts. The more moderate felt they had achieved their purpose and wanted to whistle the workers back to their slums, so that they themselves could settle down to reap the benefits. At the other end of the scale, the inarticulate masses who had believed revolution would bring them manna from heaven were shocked to discover that they were condemned to remain as hungry, miserable and downtrodden as before, and they reacted with fury. This in turn alarmed moderates naturally sympathetic to the downtrodden but not prepared to countenance violent social upheaval; they closed ranks with the authorities and enthusiastically participated in the counter-revolution. In rural areas, local interests or religious affiliation often kept the poorest classes firmly behind the existing order, and sometimes savagely hostile to the revolutionaries. Armies, when properly led, did their duty and did not fraternise with revolutionaries. The officers had their own world-view, caring more for their regiments, their families, their horses and dogs than for politics of any kind, and while they nurtured a deep dislike of policemen and officials, particularly those applying fiscal regulations, they had no fondness for writers or demagogues, and little understanding of political theory.

By the end of April, Struve was in gaol, and Hecker and Herwegh had fled to the safety of Switzerland, their legions having been scattered by loyal troops. The Austrian army bombarded an incipient rising in Kraków into submission. In July Field Marshal Radetzky defeated the Sardinian forces at Custozza and Charles Albert sued for peace, leaving the Milanese and Venetian rebels to their fate. In August the emperor was back in Vienna, and in the course of the next three months the counter-revolution triumphed in Austria and Prussia, emboldening the other rulers in Germany to repeal the reforms they had conceded and claw back prerogatives they had abdicated.

In November, the pope, who had been overtaken by the momentum of the reforms he had put in train, left Rome, where a republic came into being in February 1849. It drew to itself nationalists from all over Italy, and revolutionaries and Romantics from all over Europe, with the flamboyant Giuseppe Garibaldi at the forefront. Venice was still holding out heroically against an Austrian siege, and the Hungarians under Kossuth were valiantly defending their independence against Austrian and Russian armies. But by the summer of 1849 it was all over. The Roman Republic was extinguished by, of all things, an army despatched by the French Republic, acting jointly with Austrian troops. On his return to Paris once the trouble was over, the composer Hector Berlioz noticed that even the Spirit of Liberty atop the column on the place de la Bastille had a bullet-hole in it.[27]

When the dust settled it became clear that the events of 1848 had changed nothing much. The only monarchy which had fallen, that of Louis-Philippe, had been the most liberal in Europe. It was replaced, in 1852, by a far more reactionary Napoleonic empire. The only difference between this one and that destroyed at Waterloo was, as Herzen, now an émigré, quipped, that a *grande police* had replaced the *Grande Armée*.[28]

'It is shameful,' Princess Metternich wrote to Countess Nesselrode from Brighton in September 1848, describing the abject state to which the sovereigns of Germany had been reduced, 'when one knows how few the perfidious agitators are, merely a few nasty Jews and some miserable professors!' It had taken but a small leap of the imagination to get from the bankers to the Jews, who were henceforth part of the grand conspiracy. Preposterous as the princess's statement may have been, the fact was that although 1848 is generally called the Year of Revolution, it is arguable whether any of the multiple disorders actually added up to anything one could call a revolution.[29]

Between January 1848 and the middle of 1849, a series of randomly opportunistic riots with wildly differing motivations had coincided with equally opportunistic attempts by the King of Sardinia to enlarge his realm and the Hungarian nobility to wrench their land from Austrian rule. The hopes of the Mazzinians who had started it all in Palermo in January were incomprehensible to the men they stirred up, who did not know what the word '*Italia*' meant. The demands of the Parisians who fought on the barricades were for the right to work and to organise unions, for a ten-hour day, the abolition of debtors' prisons, extension of the suffrage, and so on. But in Alsace the 'revolutionaries' had attacked Jewish homes and synagogues; at Bourg it was a monastery; at Besançon the *mairie*; elsewhere customs houses; in the country, people helped themselves to wood from state forests while Luddites tore up railway lines and destroyed bridges, power looms and textile mills.[30]

In Germany, the only nationwide urge was the wish for a unitary state, and overwhelmingly for a German empire rather than a republic. Most of the demands made – for constitutions, the lifting of censorship, trial by jury, and so on – were fully concordant with the provisions of the Vienna settlement of 1815. Otherwise, motivation varied by area, and was often entirely localised or restricted to specific interests, and in rural areas included looting, stealing firewood and score-settling. Much of this was the expression of anger at regulation, taxation and officialdom. In Crefeld, it was silk workers who wanted to create a guild. In Vienna, the sloganeering students had nothing in common with the workers they had helped whip up, and both were despised by the moderate liberals. In Berlin, most historians are agreed, it was the exceptionally fine weather which brought out the crowds, and there would have been no revolution if it had been pouring with rain. Many of the revolts were characterised by a carnival atmosphere and a degree of levity, and their original success was due entirely to the incapacity and weakness of the rulers, whose thoughts turned to 1789 every time they were faced with a riot.[31]

With his ponderous urge to classify, Karl Marx delivered his own verdict on the causes. 'The eruption of the general discontent was finally accelerated and the sentiment for revolt ripened by *two economic world events*,' he wrote in his *Class Struggles in France*. 'The *potato blight* and the *bad harvests* of 1845 and 1846 increased the general ferment among the people.' It had been a 'struggle of the people for the first necessities of life!' This was nonsense, and does not explain why the barricades in Dresden were manned by Marx's capitalist friend Friedrich Engels, the anarchist Mikhail Bakunin and the composer Richard Wagner, none of whom would have agreed on a single policy, and all of whom certainly did not lack for the first necessities of life. In Lombardy-Venetia, while the nationalists waved their tricolour, in rural areas much of the disorder was no more than the expression of discontent over state interference in property rights, land-use and taxation. In Poland and Hungary the motivation was exclusively nationalist, and directed by moderately liberal nobility who had no intention of upsetting the social order. In Germany, the interference of radicals, and particularly of outsiders, often distorted the original motivation or overtook it completely, turning what had been an explosion of anger over economic conditions or some local issue into an attempt to bring about upheaval that might favour their own cause, be it world anarchy in the case of Bakunin, or the liberation of Poland in that of the many unattached Polish émigrés with nowhere to go and nothing to do except join in the action.[32]

One thing is self-evident: it had not been what the rulers and their ministers all over Europe had been anticipating with horror since the 1790s. 'The revolution of 1848 had everywhere the character of hastiness and precipitate action,' noted Herzen, who had witnessed the events in Paris and in many parts of Germany, adding that there 'it had a farcical character'. He was struck by the number of 'actors' apparently leading the disturbances, poseurs with no conviction or attachment to any particular cause. Far from leading events, both Marx and Engels were caught unawares. With their *Communist Manifesto* they attempted to impose a programme, but they spent the year chasing the various outbursts, desperately trying to get to the scene of the action, and mostly arriving when it was all over. Nowhere was there any sign of anyone, let alone any body, directing anything. There was no transnational cooperation. There was no attempt to overthrow the social order. There had never been any great conspiracy or any *comité directeur* – but the forces of repression had been given a golden opportunity to consolidate, and the police were there to stay.[33]

Aftermath

Beginning in the early 1790s, the British cabinet, the Habsburg monarchy and the rulers and ministers of Russia, Prussia and virtually every other state in Europe consistently misled and repressed those they governed, invoking a threat which they failed to substantiate. In some instances they appear to have believed in it, in others they patently did not. Mostly, one suspects, they fell into that grey area of self-delusion in which politicians come to believe anything they have invented out of expediency. But whether they believed in the threat or not is ultimately immaterial: the damage was done.

Perhaps the most damaging legacy is a wholly imaginary vision of the political and therefore the social sphere as a permanent conflict between the privileged and the underprivileged; a paradigm of the rich and influential ensconced in their citadels besieged by a violent, anarchic mass of the poor and deprived, led by mad-dog terrorists bent on storming those citadels and overturning the social order. This notion has bedevilled European and worldwide political discourse ever since.

More immediately, the unnecessary repression of moderate liberal tendencies arrested the natural development of European society, more in some countries than in others, and helped to create a culture of control of the individual by the state. In the more repressive states, it led to the alienation of generations of young people, resulting in the growth of real terrorist movements in the second half of the nineteenth century.

In Austria, the threat of the grand conspiracy was used to justify the preservation of an order which acted as a brake on economic development, as did the ruinous expenditure on the army needed to maintain it. The long-term consequence was that the Habsburg dominions were left far behind other parts of Europe, and while the provinces of Venetia and Lombardy flourished economically after they broke away from Austrian domination in 1860, the rest of the monarchy remained economically backward as well as politically supine.

In Russia, Alexander's and Nicholas's attempts to mould society into an obedient instrument of the state had the effect of driving thinking young people into opposition – moral, intellectual and artistic at first, murderous from the 1860s onwards. They introduced much that would later form the basis of the Soviet model of control: the benevolent menace of Benckendorff's *Gendarmerie* would shape the invasive and sinister power of the Cheka and the NKVD. In 2010, Nikolai Patrushev, director of their descendant, the FSB, described his force in terms Benckendorff would have recognised, referring to it as 'our new nobility'.[1]

In Germany, the repression of national aspirations, following as it did on Napoleon's humiliation of German national pride, turned legitimate patriotism and national feeling into a defensive, embittered subculture which, denied legitimate expression, grew increasingly angry and aggressive, with disastrous consequences for the whole world in the twentieth century.

As Mazzini put it, writing in 1849: 'The masters of the world had united against the future.' But they had also left a poisoned chalice no less toxic than the *acqua tofana* whose menace exerted such a spell. When the future caught up with them, in 1917–18, it detonated a series of events which would cost the lives of untold millions and lead to the near-destruction of European civilisation.[2]

Notes

Abbreviations

AAE – Archives du Ministère des Affaires Étrangères, Paris
AN – Archives Nationales, Paris
APP – Archives de la Préfecture de Police, Paris
BdS – Bertier de Sauvigny
CP – Correspondance Politique
HHSA – Hof- Haus- und StaatsArchiv
HHStAW – Hessischesches Haupstaatsarchiv, Wiesbaden
HStAD – Hessisches Staatsarchiv, Darmstadt
HStAS – Landesarchive Baden-Württember, Hauptstaatsarchiv, Stuttgart
MD – Mémoires et Documents
MM – Metternich, *Mémoires*
ÖStA, AVA – Österreichische StaatsArchiv, Allgemeine Verwaltungsarchiv, Vienna
PHSt – Polizeihofstelle
PRONI – Public Record Office of Northern Ireland, Belfast
TNA – The National Archives, Kew

Chapter 1: Exorcism

1. Maistre, *Lettres et opuscules*, I/274
2. Noailles, I/143; Cockburn, 11, 19; Shorter, 60
3. Cockburn, 5; Garros, 483
4. *Le Camp de Vertus*, 20–1
5. Edgcumbe, 151ff, 157
6. Zorin, 306–7, 312–13, 316, 321; Empaytaz, 40; Mikhailovskii-Danilevskii, 264–6; Shilder, *Imperator Aleksandr*, III/341–2; Krüdener, 5, 10
7. Empaytaz, 41; Angeberg, 1547–9; Zorin, 299
8. Droz, 217; Rudé, *Revolutionary Europe*, 285
9. Rey, 54–7
10. Rey, 53, 61
11. Rey, 104
12. Ley, 62
13. Ley, 100, 103, 139, 229; Zorin, 306–7

Chapter 2: Fear

1. Fox, II/361
2. Ségur, III/508; Rey, 86
3. Romilly, I/272
4. Schenk, 73
5. Fairchild, 50; Wollstonecraft, VI/140; Wordsworth, *Prelude*

6. Wangermann, 46; Zamoyski, *Holy Madness*, 75
7. Gooch, 317; Burke, *Letters*, VI/459; Cleves, 59
8. Maistre, *Soirées*, I/269, 329; Maistre, *Considérations*, 65, 69
9. Bonald, *Oeuvres*, I/1–4
10. *Essai*, 50–67
11. Ziolkowski, 69–74, 84; Wilson, in Bahr & Saine, 33–4
12. Roberts, 168; Rogalla von Bieberstein, 18–155
13. Barruel, I/39, 42
14. Barruel, II/33
15. Barruel, II/39–41, I/43, II/519, 524–5
16. Grenby, 66
17. Broers, *Napoleon's Other War*, 20
18. Barruel, II/527

Chapter 3: Contagion

1. La Mare, I/268
2. Cobb, *The Police and the People*, 22; Manuel, II/299ff, 312–13
3. See Birn, Darnton
4. Emsley, *Policing*, 1; Manuel, I/292, II/86
5. Cobb, *The Police and the People*, 14
6. Bibl, *Die Wiener Polizei*, 233
7. Bibl, *Die Wiener Polizei*, 234
8. Bibl, *Die Wiener Polizei*, 235–7, 271; Gebhardt, 60–1
9. Hughes, 12–13
10. Armitage; Archer, 58–9; Colquhoun, III/9–10, 316–17
11. Wangermann, 40; *Repercusiones*, 125, 123; Aris, 62
12. Bibl, *Die Wiener Polizei*, 257
13. Wangermann, 62; ÖStA, AVA, Pergen Akten, Karton 13; Karton 15, konvolut 1; Wegert, 42ff
14. Bibl, *Die Wiener Polizei*, 262–3, 266–7
15. Roider, 118–9
16. Bibl, *Die Wiener Polizei*, 278
17. Bernard, 180–1
18. Wangermann, 118
19. Wangermann, 122–6
20. Bibl, *Die Wiener Polizei*, 285–9; Wangermann, 127
21. Bibl, *Die Wiener Polizei*, 270–1, 297; Wangermann, 173–4
22. Bibl, *Die Wiener Polizei*, 274–7
23. Brauer, 5–7; Wangermann, 142–3
24. Roider, 86, 141
25. Miles, II/345; Nicolson, 87

Chapter 4: War on Terror

1. Polovtsov, *Gertsog*, 125; Roider, 129
2. Zamoyski, *Holy Madness*, 91
3. Roider, 150; ÖStA, AVA, Pergen Akten, Karton 15, konvolut 7
4. Bernard, 201; Wangermann, 171–2
5. Bernard, 201, 211; Brauer, 9; Wangermann, 128ff, 133–52, 156–9
6. Wangermann, 170; Brauer, 6
7. Wangermann, 171–2
8. Haag, in Brauer, 112–13
9. TNA, TS 24/1/9, 952; 11/95
10. Mori, *Pitt*, 86, 90–1
11. Burke, *Reflections*, 86, 131, 173, 166; Mori, *Britain in the Age of the French Revolution*, 40; Brown, P.A., 77
12. Brown, P.A., 80–1; Archer, 60–1
13. Cobbett, *The Parliamentary History*, 826
14. Burke, *Letters*, VII/489, VI/211, 218, VII/177, VI/81–3, 100, 451, VII/119, 170, 229, 260, 357, 489
15. Romilly, I/351, 349
16. Emsley, *Repression*, 802–3; Brown, 83, 94; Stevenson, *Popular Disturbances*, 178
17. Brown, P.A., 168, 171; Emsley, *Insurrection*, 68–77; Mori, *Pitt*, 128
18. Mori, *Pitt*, 176, 123
19. Hilton, 62; Emsley, *Insurrection*, 85
20. Hilton, 65; Sparrow
21. Sparrow
22. Brown, P.A., 67
23. Stevenson, *Popular Disturbances*, 178, 41

24. Brown, P.A., 133–4
25. Brown, P.A., 138–9, 62: TNA, TS 952–7
26. Emsley, *Britain*, 32; Brown, P.A., 137, 142–6; Stevenson, *Popular Disturbances*, 160–7; Emsley, *Britain*, 38; Mori, *Pitt*, 180
27. *Second Report from the Committee of Secrecy of the House of Commons*, 1794, 2; Brown, P.A., 142–6, 135–6
28. Mori, *Pitt*, 191–2, 241; Hansard, XXXI/502; TNA, TS 24/1/9, p.5
29. *First Report from the Committee of Secrecy of the House of Commons*, 1794
30. *Second Report from the Committee of Secrecy of the House of Commons*, 1794, 13
31. *Second Report from the Committee of Secrecy of the House of Commons*, 1794, 6–7
32. *Second Report from the Committee of Secrecy of the House of Commons*, 1794, 72
33. Brown, P.A., 118, 141
34. Mori, *Pitt*, 242; Brown, P.A., 125–6
35. Emsley, *The Home Office*, 552
36. Brown, P.A., 136, 126–9; TNA, TS 24/1/9, 4; TS 952, 14; TS 11/951, no. 3

Chapter 5: Government by Alarm

1. Thale, xxiv; Mori, *Pitt*, 250; Harrison, 4
2. Emsley, *Repression*, 804
3. Mori, *Pitt*, 226, 261, 275–6; Sparrow; Stevenson, *Popular Disturbances*, 183–4
4. Stevenson, *Popular Disturbances*, 186; Chorley, 131–3
5. Brown, P.A., 146; Royle, 27
6. Burke, *Letters*, VIII/93, 131, 242, 245, passim
7. Stewart, 25
8. Royle, 31; McCalman, 10
9. *Report from the Committee of Secrecy of the House of Lords in Ireland*, 1798, 7
10. Hilton, 81; Stewart
11. *Report from the Committee of Secrecy of the House of Commons in Ireland*, 1798, 6
12. *Report of the Committee of Secrecy of the House of Commons*, 1799, xli
13. Thale, xxiv
14. Hone, *For the Cause of Truth*, 60–1, 78
15. Emsley, *Britain*, 37; Brown, P.A., 154–5
16. Johnston, 162, 19, 113, 36–7
17. See Beaurepaire
18. Brown, P.A., 168, 171; Moylan, 18–21, 3–5
19. Burke, *Works*, VIII/214–15, 256, 185–7, 188
20. Burke, *Works*, VIII/141, IX/110
21. Burke, *Works*, IX/103–5, 109, 110, 118ff
22. Archer, 62–4; Stevenson, *Popular Disturbances*, 313
23. Cleves, 86–9, passim; Cobbett, *Peter Porcupine*, 18–20, 99, 241, 256
24. Wilson, 15–16
25. Wilson, 255, 16, 57ff
26. McCalman, 60
27. Grenby, 41, 57
28. Grenby, 67–9, 90, 115; Wallace, 189, 223
29. De Quincey; TNA, TS 11/285; Gilmartin, in Clemit, 140; Burke, *Letters*, VIII/254; Payson; Playfair; *Jacobinism Displayed*; Gilmartin, in Clemit, 140, 142; Reith, 105
30. Burke, *Letters*, VII/387, 552–3
31. Worral, 53; TNA, TS 11/122/333, HO 42/66
32. Hilton, 100–1

Chapter 6: Order

1. Cobb, *The Police and the People*, 50
2. Cobb, *The Police and the People*, 50–1
3. Cobb, *Reactions*, 79, 44

4. Cobb, *Reactions*, 41
5. Cobb, *Reactions*, 69, 75, 65–6
6. Lignereux, 13, 23, 97–8; Broers & Guimera, 52–3
7. Hauterive, *Napoléon et sa Police*, 43, 46, 48; Castanié, 26–7
8. Fouché, I/79, 320, 323; Aubouin, 286
9. Vaillé, 213, 231, 244
10. Aubouin, 286; Canler, 73
11. Fouché, II/8, I/411
12. *The Annual Register 1844*, 450
13. Darvall, 19–21, 54
14. Alison, III/21–2
15. Darvall, 64–5, 76–80
16. Hansard, XXIII, 1035
17. Wordsworth, 148
18. Pellew, III/84; White, 116, 119
19. Hansard, XXIII, 953–4, 1029–37; Palmer, 178; Darvall, 260
20. White, 99, 118
21. White, 118; Pellew, III/87–8, 94–5
22. Fraser, 13
23. Schenk, 122

Chapter 7: Peace

1. Mazour, 15; Sked, *Metternich*, 120
2. Pellew, III/132
3. Polovtsov, *Gertsog*, 370ff, 379
4. Montlosier, III/1
5. Boigne, II/5, 82; Romilly, II/390–1; Maistre, *Correspondance diplomatique*, II/193, 348
6. Maistre, *Corrrespondance diplomatique*, II/116
7. Uvarov, *L'Empereur Alexandre*, 37; Talleyrand, III/217
8. Broglie, I/262
9. Maistre, *Lettres & opuscules*, I/261; Maistre, *Correspondance Diplomatique*, II/92; Villèle, I/239, passim
10. Maistre, *Correspondance diplomatique*, II/351–2
11. Sturdza, 15; Bonald, I/4
12. Bonald, II/517

Chapter 8: A Hundred Days

1. Wilson, 14–15
2. Boigne, II/34–5; Vaillé, 349–50; Zamoyski, *Rites of Peace*, 449–51
3. Polovtsov, *Correspondance*, I/155; Marmont, VII/87, 92
4. Broglie, I/295, 297
5. Alexander, *R.S.*, 84–5
6. Waresquiel, *Talleyrand*, 491
7. Alexander, *R.S.*, 222–7
8. Castellane, I/309; Marmont, VII/200
9. Marmont, VII/188; Broglie, I/331; Noailles, II/68–82; Boigne, II/134–5
10. Marmont, VII/193ff
11. Polovtsov, *Correspondance*, I/77
12. Chevalier, 225; Polovtsov, *Correspondance*, I/367, 377, 379, 382; Richelieu, 4
13. Waresquiel, *Richelieu*, 265
14. *Mémoires d'une femme de qualité*, II/47
15. Polovtsov, *Gertsog*, 461, 466
16. Pasquier, IV/99; Polovtsov, *Correspondance*, I/364

Chapter 9: Intelligence

1. Castlereagh, XI/232, 230–1
2. Castlereagh, XI/223–4
3. Langeron, 63
4. Castanié, 1; Fouché, I/200
5. Daudet, *Police Politique*, 246; *Mémoires d'une femme de qualité*, III/311–13
6. Daudet, *Police Politique*, 152, 156
7. Boigne, II/200–1
8. Daudet, *Police Politique*, 173
9. AN, F/7/3028, 3029, 9762, 9763, 9764, 3838; Hazareesingh, 97–8
10. AN, F/7/6727; Hazareesingh, 124, 131; Merriman, 33; Lignereux, 100
11. AN, F/7/3824; Lignereux, 100–1, 109
12. Vidocq, III/355–6
13. Villèle, II/215; Merriman, 33
14. Aubouin, 312; Peuchet, VI/63–5; Daudet, *Police Politique*, 2–3;

Froment, I/35; Spitzer, 64–5; Peuchet, V/312, VI/61–3, 178
15. Peuchet, VI/65–7
16. Peuchet, V/328–33
17. Ploux, 131–3; Hazareesingh, 47
18. AN, F/7/3054, 9908; Hazareesingh, 45–7, 50, 60–2
19. Hazareesingh, 542, 54–5, 57–8; AN, F/7/6668, 6816
20. Hazareesingh, 45; Peuchet, VI/143
21. AN, F/7/3029; Hazareesingh, 84–5, 87, 147
22. Daudet, *Police Politique*, 103, 113; *Carte Segrete*, I/226; BdS, *Metternich et Decazes*, 66
23. Daudet, *Police Politique*, 118–22
24. Daudet, *Police Politique*, 136
25. Daudet, *Police Politique*, 138, 142; AN, F/7/3029, 6668
26. Richelieu, 46, 148, 152
27. Richelieu, 133–4, 62, 149, 183; Castlereagh, XI/381, XII/240–1
28. Richelieu, 186; Benhamou, 146
29. Richelieu, 46, 151, 189, 190, 195, 223–4; Montchenu, 49, 125–6; Stürmer
30. Guillon, 43; APP, AA/328–9, 333, 340; Spitzer, 23
31. Berton, 27, 29–30
32. Raisson, 292–5
33. Froment, II/146–7, 174, 376, 390, 392; Peuchet, IV/335–6; Guizot, *Des Conspirations*, 62, 56–7; Raisson, 243, 246
34. Richelieu, 9, 36; Polovtsov, *Correspondance Diplomatique*, I/398; Guillon, 85; Ducoin; Pasquier, IV/111–14
35. APP, AA/333; AN, F/7/6816; Richelieu, 30–1, 33
36. AN, F/7/6667; Guillon, 82–3; Canler, 111; Grasilier, *Un Secretaire*, 24
37. Polovtsov, *Gertsog*, 490; Richelieu, 109
38. Guillon, 91, 102
39. Guillon, 95ff; Marmont, VII/233–43; APP, AA/340
40. Pozzo di Borgo, III/253; Wellington, *Supplementary Despatches*, XII/271–92, 302–3, 329–30, 601; AAE, 7 MD Angleterre/61, no. 24; APP, AA/342; Noailles, III/240; AN F/7/3839
41. Guillon, 99–103; AN, F/7/3054; Noailles, III/289–97, 302–3, 316; Langeron, 181; Polovtsov, *Correspondance Diplomatique*, I/747; Wellington, *Supplementary Despatches*, XII/600
42. Peuchet, VI/108–24, 177–8; Noailles, III/115; Pasquier, IV/172–82
43. Wellington, *Supplementary Despatches*, XII/380, 397, 213

Chapter 10: British Bogies

1. Wellington, *Supplementary Despatches*, XI/561; Alison, III/50–2
2. Southey, IV/145, 147, 210
3. Martineau, *The History of England*, I/243
4. Pellew, III/148
5. Hunt, Henry, III/348ff, 344, 366ff; Martineau, *The History of England*, I/53; TNA, TS 11/204, 11/197, 11/203, 3; Bamford, 25; Gronow, 198–9, who commanded a company of Guards at the Spa Fields meeting of 15 November, considered it 'a most dangerous period' and thought the speeches could not have been 'more violent and treasonable'
6. Pellew, III/165–6; White, 97
7. Hunt, Henry, III/429
8. *The Annual Register 1817*, 5–12
9. *The Annual Register 1817*, 13–18
10. *The Annual Register 1817*, 10, 17–19
11. TNA, TS 11/204, 3, 11/199, 11/198
12. *The Annual Register 1817*, 14; TNA, TS 11/204, 3, 11/203, 2
13. TNA, TS 11/203
14. Pellew, III/169–77

15. *The Annual Register 1817*, 25–6; Hansard, XXXV, 547, 553, 554, 561, 573, 582–3; Bartlett, 183
16. TNA, TS 11/197; Romilly, II/460
17. Thomis, 51–8; White, 166; Bamford, 156–8
18. Bartlett, 186; Wallas, 121
19. Wallas, 120; White, 146; Hunt, Henry, III/366ff, 480; Porter, 49–50; McCalman, 110; Hazlitt, IV/194
20. Bamford, 37, 43, 77; Wallas, 122; White, 150–1; Marlow, 64; *An Exposure of the Spy System*
21. Martineau, *The History of England*, I/345; Brown, 172–3; Pellew, III/212–13, 217, 185–96, 211; Romilly, II/483–4
22. Thomis, 47–8
23. McCalman, 108–110; Martineau, I/53; TNA, TS 11/198; PRONI, D3030/5310; Wellington, *Supplementary Despatches*, XI/696
24. McCalman, 109; TNA, TS 11/202; Hilton, 28
25. Bamford, I/120ff

Chapter 11: Moral Order

1. Bibl, *Metternich. Der Dämon*, 47; Polovtsov, *Gertsog*, 121–6
2. Metternich, *Lettres*, 172
3. Schenk, 10
4. Stokes, in Brauer, 69, 75–6, 79–82
5. Reinerman, *Austria and the Papacy*, I/108ff
6. Rath, *The Provisional Austrian Regime*, 23–6, 74; Sked, *Metternich and Austria*, 186–8
7. Keates, 28
8. Rath, *The Provisional Austrian Regime*, 190–9
9. Reinerman, *Austria and the Papacy*, I/31–2
10. Rath, *The Provisional Austrian Regime*, 273–315
11. *Carte Segrete*, I/129, 74–150; Rath, *The Provisional Austrian Regime*, 222
12. Rath, *The Provisional Austrian Regime*, 225; for the secret societies in general, see also: Derek Beales, *The Risorgimento and the Unification of Italy*, London 1971; René Albrecht-Carrie, *Italy from Napoleon to Mussolini*, New York 1950; John Rath, 'The Carbonari', in *The American Historical Review*, vol. 69, No. 2, January 1964; Renato Soriga, *Le Società Segrete, l'emigrazione politica e i primi moti per l'independenza*, Modena 1942; *Memoirs of the Secret Societies of the South of Italy, particularly the Carbonari*, London 1821; J.M. Roberts, *The Mythology of the Secret Societies*, London 1972; Carlo Francovich, 'L'Azione rivoluzionaria risorgimentale e i movimenti della nazionalità, in Europa prima del 1848', in *Nuove Questioni della Storia del Risorgimento e dell'Unita d'Italia*, Milan 1961, vol. I
13. MM, III/27; BdS, *Metternich et son Temps*, 118
14. Bew, 430; Webster, 184
15. MM, III/88–94; Bibl, *Metternich. Der Dämon*, 219
16. Emerson, 62, 64, 69; *Carte Segrete*, I/49–50
17. *Carte Segrete*, I/179; ÖStA, AVA, Inneres, Polizei, PHst 3606, 824, 1084
18. Rath, *The Provisional Austrian Regime*, 230–5
19. Bew, 499
20. Consalvi, 128–9, 139; Emerson, 61
21. Hughes, 40–1; *Carte Segrete*, I/165
22. Hughes, 45, 47, 78
23. Hughes, 57
24. La Harpe, III/253–4; Beyle, *Rome, Naples et Florence*, 154; Shelley, I/200; Herzen, II/641
25. Origo, 103
26. Origo, 104–7

Chapter 12: Mysticism

1. Nicholas Mikhailovich, *L'Empereur Alexandre*, I/141
2. Rey, 405; Benckendorff, *Vospominania*, 269; Borovkov, 353
3. Zorin, 250–3
4. Ley, 167–72; Webster, 97; Rey, 428–9; Webster, 65, 88, 93, 96–7
5. MM, III/54; Rey, 381; Shilder, *Imperator Aleksandr*, IV/173
6. Rey, 403–4; Gentz, *Dépèches*, I/380
7. Ley, 203, 242; Nicholas Mikhailovich, *L'Empereur Alexandre*, II/224; MM, III/51–3
8. Ley, 197–8
9. Webster, 409, 419, 423, 424; Srbik, I/569–70
10. Lebzeltern, 359–60
11. Nicholas Mihkailovich, *Doniesienia*, 34; Polovtsov, *Correspondance*, I/475, 546, 222, II/95, 102; AN, F7/6667; Wellington, *Supplementary Despatches*, XI/632; PRONI, D3030/5310
12. Polovtsov, *Correspondance*, II/155, also I/405–8, 512, 385; Pozzo di Borgo, II/47, also 48–9, 64–5, 446–53
13. Polovtsov, *Correspondance*, II/772; Pozzo di Borgo, II/429; BdS, *Metternich et la France*, I/71–2, 74, 114–16; BdS, *Metternich et Decazes*, 63, 67–70, 73, 75; Boigne, II/353, 371; Pasquier, IV/220; Polovtsov, *Correspondance*, II/650; Waresquiel, *Richelieu*, 529
14. Schenk, 123–4; Srbik, I/573; Emerson, 39; Wellington, *Supplementary Despatches*, XII/261
15. Webster, 55, 143, 124; Bew, 451, 455–6; Lebzeltern, 369–71; BdS, *Metternich et son Temps*, 135–7; HHSA, Gesandschaft Archiv, St Petersburg, 073
16. MM, III/124–5
17. MM, III/127
18. Bew, 453
19. Shilder, *Imperator Aleksandr*, IV/111, 114–15, 118, 120; Nicholas Mikhailovich, *Doniesienia*, 29, 34; Nicholas Mikhailovich, *L'Empereur Alexandre*, I/200; Lebzeltern, 373
20. Webster, 151, 157
21. Webster, 142–3, 170
22. MM, III/175, 174
23. Sweet, 217–19
24. Shilder, *Imperator Aleksandr*, IV/124; AN F/7/6667
25. Metternich, *Lettres*, 17; Lieven, *Kniaginia*, 37
26. Metternich, *Lettres*, 11, 13, 19–20, 17
27. Shilder, *Imperator Aleksandr*, IV/124; Dubrovin, *Bumagi*, 433, 500–1; Wellington, *Supplementary Despatches*, XII/829, 832–4
28. Metternich, *Lettres*, 21–2, 23, 36
29. Shilder, *Imperator Aleksandr*, IV/129
30. Srbik, I/569–70, 573, 584

Chapter 13: Teutomania

1. Metternich, *Lettres*, 39, 43–50, 59–60, 63–6, 78–9, 88–90
2. Langeron, 166
3. Webster, 200; Wellington, *Despatches*, I/2, 7–8; BdS, *Metternich et la France*, II/304
4. BdS, *Metternich et la France*, I/223
5. BdS, *Metternich et la France*, I/226–7
6. Nesselrode, VI/37, 29
7. Siemann, 180; Baack, 30, 58–60
8. Clark, *The Wars of Liberation*, 559
9. Mann, 220, 246
10. Hippler, 196ff; Clark, *The Wars of Liberation*; Castlereagh, XI/106; Pozzo di Borgo, I/219–23, see also 229, 234, 236, 249; Nicholas Mikhailovich, *Doniesienia*, 1–5
11. Mann, 266
12. Simon, 120
13. Branig, *Fürst Wittgenstein*, 69
14. Obenaus, 91–7

15. Obenaus, 97–101; Hüber, 148
16. Obenaus, 93–4; Branig, *Fürst Wittgenstein*, 69; Hüber, 148; Siemann, 67
17. Obenaus, 103; Branig, *Fürst Wittgenstein*, 72; Siemann, 68; HHSA, Staatskanzlei Notenwechechsel mit der Polizeihofstelle, 56
18. Simon, 121
19. Branig, *Fürst Wittgenstein*, 8
20. Branig, *Fürst Wittgenstein*, 67, 73; Siemann, 68; Obenaus, 122–3
21. Obenaus, 107
22. Branig, *Fürst Wittgenstein*, 103–4; Obenaus, 108; Schenk, 124
23. Simon, 135; Obenaus, 122
24. HHSA, Gesandschaft Archiv, St Petersburg, 073; BdS, *Metternich et son Temps*, 161; Emerson, 114
25. Sturdza, 40–1, 65–6
26. Görres, 173; Gagern, 61–4; Turgenev, I/521;

Chapter 14: Suicide Terrorists

1. Williamson
2. MM, III/232–5
3. Metternich, *Lettres*, 301; MM, III/235
4. Sweet, 220; Gentz, *Briefe*, III/1/387; Baack, 57; MM, III/228, 185ff, 262
5. Clark, *Iron Kingdom*, 401; Levinger, 142
6. Lombard de Langres, v, ix, xi; HHStAW, Abt. 210: 1255, no 50, Abt. 211, Nr. 13679, Abt. 12553, Abt. 3541, Nr. 5.6
7. Lombard de Langres, 30, 40, 174, 254
8. Lombard de Langres, 44, 227
9. Wellington, *Despatches*, I/55, 59; Nesselrode, VI/43, 48, 54, 62, 79–80
10. Wellington, *Despatches*, I/56, 60–2, 66; BdS, *Metternich et Decazes*, 83; Polovtsov, *Diplomaticheskie snoshenia*, 183
11. BdS, *Metternich et la France*, I/227ff
12. BdS, *Metternich et son Temps*, 153; MM, III/253; Zimmermann, 259–60
13. Metternich, *Lettres*, 315; MM, III/224, 225
14. MM, III/270, 271–5; HHSA, Gesandschaft Archiv, St Petersburg, 073; Baack, 65
15. Marlow, 66; Webster, 498
16. White, 179; McCalman, 140–2
17. Marlow, 92; Bamford, 180–1; AAE, 8CP Angleterre, 612, No. 97, 186
18. Marlow, 93; Bamford, 183, 186
19. Marlow, 101–2
20. White, 182; Marlow, 118
21. Hunt, Henry, III/613; Read, 81, 135
22. Bamford, 205–13, 220–5; Pellew, III/253–61; Marlow, 118–52
23. Read, 141–2
24. Edgcumbe, 68; Pellew, III/278
25. Pellew, III/270–1, 298
26. Wellington, *Despatches*, I/76, 80–1
27. Woodward, 63; Marlow, 154
28. Martineau, *History of England*, I/239; Wellington, *Despatches*, I/87
29. Moylan, 97, 99
30. Thomis, 66, 75; *An Exposure of the Spy System*; Berry, III/190
31. MM, III/226; Schenk, 99
32. Baack, 65
33. HStAS, Bestand E 65, 1
34. MM, III/295–6; HHStAW, Abt. 211/7995; Büssem
35. Branig, *Briefwechsel*, 132; Emerson, 128; Liang, 19–20; Legge, 41; Hoffmann, 276–83
36. Branig, *Briefwechsel*, 132; Siemann, 187; Hüber, 150; Obenaus, 111, 113–14, 125
37. Legge, 42; Siemann, 78
38. Schenk, 91–2; La Harpe, III/373, 423
39. Legge, 52; Gentz, *Briefe*, III/1/482; Schenk, 99–100; Büssem, 356; Gagern, 64–6
40. Bartlett,215; Webster, 190–2; BdS, *Metternich et son Temps*, 163; *Metternich et Decazes*, 101
41. Gentz, *Dépèches*, I/421; MM, III/263

42. Nicholas Mikhailovich, *Doniesienia*, 59, 61, 63; Gentz, *Dépèches*, I/432–3; Lebzeltern, 374–83

Chapter 15: Corrosion

1. Wellington, *Despatches*, I/100; Gentz, *Dépèches*, I/19–20; Pasquier, IV/378
2. Lamartine, V/265; AN, F/7/3839
3. *Mémoires d'une femme de qualité*, III/411; Ploux, 36–43
4. APP, AA/343, 346; Boigne, III/42–3; *Conjuration Permanente*; *Histoire complète*; Guizot, *Des Conspirations*; *L'Homme de Gibeaux*
5. MM. III/335; Nicholas Mikhailovich, *Doniesienia*, 219; *L'Empereur Alexandre*, II/285, 300; Polovtsov, *Correspondance*, III/328; Wellington, *Despatches*, I/99–100; HHSA Gesandschaft Archiv, St Petersburg, 011
6. *The Annual Register 1820*, 1; Aylmer, 19
7. Porter, *Plots*, 58; Aylmer, 58, 48; TNA, TS 11/204; Martineau, *History of England*, I/244
8. Reith, 207; Hone, *For the Cause of Truth*, 306, 325, 340; Wellington, *Despatches*, I/106; Neumann, 18–19; McCalman, 139; TNA, HO 41/6, 41/26
9. Hone, *For the Cause of Truth*, 302; TNA, HO, 40/11, 41/6, 41/26, 16–17; Marlow, 158–60
10. Canler, 240–2; Pasquier, V/95
11. Wellington, *Despatches*, I/101, 107–8, 112; Polovtsov, *Correspondance*, III/330, 354ff, 346
12. BdS, *Metternich et la France*, II/307; Nicholas Mikhailovich, *Doniesienia*, 220–1, 225, 307–8; Gentz, *Dépèches*, II/54
13. Pasquier, IV/499; Polovtsov, *Correspondance*, III/330; BdS, *Metternich et la France*, II/306; Nicholas Mikhailovich, *Doniesienia*, 228; Webster, 235; see also TNA, FO 92/44; Wellington, *Despatches*, I/117
14. BdS, *Metternich et la France*, II/305
15. Polovtsov, *Correspondance*, III/384
16. Roy
17. Noailles, IV/354; Barante, II/438–9; Spitzer, 45, 55; Polovtsov, *Correspondance*, III/390ff
18. Lieven, *Letters*, 48
19. Wellington, *Despatches*, I/127, see also 141, 144–5, 146; Robins, 125–8; Greville, I/32; Palmer, 172; Lebzeltern, 389
20. Robins, 165, 236, 182–3; Hone, *For the Cause of Truth*, 318; Wellington, *Despatches*, I/144ff
21. MM, III/254
22. Webster, 260; Gentz, *Dépèches*, II/68–9
23. Gentz, *Dépèches*, II/68–9; Romani, 6
24. Castlereagh, XII/284; Origo, 203; Pasquier, IV/526; Webster, 263
25. Gentz, *Dépèches*, II/70; BdS, *Metternich et la France*, II/317, 324
26. Schroeder, 38–9
27. Schroeder, 39
28. Siemann, 81–2; Weber, 82
29. MM, III/407, 435–6; AAE, 112 CP, Russie, 161, 57; Consalvi, 268; AAE, 33 MD, Naples, 11, 13; 9 MD, Autriche, 46
30. Dubrovin, *Bumagi*, 472
31. Shilder, *Imperator Aleksandr*, IV/192
32. Consalvi, 33
33. BdS, *Metternich et la France*, II/318, 330; AAE, 33 MD, Naples, 11

Chapter 16: The Empire of Evil

1. Moriolles, 134–5
2. Mounier, 17–18
3. AN F/7/6676, 6702–3, 6991; APP, AA/353–9
4. Castanié, 288, 291; Mounier, 17–18; Marmont, VII/266–280; Guillon, 115ff; Peuchet, VI/108–24; APP, AA/353; Barante, II/502; Grasilier, *Un Secrétaire*, 36

5. Dubrovin, *Bumagi*, 16; Pasquier, IV/534–5; Schroeder, 48; BdS, *Metternich et la France*, II/361; HHSA, Gesandschaft Archiv, St Petersburg, 075, 10 September 1820
6. Gentz, *Dépèches*, II/89
7. Grimsted, 254, 272–3; *Carte Segrete*, I/185ff; Capo d'Istria, 244
8. Capo d'Istria, 251; Castlereagh, XII/301; Consalvi, 289–90
9. Polovtsov, *Doniesienia*, 548; Lebzeltern, 388
10 Webster, 283; Castlereagh, XII/311ff; Pellew, III/332
11. BdS, *Metternich et la France*, II/353–6; Webster, 277
12. Polovtsov, *Gertsog*, 552–3, 560ff
13. MM, III/373; BdS, *Metternich et la France*, II/417
14. Gentz, *Dépèches*, II/86; MM, III/373; Nicholas Mikhailovich, *Doniesienia*, 231
15. Webster, 288
16. Schroeder, 64; Webster, 524
17. Dubrovin, *Bumagi*, 22,109; Shilder, *Imperator Aleksandr*, IV/527ff; Nicholas I, *Pisma*, 263–4
18. Nicholas Mikhailovich, *L'Empereur Alexandre*, I/233; Oleinikov, 191; Shilder, *Imperator Nikolai*, I/2/603; Wellington, *Despatches*, I/491; Shilder, *Imperator Aleksandr*, IV/186–8; Greville, I/67
19. Shilder, *Imperator Aleksandr*, IV/185, 189
20. Nesselrode, VI/110–11
21. AAE, 112 CP, Russie, 142, 146; HHSA, Gesandschaft Archiv, St Petersburg, 011
22. MM, III/377
23. Polovtsov, *Gertsog*, 557ff; Grimsted, 248; Webster, 290; Polovtsov, *Correspondance*, III/493
24. Webster, 299, 303–4
25. Schroeder, 100
26. Schroeder, 77–9
27. BdS, *Metternich et la France*, II/414–15; Consalvi, 311
28. Consalvi, 326, 330, 335, passim; Capo d'Istria, 261; Lebzeltern, 396–9
29. Gentz, *Dépèches*, II/116–18; Webster 528
30. Shilder, *Imperator Aleksandr*, IV/191; BdS, *Metternich et la France*, II/415
31. Dubrovin, *Bumagi*, 29
32. MM, III/384; Rey, 436; BdS, *Metternich et la France*, II/393
33. Dubrovin, *Bumagi*, 34

Chapter 17: Synagogues of Satan

1. BdS, *Metternich et la France*, II/417
2. Gentz, *Dépèches*, II/122–3
3. Schroeder, 252
4. Sweet, 233; Polovtsov, *Gertsog*, 582–3
5. Schroeder, 107
6. Polovtsov, *Gertsog*, 586
7. Dubrovin, *Bumagi*, 37, 46; MM, III/451
8. Dubrovin, *Bumagi*, 43; Polovtsov, *Gertsog*, 587, 589, 598
9. Nicholas Mikhailovich, *L'Empereur Alexandre*, I/221–30
10. MM, III/460, 494; Polovtsov, *Gertsog*, 612
11. Baack, 83; Nicholas Mikhailovich, *L'Empereur Alexandre*, I/535
12. Moriolles, 185; Webster, 358, 360
13. Nicholas Mikhailovich, *L'Empereur Alexandre*, I/535–7
14. BdS, *Metternich et la France*, II/481, 486
15. Consalvi, 378–9, 374; Spadoni, 3, 10, 22–3, 6; Roberts, 332
16. MM, III/463; BdS, *Metternich et son Temps*, 95
17. Reinerman, *Metternich and the Papal Condemnation*, 60, 56; MM, III/481–2; BdS, *Metternich et la France*, II/506
18. MM, III/504–5, 508
19. Polovtsov, *Gertsog*, 624–6

20. Armitage, 220; Palmer, 173–7
21. Capo d'Istria, 269; Nicholas Mikhailovich, *L'Empereur Alexandre*, II/375; BdS, *Metternich et la France*, II/512
22. Baack, 83
23. Bignon, 3–4

Chapter 18: *Comité Directeur*

1. Waresquiel, *Richelieu*, 409; Hazareesingh, 68
2. Spitzer, 63; Guillon, 129; Guizot, *Des Conspirations*, 21–2, 24, 28–9; Guizot, *Mémoires*, I/24; Corcelle, 11
3. Guillon, 144
4. Corcelle, 5, 7–8, 9–12; Rémusat, II/58; AN, F/7/6667, 6684, dossier 5, 6685, 6686; Spitzer, 241; Dumas, I/446; Blanc, I/75ff
5. Guillon, 157ff, 167ff, 177, 192, 212ff
6. Blanc, I/125; *Paris Révolutionnaire*, I/275
7. Canler, 76; Peuchet, V/308–9
8. Canler, 74–5
9. Grasilier, *Un Secrétaire*, 35; AN, F/7/6969; Broglie, II/380–1; Froment, III/342–3; BdS, *La France et les Français*, 143
10. Froment, III/144; Desmarest, lxxff
11. Année, I/224
12. Gisquet, II/33, 34, 36–7
13. Canler, 243
14. Canler, 46, 243–8; Peuchet, V/312; see also Année, III/2–12
15. Année, II/115–21; AN, F/7/12292; APP, AA/333
16. Peuchet, V/356ff; Année, IV/158ff
17. Canler, 49–51
18. Annee, III/289, II/28ff
19. Année, II/117, 84, I/98; Grasilier, *Un Secrétaire*, 42
20. Grasilier, *Un Secrétaire*, 8; Desmarest, vii; Spitzer, 70
21. Grasilier, *Un Secrétaire*, 38
22. Grasilier, *Un Secrétaire*, 8, 18, 20–2, 27
23. Grasilier, *Un Secrétaire*, 23–4, 30; APP, AA/328, 329, 340
24. AN, F/7/6684, dossiers 6, 7, 9
25. Guillon, 146; Grasilier, *Un Secrétaire*, 32, 40–2, 45ff, 27, 34; Année, II/72–4; BdS, *Metternich et la France*, II/565–6; Shilder, *Imperator Aleksandr*, IV/547; AN, F/7/12292

Chapter 19: The Duke of Texas

1. Webster, 343; Greville, I/67
2. Lebzeltern 422; Nicholas Mikhailovich, *Doniesienia*, 93, 99, 112–13, 114
3. Schroeder, 200; BdS, *Metternich et la France*, II/600, 565
4. Webster, 429, 470
5. HHSA, Gesandschaft Archiv, St Petersburg, 013, No. 40, 16 May, 038, 5 June; Webster, 472–3
6. Webster, 541
7. Webster, 484
8. MM, III/556–7; Wellington, *Despatches*, I/284ff
9. HHSA, Gesandschaft Archiv, St Petersburg, 038, 22 June; MM, III/559
10. Brydges, 110
11. Chateaubriand, *Le Congrès de Vérone*, 117; Thürheim, III/322–4
12. Wellington, *Despatches*, I/332, 298
13. Schroeder, 147–8; Wellington, *Despatches*, I/210–13
14. Schroeder, 155
15. Reinerman, *Metternich, Italy and the Congress of Verona*, 284
16. Reinerman, *Metternich, Italy and the Congress of Verona*, 263–81; *Austria and the Papacy*, 110–11
17. Lieven, *Letters*, 57
18. Brydges, 127, 120–2; Chateaubriand, *Le Congrès de Vérone*, 69, 116
19. Metternich, *Lettres*, 325; Urquhart, 20–7
20. Allen, II/260–1, 278–9, 284, 286; Ley, 297

21. Wellington, *Despatches*, I/343–8, 457, 491
22. MM, III/615; Keates, 30
23. Schroeder, 232–3; Canning, I/69, 72, 86
24. Spitzer, 197–8; Emsley, *Gendarmes*, 99; Ploux, 55, 131–3, 180
25. Schroeder, 232–3
26. Corcelle, 12; MM, VII/657

Chapter 20: The Apostolate

1. MM, IV/107, 92; Nicholas Mikhailovich, *Doniesienia*, 273
2. Nesselrode, 189–91; Obenaus, 115; Wegert; Legge, 40; HStAS, Bestand E 65
3. Obenaus, 116, 112
4. HStAS, Bestand E 65; Obenaus, 116, 120–1; Nicholas Mikhailovich, *Doniesienia*, 292
5. BdS, *Metternich et la France*, II/894–5; MM, IV/143, 111
6. Liang, 21, 23; HHSA, Diplomatische Korrespondenz, Deutsche Akten, Alte serie, 135; Hüber, 154
7. Wilmot, 41; Sealsfield, 84–5
8. Sealsfield, 85
9. Sealsfield, 31–2; Wilmot, 41; HHSA, Inneres Polizei, PHSt, 26, 8446, 3906, 3755
10. Emerson, 122, 125
11. ÖStA, AVA, Inneres, Polizei, PHst 824, 9039, 8060, 9328, 603, 8446; HHSA, Diplomatische Korrespondenz, Deutsche Akten, alte serie, 135; *Carte Segrete*, II/7–138
12. HHSA, PHSt, Notenwechsel, 56/4, 5, 6; Gebhardt, 167–70; HStAS, Bestand, E 50/01; HHStAW, Abt, 211, Nr. 16210, 904
13. Bibl, *Wiener Polizei*, 314; Gebhardt, 169
14. Emerson, 51
15. Beyle, *Rome, Naples et Florence*, 101, 166, 172; Emerson, 65
16. *Carte Segrete*, II/231–64
17. Origo, 301–5; BdS, *Metternich et la France*, II/592
18. Hughes, 67–8
19. Hughes, 75–7
20. BdS, *Metternich et son Temps*, 173; *Carte Segrete*, II/271, I/402–516, 371–97; Witt, xiii, 7–8, 25, 85ff; Spitzer, 65; AN, F/7/6684, dossier 2, 6686, 6688, 6689
21. Roberts, 322; Andryane, I/104–5; AN, F/7/6667, 6685, 6686
22. Witt, 134–5
23. AN, F/7/6685
24. AN, F/7/6685
25. Confalonieri, I/153–82; Nicholas Mikhailovich, *Doniesienia*, 280

Chapter 21: Mutiny

1. Grimsted, 63
2. Hingley, 21; Oleinikov, 106; Saint Glin, 36, 24ff, 378
3. Nicholas Mikhailovich, *L'Empereur Alexandre*, I/266
4. Flynn, 100
5. Flynn, 104, 111
6. Shishkov, 1101; see also *K Istorii Russkoi Tsenzury*; Monas; 136; Shilder, *Imperator Aleksandr*, IV/267–8
7. Rey, 395–6, 447; Shilder, *Imperator Aleksandr*, I/514; Boigne, III/194–6
8. Ley, 281–2
9. Monas, 52; Shilder, *Imperator Aleksandr*, IV/252; Riasanovsky, *A Parting of Ways*, 85; Turgenev, I/101–5, 106–8; Nicholas Mikhailovich, *L'Empereur Alexandre*, II/263–4; HHSA, Staatskanzlei, Notenwechsel, 56, 1
10. Turgenev, I/119, 174–5; Mazour, 132
11. Turgenev, I/176
12. Mazour, 151, 114
13. Kulomzin; Maistre, *Correspondance diplomatique*, II/178, 233, 308; Polovtsov, *Diplomaticheskie*

Snoshenia, 65; Nicholas Mikhailovich, *L'Empereur Alexandre*, II/417–22
14. Monas, 46; Dubrovin, *Bumagi*, 157; Shilder, *Imperator Aleksandr*, IV/548–50; Oleinikov, 192–3; Gernet, I/172–3, 175
15. Shilder, *Imperator Aleksandr*, IV/203, 204–15; Gentz, *Dépèches*, III/71–3; Shilder, *Imperator Nikolai*, I/1/170
16. Shilder, *Imperator Aleksandr*, IV/337ff, 410ff; *Imperator Nikolai*, I/1/177ff; Borovkov, 331–5; Benckendorff, Zapiska, 82–6; Edelman, 44
17. Shilder, *Imperator Nikolai*, I/2/623–6
18. *Mezhdutsarstvie*, 39, 89, 16; Villamov, 96, 113; Mazour, 163ff; Edelman, 48, 50; see also Nesselrode, 270, 272
19. AAE, MD 43, Russie, 28, 122; AAE, CP 112 Russie, 169, 170; Custine, *La Russie*, II/39–44
20. Marmont, VIII/36; Lubomirski, 258
21. Lubomirski, 65; Dubrovin, *Materialy*, 21, 41, 37; *Mezhdutsarstvie*, 11; Grunwald, 23–5; Polievktov, 10
22. Grunwald, 23–5
23. Lubomirski, 202; Grunwald, 84–5; Nicholas I, *Perepiska*, 131
24. *Mezhdutsarstvie*, 87
25. Grunwald, 64; Raeff, 27; Borovkov, 335ff
26. Shilder, *Imperator Nikolai*, I/2/635–8; Monas, 76
27. Shilder, *Imperator Nikolai*, I/2/525, 434; Vock, 172–3; Borovkov, 341
28. *Mezhdutsarstvie*, 101; Shilder, *Imperator Nikolai*, I/2/423, 425–6, 521; Neumann, 132; Grunwald, 81
29. Turgenev, I/192–3; Shilder, *Imperator Nikolai*, I/2/429–430; see also Moriolles, 135–6

Chapter 22: Cleansing

1. Polievktov, 75
2. Oleinikov, 183; Benckendorff, *Vospominania*, 305
3. Oleinikov, 229–30, 235–6, 254, 274
4. Oleinikov, 104; Kulomzin, 214; Monas, 47; Squire, 46–7; Shilder, *Imperator Nikolai*, I/1/163–4, I/2/493; *Tolki i nastroienie*, 677; Nicholas Mikhailovich, *L'Empereur Alexandre*, II/271–5; May, I/99
5. Benckendorff, *Proiekt*, 104, 615–16; see also Gershenzon, 163–5
6. Oleinikov, 269, 288; Vock, 168; Monas, 101
7. Dubelt, 495; Squire, *The Third Department*, 59; Stogov, 108; Oleinikov, 267, 270; Monas, 65
8. Benckendorff, *Instruktsia*; Nicholas Mikhailovich, *l'Empereur Alexandre*, I/266
9. Vock, 183
10. Vock, 175; Trotskii, 18; Dmitriev, 259–60; Oleinikov, 106; Vock, 193; Dmitriev, 259, 261
11. Oleinikov, 233; Trotskii, 18, 21
12. Trotskii, 28–30; Monas, 66–8; Shilder, *Imperator Nikolai*, I/2/427–9
13. Vock, 185, 189; Trotskii, 31; Bokova, 591ff, 611
14. Trotskii, 34–6; Monas, 80–1
15. Trotskii, 36–8
16. Ruud, 14–15; Anisimov, 13, 26ff, 50–2, 80–1, 147; Czerska, 109–10
17. Monas, 90–1; Bokova, 591ff; Trotskii, 33; Shilder, *Dva Donosa*, 518–35; Monas, 90–1, 116
18. Shilder, *Dva Donosa*, 67–84
19. Shilder, *Dva Donosa*, 85–7, 628–9
20. Riasanovsky, *Nicholas I*, 231; Monas, 12
21. Gershenzon, 130–1, 139
22. Benckendorff, *Pismo*, 1753–8
23. Trotskii, 16–17
24. May, II/309
25. Constantine Pavlovich
26. Dubrovin, *Bumagi*, 479, 534–42; Monas, 86, 82–3

Chapter 23: Counter-Revolution

1. Broglie, II/416; Marmont, VIII/3–4; Année, II/507ff
2. BdS, *Metternich et la France*, III/1123–5, 1127; *Metternich et son Temps*, 212
3. Année, IV/1–2
4. Turgenev, I/185; BdS, *Metternich et son Temps*, 187; MM, IV/418, 350; Lebzeltern, 474–5; Gentz, *Dépèches*, III/61, 74, 76–7
5. BdS, *Metternich et son Temps*, 28
6. Merriman, 103; Lamartine, VIII/61
7. Broglie, III/157; Burleigh, 135; Cubitt, 16, 20, 25
8. AN, F/7/6997, 14282; Marmont, VIII/186–9
9. AN, F/7/6997, 1827, 6991, 6988, 6668
10. Canler, 94
11. AN, F/7/6767, 3880, 6753, 4174
12. Blanc, I/125
13. Marmont, VIII/238ff
14. AN, F/7/4174
15. Broglie, III/258
16. Haussez, II/232–3, 236; Broglie, IV/11; Blanc, I/112
17. AN, F/7/4174
18. Broglie, III/304; Béranger, 241
19. Boigne, III/342ff; Claveau, 9ff
20. Blanc, I/140ff, 193
21. Wellington, *Despatches*, VII/183; Blanc, I/199
22. Wierzbitski, 265
23. Baack, 234–6; Wegert, 108
24. Marmont, VIII/346; Lieven, *Correspondence*, II/36; Wellington, *Despatches*, VII/172
25. Wakefield, 26; Wallas, 244; TNA, HO 44/20, 21
26. Rudé, *The Crowd*, 150, 151–5; Archer, 17–18
27. Hobsbawm and Rudé, 254
28. McCalman, 28–9, 181
29. Hobsbawm and Rudé, 253, 255–6; Wellington, *Despatches*, VII/321
30. Lieven, *Correspondence*, II/74–5

Chapter 24: *Jupiter Tonans*

1. BsS, *Metternich et la France*, III/1358–62
2. Bibl, *Metternich*, 213
3. MM, V/23; Nesselrode, VII/152
4. Bibl, *Metternich. Der Dämon*, 251–5
5. Baack, 232, 166–9
6. Nicholas I, *Perepiska*, 36; Grunwald, 115
7. Shilder, *Imperator Nikolai*, II/1/318
8. Moriolles, 277
9. Sidorova, 67; Skarbek, 228; Shilder, *Imperator Nikolai*, II/2/455; Polievtkov, 121, 3; Dubrovin, *Materialy*, 12–14
10. Benckendorff, *Imperator Nikolai*, 13, 11, 5–6
11. Pienkos, 43–4, 47
12. Nicholas I, *Perepiska*, 42–3
13. Nicholas I, *Perepiska*, 36; Tatishchev, *Imperator Nikolai*, 65; Nicholas I, *Perepiska*, 67–8; Shilder, *Imperator Nikolai*, II/2/472–3; Sidorova, 69–70
14. Shilder, *Imperator Nikolai*, II/2/471; Grunwald, 129–30
15. *The Portfolio*, 3; Kosellek, 419
16. Reinerman, *Austria and the Papacy*, I/169
17. Thürheim, III/322–4
18. Lieven, *Letters*, 235, 246, 259
19. Fraser, 44; Lieven, *Letters*, 268; Wellington, *Despatches*, VII/354
20. TNA, HO 44/21, f.415
21. Ascoli, 98–9
22. Greville, II/68, 75, 77
23. Greville, II/99, 108
24. Wellington, *Despatches*, VII/355–6, 373, 375
25. MM, V/30, 46, 53, 152–4, 126–7, 138; BdS, *Metternich et son Temps*, 170
26. Emerson, 134
27. Seide, 159–60; MM, V/73, 76, 80
28. Bibl, *Metternich*, 213–14, 215
29. Apponyi, I/429

30. Sked, *Metternich*, 121; Bibl, *Metternich*, 219–23; Sweet, 300
31. Lieven, *Letters*, 289, 298, 300; Wellington, *Despatches*, VII/444, 352–3, 451
32. Nesselrode, VII/173; Lieven, *Letters*, 304, 324
33. Hobsbawm and Rudé, 259–62; Rudé, *The Crowd*, 155
34. Wellington, *Despatches*, VII/543–4, 556–7; Wallas, 295–6
35. Palmer, 389; Fraser, 169
36. Wellington, *Despatches*, VIII/30–3, 35; Fraser, xiii

Chapter 25: Scandals

1. Mann, 281–2
2. Mann, 299–300, 301–2, 304–5; Bibl, *Metternich*, 221
3. MM, V/536, 48, 58, 59, 222; Bibl, *Metternich*, 218; Lieven, *Correspondence*, II/104
4. Sked, *Metternich*, 20–1
5. Wegert, 103; Neigebaur
6. Bibl, *Metternich in neuer Beleuchtung*, 221–3; *Metternich*, 256–9; Baack, 249–53
7. Wierzbitski, I/265–6
8. Bibl, *Metternich in neuer Beleuchtung*, 303–5, 247; HHSA, Staatskanzlei, Diplomatische Korrespondenz, Deutsche Akten, alte serie, 217; Wierzbitski, I/267
9. MM, V/319
10. Bibl, *Metternich in neuer Beleuchtung*, 311
11. Wallas, 310
12. Wallas, 301ff
13. Bibl, *Metternich in neuer Beleuchtung*, 318
14. MM, V/286; Müller, 25–6; Bibl, *Metternich in neuer Beleuchtung*, 327–9; Siemann, 87; Bibl, *Metternich*, 261
15. MM, V/351, 368
16. Bibl, *Metternich*, 237
17. Wierzbitski, 267; Clark, *Iron Kingdom*, 440, 446–7
18. Siemann, 213–15; Legge, 116; HStAD, Best. G 2 A, Nr. 52/5
19. Wegert, 178
20. Wegert, 198ff; Obenaus, 118; Hüber, 153
21. Obenaus, 118–19; Hüber, 152
22. Bibl, *Metternich. Der Dämon*, 262; *Metternich in neuer Beleuchtung*, 190–2, 369, 197; Meyendorff, I/24
23. Meyendorff, I/33–7
24. Bibl, *Metternich*, 247
25. Bibl, *Metternich*, 240; see also Tatishchev, *Imperator Nikolai*, 69–78
26. Bibl, *Metternich*, 240–2
27. MM, V/603, 617
28. Duggan, 26
29. Mack Smith, *Mazzini*, 121
30. MM, IV/267
31. ÖStA, AVA, Inneres Polizei, PHSt H22, 1093; HStAD, Best. GA, Nr. 52/5; Fenner von Fenneberg, 131–2; HHSA, Staatskanzlei, Notenwechsel, 57; HHSA, Statenabteilung, Frankreich, Varia, 99
32. Bibl, *Metternich in neuer Beleuchtung*, 422; HHSA, Statenabteilung, Frankreich, Varia, 99; Noiriel, 62; Grandjonc, 12, 90–1; MM/V/599; Siemann, 130–3; Reiter, 28–32
33. Meyendorff, I/58–60
34. Squire, *Metternich and Benckendorff*, 161, 369, 370, 380; MM, VI/83
35. Squire, *Metternich and Benckendorff*, 376
36. MM, VI/52
37. Wellington, *Despatches*, VIII/368; Fraser, 264; Southey, VI/175, 213, 222; Bibl, *Metternich in neuer Beleuchtung*, 358
38. Harrison, 60, 4, 292–301; Ascoli, 104–5

39. Dino, I/185, 220, 254; Moore, 222; MM, V/292, 621–3

Chapter 26: Sewers

1. Gisquet, I/241
2. La Hodde, 12ff
3. La Hodde, 66–7; Chenu, 12
4. La Hodde, 67–8; Gisquet, I/366
5. Dumas, II/343, 508
6. Blanc, III/202
7. La Hodde, 145; Perreux, 64, 49; Gisquet, I/366; Guizot, *Mémoires*, III/205ff
8. Chevalier, xx–xxiii
9. Perreux, 19, 364
10. Gisquet, I/464, 471–3; Noiriel, 46, 50–2; AN F/7/6758, 6988
11. Gisquet, II/16–17, 29, 36; Chenu, 25–7, 29–30; Merriman, 10, 114
12. Perreux, 307–9, 361–2
13. Perreux, 310–13
14. Lieven, *The Correspondence of Lord Aberdeen*, 39; Maillé, 93; Trollope, *Paris*, I/130, 321ff
15. Joinville, 249
16. Du Camp, *L'Attentat Fieschi*, 63–6, 140, 149–51; Blanc, II/137; there were also large sections of the public who imagined his reported undying love for Lassave to have a redeeming quality that turned him into a kind of hero in their minds. See, for example, Dino, II/13
17. MM, VI/46–7, 148; Dino, II/78–9
18. Lieven, *The Correspondence of Lord Aberdeen*, 50; Girardin, I/45
19. Rémusat, III/383
20. Rémusat, III/406; Antonetti, 818; Tulard, 80
21. Aubouin, 327–8
22. Chevalier, 225
23. Rémusat, III/390
24. Girardin, II/202; Lieven, *The Correspondence of Lord Aberdeen*, 53–4, 57, 63, 74, 125; Maillé, 94
25. Guizot, *Mémoires*, VIII/1ff; Rémusat, III/377
26. Rémusat, III/382; Du Camp, *L'Attentat Fieschi*, 270–1
27. La Hodde, 402–5, 474

Chapter 27: The China of Europe

1. Royle, 183, 189
2. *The Annual Register 1838*, 204–5
3. Rudé, *The Crowd*, 156
4. Hilton, 612–13; Rudé, *The Crowd*, 182–4; Palmer, 455ff
5. Freitag, 211
6. Squire, *Metternich and Benckendorff*, 377
7. MM, VI/364
8. Squire, *Metternich and Benckendorff*, 383–5
9. Squire, *Metternich and Benckendorff*, 387–8
10. Gisquet, I/464, 471–3; Noiriel, 46; AN F/7/6758, 6988
11. ÖStA, AVA, Inneres, Polizei, PHSt 9039, 420, 821; MM, VII/209
12. BdS, *Metternich et son Temps*, 110, 115
13. Sked, *Metternich*, 167–8; Emerson, 45–6; Maistre, *Correpondance diplomatique*, II/244; Vaillé, 316
14. BdS, *Metternich et son Temps*, 117
15. Maistre, *Correspondance diplomatique*, II/242–4; Squire, *Metternich and Benckendorff*, 160
16. Vaillé, 354–5, 361–3, 376
17. Schenk, 77–8
18. Schenk, 77; Gebhardt, 171; Bibl, *Die Wiener Polizei*, 300, 302–6; Mack Smith, *Victor Emmanuel*, 7
19. La Harpe, III/590; *Carte Segrete*, II/306; MM, VII/140; Bibl, *Metternich*, 283
20. Emerson, 153; Schenk, 154–5; Bibl, *Die Wiener Polizei*, 300
21. Sked, *Metternich*, 146–9
22. Emerson, 151; Schenk, 78; Zamoyski, *Holy Madness*, 198; Sked,

Metternich, 146; Bibl, *Die Wiener Polizei*, 290
23. Bachleitner, *The Politics*, 101–3
24. Keates, 31–2
25. Keates, 32
26. Duggan, 152–4
27. Bachleitner, *Quellen*, 60–9
28. Bachleitner, *The Politics*, 98–101
29. Marx, Julius, *Die österreichische Zensur*, 15, 10; Emerson, 181

Chapter 28: A Mistake

1. Grunwald, 115–16; Blanc, IV/203; Marmont, IX/58; Tatishchev, *Vneshniaia Politika*, 12–18
2. *Nikolai Pervyi*, I/112–14; Shilder, *Imperator Nikolai*, II/2/563–4; Tatishchev, *Imperator Nikolai*, 142–55
3. Squire, *Metternich and Benckendorff*, 155; Henningsen, I/134–7
4. Marmier, I/250
5. Nesserlode, *Lettres*, VIII/243–4
6. Lieven, *The Lieven-Palmerston Correspondence*, 156, 199, 235, 238, 250; Monas, 232; Custine, *La Russie*, III/107
7. Uvarov, *Desiatiletie*, 2
8. Uvarov, *Desiatiletie*, 3
9. Riasanovsky, *Russian Identities*, 135–6
10. Whittaker, 118
11. Herzen, I/105; Riasanovsky, *Russian Identities*, 136
12. Riasanovsky, *Russian Identities*, 145; *Nicholas I*, 217–18
13. Monas, 194–5
14. Oleinikov, 305
15. Oleinikov, 273, 294–6; Gershenzon, 136–7
16. Monas, 134; Gershenzon, 135; Lemke, 50
17. Monas, 121; Riasanovsky, *A Parting of Ways*, 247; *Nicholas I*, 222–3
18. Kohn, 112
19. Riasanovsky, *Nicholas I*, 229; Monas, 12; *Okhranienie*, 24; Figes, 61; Tatishchev, *Imperator Nikolai*, 12–18
20. Herzen, I/134–5, 194, II/433; Monas, 125, 129
21. Herzen, II/436; Marmier, I/262; Trotskii, 70; Oleinikov, 300, 303–4; Monas, 122
22. Dubelt, 501
23. Trotskii, 57–8
24. Trotskii, 66, 70
25. Monas, 64; Oleinikov, 277; Trotskii, 53
26. Selivanov, 291, 299–316
27. Marmier, I/263; Squire, 216, 218–19; Herzen, II/427–8; Bloomfield, I/315–16; see also Henningsen, I/181–96
28. Golovine, I/234, 236–7
29. Herzen, II/457; Monas, 79; Brus, 239
30. Monas, 111–2
31. Milchina, 33; *Zhurnaly Komiteta*; Trotskii, 25–7; Monas, 278; Riasanovsky, *Nicholas I*, 210
32. Grunwald, 231, 233; Smirnova-Rosset, 370–1; Riasanovsky, *A Parting of Ways*, 246; Nesselrode, *Lettres*, VIII/199, 201, 234, 244

Chapter 29: Polonism

1. Tatishchev, *Vneshniaia Politika*, 25
2. Obenaus, 121; Legge, 144
3. Barclay, 49–50
4. Barclay, 63; Meyendorff, I/166
5. Meyendorff, I/205, 164, 127; Dino, III/307–8
6. Wierzbitski, II/214
7. Lüdtke, 69
8. Lüdtke, 134, 148; Best, 211
9. Townsend, 19
10. Meyendorff, I/312–13, 320; Nesselrode, *Lettres*, VIII/276
11. Hamerow, 19–20; Ludtke, 80–1
12. Hamerow, 77
13. MM, VII/52; Bibl, *Metternich*, 298
14. MM, VII/48, 47–51
15. MM, VII/89–91, 379
16. MM, VII/5, 7, passim; *The Annual Register 1844*, 454–5

17. MM, VII/169, 168, 193, 171–219, 242; Bibl, *Metternich*, 272
18. Sked, *The Survival of the Habsburg Empire*, 164ff
19. Bibl, *Metternich*, 273, 272
20. MM, VII/201, 200, 210–11, 205–6, 209
21. MM, VII/281–92
22. MM, VII/227–30
23. Mack Smith, *Victor Emmanuel*, 7, 24; Duggan, 77
24. Davis, 132–3, 137; Hughes, 138
25. Davis, 60, 110
26. Mack Smith, *Victor Emmanuel*, 8
27. MM, VII/249
28. Namier, 5; MM, VII/334, 330
29. Rath, *The Viennese Revolution*, 7; Sked, *The Survival of the Habsburg Empire*; Zamoyski, *Holy Madness*, 301; MM, VII/334, 424
30. Bibl, *Metternich*, 278

Chapter 30: Satan on the Loose

1. MM, VII/583
2. Tocqueville, 615, 603, 757–9
3. Langer, 91–2
4. Antonetti, 839, 887
5. Marie Amélie, 537–8; Gronow, 180
6. Boigne, IV/402–3
7. Gronow, 181; La Hodde, 449, Du Camp, *Souvenirs*, 21–3; Canler, 371
8. Du Camp, *Souvenirs*, 57ff
9. Barrot, I/504–5
10. Bouyssy, 80–1
11. Bouyssy, 81–2, 118, 42
12. Marie Amélie, 538–9
13. Barrot, I/218
14. Gronow, 183; Du Camp, *Souvenirs*, 109; Tocqueville, 798–9
15. Apponyi, IV/153, 159
16. Bibl, *Metternich*, 300; Riasanovsky, *Nicholas I*, 4; Barclay, 134
17. Smirnova-Rosset, 358; Grunwald, 248
18. Bibl, *Metternich*, 302
19. Bibl, *Die Wiener Polizei*, 321–9; *Metternich*, 310–11, 314
20. Nesselrode, *Lettres*, IX/70
21. Barclay, 142–3; Westmorland, Priscilla, 119, 127; Stadelmann, 4
22. Zamoyski, *Holy Madness*, 346
23. Rudé, *The Crowd*, 179; Palmer, 482ff
24. Riasanovsky, *Nicholas I*, 5
25. Monas, 239–40, 242; Riasanovsky, *Nicholas I*, 209; Grunwald, 261
26. Marx, Karl, *Class Struggles*, 52; Antonetti, 919
27. Berlioz, 51
28. Herzen, IV/249
29. Nesselrode, *Lettres*, IX/181–2
30. Rudé, *The Crowd*, 169
31. Stadelmann, 13, 68, 75ff, 42–4
32. Marx, Karl, *Class Struggles*, 38; Hughes, 63
33. Herzen, III/91–2, II/673

Aftermath

1. Lucas, 63
2. Mazzini, 117

Sources

ARCHIVAL

The National Archives, Kew

Treasury Solicitor's Papers: TS 11/197, 11/198, 11/199, 11/200, 11/201, 11/202, 11/203, 11/204, 11/285, 11/951, 11/952, 11/953/, 11/954, 11/955, 11/956, 11/993; 24/1/4, 24/1/5, 24/1/6, 24/1/7, 24/1/9, 24/3/33
King's Bench Papers: KB 33/6/1, 33/6/2
Privy Council Papers: PC 1/21/35A & B
Home Office Papers: HO 40/11, 40/17, 40/19, 40/20, 40/21, 40/22, 41/6, 41/26, 44/21, 79/2
Foreign Office Papers: FO/92/44

Public Record Office of Northern Ireland, Belfast

D3030/3531, D3030/5249, D3030/5250, D3030/5310

Archives Nationales, Paris

Série F/7 Police: 3028, État de personnes arrêtées; 3029, ditto; 3054, Police générale; 3824, Extrais de declarations de conducteurs de diligences; 3839, Rapports de commissaires …; 3850, Bulletins de Police; 3880, Bulletins des Préfets de Police de Paris; 4174, Rapports de la Gendarmerie de Paris; 6667, Complot du 27 janvier 1821; 6668, Personnes attachées aux Bonaparte; 6669, ditto; 6676, affaire du 19 août 1820; 6684–6689, Sociétés Secrètes; 6702–6703, Surveillance des officiers en non-activité; 6727, Gardes du Corps; 6753, Fonds de Police Secrète; 6758, Polonais; 6816, Patriotes de 1816; 6969, Mauvais esprit, etc; 6988, Police générale; 6991, Conspiration de Nantil; 6997, Police générale; 9764, Gendarmerie de Paris; 9908, Police générale; 12292, Circulaires; 12293, Police des journaux

Archives de la Préfecture de Police, Paris

Serie AA: 328, 329, Affaire Lavalette; 333, 334, 335, Affaire des Patriotes, Épingle Noire, etc.; 336–9, Ex-Conventionnels; 340, Conjurés de Lyon; 342, Attentat contre le duc de Wellington; 343, Affaire Louvel; 346–9, 352, Lettres anonymes; 353–9, Conspiration d'août 1820; 361, Affaire de La Rochelle

Archives du Ministère des Affaires Étrangères, Paris

Mémoires et Documents: Angleterre 7MD/61; Autriche, 9MD/46; Naples, 33MD/11, 33MD/13; Russie, 43MD/28

Correspondance Politique: 112CP Russie; 114CP Sardaigne; 8CP Angleterre; 11CP Autriche

Österreichisches StaatsArchiv, Vienna

Allgemeine Verwaltungsarchiv, Polizeihofstelle:

Pergen Akten, 11, 13, 15

Altere Polizei, 25b

Inneres, Polizei, PHst H 22, H 26, H 37, H 155, 15, 43, 70, 79, 157, 173, 251, 309, 603, 821, 824, 1030, 1084, 1093, 2374, 3357, 3606, 3755, 3877, 3906, 5243, 5961, 6884, 7038, 8060, 8446, 9039, 9328, 10.781, 11.420

Haus- Hof- und StaatsArchiv:

Notenwechsel mit der Polizeihofstelle, 55, 56, 57, 58

Staatskanzlei, Diplomatische Korrespondenz, Deutsche Akten, alte serie, 135, 217, 221

Staatenabteilung, Frankreich, Varia, 69, 99, 102, 105

Gesandschaft Archiv: St Petersburg 011, 013, 038, 073, 075

Hessisches Hauptstaatsarchiv, Wiesbaden

Abt. 210, Nr. 2701, 2908, 3541, 3780, 3796, 8317, 12552, 12553, 3541; Abt. 211, Nr. 904, 7995, 13679, 16210; Abt. 295, Nr. 22, 24, 201, 204, 16210; Abt. 1054, Nr. 1–7; Abt. 1097, Nr. B7, B17, B21, B77; Abt. 1255, Nr. 50

Hessisches Staatsarchiv, Darmstadt

Bestand G2A, Nr. 52/5

Landesarchiv Baden-Württemberg, Hauptstaatsarchiv, Stuttgart

Bestand E 50/01 Bü 600, Bü 644, Bü1248; E50/02; E 50/03; E 65 Bü 32; Bü 707; E 301, Bü 897; E 301

PUBLISHED

Agethen, Manfred. *Geheimbund und Utopie: Illuminaten, Freimaurer und Deutsche Spätaufklärung*, in *Ancien Régime, Aufklärung und Revolution*, Vol. XI, Oldenburg 1984

Alexander I, Emperor of Russia, *Correspondance de l'Empereur Alexandre Ier avec sa soeur la Grande Duchesse Catherine*, St Petersburg 1910

Alexander, R.S., *Bonapartism and Revolutionary Tradition in France. The Fédérés of 1815*, Cambridge 1991

Alison, Sir Archibald, *Lives of Lord Castlereagh and Sir Charles Stewart*, Vol. III, London 1861

Allen, William, *Life of William Allen, with Selections from his Correspondence*, 3 vols, London 1846

Alletz, *Dictionnaire de Police Moderne pour toute la France*, 4 vols, Paris 1823

An Account of the Seizure of Citizen Thomas Hardy, Secretary to the London Corresponding Society, etc., London 1794

Ancelot, M., *Six mois en Russie*, Paris 1827

Andryane, Alexander, *Memoirs of a Prisoner of State in the Fortress of Spielberg; by Alexander Andryane*, 2 vols, London 1840

An Exposure of the Spy System pursued in Glasgow in the Years 1816–17–18–19 and 20, etc., Glasgow 1833

Angeberg, Comte d' (Leonard Chodźko), *Le Congrès de Vienne et les Traités de 1815: précédé et suivi des actes diplomatiques qui s'y rattachent, avec une introduction historique par M. Capefigue*, 2 vols, Paris 1864

Anglade, Eugène, *Coup d'Oeil sur la Police, depuis son origine jusqu'à nos jours*, Agen 1847

Anisimov, Evgenii, *Dyba i Knut. Politicheskii sysk i russkoe obshchestvo v XVIII veke*, Moscow 1999

Année, Antoine, *Le Livre Noir de Messieurs Delavau et Franchet, ou Repertoire alphabétique de la police politique sous le ministère déplorable*, 4 vols, Paris 1829

Antioche, comte d', *Chateaubriand Ambassadeur à Londres (1822) d'après ses dépèches inédites*, Paris n.d.

Antonetti, Guy, *Louis-Philippe*, Paris 1994

Apponyi, Rodolphe, *Vingt-cinq ans à Paris, 1826–50. Journal du comte Rodolphe Apponyi*, Paris 1913

Archer, John E., *Social Unrest and Popular Protest in England 1780–1840*, Cambridge 2000

Aris, Reinhold, *History of Political Thought in Germany from 1789 to 1815*, London 1936

Armitage, Gilbert, *The History of the Bow Street Runners 1729–1829*, London 1932

Artz, Frederick B., *Reaction and Revolution 1814–1832*, New York 1966

Ascoli, David, *The Queen's Peace. The Origins and Development of the Metropolitan Police 1829–1979*, London 1979

Aubouin, M., Teyssier, A. and Tulard, J., *Histoire et dictionnaire de la Police*, Paris 2005

Aylmer, Edward, *Memoirs of George Edwards, alias Wards, the Acknowledged Spy, and principal instigator, in the Cato-Street Plot*, London 1820

Baack, Lawrence J., *Christian Bernstorff and Prussia. Diplomacy and Reform Conservatism 1818–1832*, New Brunswick 1980

Bachleitner, Norbert, 'The Politics of the Book Trade in Nineteenth-century Austria', in *Austrian History Yearbook*, XVIII, 1997

— *Quellen zur Rezeption des englischen und französischen Romans in Deutschland und Österreich im 19. Jahrhundert*, Tübingen 1990

Bahr, E. and Saine, T., eds, *The Internalized Revolution. German Reactions to the French Revolution, 1789–1989*, New York 1992
Bamford, Samuel, *Passages in the Life of a Radical*, 2 vols, London 1844
Barante, Amable Guillaume Baron de, *Souvenirs du Baron de Barante*, Vol. II, Paris 1892
Barclay, David E., *Frederick William IV and the Prussian Monarchy 1840–1861*, Oxford 1995
Barrot, Camille Odilon, *Mémoires posthumes*, Vol. I, Paris 1875
Barruel, Abbé Augustin, *Mémoires pour servir à l'Histoire du Jacobinisme*, 2 vols, Chiré-en-Montreuil 1973
Bartlett, C.J., *Castlereagh*, London 1966
Bayley, David H., 'The Police and Political Development in Europe', in Charles Tilly, ed., *The Formation of National States in Western Europe*, Princeton 1975
Beattie, J.M., *The First English Detectives. The Bow Street Runners and the Policing of London 1750–1840*, Oxford 2012
Beaurepaire, Pierre-Yves, *William Pitt, les Francs-Maçons Anglais et la loi sur les Sociétés Secrètes*, in *Annales de la Révolution Française*, No. 342, 2005
Belgioioso, Princess Cristina Trivulzio, *L'Italia e la Rivoluzione Italiana nel 1848: Parti Due*, Lugano 1849
— *La Rivoluzione Lombarda del 1848*, Milan n.d.
Benckendorff, A. Kh., *Pismo grafa Aleksandra Benkendorfa k Nikolaiu Aleksandrovichu Polevovomu*, in *Russkii Arkhiv*, 1863
— *Otryvok iz zapisok grafa A. Kh. Benkendorfa*, ed. Baron M. Korff, in *Russkii Arkhiv*, 1866
— *Pisma grafa Benkendorfa k N. B. Kukolniku*, in *Russkaia Starina*, 1871
— *Instruktsia Grafa Benkendorfa Chinovniku 'Tretiago Otdelenia'*, in *Russkii Arkhiv*, Vol. 7, 1889
— *Imperator Nikolai v 1828–1829gg. (iz zapisok grafa A. Kh. Benkendorfa)*, in *Russkaia Starina*, Vol. 86, April–June 1896 and Vol. 87, July–September 1896
— *Proiekt g A. Benkendorfa ob ustroistvie vysshei politsii*, in *Russkaia Starina*, Vol. 104, October 1900
— *Zapiska o sostoianii russkago voiska v 1825 godu. Iz bumag A. Kh. Benkendorfa*, ed. M. Sokolovskii, in *Russlii Arkhiv*, Vol. 3, Moscow 1904
— *Vospominania 1802–1837*, ed. M.V. Sidorova and A.A. Litvina, trs. O.V. Marinina, Moscow 2012
Benhamou, Albert, *L'Autre Sainte-Hélène. La Captivité, la maladie, la mort et les médecins autour de Napoléon*, Hemel Hempstead 2010
Béranger, P.J. de, *Ma Biographie*, Paris 1857
Berlioz, Hector, *Memoirs*, trs. David Cairns, London 1970
Bernard, Paul P., *From the Enlightenment to the Police State. The Public Life of Johann Anton Pergen*, Chicago 1991
Berry, Mary, *Extracts from the Journals and Correspondence of Miss Berry*, 3 vols, London 1866
Bertier de Sauvigny, G. de, *Metternich et Decazes, d'après leur correspondance 1816–1820*, in *Études d'histoire moderne et contemporaine*, Vol. V, 1953

— *Metternich et son temps*, Paris 1959
— *Metternich et la France après le Congrès de Vienne*, 3 vols, Paris 1968–72
— *La France et les Français vus par les voyageurs americains 1814–1848*, Paris 1982
Berton, Jean-Baptiste, *Considérations sur la police, etc.*, Paris 1820
Best, Geoffrey, *War and Society in Revolutionary Europe 1770–1870*, Stroud 1998
Beugnot, Claude Comte, *Mémoires du Comte Beugnot, ancien ministre (1783–1815)*, Vol. II, Paris 1866
Bew, John, *Castlereagh. Enlightenment, War and Tyranny*, London 2011
Beyle, Henri (Stendhal), *Rome, Naples et Florence*, Paris 1854
— *Journal*, 4 vols, Paris 1932
Bibl, Wiktor, *Die Wiener Polizei. Eine Kulturhistorische Studie*, Leipzig 1927
— *Metternich 1773–1859*, Paris 1935
— *Metternich. Der Dämon Ősterreichs*, Leipzig 1936
— *Metternich in neuer Beleuchtung. Seine geheime briefwechsel mit dem Bayerishen Staatsminister Wrede 1831–4*, Vienna 1928
Bieker, Eva. *Die Interventionen Frankreichs und Grossbritanniens Anlässlich des Frankfurter Wachensturms 1833. Eine Fallstudie zur Geschichte Völkerrechtlicher Verträge*, in *Saarbrücker Studien zum Internationalen Recht*, Vol. XXI, Baden-Baden 2003
Bignon, Louis-Pierre-Édouard Baron, *Les Cabinets et les peuples*, Paris 1822
Billinger, Robert D., *Metternich and the German Question. States' Rights and Federal Duties, 1820–1834*, London 1991
Binyon, T.J., *Pushkin. A Biography*, London 2002
Birn, Raymond, *Royal Censorship of Books in Eighteenth-century France*, Stanford 2012
Blanc, Louis, *Histoire de dix ans*, 5 vols, Brussels 1846
Bloomfield, Georgiana Baroness, *Reminiscences of Court and Diplomatic Life*, 2 vols, London 1883
Boigne, Adèle d'Osmond, comtesse de, *Récits d'une tante. Mémoires de la comtesse de Boigne*, 4 vols, Paris 1908
Bokova, V.H., *Epokha tainykh obshchestv. Russkie obshchestvennye obedinienia pervoi tretii 19 vekha*, Moscow 2003
Bonald, Louis Gabriel Ambroise vicomte de, *Oeuvres complètes*, 3 vols, Paris 1864
Borovkov, Aleksandr Dmitrievich, *Avtobiograficheskia Zapiski*, in *Russkaia Starina*, Vol. 96, October 1898
Bouyssy, Maité, ed., *Maréchal Bugeaud, le guerre des rues et des maisons*, Paris 1997
Branig, Hans, ed., *Briefwechsel des Fürsten Karl August von Hardenberg mit dem Fürsten Wilhelm Ludwig von Sayn-Wittgenstein*, Cologne 1972
— *Fürst Wittgenstein. Ein preussischer Staatsmann der Restaurationszeit*, Cologne 1981
Brauer, Kinley, and Wright, William E., *Austria in the Age of the French Revolution 1789–1815*, Minneapolis 1990
Broers, Michael, *Napoleon's Other War. Bandits, Rebels and their Pursuers in the Age of Revolutions*, Oxford 2010
— with Peter Hicks and Augustín Guimerá, *The Napoleonic Empire and the New European Political Culture*, London 2012

Broglie, A.L.V.C. duc de, *Souvenirs 1785–1870*, 4 vols, Paris 1886
Brown, Mark Liam, 'The Polish Question and Public Opinion in France 1830–1848', in *Antemurale*, Vol. XXIV, Rome 1980
Brown, Philip Anthony, *The French Revolution in English History*, London 1918
Brunschwig, Henri, *La Crise de l'État Prussien à la fin du XVIIIe siècle et la genèse de la mentalité Romantique*, Paris 1947
Brus, Anna, Kaczyńska, Elżbieta and Śliwowska, Wiktoria, *Zesłanie i Katorga na Syberii w dziejach Polaków 1815–1914*, Warsaw 1992
Brydges, Sir Egerton, *Travels of My Nightcap, or Reveries in Rhyme with Scenes at the Congress of Verona*, London 1825
Buloz, A., see Witt, Jean
Burke, Edmund, *Reflections on the Revolution in France*, in *Works*, Vol. V, London 1826
— 'Letters on a Regicide Peace', in *Works*, Vols VIII and IX, London 1826
— 'An Appeal from the New to the Old Whigs', in *Works*, Vol. III, London 1855
— *The Correspondence of Edmund Burke*, Vols VI–X, Cambridge 1967
Burleigh, Michael, *Earthly Powers. Religion and Politics in Europe from the French Revolution to the Great War*, London 2005
Burtin, P.M. Nicolas, *Un Semeur d'idées au temps de la Restauration. Le baron d'Eckstein*, Paris 1931
Büssem, Eberhard, *Die Karlsbader Beschlüsse von 1819. Die Endgültige Stabilisierung der Restaurativen Politik im Deutschen Bund nach dem Wiener Kongress von 1814–15*, Hildesheim 1974
Canler, Paul Louis Alphonse, *Mémoires de Canler, ancien chef du service de Sûreté*, Paris 1986
Canning, George, *Some Official Correspondence of George Canning*, Vol. I, London 1887
Capefigue, J.B., *Histoire de la Restauration*, 10 vols, Paris 1831
Capo d'Istria, Ionnes, *Zapiska grafa Ioanna Kapodistria o ego sluzhebnoi deatelnosti*, in *Sbornik Imperatorskogo Russkogo Istoricheskogo Obshchestva*, Vol. III, St Petersburg 1868
Carrano, Francesco, *Vita di Guglielmo Pepe*, Turin 1857
Carrot, Georges, *Histoire de la police française*, Paris 1992
Carte Segrete e Atti Ufficiali della Polizia Austriaca in Italia dal giugno 1814 al 22 marzo 1848, 3 vols, Turin 1851
Castanié, François, *Les Indiscrétions d'un Préfet de Police de Napoléon*, Paris n.d.
Castellane, Esprit Victor Elisabeth Boniface, *Journal du maréchal de Castellane*, Vols I and II, Paris 1895
Castlereagh, Robert, Viscount, *Correspondence, Despatches, and other Papers of Viscount Castlereagh*, Vols XI and XII, London 1853
Chateaubriand, René vicomte de, *Lectures des Mémoires de M. de Chateaubriand, ou recueil d'articles publiés sur ces mémoires*, Paris 1834
— *Congrès de Vérone*, Paris 1838
Chenu, A., *Les Conspirateurs*, Paris 1850
Chevalier, Louis, *Classes laborieuses et classes dangereuses à Paris pendant la première moitié du XIXe siècle*, Paris 1958

Chicherin, Boris Nikolaevich, *Vospominania*, Vol. I, Moscow 2010
Chorley, Katharine, *Armies and the Art of Revolution*, London 1943
Church, Clive H., *Europe in 1830. Revolution and Political Change*, London 1983
Clark, Christopher, 'The Wars of Liberation in Prussian Memory: Reflections on the Memorialisation of War in Early Nineteenth-century Germany', *Journal of Modern History*, Vol. 68, No. 3, 1996
— *Iron Kingdom. The Rise and Downfall of Prussia, 1600–1947*, London 2006
Claveau, A. G., *De la Police de Paris, de ses abus, et des réformes dont elle est susceptible*, Paris 1831
Clemit, Pamela, ed., *The Cambridge Companion to British Literature of the French Revolution in the 1790s*, Cambridge 2011
Cleves, Rachel Hope, *The Reign of Terror in America. Visions of Violence from Anti-Jacobinism to Antislavery*, Cambridge 2009
Cobb, Richard, *The Police and the People. French Popular Protest, 1789–1820*, Oxford 1970
— *Reactions to the French Revolution*, Oxford 1972
Cobbett, William, *Peter Porcupine in America. Pamphlets on Republicanism and Revolution*, ed. David A. Wilson, Cornell 1999
— *The Parliamentary History of England from the Earliest Period to the Year 1803*, Vol. XXIX, London 1817
Cockburn, Sir George, *Extract from a Diary of Rear-Admiral Sir George Cockburn*, London 1888
Colquhoun, Patrick, *A Treatise on the Police of the Metropolis*, London 1796
Confalonieri, Federico Count, *Memorie e Lettere*, 2 vols, Milan 1889
Coniglio, Giuseppe, ed., *Le Relazioni Diplomatiche fra il Regno delle Due Sicilie e il Regno della Prussia, I e II Serie: 1814–1848*, Rome 1977
Conjuration permanente contre la maison de Bourbon et les rois de l'Europe, Paris 1820
Consalvi, Ercole Cardinal, *Correspondance du Cardinal Hercule Consalvi avec le Prince Clément de Metternich*, ed. Charles Van Duerm, Louvain 1899
Conspiration des Chevaliers de l'Épingle Noire, Paris 1817
Constantine Pavlovich, Grand Duke, *Pisma Velikago Kniazia Konstantina Pavlovicha s grafom A. Kh. Benkendorfom 1826–1828*, in *Russkaia Starina*, Vol. 6, 1884
Corcelle, F. de, *Documents pour servir à l'histoire des conspirations, des partis et des sectes*, Paris 1831
Corti, Egon C., *Anonyme Briefe an drei Kaiser*, Leipzig 1939
Cubitt, Geoffrey, *The Jesuit Myth. Conspiracy Theory and Politics in Nineteenth-century France*, Oxford 1993
Custine, Astolphe marquis de, *La Russie en 1839*, 4 vols, Paris 1843
— *L'Espagne sous Ferdinand VII*, 4 vols, Brussels 1838
Czajkowski, Michał, *Pamiętniki Sadyka Paszy*, Lwów 1898
Czerska, Danuta, *Sobornoje Ułozenije 1649 roku. Zagadnienia społeczno-ustrojowe*, Wrocław 1970
Damas, Ange Hyacinthe baron de, *Mémoires du baron de Damas (1785–1862)*, 2 vols, Paris 1922

Darnton, R., *Poetry and the Police. Communication Networks in Eighteenth-century Paris*, London 2010
Darvall, F.O., *Popular Disturbances and Public Order in Regency England*, London 1934
Daudet, Ernest, *La Police et les Chouans*, Paris 1895
— *La Police Politique. Chronique des temps de la Restauration*, Paris 1912
Davis, John A., *Conflict and Control. Law and Order in Nineteenth-century Italy*, London 1988
De Quincey, Thomas, 'Secret Societies', 513–22 and 661–70, in *Tait's Edinburgh Magazine*, 1847
*Des conspirateurs et des conspirations, par Theodore ****, Paris 1822
Desmarest, Pierre-Marie, *Quinze ans de Haute Police sous le Consulat et l'Empire*, Paris 1900
Dino, duchesse de, *Chronique de 1831 à 1862*, 4 vols, Paris 1909–10
Dmitriev, M.A. *Glavy iz vospominanii moiei zhizni*, Moscow 1998
Droz, Jacques, *Europe between Revolutions 1815–1848*, London 1985
Dubelt, E.I., *Leontii Vasilievich Dubelt. Biograficheskia ocherki i ego pisma*, in *Russkaia Starina*, Vol. 60, October 1888
Dubrovin, N.Th., ed., *Bumagi grafa Arsenia Andreevicha Zakrevskogo*, in *Sbornik Imperatorskogo Russkogo Istoricheskogo Obshchestva*, Vol. 73, 1890
— ed., *Materialy i Cherti k biografii Imperatora Nikolaia I i k istorii ego tsarstvovania*, in *Sbornik Imperatorskogo Russkogo Istoricheskogo Obshchestva*, Vol. 98, St Petersburg 1896
Du Camp, Maxime, *Souvenirs de l'année 1848*, Paris 1876
— *Histoire et critique*, Paris 1877
— *L'Attentat Fieschi*, Paris 1877
Ducoin, Auguste, *Histoire de la conspiration de 1816*, Paris 1844
Duggan, Christopher, *The Force of Destiny. A History of Italy since 1796*, London 2007
Dumas, Alexandre, *Mes Mémoires 1802–1830*, 2 vols, Paris 1989
Edelman, O.V., *Sledstvie po Delu Dekabristov*, Moscow 2010
Edgcumbe, Richard, ed., *The Diary of Frances Lady Shelley*, 2 vols, London 1912–13
Ellis, P. Beresford, and Mac A'Ghobhainn, Seumas, *The Scottish Insurrection of 1820*, London 1970
Emerson, Donald E., *Metternich and the Political Police. Security and Subversion in the Hapsburg Monarchy (1815–1830)*, The Hague 1968
Empaytaz, H.L., *Notice sur Alexandre, Empereur de Russie*, Paris 1840
Emsley, Clive, 'The London "Insurrection" of December 1792: Fact, Fiction, or Fantasy?', in *Journal of British Studies*, Vol. 17, No. 2, Spring 1978
— 'The Home Office and its Sources of Information and Investigation 1791–1810', in *English Historical Review*, Vol. 94, No. 372, July 1979
— *Policing and its Context 1750–1870*, London 1983
— *Gendarmes and the State in Nineteenth-century Europe*, Oxford 1999
— 'Repression, "Terror" and the Rule of Law in England during the Decade of the French Revolution', in *English Historical Review*, Vol. 100, No. 397, October 1985
Essai sur la Secte des Illuminés, Paris 1789
Fairchild, H.C., *The Romantic Quest*, New York 1993

Fenner von Fenneberg, Freiherr, *Österreich und siene Armee*, Leipzig 1847
Figes, Orlando, *Crimea. The Last Crusade*, London 2010
Fitzpatrick, W.J., *Secret Service under Pitt*, London 1892
Flynn, James T., *The University Reform of Tsar Alexander I, 1802–1835*, Washington DC 1988
Fouché, Joseph, *Mémoires de Joseph Fouché, duc d'Otrante*, 2 vols, Paris 1824
Fox, Charles James, *Memorials and Correspondence*, ed. Lord John Russell, 2 vols, London 1853
Fraser, Antonia, *Perilous Question. The Drama of the Great Reform Bill 1832*, London 2013
Freitag, Sabine, ed., *Exiles from European Revolutions. Refugees in Mid-Victorian England*, New York 2003
Froment, M., *La Police Dévoilée, depuis la Restauration*, 3 vols, Paris 1829
Gagern, Heinrich von, *Deutscher Liberalismus in Vormarz, Briefe und Reden 1815–1848*, Götingen 1959
Garros, Louis, *Quel Roman que ma vie! Itinéraire de Napoléon Bonaparte, 1769–1821*, Paris 1947
Gauchais, Colonel, *Histoire de la conspiration de Saumur*, Paris 1832
Gebhardt, Helmut, *Die Grazer Polizei, 1786–1850*, Graz 1992
Gentz, Friedrich von, *Aus dem Nachlasse Friedrichs von Gentz*, 2 vols, Vienna 1867
— *Dépêches Inédites du chevalier de Gentz aux Hospodars de Moldavie*, Vols I and II, Paris 1876
Gernet, M.N., *Istoria Tsarskoi Tiurmy*, 2 vols, Moscow 1951
Gershenzon, Mikhail, *Nikolai I i ego epokha*, Moscow 2001
Gillen, Mollie, *Assassination of the Prime Minister. The Shocking Death of Spencer Perceval*, London 1972
Gilmartin, Kevin, *Writing against Revolution. Literary Conservatism in Britain, 1790–1832*, Cambridge 2007
Gin, Emilion, *Sanfedisti, Carbonari, Magistrati del Re. Il Regno delle Due Sicilie tra Restaurazione e Rivoluzione*, Naples 2003
Girardin, Sophie Gay, Mme Émile de, *Le Vicomte de Launay. Lettres Parisiennes*, 5 vols, Paris 1868
Gisquet, M. *Mémoires de M. Gisquet, ancient préfet de police*, 2 vols, Paris 1840
Golovine, Ivan, *Russia under the Autocrat Nicholas I*, 2 vols, Paris 1846
Gooch, G.P., *Germany and the French Revolution*, London 1920
Goodwin, Albert, *The Friends of Liberty. The English Democratic Movement in the Age of the French Revolution*, London 1979
Görres, Joseph, *Germany and the Revolution*, trs. John Black, London 1820
Graham, Jenny, *The Nation, the Law and the King. Reform Politics in England, 1789–1799*, 2 vols, Lanham 2000
Grandjonc, Jacques, *Marx et les communistes allemands à Paris, Vorwärts 1844*, Paris 1974
Grandmaison, Geoffroy de, *L'Expédition d'Espagne en 1823*, Paris 1928
Grasilier, Léonce, *Évasions de prisonniers de guerre favorisées par les Francs-Maçons sous Napoléon Ier*, Paris 1913

— *Un Secrétaire de Robespierre. Simon Duplay (1774–1827) et son mémoire sur les sociétés secrètes et les conspirations sous la Restauration*, Paris 1913
Grenby, M.O., *The Anti-Jacobin Novel. British Conservatism and the French Revolution*, Cambridge 2001
Greville, Charles C.F., *A Journal of the Reigns of King George IV and King William IV*, ed. Henry Reeve, 3 vols, London 1874
Griffin, Charles J.G., 'Jedediah Morse and the Bavarian Illuminati. An Essay in the Rhetoric of Conspiracy', in *Communication Studies*, Vol. 63, No. 1
Grimsted, Patricia Kennedy, *The Foreign Ministers of Alexander I. Political Attitudes and the Conduct of Russian Diplomacy 1801–1825*, Berkeley 1969
Gronow, R.H., *The Reminiscences and Recollections of Captain Gronow, etc.*, ed. John Raymond, London 1964
Grunwald, Constantin de, *La Vie de Nicolas Ier*, Paris 1946
Guillon, E., *Les Complots militaires sous la Restauration*, Paris 1895
Guizot, François, *Des Conspirations et de la justice politique*, Paris 1821
— *Des Moyens de gouvernement et d'opposition dans l'état actuel de la France*, Paris 1821
— *De la Peine de mort en matière politique*, Paris 1822
— *Mémoires pour servir à l'histoire de mon temps*, 8 vols, Paris 1858–67
— *Lettres de François Guizot et de la princesse de Lieven*, 3 vols, Paris 1963
Hamerow, Theodore S., *Restoration, Revolution, Reaction. Economics and Politics in Germany 1815–1871*, Princeton 1958
Hammond, J.L. and B., *The Skilled Labourer 1760–1832*, London 1927
Harrison, Mark, *Crowds and History. Mass Phenomena in English Towns, 1790–1835*, Cambridge 1988
Haussez, C. Lemercier de Longpré, Baron d', *Mémoires*, 2 vols, Paris 1896
Hauterive, Ernest d', *Mouchards et policiers*, Paris 1936
— *Napoléon et sa police*, Paris 1943
Haywood, I., 'The Dark Sketches of a Revolution', in *European Romantic Review*, Vol. 22, No. 4, 2011
Hazareesingh, Sudhir, *The Legend of Napoleon*, London 2004
Hazlitt, William, *Selected Writings*, ed. Duncan Wu, Vol. IV, London 1998
Henningsen, Charles Frederick, *Eastern Europe and the Emperor Nicholas*, 2 vols, London 1846
— *Revelations of Russia in 1846, by an English Resident*, 2 vols, London 1846
Herzen, Alexander, *My Past and Thoughts*, trs. Constance Garnett, 4 vols, London 1968
Hilton, Boyd, *A Mad, Bad, and Dangerous People? England 1783–1846*, Oxford 2006
Hingley, Ronald, *The Russian Secret Police. Muscovite, Imperial Russian and Soviet Political Security Operations 1565–1970*, London 1970
Hippler, Thomas, *Citizens, Soldiers and National Armies. Military Service in France and Germany, 1789–1830*, London 2008
Histoire complète du procès de Louis-Pierre Louvel, etc… par M. G… ex-officier d'Infanterie, Paris 1820
Hobsbawm, Eric, and Rudé, George, *Captain Swing*, London 1970
Hoffmann, E.T.A., *Juristische Arbeiten*, Munich 1973

Hone, J. Ann, 'Radicalism in London, 1796–1802', in J. Stevenson, ed., *London in the Age of Reform*, Oxford 1977
— *For the Cause of Truth. Radicalism in London 1796–1821*, Oxford 1982
Howe, Daniel Walker, *What Hath God Wrought. The Transformation of America, 1815–1848*, Oxford 2007
Hüber, E.R., *Nationalstaat und Verfassungsstaat*, Stuttgart 1965
Hughes, Steven C., *Crime, Disorder and the Risorgimento. The Politics of Policing in Bologna*, Cambridge 1994
Hunt, Henry, *Memoirs of Henry Hunt, Esq.*, 3 vols, London 1820
Hunt, Tristram, *The Frock-Coated Communist. The Revolutionary Life of Friedrich Engels*, London 2009
Ilse, Leopold Friedrich, *Geschichte der Politischen Untersuchungen, Welche Durch die Neben der Bundesversammlung Errichteten Commissionen, der Central Untersuchungs-Commission zu Mainz und der Bundes-Central-Behörde zu Frankfurt in den Jahren 1819 bis 1827 und 1833 bis 1842 Geführt Sind*, Frankfurt am Main 1860
Jackman, S.W., ed., *Romanov Relations. The Private Correspondence of Tsars Alexander I, Nicholas I and the Grand Dukes Constantine and Michael with their Sister Queen Anna Pavlovna 1817–1855*, London 1969
Jacobinism Displayed, Birmingham 1798
Jewson, C.B., *The Jacobin City. A Portrait of Norwich in its Reaction to the French Revolution 1788–1802*, Glasgow 1975
Johnston, Kenneth R., *Unusual Suspects. Pitt's Reign of Alarm and the Lost Generation of the 1790s*, Oxford 2013
Joinville, François Ferdinand d'Orléans, prince de, *Vieux souvenirs 1818–1848*, Paris 1986
Junius, *American Democracy*, New York 1840
K Istorii russkoi tsenzury (1814–1820), in *Russkaia Starina*, Vol. 104, October 1900
Kann, Robert A., *A Study in Austrian Intellectual History. From Late Baroque to Romanticism*, New York 1960
Kassandrus, N.B., *Die Entlarvung der Reactionairen Umtriebe vom Wiener Kongress bis zum Frankfurter Wachensturm. Aspekte zu Einer Verteidigung der Liberal-demokratischen Bewegung*, Giessen 1987
Katz, Jacob, and Oschry, Leonard, *Jews and Freemasons in Europe 1723–1939*, Cambridge, Mass. 1970
Kauchtschischwili, Nina, *Silvio Pellico e la Russia*, Milan 1963
Keates, Jonathan, *The Siege of Venice*, London 2005
Kelly, Gary, *The English Jacobin Novel 1780–1805*, Oxford 1976
Kohn, Hans, *Pan-Slavism. Its History and Ideology*, Notre Dame, Ind. 1953
Komitet, Vysochaishim reskriptom 6 dekabria 1826g uchrezhdenny, in *Sbornik Imperatorskogo Russkogo Istoricheskogo Obshchestva*, Vols 74, 1891 and 90, St Petersburg 1898
Körner, Alfred, *Die Wiener Jakobiner*, Stuttgart 1972
Kosellek, Reinhart, *Preussen zwischen Reform und Revolution. Allgemeines Landnecht, Verwaltung und Sociale Bewegung von 1791 bis 1848*, Stuttgart 1967

Koubrakiewicz, M., *Revelations of Austria*, Vol. I, London 1846
Krüdener, Baroness Julie von, *Le Camp de Vertus, ou La Grande Revue de l'armée russe, dans la plaine de ce nom*, Lyon 1815
Kulomzin, A.N., ed., *Finansovie Dokumenty Trsarstvovania Impratora Aleksandra I*, in *Sbornik Imperatorskogo Russkogo Istoricheskogo Obshchestva*, Vol. 45, St Petersburg 1885
Lachenicht, Susanne, *Information und Propaganda. Die Presse deutscher Jakobiner in Elsass (1791–1800)*, Munich 2004
La Harpe, Frédéric-César de, *Correspondance de Frédéric-César de La Harpe et Alexandre Ier*, Vol. III, Neuchâtel 1980
La Hodde, Lucien de, *Histoire des sociétés secrètes et du Parti Républicain de 1830 à 1848*, Paris 1850
La Mare, Nicolas de, *Traité de la police*, 4 vols, Paris 1705–38
Lamartine, Alphonse de, *Histoire de la Restauration*, 8 vols, Paris 1851–52
Lamennais, Félicité de, *De la Religion considérée dans ses rapports avec l'ordre politique et civil*, Paris 1826
Land, Isaac, *Enemies of Humanity. The Nineteenth-century War on Terrorism*, London 2008
Langer, William L., 'The Pattern of Urban Revolution in 1848', in E.M. Anscomb and M.L. Brown, eds, *French Society and Culture Since the Old Regime*, New York 1966
Langeron, Roger, *Decazes, Ministre du Roi*, Paris 1960
Laven, David, 'The Age of Restoration', in John A. Davis, ed., *Italy in the Nineteenth Century*, Oxford 2000
Lebzeltern, Louis-Joseph Count, *Mémoires et papiers*, Paris 1949
Le Cabinet Noir et M. de Vaulchier, Paris 1828
Le Camp de Vertus. Revue de l'Armée Russe sur le Mont-Aimé (10 septembre 1815), Epernay 1896
Legge, J.G., *Rhyme and Revolution in Germany. A Study in German History, Life, Literature and Character 1813–1850*, London 1918
Leininger, Franz, and Haupt, Herman, *Zur Geschichte des Frankfurter Attentats*, in Herman Haupt, ed., *Quellen und Darstellungen zur Geschichte der Burschenschaft und der Deutschen Einheitsbewegung*, Vol. V, Heidelberg 1920
Lemke, M., *Nikolaevskie Zhandarmy i literatura 1826–1855gg*, Moscow 1909
Lennhoff, Eugen *Politsche Geheimbunde*, Vienna 1931
Le Pont d'Arcole et la Police Gisquet, Paris 1833
Leśnodorski, B., *Polscy Jakobini*, Warsaw 1960
Levinger, Matthew, *Enlightened Nationalism. The Transformation of Prussian Political Culture 1806–1848*, Oxford 2000
Ley, Francis, *Alexandre Ier et sa Sainte Alliance*, Paris 1975
L'Heuillet, Hélène, *Basse politique, haute police. Une approche philosophique et historique*, Paris 2001
L'Homme de Gibeaux, ou nouvelles preuves de la conjuration de M. Élie de Cazes et consorts, contre la Légitimité, Paris 1820
Liang, His-Huey, *The Rise of Modern Police and the European State System from Metternich to the Second World War*, Cambridge 1992

Lieven, Dorothea, Princess, *Correspondence of Princess Lieven and Earl Grey*, 3 vols, London 1890
— *Kniaginia D. Kh. Liven i eia perepiska s raznymi litsami*, in *Russkaia Starina*, Vols 113–17, January 1903–January 1904
— *The Correspondence of Lord Aberdeen and Princess Lieven 1832–1854*, Vol. I, ed. E. Jones Parry, Royal Historical Society, Camden Third Series, Vol. LX, London 1938
— *The Lieven–Palmerston Correspondence 1828–1856*, ed. Lord Sudley, London 1943
— *Letters of Dorothea, Princess Lieven, during her Residence in London, 1812–1834*, ed. Lionel G. Robinson, London 1944
Lignereux, Aurélien, *La France rébellionnaire. Les résistances à la gendarmerie (1800–1859)*, Rennes 2008
Linklater, Andro, *Why Spencer Perceval Had to Die. The Assassination of a British Prime Minister*, London 2012
Lomachevskii, A., *Raskazy iz prezhnei politseiskoi sluzhby v Peterburge*, in *Russkaia Starina*, Vol. 9, 1874
Lombard de Langres, V., *Des Sociétés Secrètes en Allemagne, et en d'autres contrées, etc.*, Paris 1819
Lubomirski, Prince Józef, *Souvenirs d'un page du Tsar Nicolas*, Paris 1869
Luc, Jean-Noel, *Gendarmerie, état et société au XIXe siècle*, Paris 2002
Lucas, Edward, *Deception. Spies, Lies and How Russia Dupes the West*, London 2012
Lüdtke, Alf, *Police and State in Prussia, 1815–1850*, trs. Pete Burgess, Cambridge 1989
McCalman, Iain, *Radical Underworld. Prophets, Revolutionaries and Pornographers in London 1795–1840*, Cambridge 1988
McDowell, R. B., *Ireland in the Age of Imperialism and Revolution 1760–1801*, Oxford 1979
Mack Smith, Denis, *Victor Emmanuel, Cavour and the Risorgimento*, Oxford 1971
— *Mazzini*, Yale 1994
Madelin, Louis, *Fouché 1759–1820*, Paris 1969
Maillé, Blanche-Joséphine, duchesse de, *Mémoires 1832–1851*, Paris 1989
Maistre, Joseph de, *Les Soirées de Saint-Pétersbourg*, 2 vols, Lyon 1836
— *Considérations sur la France*, Brussels 1838
— *Lettres à un Gentilhomme russe sur l'Inquisition en Espagne*, Brussels 1838
— *Lettres et opuscules inédits*, 2 vols, Paris 1851
— *Correspondance diplomatique*, 2 vols, Paris 1860
Małachowski-Łempicki, Stanisław, *Raporty Szpiega Mackrotta o wolnomularstwie polskim, 1819–1822*, Warsaw n.d.
Mann, Golo, *Secretary of Europe. The Life of Friedrich Gentz, Enemy of Napoleon*, trs. William H. Woglom, Yale 1946
Manuel, Pierre, *La Police de Paris dévoilée*, 2 vols, Paris 1791
Marancourt, *Eugène Sue et Le Juif Errant à la recherche des horreurs sociales, etc.*, Paris 1845
Marie-Amélie, Reine des Français, *Journal*, ed. S. Huart, Paris 1981
Marlow, Joyce, *The Peterloo Massacre*, London 1969
Marmier, X., *Lettres sur la Russie, la Finlande et la Pologne*, 2 vols, Paris 1843

Marmont, Auguste, duc de Raguse, *Mémoires du Maréchal Marmont, duc de Raguse de 1792 à 1841*, 9 vols, Paris 1857

Martineau, Harriet, *The History of England during the Thirty Years' Peace 1816–1846*, 3 vols, London 1849

— *Introduction to the History of the Peace. From 1800 to 1815*, London 1851

Marx, Julius, *Die Zensur der Kanzlei Metternichs*, in *Österreichische Zeitschrift für Öffentliches Recht*, Vol. 4, 1951

— *Die österreichische Zensur im Vormärz*, Vienna 1959

Marx, Karl, *Class Struggles in France (1848–1850)*, London 1942

— *The Eighteenth Brumaire of Louis Bonaparte*, New York 1926

May, J.-B., *Saint-Pétersbourg et la Russie*, 2 vols, Paris 1830

Mayr, Joseph Karl, *Metternichs Geheimer Briefdienst, Postlogen und Postkurse*, Vienna 1935

— *Geschichte der österrieichischen Staatskanzlei im Zeitalter des Fürsten Metternichs*, Vienna 1935

Mazour, Anatole G., *The First Russian Revolution*, Berkeley 1937

Mazzini, Giuseppe, *A Cosmopolitanism of Nations. Giuseppe Mazzini's Writings on Democracy, Nation Building, and International Relations*, ed. Stefano Recchia and Nadia Urbinati, Princeton 2009

Mémoires d'une femme de qualité sous Louis XVIII, 6 vols, Paris 1829

Mérimée, Prosper, *H.B.*, Paris 1935

Merriman, John, *Police Stories. Building the French State, 1815–1851*, Oxford 2006

Metternich, Klemens Lothar von, *Mémoires, documents et écrits divers laissés par le prince de Metternich*, ed. A. de Klinkowstroem, 10 vols, Paris 1880

— *Lettres du prince de Metternich à la comtesse de Lieven 1818–1819*, Paris 1909

— *Mémoires du prince de Metternich*, Vol. IV: *Lettres inédites du prince de Metternich au baron Hübner, 1849–1859*, Paris 1959

Meyendorff, Peter von, *Ein russischer Diplomat an den Höfen von Berlin und Wien. Politischer und Privater Briefwechsel 1826–1863*, 2 vols, Berlin 1923

Mezhdutsarstvie 1825 goda i Vosstanie Dekabristov v perepiske i memuarakh chlenov tsarskoi semi, ed. B.E. Syroechkovskii, Moscow 1926

Mikhailovskii-Danilevskii, A.I., *Iz vospominanii A. I. Mikhailovskogo-Danilevskogo*, in *Russkaia Starina*, Vol. 104, October 1900

Milchina, V., *Rossia i Frantsia. Diplomaty, Literatori, Shpiony*, St Petersburg 2004

Mildmay, Sir William, *The Police of France*, London 1763

Miles, William Augustus, *Letters on the French Revolution, 1789–1817*, 2 vols, London 1890

Monas, Sidney, *The Third Section. Police and Society in Russia under Nicholas I*, Cambridge, Mass. 1961

Montcalm, marquise de, *Mon Journal 1815–1818 pendant le premier ministère de mon frère*, Paris 1936

Montchenu, marquis de, *La Captivité de Sainte-Hélène d'après les rapports inédits du marquis de Montchenu*, Paris 1894

Montlosier, Reynaud, comte de, *De la Monarchie française*, 7 vols, Paris 1814–24

Moore, Thomas, *The Journal of Thomas Moore 1818–1841*, ed. Peter Quennell, London 1964

Mori, Jennifer, *William Pitt and the French Revolution 1785–1795*, Keele 1997
— *Britain in the Age of the French Revolution 1785–1820*, Harlow 2000
Moriolles, Alexandre Nicolas de, *Mémoires sur l'émigration, la Pologne et la cour du grand duc Constantin*, Paris 1902
Morris, Marilyn, *The British Monarchy and the French Revolution*, New Haven 1998
Mounier, Baron, *Souvenirs et notes intimes du baron Mounier, secrétaire de Napoléon Ier, Pair de France, Directeur Général de Police*, Paris 1896
Moylan, D.C., ed., *The Opinions of Lord Holland, as Recorded in the Journals of the House of Lords, from 1797 to 1841*, London 1841
Müller, Harald, *Der Weg nach Münchengraetz. Voraussetzungen, Bedingungen und Grenzen der Reaktivierung des reaktionären Bündnisses der Habsburger und Hohenzollern mit den Romanows im Herbst 1833*, in *Jahrbuch für Geschichte 21*, Berlin 1980
Namier, Lewis, *1848. The Revolution of the Intellectuals*, London 1946
Neiberg, Michael S., *Dance of the Furies*, Cambridge, Mass. 2011
Neigebaur, Johann Ferdinand, *Geschichte der geheimen Verbindungen der neuesten Zeit*, Leipzig 1831
Nesselrode, Karl von, *Lettres et papiers du Chancelier comte de Nesselrode 1760–1850*, 11 vols, Paris 1904–11
Neumann, Philipp von, *The Diary of Philipp von Neumann 1819–1850*, London 1928
Nicholas I, Emperor of Russia, *Perepiska Imperatora Nikolaia Pavlovicha s velikim kniazhem Konstantinom Pavlovichom*, in *Sbornik Imperatorskogo Russkogo Istoricheskogo Obshchestva*, Vol. 131, St Petersburg 1910
— *Pisma Imperatora Nikolaia Pavlovicha k grafu A. Kh. Benkendorfu 1837 goda*, in *Russkaia Starina*, Vol. 1, 1884
Nicholas Mikhailovich, Grand Duke, *L'Empereur Alexandre Ier. Essai d'étude historique*, 2 vols, St Petersburg 1912
— ed., *Doniesienia avstriiskovgo poslannika pri russkom dvore Lebzelterna za 1816–1828 gody*, St Petersburg 1913
Nicolson, Harold, *The Desire to Please. A Story of Hamilton Rowan and the United Irishmen*, London 1943
Nikolai Pervy i ego vremia. Dokumenty, pisma, dnevniki, memuary, svidetelstva sovremennikov i trudy istorikov, 2 vols, Moscow 2000
Noailles, H., marquis de, *Le Comte Molé 1781–1855. Sa vie – ses mémoires*, 6 vols, Paris 1922–30
Nodier, Charles, *Histoire des Sociétés Secrètes de l'Armée et des Conspirations Militaires qui ont eu pour objet la destruction du gouvernement de Bonaparte*, Paris 1815
Noiriel, Gérard, *La Tyrannie du National. Le droit d'asile en Europe 1793–1993*, Paris 1991
Obenaus, Walter, *Die Entwicklung der Preussischen Sicherheitspolizei bis zum Ende der Reaktionszeit*, Berlin 1940
Okhranienie Nikolaia I v ego puteshestvii za granitsu, in *Russkaia Starina*, Vol. 100, October 1899
Oksman, Yu.G. and Chernov, S.N., *Vospominania i Raskazy Deatelei Tainykh Obshchestv 1820 godov*, 2 vols, Moscow 1931

Oleinikov, Dmitrii, *Benkendorf*, Moscow 2009
Origo, Iris, *The Last Attachment. The Story of Byron and Teresa Guiccioli as Told in their Unpublished Letters and Other Family Papers*, London 1949
Orlik, O.V., *Rossia v mezhdunarodnykh otnosheniakh 1815–1829*, Moscow 1998
Orloff, G.V., *Mémoires historiques, politiques et littéraires sur le royaume de Naples*, 5 vols, Paris 1821–25
Palmer, Stanley H., *Police and Protest in England and Ireland 1780–1850*, Cambridge 1988
Paris Révolutionnaire, 4 vols, Paris 1838
Parliamentary Reports:
— *First Report from the Committee of Secrecy of the House of Commons*, London 1794
— *Second Report from the Committee of Secrecy of the House of Commons*, London 1794
— *First Report from the Committee of Secrecy of the House of Lords*, London 1794
— *Second Report from the Committee of Secrecy of the House of Lords*, London 1794
— *Report from the Committee of Secrecy of the House of Lords in Ireland*, London 1798
— *Report of the Committee of Secrecy of the House of Commons*, London 1799
Parolin, Christina, *Radical Spaces. Venues of Popular Politics in London, 1790–c. 1845*, Acton 2010
Pasquier, E.D., *Mémoires du Chancelier Pasquier*, Vols IV and V, Paris 1894
Payson, Seth, *Proofs of the Real Existence, and Dangerous Tendency, of Illuminism, etc.*, Charlestown 1802
Pellew, George, *The Life and Correspondence of the Right Honble Henry Addington, First Viscount Sidmouth*, Vol. III, London 1847
Perreux, Gabriel, *Au Temps des Sociétés Secrètes. La propagande républicaine au début de la monarchie de juillet (1830–1835)*, Paris 1931
Petzold, Albert, 'Die Zentral-Untersuchungs-Kommission in Mainz', in Herman Haupt, ed., *Quellen und Darstellungen zur Geschichte der Burschenschaft und der Deutschen Einheitsbewegung*, Vol. V, Heidelberg 1920
Peuchet, Jacques, *Mémoires tirés des Archives de la Police de Paris*, 6 vols, Paris 1838
Pienkos, Angela T., *The Imperfect Autocrat. Grand Duke Constantine Pavlovich and the Polish Congress Kingdom*, Boulder 1987
Pii, Eugenio, *Idee e parole nel giacobinismo italiano*, Florence 1990
Pinkney, D.H., 'The Myth of the Revolution of 1830', in D.H. Pinkney and D. Ropps, eds, *A Festchrift for Frederick B. Artz*, Durham, NC 1964
Plamenatz, John, *The Revolutionary Movement in France 1815–71*, London 1952
Playfair, William, *The History of Jacobinism, its Crimes, Cruelties and Perfidies*, 2 vols, London 1798
Ploux, François, *De Bouche à oreille. Naissance et propagation des rumeurs dans la France du XIXe siècle*, Paris 2003
Polidori, J.W., *The Diary of Dr John William Polidori 1816, Relating to Byron, Shelley, etc.*, London 1911
Polievktov, M., *Nikolai I. Biografia i Obzor Tsarstvovania*, Moscow 1918
Polišenský, Josef, *Aristocrats and the Crowd in the Revolutionary Year 1848*, Albany 1980

Polovtsov, A., *Gertsog Armand-Emmanuel Richelieu. Dokumenty i bumagi o ego zhizni i deatelnosti*, in *Sbornik Imperatorskogo Russkogo Istoricheskogo Obshchestva*, Vol. 54, St Petersburg 1886
— *Diplomaticheskie snoshenia Rossii i Frantsii. Doniesenia frantsuskikh predstavitelei pri russkom dvore i Russkikh predstavitelei pri frantsuskom dvore*, in *Sbornik Imperatorskogo Russkogo Istoricheskogo Obshchestva*, Vol. 112, 1901
— *Correspondance diplomatique des ambassadeurs et ministres de Russie en France et de France en Russie avec leurs gouvernements*, 3 vols, St Petersburg 1902–03
Ponteil, Félix, *L'Éveil des nationalités et le Mouvement Libéral (1815–1848)*, Paris 1960
Porter, Bernard, *The Refugee Question in mid-Victorian Politics*, Cambridge 1979
— *Plots and Paranoia. A History of Political Espionage in Britain 1790–1988*, London 1989
Pozzo di Borgo, Charles-André, *Correspondance diplomatique du comte Pozzo di Borgo et du comte de Nesselrode*, 2 vols, Paris 1890
Presniakov, A.Ye., *Apogei samoderzhavia: Nikolai I*, Leningrad 1925
Price, Munro, 'The "Foreign Plot" in the French Revolution: A Reappraisal', in B. Coward and J. Swann (eds), *Conspiracy and Conspiracy Theory in Early-Modern Europe*, Aldershot 2004
Prochaska, Alice, 'The Practice of Radicalism. Educational Reform in Westminster', in J. Stevenson, ed., *London in the Age of Reform*, Oxford 1977
Raeff, Marc, *The Decembrist Movement*, London 1966
Raisson, Horace, *Histoire de la police de Paris*, Paris 1844
Rath, R. John, *The Viennese Revolution of 1848*, New York 1969
— *The Provisional Austrian Regime in Lombardy-Venetia 1814–1815*, Austin, Tex. 1969
Read, Donald, *Peterloo. The 'Massacre' and its Background*, Manchester 1958
Reinerman, Alan, 'Metternich and the Papal Condemnation of the Carbonari, 1821', in *Catholic Historical Review*, Vol. 54, No. 1, April 1968
— 'Metternich, Italy and the Congress of Verona, 1821–1822', in *Historical Journal*, Vol. 14, No. 2, June 1971
— *Austria and the Papacy in the Age of Metternich*, 2 vols, Washington 1979–89
Reitblat, A.I., ed., *Vidok Figliarin. Pisma i agenturnie zapiski F.V. Bulgarina v III Otdelenie*, Moscow 1998
Reiter, Herbert, *Politisches Asyl in 19 jahrhundert*, Berlin 1992
Reith, Charles, *The Police Idea. Its History and Evolution in England in the Eighteenth Century and After*, Oxford 1938
Rémusat, Charles de, *Mémoires de ma vie*, 4 vols, Paris 1958
Repercusiones de la Revoluciòn Francesa en España, Actas del Congreso Internacional celebrado en Madrid 27–30 noviembre 1989, Madrid 1990
Rey, Marie-Pierre, *Alexandre Ier*, Paris 2009
Riasanovsky, Nicholas V., *Nicholas I and Official Russian Nationality in Russia, 1825–55*, Berkeley 1959
— *A Parting of Ways. Government and the Educated Public in Russia 1801–1855*, Oxford 1976
— *Russian Identities. A Historical Survey*, Oxford 2005

Richelieu, Armand-Émmanuel du Plessis, duc de, *Lettres du duc de Richelieu au marquis d'Osmond 1816–1818*, Paris 1939
Roberts, J.M., *The Mythology of the Secret Societies*, London 1972
Robins, Jane, *Rebel Queen. How the Trial of Caroline Brought England to the Brink of Revolution*, London 2007
Rogalla von Bieberstein, Johannes, *Die These von der Verschwörung, 1776–1945: Philosophen, Freimaurer, Juden, Liberale und Sozialisten als Verschwörer Gegen die Sozialordnung*, in *Europäische Hochschulschriften*, Vol. LXIII, Frankfurt 1976
Roider, Karl A., Jr., *Baron Thugut and Austria's Response to the French Revolution*, Princeton 1987
Romani, George T., *The Neapolitan Revolution of 1820–1821*, Evanston 1950
Romilly, Sir Samuel, *Memoirs of the Life of Sir Samuel Romilly*, 2 vols, London 1841
Rössler, Helmut, *Zwischen Revolution und Reaktion. Ein Lebensbild der Reichsfreiherrn Hans Christoph von Gagern 1766–1852*, Göttingen 1958
Roy, J.J., *Tableau de Paris dans les quinze premiers jours de juin 1820*, Paris 1820
Royle, Edward, *Revolutionary Britannia? Reflections on the Threat of Revolution in Britain 1789–1848*, Manchester 2000
Rudé, George, *The Crowd in History. A Study of Popular Disturbances in France and England 1730–1848*, New York 1964
— *Revolutionary Europe, 1783–1815*, London 1985
Ruud, Charles A., and Stepanov, Sergei A., *Fontanka 16. The Tsars' Secret Police*, Stroud 1999
Saint Glin (Sanglen), Yakov Ivanovich de, *Zapiski Yakova Ivanovicha de-Sanglena 1776–1831*, in *Russkaia Starina*, Vol. 37
Schenk, H.G., *The Aftermath of the Napoleonic Wars*, London 1947
Schroeder, Paul W., *Metternich's Diplomacy at its Zenith 1820–1823*, New York 1969
Sealsfield, Charles, *Austria as it is: or, Sketches of Continental Courts*, London 1828
Ségur, comte de, *Mémoires, ou souvenirs et anecdotes*, Vol. III, Paris 1824
Seide, Gernot, *Regierungspolitik und öffentliche Meinung im Kaisertum Österreich anlasslich der polnischen Novemberrevolution (1830–1831)*, Wiesbaden 1971
Selivanov, I.V., *Zapiski Dvorianina-pomieshchika*, in *Russkaia Starina*, Vol. 28, 1880
Shelley, Mary, *The Journals of Mary Shelley 1814–1844*, 2 vols, Oxford 1987
Shilder, N.K., *Imperator Aleksandr Pervii. Ievo zhizn i tsarstvovanie*, 4 vols, St Petersburg 1897–98
— *Dva Donosa v 1831 godu*, in *Russkaia Starina*, Vol. 96, December 1898 and Vol. 97, February 1899
— *Imperator Nikolai Pervyi. Ego Zhizn i Tsarstvovanie*, 2 vols, St Petersburg 1903
Shishkov, A.S., *Mnenie Admirala i Prezidenta Rossiiskoi Akademii A.S. Shishkova o rassmotrivanii knig, ili o tsenzurzhe*, in *Russkii Arkhiv*, 1865
Shoemaker, Robert B., *The London Mob. Violence and Disorder in Eighteenth-century England*, Hambledon 2004
Shorter, Clement, ed., *Napoleon and his Fellow Travellers. Being a Reprint of Certain Narratives of the Voyages of the Dethroned Emperor on the Bellerophon and the Northumberland, etc.*, London 1908

Sidorova, M.V., and Shcherbakova, E.I., eds, *Rossia pod Nadzorom. Otchety III Otdelenia 1827–1869*, Moscow 2006
Siemann, Wolfram, 'Die Mainzer Zentraluntersuchungskommission 1819–1828', in *Deutschlands Rühe, Sicherheit und Ordnung. Die Anfänge der Politischen Polizei 1806–1866*, Tübingen 1985
Simon, Walter M., *The Failure of the Prussian Reform Movement 1807–1819*, Ithaca 1955
Skarbek, Fryderyk, *Pamiętniki*, Warsaw 2009
Sked, Alan, *The Survivial of the Habsburg Empire. Radetzky, the Imperial Army and the Class War, 1848*, London 1979
— *Metternich and Austria. An Evaluation*, London 2008
Smirnova-Rosset, Aleksandra Osipovna, *Vospominania, Pisma*, Moscow 1990
Sollogub, V.A., *Vospominania*, Moscow 1931
Southey, Robert, *The Life and Correspondence of the Late Robert Southey*, Vols IV–VI, London 1850
Spadoni, Domenico, *Una Trama e un Tentativo Rivoluzionario nello Stato Romano nel 1820–21*, Rome 1910
Sparrow, Elizabeth, 'The Alien Office', in *Historical Journal*, No. 33, 1990
Spence, Peter, *The Birth of Romantic Radicalism. War, Popular Politics and English Radical Reformism, 1800–1815*, Aldershot 1996
Spies and Bloodites!!! The Lives and Political Hisotry of Those Arch-fiends Oliver, Reynolds, & Co., etc., London n.d.
Spitzer, Alan B., *Old Hatreds and Young Hopes. The French Carbonari against the Bourbon Restoration*, Cambridge, Mass. 1971
Squire, P.S., 'Metternich and Benckendorff, 1807–1834', in *Slavonic and East European Review*, Vol. 45, No. 104, January 1967
— 'The Metternich—Benckendorff Letters, 1835–1842', in *Slavonic and East European Review*, Vol. 45, No. 105, July 1967
— *The Third Department. The Establishment and Practices of the Political Police in the Russia of Nicholas I*, Cambridge 1968
Srbik, Heinrich von, *Metternich. Der Staatsmann und der Mensch*, 2 vols, Darmstadt 1957
Stadelmann, Rudolph, *Social and Political History of the German 1848 Revolution*, trs. James Chastain, Athens, Ohio 1975
Stanhope, John, *The Cato Street Conspiracy*, London 1962
Stead, John Philip, *The Police of Paris*, London 1957
Stevenson, John, 'The Queen Caroline Affair', in J. Stevenson, ed., *London in the Age of Reform*, Oxford 1977
— *Popular Disturbances in England, 1700–1832*, London 1992
Stewart, A.T.Q., *The Summer Soldiers. The 1798 Rebellion in Antrim and Down*, Belfast 1995
Stogov, E.I., *Zapiski Zhandarmskovo shtabs-ofitsera epokhi Nikolaia I*, Moscow 2003
Sturdza, Alexandru, *Mémoire sur l'état actuel de l'Allemagne*, n.p. 1818
Stürmer, Baron Bartholmeus von, *Napoléon à Sainte-Hélène*, ed. Jacques St Cere and H. Schlitter, Paris n.d.

Sweet, Paul R., *Friedrich von Gentz. Defender of the Old Order*, Madison 1941
Système de legislation, d'administration et de politique de la Russie en 1844, par un homme d'état russe, Paris 1845
Talleyrand-Périgord, Charles-Maurice, prince de, *Mémoires du prince de Talleyrand*, Vol. III, Paris 1891
Tanshina, Natalia, *Kniaginia Liven*, Moscow 2009
Tatishchev, S.S., *Vneshniaia Politika Imperatora Nikolaia Pervogo*, St Petersburg 1887
— *Imperator Nikolai I i Inostrannie Dvory*, St Petersburg 1889
Taylor, David, *The New Police in Nineteenth-century England*, Manchester 1997
Thale, Mary, ed., *Selections from the Papers of the London Corresponding Society 1792–1799*, Cambridge 1983
The Annual Register, 1812, 1817, 1818, 1819, 1820, 1838, 1844 London 1813–45
The Parliamentary History of England, Vol. XXXI, London 1818
The Parliamentary Debates from the Year 1803, to the Present Time (Hansard), Vol. XXIII, London 1812; Vol. XXXV, London 1817
The Portfolio; or a Collection of State Papers, etc. etc. illustrative of the History of Our Times, 5 vols, London 1836–37
The Trial of James Wilson for High Treason, with an account of his execution at Glasgow, August 1820, Glasgow 1834
Thomis, Malcolm I., *The Luddites. Machine-Breaking in Regency England*, Newton Abbot 1970
— and Holt, Peter, *Threats of Revolution in Britain, 1789–1848*, Hamden, Conn. 1977
Thürheim, L. von, *Mein Leben*, 4 vols, Munich 1914
Tissot, Victor, *La Police Secrète Prussienne*, Paris 1884
Tocqueville, Alexis de, *Lettres choisies, souvenirs 1814–1859*, Paris 2003
Tolki i nastroienie umov v Rossii po doniesieniam vyzshei politsii v S.-Peterburgie s avgusta 1818 po 1 maia 1819g, in *Russkaia Starina*, Vol. 22, 1881
Townsend, Mary Lee, *Forbidden Laughter. Popular Humor and the Limits of Repression in Nineteenth-century Prussia*, Ann Arbor 1992
Trefolev, L., *Benkendorfovskie 'shaluny'*, in *Russkii Arkhiv*, Vol. 8, 1896
Trial of James Watson, Senior, for High Treason, etc., London 1817
Trollope, Frances, *Paris and the Parisians*, 2 vols, London 1836
— *Vienna and the Austrians*, 2 vols, London 1838
Trotskii, I., *Tretie Otdelenie pri Nikolae I*, Leningrad 1990
Tulard, Jean, *La Préfecture de Police sous la monarchie de juillet*, Paris 1964
Turgenev, Nikolai, *La Russie et les Russes*, 3 vols, Paris 1847
Urquhart, Diane, *The Ladies of Londonderry*, London 2007
Uvarov, S.S., *L'Empereur Alexandre et Buonaparte*, St Petersburg 1814
— *Esquisses politiques et littéraires*, Paris 1848
— *Desiatiletie Ministerstva Narodnogo Prosveshchenia 1833–1843*, St Petersburg 1864
Vaillé, Eugène, *Le Cabinet Noir*, Paris 1950
Varnhagen von Ense, K.A., *Denkvurdigkeiten und Vermischete Schriften*, 6 vols, Mannheim 1837–42
Vaulabelle, Achille de, *Chute de l'empire et histoire des deux Restaurations*, 8 vols, Paris 1847

Veit, Ursula, *Justus Grüner als Schöpfer der Geheimen Preussischen Staatspolizei*, Coburg 1937
Vidocq, François Eugène, *Mémoires*, 4 vols, Paris 1828–29
Viel-Castel, Louis de, *Histoire de la Restauration*, 20 vols, Paris 1860–78
Villamov, G.I., *Votsarenie Imperatora Nikolaia I-go*, in *Russkaia Starina*, Vol. 97, February 1899
Villèle, comte de, *Mémoires et correspondance*, 5 vols, Paris 1888–90
Vivien, Auguste, *Le Préfet de Police*, Paris 1842
Vock, M.M. von, *Peterburgskoe Obshchestvo pri voshestvii na prestol imperatora Nikolaia, po doniesieniam M.M. Vocka A.Kh. Benkendorfu*, in *Russkaia Starina*, Vol. 32, Vol. 9, 1881
Wakefield, Edward Gibbon, *Swing Unmasked; or, the Causes of Rural Incendiarism*, London 1831
Wallace, Miriam L., *Revolutionary Subjects in the English 'Jacobin' Novel*, Lewisburg 2009
Wallas, Graham, *The Life of Francis Place 1771–1854*, London 1925
Wangermann, Ernst, *From Joseph II to the Jacobin Trials. Government Policy and Public Opinion in the Habsburg Dominions in the Period of the French Revolution*, Oxford 1959
Waresquiel, Émmanuel de, *Le duc de Richelieu 1766–1822*, Paris 1990
— *Talleyrand. Le Prince immobile*, Paris 2003
Weber, Eberhard, *Die Mainzer Zentraluntersuchungskommission*, in *Quellen und Darstellungen zur Geschichte des Deutschen Verfassungsrechts*, Vol. 8, Karlsruhe 1970
Webster, C.K., *The Foreign Policy of Castlereagh 1815–1822*, London 1925
Wegert, Karl H., *German Radicals Confront the Common People. Revolutionary Politics and Popular Politics 1789–1849*, Mainz 1992
Weiss, John, *Conservatism in Europe 1770–1945*, London 1977
Wellington, Arthur Wellesley, Duke of, *Despatches, Correspondence, and Memoranda*, Vol. I, London 1867
— *Supplementary Despatches, Correspondence, and Memoranda*, Vol. XI, London 1864; Vol. XXII, London 1865
Wells, Roger, *Insurrection. The British Experience 1795–1803*, Gloucester 1983
Welschinger, Henri, *La Censure sous le Premier Empire*, Paris 1882
Westmorland, John Fane, Earl of, *Memoirs of the Great European Congresses of Vienna–Paris, 1814–1815 - Aix-la-Chapelle, 1818 - Troppau, 1820 - and Laybach, 1820–21*, London 1860
Westmorland, Priscilla Countess of, *The Correspondence of Priscilla, Countess of Westmorland*, London 1909
White, R.J., *Waterloo to Peterloo*, London 1957
Whittaker, Cynthia, *The Origins of Modern Russian Education. An Intellectual Biography of Count Sergei Uvarov 1786–1855*, DeKalb 1984
Wierzbitski, K., *A Life of Adventure. An Autobiography. By Colonel Corvin*, 3 vols, London 1871
Williams, Alan, *The Police of Paris 1718–1789*, Baton Rouge 1979

Williamson, George S., 'What Killed August von Kotzebue? The Temptations of Virtue and the Political Theology of German Nationalism, 1789–1819', in *Journal of Modern History*, Vol. 72, No. 4, Chicago 2000

Wilmot, Martha, *More Letters from Martha Wilmot. Impressions of Vienna, 1819–1829*, London 1935

Wilson, Ben, *Decency and Disorder. The Age of Cant 1789–1837*, London 2007

Witt, Jean, *Les Sociétés Secrètes de France et d'Italie*, Paris 1830

Wollstonecraft, Mary, *Works*, ed. Janet Todd and Marilyn Butler, Vol. IV, London 1989

Woodward, E.L., *The Age of Reform*, Oxford 1946

Wordsworth, William and Mary, *The Love Letters of William and Mary Wordsworth*, ed. Beth Darlington, London 1982

Worrall, David, *Radical Culture. Discourse, Resistance and Surveillance, 1790–1820*, Hemel Hempsted 1992

Zamoyski, Adam, *Holy Madness*, London 1999

— *Rites of Peace*, London 2007

Zhizneopisanie, vsepoddanneishie doklady i perepiska kniazia Aleksandra Ivanovicha Chernysheva, in *Sbornik Imperatorskogo Russkogo Istoricheskogo Obshchestva*, Vols 121 and 122, St Petersburg 1905

Zhurnaly Komiteta uchrezhdennago vysochaishym reskryptom 6 Dekabria 1826 goda, in *Sbornik Imperatorskogo Russkogo Istoricheskogo Obshchestva*, Vol. 74, St Petersburg 1891

Zimmermann, Harro, *Friedrich Gentz – Die Erfindung der Realpolitik*, Paderborn 2012

Ziolkowski, Theodore, *Lure of the Arcane. The Literature of Cult and Conspiracy*, Baltimore 2013

Zorin, Andrei, *Kormia Dvuglavogo Orla*, Moscow 2004

Index